PRINCIPLES OF
ENGINEERING PRODUCTION

Anthony O Sullivan

Strawhall,

Monkstown,

Co. Cork.

Cork RTC.

Principles of Engineering Production

A. J. LISSAMAN
C.Eng., M.I.Mech,E., F.I.Prod.E.
Formerly Head of Department of Production Engineering
North Gloucestershire College of Technology, Cheltenham

S. J. MARTIN
C.Eng., F.I.Mech., F.I.Prod.E.
Formerly Principal Lecturer in Production Engineering
North Gloucestershire College of Technology, Cheltenham
Examiner, C.G.L.I.

Edward Arnold
A division of Hodder & Stoughton
LONDON MELBOURNE AUCKLAND

© 1982 A.J. Lissaman and S.J. Martin

First published in Great Britian 1964
Second edition 1982
Third impression 1986
Fourth impression 1987
Fifth impression 1989

British Library Cataloguing in Publication Data

Martin, S.J.
    Principles of engineering production. — 2nd ed.
    1. Engineering instruments   2. Mechanical engineering.
    I. Title   II. Lissaman, A.J.
    621.9   TA165

    ISBN 0 340 28173 1

Typeset in 10/11 pt Times Roman (Monophoto) by Macmillian India Ltd. Bangalore
Printed and bound in Hong Kong for Edward Arnold, the educational academic
and medical publishing division of Hodder and Stoughton Limited, 41 Bedford
Square, London WC1B 3DQ by Colorcraft Ltd.

Preface to Second Edition

This book treats technical aspects of manufacturing with respect to metal machining and press-forming. Starting from a consideration of specification and standardisation, it goes on to deal analytically with the main aspects of the manufacturing processes giving due attention to the crucial matters of quality and cost.

The new edition, in SI units, is an enlarged revised version of the original book which first appeared in 1964. It incorporates the many changes necessitated by the metrication and revision of British Standards; all the relevant standards up to 1980 have been consulted.

Since the book first appeared there have been major developments in machine tools. This edition incorporates a new chapter, 'Control of Machine Tools' which gives a substantial introduction to numerical control and programming. A further new chapter deals with electro-discharge and electro-chemical methods of machining, and the chapter on 'Statistical Methods of Process Control' has been extended to cover control by attributes. A bibliography is added at the end of the book, listing further reading likely to be of interest to students.

Eight printings of the original work show that it met a real need. While courses leading to the higher engineering qualifications have changed considerably since 1964, there is now a growing awareness that such courses ought to include some consideration of manufacturing technology in order better to meet the needs of industry. Since this is a diverse subject involving considerable practical detail students may have difficulty in gaining a useful knowledge of the basic principles within the limited time available.

This book is designed to help 'A' level entrants to higher diploma and degree courses obtain a first appreciation of some important aspect of engineering manufacture. It should also be of service during their periods of industrial experience.

It is hoped that the extensive updating of this edition with respect to British Standards will again make the book useful as a reference for mature engineers.

The authors and publishers would like to express their thanks to firms which have supplied data and illustrations. They are particularly indebted to the British Standards Institution, 2 Park Street, London W1A 2BS, for permission to reproduce extracts from their publications. Copies of Standards may be obtained on application to the Institution.

The specially drawn diagrams featured in the book have been prepared by Mrs E. M. Harris and the authors are extremely grateful for her valuable assistance. They also thank the Principal and Librarian of the North Gloucestershire College of Technology for allowing access to British Standards and other reference material held in the College library.

A. J. Lissaman
S. J. Martin

Cheltenham

Extract from the Preface to the First Edition

ENGINEERING manufacture is a diverse economic activity embracing all the work lying between a design and its execution. It calls for decisions which, if they are to be wisely made, ought to have a rational basis.

The Principles of Engineering Production ought to satisfy two criteria:

(i) they should be developed logically from the elements of manufacturing activities;

(ii) their application should tend to improve the quality of the work produced, or to lower its cost.

This book aims to develop and illustrate some important principles underlying engineering manufacture, principles which the authors believe come near to satisfying the above criteria. They are principles of wide application and apply equally to batch work and to large quantity production involving automatic machinery.

The text has been developed mathematically wherever appropriate, and it is hoped that the treatment will stimulate the teaching of the subject, as well as capture the interest of students. Mature engineers engaged in manufacture should find in this book much to guide and assist them in the analysis and solution of their day-to-day problems.

In a work deliberately planned to introduce greater rigour into the treatment of its subject, two difficulties of presentation have confronted the authors. A reasonably consistent set of symbols has had to be adopted for use throughout the book, and this has led to certain topics, e.g. Merchant's Theory of Cutting, appearing in symbols which differ from those of the original research papers. In order to illustrate certain points by means of worked examples, it has sometimes been necessary to over simplify practical detail in the interest of conciseness. It is hoped that readers will accept that the authors have pondered a great deal over both difficulties and that their decisions, however imperfect, solve in some degree both problems of presentation.

A. J. Lissaman
S. J. Martin

Cheltenham

CONTENTS

CHAPTER 1
Specification and Standardisation for Production

1.1 Specification and Drawing

The object of manufacturing is to produce saleable goods. To be saleable the goods must function satisfactorily, and this is primarily the concern of the designer; they must further satisfy purchasers by giving value for money. Manufacturing methods need to be considered at the design stage. To give value for money attention must be given, among other things, to

(a) production costs,
(b) quality, which includes reliability, of the resulting product.

The efficiency of, say, a petrol engine can be expressed as the ratio of energy output to energy input. Its efficiency in terms of manufacture is a more complex matter involving the cost of manufacture and the resulting quality of the product measured in such terms as finish, reliability and useful life. Cost and quality are perhaps the two most important criteria for judging a manufacturing method, but production rate and availability as required by the market are important commercial factors.

Manufacturing is based on production drawings and specified details such as quality and delivery date. The production drawing usually incorporates dimensional tolerances and specifies the material, surface finishes, any heat treatments, etc. So much information is needed for a complete specification that the drawing cannot possibly include it all; the problem is generally solved by reference to published **standards**. For British Industry the standards most widely used are those provided by the British Standards Institution (2, Park Street, London W1A 2BS) and are identified by their BS number. The following Sectional Lists of British Standards are available and have been consulted in the revision of this book:

SL 6 *Mechanical Engineering*
SL 20 *Machine Tools*
SL 37 *Drawing Practice*
SL 44 *General Management, Quality Assurance, Quality Control and Statistics.*

1

Principles of engineering production

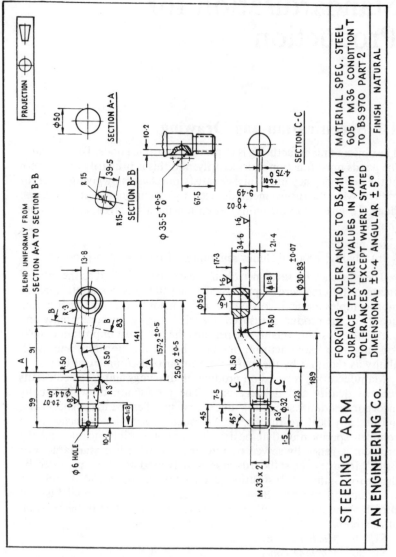

Fig. 1.1 (Courtesy of British Standards Institution)

Fig 1.1, reproduced by kind permission of the British Standards Institution, gives the drawing and specification for machining a steering arm made from a drop forging. The drawing conforms to BS308 Engineering Drawing Practice; its interpretation becomes more explicit by reference to further standards.

(1) *BS970 Part 2*. This standard amplifies the material specification—Steel 605 M36 Condition T. This is a $1\frac{1}{2}\%$ manganese molybdenum alloy of stated chemical composition. Condition T, for a ruling section below 63.5 mm ($2\frac{1}{2}$ inches), requires that a standard test piece conform to specified mechanical properties of tensile strength, yield stress, elongation, impact value (Izod test) and hardness. These properties are to be obtained from the following heat treatment: harden in oil from 840 to 870°C, temper between 550°C and 680°C. The mechanical tests for properties are standardised in BS18 (Tensile testing) and BS240 (Hardness testing).

(2) The drawing requires the forging to conform to BS4114. This specification covers drop forgings giving permitted tolerances. These tolerances depend on weight, shape of die line, type of steel and on a shape complexity factor. The specification also controls quality in respect of mismatch (of the two halves of the die), amount of residual flash and straightness and flatness where applicable.

(3) The symbolic thread dimension M33 × 2 at one end of the steering arm would be meaningless without the information contained in BS3643 (*ISO Metric Screw Threads*). Reference to the standard shows it to be from the "fine thread" series. As shown on this drawing it is not a full specification because tolerances are not stated. Since the "medium fit" would probably give a suitable thread the drawing could specify M33 × 2—6g; a 60° angle vee thread, nominal diameter 33 mm, pitch 2 mm manufactured to 6g tolerances (see Chapter 14).

(4) The **Woodruff** keyway in the tapered diameter would present manufacturing problems because a standard cutter is not available for the dimensions given. The drawing was evidently made before BS4235 Part 2: *Woodruff Keys and Keyways* became available. The dimensions of Fig 1.1 may arise from conversion of previous inch units; they do not arise from metric basic sizes. The nearest keyway shown in BS4235 is based on a standard cutter of diameter 32 mm and width 10 mm as the basic sizes.

(5) Two important standard symbols appear on the drawing. Symbol ▽ specifies surface finish in accordance with BS308; the accompanying numbers, 0·8 and 1·6, state the required degree of finish in μm units.

Symbol ◄— 1:8 specifies a taper of one in eight on the diameter in accordance with BS308.

(6) Notes at the foot of the drawing lay down further conditions relative to the acceptable quality in a finished component.

This example makes it clear that production drawings require the support of relevant British Standard in order to more accurately define the required quality of the product.

Standardisation. Following the decision to adopt the metric system, there was considerable revision of:

(a) the physical units employed by engineers, e.g. the newton (N) is now used for force;
(b) British Standards reflecting the use of metric linear dimensions.

Many countries now support the Système International des Unités (SI) which has led to a common set of standards, the work of the International Organisation for Standards (ISO). The advantages for international trade of common units and standard specifications should ultimately outweigh the cost and inconvenience of the changes involved. The British Standards Institution has issued many metric standards based upon ISO recommendations to replace standards based on the inch unit. However, it may be many years before all the consequences of our use of the inch unit disappear. For example, farm tractors are fitted with a splined hole on a shaft drive for attachment of agricultural implements. These splines generally had basic sizes in terms of the inch unit and any change will be difficult due to the considerable capital investments of the past. In such cases it seems likely that metrication may only involve a change in the unit employed as basic sizes cannot be readily changed.

It is most important to recognise that metrication involves more than a change from inches to millimetres; only as standard metric basic sizes become established will the full advantages of a common international system be realised.

Standardisation. Reference has already been made to the use of **standards.** The full economic implications are worth considering in some detail.

Suppose it is required to produce an M30 × 2 screw thread, medium fit tolerance, on a component which is to be machined on a capstan lathe. The essential tooling and equipment could be purchased from stock if not already available.

(1) Set of dies for self-releasing diehead.
(2) Screw thread calliper gauge; medium fit tol.

An order for the equipment would be very brief and reference to BS3643: *ISO Metric Threads* would completely define what was required.

Now consider a special thread of non-standard form and dimensions, as an alternative to the above thread. The dies for the die-head, and the calliper gauge anvils, will have to be specially made. Detail drawings of the thread form, showing the permitted tolerances, will have to be prepared and quotations requested from possible manufacturers. Work cannot commence until a quotation has been accepted and will await certain necessary preparatory steps such as the manufacture of equipment to dress the special "form" on to grinding wheels, and the drawing of large-scale layout charts for optical projection. The chance of error at some stage of the proceedings is an additional hazard which may delay the completion of the special equipment.

It is obvious that the cost of such equipment will be much higher than the cost of standard equipment made in batches of moderate size; also that the time delay before production can commence will be much greater for the special thread. Quite a serious additional factor of the economic comparison lies in the different level of the technical demands which are made. To work out a satisfactory tolerancing system and design gauges for the special thread is not an elementary matter, and demands upon manpower of a high level of technical knowledge and skill will be made, in order to manufacture the special equipment. There must be a very compelling reason before the use of the non-standard thread is justified.

1.2 Interchangeable Manufacture

Present methods of quantity production have arisen because the interchangeable system has certain important economic advantages:

(*a*) Parts can be made in quantity with less demand upon skill and effort if suitable gauges and tooling are employed. The quantity must, however, be sufficient to recover the special tooling costs, as is discussed in Chapter 17.

(*b*) Parts can be *assembled* instead of *fitted*, i.e. they will not need final adjustments of a skilled character in order to produce satisfactory assemblies.

(*c*) Assemblies so made can be serviced by a simple system of replacement parts drawn from stock. This is convenient for the user and is cheaper than reconditioning involving the manufacture of new parts to special sizes.

Before a system of interchangeable assembly can be operated, certain fundamental conditions must be met:

(i) the permissible variation (tolerance) of each dimension must be fixed;

(ii) the mating condition of each pair of parts assembled must be decided.

These conditions are generally satisfied by use of a system of limits and fits. The object of such a system is to make the decisions required under (i) and (ii) conform to a rational pattern. For reasons given above, a **standard** system should be employed.

Interchangeable manufacture requires that the parts made should be as nearly identical as possible. The manufacturing processes to be employed must be chosen accordingly. The procedure will involve the following:

(1) Process Planning. A schedule of the individual operations and their sequence must be drafted.

(2) Jig and Tool Design. Special tooling and equipment must be designed in accordance with the process plan. Choice of the datum faces for the consecutive locations of the part while individual operations are performed is very important. Functional datums must be considered.

(3) Limit gauges and gauging equipment must be designed in order to control the accuracy of the work. The accuracy of the gauges and special tooling must be checked to high precision standards.

A component designed and dimensioned by someone aware of the implications of interchangeable manufacture is likely to be produced much more cheaply and accurately than one designed by someone who has a poor appreciation of quantity manufacturing techniques.

1.3. Dimensioning

The metric system uses decimal fractions only of the basic unit (mm up to 1000 mm). The millimetre, approximately $\frac{1}{25}$ inch, enables small increments to be expressed using fewer decimal places than the inch system. Frequently open dimensions can be expressed in whole numbers; measurement of these by rule can be made to an accuracy of about ± 0.5 mm.

Two quite difference circumstances apply when metric dimensions are being chosen;

(i) conversion from inch dimensions for an existing design,

(ii) metric dimensioning where no relationship to previously employed inch sizes is involved.

(i) *Conversion of inch units* (see BS2856). Precise conversion based on 1 inch = 25.4 mm is rarely sensible; a 17/64 inch clearance hole for a $\frac{1}{4}$ inch bolt would become 6.746 875 mm. Consider an open dimension of 6.25 inches. Unless otherwise toleranced an accuracy of ± 0.01 in is implied. Since 6.25 in = 158.75 mm a conversion to 159 mm is within the implied tolerance but 160 mm, a preferred size from the R5 series, is probably a better conversion.

For closely toleranced dimensions greater accuracy would be necessary and BS2856 would apply. At this point it is worth considering the degree of accuracy likely to be achieved by common workshop methods of measurement.

TABLE 1.1

Workshop instrument used	Smallest increment for which the instrument is reliable
Vernier calliper	0·002 inch or 0·05 mm
Micrometer	0·0004 inch or 0·01 mm
Sensitive dial indicator	0·0001 inch or 0·0025 mm

Example 1.1
Convert $1·734^{-0·001}_{-0·002}$ inch to mm in accordance with BS2856.

Solution
Limits of size   1·733/1·732, tol 0·001
Precise conversion 1·733 inch = 44·0182 mm
                    1·732 inch = 43·9928 mm

As the tolerance is between 0·001 and 0·01 inch, the BS rules require the metric sizes to be rounded to the nearest 0·001 mm. The required conversion becomes 44·018/43·993 mm and these **limits** should appear on the drawing because it is impossible to show deviations from a basic size as the 1·734 dimension converts to 44·0436 mm.

(ii) *Metric dimensioning of new designs.* The starting point is the choice of basic sizes. Progress towards an agreed list of standard basic sizes is slow but reference to BS2045: *Preferred Numbers* is often helpful. BS Handbook 18: *Metric Standards for Engineering* covers such items as screws, gears, fasteners, cutting tools, machine tool details, measuring tools and instruments. Only as these standards come fully into use will problems of selecting rational basic sizes be simplified.

Size-ranges. The advantages of standardisation are lost if too many gradations of size occur within a specified range. This is not just a matter of linear dimensions; weights, volumes, horsepower, electrical resistances or other physical properties may determine the size of a product, e.g. a 3-hp electric motor (= 2·2 kW approx.)
The sizes within a range are generally required to increase at an approximately constant rate. A size-range of electric motors might contain a ½-hp and a ¾-hp size at the lower end, i.e. a 50% increase in size; such a range is also likely to include a 5-hp and a 7½-hp motor, again an increase of 50%. It would be an unnecessary duplication of sizes to include a 5¼-hp motor in the range (a 5% increase in size). The manufacture of large quantities of each size in a limited size-range will enable motors to be supplied at a lower price than if a wider choice is given. The full economic advantages of quantity manufacturing methods can then be exploited.
Similar reasoning can be applied to the dimensional aspects of many products, e.g. the diameters of bolts, the thicknesses of steel sheet, etc. A

rational series of standard sizes will tend to follow a geometric series:

$$a, ar, ar^2, ar^3, \ldots ar^n$$

where r is the constant rate of increase. Due to traditional developments, many of the standard sizes arrived at empirically, such as the BS Whitworth threads, do not follow the geometric rate of increase exactly, but the closeness of agreement is sometimes surprising. The sizes of new products should, however, be related to a suitable series of preferred numbers in order to avoid unnecessary duplication and to obtain the maximum advantages of standardisation.

Preferred Numbers (BS2045)
These number series are based on ISO Recommendation R3 which has received international agreement. The series is based on the ideas of the French engineer, Col. Charles Renard and are designated R5, R10, R20 etc. The geometric ratios are shown in Table 1.2.

TABLE 1.2

Series	Ratio	Percentage rate of increase
R5	$\sqrt[5]{10} = 1{\cdot}58$	58
R10	$\sqrt[10]{10} = 1{\cdot}26$	26
R20	$\sqrt[20]{10} = 1{\cdot}12$	12
R40	$\sqrt[40]{10} = 1{\cdot}06$	6
R80	$\sqrt[80]{10} = 1{\cdot}03$	3

Additional series can be formed by taking every third term of the basic series; e.g. R40/3, ratio $= \sqrt[40]{10^3} = 1{\cdot}188$.

Examples of the use of such series are given in Tables 2.5 and 2.6 spindle speeds and feeds for machine tools.

In an earlier BS, now withdrawn, the late Mr J. E. Spears discussed the technical advantages and practical uses of preferred numbers. Extracts are given in BS2045 and the main points are summarized below.

'The object of formulating an agreed series of preferred numbers is to provide the designer with a guide which, while not operating to restrict the liberty of his choice, will serve to minimize unnecessary size variations. In a majority of cases the designer, having calculated or selected a preliminary value, would not prejudice his final design by adopting instead the nearest size in a pre-selected (preferred) series. The adoption of preferred numbers in grading a series of articles enables the requisite range to be covered with a minimum of different sizes with resulting economy to both maker and user'.

Example 1.2
It is required to standardise parallel keyways ranging from 2 mm to 28 mm. The first seven sizes are to follow the R10 series, the remainder to follow the R20 series. Develop a suitable range of key widths.

Solution
For the R10 series, geometric ratio $r = 10^{0.1} = 1.259$

Calculated values	2	2·52 3·17	3·99	5·02	6·33	7·96	10·02

Nom. (rounded) values	2	3	4	5	6	8	10

For the R20 series, $r = 10^{0.05} = 1.22$

Calculated values	10	11·22*	12·59	14·12	15·84	17·78	19·95	22·38	25·12	28·18

Nominal widths	10	12	14	16	18	20	22	25	28

Summarising, the result shows that the rounded values result in three arithmetic series i.e.

2 mm to 6 mm in 1 mm steps
6 mm to 22 mm in 2 mm steps
22 mm to 28 mm in 3 mm steps

If plotted the three straight lines of the arithmetic series will approximate to the curves of the geometric series, a common situation where sizes are rounded as is necessary for such items as bolts and twist drills. Such a series of sizes can be written down directly from tabular values given in Table 1.3:

1.4. Limits and Fits

Several standard limit systems have been in previous use with partial success. One of the earliest, the Newall system, was widely used but is now of diminishing importance. The current metric system is BS4500 which incorporates changes made in ISA Bulletin 25 now reissued in its up-dated form as ISO Recommendation R286.
Fig 1.2 shows:

(A) The designer's concept of a fit; the diameter of the shaft and the running clearance are his main concern.
(B) The manufacturing specifications for the fit; an acceptable amount of variation in the sizes of both elements has to be included in the specification.
(C) A conventional diagram of fits based upon (B), which shows graphically all the possible relationships between holes and shafts resulting from the specification. Once an acceptable amount of variation in the sizes of hole and shaft has been fixed, it becomes

---

* It would be illogical to include an 11 mm size because the last step in the R10 series gives a 2 mm interval.

TABLE 1.3
Basic Series of Preferred Numbers

1	2	3	4	5
	Basic series			
Serial number	R5	R10	R20	R40
0	1·00	1·00	1·00	1·00
1				1·06
2			1·12	1·12
3				1·18
4		1·25	1·25	1·25
5				1·32
6			1·40	1·40
7				1·50
8	1·60	1·60	1·60	1·60
9				1·70
10			1·80	1·80
11				1·90
12		2·00	2·00	2·00
13				2·12
14			2·24	2·24
15				2·36
16	2·50	2·50	2·50	2·50
17				2·65
18			2·80	2·80
19				3·00
20		3·15	3·15	3·15
21				3·35
22			3·55	3·55
23				3·75
24	4·00	4·00	4·00	4·00
25				4·25
26			4·50	4·50
27				4·75
28		5·00	5·00	5·00
29				5·30
30			5·60	5·60
31				6·00
32	6·30	6·30	6·30	6·30
33				6·70
34			7·10	7·10
35				7·50
36		8·00	8·00	8·00
37				8·50
38			9·00	9·00
39				9·50
40	10·00	10·00	10·00	10·00

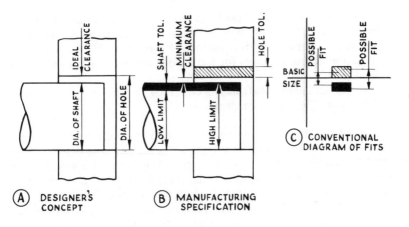

Fig. 1.2 Fundamentals of a limit system

impossible to guarantee that assemblies will have the ideal running clearance as laid down by the designer. The clearance will vary in amount by the sum of the tolerances. The minimum clearance must not be too small.

Systems of Limits and Fits. Fig 1.3 illustrates different arrangements of the tolerance bands in relationship to the basic size (i.e. the bands are given differing fundamental deviations, FD (see p. 14):

(D) Unilateral and bilateral tolerances are shown. The unilateral system is now preferred. In this system the basic size becomes the **go** size of a limit gauge, which is a convenient arrangement. Changes in tolerance magnitude only involve the change of one limit, and of one gauge dimension, the **not-go** gauge size.

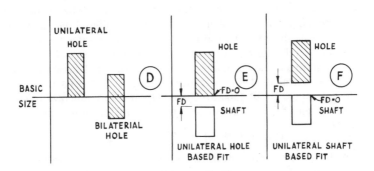

Fig. 1.3 Hole/shaft bases

(E) A unilateral **hole-based** clearance fit; the clearance is achieved by moving the tolerance band of the shaft away from the basic size. The minimum clearance is equal to the FD of the shaft. Hole-based fits have practical advantages for most work and are the ones normally used.

(F) A unilateral **shaft-based** clearance fit; the FD of the hole determines the minimum clearance.

Classes of Fit. Fig 1.4 illustrates the classes of fit which can be obtained from a system of limits and fits. (G) shows the fits on a hole-based system; (J) shows the fits on a shaft-based system. The various fits which result from variations in the magnitude and direction of the FD of the non-basic element are: (i) Clearance; (ii) Interference; (iii) Transition.

Transition indicates that the specified limits may give assemblies which have either clearance or interference. Transition fits are often specified for locating purposes.

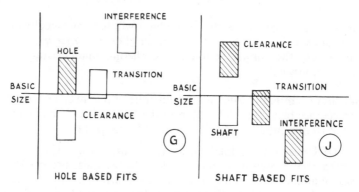

Fig. 1.4 Classes of fit

Tolerance. Tolerance is a permitted variation of the size of a part to allow for variation in the manufacturing process. Tolerance is indirectly a measure of quality, the smaller the tolerance, the higher the quality; it is also related to the cost of production. Fig 1.5 illustrates the tolerance (quality) cost relationship for manufacturing processes.

To maintain a constant quality over a wide range of sizes, there must be some adjustment of the tolerance in relation to the basic size.

The tolerances of BS4500 are based upon a fundamental tolerance unit. For grades IT5 to IT16, sizes up to 500 mm, this unit is given by the formula,

$$i\,(\text{micrometres}) = 0 \cdot 45 \sqrt[3]{D} + 0 \cdot 001\,D$$

where D is the geometric mean (in millimetres) of the size range having the constant tolerance. The term $0 \cdot 001\,D$ is introduced to ensure a reasonable tolerance when D is large and temperature differences have a

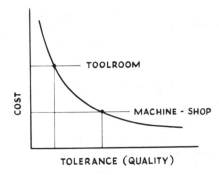

Fig. 1.5 *Economic aspect of tolerance*

significant influence upon the size. Changes of tolerance for work of constant quality, occur at certain diameters; the arrangement is shown in Fig 1.6.

Standard tolerances for the 18 grades covering sizes up to 3150 mm are given in BS4500. It is not intended that they should be calculated from the explanatory details given in appendix A of the standard. The following example is included to illustrate the rational basis of the system.

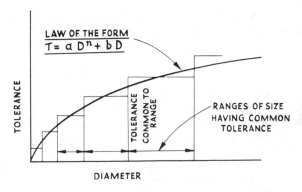

Fig. 1.6 *Tolerance–diameter relationship for constant quality, and diameter steps*

Example 1.3

Working from the basic principles find suitable tolerances for (a) 82 mm IT6, and (b) 440 mm IT12. Compare the calculated values with the rounded values given in BS4500.

Solution

82 mm   is in the size range   80–120
440 mm   „ „ „   „   „   400–500

From BS4500 appendix A, IT6 $= 10\,i$ and the tolerances increase in accordance with the R5 series as the IT number increases, hence:

IT series 6 7 8 9 10 11 12 13 etc.

R5 series 1 1·6 2·5 4 6·4 10 16 25

∴ IT12 tolerances are 16 times IT6 tolerances

82 mm IT6. D for range $= \sqrt{(80 \times 120)} = 98$

$i = 0\cdot45\ \sqrt[3]{98} + (0\cdot001 \times 98) = 2\cdot173\,\mu m$

IT6 $= 10\,i = 21\cdot73\,\mu m$ (BS4500 gives $22\,\mu m$)

440 mm IT12. D for range $= \sqrt{(400 \times 500)} = 447$

$i = 0\cdot45\ \sqrt[3]{447} + (0\cdot001 \times 447) = 3\cdot888\,\mu m$

IT12 $= 16 \times$ IT6 $= 160\,i$

$$\text{IT12} = 160 \times 3\cdot888 = 622\,\mu m$$
$$(\text{BS4500 gives } 630\,\mu m)$$

Fundamental Deviation. The disposition of the tolerance band with respect to the basic size determines the class of fit. The disposition is fixed by the fundamental deviation (FD) selected for the fit. The FD is designated by letter symbol

For holes: A B C D E F G H J K M N P R S T U V X Y Z etc

For shafts: a b c d e f g h j k m n p r s t u v x y z etc

The rules for determining all of the 27FD magnitudes are rather involved, see BS4500, Appendix A. Typical examples are:

$$\text{f, F} = 5\cdot5\ D^{0.41} \text{ where f is } -\text{ve and F is } +\text{ve,}$$
$$\text{m, M} = \text{IT7} - \text{IT6 where m is } +\text{ve and M is } -\text{ve.}$$

There are certain other restrictions too lengthy to reproduce here.

BS4500 provides fits for either a hole-based or a shaft-based system. The fundamental deviations are of equal magnitude for holes and shafts for all the clearance fits but are disposed on the opposite sides of the basic size. For this reason the hole-based fit H7/f6 will give the same range of clearance as the shaft-based F7/h6 fit. For interference and transition fits where holes and shafts are not to the same tolerance grades special rules apply (see BS4500 Appendix A). While clearance fits can be satisfactorily achieved by applying mathematical rules, interference and transition fits tend to require a compromise between some basic law and practical conditions proved by experience.

Example 1.4

For the diameter range 30/50 mm, IT6 $= 0\cdot0016$ mm, IT7 $= 0\cdot0025$ mm, and the fundamental deviation g $= -0\cdot009$ mm. Determine limits for a 31·5 mm diameter H7/g6 assembly, and for a G7/h6 assembly. Illustrate the fitting conditions in a scale and give the mean and maximum clearance fits which are possible.

Solution
(see Fig. 1.7)

H7/g6	G7/h6
Limits	*Limits*
Hole, 31·525/31·5	Hole, 31·535/31·509
Shaft 31·491/31·475	Shaft, 31·5/31·494

Mean clearance = $\frac{1}{2}$(sum of tols) + FD = 0·0295 mm

Max clearance = sum of tols + FD = 0·05 mm

These fits are identical for either a unilateral hole basis or a unilateral shaft basis. This is not true of all the fits obtainable from BS4500, but any difference which may arise from a change of basic member is quite small.

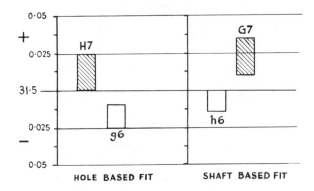

Fig. 1.7 Scale diagram of fits

Selection of Fits. We have shown that the fits to be obtained from BS4500 are derived from the association of two apparently independent variables:

    (i) the 18 tolerance grades;
    (ii) the 27 fundamental deviations.

There are strong practical reasons why certain tolerance grades and fundamental deviations are much more likely to be associated than others; light interference fits, for example, can be achieved only if the tolerances are suitably small.

It is not intended that *any* possible association of tolerance and FD should be used regardless of other considerations, because to do so would be to lose most of the economic advantages of standardisation. In this respect two important facts should be noted:

    Only certain of the IT grades are intended for fits.
    IT01 to IT5 are intended for precision standards, gauges etc.;
    IT6 to IT11 may be used for fits;
    IT12 to IT16 are not intended for fits.

Experience has shown that a majority of the normal engineering fits can be obtained from a fairly limited range of those contained in BS4500. These are referred to as the **selected fits** and may be either hole-based or shaft-based. Fig. 1.8 shows these fits on a hole basis, Table 1.4 shows the fits on a shaft basis designated symbolically.

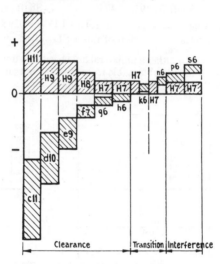

Fig. 1.8 BS4500 Selected fits – hole basis

Example 1.5

Fig 1.9 shows a knuckle joint in which a centreless ground pin is to be an interference fit in part A and a clearance fit in part B. Select suitable fits and give the limits for the pin and holes:

    (i) on a unilateral shaft basis;
    (ii) on a unilateral hole basis for the clearance fit.

Compare the two arrangements from the point of view of tooling costs.

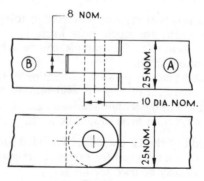

Fig. 1.9

TABLE 1.4
Shaft-based Fits

Type of fit	Hole tolerance	Shaft tolerances			
		h6	h7	h9	h11
Clearance	C11				////
	D10			////	
	E9			////	
	F8		////		
	G7	////			
Transition	H7	////			
	K7	////			
	N7	////			
Interference	P7	////			
	S7	////			

Solution

By reference to Fig. 1.8, a suitable pair of hole based fits are:

Clearance   H8   f7
Interference   H7   p6

Converting to a unilateral shaft basis, a suitable arrangement is:

Shaft, h7   Hole in A, P7
                 Hole in B, F8

To convert to a hole basis, one only of the holes can be of FD = H, because it is not convenient to have two different diameters on the centreless ground pin. A suitable arrangement is:

Hole in B, H8   Shaft,   f7
                     Hole in A, S7

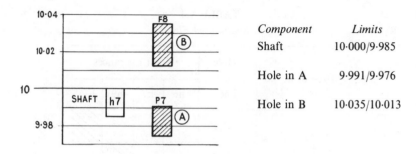

Fig. 1.10 Shaft-based fits

Component	Limits
Shaft	10·000/9·985
Hole in A	9·991/9·976
Hole in B	10·035/10·013

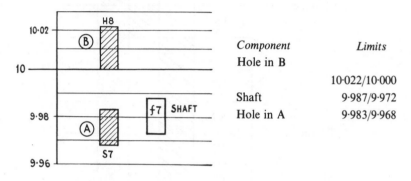

Fig. 1.11 Hole-based fits

Component	Limits
Hole in B	10·022/10·000
Shaft	9·987/9·972
Hole in A	9·983/9·968

For the shaft-based fits neither of the reamed holes are standard, and special reamers and gauges will be required for both.

For the hole-based fits the H8 hole is a standard reamed hole, and the equipment for this will probably be available in the tool stores. The S7 hole can be reamed using a standard reamer ground down to the required size. The centreless ground pin will be checked using slip gauges and a comparator, so that there are no special tool costs for this whatever its size. The tooling costs will be lower for the second arrangement.

Fig 1.12, reproduced from BS 1916 Part 2 by kind permission of the British Standards Institution, shows fits suitable for a belt-drive unit. These come from the previously given selected fits. Fit H7–h6 represents a little higher standard of work than the fit H8–h7. The H11–c11 is not, of course, a normal working fit.

1.5 Dimensions and Tolerance Build-up

Consider the dimensional limits shown in Fig 1.13. No value is given for dimension x because this has been fixed indirectly. The maximum

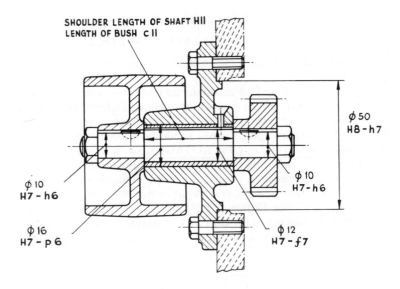

SHOULDER LENGTH OF SHAFT H II
LENGTH OF BUSH C II

ϕ 50
H8 - h7

ϕ 10
H7 - h6

ϕ 16
H7 - p 6

ϕ 10
H7 - h6

ϕ 12
H7 - f 7

Fig. 1.12 Belt drive unit showing appropriate fits

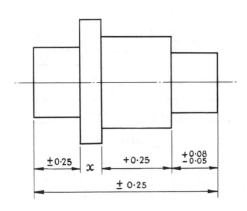

± 0.25

x

$+0.25$

$^{+0.08}_{-0.05}$

± 0.25

Fig. 1.13

possible variation in the size of x will be the algebraic sum of the tolerances of the dimensions shown:

$$0.50 + 0.25 + 0.13 + 0.50 = 1.38 \,\text{mm}$$

The maximum value of x above nominal is

$$+0.25 - (-0.25 - 0.05) = +0.55 \,\text{mm}$$

The maximum value of x below nominal is

$$-0.25 - (0.25 + 0.25 + 0.08) = -0.83 \text{ mm}$$

It is unlikely that these extremes will be realised for reasons given on pp. 495–6.

Suppose it is required to maintain dimension x to a tolerance of 0·48 mm. Since there are four separate tolerances which "build-up" to give the tolerance on x, their average value must not exceed 0·12 mm. A change in the dimensioning method would be a more effective way of controlling variation of size x. Fig 1.14 (A) shows how this might be done by making the end faces into the datum faces for dimensioning. There are now only three dimensions involved in fixing dimension x.

Fig 1.14 (B) shows how the part might be dimensioned for manufacture on a capstan lathe. Datum face (1) is produced by facing the end of the bar after feeding out to the stop, and datum face (2) is produced by a further facing cut taken at the same work setting. After a parting-off

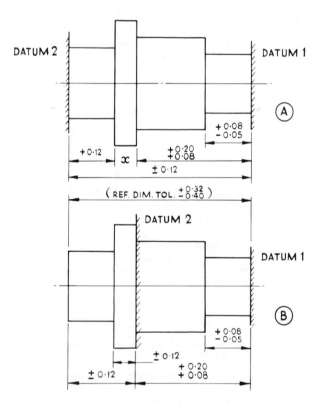

Fig. 1.14 Dimensioning in relation to various datum faces

operation, the part is located in a dead-length collet from datum (2). Dimension x can be produced from datum (2) to a tolerance of ± 0.12 mm. The overall length is now the indirectly determined dimension, but it has been held to a closer tolerance than the original without undue difficulty.

The choice of datum faces for dimensioning tends to follow the assembly requirements, i.e. they are functional datums, but the dimensioning may need revision when working out the manufacturing processes of components in detail.

Fig 1.15, reproduced by permission from BS308, shows how the parts of an assembly may be dimensioned on a functional basis and how redimensioning is used to facilitate manufacture. If the functional datum is retained the $6.05/6.00$ dimension will require an expensive form of receiver gauge in order to check it. Redimensioning splits the tolerance, but it simplifies the measurement and the manufacturing methods.

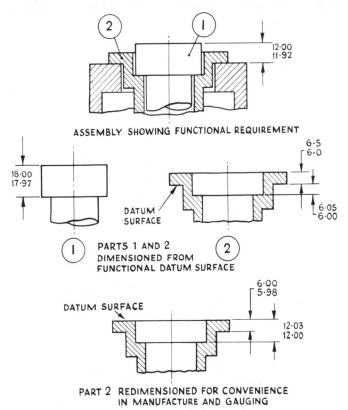

Fig. 1.15
(From BS308 Part 2: 1972 by Courtesy of British Standards Institution)

A solution to this problem not shown in BS308 would be to finish machine the face of item (1) after assembly, a method frequently used to avoid tolerance build-up on precision assemblies and in gauge and tool manufacture. Replacement parts cannot then be supplied separately.

1.6 Geometrical Tolerances

Tolerance has, so far, been considered in relation to linear dimensions. It is often necessary to set limits to the variation permissible in other features of the geometry of a component, such as roundness, squareness and symmetry. This is not as easy as tolerancing linear dimensions; in BS308 a considerable effort has been made to provide conventions for expressing such tolerances clearly and unambiguously.

Fig 1.16 shows one method of dimensioning a taper part, and the interpretation to be given to this. Two perfect and concentric cones are specified, and the work is acceptable so long as its surface lies between these cones, i.e. within a defined **zone**. Fig 1.17 illustrates possible errors

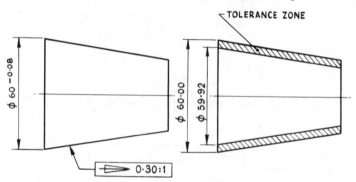

Fig. 1.16 *Taper specification and its interpretation*

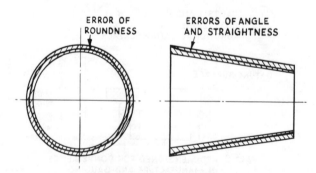

TYPES OF ERROR PERMITTED
BY TOLERANCE ZONE

Fig. 1.17

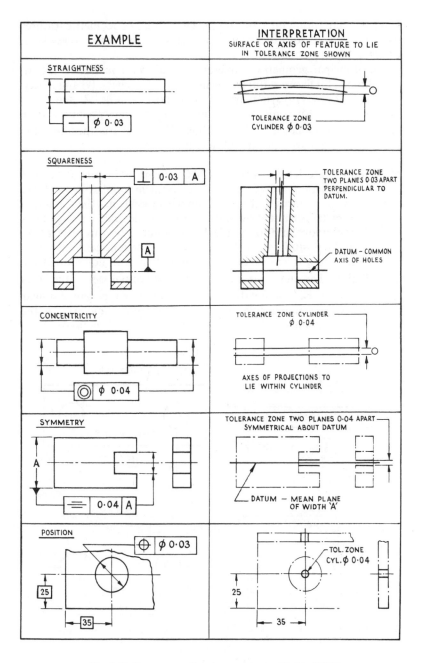

Fig. 1.18 Some geometric tolerances as specified in BS308
(Courtesy of British Standards Institution)

of a part lying within the limits given. The control of geometric features by specifying a tolerance zone is discussed for screw threads in Chapter 14.

The principal geometrical tolerances dealt with in BS308 are: (i) straightness; (ii) flatness; (iii) parallelism; (iv) squareness; (v) angularity; (vi) concentricity; (vii) symmetry; and (viii) position. Fig 1.21 shows the BS conventions for some of these, indicating the interpretation to be given to each. Dimensions boxed thus $\boxed{25}$ define true position: the symbol $\oplus$ signifies a positional tolerance.

Maximum Material Condition (MMC). From both functional and gauging considerations it is frequently convenient to relate geometrical or positional tolerances to the condition where a part has the maximum amount of metal permitted by the dimensional tolerance, e.g. high limit for a shaft and low limit for a hole. Fig 1.19 illustrates this principle in relation to the position of the holes in part B. The hole centre distance must be held to a tolerance of ± 0.1 mm only if both holes are at the lower limit of diameter. This is the meaning of symbol (M). If the holes are larger the work is acceptable provided a receiver-type gauge similar to part A will enter the holes, and provided neither hole exceeds the upper limit of diameter. The arrangements has two attractions:

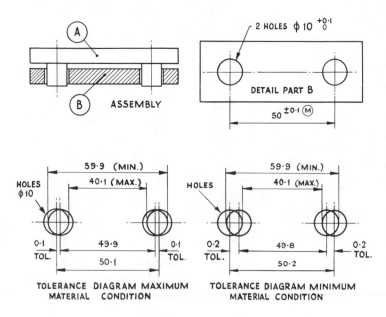

Fig. 1.19 MMC specification as BS308 Part 3: 1972
(Courtesy of British Standards Institution)

(i) the fullest possible tolerance is available to the workshops commensurate with the required accuracy of location of part A in part B;

(ii) a gauging system based upon Taylor's principles (p. 427) will control work exactly to the given specification.

If the symbol Ⓜ is removed, it is not possible to make simple limit gauges which will test the work exactly to the drawing specifications, as a careful investigation of the conditions will show.

A more complicated example of positional tolerancing is shown, by kind permission of the British Standards Institution, in Fig 1.20 reproduced from BS308 Part 3. Positions of the slots and tongue are defined relative to the bore A and keyway B. The median planes of the two slots and of the tongue are indicated by centre lines. For an actual component the real median plane of each feature would be equidistant from the machined surfaces and so not necessarily perpendicular to face C. The slots have true positions defined by $\boxed{60°}$ and $\boxed{90°}$ and positional tolerances conveyed by symbols attached to the 24·9/24·8 and 16·05/16·00 dimensions. Symbol Ⓜ appearing in three places shows that the 0·125 mm tolerance zone applies when the slot width, bore diameter and keyway width are all at maximum material condition. Should any feature depart from MMC (but remain of course within its

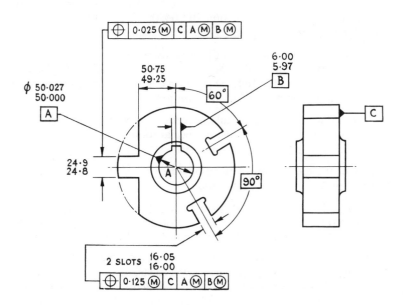

Fig. 1.20 Examples of positional tolerancing
(Courtesy of British Standards Institution)

specified tolerance) an increase in the permitted departure from the true positions of the slots is automatically allowed by this specification.

Notice how this specification simplifies gauging procedure. A receiver type gauge locating from A, B and C, used to check the positions of the slots and tongue, would be made to conform to the maximum material conditions stated and would be, in effect, a full form G0 gauge. NOT-G0 gauges for the slot and tongue widths would then give a complete dimensional check of the part.

Such a specification may appear unnecessarily complicated. The fifteen symbols now appearing in BS308 Part 3 can replace matter previously printed on many drawings, saving time and space. There arises however a problem for shop floor workers who have less opportunity to familiarise themselves with the precise meaning of so many symbols. Obviously elaborate geometrical and positional tolerancing should only be used where normal production methods may fail to achieve the required degree of accuracy. Fuller use of the conventional methods of BS308 Part 3 have advantages if work is subcontracted. They enable a "tight" specification to be drawn up as the contractual basis of such business.

1.7 Economic Aspects of Tolerancing

Designers and draughtsmen responsible for production drawings are advised to consult BS publication PD 6470:
The Management of Design for Economic Production

Consider possible methods of producing the slot shown in Fig 1.21. The tolerance on the width of the slot is too small to be held by production milling, although the position could be held by this method. The alternative methods of production are:

(a) surface broaching, suitable only if a very large quantity is required due to the high cost of special tooling;
(b) mill to 5·75/5·67 mm, finish to width by a grinding operation.

The second method is expensive because each side of the slot must be finished by a "cut-and-try" method:

(i) grind to produce dimension x using a limit gap gauge;
(ii) grind to produce $6^{+0.03}$ mm using a limit slip gauge. It will not be possible to maintain sharp corners at the bottom of the slot.

Rather than use method (b) it is likely that the production workshop will appeal to the drawing office for a revision of the tolerance. A 0·05 mm tolerance could be held on the milling operation if a machine in good condition and a well-ground cutter are used. More care will be required than if the normal 0·07 mm tolerance on the slot were available, but the saving in cost which would result from a 0·02 mm increase in

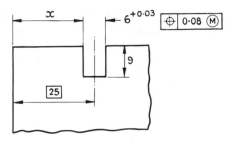

Fig. 1.21

tolerance would be substantial, and the quality of the product is hardly likely to be seriously impaired by the change.

Some examination of the method of dimensioning the position of the slot is perhaps necessary. As dimensioned, x has a tolerance of 0·08 mm minimum, more if the slot exceeds 6 mm in width. Suppose the $\boxed{25}$ true position dimension and positional tolerance of 0·08 ⓜ are omitted, limits must then be given for dimension x. The position of the centre of the slot is now subject to tolerance build-up, and the tolerance for x will be $0·08 - 0·015 = 0·065$. The limits of x are found as follows:

$$x_{max} + 3·015 = 25·04$$
$$x_{max} = \underline{22·025} \text{ mm}$$

$$x_{min} + 3·00 = 24·96$$
$$x_{min} = \underline{21·96} \text{ mm}$$

Limits of $x = 22·025/21·96$; tolerance 0·065 mm. The method of dimensioning given in Fig 1.21 is superior to a method giving limits of x if the work is to be made in quantity and controlled by limit gauging.

Economic Tolerance. 1.7 has shown that production costs are closely linked to the tolerances specified. It may be an invitation to criticism to lay down in very precise terms what tolerances can reasonably be held by the common manufacturing processes. Table 1.5 is included as a guide only, and the actual values which may be worked to in industry will reflect the quality of the equipment and skill of the operators, both of which vary considerably.

Example 1.6

Fig 1.22 gives details of an assembly. Shaft C is to be ground parallel, the holes of A and B are to be bored, the tongue and slot are to be produced by milling. A is to be a press fit on C, B is to be an easy sliding fit on C. The tongue of B is to engage in the slot of A in either possible position with a minimum of "play".

Set suitable limits to the basic dimensions given and make a dimensioned drawing of part B suitable for quantity manufacture.

TABLE 1.5
Tolerances Associated with Manufacturing Processes

Process	Tolerance (mm)	Tol grade
Sand casting: Small Large	± 0.3 ± 1.6	IT16
Forging and drop forging: Small Large	± 0.8 ± 1.5	IT15–IT16
Die-casting, plastic moulding Precision die-cast zinc alloys	General ± 0.4 0.05–0.2	IT14 IT10–IT12
Press work, tube drawing and extrusion	0.1–1.4	IT10–IT13
Planing and shaping	0.1–0n3	IT10–IT11
Drilling: 6–12 mm 12–20 mm	0.1 0.18	IT11–IT12
Reaming: 6–25 mm Over 25 mm	0.02 0.035 upwards	IT7–IT8
Milling: Gang milling Small slots	0.08–0.12 0.05–0.08	IT8–IT10
Turning: capstan and turret lathes, roller box to 18 mm dia Turning: 25–50 mm dia Over 50 mm dia	0.05 0.10 0.12 upwards	IT8–IT10
Broaching: Up to 25 mm dia 25–50 mm dia	0.02 0.04	IT7–IT8
Honing, up to 50 mm dia	0.01–0.016	IT6
Grinding: Up to 25 mm dia 25–50 mm dia	0.007–0.012 0.012–0.016	IT5–IT6
Lapping, machine	0.002–0.01	IT4–IT5
Lapping, standards, reference guages etc.	Less than 0.002	IT01–IT3

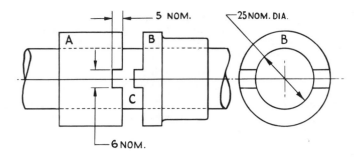

Fig. 1.22

Solution
The hole and shaft fits are shaft based because the shaft is parallel and the holes must differ to give the required fits. Suitable fits from the selected range are:

Shaft h6   Hole A, P7
       Hole B, F8

The reader can find the limits in BS4500.

The slot in A will be milled with a standard side and face cutter of 6 mm width, suitable limits are 6·00 + 0·07. There must also be a positional tolerance for the slot, say 0·05 Ⓜ , from **datum-bore** D Ⓜ

The tongue of B must have a positional tolerance, say same as for the slot in A. The maximum mis-alignment of the centre line of tongue and slot at Ⓜ will be 0·05 and the tongue will need to be − 0·01 in width to accommodate this in both possible positions.

The tongue will need a tolerance on width, for straddle milling, say 0·07.

Limits for the tongue are: 6 − 0·10 and 6 − 0·10 − 0·07, i.e. 5·90/5·83. Note that there are no special cutters required for this work. An adjustable type of arbor collar can be used for spacing the cutters of the straddle milling operation. The dimensioning of part B is shown in Fig 1.23

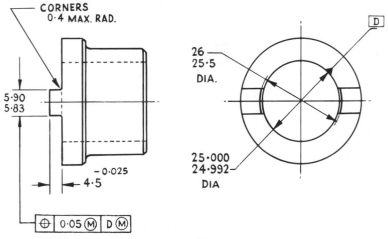

Fig. 1.23

The solution has been worked without detailed reference to BS4500, and for purely exercise purposes this is satisfactory. It is generally desirable to use the standard limits where appropriate, and for the example given a 6 mm H11/c11 fit would be satisfactory, limits:

$$\begin{array}{lll} \text{H11} & \text{slot} & 6\cdot075/6\cdot000 \\ \text{C11} & \text{tongue} & 5\cdot930/5\cdot855 \end{array}$$

For such work it is unlikely that gauges will be obtainable from stock, but use of the standard system saves considerable clerical work when ordering gauges and reduces the likelihood of clerical errors.

Example 1.7
A shaft is to be hard chrome plated and finished ground to 32 mm g6 diameter. The minimum thickness of plating deposit remaining is to be 0·05 mm the maximum grinding allowance to be 0·20 mm on diameter; the tolerance on the initial grinding is to be 0·02 mm, and on the plating to be 0·05 , on diameter. Find the process limits and illustrate the relationships involved in a diagram of fits.

Solution
The easiest method of solution is to sketch a tolerance diagram building up the limits as follows.

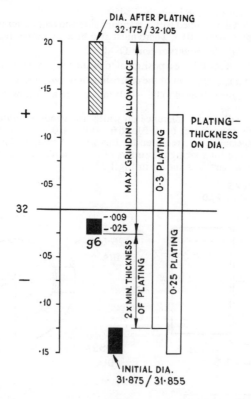

Fig. 1.24 Tolerance diagram for Example 11.7

Final limits of shaft, 31·991/31·975 mm
If the maximum grinding allowance is to be 0·20 mm the maximum diameter before final grinding must be 32·175 mm.
If the minimum plating thickness is to be 0·05 mm the maximum dia of the initial grinding must be 31·975 − 0·1 = 31·875. The initial grinding dia is 31·875/31·855 mm.
For a 0·05 mm tol on the plating, the limits after plating will be 32·175 − 0·07 = 32·105 mm dia (tolerance build-up). The relationships are clearly shown in Fig 1.24.

EXERCISES 1

1. Describe ways in which the production engineer can co-operate with the design engineer in a common endeavour to produce mass-produced engineering equipment of good quality at a low price and in accordance with the majority demands of the potential customers.
2. (a) State the principles and advantages of standardisation.
(b) Indicate how standardisation can be applied within a company.
(c) What are the advantages of preferred numbers? Give an example of their application.
3. (a) Give reasons why a system of interchangeable manufacture of the component parts of assemblies required in quantity is economically advantageous.
(b) By reference to an 18 mm nominal close running fit, discuss the requirements of such a system under the following headings:

    (i) size specification on the workshop drawings;
    (ii) component inspection;
    (iii) standards of length and precision measurement.

4. (a) Give a brief explanation of "preferred sizes". A product is to be marketed in a range of sizes, from 1 to 4 kW inclusive, based upon the R10 series rounded to the nearest $\frac{1}{4}$ kW. Determine the sizes.
(b) A hole and shaft fit, nominal size 44·5 mm, is designated H7/g6. The maximum possible clearance is 0·05 mm; the minimum 0·009 mm. The hole tolerance is 1·6 times the shaft tolerance. Find the hole and shaft limits. Represent the same fit symbolically on a shaft basis and write the new limits.
5. (a) Explain how dimensional tolerance affects the economy of manufacturing processes with reference to: (i) the machine used; (ii) the method of inspection.
(b) In BS4500 the fundamental tolerance unit (0·001 mm) is derived from,

$$i = 0.45 \sqrt[3]{D} + 0.001 D \qquad D \leqslant 500$$

where D is the geometric mean (in mm) of the diameter steps. Comment upon the significance of the terms in this expression.
Why is a different formula used for i when D exceeds 500 mm?
6. Fig 1.25 shows an assembly of cylindrical parts giving the nominal lengths and the tolerances to be achieved on assembly. Sketch the parts A, B and C separately and on each sketch dimension the lengths required to achieve the fitting conditions. The minimum tolerance on any length is to be 0·10 mm, tolerances are to be specified in multiples of 0·05 mm, and dimensions must be given from suitable datum faces.
7. Fig 1.26 shows a specification for a taper seating. Find the nominal value of diameter D and, to the nearest 0·02 mm, the maximum variation which can occur in this dimension.

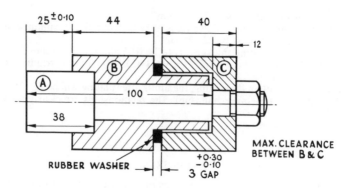

Fig. 1.25

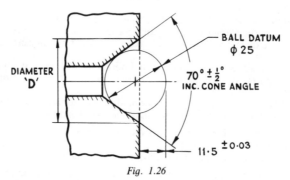

Fig. 1.26

Comment on the tolerance of the 11·5 mm dimension in relation to the angular tolerance.

What particular value is there in this method of dimensioning a taper seating?

8. The specification for a jig-boring machine includes guarantees of accuracy as set out below:

(i) travel of main table is straight over 600 mm to within 0·0025 mm;
(ii) travel of auxiliary table is straight over 450 mm to within 0·0025 mm;
(iii) mean travel of auxiliary table is at right angles to the mean travel of the main table within 2 sec of arc;
(iv) the main and auxiliary tables may be positioned to an accuracy of 0·0012 mm over any 50 mm and 0·0025 mm over any 250 mm.

If the above equipment is used to bore the holes shown in Fig 1.27, calculate the maximum possible error between any two adjacent holes. With the above data as a basis, specify positional tolerances for the six holes.

9. Fig 1.28, reproduced by kind permission of the BSI, shows four geometric tolerances. (The symbol ⤴ signifies "run out").

(a) Using notes and sketches explain what each means.
(b) Find the maximum permitted distances of the 6·5/6·4 mm diameter holes from the centre line of datum A when;
(i) their diameters (including datum A also) are at maximum material condition;
(ii) the diameters are at minimum material condition.

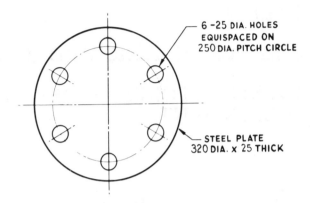

Fig. 1.27

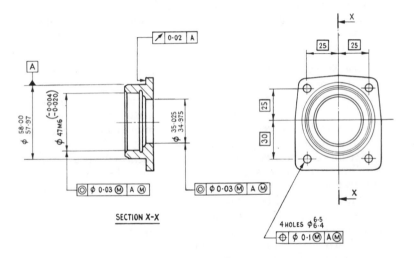

Fig. 1.28

10. A bore is required to be hard chrome plated and finished ground to 57·805/57·790 mm dia. The minimum plating thickness after grinding is to be 0·10 mm the minimum grinding allowance after plating is to be 0·15 mm on dia. The maximum plating thickness to be deposited is 0·28 mm and this can be achieved within a tolerance of 0·08 mm on thickness.

Determine the limits of size of the bore: (i) before plating; (ii) after plating. What is the maximum thickness of plating possible on a finished component? A diagram is expected.

CHAPTER 2
Mechanics of Machine Tools
PART A STRUCTURES, SLIDEWAYS AND ALIGNMENTS

2.1 Basic Features of a Machine Tool

A machine tool provides the means for cutting tools to shape a workpiece to required dimensions; the machine supports the tool and the workpiece in a controlled relationship through the functioning of its basic members, which are as follows:

(a) *Bed, Structure or Frame.* This is the main member which provides a basis for, and a connection between, the spindles and slides; the distortion and vibration under load must be kept to a minimum.

(b) *Slides and Slideways.* The translation of a machine element (e.g. the slide) is normally achieved by straight-line motion under the constraint of accurate guiding surfaces (the slideway).

(c) *Spindles and Bearings.* Angular displacements take place about an axis of rotation; the position of this axis must be constant within extremely fine limits in machine tools, and is ensured by the provision of precision spindles and bearings.

(d) *Power Units.* The electric motor is the universally adopted power unit for machine tools. By suitably positioning individual motors, belt and gear drives are reduced to a minimum.

(e) *Transmission Linkage.* Linkage is the general term used to denote the mechanical, hydraulic, pneumatic or electric mechanisms which connect angular and linear displacements in defined relationships.

2.2 Forces in a Machine Tool

Stresses which tend to deform the machine tool or workpiece are caused by the following:

(*a*) Static loads, i.e. the weight of the machine and its various parts as considered on p. 40.

(*b*) Dynamic loads, i.e. forces induced by rotating or reciprocating masses.

(*c*) Cutting forces, as discussed in Chapters 6–9.

There are two broad divisions of machining operations:

(*a*) Roughing, for which the metal removal rate and consequently the cutting force is high, but the required dimensional accuracy relatively low.

(*b*) Finishing, for which the metal removal rate, and consequently the cutting force, is low, but the required dimensional accuracy and surface finish relatively high.

It follows from the foregoing considerations that static loads (the position of which may vary as slideways are displaced) and dynamic loads such as result from an unbalanced grinding wheel are more significant in finishing operations than in roughing operations. The degree of precision achieved in any machining process is usually influenced by the magnitude of the deflections which occur as a result of the forces acting.

Machine tools are regularly required to work to 0·02mm and often to 0·002 mm in dimensional accuracy. The permissible amounts of elastic flexure of the main frame and its subsidiary units must be small to achieve this degree of accuracy. The machine as a structure cannot be designed by normal stressing methods where load-carrying capacity is the criterion, but must be designed to have negligible deflection and provide generous bearing surfaces so as to diminish wear. To achieve this, the section modulus must be made as large as possible without giving rise to excessive weight. This leads to the employment of very deep sections, such as shown in Fig 2.1.

Symbolically, for the given section:

Deflection, $\qquad\qquad \Delta y \propto 1/I$

where I = 2nd moment of area

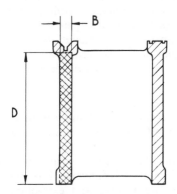

Fig. 2.1 Cross-section through slideways of grinding machine

The depth of section, D, is substantial to ensure maximum resistance to deflection.

Now, for a rectangular section $I = BD^3/12$

$\therefore$ $I \propto D^3$ when thickness of casting is constant

hence, $\Delta y \propto 1/D^3$

The proportions of the section in Fig 2.1 give a high resistance to bending for moderate metal thickness; a large aperture (say, for a cupboard) in beds having this type of section would reduce the value of D and permit greater deflection, and therefore should be avoided.

2.3 Structural Elements

Machine tool frames are generally made in cast iron, although some may be steel castings or mild-steel fabrications. Cast iron is chosen because of its cheapness, rigidity, compressive strength and capacity for damping the vibrations set up in machining operations.

The cost factor deserves more than a passing mention and the following points should be noted:

(*a*) the price of cast iron is about twice that of mild-steel plate, but it includes the cost of moulding.

(*b*) Cast iron is the cheapest metal, consistent with strength, which can be used to produce *castings*. Steel castings are much more costly to produce.

(*c*) The cost of pattern and core boxes must be spread over the number of castings produced.

(*d*) The greater strength in tension of mild steel often permits thinner sections than those required in cast iron, but this lower cost of material is offset by the expense of cutting and welding.

From a consideration of the above factors it is apparent that steel fabrications have certain advantages to offer, particularly when the cost of the pattern has to be borne by a single casting or when time cannot be spared for making a pattern. Two reasons why steel is not more widely used for machine-tool frames is because of its greater resonance and because castings can be more easily produced in aesthetically pleasing shapes.

To avoid massive sections in casting, carefully designed systems of ribbing are used to offer the maximum resistance to bending and torsional stresses.

Two basic types of ribbing are (*a*) box, and (*b*) diagonal, as illustrated in Fig 2.2. The box formation is convenient to produce, apertures in the walls permitting the positioning and extraction of cores. Diagonal ribbing provides greater torsional stiffness and yet permits swarf to fall between the sections; it is frequently used for lathe beds.

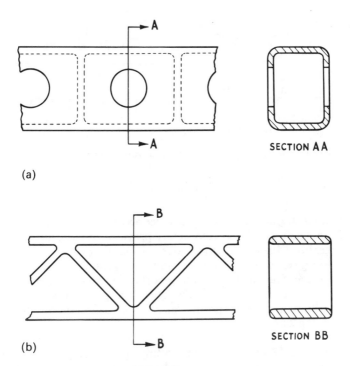

Fig. 2.2 *Basic sections for cast structural members*
(a) Box ribbing
(b) Diagonal ribbing

Support of Frames. Structural members of machine-tool frames are supported to conform as closely as possible with the Kinematic Principles outlined in Chapter 3, but for a large member additional points of support are needed to avoid the "sag" caused by its own weight plus the applied loads. Such conditions can occur in the foundation supports of a machine, e.g. small cylindrical grinding machines can be supported at three points, Fig 2.3(a), whereas a very large machine would need support at a greater number of points, Fig 2.3(b). In the latter case periodic checks should be made to ensure that the straightness and accuracy of slideways have been maintained.

Two other considerations affecting the method of support for frame members are:

(a) adequate space for the workpiece;
(b) accessibility of the workpiece for operator convenience.

These are often complementary factors, but they may be opposed to the type of support which gives the greatest resistance to deflection. An

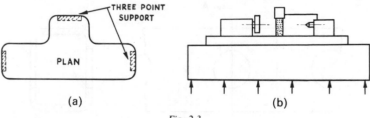

Fig. 2.3

(a) Kinematic principles applied to the method used in supporting a small external grinding machine

(b) Multi-point support applied to a large external grinding machine to prevent sag of machine bed

example illustrating the alternative choice occurs in a jig boring machine. Some designers prefer the accessibility provided by the cantilever-type machine, Fig 2.4(a), while others consider that the portal frame design, Fig 2.4(b), gives reasonable accessibility and a greater degree of support for the beam. Should the beam in a portal frame sag, its slope is zero midway between the supports, consequently a spindle situated near the centre will maintain a perpendicular axis (see deflection of equivalent beam in Fig 2.6).

Deflection of Machine Elements. Many spindles, Fig 2.5, and structural members of machine tools can be considered as cantilever, simply

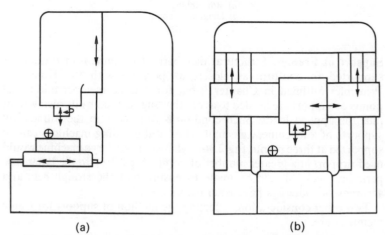

Fig. 2.4 Alternatives in the basic design of jig boring machines illustrating typical methods of supporting structural members of a machine tool

(a) Column-type machine
(b) Portal beam type machine

(⊕ indicates translation of slide in direction perpendicular to the page.)

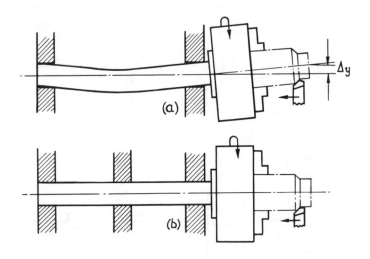

Fig. 2.5 Lathe spindle considered as a beam

(*a*) Deflection (Δy) at tool point caused by bending of inadequately supported spindle
(*b*) The introduction of an intermediate bearing greatly reduces deflection of long
spindles

supported or built-in beams. Although text-book conditions rarely apply in practice, the effectiveness of these designs from the point of view of resistance to deflection can be compared by reference to expressions giving the deflection of beams. Examples are shown in Fig 2.6 together with idealised applications from common types of machine tool. Examples of modifications to the designs shown in the idealised diagrams so as to improve performance are:

(*a*) increase in section depth proportionate to the bending moment for the drilling machine arm;

(*b*) widening the legs of the lathe and so approximating the bed to a built-in beam.

A device used to minimise deflection and give a balanced load is the counter-weight shown in Fig 2.7; also the force required for vertical movement of the slide is reduced by this means. An example of the use of this method is found on horizontal boring machines.

2.4 Slides and Slideways

The slides and slideways of a machine tool locate and guide members which move relative to each other, usually changing the position of the tool relative to the workpiece. The movement generally takes the form of translation in a straight line, but is sometimes angular rotation, e.g.

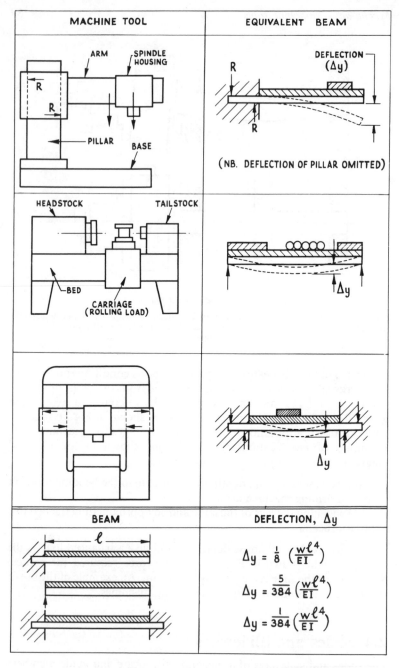

MACHINE TOOL	EQUIVALENT BEAM
ARM — SPINDLE HOUSING — R — R — PILLAR — BASE	DEFLECTION — (Δy) — R — R (NB. DEFLECTION OF PILLAR OMITTED)
HEADSTOCK — TAILSTOCK — BED — CARRIAGE (ROLLING LOAD)	Δy
	Δy

BEAM	DEFLECTION, Δy
ℓ	$\Delta y = \frac{1}{8}\left(\frac{w\ell^4}{EI}\right)$
	$\Delta y = \frac{5}{384}\left(\frac{w\ell^4}{EI}\right)$
	$\Delta y = \frac{1}{384}\left(\frac{w\ell^4}{EI}\right)$

Fig. 2.6 Machine-tool members considered as beams

(Note the relative magnitudes of Δy for the three basic beams shown at the bottom of the diagram.)

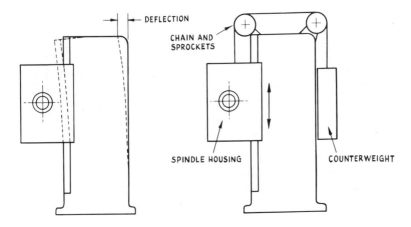

Fig. 2.7 Counterweight balancing of an asymmetrical load to prevent deflection of column and to reduce the effort needed to move the sliding unit

tilting the wheel-head of a universal thread-grinding machine to an angle corresponding with the helix angle of the workpiece thread.

Features of slideways are as follows:

(a) *Accuracy of Movement.* Where a slide is to be displaced in a straight line, this line must lie in *two* mutually perpendicular planes and there must be no "crosswind", i.e. slide rotation (the principles of slide movements are analysed in Chapter 3). The general tolerance for straightness of machine tool slideways is 0–0·02 mm per 1000 mm; on horizontal surfaces this tolerance may be disposed so that a convex surface results, thus countering the effect of "sag" of the slideway.

(b) *Means of Adjustment.* To facilitate assembly, maintain accuracy and eliminate "play" between sliding members after wear has taken place, a strip is sometimes inserted in the slides. This is called a gib-strip, and a simple design using this device is shown in Fig 2.9(*b*). In this example the gib is retained by socket-head screws passing through elongated slots and is adjusted by grub-screws secured by lock-nuts. Minimum slideway wear is achieved by low-pressure conditions (assuming lubrication is adequate), i.e. for a given load, the greater the contact area, the lower will be the wear rate.

(c) *Lubrication.* Slideways may be lubricated by either of the following systems:

(i) Intermittently through grease or oil nipples, a method suitable where movements are infrequent and speeds low.

(ii) Continuously, e.g. by pumping through a metering valve and pipework to the point of application; the film of oil introduced between surfaces by these means must be extremely thin to avoid the slide "floating" (see Hydrostatic Slideways, p. 48). If sliding surfaces

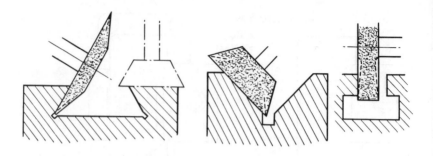

Fig. 2.8 Methods employed for surface grinding machine tool slideways

Note: Line contact, e.g. edge of cup wheel, between wheel and slide surface is extensively employed.

were optically flat oil would be squeezed out, resulting in the surfaces "wringing" together like slip gauges, and resisting movement. Hence, in practice slide surfaces are either ground using the edge of a cup wheel, Fig 2.8, or scraped. Both processes produce minute surface depressions which retain "pockets" of oil, and complete separation of the parts may not occur at all points; positive location of the slides is thus retained.

(d) *Protection.* To maintain slideways in good order, the following conditions must be met:

(i) Ingress of foreign matter, e.g. swarf, must be prevented. Where this is not possible, it is desirable to have a form of slideway which does not retain swarf, e.g. the inverted vee.

(ii) Lubricating oil must be retained. The adhesive property of oil for use on vertical or inclined slide surface is important; oils are available which have been specially developed for this purpose. The adhesiveness of an oil also prevents it being washed away by cutting fluids.

(iii) Accidental damage must be prevented by protective guards. These can be of the rigid, sliding, "concertina" bellows or roller-blind type.

Basic Types of Slideways. The basic geometric elements of slides are the flat, vee, dovetail and cylinder. These elements may be used separately or combined in various ways according to the application. The design shown in Fig 2.9(a) provides a simple, effective slide, free of unnecessary constraints, straightforward to manufacture and one which permits regrinding or rescraping of the slide surfaces. If two vees are used redundant constraints are present, and the difficulties of manufacture considerably increased, because a high degree of accuracy is required in order to obtain a perfect fit between the two sets of vees.

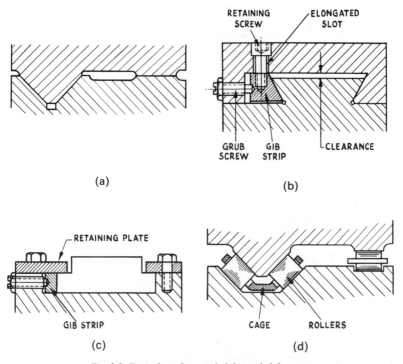

Fig. 2.9 *Typical machine tool slides and slideways*

(*a*) Vee and flat
(*b*) Dovetail (with gib strip)
(*c*) Square edge (with gib strip)
(*d*) Vee and flat using rollers

Dovetail slides, Fig 2.9(*b*), are used where an upward movement of the slide must be prevented. The effect of tightening the adjusting gib-strip is to pull the sliding members into closer contact, thus eliminating "lift" and reducing vibrational tendencies. The square-edge slide shown in Fig 2.9(*c*) is provided with adjustment on one side, the two retaining plates prevent lifting of the slide.

An extension of the vee-and-flat slideway is illustrated in Fig 2.9(*d*). Rollers retained in brass cages are interposed between the sliding members; by this means rolling friction is substituted for sliding friction. The method has been in use for many years on the wheelhead sideways of Matrix thread-grinding machines. The heavy wheelhead unit of such a machine is required to make very small displacements (often as little as a few thousandths of a millimetre) positively and with a light control. The rolling motion of this type of slideway provides the necessary sensitiveness of response and movement.

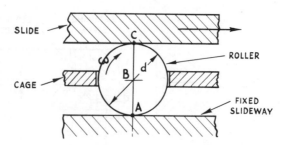

Fig. 2.10 Relative movements of slide, roller and cage

Slide displacement = 2 × linear displacement of roller and cage.

One point in regard to roller cages which should be noted is that their linear displacement is only half the displacement of the slide. This is made clear by reference to Fig 2.10.

Let *A* be the instantaneous centre, then

$$\text{Velocity of } B = \omega d/2 \quad \text{and} \quad \text{Velocity of } C = \omega d$$

Hence in any time interval, *t*, *C* will move twice as far as *B*.

The principle of rolling slideways has been extended to the use of slide units of the roller recirculating type, Fig 2.11 (cf. recirculating ball and

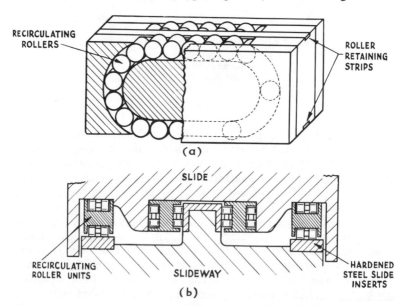

Fig. 2.11

(*a*) Recirculating-roller slide unit
(*b*) Application of units to a machine tool slideway

nut, p. 64). In addition to advantages of minimum friction and wear, and the elimination of "stick-slip" (p. 48), the length of slide travel is not limited by the use of these recirculating type roller-ways.

Narrow Guide Principle. This important principle is illustrated by the vee guide and to a lesser extent by the dovetail and square-edge slides. To prevent "jamming" of slides (cf. with the jamming of a sash window) the width between the guiding surfaces must be limited relative to the length of the guide. The application of the narrow guide principle is particularly important when the feed force of the sliding member is applied eccentrically.

Example 2.1
A slide, Fig 2.12, of weight W is caused to move by force F acting parallel to the slideway and distance e from the centre line. Obtain expressions for

    (a) magnitude of force F;
    (b) the minimum value of e for which jamming will occur.

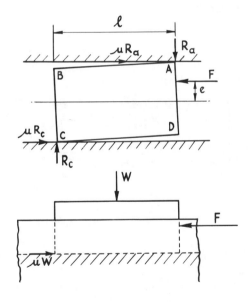

Fig. 2.12

Solution
    (a) If the eccentricity of force F is assumed to slightly tilt the slide, then reaction of sides of slideway will act at A and C respectively; since $R_a = R_c$ the reactions may be represented by R.

    ∴   The resistance due to friction, at each side of slideway = $\mu . R$

    Also, frictional resistance to slide motion on lower surface = $\mu . W$

Hence, for equilibrium at the limiting conditions,

$$F = \mu W + 2\mu R \tag{2.1}$$

Taking moments about a point on the centre line (μR then has no moment)

$$Rl = Fe$$
$$\therefore \quad R = Fe/l \tag{2.2}$$

Substitute for R in Eqn (2.1)

$$F = \mu W + 2\mu Fe/l$$
$$F(1 - 2\mu e/l) = \mu W$$
$$\therefore \quad F = \frac{\mu W}{1 - 2\mu e/l} \tag{2.3}$$

(b) From Eqn (2.3) it can be seen that if $e = l/2\mu$ the denominator becomes zero and hence F is infinite,

$$\therefore \quad \underline{\text{When } e \geqslant l/2\mu \text{ the slide will jam}} \tag{2.4}$$

A similar analysis applied to a vee and flat slide, Fig 2.13, gives the following relationships.

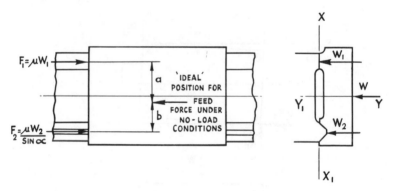

Fig. 2.13 Forces acting on a simple slide

The distribution of weight W will be W_1 and W_2 on the flat and vee slides respectively.

Resolving W_2 to obtain forces normal to the vee surfaces, Fig 2.14

$$R_1 + R_2 = W_2/\sin \alpha$$

where α = semi-angle of vee

$\quad \therefore \quad$ Frictional resistance of vee slideway $\quad F_2 = \mu W_2/\sin \alpha$

$\quad$ Also, Frictional resistance of flat slideway $\quad F_1 = \mu W_1$

$\quad \therefore \quad$ Under no-load conditions, feed force $\quad F = F_1 + F_2$

$$= \mu(W_1 + W_2/\sin \alpha)$$

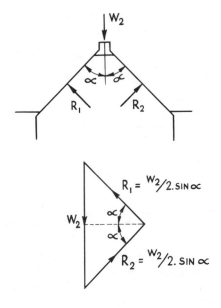

Fig 2.14

The ideal point of application for the feed force under these conditions is the position for which no turning moment acts on the sliding member, i.e. when

$$a \times F_1 = b \times F_2 \quad \text{(see Fig 2.13)}$$

For any other position of the feed force the vee slide must provide a restraining couple, thus increasing frictional resistance and the magnitude of the feed force.

When slideways support approximately symmetrical loads, e.g. the table slideways of a jig boring machine, "ideal" position for the feed force is easily determined, but where unsymmetrical loads are supported, the position is less readily found.

Fig 2.15 shows the resultant cutting force which acts on a lathe saddle. Its magnitude and point of application will vary according to the dimensions of the cut and the diameter turned. Thus, it is not possible to fix an ideal position for the application of the feed force because of these variations in the cutting force, and the position finally chosen, may be influenced as much by design convenience as by a consideration of the forces met in operation.

Slideways for Programme-controlled Machines. The operation of tape-controlled machines makes functional demands which go beyond the requirements for a machine handled by an operator. One of these

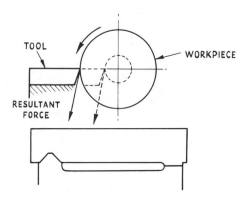

TOOL

WORKPIECE

RESULTANT
FORCE

*Fig. 2.15 Position (and direction) of the resultant cutting force acting on the
tool when turning, depends upon many factors, including size of workpiece*

demands is that the response of a slide to a signal shall be positive and
almost instantaneous. Because of the weight of the average slide, this
requirement is not met by conventional slideway construction, and as a
result slideways have been developed to keep the frictional resistance as
low as possible.

(*a*) Slides may be mounted on rollers, see pp. 43–44 and Figs 2.9(*d*)
and 2.11.

(*b*) In hydrostatic or aerostatic slideways, the principle of which is
illustrated in Fig 2.16, the slide floats on a film of pressurised oil or air.
Maximum stiffness and damping is obtained by using a very thin fluid
film which must remain constant in thickness under varying conditions of loading in order to maintain accuracy in the position of the
slide.

(*c*) Low friction materials may be employed for sliding surfaces in
places of the usual cast iron or steel, e.g. sintered bronze impregnated
with the plastic PTFE (polytetrafluoroethylene, C_2F_4). The coefficient of friction of PTFE on ground steel surfaces is 0·04.

Stick–Slip. An important advantage possessed by low friction slideways is uniformity of motion at low speeds and the elimination of
stick–slip.

Stick–slip is the alternate sticking and slipping which occurs when
partially lubricated slides operate at low speed. This produces a saw-
tooth form of friction force variation in the stick–slip range illustrated by
the graph Fig 2.17. Under these conditions a machine-tool slide will
remain stationary until the feed force has reached a magnitude sufficient
to overcome static friction, the slide will then be accelerated by the
applied force, but this movement will be immediately followed by a
tendency for the slide to decelerate or come to rest. This unstable motion

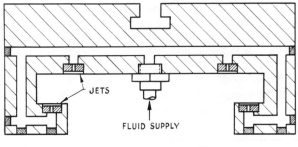

SECTION THROUGH **XX**

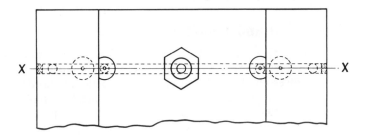

Fig. 2.16 Principle of the hydrostatic slide for machine tools

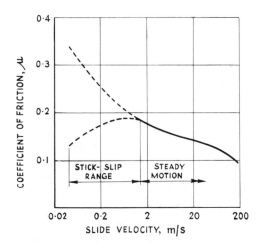

Fig. 2.17 Variation in coefficient of friction during movement of a slide

is repeated in rapid succession, often being so pronounced as to cause a noticeable low frequency vibration of the slide.

Stick–slip motion is one of the factors which makes fine adjustment of a slide difficult. For example, if the wheelhead of a grinding machine is to be adjusted to remove 0·01 mm from the diameter of a workpiece the slide must move 0·005 mm. If sticking occurs in the slide, no cut will result, and if the operator makes a second adjustment, the sticking may be overcome but the wheelhead may move forward the total adjustment of 0·01 mm, thus removing 0·02 mm from the workpiece diameter instead of the intended 0·01 mm.

When such trouble occurs on conventional machines it can be mitigated by the use of one of the special lubricants developed for the specific purpose of reducing static friction.

2.5 Vibration and Chatter

Chatter in machining operations is an objectional manifestation of vibration in the machine, tool or workpiece; it affects surface finish, accuracy, and adversely affects the life of carbide or ceramic-tipped tools.

Research into the vibrational characteristics of machine tools is a complex matter calling for advanced experimental techniques. Investigations on a vertical milling machine carried out by Dr Tobias at Cambridge University showed the behaviour of this machine under vibrations induced by an exciting force, and also related the severity of chatter to the relative cutter/workpiece position.

Excitation of the machine table in a vertical plane produced conditions from which the resonance curve, Fig 2.18, was plotted; the relative

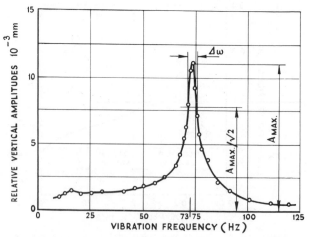

Fig. 2.18 Resonance curve for vertical excitation of milling machine
(Exciting force = 122N rms)
(Courtesy I.Mech.E.)

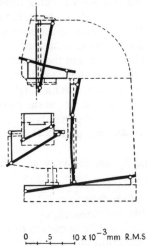

0   5 10×10^{-3}mm R.M.S
AMPLITUDE SCALE

Fig. 2.19 *Vertical mode of vibration of milling machine*
(*Courtesy I.Mech.E.*)

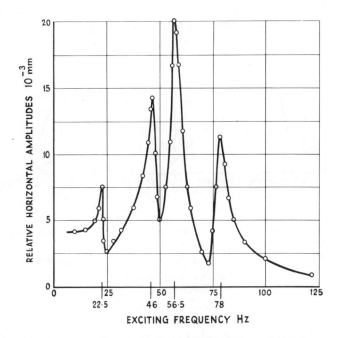

Fig. 2.20 *Resonance curve for horizontal excitation of milling machines*
(*Exciting force = 122N rms*)
(*Courtesy I.Mech.E.*)

amplitudes between table and spindle being measured by a capacitance pick-up. The vibration mode produced by an induced vibration at 73 Hz is illustrated in Fig 2.19. The thin continuous lines represent surfaces from which the amplitudes were measured, and the thick lines the maximum deflection. The distance of the circles from the thin base lines represents the amplitude of the dynamic deflection.

Horizontal excitation of the machine table produced vibrations represented by the curve, Fig 2.20, which shows peaks corresponding to four modes of vibration. The alignments of spindle and table at the excitation frequencies of 46, 56·5 and 78 Hz are illustrated in Fig 2.21.

Factors determining the modes vary at different frequencies, but included among them are:

(*a*) stiffness of the foundation;
(*b*) stiffness of table and cross-slides;
(*c*) bending and torsional deformation of knee, column and head;
(*d*) strength of connection between knee and column.

The behaviour of the machine tested led to the recommendations:

(i) slides, slideways and retaining strips need to be of substantial proportions to ensure stiffness, and where retaining strips are used there should be an adequate number of retaining bolts, otherwise flexure may result from elasticity at this source;

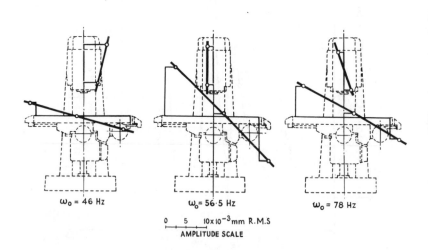

$\omega_0 = 46$ Hz $\omega_0 = 56·5$ Hz $\omega_0 = 78$ Hz

0   5 10×10^{-3} mm R.M.S
AMPLITUDE SCALE

Fig. 2.21 Alignment of spindle and table of milling machine in the horizontal modes
(Courtesy I.Mech.E.)

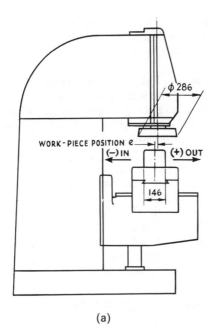

(a)

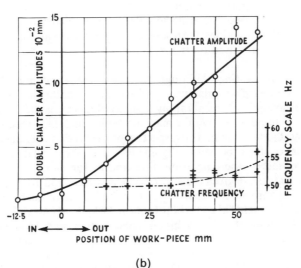

(b)

Fig. 2.22 The effect on chatter of relative workpiece and cutter position

(a) Details of the milling machine set-up:
    No. of teeth = 32, Workpiece material = CI, Cutter speed = 126 rev/min,
        Cutter feed rate = 584 mm/min, Depth of cut = 1·9 mm
(b) Variation of chatter amplitude and frequency as a function of workpiece position
                condition stated at (a)   (*Courtesy I.Mech. E.*)

(ii) apertures in the column, e.g. for the motor, should be kept as small as possible as the flexure of the column of the machine under test was largely determined by such an aperture.

Effect of Cutter Position Relative to Workpiece. The conditions used to test the relationship between chatter in vertical milling and the eccenetricity of the workpiece position relative to the cutter axis are shown in Fig 2.22(*a*). The graph, Fig 2.22(*b*), plotted from results obtained in the test, clearly shows an increase in chatter amplitude as the table is moved outwards. The report also states that during the investigations newly sharpened cutters gave rise to increased chatter until the initial sharpness was removed. With very dull cutters chatter of a higher frequency was experienced.

For detailed findings of the investigation reference should be made to the paper "Vibrations of Vertical Milling Machines Under Test and Working Conditions" by Dr S. A. Tobias, published by the Institution of Mechanical Engineers, which has has kindly given permission to reproduce the diagrams in this section.

2.6 Machine-tool Alignments

Machine-tool alignments are tested to ensure the machine is capable of consistently producing components to the accuracy demanded by standard tolerances. The method of testing is related to the type of machine and its functions; the tolerance magnitudes to its quality and the class of work produced on the machine.

Principles of Testing. Although there are many different types of machine tool each with its own arrangement of spindles and slideways, certain elemental alignments apply to many of them; e.g. the perpendicularity of a spindle axis with a machine table. Such alignments can be tested by standard methods irrespective of the type of machine, but the inter-relationships between alignments—and their relative importance—depend on the type of machine and its function.

These factors are given the appropriate emphasis and arrangement in standard alignment test charts, but in the absence of such charts **the essential alignments of a machine tool can be logically established from a consideration of the machine's construction and its method of functioning.**

Basic Alignment Tests. The basic alignment tests may be sectionalised under the following headings:

1. Tables and Slideways.
2. Spindles.
3. Spindle-axis alignment with another feature.
4. Performance Tests.

BS3800, Methods for Testing the Accuracy of Machine Tools, gives details of suitable tests.

Some suitable tests are given in Tables 2.1–2.3. Tolerances are quoted to give the student some concept of the accuracy involved in the alignments of high-quality machine tools. It will be appreciated that tolerances will be increased for large machines and that tolerances for grinding machines will, in general, be less than those permitted on, say, horizontal boring machines. Hence, the figures given for tolerances in the following section are for general guidance—when alignment tests are actually carried out, reference should be made to standard test charts such as those contained in the relevant parts of BS4656, or to "Testing Machine Tools" by Georg Schlesinger (Machinery Publishing Co. Ltd.).

TABLE 2.1

Table and Slideways

	Description of test	Example of tolerance magnitude	Diagram illustrating method of testing
(a)	Straightness	$\pm0.02/1000$	
(b)	Flatness (In the case of parallel slideways, flatness implies the absence of "twist") *Note:* For details of the techniques employed for straightness and flatness testing see 12·8 and 12·9	$\pm0.02/1000$	
(c)	Perpendicularity of Two Slideways (It is important to realise that this test must be carried out in *two* planes as shown in each of the diagrams)	$0.02/300$	Fig 2.23 (a) and (b)

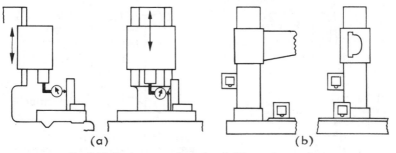

(a)   (b)

Fig. 2.23 Testing perpendicularity of slideways in two planes

(a) Dial indicator method   (b) Spirit level method

Note: (i) Machines must be satisfactorily supported and level before alignment tests are commenced, otherwise twist or deformation may be induced in the frame or its members. A spirit level is used for this purpose, and the test should be made in both transverse and longitudinal directions.

(ii) The sensitivity of a spirit level suitable for testing machine-tool alignments is 0·04 mm/1000 mm per division.

TABLE 2.2

Spindles

Description of test	Example of tolerance magnitude*	Diagram illustrating method of testing
Note: Before tests are carried out the spindle must have attained normal working temperature	Precision	
(a) Axial "Float". (This may be caused by non-parallel thrust faces or incorrect bearing adjustment)	0·005 mm Average 0·010 mm Large machines 0·020 mm	Fig 2.24
(b) True Running of Location Faces and Diameters (Faces must be tested to positions 180° apart)	Precision 0·005 mm Average 0·010 mm	Fig 2.25

* Total indicator reading.

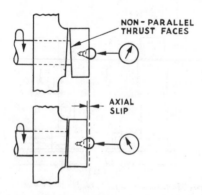

Fig. 2.24 Testing for axial float

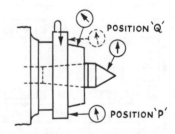

Fig. 2.25 Testing concentricity of location diameters and true running of location faces

(Faces must be tested at two positions, P and Q, separated by 180°.)

TABLE 2.3

Alignment of Spindle Axis

	Description of test	Example of tolerance magnitude	Diagram illustrating method of testing
(a)	Parallelism between Axis and Another feature Parallelism in one plane Parallelism in two planes	0·02/300*	Fig 2.27(a) Fig 2.27(b)
(b)	Perpendicularity between Axis and Another Feature The tolerance for this alignment varies considerably according to the size of machine and the class of work it performs, e.g. vertical milling machine, axis perpendicular to the table Perpendicularity of axis to slideway is tested by setting a straight-edge perpendicular to the spindle using the "turn-round" method, as shown by positions P and Q; errors of perpendicularity will be observed as the cross-slide is moved to traverse the straight-edge past the dial gauge	0.02/300	Fig 2.28(a) Fig 2.28(b)
(c)	Alignment between spindle axis and some other axis	0.03 mm	Fig 2.29

* Some tolerances are directional in character, e.g. headstock spindle of a centre lathe is permitted to slope upwards towards the free end of the test mandrel. Where these conditions apply, the direction of the slope is such that it tends to counter the normal deflection or wear of the machine (the direction of the slope is always stated in the general description of the alignment being tested).

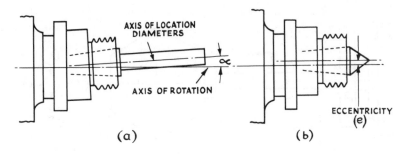

Fig. 2.26 Types of error in concentricity
Inclination (a) and eccentricity (b) of an axis relative to the axis of rotation.

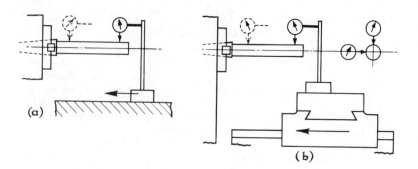

Fig. 2.27 *Testing parallelism between spindle and* (a) *table* (*one plane*)
(b) *slideway* (*two planes*)

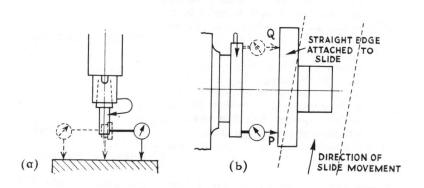

Fig. 2.28 *Testing perpendicularity between spindle and* (a) *table,* (b) *slideway*

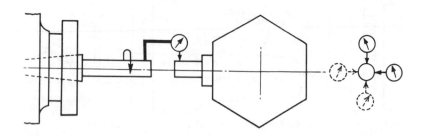

Fig. 2.29 *Testing alignment in two planes between axis of spindle and some
other axis*

If a location face has been machined with the spindle in position and the dial indicator touches the spindle on the same point no error will be apparent, hence two readings are taken as stated in Table 2.2(*b*).

The errors encountered in location faces and diameters are illustrated in Fig 2.26(*a*) and (*b*), and may be classified as follows:

    (i) Inclination (α) of spindle axis in relation to the axis of rotation.
    (ii) Eccentricity (e) of spindle axis.

Performance Tests. At the present time performance tests are subject to agreement between the purchaser and the maker of a machine tool, the agreement preferably being made during the negotiations which precede the placing of an order. An agreement made at such a time not only avoids possible disagreement at a later date but also gives the manufacturer an opportunity to ensure the machine will reach the required standards.

Certain well-known performance tests are applied to standard machine tools, some of these are illustrated in Fig 2.30.

Example 2.2
Explain with the aid of diagrams the principal alignment checks for a duplex spindle surface milling machine of the type shown in Fig 2.31.

Solution
Note: **Problems dealing with alignments are best approached from a consideration of the general to a consideration of the particular. In other words, plan the overall sequence of the tests before considering the detail testing.**

In this type of machine it is clear that a basis for the tests is provided by the table and its slideways. The next most basic feature is the slideway of the upright columns, and these should be tested next, followed by tests of the spindles. Once the accuracy of the fundamentals has been determined, the relationships between the spindles and the other machine features should be checked. A detailed analysis of the testing procedure can be tabulated as follows:

1. *Slideways and Worktable*

	Description of test	Diagram (or Equipment used)	Tolerance
(*a*)	Flatness of worktable in longitudinal and transverse directions	Spirit level	$\pm 0\cdot04/1000$
(*b*)	Rise and fall of worktable longitudinally	Fig 2.32(*a*)	$0\cdot03/1000$
(*c*)	Slideways of column perpendicular to table in plane of spindle axes	Fig 2.23(*a*)	$0\cdot02/300$
(*d*)	Slideways of column in plane perpendicular to spindle axes	Fig 2.23(*a*)	$0\cdot02/300$

2. Spindles

	Description of test	Diagram (or equipment used)	Tolerance
(a)	Internal taper of spindles runs true: (i) near spindle nose (ii) 300 mm from spindle nose	Set-up as Fig 2.27(a) but with spindle rotating	(i) 0·01 mm (ii) 0·02 mm
(b)	Location diameter of spindle nose runs true	Fig 2.25	0·01 mm
(c)	Location face of spindle nose runs true	Fig 2.25	0·01 mm
(d)	Axial float of spindles	Fig 2.24	0·02 mm

3. Spindle Alignments

	Description of test	Diagram (or equipment used)	Tolerance
(a)	Spindles square with slideways of upright	Fig 2.32(b)	0·02/300
(b)	Spindles square with slideways of table	Fig 2.28(b)	0·04/300
(c)	Spindles parallel with worktable	Fig 2.27(a)	0·02/300
(d)	Axial movement of spindle slide parallel with worktable	Fig 2.32(c)	0·04/1000
(e)	Spindles co-axial in vertical plane	Fig 2.32(d)	0·01 mm
(f)	Tee slots square with spindle (turn-round method)	Similar to Fig 2.32(b)	0·05/1000

2.7 Straight-line Motion

Some common methods for obtaining straight-line motion are illustrated in Fig 2.33.

The thread form used for leadscrews, Fig 2.33(b), is usually acme or square thread: the efficiency of this type of screw is low, as can be seen from the following example:

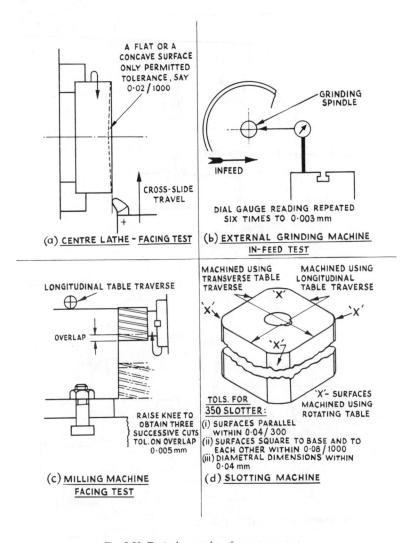

Fig. 2.30 Typical examples of acceptance tests

Example 2.3
Determine the efficiency of a 5 mm pitch acme screw, thread angle 29°, of 44·5 mm effective diameter when the coefficient of friction is 0·05.

Solution
From mechanics, efficiency for an acme screw thread is:

$$\eta = \frac{\tan \alpha (1 - \mu \sec \theta \tan \alpha)}{\tan \alpha + \mu \sec \theta}$$

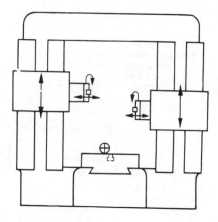

Fig. 2.31

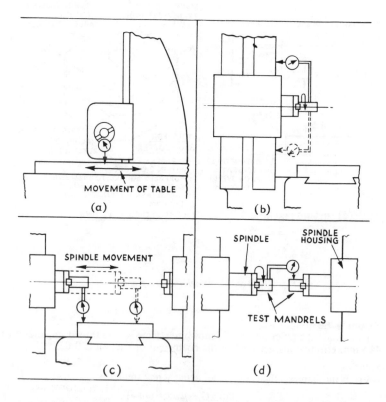

Fig. 2.32 Some of the alignment tests for the duplex spindle milling machine

Mechanics of machine tools

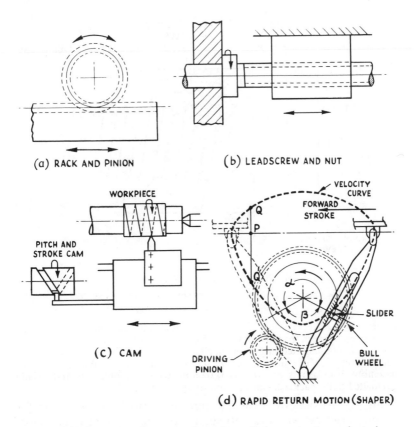

Fig. 2.33 *Conversion of rotary motion to linear displacement using mechanical methods*

where

$$\theta \ (\text{semi-angle}) = 29°/2$$

α (helix angle) is given by,

$$\tan \alpha = \frac{5}{44 \cdot 5\pi} = 0 \cdot 03577$$

$$\sec \theta = 1 \cdot 033$$

$$\therefore \quad \eta = \frac{0 \cdot 03577 \{1 - (0 \cdot 05 \times 1 \cdot 033 \times 0 \cdot 03577)\}}{0 \cdot 03577 + (0 \cdot 05 \times 1 \cdot 033)} = 0 \cdot 4084$$

$$\therefore \quad \text{Efficiency}, \ \eta \simeq 41\%$$

Note: The recirculating ball and nut, Fig 2.34, greatly improves upon the performance of an acme thread, the minimum efficiency being above 90%. The assemblies comprise a shaft with a semicircular helical groove and a nut with a

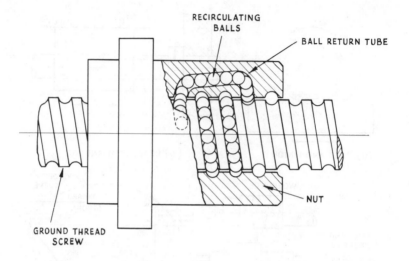

Fig. 2.34 Recirculating-ball screw and nut

The minimum efficiency of this mechanism is greater than 90%.

corresponding helical groove. A stream of balls fits into the groove, so forming a connection between the nut and screw. When in operation, the balls at the end of the stream are deflected into a return channel, thus ensuring a continuous and recirculating flow of balls when either screw or nut is turned. With a single nut assembly, backlash is as little as 0·02 mm; with a double nut and axially preloaded balls, backlash can be completely eliminated.

Fig 2.33(*d*) shows the basic features of a rapid return motion for shaping machines with a velocity curve superimposed upon it. The radial position of the slider on the "bull" wheel may be varied and determines the length of stroke. The forward stroke occurs while the bull wheel rotates at constant speed through angle α, and the return stroke during rotation through angle β. The ram velocity at any position P is determined from the velocity curve by length PQ for the forward stroke and PQ^1 for the return stroke.

2.8 Hydraulic Operation of Machine Tools

The use of hydraulic power in the operation of machine tools offers the following advantages:

(*a*) infinitely variable speeds up to the maximum speed;
(*b*) a fairly rapid and shockless reversal in reciprocating motions;
(*c*) quiet operation;
(*d*) straightforward design and simple maintenance;
(*e*) improved tool life, especially with cemented carbide tools;
(*f*) relief valves provide a safety factor.

Hydraulic operation may not be directly competitive with mechanical or electrical units in all cases, its limitations being:

(i) cost may be higher than for the equivalent mechanical equipment;

(ii) a fixed ratio between co-ordinated motions cannot be guaranteed;

(iii) oil viscosity varies with temperature and may cause fluctuations in feed or speed rates, although compensating devices can be introduced to deal with this difficulty.

Elements of Hydraulic System. A hydraulic system has four elements:

(*a*) the power producing unit, i.e. pump;

(*b*) the element making use of the pressure, e.g. cylinder, hydraulic motor;

(*c*) controlling elements, e.g. valves;

(*d*) storage and transmission elements, e.g. tank, pipeline, etc.

The circuit of a hydraulic system may be either closed, Fig 2.35(*b*), in which the exhaust oil returns directly to the pump for recirculation, the reservoir being used only to make good oil losses; or it may be an open circuit, Fig 2.35(*a*), in which the exhaust oil returns to the reservoir. This latter method has the advantage that oil is kept cooler due to the greater volume employed but has the disadvantage that air may enter the system more easily.

A fixed displacement pump is used to make good losses due to leakage in the closed circuit.

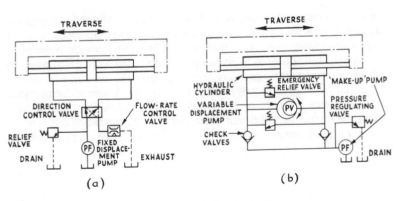

Fig. 2.35 Simple hydraulic circuits

(*a*) Open circuit using fixed displacement pump—piston speed is controlled by throttle valve in return line

(*b*) Closed circuit using a variable displacement pump to give the different rates of table traverse

The pumps may be of the following general types:

(*a*) Constant delivery pumps for light and medium duty. Vane pumps or gear pumps, Fig 2.36(*a*), are often used, being reliable and relatively inexpensive.

(*b*) Variable delivery pumps, Fig 2.36(*b*), for pressures above, say, 7 N/mm^2. These pumps are much more expensive and frequently make use of the eccentric principle to vary the flow, e.g. eccentrically operated plungers, swashplate operation, etc.

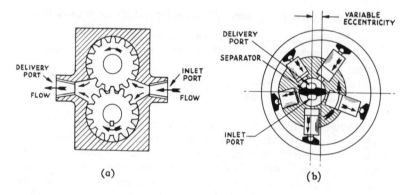

Fig. 2.36 Two types of hydraulic pump

(*a*) Constant delivery gear pump
(*b*) Variable delivery plunger pump (arrows show direction of piston displacement for the instantaneous position shown)

Oil is almost incompressible and provides the medium for a positive response to control signals. In contrast, air is easily compressed, hence if air gets into the line positive control may be lost and a jerky movement or a noisy hydraulic pump is likely to result. If the exhaust line is allowed to fall below atmospheric pressure, air may enter the system; this can be prevented by a throttle valve in the exhaust line keeping the pressure above ambient pressure or by immersing the end of the exhaust line. When the former arrangement is used in a circuit operating a hydraulic cylinder a more positive control is exerted because the oil pressure acts on both sides of the piston.

Mechanics of Machine Tools (*contd.*)

PART B MOTORS, SPINDLES AND BEARINGS

2.9 Motors

The use of individual electric motors for separate drives within a machine tool has meant the elimination of linking mechanisms, simplification of design and the opportunity to choose motors having characteristics suited to particular purposes. The majority are induction motors, since these are the simplest and least expensive. Two typical a.c. motors are:

(*a*) Squirrel-cage motors having solid copper or aluminium conductor bars through the rotor slots. The bars are joined to end rings and so form the "squirrel-cage".

(*b*) Slip-ring motors having 3-phase windings instead of solid bars in the rotor slots.

The stator is identical for both types of machine. The squirrel-cage motor with its solid conductor bars is both cheaper and more robust than the slip-ring motor.

Induction motors can run for short periods at torques greater than their full-load rating; the output torque may be as much as 250% of full load. A typical torque–speed curve for a squirrel-cage motor is shown in Fig 2.37.

The wound-rotor slip-ring machines can have the position of maximum torque displaced during operation by suitable control gear, as shown in Fig 2.38. If the motor is to start against full load the starting gear is so arranged that the motor gives $1\frac{1}{2}$–$2\frac{1}{2}$ full-load torque. This provides excess torque for acceleration, and as the motor speed increases, external resistances are reduced to zero until the motor runs much as a squirrel-cage machine.

Alteration to the rotor design will result in a different torque curve and in modified motor characteristics, e.g. a double squirrel-cage rotor, Fig 2.39(*a*), provides a high starting torque and good running characteristics as shown at (*b*).

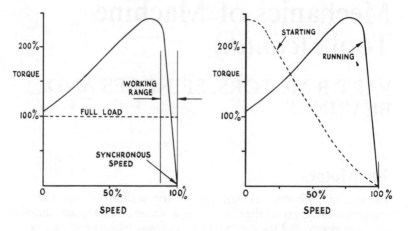

Fig. 2.37 Typical torque–speed curve
for squirrel-cage motor

Fig. 2.38 Torque–speed curve for
slip-ring motor

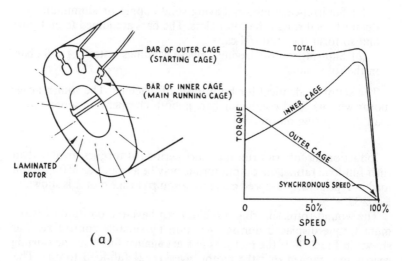

(a)   (b)

Fig. 2.39

(a) Double squirrel-cage rotor
(b) Torque characteristic of a double squirrel-cage motor

Within the working range of a motor (see Fig 2.37) the torque–speed
curve approximates to a straight line, hence in this range torque is
proportional to slip (i.e. speed reduction). For example, if a motor of
1500 rev/min synchronous speed runs at 1450 rev/min under full-load
conditions it will rotate at 1400 rev/min under 200 % of full-load torque.

Speed variation. Change of speed may be obtained in a number of ways, including the use of the following a.c. motors.

(a) *Pole Change Motors*. These are usually squirrel-cage induction motors. By switching arranged to change the number of poles, several fixed speeds can be obtained: the general relationship is

$$N = 60f/p \qquad (2.5)$$

where N = rev/min

f = cycles/s

p = number of pairs of poles.

Numbers of poles	2	4	6	8	12
Synchronous speed (rev/min) 50 Hz supply	3000	1500	1000	750	500

The principle of switching to change from 4- to 8-pole windings is shown in Fig 2.40.

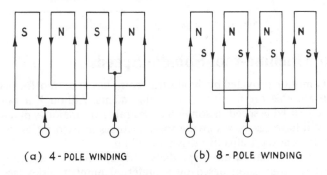

(a) 4 - POLE WINDING (b) 8 - POLE WINDING

Fig. 2.40 Change in supply connections to alter the number of poles in a pole-change motor

(b) *Schrage Motor*. This is a variable-speed machine, and for its constructional details the reader is referred to a text-book on electrical machines. The speed range is usually from $\frac{1}{2}$ to $1\frac{1}{2}$ times the synchronous speed, i.e. from 750 to 2250 rev/min in a 4-pole motor.

(c) *D.C. Motors*. While involving conversion of an a.c. power supply to direct current, these motors can be designed to give infinitely variable speeds with their range. Many N.C. lathes are now fitted with this arrangement.

(d) *a.c. Inverters*. The use of a 3-phase rectifier coupled to 3 banks of forced commutated thyristors and controlled electronically makes it possible to convert standard a.c. to a.c. of varying frequency. Standard a.c. motors supplied via an inverter can run at infinitely variable speeds up to their maximum and some N.C. machine tools employ this system.

A summary of the characteristics of the motors mentioned above and their approximate relative cost (squirrel-cage motor taken as 100%) is given in Table 2.4.

TABLE 2.4
Comparison of Motor Characteristics

Type of motor	Approximate relative cost (%)	Speed control	Starting torque*
Squirrel-cage induction	100	None	100
Slip-ring induction	200	None	250
Pole-change induction	200	Four fixed speeds	100
Schrage	700	Variable	250

* Stated as a percentage of full-load torque.

2.10 Machine-tool Spindle Speeds

Rotary motion provided by the electric motor has to be transformed into speeds suitable for machine-tool requirements. Although a range of infinitely variable speeds is sometimes desirable, the majority of machine tools still have gearboxes giving speed changes in fixed ratios, because this is the cheapest effective driving method.

A system of standardised spindle speeds and feed rates arranged in geometric progression based on a preferred number series (see p. 8) has been internationally accepted and is published by the International Organisation for Standardisation in the recommendation ISO/R229. Tables 2.5 and 2.6 are reproduced from ISO/R229 by permission of the British Standards Institution. The adoption of standardised spindle speeds and feed rates is of considerable help in production engineering, since once speeds and feeds for a given machining process are established, they can be maintained and used on any machine which has gear ratios based on the standardised system.

Spindle Speeds in Geometric Progression. If spindle speeds were in arithmetic progression the steps between one spindle speed and the next would be too far apart at low speeds and too close together at high speeds. Spindle speeds in geometric progression provide a more even range of cutting speeds at each step.

TABLE 2.5
Speeds: Number of Rev/Min or Strokes/Min

Basic value R 20	Limits corresponding to the total tolerance; electrical + mechanical $-2\%\atop+6\%$ } approx.		Limits for calculating the mechanical tolerance* $-2\%\atop+3\%$ } approx.	
	Minimum	Maximum	Minimum	Maximum
1	2	3	4	5
100	98	106	98	103
112	110	119	110	116
125	123	133	123	130
140	138	150	138	145
160	155	168	155	163
180	174	188	174	183
200	196	212	196	206
224	219	237	219	231
250	246	266	246	259
280	276	299	276	290
315	310	335	310	326
355	348	376	348	365
400	390	422	390	410
450	438	473	438	460
500	491	531	491	516
560	551	596	551	579
630	618	669	618	650
710	694	750	694	729
800	778	842	778	818
900	873	945	873	918
1000	980	1060	980	1030

To extend the table upwards or downwards, divide or multiply the given values by 10 or a power of 10.

* For the calculation of the transmission ratio of the driving equipment, the speed at the input is taken as lower by 6% than the synchronous speed of the motor. (The quotient of the speed at the input by each of the two tabulated limits gives the extreme values of the transmission ratio.)

TABLE 2.6

Feeds in millimetres

Basic value R20	Feeds per minute*		Feeds per revolution (or per stroke)†	
	Limits of the tolerance −2 per cent +6 per cent approximately		Limits of the tolerance −2 per cent +3 per cent approximately	
	minimum	maximum	minimum	maximum
1	2	3	4	5
1	0·98	1·06	0·98	1·03
1·12	1·10	1·19	1·10	1·16
1·25	1·23	1·33	1·23	1·30
1·4	1·38	1·50	1·38	1·45
1·6	1·55	1·68	1·55	1·63
1·8	1·74	1·88	1·74	1·83
2	1·96	2·12	1·96	2·06
2·24	2·19	2·37	2·19	2·31
2·5	2·46	2·66	2·46	2·59
2·8	2·76	2·99	2·76	2·90
3·15	3·10	3·35	3·10	3·26
3·55	3·48	3·76	3·48	3·65
4	3·90	4·22	3·90	4·10
4·5	4·38	4·73	4·38	4·60
5	4·91	5·31	4·91	5·16
5·6	5·51	5·96	5·51	5·79
6·3	6·18	6·69	6·18	6·50
7·1	6·94	7·50	6·94	7·29
8	7·78	8·42	7·78	8·18
9	8·73	9·45	8·73	9·18
10	9·80	10.6	9·80	10·3

To extend the table downwards or upwards, divide or multiply the given values by 10 or a power of 10.

* The limits given for the actual values of feeds per minute in columns 2 and 3 correspond to the sum of electrical and mechanical tolerances. The mechanical tolerance is calculated as for feeds per revolution (or per stroke) from values in columns 4 and 5, but, for the calculation of the transmission ratio of the driving equipment, the speed at the input is taken as lower by 6 % than the synchronous speed of the motor. (The quotient of the speed at the input by each of the two tabulated limits gives the extreme values of the transmission ratio.)

† The actual limits of feed per revolution (or per stroke) in columns 4 and 5 correspond to a mechanical tolerance only.

The desirability of using speeds in geometric progression may be demonstrated in the following way:

Let the range of n spindle speeds be $N_1, N_2, N_3, \ldots N_n$.

For any given spindle speed, a change in work (or cutter) diameter will produce a proportionate change in cutting velocity, i.e. a reduction in work diameter will give cutting velocity V_{min} and an increase in diameter will give cutting velocity V_{max}. Beyond these values a gear change would be made.

For the cutting velocity to lie between the limits V_{min} and V_{max} (m/min) at 1st spindle speed, N_1,

$$\text{Max dia of work (or cutter) (in mm)} = \frac{10^3 \cdot V_{max}}{\pi N_1}$$

$$\text{Min dia of work (or cutter)} = \frac{10^3 \cdot V_{min}}{\pi N_1}$$

at N_2,

$$\text{Max dia of work (or cutter)} = \frac{10^3 \cdot V_{max}}{\pi N_2}$$

$$\text{Min dia of work (or cutter)} = \frac{10^3 \cdot V_{min}}{\pi N_2}$$

and so on.

For constant cutting velocity, minimum diameter at N_1 rev/min will be the same as the maximum diameter at N_2 rev/min.

$$\therefore \quad \frac{10^3}{\pi} \cdot \frac{V_{min}}{N_1} = \frac{10^3}{\pi} \cdot \frac{V_{max}}{N_2}$$

i.e. $\dfrac{V_{max}}{V_{min}} = \text{constant ratio} = \dfrac{N_2}{N_1} = \dfrac{N_3}{N_2} = \cdots = \dfrac{N_n}{N_{n-1}}$ and this is a series in geometric progression.

Let $r = $ the constant ratio,

then $r^{n-1} = \dfrac{N_2}{N_1} \times \dfrac{N_3}{N_2} \times \dfrac{N_4}{N_3} \times \cdots \times \dfrac{N_n}{N_{n-1}}$

Cancelling terms on RHS and taking the root,

$$r = \sqrt[n-1]{\left(\frac{N_n}{N_1}\right)} \tag{2.6}$$

Example 2.4

A machine spindle is required to have 8 speeds in GP and to operate on ferrous metals at 28 m/min. If the spindle accommodates HSS cutters ranging from 10 mm to 50 mm dia, determine the spindle speeds and rationalise them in accordance with the preferred number series (see Table 2.5)

Plot a graph of cutting velocity (V) against cutter diameter (D) for each spindle speed. Find the spindle speed for operating with cutters of (a) 12·5 mm dia., (b) 40 mm dia. Find, for each cutter, the fall in cutting speed caused by dropping to the next lower spindle speed.

Solution

$$N_1 = \frac{10^3 \cdot V}{\pi D_{max}} = \frac{10^3 \times 28}{\pi \times 50} = 178 \cdot 3 \text{ say } 178 \text{ rev/min}$$

$$N_n = \frac{10^3 \cdot V}{\pi D_{min}} = \frac{10^3 \times 28}{\pi \times 10} = 891 \cdot 3 \text{ say } 891 \text{ rev/min}$$

$$\therefore \text{ Common ratio, } r = {}^{n-1}\!\!\sqrt{(N_n/N_1)} = \sqrt[7]{(891/178)}$$
$$= \underline{1 \cdot 2587} \quad (\text{ratio } R10 = 1 \cdot 26, \text{ see Table 1.1})$$

From the above data the following table can be compiled and the graph (Fig 2.41) plotted.

Speed ratio	N_1	N_2	N_3	N_4	N_5	N_6	N_7	N_8
Spindle speed, calculated (rev/min)	178	224	282	355	447	562	708	891
*Spindle speed, rationalised (rev/min)	180	224	280	355	450	560	710	900
Cutter dia (mm) to produce $V = 28$ m/min	49·5	39·9	31·8	25·1	19·8	15·9	12·6	9·9

* Note, every second value of R20 series gives an R10 series

(a) For 12·5 mm dia cutter, $V_{min} = 22 \cdot 1$ m/min $\qquad V_{max} = 27 \cdot 9$ m/min
$$\therefore \text{ Range} = 27 \cdot 9 - 22 \cdot 1 = \underline{5 \cdot 8 \text{ m/min}}$$

(b) For 40 mm dia cutter, $\qquad V_{min} = 22 \cdot 3$ m/min $\qquad V_{max} = \underline{28 \cdot 1 \text{ m/min}}$
$$\therefore \text{ Range} = 28 \cdot 1 - 22 \cdot 3 = \underline{5 \cdot 8 \text{ m/min}}$$

i.e. the step between one speed and the next remains consistent when spindle speeds are arranged in GP.

2.11 Spindle Speed-change Mechanisms

Some typical examples of mechanical methods for obtaining spindle speed changes are illustrated in Fig 2.42. The use of cone pulleys and belt drives as shown at (A) needs no explanation. It is simple and inexpensive, but should be used only when a completely positive drive is not essential; if it is necessary to eliminate slip and maintain a positive ratio in the drive, toothed pulleys and stepped belts may be used (see inset). Variable-speed drives based on the principle shown at (B) are available as a unit and overcome the limitation of the fixed ratios of a normal belt drive. The

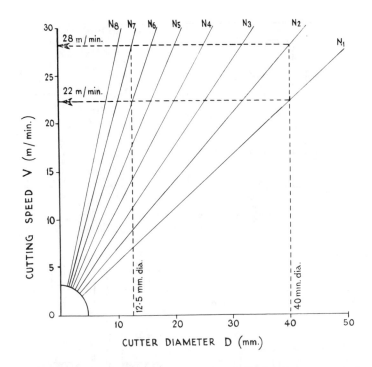

Fig. 2.41 Graph showing spindle speed ratios in geometrical progression

This type of graph can be used as a chart for selecting appropriate speed ratios for a given diameter of work or cutter and a given cutting speed.

conical pulleys may be separated to allow the belt to operate at a reduced radius, or closed together to increase the radius. The ratio N_a/N_b is infinitely variable between the limits r_1/r_2 and r_3/r_4.

For spindle speed changes within the headstock of a lathe, or in a main drive gearbox, the methods shown in Fig 2.42(C) and (D) are commonly used. Because of the smooth "take-up" of plate clutches, and because the gears in drive (C) are in constant mesh, rapid gear changes without stopping the spindle are possible. When the sliding gear method (D) is used the spindle must be synchronised or stopped before a gear change is made, to avoid "crashing" the gears.

In machine tool feed gearboxes the power transmitted is usually not great, but a range of speeds in close ratio is needed. These basic conditions are met by the speed-change mechanisms shown in principle in Fig 2.42(E) and (F); the cone of gears in each case can be extended considerably from the numbers shown, a cone of ten to twenty gears is not uncommon. In the Norton type gearbox (E) connection between the

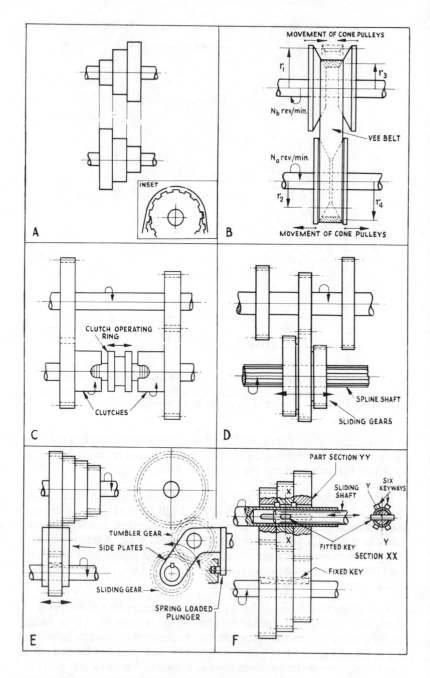

Fig. 2.42 Principles of speed-changing mechanisms

gears on the cone, and the driven shaft, is made through a tumbler gear and the sliding gear keyed to the shaft. Pivoting the tumbler device about the axis of the driven shaft and fixing its position with the spring-loaded plunger overcomes the problem presented by different gear diameters on the cone of gears. In the sliding-key change-speed mechanism, Fig 2.42(F), the gears of the lower cone are keyed to the shaft while the gears of the upper cone (each with six keyways for ease of engagement) rotate freely on their shaft. The gear required to obtain a given ratio is selected by moving the sliding shaft until its fitted key engages in the keyways of the chosen gear.

2.12 Machine-tool Spindles

The material used for machine-tool spindles is normally a low-carbon alloy steel, heat treated to give a case-hardened surface. Such a spindle possesses resistance to wear combined with a tough core for strength in torsion. Where high-precision spindles with maximum stability are required, e.g. spindles for external grinding machines, Nitralloy steel is used. The hardness of the case achieved by the nitriding process is greater than that obtained by carburising and hardening, and since nitriding is carried out at a temperature (500–550°C) which is below the critical range, the structural equilibrium of the steel is not affected and secular changes due to retained austenite cannot occur.

Allowance must be made for the thermal expansion of spindles. This may be done by preventing axial float by means of bearings situated close together at one end of the spindle, and allowing the other end to expand freely in bearings which provide radial location, but permit axial movement, e.g. cylindrical roller bearings. The spindle of a Swift type "C" lathe illustrating these principles is shown in Fig 2.43.

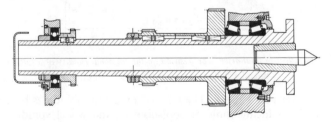

Fig. 2.43 Bearings and drive-gear arrangement on spindle of Swift Type "C" lathe (Courtesy G. Swift Ltd.)

Example 2.5
  A machine-tool spindle is supported between bearings 560 mm apart. The lowest temperature at which the machine is used is 10°C and the working temperature of the spindle is found to be 45°C, while the average temperature of

the spindle housing casting is 35°C. Determine the necessary allowance in the bearings for expansion. (α_s for spindle = 0·000 015, α_n for housing = 0·000 01, per deg C).

Solution

Expansion of spindle	= Length $\times \alpha_s \times$ Temp change
	= $560 \times 0·000 015 \times (45 - 10) = 0·294$ mm
Expansion of housing	= $560 \times 0·000 01 \times (35 - 10) = 0·140$ mm
Difference in expansion	= $0·294 - 0·140$
	= $0·154$ mm

It is clear that 0·154 mm "play" would be unacceptable in a machine-tool spindle and the provision for expansion mentioned above must be made without allowing axial "float" in the bearings.

In heavy duty spindles and where a high torque is transmitted the final-drive gear should be positioned as close to the cutting force as the design will permit, in order to keep torsion of the spindle to a minimum. By reference to Fig 2.44, it can be seen that if the final-drive gear is positioned at A the spindle length between the gear and the cutting force is as small as possible. If the gear was situated at B, where $l_2 = 4l_1$, the angle of twist of the shaft would be quadrupled, since it is proportional to the length l.

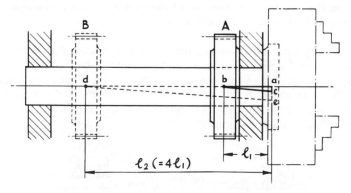

Fig. 2.44 Effect of final-drive gear position on the torsional rigidity of a lathe spindle

Angular deflection ae = 4 × angular deflection ac

Spindle Noses and Tapers. The nose of a machine spindle is bored out to receive and locate tools or tool-holders; the wheel spindle of an external grinding machine has an external taper to locate the wheel adapter. The advantages of the taper for location purposes are:

    (i) accurate location ensuring concentricity with spindle journals;
    (ii) the taper seating eliminates all "play";
    (iii) assembly and disconnection of tapered parts is easily performed.

The tapers used may be classified into two groups.

(a) *Self-Holding Tapers*, e.g. Morse taper and 5% metric taper (BS1660). These are used where parts are to be retained in position and withstand the application of a moderate torque by means of the friction between the taper surfaces, e.g. taper shank drill.

(b) *Self-Release Tapers*, e.g. taper ratio 7/24 (BS1660). Where the torque is too great to be transmitted by the friction of a taper, positive drive by means of two keys is employed, and the taper angle increased to avoid difficulty in releasing the mating parts.

Because of their widespread international use, the original Morse taper and the self-releasing taper of $3\frac{1}{2}$ in/ft ($= 7/24$) provide the bases of the current metric standard (BS1660: 1972)

Holding and Releasing Forces for Taper Fits

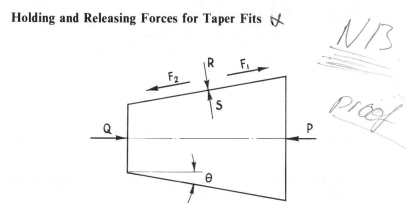

Fig. 2.45 Forces acting on a taper spindle when inserted in a taper bore

Let P = force to drive in;
$\quad Q$ = force to drive out;
$\quad S$ = total normal thrust of shank on socket;
$\quad R$ = total normal reaction of socket on shank;
$\quad F_1$ = frictional resistance when driving in;
$\quad F_2$ = frictional resistance when driving out;
$\quad F_3$ = frictional resistance of taper acting tangential to mean diameter;
$\quad \theta$ = semi-angle of taper;
$\quad t$ = taper ratio, change of diameter/length;
$\quad \mu$ = coefficient of friction.

$$F_1 = F_2 = \mu R \qquad (2.7)$$

By resolving forces horizontally

$$P = F_1 \cos \theta + R \sin \theta$$

Substituting from Eqn (2.7) and rearranging

$$P = R \sin \theta (\mu \cot \theta + 1) \qquad (2.8)$$
$$Q = F_2 \cos \theta - R \sin \theta$$

Substituting from Eqn (2.7) and rearranging

$$Q = R \sin \theta (\mu \cot \theta - 1) \qquad (2.9)$$

Now

$$Q = P\left(\frac{Q}{P}\right)$$

$\therefore$ From Eqn (2.8) and Eqn (2.9),

$$Q = P\left[\frac{R \sin \theta (\mu \cot \theta - 1)}{R \sin \theta (\mu \cot \theta + 1)}\right]$$
$$= P\frac{(\mu \cot \theta - 1)}{(\mu \cot \theta + 1)}$$

hence, by division, $\quad Q = P - \left(\dfrac{2P}{(\mu \cot \theta + 1)}\right) \qquad (2.10)$

From Eqn (2.10) it follows that Q increases as the taper semi-angle (θ) decreases and that $P = -Q$ when $\theta = 0$, i.e. shank is parallel.

Similarly, for shank and socket of a known coefficient of friction there will be a value of θ at which the taper will become self-releasing.

The value of θ at which a taper becomes self-releasing, i.e. the value at which the releasing force, Q, just equals zero, is determined as follows. Equation (2.9) may be rewritten as $Q = R \ (\mu \cos \theta - \sin \theta)$ and since, for self-releasing tapers, $Q = 0$, but $R \neq 0$,

$$\mu \cos \theta = \sin \theta$$
$$\therefore \quad \mu = \tan \theta \qquad (2.11)$$

The taper ratio (t) is $2 \times \tan \theta$ and substituting from Eqn (2.11) a taper is self-releasing when $t = 2\mu$. If we take $\mu = 0 \cdot 146$ for steel tapers in steel sockets ($0 \cdot 15$ is considered an average value for μ, steel on steel), then the taper ratio for self-releasing action,

$$t = 0 \cdot 292 \text{ or } 7/24$$

(equivalent to $3\frac{1}{2}$ inches/ft on diameter.)

This is the value specified for self-release machine tapers in BS1660.

Torque Transmitted by Self-holding Tapers. The maximum torque which can be transmitted through the friction of a self-holding taper will be limited by the accuracy in matching of the sleeve and shank. For accurately fitting tapers, the actual transmitted torque is reasonably close to the value shown below.

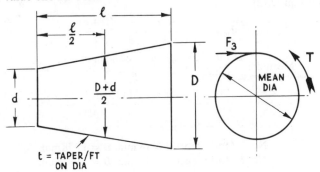

Fig. 2.46 *Frictional torque transmitted by a taper*

Max value of transmitted torque,

$$T_{max} = F_3 \times \frac{\text{Mean dia}}{2}$$

$$= \mu R\left(\frac{D+d}{4}\right)$$

Rearranging Eqn (2.8) and substituting for R,

$$T_{max} = \frac{\mu P}{\mu\cos\theta + \sin\theta}\left(\frac{D+d}{4}\right) \qquad (2.12)$$

NB.

From Eqn (2.12) it will be noted that the maximum torque transmitted can be increased by:

   (i) increasing mean radius, R_m;
   (ii) increasing value of P;
   (iii) decreasing value of θ.

All three of these expedients are used in the design of taper shanks for cutting tools; θ is given a low value for self-holding tapers, P is increased by the provision of draw bars, R_m is increased for the shanks of large diameter drills and other heavy duty cutters.

Example 2.6
  The following data is taken from a series of practical tests on drilling.
  Material, cast iron. Cutting speed, 20 m/min. Dia of drill, 24 mm
  Feed = 0·33 mm/rev. Axial thrust = 4500 N
  Torque = 37·6 Nm
  Determine whether a No. 2 or a No. 3 Morse taper shank is suitable for this drill. (Take taper ratio as 5% for both sizes and $\mu = 0·15$.)

Solution

$$\tan \theta = \frac{0 \cdot 05}{2}$$

$$\therefore \quad \theta = 1°\,26'$$

From Eqn (2.12)

$$T_{\max} = \frac{\mu \cdot P}{\mu \cdot \cos \theta + \sin \theta} \times \frac{(D + d)}{4}$$

$$\therefore \quad \text{Mean dia,} \frac{D + d}{2} = \frac{2 \times T_{\max}\,(\mu \cdot \cos \theta + \sin \theta)}{\mu \cdot P}$$

$$= \frac{2 \times 37 \cdot 6 \times 10^3\,(0 \cdot 15 \cos 1°\,26' + \sin 1°\,26')}{0 \cdot 15 \times 4500}$$

$$= 19 \cdot 5 \text{ mm}$$

Now   No. 2 Morse taper $d = 14$ mm, $D = 17 \cdot 78$ mm
             No. 3 Morse taper $d = 19$ mm, $D = 23 \cdot 825$ mm

$$\therefore \quad \underline{\text{A No. 3 Morse taper is required.}}$$

2.13 Plain Bearings

A plain bearing is formed when a shaft rotates in a bush, liner or the bore of a housing. The frictional loss is greater than in rolling bearings, and the use of plain bearings is confined to applications where simplicity and cheapness are required, or where such a high standard of precision or rigidity is demanded that a plain bearing is preferred to a rolling bearing.

The bearings may be:

   (*a*) journal bearings, capable of carrying radial loads;
   (*b*) thrust bearings, for carrying axial loads; or
   (*c*) a bearing combining (*a*) and (*b*), e.g. as illustrated in Fig 2.47.

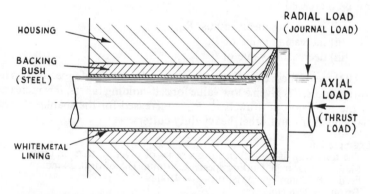

Fig. 2.47 White-metal-lined plain bearing for combined thrust and journal loads
(method of lubrication omitted)

Lubrication of Plain Bearings. Provision for lubrication of plain bearings is essential except for nylon, P.T.F.E., or oil-impregnated bearing bushes. The latter type of bush is produced by sintering compressed powder metal to create a porous metal structure which then absorbs up to 35 % oil by volume. The oil in the bush provides a reservoir from which oil is drawn during the life of the bearing.

For plain bearings in machine-tool spindles pressure-fed oil provides the most effective method of lubrication, although such bearings are more liable to oil leakages, particularly in the case of vertical spindles. To reduce oil leakage, oil seals, throwers and suitably placed oil-return holes are used.

Machine-tool bearings are lubricated with mineral oils having a viscosity selected to suit the conditions of operation, e.g.:

(*a*) a light oil (i.e. low viscosity) for high-speed bearings with a fine clearance between shaft and bearing;

(*b*) a heavy oil (i.e. high viscosity) for heavily loaded low-speed bearings.

Note: Viscosity may be defined as the resistance of a fluid to shear or flow. It may be specified by reference to the time in seconds which a given quantity of oil at a standard temperature takes to flow through a hole of fixed size.

The properties required of a spindle oil are:

(i) must be non-corrosive;

(ii) must not readily oxidise under conditions of mist or spray in contact with the air (these conditions occur at high speeds or when churning takes place);

(iii) should assist in cooling the bearings.

According to the conditions of operation and lubrication, a bearing may run dry, partially lubricated or fully lubricated.

(a) *Dry.* If a metal-to-metal contact exists, the wear rate will be rapid and the coefficient of friction (μ) will lie between $0 \cdot 15$ and $0 \cdot 4$ according to the materials in contact. Some cast irons contain free graphite in their composition, e.g. grey cast iron, Fig 2.48(*a*), and are used for cheap bearings, the graphite itself being a lubricant. Bearing metals which have hard cuboids of an intermetallic compound embedded in a soft matrix, e.g. white metal, Fig 2.48(*b*), will rapidly "seize-up" if lubrication breaks down.

Metal-to-metal contact occurs in machine-tool bearings after the spindles have been stationary for a period. Due to leakage, oil drains from the bearings and the weight of the spindle causes it to drop and rest in direct contact with the bearing metal, Fig 2.50(*a*), thus creating the non-lubricated conditions which give a high rate of wear for a brief period immediately after starting-up the spindle.

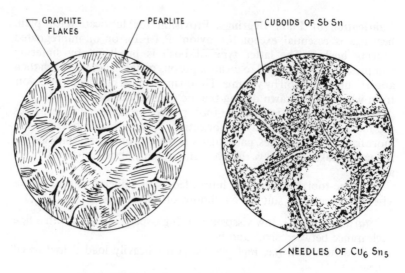

Fig. 2.48 Microstructure of metals used for plain bearings

(*a*) Grey cast iron

   Graphite flakes in a matrix of pearlite.

(*b*) Bearing metal containing 10 % antimony; 60 % tin; 27 % lead; 3 % copper

   Cuboids of SbSn (light) and needles of Cu_6Sn_5 (light) in a matrix consisting of a eutectic of tin-rich and lead-rich solid solutions.

(b) *Partial Lubrication:* In semi-fluid (i.e. partial) lubrication the bearing elements are not completely separated by an oil film, but some oil or grease is present. The coefficient of friction in these circumstances varies considerably, and in general is from about 0·02 to 0·1. The conditions often occur in machine-tool slideways, but are also found in bearings where:

     (i) oil grooves are badly designed or not properly situated;
     (ii) the spindle is bent, see Fig 2.49;
     (iii) the oil supply is inadequate;
     (iv) flat surfaces are in contact, e.g. in a thrust bearing.

(c) *Full Lubrication.* Under these conditions the bearing surfaces are completely separated by a fluid film, as shown in Fig 2.50(*c*), thus reducing friction to a minimum. Wear is almost eliminated, but to be effective the fluid must be forced into the bearing under pressure to provide consistent conditions and replace the fluid lost by leakage.

As can be from Fig 2.50(*c*) and (*d*) the spindle does not run co-axially with the bearing; this condition occurs through the creation of a hydrodynamic wedge by the rotating spindle. The action takes place as follows. Lubricating fluid adheres to the surface of the rotating spindle,

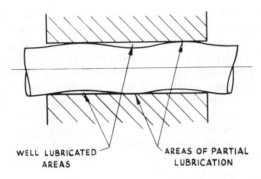

Fig. 2.49 *Areas of partial lubrication caused by bent spindle*

Note: Amount of error need not be very great to produce this effect.

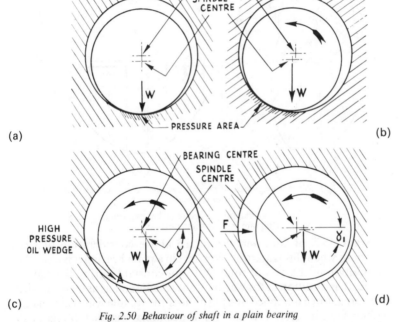

Fig. 2.50 *Behaviour of shaft in a plain bearing*

(a) *Shaft at rest* During a period of idleness, oil will drain from the bearing leaving the shaft in metal-to-metal contact with the bearing

(b) *Starting-up* As shaft starts to rotate and oil is fed to the bearing the shaft begins to "climb" up the side of the bearing

(c) *Full speed* Lubricating oil is drawn into the pressure area A though friction caused by shaft rotation

(d) *Effect of an externally applied force* The position of the shaft again alters when external force F is applied. Angle γ_1 will vary according to the magnitude and direction of force F

and this layer is drawn into the space "A", Fig 2.50(c). Since inter-molecular friction (i.e. viscosity or resistance to shear) exists in the fluid, other layers are drawn into the space. However, if the bearing is stationary a fluid layer will adhere to the bearing wall and try to remain stationary, hence creating a velocity gradient between the fluid layers and causing a state of shear in the fluid. In the narrowing gap of the wedge a high pressure is developed normal to the bearing surfaces, thus supporting the spindle and its load. The relative magnitudes of normal pressure are shown by the vectors in a typical polar diagram, Fig 2.51(a); at point B a divergent wedge creates reduced pressure, and if this falls below atmospheric pressure air may enter the bearing and mix with the lubricating medium.

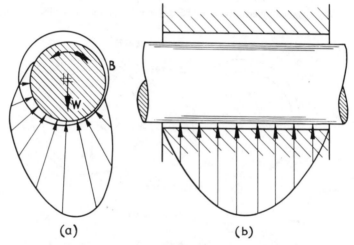

Fig. 2.51 *Relative magnitude of pressures normal to the surface of a plain bearing spindle*

(a) Polar diagram at centre of bearing length
(b) Diagram in transverse direction

Constant Axis of Rotation. From the above consideration of shaft behaviour when this is starting from rest in a plain bearing it is clear that the position of the axis of rotation is not constant during the starting period. If, in addition to the weight of the spindle and its associated parts, an external force is applied, the position of the spindle will again change, as shown in Fig 2.50(d). Although this positional change is not large for bearings with small clearance ratios, a movement as small as 0·002 mm would be unacceptable in bearings with the degree of precision required for the wheel-head of an external grinding machine. The effect of an out-of-balance grinding wheel in producing a disturbing force affecting work accuracy and surface finish can be readily appreciated in this context. A numerical example showing the magnitude of such forces is given on p. 285.

Bearings with Pivoted Segments. Bearings using tilting pads to make use of the hydrodynamic wedge principle were developed by Michell (UK) and Kingsbury (USA) independently, and bearings of this type are often referred to by the names of the originators. The idea has been adapted to machine tools, and bearings with pivoted segments are used in the wheelhead spindles of some external grinding machines.

The basic principle is illustrated in Fig 2.52. A number of pivoting segments, equally spaced and secured in the bearing housing, contain the

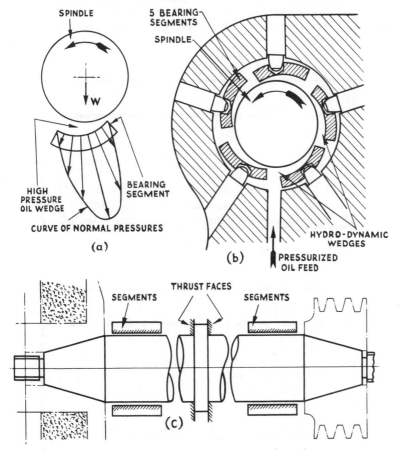

Fig. 2.52 Application of pivoting segments to spindle bearing of grinding machine

(a) Principle of pivoting segment
(b) Section through segment showing application
(c) Elevation showing position of segments in grinding-machine spindle (axial location is provided by a flange on the spindle held between bearing thrust faces)

wheelhead spindle within their circle. When the spindle rotates, *several* hydrodynamic wedges are formed, creating an equispaced series of normal pressures which centralise the spindle and provide a constant axis of rotation.

To ensure the spindle achieves its working position immediately the machine is switched-on, oil is fed under pressure to the bearing and the spindle does not start rotating until sufficient pressure is built-up to maintain the spindle in position. A comparison between the spindle "flutter", i.e. variation in position of spindle axis, of plain and pivoted segment bearings is shown in the oscillographs, Fig 2.53. The importance of eliminating spindle flutter in terms of component surface finish and efficiency of metal removal should need no further emphasis.

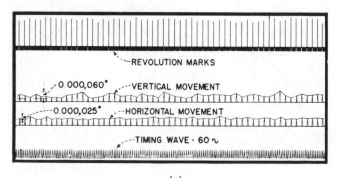

(a)

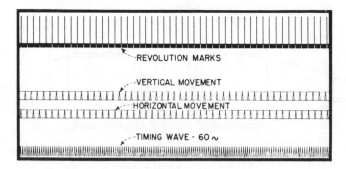

(b)

Fig. 2.53 Oscillograms of spindle rotation

(a) Flutter in old style bearings indicated by wave peaks
(b) Unwavering dead-centre rotation of spindle running in Filmatic bearings
(*Courtesy Cincinnati Milling Machine Co. Ltd.*)

2.14 Rolling Bearings

The great advantage of rolling bearings lies in the substitution of rolling friction (the theory of which is discussed on p. 91) for sliding friction. The coefficient of friction for rolling bearings is $\mu = 0.001 - 0.0015$, although needle roller bearings are a little less efficient and $\mu \simeq 0.004$. Other advantages of rolling bearings include reduced torque for starting from rest, reliability, ease of lubricating, easy replacement and low maintenance costs—although to obtain these advantages correct design and assembly is essential.

Selection of Bearing. Basic considerations in the selection of bearings are as follows:

(*a*) Direction of load relative to bearing axis: the bearing may be required to meet axial thrust, radial load or a combination of both.

(*b*) Magnitude and type of load: ball bearings will sustain considerable loads, but for severe conditions and shock loads roller bearings with their line contact are to be preferred.

(*c*) Shaft stiffness: rigid bearings may be used for stiff well-aligned shafts, but shafts subject to flexure or misalignment require self-aligning bearings.

(*d*) Speed of rotation: speed and load are inter-connected; for a given life, speed must be reduced as load is increased, and vice versa, i.e.

$$\text{Life} \propto \frac{1}{(\text{Speed})^a \, (\text{Load})^b}.$$

Basic Types of Bearing (Fig 2.54)

(a) *Single-row Radial Ball Bearings.* This type of bearing will accept pure thrust in either direction, pure radial load or a combination of both; the maximum thrust load is less than the maximum radial load. In common with other rolling bearings, the permissible load decreases with increasing speeds, and its life is reduced by elevated operating temperatures.

(b) *Single-row Angular Contact Bearings.* These bearings will accept a greater thrust load than (*a*) above, but in one direction only; in consequence, they are used in pairs. The angle of contact (α) may be selected according to the amount of thrust the bearing is to sustain.

(c) *Single-row Thrust Bearings.* The applied load should be pure thrust only, as a journal load affects the concentricity of the rings. The balls are subject to centrifugal force, and very high speeds must be avoided.

(d) *Cylindrical Roller Bearings.* These bearings are used for applications where a high radial or shock load is encountered. The inner race may move axially relative to the outer race, and this property is utilised in

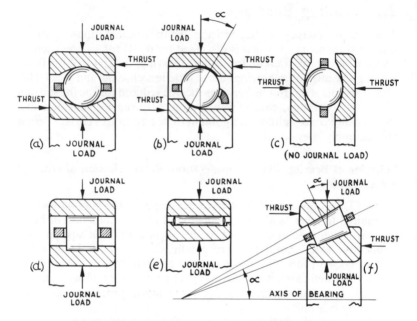

Fig. 2.54 Basic types of rolling bearings

(a) Single-row ball bearing   (d) Cylindrical-roller bearing
(b) Angular-contact bearing   (e) Needle-roller bearing
(c) Single-row thrust bearing   (f) Taper-roller bearing

machine-tool spindles to permit expansion due to temperature effects without loss of radial location, see p. 77.

(e) *Needle Roller Bearings.* For a given bore size, less room is taken up by needle roller bearings than by the standard cylindrical type, although needle rollers are less efficient. The bearings are used for the lower speeds and as bearings for oscillating motions.

(f) *Taper Roller Bearings.* This type of bearing has a wide field of usefulness, especially in connection with machine-tool spindles, gear-shafts, etc., where high axial and radial forces are combined. The angle α, Fig 2.54(f), can be selected according to the relative magnitudes of the axial and radial forces, the usual range being from $7\frac{1}{2}°$ to $25°$, the steep angle bearings being suited to heavy thrust conditions.

In all cases basic bearing types have variants to suit particular conditions. Makers' catalogues not only give details of the wide range of types and sizes which are available but also provide data relating speed, load and life factors.

Rolling Friction. If an inelastic ball or roller rolls over an inelastic plane surface, Fig 2.55(a), the ball is in point contact and the roller in line contact: under such theoretical conditions the stress is infinite;

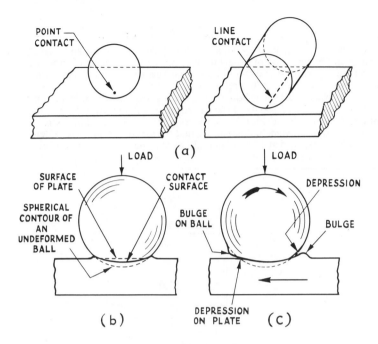

Fig. 2.55 Contact conditions between a plane and a rolling element

    (*a*) Inelastic elements
    (*b*) Elastic elements (stationary)
    (*c*) Elastic elements (rolling)

Stress = load/area, but when area = 0, stress = ∞. However, the materials used for rolling bearings are elastic and deform under load, Fig 2.55(*b*); this enables them to withstand loads without fracturing due to excessive stress.

Since the deformation of rolling bearings in practice is of significant size, it is clear that relative movement between the inner and outer races can take place due to this factor, and, additionally, that energy is absorbed by the process of deformation. This energy is an important factor in the total energy absorbed by "rolling friction".

A further aspect of the deformation process relates to endurance: in use, the metallic crystals of the bearing are subjected to repeated stresses which, even if they do not reach the ultimate strength of the material, can eventually lead to failure by fatigue of the metal.

In dealing with rolling bearings it is desirable to know their load-carrying capacity and, in precision applications, to have a concept of the magnitude of the deformation which can occur in bearing elements. These matters have been treated in research carried out by Hertz, Stribeck, Palmgren and others. A study of rolling bearings has been published under the title of *Rolling Bearings* by R. K. Allen (Pitman), to which the reader is referred for detailed information.

EXERCISES 2

1. Analyse the effect of dynamic forces induced by rotating and reciprocating masses in the operation of a machine tool. Discuss the relevant factors and their effects in regard to one of the following: (*a*) centre lathe; (*b*) planing machine; (*c*) external cylindrical grinding machine.

2. The wheelhead slide shown, Fig 2.56, is supported on rollers retained in a cage. If the centre of gravity of the wheelhead is 145 mm from the left-hand end of the slide, and the position of the rollers when the slide is at the extreme right-hand end of its movement is as shown, find the maximum slide movement (*L*). If the rollers are spaced at 43 mm intervals, what is the maximum number of rollers the slide will accommodate?

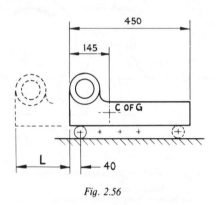

Fig. 2.56

3. A machine slide of height *h* is counterbalanced as shown in Fig 2.57. Show that it can be raised by a vertical feed force if its point of application is not greater than $h/2 \cot \phi$ from the centreline (ϕ = angle of friction).

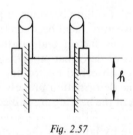

Fig. 2.57

4. A vee slide, Fig 2.58, moves in its slideway under the action of force *P*. If the vertical force acting on the slide is *W*, show that $P = \mu W \sqrt{2}$.

5. Determine the feed force at the leadscrew required to displace the slide shown in Fig 2.59 ($\mu = 0.12$). Find the position for applying the least possible feed force, and the magnitude of this force.

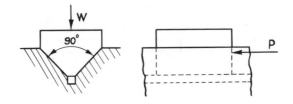

Fig. 2.58

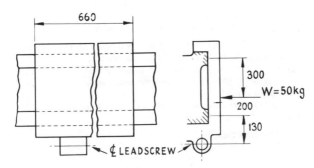

Fig. 2.59

6. Illustrate the principle of a device to eliminate the effect of backlash in the table screw and nut on a milling machine. Why is this essential in the down-cut process?

7. How are the following relations established in machine-tool alignment?

(i) Squareness of two or more machine surfaces.
(ii) Flatness and straightness of a machine bed.
(iii) Alignment of a spindle with a surface.

The general characteristics of the instruments used should be stated.

8. (a) What equipment would you use to check the straightness of the slideways of a large slideways grinding machine?

(b) How would you check the vertical slide for squareness?

(c) How would you check the bed for cross-wind, and

(d) What accuracy could be achieved in each of the above measurements?

9. (a) What principal alignment checks are necessary for a first-grade centre lathe, and what tolerances should be met?

(b) What equipment is necessary to check the alignments?

10. The vertical and horizontal cutting forces acting on the boring bar shown in Fig 2.60 are 900 N and 270 N respectively. If the tool is set at a radius of 19 mm determine:

(a) Torsional deflection due to the 900 N component. (*Note*: torsional deflection).

$$\theta° = \frac{584 . T . L}{G . D^4},$$ where T = torque, Nm, and modulus of rigidity,

$G = 82 \times 10^9 \text{ N/m}^2$, D and L in m.

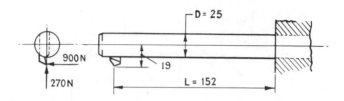

Fig. 2.60

(*b*) Deflection as a cantilever due to—

    (i) vertical component of cutting force;
    (ii) horizontal component of cutting force.

Hence determine the final position of the tool point and the size of hole which will be produced by the boring tool ($E = 206 \times 10^9$ N/m^2).

11. Explain by means of a clear sketch how the various feeds and speeds are obtained on a fixed-spindle drilling machine and also how reversal of the spindle rotation is brought about.

12. The spindle speed-change gear for a drilling machine has to comply with the following specification:

Max diameter of drill	= 12 mm
Min diameter of drill	= 3 mm
Max cutting speed of smallest drill	= 30 m/min
Min cutting speed of largest drill	= 20 m/min
Six spindle speeds.	
Motor speed	= 2800 rev/min

Make a line diagram of a suitable layout for the spindle drive and determine the gear ratios.

13. Make a diagrammatic sketch suitably annotated of a typical transmission from the headstock of a lathe, through the feed box to the rack for sliding, the saddlescrew for surfacing and the leadscrew for screwcutting.

14. (*a*) The design requirements for the main spindle of a lathe are that it must be constrained in a manner which will ensure that it is rigid in all directions, except that it is very important for it to rotate about a fixed axis. Enumerate the minimum number of constraints which must be provided in an ideal pneumatic bearing arrangement and indicate how these ideal requirements are modified to provide a design which will be satisfactory in service.

(*b*) What arrangements can be made to ensure that the main spindle of a lathe with a very wide speed range will:

    (i) not be subject to serious angular oscillations during heavy machining operations, which may include intermittent loading;
    (ii) not be subject to high-frequency vibrations during high-speed finish machining?

15. Show that a taper ratio of 7/24 is the most suitable taper to be used for a "non-stick" taper fit. ($\mu = 0.145$.)

Make a neat sketch of the type of arbor end and spindle nose used on a milling machine having a "non-stick" taper and add notes explaining the design.

16. A cutting test on cast iron conducted on a drilling machine gave the following results:

Drill diameter = 19 mm   Spindle speed = 302 rev/min
Feed/rev   = 0·3 mm   Torque   = 21 Nm
Axial thrust = 3400 N

Using an average value of 5 % for the taper, and allowing a safety factor of 1·25 on the torque and thrust values, determine a suitable size Morse taper shank for this drill. ($\mu = 0.15$.)

17. Analyse the forces acting on the spindle of a conventional vertical milling machine, and by reference to this analysis draw a cross-section through the spindle to show the type and disposition of the bearings you suggest to meet the conditions.

Clearly explain what provisions are made in the design to allow for temperature variations of the spindle due to speed and load conditions.

CHAPTER 3
Kinematics of Machine Tools

3.1

The shape of many engineering components is derived from common geometric solids. One useful approach to the machining of such shapes is to analyse motions capable of producing them.

There are alternative ways of machining each geometric form; traditional machine tools have evolved to provide the most convenient way for machining the general run of work. Where however special component forms are required to be machined in large quantities, it is first desirable to consider possible generating motions and then to base manufacturing methods and equipment, including in some instances specially designed machine tools, on the generating system likely to give the lowest cost for the quality required.

3.2 Geometric Form of Engineering Components

As a basis for analysing elements of movement of machine tools some of the common geometric figures used in engineering components will be considered.

(i) *Plane*. This is the basic element of prismatic shapes, and it is used as a datum from which component dimensions are given. It is a feature which is sometimes required to a high order of accuracy, and the methods used in its production must be capable of achieving whatever degree of accuracy is required for functional purposes, both as regards flatness and angular relationship with adjacent planes.

(ii) *Cylinder*. This appears in very many components and may have an external surface (shafts) or an internal surface (holes).

(iii) *Cone*. In relation to the production of components a cone is more commonly referred to as a taper, chamfer or bevel (as in bevel gears).

(iv) *Sphere*. The ball bearing is the most common example of the spherical shape, but spherical surfaces are also used for applications such as spherical seatings.

(v) *Helix*. This appears in the form of screw threads, oil grooves, drill flutes, etc.

Shapes more complex than standard geometric forms occur in component profiles and contours, and dimensions for these may lie in two or three planes. For example, a point on the profile of a plate cam will be defined by two dimensions, each taken from a datum and expressed in either rectangular or polar co-ordinates.

These two methods of dimensioning are shown in Fig 3.1.

Similarly, relationship with a point on the flank of a tooth of a helical gear would need to be defined by dimensions in three planes, one of which would be an angular dimension.

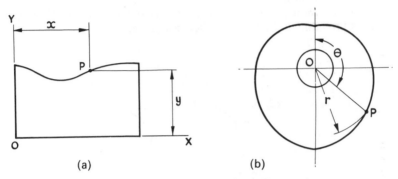

Fig. 3.1 Plate cam profiles defined by: (a) rectangular co-ordinates;
(b) polar co-ordinates

In order to produce these geometric figures on a machine tool, surplus material must be cut away as chips or swarf until the original piece is reduced to the required form and size. This requires that the machine tool be capable of reproducing controlled movements of workpiece or tool or both in such a way that geometric shapes result. Quite apart from the questions of cutting action and the power required to remove material from a component, the machine must be able to perform accurately its basic functions of motion.

3.3 Kinematics in Machine Tools

Kinematics is the branch of science treating position and movement. Since components are machined by movement of tools and are produced to a size by the accurate relative position of tool and workpiece, kinematics is clearly important as far as machine tools are concerned.

Alignments are closely related to the kinematics of a machine both as regards straight-line motion and accuracy of rotation about a fixed axis. The machine must be capable of maintaining its alignments under conditions of:

(a) static loading—it must be strong enough to bear applied forces without undue flexure;

(b) dynamic loading—it must accept stresses set up by moving parts without the effects of vibration or deformation affecting its function.

Fundamental Aspects of Movement. Consider the basic problem of constraining a body—whether it be a machine slide, a cutter or an abstract mass is immaterial to our present purpose. Such a body is shown in Fig 3.2, and it may be seen that the "pure" movements of the body can be classified as follows:

(*a*) Linear movement along any one of the three conventional axes, i.e. XX, YY or ZZ. Thus the body has three degrees of freedom by means of axial translation.

(*b*) Rotational movement about any one of the axes, XX, YY or ZZ, thus providing a further three degrees of freedom.

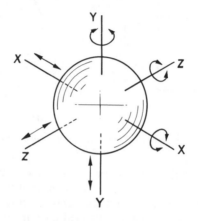

Fig. 3.2 Six degrees of freedom of a body in space

Hence it is seen that **an unrestrained body in space has six "pure" or precise degrees of freedom.** All other movements of the body may be achieved by combining two or more of the precise movements to obtain the required motion. Thus, the path of the sphere in a given plane, Fig. 3.3, is defined by relating ordinates x_1y_1, x_2y_2, etc.

It can be shown that a body will be constrained from movement by six locations suitably applied and which take into consideration kinematic principles. The removal of one location will then permit one degree of freedom, the removal of two locations will permit two degrees of freedom and so on.

Fig 3.4(*a*) represents the location of two separate bodies—one having three ball feet, the other three radially disposed vees. Six location points occur, numbered 1 to 6, constraining movement of the body. Important aspects of kinematic design can be observed in this example:

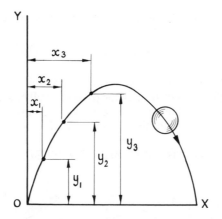

Fig. 3.3 Movement of a body in one plane (without rotation)

The movement consists of translation along two axes, OX $(x_1 x_2 x_3 \dots)$ and OY $(y_1 y_2 y_3 \dots)$.

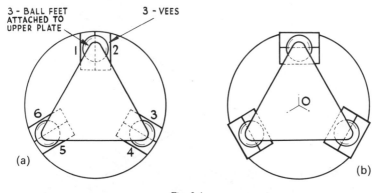

Fig. 3.4

(*a*) Simple kinematic design for location of two bodies—the six points of constraint are numbered 1 to 6

(*b*) Degenerate design. Constraints are tangential to a circle and do not prevent rotation about a vertical axis through O. The three ball feet must also be accurately positioned relative to the vees to ensure contact at six points.

(*a*) The two bodies can be separated and replaced in the same relationship as frequently as is necessary.

(*b*) A high degree of accuracy in construction is not needed, e.g. the diameter of the pitch circle of the feet may vary considerably and yet be accommodated by the vees.

(*c*) The six locations are all "point" contact, there are no redundant locations, i.e. none of the locations can be dispensed with.

(*d*) Wear of locations will not cause slackness to occur between the mating parts.

A similar but degenerate design for locating two bodies is illustrated in Fig 3.4(*b*).

Notes: (i) It is apparent that while the two parts of a kinematic pair are fully constrained by six restraints, the parts can still be separated unless a closing force is applied. Frequently gravity is the only force necessary to close the system, in other designs some form of retention (e.g. clamping) may be necessary.

(ii) "Point" contact is not normally feasible in machine-tool appli-

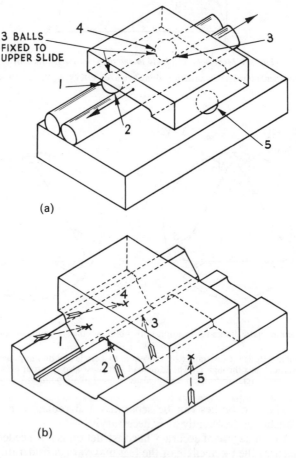

Fig. 3.5

(*a*) Kinematic slide (point contacts) with five restraints, permitting one degree of freedom (indicated by arrow)

(*b*) Slideway based on kinematic principles and having one degree of freedom

cations because of the substantial forces which are invariably present. These forces must be supported over suitably large areas of contact to keep the pressure between surfaces within reasonable limits, if this were not done the pressure would be infinitely high (p. 91). A comparison between a fully kinematic slide and the equivalent type of slide used on machine tools and based on kinematic principles is shown in Fig 3.5.

Example 3.1
State the degrees of freedom possessed by the parts given below, indicate translation by T, rotation by R.

(*a*) Threaded nut on stationary screw.
(*b*) Plug gauge in component bore.
(*c*) Scribing block on marking-out table.
(*d*) Arm of radial drill.
(*e*) Single-point tool operating in lathe tool-post.

Solutions
(*a*) $1T$, $1R$; (*b*) $1T$, $1R$; (*c*) $2T$, $1R$; (*d*) $1T$, $1R$; (*e*) $2T$.

Note:
(i) Two planes in contact provide four constraints, one of which is redundant. To obtain similar results using true kinematic location the scribing block in (*c*) should be supported at three points. A simple example illustrating the existence of a redundant location is the case of the four-legged chair, which will rock on an uneven surface and a three-legged stool which will not rock.

(ii) A cylinder enveloped in a bore as (*a*), (*b*) and (*d*) has two degrees of freedom ($1T$, $1R$) and four constraints, i.e. to obtain similar results kinematically the cylinder should be supported at four points of contact as illustrated in Fig 3.6.

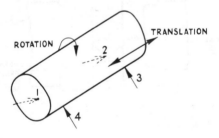

Fig. 3.6 A kinematically constrained cylinder showing four points of restraint and two degrees of freedom (i.e. $1R$, $1T$)

3.4 Kinematics and Machining Geometric Forms

The geometric requirements of machining are derived from two basic elements:

(*a*) rotation about an axis which has a fixed position;
(*b*) translation in a straight line.

Fig 3.7 gives the conventional symbols for linear and rotary displacements in accordance with BS3635: *The Numerical Control of Machine Tools.*

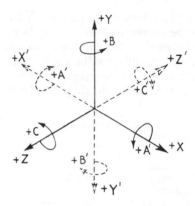

Fig. 3.7 Conventional symbols in accordance with BS3635

When considered kinematically each of these motions occur in systems having five location points and one degree of freedom. This is illustrated by the rotation of a lathe spindle and by the single translatory movement of a lathe saddle shown in diagrammatic form in Fig 3.8.

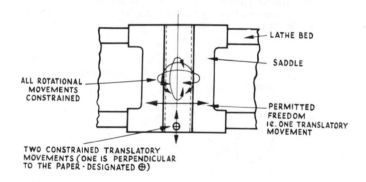

Fig. 3.8 The single degree of freedom of a lathe saddle

For an axis of rotation to have a constant position in space, the rotating element must be exactly cylindrical (e.g. bearing surfaces of a machine-tool spindle) and there must be no axial "float" (endwise motion of the axis).

For translation to be in a straight line, the motion at all points of the moving element must be in two mutually prependicular planes. Any "cross-wind" about the line of translation produces a rotation of the sliding member. This is shown in Fig 3.9, where a cylinder rolls on two separate surfaces. If planes A and B do not lie in a common true plane,

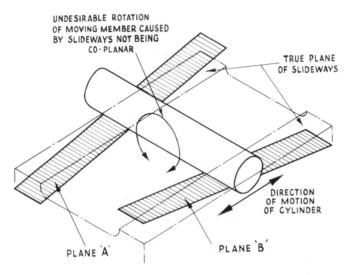

UNDESIRABLE ROTATION
OF MOVING MEMBER CAUSED
BY SLIDEWAYS NOT BEING
CO-PLANAR

TRUE PLANE
OF SLIDEWAYS

DIRECTION
OF MOTION
OF CYLINDER

PLANE 'A'

PLANE 'B'

Fig. 3.9 The rotational effect on a moving member caused by cross-wind in machine slideways

but are inclined as indicated, then the cylinder will have an additional freedom.

Symbolic Notation of BS3635. To apply the notation of Fig 3.7 in accordance with rules given in BS3635, the following conventions must be followed:

Z-axis   The principal axis of rotation of the machine (e.g. spindle of a lathe) is designated as the Z-axis. A displacement of either workpiece or tool, made parallel to this axis, is a z displacement.

For machines without a rotating spindle (e.g. planing machine) the Z-axis is perpendicular to the workholding surface.

X-axis   This axis is always horizontal, parallel to the workholding surface and perpendicular to the Z-axis.

Y-axis   An axis perpendicular to the Z- and X-axes.

Some machine tools have elements which can rotate about one or more of the above axes, such as circular tables. These rotations are symbolically designated in relation to their axes as shown in Fig 3.7. Note that the directions of displacement along the axis and the direction of the associated rotation follows the well known 'right hand screw' rule enabling +ve and −ve directions to be standardised.

Standardisation of these features has become essential since it

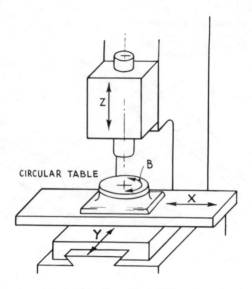

Fig. 3.10 Conventional symbols for axes of single column drilling and boring machines

facilitates numerical control programming. Fig 3.10 shows the application of the above rules for a particular machine tool.

Rotations A, B and C are primarily intended for feed motions under numerical control. In discussing the kinematics of generating, θ has been used to indicate rotation as an essential part of the cutting process, e.g. work rotation during turning; (see **3.5**).

In producing the geometric forms discussed in **3.2**, machine tools use systems based on (*a*) or (*b*) (p. 101), or combinations of these elementary movements. **Machine tools normally have two kinematic systems of freedom and constraints, one controlling the workpiece and the other controlling the medium through which cutting is effected, e.g. cutting tool, grinding wheel.**

These two systems are linked to obtain the relative movements necessary to produce a geometric shape. The form of this linkage may be as follows:

(*a*) Mechanical, e.g. gear train, leadscrew and nut, etc.
(*b*) Hydraulic, e.g. hydraulic systems of valves and cylinders as used on tracer mechanisms.
(*c*) Electronic, e.g. punched or magnetic tape control.

Sometimes it is essential for this linkage to give a fixed and definite ratio in order to produce a required shape. In other cases the relationship is not critical, i.e. the ratio can be changed without affecting the geometry of the parts produced, e.g. changing the feed rate when turning a cylinder will not affect the geometric shape of the solid body produced, but changing the traverse rate when screw cutting would most certainly affect the accuracy of the screw thread. **In this latter case the linkage-ratio is said to be critical.**

3.5 Classification of Generating Systems

In the following examples the notation used will be as follows:

θ_w = Rotation of workpiece.
θ_t = Rotation of tool.
x = Translation along XX axis.
y = Translation along YY axis.
z = Translation along ZZ axis. (*Note*: displacement parallel to a spindle axis is usually designated as z.)
$\oplus$ = Linear motion of machine element in a direction perpendicular to the plane of the diagram.

The generation of geometric shapes on a machine tool may be classified as follows:

(a) 1*st Order Generation.* In this group the separate kinematic systems of the tool and workpiece are linked with a *non-critical ratio.* This order of generation may be subdivided into the following classes:

Class 1. No critical relationship exists within the kinematic system of the tool, nor within the kinematic system of the workpiece. Examples of this class of 1st Order Generation are the machining of plane and cylindrical workpieces, Fig 3.11

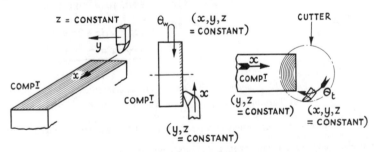

Fig. 3.11 Examples of 1st Order, Class 1, generation

(*a*) Motions of translation (y and z) must be in a straight line—for convenience they are usually perpendicular to each other. The component and tool may each have one degree of freedom (e.g. planing), or the tool may have two freedoms and the component none, or the tool none and the component two, freedoms

(*b*) and (*c*) The essential conditions for producing a plane surface under the conditions shown are: (i) translation (x) must be in a straight line, and (ii) axis of rotation must be perpendicular to x

Class 2. A critical relationship exists within either:

    (i) the kinematic system of the tool; or
    (ii) the kinematic system of the workpiece.

Examples of machining which fall into this group are the production of a spherical or conical surface on a lathe, Fig 3.12, or a helix on a milling machine.

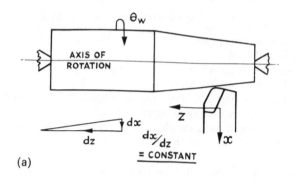

(a)

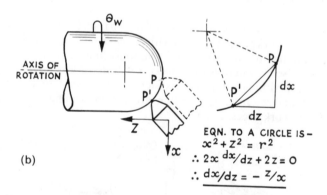

(b)

Fig. 3.12 Examples of 1st Order, Class 2, generation

    (*a*) Turning a cone   (*b*) Turning a sphere

The relationship dx/dz may be achieved by the following methods:
  (i) mechanical (e.g. taper turning attachment, Fig. 3.21 link mechanism, Fig. 3.15(*a*));
 (ii) hydraulic (see p. 130);
(iii) electronic (e.g. punched or magnetic tape control).

(b) *2nd Order Generation.* The two kinematic systems (i.e. of workpiece and of tool) *are linked with a critical ratio*, which if altered or varied, would affect the geometric form produced. Again, this order of generation may be subdivided into classes as for 1st Order Generation.

Class 1. Examples of machining in which the kinematic systems of tool and workpiece are linked with a critical ratio are the production on a lathe of a helix, or a spiral (as, for example, the relief curve of a form-relieved cutter).

Class 2. This is a complex form of generation in which a critical relationship exists within the kinematic system of the tool (or workpiece) in addition to the critical relationship between the kinematic system of the tool and the kinematic system of the workpiece. Examples of machining which fall into this group are the production on a lathe of a taper helix (taper thread) and the imposition of a spiral upon a helix which occurs when machining the relief curve on the teeth of a gear-cutting hob.

This classification of the generating systems employed on machine tools will now be illustrated by worked examples, some of which are problems related to conditions of alignment and serve to emphasise the connection between the kinematics of a machine tool, and its alignments.

Example 3.2
(1st Order Generation. Class 1)

Illustrate methods of generating a cylindrical surface and state the essential kinematic conditions for producing an accurate form. In separate diagrams show inversions of the methods.

Solution
(1) Rotation θ_w and translation z (see Fig 3.13(a)) are linked, usually by mechanical methods, in a non-critical ratio, i.e. the feed rate. Considered from a kinematic point of view, the boring of a hole by rotation of the work, θ_w, and translation of the tool, z, uses the same principle and is merely a variation (Fig 3.14(i)).

On the other hand, machining a spigot using a boring head as shown in Fig 3.14(ii) is an inversion of the turning process, and has a variation shown in (iii).

(2) Translation, z, and rotation, θ_w (see Fig 3.13(b)) are linked by a hand or mechanical feed in a non-critical ratio. This method is used on slotting machines, and a variation may be seen in Fig 3.14(iv), where the grinding of the root of a spline shaft is shown.

Producing a cylinder in this way will take longer than the methods in (1), and hence will be used only if technical difficulties prevent the use of the quicker method.

(3) The essential kinematic conditions for producing a true cylinder are:

(a) Rotation (θ_w or θ_t) must be about a constant axis.

(b) Translation, z, must be in a straight line *parallel to the axis of rotation and lying in a plane containing the axis.* The significance of this condition is shown in Example 3.6, which has been chosen to illustrate the effect of translation, z, taking place in a plane inclined to the plane containing the axis of rotation.

Example 3.3
(1st Order Generation—Class 2)
Analyse the motions capable of generating spherical surfaces.

Solution
Spherical surfaces may be produced by tool movements using continuous co-ordinate settings based on systems of: (a) polar co-ordinates; (b) Cartesian co-ordinates.

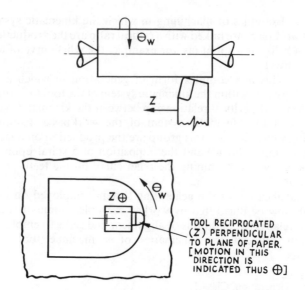

Fig. 3.13 Basic methods of generating cylindrical surfaces
(1st Order generation, Class 1)

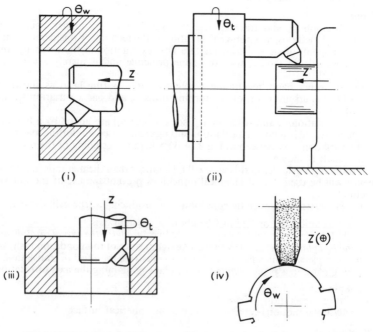

*Fig. 3.14 Variations and inversions of basic methods of producing cylindrical
surfaces*

For both these methods, the workpiece must rotate (θ_w) about a constant axis ZZ and the locus of the tool point should follow a circular path, origin at the centre of the sphere.

(a) When using polar co-ordinates the tool is maintained at a constant radius from the sphere centre by means of a mechanical linkage. The principle is illustrated in Fig 3.15(a), and any one of several alternative mechanisms might be used to achieve these conditions. For example, if on a lathe the saddle and cross slide were locked and the conventional tool-post replaced by a form of circular table capable of holding the tool the necessary movement could be achieved.

(b) To produce a spherical surface using Cartesian co-ordinate settings for the tool point the relationship of the tool movement along the XX and ZZ axes must be carefully controlled, see Fig 3.15(b). When a locus of the tool point traces a

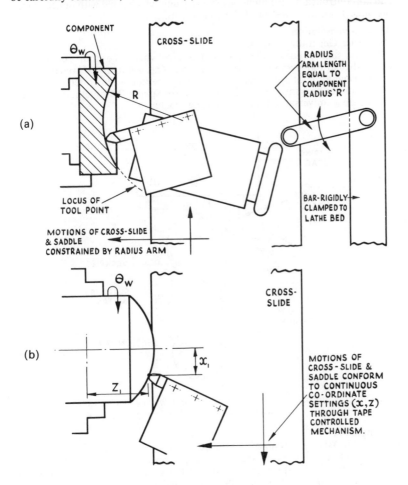

Fig. 3.15 Generating spherical surfaces

(a) Polar co-ordinate method
(b) Cartesian co-ordinate method

circle, origin at the centre of the spherical surface, the equation to the locus will be:

$$x^2 + z^2 = R^2$$

i.e.
$$2x \cdot dx/dz + 2z = 0$$
$$\therefore \quad dx/dz = -z/x$$

The relationship dx/dz cannot be achieved satisfactorily by manual operation of the tool movement. If the work is to be performed on a lathe the relationship may be ensured by electronic control using punched or magnetic tape to feed instructions to motors controlling saddle and cross-slide movements. Lathes of this type dispense with the usual handwheel controls, gear-change levers, etc., and are controlled from a numerical control unit which is fed with punched tape prepared from the drawing of the component.

Alternative Solution
(1st Order Generation—Class 1)

In the first solution the axis (Y) about which the tool rotated was perpendicular to the axis (Z) of the workpiece. This is not an essential condition for the generation of a spherical surface, and a method is illustrated in Fig 3.16, where oblique axes intersect at the centre of the sphere. This method is suitable for use on a universal milling or a boring machine.

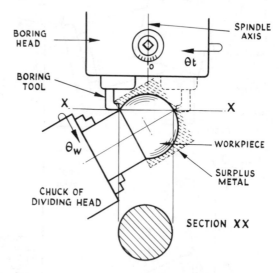

Fig. 3.16 Generating spherical surfaces on boring or milling machine. Internal spherical surfaces can also be produced this way

Example 3.4

Fig 3.17(a) shows the contour of the bore of a component which is required in large quantities. It is proposed to develop a special machine with slides in directions A and B displacing simultaneously to cause the tool nose shown to bore the desired profile. Slide A is to be actuated by means of a 6 mm pitch leadscrew and slide B by means of a cam.

Show in a line diagram a suitable mechanism for relating the motions of A and B.

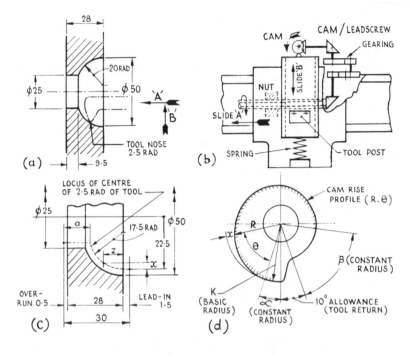

Fig. 3.17

(*a*) Internal profile to be produced by single-purpose machine
(*b*) Diagram of cam-operated and leadscrew-operated slides
(*c*) Locus for centre of tool nose-radius
   Note the allowances for tool lead-in and over-run
(*d*) General form of cam for cross-slide operation

Develop mathematical expressions from which the shape of the cam can be determined.

Solution
   A suitable mechanism is shown in Fig 3.17(*b*).
   The cam will have four parts, see Fig 3.17(*c*) and (*d*), as follows:

(*a*) The initial constant radius lobe for the 1·5 mm lead-in.
(*b*) A cam fall to control slide movement B during machining of the 20 mm radius.
(*c*) The final constant radius lobe for the parallel bore and 0·5 mm over-run.
(*d*) The allowance for the tool return.

To simplify the calculations, consider the path followed by the centre of the 2·5 mm tool-point radius.

Total distance travelled by slide A = 1·5 + 28 + 0·5 = 30 mm

Angle through which cam will turn during 30 mm in travel of A

$$= 360° - \text{Angle allowed for tool return (say 10°)}$$
$$= 350°$$

$\therefore$ For z_1 mm travel of A, cam will rotate through $\dfrac{350 \times z_1}{30}$ degrees

Hence:

(a) To produce 1·5 mm lead-in, cam will have a constant radius, K, acting during rotation through α degrees.

$$\alpha = \frac{1·5 \times 350}{30} = 17\tfrac{1}{2}°$$

(b) The cam profile required during the machining of the 20 mm radius may be determined as follows:

Let z = displacement of slide from front face of component

              x = displacement of slide in direction "B"

From Fig 3.17(c) $x = 17·5 - \sqrt{(17·5^2 - z^2)}$

Now, radius of cam profile, $R = K - x$

Substituting for x,

$$\therefore \quad R = K - [17.5 - \sqrt{(17.5^2 - z^2)}] \tag{1}$$

also
$$\theta = \frac{350 \times z}{30} \tag{2}$$

In equations (1) and (2), K is constant and z is a parameter. Hence, if z is given a series of values then the expressions may be used to calculate the co-ordinates R and θ for the cam profile.

Example 3.5

The spindle of a vertical milling machine is inclined at 20° to the vertical, and a boring head fitted with the tool set at a radius of 50 mm is used to bore a component having a previously drilled hole. If the spindle traverse is locked during the operation and the vertical feed of the machine knee used in its place, determine the geometric form and dimensions of the bore produced.

Solution

In the plane AA_1 normal to the spindle axis (see Fig 3.18) the locus of the tool point is a circle which meets the plane BB_1 of the work at angle α as the work is fed vertically upwards (motion z).

By reference to the projection of $\triangle$s OPQ and $O_1 P_1 Q_1$ it will be seen that—

$$x = x_1 \cos \alpha$$

$$\therefore \quad x_1 = \frac{x}{\cos \alpha}$$

also
$$y_1 = y$$

Since the locus of the tool point in plane AA_1 is a circle, it may be represented by the equation

$$x_1^2 + y_1{}^2 = R_1{}^2 \tag{1}$$

substituting for x_1 and y_1

$$\frac{x^2}{\cos^2 \alpha} + y^2 = R_1{}^2$$

Divide by $R_1{}^2$

$$\frac{x^2}{R_1{}^2 \cos^2 \alpha} + \frac{y^2}{R_1{}^2} = 1 \tag{2}$$

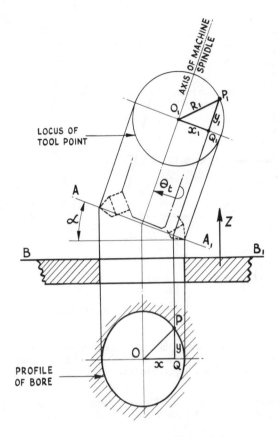

Fig. 3.18 Generating an elliptical hole

but (R_1 . cos α) and (R_1) are constants, and may be represented by *a* and *b* respectively
∴ Eqn (2) becomes

$$\frac{x^2}{a^2} + \frac{y^2}{b^2} = 1,$$

which is the equation to an ellipse. Hence the profile of the bore produced is an ellipse.

The dimensions of the ellipse will be:

semi-major axis, OY = radius of tool $\quad\quad$ = <u>50 mm</u>
semi-minor axis, OX = radius of tool × cos α = 50 cos 20°
$\quad\quad\quad\quad\quad\quad\quad\quad\quad\quad\quad\quad\quad\quad\quad\quad$ = 46·98 mm

Example 3.6

A workpiece rotates about a constant axis AB and is cut by the point of a tool moving in a straight line CD contained in a plane parallel to AB and distance *p* from it, Fig 3.19(*a*).

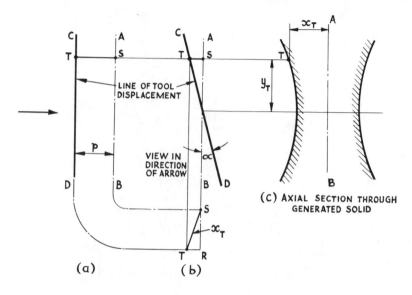

Fig. 3.19 Generation of a hyperboloid

Viewed perpendicular to these planes, the line of displacement CD of the tool point is inclined to axis AB at angle α; see Fig 3.19(*b*). Show that an axial section of the surface generated is a hyperbola $(x^2/p^2 - y^2/q^2 = 1)$.

Solution

Let co-ordinates of some point T on the generated surface be $(x_T\, y_T)$. By projection, draw $\triangle$ RST, and with reference to this triangle

$$SR = p$$

$$RT = y_T \tan \alpha$$

$$\therefore \quad x_T^2 = p^2 + y_T^2 \cdot \tan^2 \alpha \text{ for point T}$$

and, in general,
$$x^2 = p^2 + y^2 \cdot \tan^2 \alpha$$

or
$$x^2/p^2 = 1 + y^2 \cdot \tan^2 \alpha/p^2$$

but $\tan^2 \alpha/p^2$ is a constant, say $1/q^2$

$$\therefore \quad \underline{x^2/p^2 - y^2/q^2 = 1} \text{ which is the desired equation.}$$

Example 3.7

A workpiece rotates (θ_w) about a constant axis, and a rotating cutting tool (e.g. end mill) of small diameter (d), with its axis parallel to the workpiece axis moves in a straight line, AB, in a plane perpendicular to the workpiece axis, see Fig 3.20. At the nearest position, AB is distance h from the workpiece axis and the relationship between the rotation θ_w of the workpiece and the displacement x of the cutter in line AB is given by the equation $x = K\theta_w$, where K is a constant.

(*a*) Form an equation in polar co-ordinates for the contour generated assuming distance h to be small.

(*b*) State the condition which would make this an Archimedean spiral.

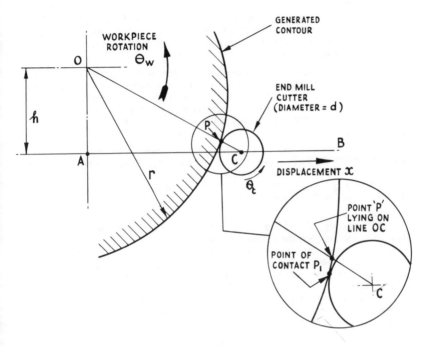

Fig. 3.20 Generating a cam contour using an end mill

Solution

(a) Let $\theta_w = 0$ when centre (C) of cutter is distance h from workpiece axis O
Then for all greater values of θ_w,

$$OC^2 = h^2 + x^2$$

but $x = K\theta_w$ (given)

$$\therefore \quad OC^2 = h^2 + K^2\theta_w^2 \qquad (1)$$

If distance h is small, then

$$OP = OC - \frac{d}{2} \text{ (nearly)} \qquad (2)$$

(the contour being generated is not a circle, and consequently the centre of curvature is not at O, thus point of contact P_1 between workpiece and cutter does not lie on the line joining centres O and C, see inset to Fig 3.20.)

Substituting (1) in equation (2),

$$OP = \sqrt{(h^2 + K^2\theta_w^2)} - \frac{d}{2} \text{ (very nearly)}$$

Thus, in polar co-ordinates, where r is the radius from O of any point on the contour, the equation may be stated

$$r = \sqrt{(h^2 + K^2\theta_w^2)} - \frac{d}{2}$$

(b) The equation to an Archimedean spiral is $r = K\theta$, and the condition necessary in (a) above to ensure that such a curve is produced would be that h must be zero, i.e. that the path of displacement AB must intersect the axis of workpiece rotation.

Note: Since the centre of curvature of an Archimedean spiral is not at O, the method of cam milling commonly employed does not give an exact Archimedean spiral. However, if d is small relative to r, and K is small, the departure from the exact spiral is negligible. **For milling constant-rise cams, the cutter diameter should be the same diameter as the roller follower of the cam.**

Example 3.8

(a) Discuss with the aid of a diagram, the mechanical linkage required to produce a taper thread on a conventional tool-room lathe using a taper-turning attachment. Sketch a typical taper thread form.

(b) Show why a taper thread produced by the offset tailstock method will be "drunken", i.e. have a non-constant slope.

Solution

(a) Refer to Fig 3.21. As in the case of screw cutting parallel threads, a critical linkage exists between the kinematic system of the lathe spindle (θ_w) and the longitudinal tool translation (z). In order to produce a true helix the linkage must ensure that the relationship between θ_w and z is constant. The leadscrew and the gear train between machine spindle and leadscrew ensures this constant relationship.

The second critical linkage occurs in the kinematic system of the tool movement. In order to produce the taper helix, the translatory movement (x) perpendicular to the workpiece axis must bear a constant relationship to the

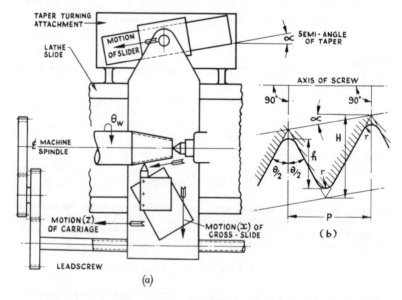

Fig. 3.21

(a) Producing a taper screw thread on a lathe using a taper turning attachment
(b) Typical taper thread form
    Note that the thread form is perpendicular to the axis of the screw

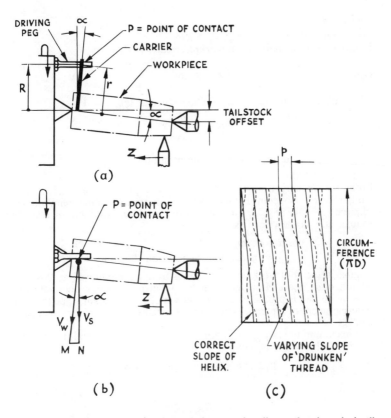

Fig. 3.22 *Producing a taper thread on a lathe using the off-set tailstock method will result in a "drunken" thread*

The development of a (parallel) screw thread is shown at (c); a correctly produced thread has a constant slope to the helix, whereas a "drunken" thread has a variable slope to the helix.

movement z, **i.e. $dx/dz =$ constant,** as for the generation of a simple cone. The taper-turning attachment fulfils this function and is set to the semi-angle (α) of the taper.

(b) With reference to Fig 3.22

Let $V_s =$ linear velocity of driving peg.
$\quad V_w =$ linear velocity of work carrier at P.
$\quad \omega_s =$ angular velocity of lathe spindle.
$\quad \omega_w =$ angular velocity of workpiece.
$\quad r =$ radius from workpiece axis to point P.
$\quad R =$ radius from spindle axis to driving peg.
$\quad \alpha =$ angle between spindle axis and workpiece axis.

When turning or screw cutting using the offset tailstock method, the workpiece is rotated by the action of the driving peg against the carrier clamped to the workpiece. Fig 3.22 shows the driving peg at two positions 90° apart.

Consider Fig 3.22(a)

Linear velocity of driving peg, $V_s = R\omega_s$
Linear velocity of point P on workpiece carrier, $V_w = r\omega_w$

Now $\qquad\qquad r = R/\cos\alpha \qquad\qquad \therefore\quad V_w = \dfrac{R\omega_w}{\cos\alpha}$

∴ For the instantaneous position as shown at (a), $V_s = V_w$

i.e. $\qquad\qquad\qquad R.\omega_s = \dfrac{R.\omega_w}{\cos\alpha}$

∴ $\omega_w = \omega_s.\cos\alpha$ at the position shown at (a).

Consider Fig 3.22(b)

From the velocity triangle PMN, $\cos\alpha = V_s/V_w$ for the instantaneous position shown. Also, point P is equidistant from the axes of the spindle and the workpiece hence the angular rotation of workpiece and of spindle are related in the same ratio as the velocities.

i.e. $\qquad\qquad\qquad \cos\alpha = \omega_s/\omega_w$

∴ $\omega_w = \omega_s/\cos\alpha$ at the position shown at (b).

Angular velocity of workpiece, ω_w, varies from a minimum of $\omega_s.\cos\alpha$ to a maximum of $\omega_s/\cos\alpha$. However, since the tool displacement, z, does not vary, a "drunken" thread is produced, i.e. the helix is of non-constant slope $(z \neq K\theta)$. The development of a parallel screw thread is shown in Fig 3.22(c) to illustrate this effect.

The maximum pitch (p_{max}) will occur when $\omega_w = \omega_s\cos\alpha$ and the minimum pitch (p_{min}) when $\omega_w = \omega_s/\cos\alpha$

i.e. $\qquad\qquad\qquad p_{max} = p/\cos\alpha$ and $p_{min} = p\cos\alpha$

EXERCISES 3

1. (a) A high-precision rectangular bar 1 m long × 150 mm wide × 100 mm deep forms the stationary member in a slide unit. A slide, 250 mm long, is to be constructed with location points based on true kinematic principles. The slide must be free to move along the fixed members in a straight line without slackness or redundant locations. Make a sketch of a suitable slide.

(b) Consider a high-precision ring 50 mm internal diameter × 100 mm long × 100 mm external diameter with the bore truly circular and parallel and one end face flat and truly normal to the bore. Illustrate by a sketch how the bush may be supported by the bore and the flat end face, so that it could be caused to rotate about a fixed axis without axial or diametral slackness or redundant locations.

2. State the machine to be used and the conditions to be satisfied for controlling the relative movement of the cutting medium and workpiece for the production of the following parts to a high standard of accuracy for size and geometric shape:

(a) Finish machine 50 mm diameter bore and face of a brass bush, 100 mm outside diameter × 75 mm long (tolerance ± 0.005 mm).

(b) Finish machine the four sides (100 mm × 50mm) of a square block 100 mm × 100 mm × 50 mm so that the opposite sides are parallel and adjacent sides are at 90° to each other (tolerance ± 0.003 mm).

3. Describe the methods which may be used for generating a spherical surface on the outside diameter of a disc 50 mm thick and 150 mm diameter.

4. Make a line diagram of the mechanical linkage available on a horizontal milling machine (with vertical head attachment) and dividing head, which may be used to generate a constant-rise spiral. If the rise of spiral required is less than the lead available on the machine, show how the vertical head and dividing head may be set to achieve the required rise. Use a vector displacement diagram to show the relationship between the lead available on the milling machine and the rise/rev of the spiral produced.

5. A flycutter at radius 190 mm is set in the spindle of a vertical milling machine with its axis on the workpiece centreline and is used to machine a plane surface 250 mm wide, the workpiece having a linear displacement, x, to provide the feed motion.

If the axis of rotation of the flycutter is inclined at $0° 20'$ to a perpendicular with the line of displacement, x, determine the maximum amount by which the machined surface will be concave.

6. Make a line diagram of the mechanical linkage representing the relationship $z = K \cdot \theta_w$ when helical milling, where

$$z = \text{translation parallel to dividing head axis;}$$

$$\theta_w = \text{rotation of work (radians);}$$

$$K = \text{constant.}$$

If the table leadscrew is 6 mm pitch and the dividing head has a 40/1 ratio, show how the change gears 48, 56, 64 and 100 teeth must be set to produce a helix of 100·8 mm lead.

What change in the alignment conditions is necessary to enable an approximate Archimedean spiral, $r = k\theta_w$ (where r = radius of cam form) to be milled using an end milling cutter? Find k for the above lead if θ_w is in radian measure.

7. A 2 mm pitch screw thread has to be produced for the insert of a plastic mould. To compensate for shrinkage of the plastic when removed from the mould the thread has to be produced 0·8 % long in pitch.

Show, with the aid of sketches, that this may be done on a tool-room lathe fitted with a taper-turning attachment if the workpiece is set between centres with its axis slightly inclined to the spindle axis. Determine the required taper settings for this work. (The "drunken thread" effect produced by off-setting the tailstock may be neglected.)

8. Illustrate and define the conditions necessary to produce a taper bore with a rotating tool, the workpiece to remain stationary. The machined surface of a bore so produced is found to follow a hyperbolic curve (instead of a straight line) in a plane containing the axis. Show how a positional error of the directions of motion could cause this. If the feeds available along the axis are 0·10, 0·16, 0·25, 0·40, 0·63 mm per rev, and the feeds on the cutter head cross slide are $\frac{2}{3}$ of these, what are the largest and smallest included angles of taper which can be bored?

9. A machine has tape controlled slides for x and y displacements, see Fig 3.23.

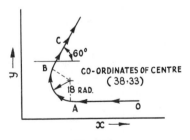

Fig. 3.23

Construct mathematical expressions giving the x and y co-ordinate systems for the three parts of the contour OA, AB and BC.

10. What are the methods used for controlling the movement of the cutter on:

    (a) an engraving machine;
    (b) a large automatic die-sinking machine of the type used for producing the dies used for the manufacture of car bodies?

In both cases, state the conditions which influence the accuracy of the part produced in relation to the master.

11. A universal milling machine is to be set to mill a plate cam for use on an automatic lathe. The cam is to have constant rise lobes as follows:

    (i) a rise of 23·6 mm over 15/100 of the profile;
    (ii) a rise of 22·2 mm over 20/100 of the profile;
    (iii) a rise of 19·0 mm over 12·5/100 of the profile.

If the dividing head spindle is not to be inclined at an angle (α) from the machine table of less than 30°, and gears of 24(2), 72, and 100 teeth are to be used, show how the machine must be set to produce the three lobes. Lead of the machine = 240 mm.

CHAPTER 4
Control of Machine Tools
PART A MECHANICAL, ELECTRICAL AND HYDRAULIC SYSTEMS

4.1 The Need for Automatic Control

In those processes of manufacturing which include machining operations, several types of machine tool may be involved sequentially, e.g. turning, milling, grinding. Manual control of such operations becomes uneconomic as the required output rises and alternatives of an automatic or semi-automatic (manual loading and unloading) nature have long been available. These trends are now further advanced by numerical control (NC), applicable to more complex machining, and by in-process measurement with feed-back to compensate for tool wear or other minor variables affecting a critical dimension.

Manually controlled machining operations involve three distinct steps: planning, machine settings, machining and, for one-off jobs, these may be done on the shop floor by a skilled craftsman. For automatic or semi-automatic operation a work's organisation generally has separate groupings; a production planning department does the operation planning, skilled tool setters prepare the machines and machine operators/loaders tend the machines while they produce the work.

From early times machine tools were fitted with devices to reduce manual labour, e.g. automatic traverse of slides. A considerable range of mechanical hydraulic and electrical devices have contributed to the development of automatic operation and control, some of which are treated below.

4.2 Mechanical Control

Fig 2.33(a), (b) and (c) illustrate common mechanisms used to propel slides. By linking these to some device which engages and disengages them at the required points within a cycle, a simple automatic form of operation is achieved.

Fig 4.1 shows a trip and clutch mechanism used on some automatic lathes. The angular setting of the trip dog on the disc gives control of operation timing. The arrangement shows how a trip-displaced lever can

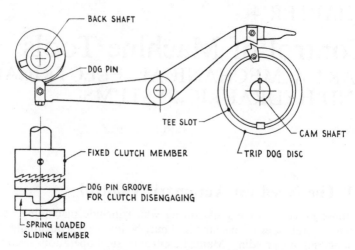

Fig. 4.1 Trip and clutch mechanism

operate a spring loaded clutch which incorporates a device for disengaging the same clutch after a short period of action. Such mechanically controlled clutches can be used to drive other items of an automatic lathe such as the Geneva indexing turret mechanism shown schematically in Fig 4.2. When the index plate is driven its rotation has two consequences. By the partial rotation of the connecting rod about D, the sub-slide is rapidly retracted and then returned to its former position. Simultaneously, pin A, after most of the slide retraction has occurred, engages slot B of the Geneva plate and rotates it to position C, thus

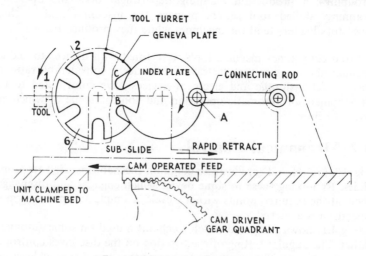

Fig. 4.2 Geneva indexing mechanism

indexing the tools mounted within the turret. In small high-speed single spindle automatic lathes the entire action can be completed in as short a time as 0·5 s.

The turret feed is driven by a geared quadrant driving a rack, the quadrant being part of a cam-operated lever mechanism as shown in Fig 4.3.

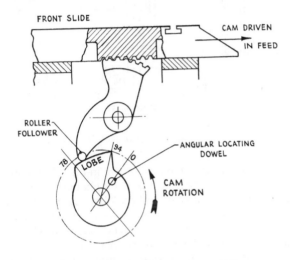

Fig. 4.3 Cam mechanism for advance of slide

The mechanism in Fig 4.3 gives the typical method for cam-operated slides where a specially designed and manufactured plate cam is used. The cam, its timing location fixed by means of a dowel as shown, brings the slide into action at 78/100 of the cycle, and advances the slide at a feed rate fixed by the rate of cam rise until the operation element is completed at 94/100 of the cycle.

The equivalent cam for operating the turret could of course be six-lobed to make use of all six tooling stations on the turret.

4.3 Single Spindle Bar Automatic Lathe (SS Auto)

This machine, often called a **screw machine** because of its widespread use for rapid manufacture of turned and die-threaded small screws from bar-stock, is representative of the majority of the ideas incorporated in mechanically controlled automatic machines.

Fig 4.4 gives a schematic arrangement of an SS Auto. Mechanical control of this machine depends upon the drive to the back shaft on

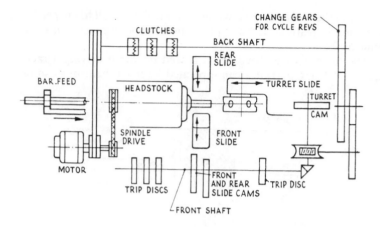

Fig. 4.4 Layout of drives on single spindle automatic

which clutch mechanisms of the type shown in Fig 4.1 and other devices are mounted. The back shaft is linked by change gears and a worm reduction gear to the front shaft and the turret cam shaft. These shafts are arranged to make one complete revolution while the headstock spindle makes the number of revolutions needed for machining the part. The front shaft rotates the front and rear slide cams and, via trip mechanisms, operates collet opening, spindle speed changes, turret indexing etc. Data are given in the machine handbook for preparing an operation layout with timing based on headstock spindle revolutions, and for the design of the special cams where the unit used is 1/100 of the cam circle. Such a machine is automatic in operation except for the manual loading of bar stock as it is consumed.

Single spindle **chucking** autos operate on similar principles but require manual loading and unloading unless specially designed equipment is fitted. Some of these machines can be set-up from standard parts, thus avoiding the expense of special cams, but this method normally causes a larger proportion of idle time and consequently a lower rate of production.

4.3 Multi-tooling

By skilful planning, cycle times for the above machines can be reduced by overlapping operations; see Chapter 16. When very high output is needed there is an obvious advantage in having as many tools cutting simultaneously as is possible. Two different developments of the automatic lathe exploit this principle.

Fig 4.5 shows the basic features of an **automatic centre lathe**; front and rear toolblocks enable parts to be machined using simple cam-

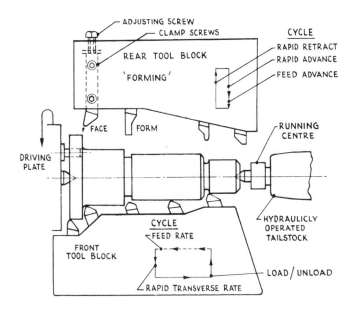

Fig. 4.5 Tool blocks and operating cycle of automatic centre lathe

controlled cycles. Special toolblocks must be manufactured for each component, an expensive matter; each tool fits into a square sectioned slot and is backed up by a screw for adjusting the amount it projects. To make the process completely automatic specially designed loading/unloading devices are also needed. Due to the high driving torque required, bar is gripped in two serrated jaws which increase their grip as the torque rises, and parts (such as that shown) having bolt holes in the end flange or having projections are driven via a specially arranged driving plate. A typical component would be a drop forged stub axle.

Simultaneous cutting by a number of tools is a feature of **multi-spindle automatics**, the principle of which is shown in Fig 4.6. The headstock incorporates a number of equi-spaced work spindles each with its own cross slide. The central toolblock has a tooling position for each spindle serving the function of the turret of the SS Auto. Traditionally, cams are used to control the slide and central toolblock motions and are either specially designed or selected from a standard range at some sacrifice of optimum output. Other forms of control, including NC, are now available for this type of machine.

As the headstock indexes, spindles move round to consecutive tooling positions, the cycle being completed by parting-off the job at spindle 5 and feeding bar to a stop. Ideally, given the same speed and feed rates, the machine should turn a part in 1/5 of the time required on the SS Auto.

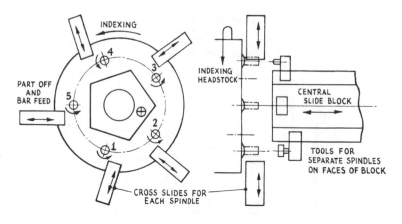

Fig. 4.6 Arrangement of multi-spindle automatic lathe

This however requires the operation to be sub-divided into five elements of equal duration. More realistically there is likely to be one operation element which cannot be split but which takes a little more time than is needed at other positions; hence one five-spindle machine has an output about equal to four SS Autos. There are also chucking versions of this machine type.

The practical advantages of multi-spindle machines are more tooling positions, more space for the tooling so that clearing the tools takes less time, and a more economical use of floor space where continuous high output is required.

4.4 Economics of Automatic Lathes

Accurate comparison of costs for a particular component requires detailed operation planning by reference to the handbooks of the machines to be compared. Chapter 16 treats time and cost estimates in a general manner and shows how "break-even" quantities are found. Fig 4.7 shows, tentatively, the approximate relationships between various types of lathes in terms of break-even points.

Note that the initial costs increase with the complexities of special equipment and setting of the machine, while high output with low direct labour cost reduces the price per piece as presented by the slope of the graph.

    (i) Cost of getting into production includes:
planning and tool design—manufacture of special tools and cams—time spent in setting-up the machine etc.

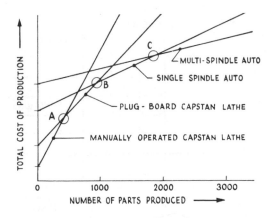ConCont

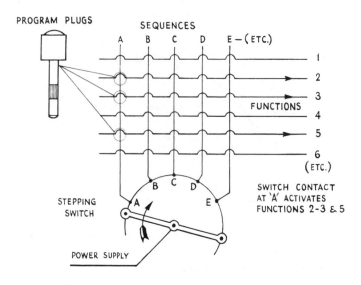

Fig. 4.8 Principle of plug-board sequence control

functions. If plugs are inserted into sockets 2, 3 and 5 of column A, their separate functions will be brought into action when the stepping switch rotates to contact at A.

Fig 4.9 illustrate one kind of functional mechanism, namely for slide displacement. Power received from the plug board operates an hydraulic valve via the solenoid. The piston is displaced at a feed rate controlled by the rate of oil flow until the slide contacts a stop. This actuates a microswitch, causing the hydraulic valve to reverse the flow and return the piston, at rapid traverse rate, to its original position. As the original position is reached the signal switch is operated. When all the functions on that line of the stepping switch have returned their "function completed" signal, the wiper arm rotates to the next position.

Practical systems have as many as 30 × 40 intersections on their plug board. Inserting plugs needs care and takes time; where regular batches

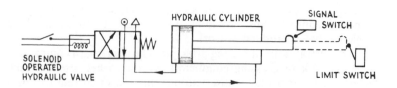

Fig. 4.9 Slide displacement of plug-board lathe

of work are needed a punched card can be made. This masks the plugboard sockets except for those holes where plugs must be inserted and provides a rapid and error free method of setting a frequently repeated sequence.

In the following example only a limited portion of the actual plug board is shown. The *home* signal at the end of the sequence causes the wiper arm of the stepping switch to return to its initial position for a restart of the cycle.

Example 4.1
Write an operation layout and show how the board should be plugged for machining the pin shown in Fig 4.10 on a plug-board capstan lathe.

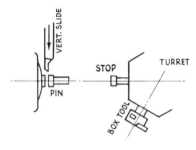

Fig. 4.10

Solution
The operation layout and signals are shown in Table 4.1, and the position of the plugs in the plug board in Table 4.2.

TABLE 4.1

Number	Motion	Signal
1	Turret forward; hydrofeed 1	Turret forward
2	Turret forward; hydrofeed 1	Collet open
3	Turret forward; hydrofeed 1	Collet close
4	(Index turret)	Turret back
5	Turret forward; hydrofeed 2	Turret forward
6	(Index turret)	Turret back
7	Vert. slide down; hydrofeed 1	Vert. slide down
8		Home

TABLE 4.2
Position of Plugs in Plug-board

		MOTIONS							
		1	2	3	4	5	6	7	8
Turret	Forward	•	•	•		•			
	Hydro-feed 1	•	•	•				•	
	Hydro-feed 2					•			
Collet	Open		•						
Slides	Front in								
	Rear in								
	Vert. down							•	
		SIGNALS							
Turret	Forward	•				•			
	Back				•		•		
Collet	Open		•						
	Close			•					
Slides	Front in								
	Vert. down							•	
	Home								•

4.6 Servo system control of slides

With exceptions arising from the use of cams, mechanically driven slides operate on a linear relationship. Reference to Chapter 3 will show that generating contours involving curves requires two slides in simultaneous motion but having a non-uniform ratio of displacements.

As explained later in this chapter, numerical control can meet these requirements but an alternative is the use of a servo copying system. The principle is shown schematically in Fig 4.11. A stylus, moving over the surface of a form plate, is displaced in or out under light spring pressure to supply error signals to a slide via the servo system. This system has two functions;

(i) to keep the tool displacement in agreement with the shape of the form plate,

(ii) to enable the slide displacement force to overcome the cutting forces.

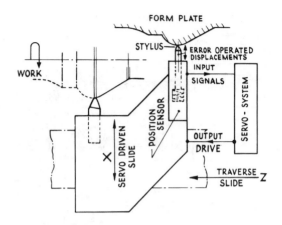

Fig. 4.11 Principle of servo-copying

The system is error operated (without feed-back) and the "copied" profile will be affected by small lags and by any differences between the stylus point and the cutting tool nose radius. Fig 4.11 shows clearly how the relationships between the *x* and *z* displacements are achieved via the stylus displacements and servo drive to the *X* slideway.

Hydraulic Servo Control. Hydraulics are applied to the control of machine tools through servo mechanisms, i.e. a device enabling a large power output to be controlled by simple control movements at low power levels.

The example of an hydraulic servo mechanism which follows has been chosen for its simplicity, and as in many other cases, the satisfactory functioning of the system is made possible by the servo spool valve.

Fig 4.12 shows the principle of a hydraulic profiling attachment fitted to the rear of an otherwise standard Harrison centre lathe.

The lathe saddle is connected to the hydraulic piston and supports the hydraulic slide, on which is positioned the rear tool post. Since the piston is attached to the saddle, its position is fixed, and the pressure exerted by the hydraulic fluid displaces the *cylinder*, the cutting-tool position changing accordingly.

The template—which is often a turned component—establishes the tool position through operation of the valve in the following manner. Suppose the stylus in following the template moves to the left: the piston of the spool valve will uncover the opening at R_4, allowing oil to return to exhaust. The flow of oil will cause the hydraulic cylinder and the hydraulic slide to move to the left and the tool to cut the workpiece to the required shape. As this occurs, the valve will return to neutral unless further difference in template size imparts movement to the spool valve via the stylus.

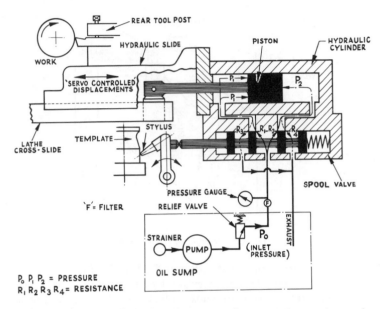

Fig. 4.12 Principle of hydraulic copying system for copy turning attachment of Harrison centre lathe

Should the stylus move to the right, piston movement will permit oil to flow:

    (i) through the opening at R_2, increasing the pressure at P_2;
    (ii) to exhaust through the port at R_3.

It is essential that the force moving the hydraulic slide is greater than the radial cutting force, and the tool response must immediately follow the stylus displacement for accurate reproduction.

To produce a square shoulder the hydraulic slide is set at an angle as shown in Fig 4.13 The vector diagram represents the tool feed, f, and the hydraulic slide withdrawal motion, s. If the ratio f/s were $\frac{1}{2}$ and the slide angle 30° the combined effect of f and s would be to produce a tool displacement perpendicular to the workpiece axis.

Valve Operation in Hydraulic Servo-system. The spool valve shown in Fig. 4.14 (a) must have exact shoulder lengths relative to the ports and equal chamfers or radii such that the resistance to flow at a slight displacement of the spool are equal, i.e. that $R_1 = R_4$ and $R_2 = R_3$. This is readily achieved in manufacture of the valve by making the spool with an adjustment allowance on each shoulder, assembling with the valve body and testing the flow through each port for a given displacement of the spool. The amount to be removed from the shoulders can then be

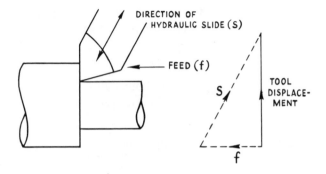

Fig. 4.13 *Method of generating a square shoulder using a hydraulic copy-turning slide*

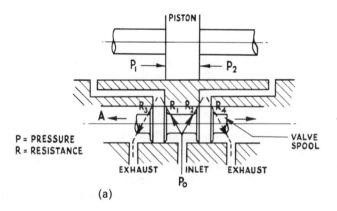

(a)

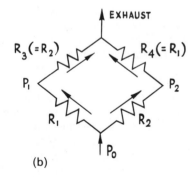

(b)

Fig. 4.14
(a) Principle of hydraulic spool valve
(b) Analogy of spool valve with Wheatstone bridge

calculated and the adjustment carried out by a grinding operation.

The operation of the valve can be explained by an analogy with a Wheatsone Bridge for d.c.

Now $$V = IR$$

$$\therefore \quad \text{Current} = \frac{\text{Potential}}{\text{Resistance}}$$

and by analogy, in the spool valve,

$$\text{Flow} = \frac{\text{Pressure}}{\text{Resistance}}$$

By reference to Fig 4.14(b),

$$P_1 = P_0 - IR_1 \text{ and } P_2 = P_0 - IR_2$$
$$\therefore \quad P_1 - P_2 = (P_0 - IR_1) - (P_0 - IR_2) = I(R_2 - R_1)$$

But $$I = \frac{P_0}{R_1 + R_2} \qquad \therefore \quad P_1 - P_2 = \frac{P_0(R_2 - R_1)}{(R_1 + R_2)}$$

This result may be applied to the spool valve, Fig 4.14(a). If the spool is moved a small amount in direction A, then R_2 and $R_3 \longrightarrow \infty$. Hence

$$\frac{R_2 - R_1}{R_2 + R_1} \longrightarrow 1$$

and $P_1 - P_2 \longrightarrow P_0$, i.e. for a small displacement of the spool the pressure rises rapidly towards the inlet pressure in a direction tending to displace the hydraulic cylinder to the neutral position. Since the cylinder is attached to the hydraulic slide as shown in Fig 4.12, the cutting tool is displaced, thus reproducing the shape of the template on the workpiece.

Electrical Servo Control. In this system error detected by the stylus is used to close one of two switches. The current energises one of two magnetic clutches and so drives a geared system linking an electric motor to the leadscrew of the X axis slide. Clutch engagement causes either forward or backward slide displacement according to the direction of the transmitted rotation.

The systems described above are designed to copy plane profiles. However, in the case of die sinking and similar machines it is necessary to produce three-dimensional forms. The third dimension is obtained from the basic two-dimensional arrangement by traversing the stylus and cutting tool (commonly an end mill) along a sequence of such planes. At the end of each pass the copying system is displaced by a small (feed) increment on a third slide (Y axis). The three dimensional form is thus built up from a series of parallel two-dimensional sections of the master shape.

PART B THE NUMERICAL CONTROL OF MACHINE TOOLS

4.7 The Advantages of Numerical Control

As an alternative to the control of machine tools by mechanical, hydraulic, or other conventional means, numerical engineering provides considerable attractions in suitable manufacturing applications. Numerical control, as applied to machine tools and other equipment, is versatile in that it can be employed for a wide variety of processes and used on components of widely differing characteristics. It is flexible, for whilst it may be used for high production quantities, it is of particular value in the production of small and medium-sized batches of components, since the need for jigs and fixtures—and the very high cost these involve—is almost eliminated. The computer is a very powerful tool in the preparation of programs for NC, and the development of mini-computers has enabled machine control units (MCU) of compact size to be dedicated to individual machines. An MCU will often incorporate extended facilities, e.g. keyboard, visual display unit (VDU), memory etc. which are invaluable in realising the full potential of a machine tool.

In keeping with the aims of this book, NC will be dealt with in terms of its principles, keeping to a minimum unfamiliar terms which inevitably spring up around technologies covering new ground, where words are coined to provide precise and specific meanings for new concepts. However, if a reader feels the need to develop his vocabulary to include these terms, he will find them defined in the 'Glossary of Terms Used in NC' which forms an appendix to *Numerical Control of Machine Tools* by S. J. Martin (Hodder and Stoughton)

4.8 Analysis of the Functions of an NC Machine Tool

Application of NC to a machine tool enables the functions normally performed by an operator in conventional situations to be taken care of by the NC system. For present purposes these functions may be separated into two groups.

(a) *The primary function*—namely the displacement of the machine slides to maintain a relationship between the cutting tool and the workpiece which will result in the desired geometric shape of the component to the required degree of accuracy.

The conventions adopted to identify slide displacements are illustrated in Fig 4.15. In addition to the primary linear displacements X, Y

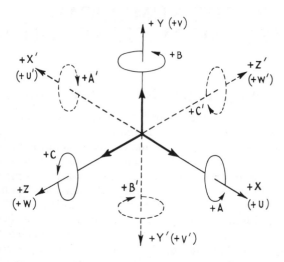

Fig. 4.15 Convential notation for linear translation along machine axes (notation for secondary displacements shown in brackets) and for rotational displacement about each axis

and Z, certain types of machine may possess secondary slides operating in directions parallel to those of the primary slideways e.g. capstan lathes Fig 4.16. Displacements of such secondary slides are identified by the letters U, V and W. Occasionally tertiary slides exist and corresponding displacements are referred to as P, Q and R. The Z axis of an NC machine is always in line with the axis of the principal spindle of the machine whether that axis is vertical or horizontal. The X axis is always horizontal and parallel to the work-holding surface, and the Y axis is perpendicular to the X and Z axes.

(b) *The secondary functions—* that is, those supporting functions which are necessary for the normal operation of the machine. The functions will vary according to the type of machine or equipment, e.g. the requirements for the operation of, say, an NC lathe will differ from those of an NC electro-discharge machine. Common examples of secondary functions include some or all of the following:

(i) Spindle, start/stop/reverse
(ii) Cutting fluid, on/off
(iii) Select desired spindle speed
(iv) Select desired feed rate for slides
(v) Index/rotate circular table
(vi) Exchange cutting tools
(vii) Lock slides when desired position is reached.

The extent of the range of secondary functions is determined not only by the type of machine, but also by the degree of sophistication

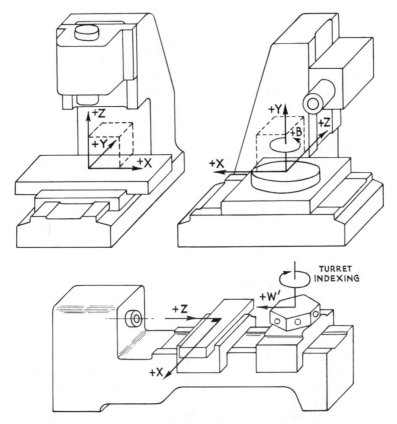

Fig. 4.16 Convential notation for slide displacements in some common types of NC machines.

Note: (i) the Z axis is always in line with the spindle;
(ii) the X axis is always parallel to the work table

considered necessary in the machine for a particular application, e.g. the desirability or otherwise of providing automatic tool-changing. Many extra functions are offered by machine tool manufactures as additional options which the machine user can select—at extra cost—according to the nature of the work the machine is to perform. Clearly, before adding to the purchase cost of a machine by demanding a wide range of extra options, an investigation into the particular needs of the manufacturing organisation must be carried out.

4.9 Inputs to the Machine Control Unit

Operating instructions to an NC machine are conveyed through the machine control unit. The operating instructions are devised by the process planning engineer (or programmer) in the form of a part-program and are then converted into a physical medium acceptable as an input by the MCU—e.g. punched (or magnetic) tape.

Originally, MCUs were of the "hard-wire" type i.e. they were constructed to initiate a series of set functions when requested to do so by the input of a particular code specified on the tape; for example, G81 is an alpha-numeric code which signifies a complete sequence of machine movements needed to perform a drilling or reaming operation. The MCU would recognise this signal and the control system would initiate the necessary responses from the machine tool. For most "hard-wire" type MCUs the tape is run once through the tape reading head each time a component is machined.

Machine control units using a system based on the computer and referred to as CNC (computer numerical control) are more flexible than the hard-wire units in that they can be prepared to meet operating requirements by means of software, e.g. a compiler, in a manner similar to that used for computers.

Unlike basic hardware NC units, CNC machine control units possess storage, i.e. memory, facilities. This facility can enable the contents of the tape to be put into store on its first run through the tape reading head. Thereafter the operation of the machine tool can be controlled from the memory each time a component is machined without re-running the tape. The tape may then be retained as a permanent record, and for use on future occasions if repeat components are required. Taking the information direct from the memory of a CNC unit is faster than reading and re-reading tape each time a component is machined, and errors or hold-ups due to damaged tape are eliminated.

CNC machine tools do not necessarily need the program information input to be in the form of punched tape. Input data may be dialed straight into the memory by means of a keyboard (similar to that of a typewriter) incorporated in the MCU. In some advanced systems the input data may be received by the MCU from a separate computer located at a distance from the machine tool. This method of control is termed DNC (direct numerical control) and the computer may concurrently control several machine tools. In more advanced DNC applications, the computer is not confined to controlling machine tools but may control the entire manufacturing system.

Other benefits of CNC include the following:

(i) *Editing.* The data on the tape can be modified by overriding, during which new information is keyed into the MCU by the operator or programmer. Feed rates can be optimised, over-runs eliminated, cutter paths shortened etc.

(ii) *Optimised tapes.* Once the program has been optimised by editing, a high-speed tape punch is plugged to the MCU to produce the new, modified tape.

(iii) *Display.* A visual display unit (VDU) employing a small cathode ray screen provides a medium for communication between the machine and the operator.

(iv) *Diagnostics.* A series of standard test procedures are held in store, and may be called-up to check the operational state of various parts of the system.

4.10 The Program and Tape Preparation

The use of NC machine tools increasingly transfers responsibility for the machining processes from the shop floor to the process planning office and requires more detailed work at this stage than when conventional (i.e. non-NC) machines are employed for batch production. For example, in addition to specifying the normal sequence of operations on a process planning sheet, NC programming also necessitates the definition of workpiece geometry, the calculation of co-ordinate positions and points of intersection, the specification of tool types and sizes, spindle speeds, feed rates and miscellaneous functions e.g. cutting fluid, mist/flood, supply on/off, etc.

The complete information for producing the component is entered on a part program sheet. There are several different classes of programming, i.e. manual and differing types of computer-based methods. According to which method is used, it will be necessary for the programmer to ensure the appropriate procedure is followed in preparing the tape (see Fig 4.17)

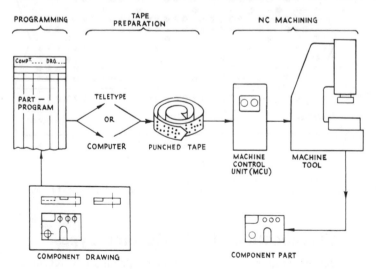

Fig. 4.17 Stages in NC machining from component drawing to finished part

A simple example of a single line taken from a manually prepared program (i.e. a program not requiring the use of a computer to prepare the tape) is shown in Fig 4.18(*a*). The complete program comprises many such lines to take the operation of the machine step by step through the process of part manufacture.

This program is reproduced in coded format on punched tape, each line of the program forming a corresponding block of information as shown in Fig 4.18(*b*). The format for the punched holes, in this example, uses the ISO system. This system is computer compatible and employs track No. 8 for obtaining even parity i.e. each line across the tape must contain an even number of holes otherwise an error is present. Writing programs in such detail is time consuming and costly; the method is suitable for simple components on relatively basic NC machines but more sophisticated programming methods are essential for advanced work. These methods will be described later.

SEQUENCE No.	PREPARATORY FUNCTION	CO-ORDINATES				FEED RATE	SPINDLE SPEED	MISC. FUNC.
		X	Y	Z	R			
N 001	G 81	X 12500	Y04800			F611	S 517	M 03

(*a*)

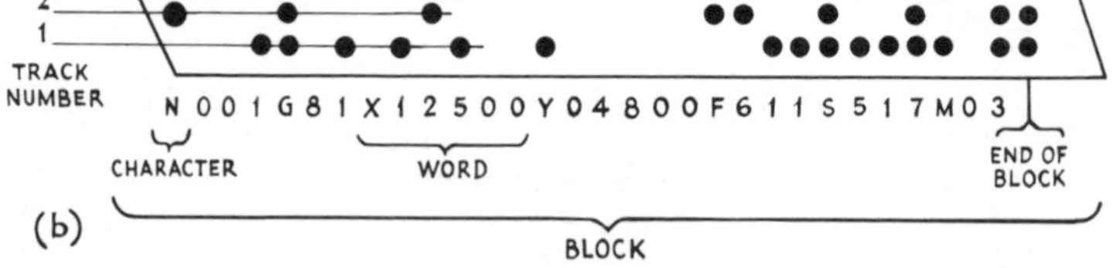

(*b*)

Fig. 4.18

(*a*) A line of information on a part-program
(*b*) The corresponding block of information on punched tape using ISO format (even parity)

4.11 Classification of NC Machine Types

Consideration of the geometry of components produced by NC machine tools (see Fig 4.19) shows that the basic requirements in slide control are

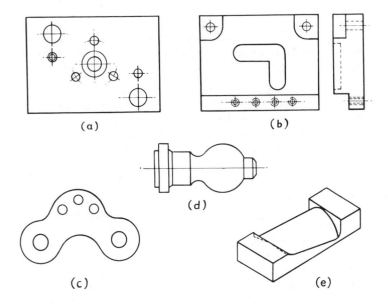

Fig. 4.19 *Examples of workpieces produced on NC machine tools:*

(*a*) positional;
(*b*) line-motion control;
(*c*) contouring (2 CL);
(*d*) contouring (2 C);
(*e*) contouring (3 C)

for positional, linear and contouring capabilities. Examples of machine types and equipment falling into these categories are shown in Fig 4.20. Note that some processes, e.g. welding, can fall into more than one group.

(a) *Positional Control.* Two orthogonal slides move rapidly to a fixed position at which machining takes place, e.g. drilling, boring, hole punching. The path taken by the slides to reach the desired position should be the quickest possible route, but is otherwise of no importance

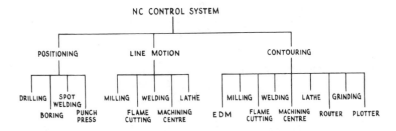

Fig. 4.20 *Classification of types of control for slide displacements on a range of NC machine tools and equipment*

unless obstructions, e.g. a clamp, need avoiding. This class of slide control is referred to as 2PL when the spindle feed motion is controlled by the tape, but 2P when cams, trips and stops mechanically control the spindle feed motion.

(b) *Line Motion Control.* The slides can be displaced at rapid rates for positioning purposes, as for (a), but they are also capable of being controlled to move at feed rate, individually or concurrently, to enable straight cuts to be made. The designation is 2L or 3L for linear control in two or three axes respectively, and may be extended to 4L, etc.

(c) *Contouring Control.* The machining of some components requires that slides move concurrently in a non-linear relationship, and need control systems able to accept and process detailed and complex data. These data are necessary to define the cutter path required to produce the desired geometric shape. This process involves controlling the velocities, accelerations and decelerations of the slides along their respective axes. A simple example of constantly changing slide velocities when machining an arc is illustrated in Fig 4.21. The commonest example of this type of control is designated 2CL; i.e. the spindle in the Z axis has a linear control system (L), but the other two axes, X and Y, have a continuous type control system (2C) capable of dealing with non-linear data. Continuous control of motion for contouring processes is extended to three axes (3C) or more for complex machines and equipment.

The geometry of many engineering components is developed from flat surfaces and circular arcs. To machine profiles of this kind a full contouring capability is not essential; however, line motion control alone is unable to produce circular arcs. In consequence, to manufacture such components without incurring the expense of a full contouring control system, machines with line motion control can be equipped with an additional control facility which will enable them to machine surfaces (slopes) at an angle to the main axes, and circular arcs, by employing interpolation methods.

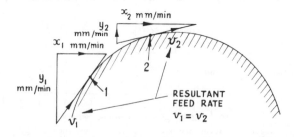

Fig. 4.21

To maintain a constant feed rate when milling a curve it is necessary that slide velocities in X and Y are varied; i.e. X, to X_2, Y to Y_2, etc.

4.12 Interpolation for Contour Generation

To produce smooth curves when contour machining using NC, points on the surface are followed in a sequence of slide movements made possible by a system of interpolation. The control system of an NC machine of contouring capability ensures related slide motions at the velocities necessary to achieve the desired geometrical shape of the component. Slopes and circular arcs are among the most common features needing this facility and the two common interpolation systems used are linear and circular interpolation, defined in BS3635 as follows:

(i) *Linear interpolation.* A mode of contouring control that causes a slope or straight-line operation, using data in a single block to produce velocities proportional to the distances to be moved in two or more axes simultaneously.

(ii) *Circular interpolation.* A mode of contouring control that uses the data in a single block to produce an arc of a circle, the velocities of the motions in two axes used to generate this arc being varied by the control system.

Example 4.2

Examine the differences in the linear cut vectors when using (i) chords, (ii) tangents, (iii) secants, to approximate a 25 mm external radius through a 90° arc, if the maximum variation from a true radius is not to exceed 0·025 mm. What will be the length of the cut vector in each case?

Solution

The three methods of approximating the arc are shown in Fig 4.22.

R = true radius of the arc

ϕ = angle subtending a cut vector

t = tolerance, i.e. maximum permitted deviation from true arc.

The tolerance t is negative for the chordal method, positive for the tangents, and both positive and negative for the secants.

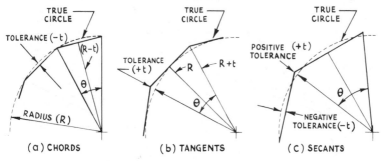

METHODS OF APPROXIMATING CIRCULAR ARCS

Fig. 4.22 Three methods of approximating a circular are by cut vectors:
(a) chords; (b) tangents; (c) secants

(i) $\theta = 2 \arccos[(R-t)/R] = 2 \arccos[(25-0.025)/25] = 5.125°$

∴ Number of cut vectors in 90° of arc = $90°/5.125° = 17.56$

Length of cut vector = $2\sqrt{[t(2R-t)]} = 2\sqrt{[0.025(50-0.025)]}$
$= 2.235\,\text{mm}$

(ii) $\theta = 2 \arccos[R/(R+t)] = 2 \arccos[25/(25+0.025)] = 5.122°$

∴ Number of cut vectors in 90° of arc = $90°/5.122° = 17.57$

Length of cut vector = $2\sqrt{[t(2R+t)]} = 2\sqrt{[0.025(50+0.025)]}$
$= 2.237\,\text{mm}$

(iii) $\theta = 2 \arccos[(R-t)/(R+t)] = 2 \arccos[(25-0.025)/(25+0.025)]$
$= 7.245°$

∴ Number of cut vectors in 90° of arc = $90°/7.245° = 12.422$

Length of cut vector = $4\sqrt{(Rt)} = 4\sqrt{(25 \times 0.025)} = 3.162\,\text{mm}$

4.13 The Displacement of Machine Tool-Slides

To displace a machine tool slide by means of a control system, a rapid response by slides and rotating drive members to the input signals is essential, see Fig 4.23, and yet, in order to withstand heavy loads and forces in the cutting of metal, rugged machine construction is needed.

To meet these conflicting requirements, traditional machine tool design is modified and developed, e.g. frictional forces are reduced by the substitution of rolling for sliding friction in slideways and leadscrew nuts, thus reducing loads and enabling components in the drive system, e.g.

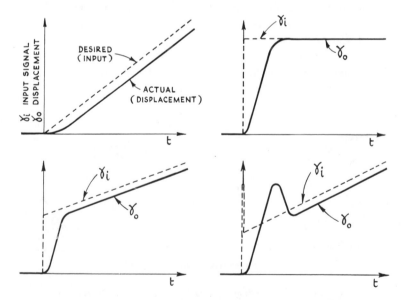

Fig. 4.23 Examples of input signals and actual response conditions

clutches, gears, shafts, to be reduced in size. By such means, inertia in the system is diminished, drive systems of smaller power are used and the cost of components of sophisticated design minimised.

In the control of slide elements, a distinction must be made between **drive systems** for physically displacing the slide, and **feed-back systems** for monitoring the slide position (closed-loop systems). This distinction is illustrated in Fig 4.24, and examples of open—and closed-loop control shown in Fig 4.25. A transducer is required to monitor displacement of

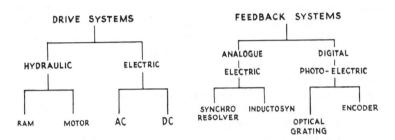

Fig. 4.24

(*a*) Types of drive systems used to displace machine tool slides
(*b*) Examples of analogue and digital methods for providing feedback on slide position

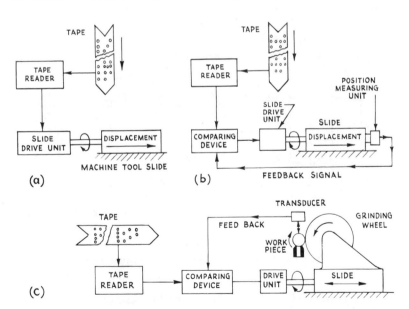

Fig. 4.25 Open- and closed-loop systems for machine tool slide control;

(*a*) open-loop;   (*b*) closed-loop;   (*c*) closed-loop based on inprocess workpiece
measurement

slides. It may receive its input from a rotating member of the drive system, e.g. leadscrew, in which case accuracy may be affected by leadscrew errors, wind-up, axial slip etc.; or from a linear transducer, e.g. optical gratings or laser interferometers, and may monitor displacements directly from the slide itself. In all cases, the system must be capable of monitoring slide displacement (and velocity in the case of contouring machines) over long distances of travel and to a high degree of accuracy.

Stepping-Motor Drive System. A stepping-motor drives a leadscrew either directly, or indirectly through gearing, in a series of incremental movements. The principle of its design is illustrated in Fig 4.26, which shows three sets of co-axial stator laminations (s_1, s_2, s_3) arranged with their slots in exact angular correspondence. Three sets of rotor laminations (r_1, r_2, r_3) are positioned on the motor shaft to coincide axially with the stators, but are disposed radially such that their slots are displaced relative to each other by one-third of the radial pitch of the slots, i.e. in the diagram, $360°/24 \div 3 = 5°$. The stator windings (W_1, W_2, W_3) receive pulses from the supply in sequence, causing the rotor to turn in $5°$ steps clockwise or anticlockwise according to the order in which the windings receive the pulses. The speed of rotation is a function of the pulse frequency. The magnitude of the angular displacement (and hence the displacement of the machine slide) is dependent on the total number of pulses received.

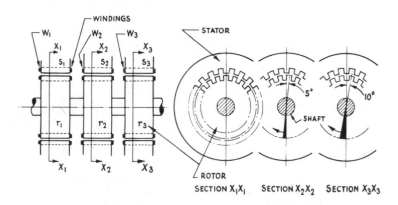

Fig. 4.26 Principle of operation of stepping motor
Note the relative radial displacement of the rotor slots

The Synchro-resolver (Fig 4.27). A synchro-resolver is an electro-magnetic position transducer comprising a stator and a rotor connected to an output shaft or leadscrew. The stator has two coils at $90°$ to each other, the single phase winding of the rotor turns with the output shaft.

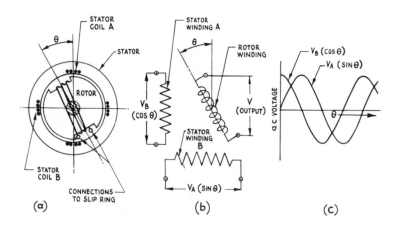

Fig. 4.27 Principle of operation of synchro-resolver

(a) cross-section; (b) relationship between rotor-position and voltages of stator windings; (c) phase difference in stator voltages

By accurately controlling the angular rotation of the rotor relative to the stator, a machine slide can be displaced to its desired position via a mechanical linkage, e.g. gears, clutches and leadscrews.

The positional input data are converted from digital to analogue form and the resulting a.c. voltage signal is resolved into two sinusoidal components of 90° phase difference, i.e. $\sin \theta$ and $\cos \theta$, where θ represents the angular position of the rotor necessary to give the required slide position of the machine via the leadscrew drive.

In the resolver, the voltage induced in the coil of the rotor varies sinusoidally as the rotor turns through 360°; when the angle turned by the rotor (ϕ) corresponds to the desired angle (θ), the voltage magnitude reduces to zero (i.e. the null). Thus, $\theta - \phi$ is the angular error between the desired and actual positions of the rotor, and when $\theta = \phi$ the error is zero and the machine slide is in the position required by the input signal. Due to the voltage in the rotor coil varying sinusoidally according to its angular position, a null will occur every 180° and a phase sensor is employed to identify the correct phase change.

Since a null also will occur for each 180° turn of a leadscrew directly connected to a rotor, it is necessary to connect several resolvers together through gears and clutches to extend the range of the system. Fig 4.28 illustrates the part-cycle sine curves of a three-stage resolver and shows the positions at which control passes from the resolver with coarse gearing to the medium stage and then to the fine resolver.

The Inductosyn (Fig 4.29). Effectively, the Inductosyn is a linear resolver. It employs the principle of inductive coupling between two

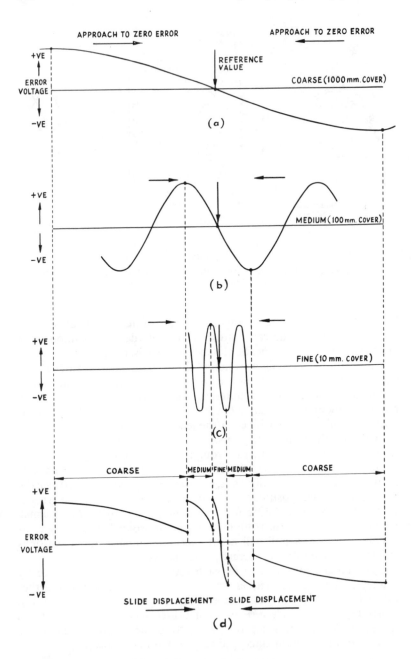

Fig. 4.28 Error voltages at coarse medium and fine stages of a three-stage resolver. The slide movement is directed towards the reference value in order to reduce the error voltage to zero

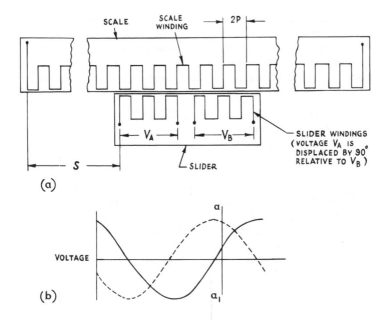

Fig. 4.29 Principle of the Inductosyn:
(a) arrangement and relationship of scale and slider printed circuits;
(b) phase differences in voltages V_A and V_B of slider windings

conductors to provide a signal analogous to the linear position of a machine tool slide. It has two windings, the long (scale) winding extending the length of the slideway, the short (slider) winding is usually fitted to the slide. A gap of 0.2 mm separates the two elements.

As illustrated in Fig 4.29(a) the windings are in "hairpin" formation; the scale winding is single phase and analogous to a resolver rotor, the slider has two sets of windings, one set displaced $P/2$ relative to the other. When an a.c. signal is applied to the scale winding the voltages induced into the two slider windings will be displaced by 90°, i.e. they will be proportional to sin ϕ and cos ϕ respectively.

    If S = linear displacement of the slider,

      P = spacing of the poles,

    then $\phi = \dfrac{2\pi S}{P}$

If a line aa_1 is drawn, cutting the two curves shown in Fig 4.29 (b), two voltages will be identified, which, taken together, will be unique for the curves illustrated and hence may be used to identity the position of the slider relative to a pole in the scale winding. Alternatively, if these same two voltages are fed to the windings of the slider, a voltage will be induced into the scale winding which will be at a maximum for the same unique position.

These principles provide the basis of a system to identify the position of a machine tool slide, but, as in the case of the synchro-resolver, because the identified position is unique only so far as each cycle winding is concerned, it is also necessary to:

(i) provide means of identifying the cycle, and
(ii) establish a range sufficient to accommodate the full linear displacement of the slide.

The Rotary Encoder (Figs 4.30 and 4.31). The basis of this type of transducer is an encoder disc mounted at the end of the slide leadscrew. The disc is divided into segments which are transparent/opaque for use in photocell scanning techniques, or alternatively, conductive/non-conductive for scanning by commutator-type brushes.

The coding of the disc is analogous to the coding used on punched tape. If the disc segments are "straightened out" as shown in Fig 4.30(*ii*) it

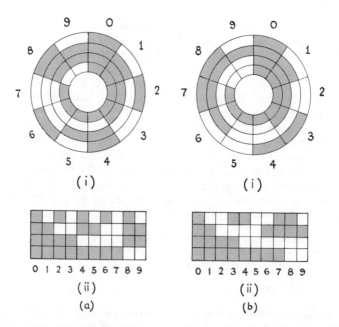

Fig. 4.30 Rotary shaft encoders: (i) discs; (ii) development of coded segments demonstrating the analogy between coding for discs and coding for punched tape – unshaded areas correspond to holes in punched tape.

Codes shown are (*a*) natural binary;   (*b*) Gray code

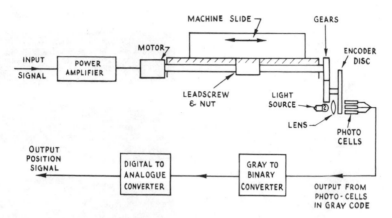

Fig. 4.31 Principle of the rotary shaft encoder system applied to a NC machine tool

can be seen that the unshaded areas correspond to a hole in punched tape. By scanning the disc as it is rotated via the leadscrew, pulses are fed into the system. After suitable decoding, these output signals are compared with the input for correction to take place if a difference, i.e. error, exists between the desired and the actual slide positions.

Optical Gratings. The principle of one method employed in the application of linear gratings for monitoring machine tool slide displacement is shown in Fig 4.32. The lines of the short index grating are inclined at a slight angle to the lines of the scale grating which extends for the length of the slideway.

The intersections of these two sets of lines create an interference effect, giving rise to the Moiré-fringe pattern. When one scale is displaced relative to the other, the dark interference fringes pass across the width of the grating at right angles to the direction of travel; see Fig. 4.32(*b*). The dark fringes give rise to a variation in the light intensity received by the photocells, as shown by the waveforms in the diagram. The de-energising of each photocell in turn generates pulses in direct proportion to the magnitude of slide displacement. The order in which the photo-cells are de-energised provides the information necessary to discriminate in the sense of direction of slide movement. Once again, the pulses provide the output signal which can be de-coded and compared with the position input signal for the slide of the machine tool.

4.14 Programming

Clearly it is not possible to give anything other than a brief summary of programming in this text, with accompanying examples for illustration.

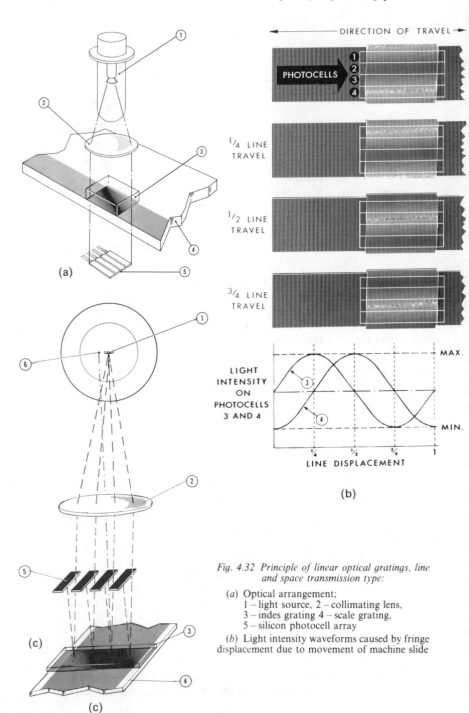

Fig. 4.32 Principle of linear optical gratings, line and space transmission type:

(a) Optical arrangement;
    1 – light source, 2 – collimating lens,
    3 – indes grating 4 – scale grating,
    5 – silicon photocell array

(b) Light intensity waveforms caused by fringe displacement due to movement of machine slide

For further details the reader is referred to *Numerical Control of Machine Tools* by S. J. Martin (Hodder and Stoughton) in which manual and computer methods of programming are dealt with at some length (Chapters 8–10).

4.15 Manual Programming

The procedure adopted in basic (manual) programming (see Fig 4.18) is to set down by hand, in machine code, each detail of a required program, specifying sequence of operation, co-ordinates in each axis, machine functions, feed rates, spindle speeds etc. The program is then typed on a teletypewriter which simultaneously produces the corresponding punched tape.

This programming procedure uses a low level language and is slow and cumbersome to write. The machine manufacturers adopt different formats, i.e. styles, for their programs and the format for a given machine must be followed exactly.

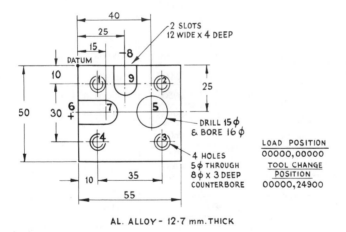

Fig. 4.33 Aluminium end plate (Co-ordinates of datum point: 05000, 05000)

Example of Manual Programming I (Fixed Block Format). A simple component requiring machining by drilling, milling, boring, and counterboring is shown in Fig 4.33. The program for machining this component is written in fixed block format, i.e. each line of the program (and hence each block of information on the tape) contains the same number of alpha-numeric characters (see Fig 4.34). Given the following information regarding the code, the program should be self-explanatory.

Part Description End Plate   (12.7 Thick Alum^N)   Machine Model   1000TP

Reference	Location No	Prep. Func.	X Dimn. or Z Rapid	Y Dimn. or Z Final	Res.	Tool No	Misc. Func.
Load	000	0	00000	00000	0	00	02
TC1 15ϕ Drill	001	0	00000	24900	0	01	06
⑤ ,,	002	4	09000	07500	0	01	08
⑤ Z ,,	003	9	05500	08000	0	01	80
TC2 16ϕ Boring bar	004	0	00000	24900	0	02	06
⑤ ,,	005	7	09000	07500	0	02	80
⑤ Z ,,	006	9	06000	08000	0	02	80
TC3 5ϕ Drill	007	0	00000	24900	0	03	06
① ,,	008	4	06000	06000	0	03	80
① Z ,,	009	9	09000	11000	0	03	80
② ,,	010	4	09500	06000	0	03	80
③ ,,	011	4	09500	09000	0	03	80
④ ,,	012	4	06000	09000	0	03	80
TC4 8ϕ C/bore	013	0	00000	24900	0	04	06
① ,,	014	5	06000	06000	0	04	80
① Z ,,	015	9	10000	10400	0	04	80
② ,,	016	5	09500	06000	0	04	80
③ ,,	017	5	09500	09000	0	04	80
④ ,,	018	5	06000	09000	0	04	80
TC5 12ϕ slot drill	019	0	00000	24900	0	05	06
⑥ ,,	020	5	04000	07500	0	05	80
⑥ Z ,,	021	9	10500	11000	0	05	80
⑦ Mill	022	6	06500	07500	0	05	80
⑧ Mill	023	5	07500	04000	0	05	80
⑨ Mill	024	6	07500	06000	0	05	80
unload	025	0	00000	00000	0	00	02
	6				0		
	7				0		
	8				0		

Fig. 4.34 Program in fixed-block format for machining the End Plate shown in Fig. 4.33

Reference column.   For information only, not included on the tape (TC indicates a tool-change)

Location No.   The sequence number of the block. It is displayed on the machine console as machining is in progress to indicate the operation reached.

Prep. Function.   The code number representing a set sequence of events the machine is required to perform (i.e. a "canned cycle"). Examples of preparatory function codes used in the program.

0 = machine table moves rapidly to its programmed position

4 = Table moves rapidly to position, spindle descends rapidly, changes to feed rate just above workpiece surface (this position is defined as Z-rapid in the next column), commences drilling using peck-feed until drill reaches specified Z-final position. Spindle retracts rapidly. See Fig 4.35(b).

5 = as 4, but with normal (not peck) feed. See Fig 4.35(a).

6 = end-milling cycle.

7 = bore cycle

9 = indicates that the co-ordinate data on this line of the program refers to the Z axis (in all other instances, i.e. where 9 is not specified, the co-ordinates refer to X and Y axes respectively)

Misc. Function   The code number representing one of the supporting functions necessary for the normal operation of the machine e.g.

02 = end of program

06 = denotes a manual tool change, spindle stops rotating, cutting-fluid flow ceases.

08 = mist coolant switched on

80 = no alteration is required, procedure as miscellaneous function on previous line.

In this type of format, because every block of information on the tape contains the same number of characters in a fixed order, the machine control unit can be of relatively simple construction.

An example now follows of a format which diminishes the time required for writing a manual program by reducing the amount of data that needs to be written down and typed; it also shortens the length of the tape.

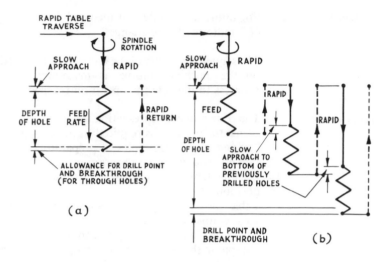

Fig. 4.35 Drill cycle diagrams:

(a) nominal drilling cycle (cycles identical for drilling and reaming)
(b) peck-feed (woodpecker) drilling cycle for clearing swarf when drilling a deep hole.

Example of Manual Programming II (Word Address Format). Preceding each piece of numerical information on the program by an identifying letter (the "address") ensures that the data immediately following the letter are recognized by the machine control system and are sent through the circuitry via the appropriate "route". By this means the data do not need to be in a fixed block, and data already in the system need not be repeated (but they must be stored for subsequent use; hence the system must possess a memory).

The program, written in word address format, for machining the profile of the simple component shown in Fig 4.36 using a machine with line-motion control, is given in Fig 4.37. The end-milling cutter used is 30 mm diameter. The basic machine datum position $x = 0$, $y = 0$ is taken as the starting point for the programmed co-ordinates which are stated in the absolute mode i.e. all co-ordinates are specified from 0, 0.

It is necessary for the cutter diameter to be specified since the program represents the displacement of the cutter axis with respect to the fixed position of the component on the machine table. For outside corners, the length of travel is increased by an amount equal to the cutter radius. If the cutter used varies in diameter from that specified in the program, e.g. because of re-grinding, then this variation will result in the component being machined over- or under-size unless the machine control system includes a facility known as the *cutter radius offset option*. By means of a simple adjustment to the cutter radius offset control, small variations in

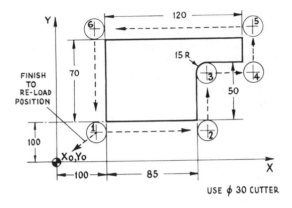

Fig. 4.36 Plate in mild steel

cutter diameter can be allowed for. A similar facility to accommodate variation in the length of an end-mill is also employed.

In the program, Fig 4.37, m03 is the codeword to start the spindle rotating in a clockwise direction, g78 is the code for rapid approach to the specified co-ordinate positions, g79 calls up the milling mode at the

n	g	x	y	z	r	f	m	Remarks
n001	g78	x008500	y008500				m03	Use φ 30
n002	g79	x020000				f010000		end-mill
n003			y013500					and set
n004		x023500						micro-switches
n005			y018500					for spindle
n006		x008500						motions
n007			y008500					
n008	g80							
n009		x000000	y000000			f524000		

Fig. 4.37 Program in word address format for milling profile of plate shown in Fig. 3.36

feed rate stated and g80 cancels the previous g function. In this example f signifies feed-rate and f 010000 represents 100 mm/minute. Both of these latter codes are modal in the particular system considered, i.e. they remain effective until a new g or f word is programmed. No co-ordinates in the Z axis are given because the example is taken for a machine with two-axis (2L) control—the third (Z) axis is controlled by physically setting micro-switches on the machine, as shown in Fig 4.38. The changeover from rapid approach to feed rate in the Z axis takes place at the position specified by the programmer as an r co-ordinate.

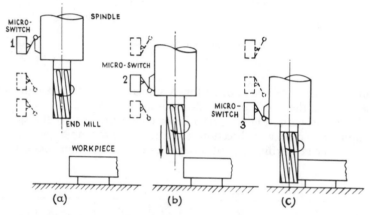

Fig. 4.38 Arrangement of limit switches used in the control of the spindle in the Z-axis, tape control confined to X and Y axes, eg 2L or 2P

(a) Spindle fully retracted, backstop position
(*b*) Clearance plane (r co-ordinate), changeover trip from rapid traverse to feed rate
(c) Full depth stop (z)—followed by spindle retraction

4.16 Computer-Assisted Part Programming

If a component is complex and requires many features to be machined, manual programming is not economic and a computer-assisted method is used. This type of part programming makes use of repeated geometric patterns which occur in engineering components. Instead of the part program specifying each individual element in the sequence needed to perform an operation:

  (i) the geometry of the component is specified, e.g. in terms of lines and circular arcs; and
  (ii) the technical machining instructions are specified.

This information is fed into a computer which then makes the computations necessary to produce the "cutter location file", i.e. stored data giving the general solution to the machining operations. This is the processor stage. The post-processor stage involves taking the general solution and making it compatible with the capabilities of the particular machine tool on which it is intended to carry out the machining, and the characteristics of the MCU associated with that particular machine.

Example in Computer-assisted Part Programming. The example, by courtesy of British Olivetti Ltd, selected as an illustration of computer-assisted programming (Fig 4.39) deals with the machining of a component requiring a machine tool with both positional (point-to-point) and contouring capabilities. Note that dimensions in this drawing are, where possible, given from $X = 0$, $Y = 0$; this method simplifies programming.

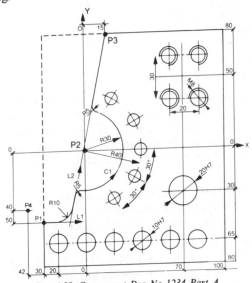

Fig. 4.39 Component Drg No 1234 Part A

Part Program for Component Fig 4.39

```
10 SYS/CPR, PRES 120, TIME          } 1. Control Statements
20 PART/MAT 1, DP20, COMP
```

```
30 SET 1/LIN 6, 20, X-20, Y-65, A0  ⎫
40 SET 2/RECT, 20, 30, X70, Y50, A0  ⎪
50 SET 3/CIR 5, −60, 30, X0, Y0, R40 ⎪
60 P10/X70, Y-30                     ⎬ 2. Positional Operations
70 E1/REAM, D10, SET 1               ⎪
80 E2/FODR, D8, SET 3                ⎪
90 E3/REAM, D20 P10                  ⎪
100 E4/TAMA, D8, SET 2               ⎭
```

110 P1/X-30, Y-50
120 P2/X0, Y0
130 P3/15, Y80
140 P4/X-42, Y-40
150 C1/X0, Y0, R30
160 L1/P1, A0
170 L2/P2, P3
180 V2 = − 5
190 PF1/P1, L1, R10, L2, V2, C1, V2, L2, P3

3. Geometric
Definitions

200 TOOL/D20, CL35
210 GOTO/P4, RAP
220 GOTO/Z21, RAP
230 MILL/PF1, LFT, OVS1, CORR
240 TOOL/D8, CL65
250 GOTO/X-35, Y-46, RAP
260 GOTO/Z21, RAP
270 MILL/PF1

4. Profile
Machining

Explanation of Part Program

1. *Control Statements.* SYS/CPR, PRES 120, TIME indicates that all geometrical forms are to be printed (CPR); that the tool length compensation is to be calculated from the lengths of tools used, with the longest tool pre-set at 120 mm above the workpiece; and that the machining time for each tool is to be computed and printed.

PART/MAT 1, DP20, COMP—the material for the component is Type 1 (exact specification has been previously filed in a memory store), depth of workpiece is 20 mm, and tool length compensation, COMP, is required.

2. *Positional Operations.* SET 1/LIN 6, 20, X-20, Y-65, AO defines a set of 6 points (holes) at a pitch of 20 mm in a line, starting at X-20, Y-65 and inclined at an angle of zero degrees, AO.

SET 2/RECT, 20, 30, X70, Y50, AO defines a set of four points at the corners of a rectangle of sides 20 by 30 and having its centre at X70, Y50.

SET 3/CIR 5, − 60, 30, XO, YO, R40 defines a set of 5 points on the circumference of a circle of radius 40 mm, centre XO, YO, from − 60° and in increments of 30°.

P10/X70, Y-30 defines a point at co-ordinates X70, Y-30.

E1/REAM, D10, SET 1; Indicates execution of reaming of holes at
E2/FODR, D8, SET 3;   positions defined in SET 1 and P10; drilling
E3/REAM, D20, P10;   at SET 3 and tapping at SET 2. The
E4/TAMA, D8, SET 2;   computer will call up and print out neces-
sary drill sizes to be used prior to the reaming and tapping processes.

3. *Geometrical Definitions*

P1/X-30, Y-50;
P2/XO, YO;
P3/X15, Y80;
P4/X-42, Y-40;   These are the definitions of four points in Cartesian co-ordinates.

C1/XO, YO, R30;   defines circle 1 of the contour.

L1/P1, AO;
L2/P2, P3;   Definitions of lines 1 and 2

V2 = − 5;   The definition of a fillet radius using a variable (fillet radii can be generated automatically)

PF1/P1, L1, R10, L2, V2, C1, V2, L2, P3 is the definition of the profile (PF1) from P1 to P3 composed of pre-defined elements, see Fig 4.40.

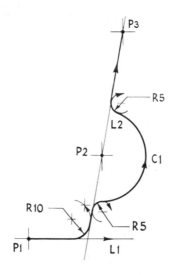

Fig. 4.40 Identified and pre-defined elements in program for contour milling of component Drg No 1234 Part A

4. *Machining the Profile*
  TOOL/D20, CL35; defines the tool for a roughing cut.
  GOTO/P4, RAP; the tool moves at rapid travel to P4.
  GOTO/Z21, RAP; the tool moves at rapid travel to working depth.
  MILL/PFI, LFT, OVS 1, CORR; the tool mills the profile with the tool on the left, leaving 1 mm oversize and requests tool radius compensation.
  TOOL/D8, CL65; defines the tool for the finishing cut.

GOTO/X-35, Y-46, RAP; tool moves at rapid traverse rate.
GOTO/Z21, RAP; as previously.
MILL/PFI; tool mills the profile with the finishing cut.
For both diameters (D20, D8) of the milling cutters the spindle speed
(SP) and feed rate (FR) are calculated by the computer from data already
in store, e.g. material type, diameter and type of tool. The processing and
post-processing for this program can be carried out on a desk-top
minicomputer.

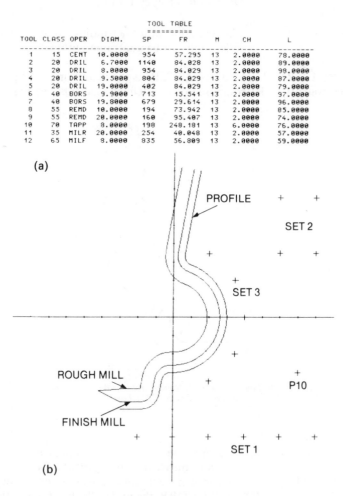

TOOL TABLE
==========

TOOL	CLASS	OPER	DIAM.	SP	FR	M	CH	L
1	15	CENT	10.0000	954	57.295	13	2.0000	78.0000
2	20	DRIL	6.7000	1140	84.028	13	2.0000	89.0000
3	20	DRIL	8.0000	954	84.029	13	2.0000	98.0000
4	20	DRIL	9.5000	804	84.029	13	2.0000	87.0000
5	20	DRIL	19.0000	402	84.029	13	2.0000	79.0000
6	40	BORS	9.9000	713	15.541	13	2.0000	97.0000
7	40	BORS	19.8000	679	29.614	13	2.0000	96.0000
8	55	REMD	10.0000	194	73.942	13	2.0000	85.0000
9	55	REMD	20.0000	160	95.407	13	2.0000	74.0000
10	70	TAPP	8.0000	198	248.181	13	6.0000	76.0000
11	35	MILR	20.0000	254	40.048	13	2.0000	57.0000
12	65	MILF	8.0000	835	56.809	13	2.0000	59.0000

(a)

PROFILE

SET 2

SET 3

ROUGH MILL

P10

FINISH MILL

SET 1

(b)

Fig. 4.41

(a) Print-out of tool table compiled in processing phase
(b) Plot produced by XY plotter as a visual check of the geometry called for in the
program—hole and centre positions indicated thus +

```
                                    POST PROCESSOR
                                    ==== =========

DRAWING NO.  1234   (PART A)    %

********  TOOL * 1   CENTRE DRILL   DIAM.  10.0000  GAUGE HT.  2.0000

:001.........................................................................T00100M06
N002G00...................R+0000000.......................................S695......M13
N003...X-0020000Y-0065000
N004...................R-0168000
N005G81...................Z-0171500...........................................F00570
N006...X+0000000
N007...X+0020000
N008...X+0040000
N009...X+0060000
N010...X+0080000
N011...X+0020000Y-0034641
N012...X+0034641Y-0020000
N013...X+0040000Y+0000000
N014...X+0034641Y+0020000
N015...X+0020000Y+0034641
N016...X+0070000Y-0030000
N017...X+0060000Y+0035000
N018...X+0080000
N019..........Y+0065000
N020...X+0060000
N021G80.................R+0000000................................................M05

******** TOTAL TIME REQUIRED BY TOOL    1.50  MIN

******** TOOL * 2   TWIST DRILL   DIAM.  6.7000  GAUGE HT.  2.0000

:022..........................................................................T00200M06
N023G00...................R+0000000.......................................S711......M13
N024...X+0060000Y+0035000
N025...................R-0128000
N026G81...................Z-0153512...........................................F00810
N027...X+0080000
N028..........Y+0065000
N029...X+0060000
N030G80.................R+0000000................................................M05

******** TOTAL TIME REQUIRED BY TOOL    1.51  MIN
```

```
******** TOTAL TIME REQUIRED BY TOOL    4.39  MIN

******** TOOL * 12  FINISH MILL   DIAM.  8.0000  GAUGE HT.  2.0000

:120...........................................................................T01200M06
N121G00.................R+0000000.........................................S689......M13
N122...X+0035000Y-0040000
N123....................R-0141000
N124G29X-0030000..............................................................F00605
N125G01X-0017674
N126...X-0017355Y-0045991.....................................................F00588
N127G03X-0011844Y-0041418..........I-0017674J-0040000.........................F00605
N128G01X-0011777Y-0041106
N129...X-0010315Y-0033311
N130...X-0010233Y-0032919
N131G02X-0001493Y-0025971..........I-0001470J-0034969
N132G01X-0001092Y-0025977
N133...X-0000378Y-0025997
N134G03X+0009865Y+0024368..........I+0000000J+0000000
N135G01X+0008393Y+0024608
N136...X+0008016Y+0024746
N137G02X+0002387Y+0034389..........I+0011298J+0033126
N138G01X+0002452Y+0034785
N139...X+0011060Y+0080693
N140G29X+0011069Y+0080737
N141....................R+0000000................................................M05
N142G53.................R+0000000
N143G00X+0000000Y+0000000
N144............................................................................M30
%

******** TOTAL TIME REQUIRED BY TOOL    3.16 MIN

******** TOTAL MACHINING TIME         25.72 MIN
******** TOTAL TAPE LENGTH (METERS)   10.78
```

Fig. 4.42 Extract from print-out after post-processing in the program for producing component Drg No 1234 Part A (Fig. 4.39)

The Processor Output for the Program. At the completion of processing, the computer prints a tool table for all the programmed operations, together with the calculated parameters. If necessary, the machine operator can modify the parameters to suit conditions at the machine. The geometry defined in the program is plotted as a visual check. These two print-outs are shown in Fig 4.41(*a*) and (*b*) respectively.

The Post-processor Output for the Program. As stated on p. 159 the general solution to the program is prepared during the processing stage and produces the *cutter location file*. The general solution is then developed at the post-processing stage to make the final output (tape) compatible with the characteristics of the particular machine tool and its associated control system. Fig 4.42 gives an extract from the post-processor print-out for the program considered above.

4.17 Economic Considerations in the Application of NC

A basic tenet in the selection of economic methods of manufacture is identifying the process of least cost compatible with maintaining the component specification. This task is not difficult when confined to an economic comparison between alternative methods in conventional machining, because the cost factors are in similar areas and directly comparable. However, when investigating the relative economic advantages of using NC machines, new factors emerge, e.g. the cost of using a computer for programming.

Additionally, although the use of NC involves new areas of cost, compensating savings are made, often in directions which are not immediately apparent and sometimes in directions which may be difficult to quantify; e.g. the accuracy and consistency in the components produced may lead to a reduction in inspection costs. Some of the many factors involved are considered bwlow.

Before considering the economic aspects in manufacture, reference must first be made to the important area of product design. For the maximum advantage to be gained from NC manufacturing methods, the components must be designed and dimensioned with the capabilities of the NC method in view. Some points worth considering are:

(i) dimensioning of detail parts from suitable *X* and *Y* datum positions to facilitate programming:

(ii) standardisation in the sizes of design detail features—e.g. hole diameters and depths, slot widths, fillet radii, etc.—to eliminate unnecessary tool-setting and tool-changing;

(iii) machining of components from the solid instead of using built-up assemblies may be economic in appropriate cases when using NC machines:

(iv) using profiles which can be defined mathematically, e.g. the ellipse can be readily machined on NC machines having contouring capabilities.

Although the subject is beyond the scope of this book, the attention of the reader is drawn to the natural connection between CAD (computer-aided design), CAM (computer-aided manufacture) and CNC.

Economic factors involved in the use of NC are now considered in relation to particular areas of cost.

(a) *Capital costs.* The purchase of an NC machine involves a very high capital outlay and requires further heavy expenditure on expensive tooling. Proper back-up facilities are essential, and this necessitates a further financial commitment especially in the early stages of an NC installation.

To spread the effect of a high rate of amortisation which is due, in part, to a combination of the high capital cost and the need to depreciate the asset over a short period (to avoid the consequences of a possible rapid technological obsolescence), double shift working is frequently adopted. The increased productivity of an NC machine may enable several conventional machines to be replaced, thus reducing manpower requirements and the demand on floor space.

(b) *Pre-production costs.* The costs of process planning for conventional machining are usually lower than the combined costs of process planning, programming and tape preparation for NC work. However, since drill jigs, milling fixtures etc. are not needed for NC work (which usually requires relatively simple workholding fixtures only), considerable savings are to be made by the elimination of the design and manufacture costs of such equipment. To these savings can be added the advantage that capital is not tied up in jigs and fixtures and their relatively high cost of storage is eliminated.

(c) *Set-up and tape-proving costs.* It takes very little time to change over the settings of some NC machines from producing one component to another—not much more time than is required to change the tape in some cases—although such rapid change-over is unusual. Speedy change-over is achieved by pre-setting and pre-loading all cutting tools, and by employing a series of moving platens on which components are pre-set, instead of the conventional machine table. However, the principles behind the use of pre-set tools and pre-set workpieces on platens or duplex machine tables are often applied on NC machines to keep idle machine time to a minimum. The operator can perform the preparatory work whilst components are being machined (see Fig 4.43). Proving a new tape is often a time-consuming exercise during which the

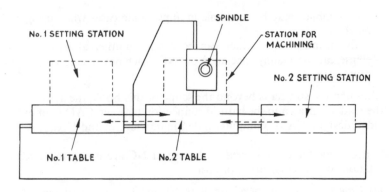

Fig. 4.43 Arrangement of typical twin-table machine. The workpiece is machined at one station while loading and unloading takes place at the setting stations

machine tool is not producing components. The use of XY plotters (see Fig 4.41(b)) at the pre-production stage to assess the accuracy of the program in respect of the tool-path, helps to minimise programming errors and tape-proving costs.

(d) *Machining costs.* An important factor in making NC machining methods economic is that the cutting tool is in contact with the workpiece and removing metal for a greater proportion of the floor-to-floor time than in conventional machining. The reduction in idle time during the machining sequence is achieved in a number of ways.

(i) There is no hand manipulation of the machine; motion of the slides in non-cutting movements is in the rapid mode (it follows that the tape, or other input, is consistent, the cycle time is known and the theoretical daily output of the machine is predictable).

(ii) The machine need not be stopped for measurement or gauging of the component to take place.

(iii) Automatic tool-changing is much faster than manual methods.

(iv) Repeat cuts are rapidly performed keeping cycle times short, especially in turning operations (see Fig 4.44).

(v) Adaptive control is increasingly being used to maintain optimum cutting conditions on a consistent basis (Fig 4.45) e.g. when machining the face of a turned component at a constant cutting speed.

(e) *Post-machining costs.* Once a tape has been proved correct by the machining of a workpiece which satisfactorily meets all inspection criteria, the components subsequently machined may be accepted after a limited inspection, e.g. checks on hole sizes. More rigorous inspection requirements can be economically met by employing inspection machines (see Fig 13.25) to check hole centre positions and other features. The machine checks positions through the orthogonal displacement of a

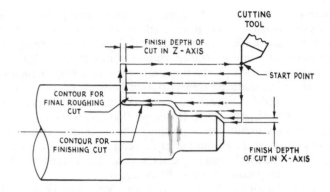

Fig. 4.44 Repeat cuts in an area clearance cycle for a typical turning operation

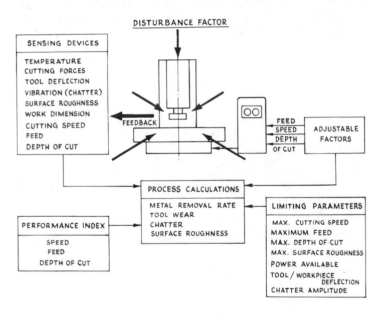

Fig. 4.45 Application of adaptive control to a machining process. The effect
of factors disturbing the process are monitored and corresponding kinematic or
geometric corrections introduced into the system

probe held in a measuring head. The magnitude of the displacement in
each axis is registered by means of transducers and is visually displayed
in digital mode. Assembly of parts is greatly facilitated by the accuracy
and consistency of NC machining which eliminates or reduces the
amount of fitting work and consequent adjustments.

(f) *Other economic factors.* Machining centres which perform machining processes which would require several types of conventional machine tool (e.g. drilling, milling, horizontal- and jig-boring machines) clearly reduce the need for internal transportation from section to section. They also minimise the non-productive time spent in set-up sequences on several machines. Reduced transportation between processes also implies a lesser need for the activities of production control personnel— and the associated paperwork. It follows that less work-in-progress is involved in the circumstances outlined above, thus effecting further savings by reducing the amount of capital employed. Due to the control exercised over the machining processes, savings due to a reduction in the amount of scrap produced are to be expected.

One further factor which can be advanced in favour of the use of NC in manufacturing engineering is that a reduced amount of lead-time is needed for getting work into production. Because jigs and fixtures do not have to be designed and manufactured before production can start, lead-time is saved, and this can be a vital element in the fulfillment of orders according to a time schedule.

CHAPTER 5

Tool Geometry And Chip Formation— Single-point Tools

5.1 Cutting Tool Angles

Metal cutting by chip formation occurs when a workpiece moves relative to a cutting edge which is positioned to penetrate its surface. The cutting edge has a precise geometrical form determined by the grinding of the tool; the chip produced has a form dependent upon the shape of the cutting tool and upon the behaviour, under the action of the cutting forces, of the material cut.

Consider the tool as a wedge, its cutting edge the intersection of two plane surfaces. Cutting requires a relative velocity between tool and workpiece which can be represented by a straight line meeting the cutting edge at the point being considered i.e, the velocity vector. Fundamentally the geometry of cutting tool angles arises from the spatial relationships between this vector, the tool edge and the two surfaces which intersect to give the edge.

When the tool edge is perpendicular to the velocity vector as Fig 5.1, a plane P_n, perpendicular to the edge, will contain the vector. A section of the wedge in this plane will contain the angles which have the greatest physical significance for the cutting process.

(a) The cut surface will slide past the clearance face of the tool which is represented by ST (lying in plane P_n). The angle in plane P_n between vector V and face ST is the clearance angle α.

(b) The cut chip will slide down the rake face of the tool which is represented by SU (lying in plane P_n). The angle in plane P_n between plane P_r and face SU is the rake angle γ.

(c) Angle β in plane P_n is the tool wedge angle and it follows from the angular relationships that

$$\alpha + \beta + \gamma = 90°$$

These conditions are the simplest geometrical ones for cutting and are generally referred to as **orthogonal**. They represent, in fact, a special case of the general condition.

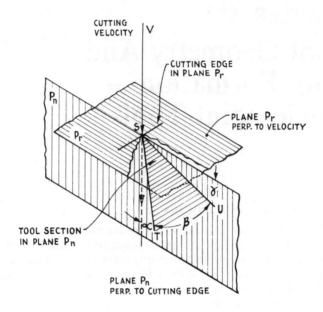

Fig. 5.1 Basic geometry of cutting angles

Suppose now that the cutting edge is inclined at some angle relative to the velocity (no longer lying in plane P_r). The principal effect will be to change the direction in which the chip slides down the tool rake face. Plane P_n in which the tool angles have been measured will no longer be perpendicular to plane P_r, nor will it contain the velocity vector. These are the general conditions for cutting and, where the inclination of the cutting edge is of a significant magnitude, they are referred to as **oblique.**

A practical problem of specifying tool angles arises from the fact that two distinct elements are involved, the angles ground on the tool to produce the wedge and, further, the location of that wedge relative to the motions of the machine. The current British Standard, BS 1296: *Single Point Cutting Tools Part 2 Nomenclature*, distinguishes these by reference to:

    (i) "tool-in-hand" system; the so-called tool angles;
    (ii) "tool-in-use" system; the so-called working angles.

In attempting to provide a more rigorous basis for cutting geometry than BS 1886 (now withdrawn), BS 1296 uses 51 different symbols and its complexity limits its usefulness at workshop levels. In this text an attempt will be made to show the more significant aspects of BS 1296 but for a complete picture the standard itself must be consulted.

Fig. 5.2 shows a method of specifying tool angles relative to the tool shank, a convenient system when using certain types of tool grinding jig and one widely used in America. Its disadvantage is that the angles in planes BB and CC are not angles having direct physical meaning in relation to cutting. Their combined effect depends on the approach angle ψ (see 5.2 p. 175).

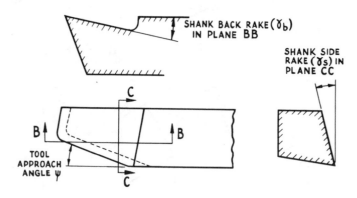

Fig. 5.2 Cutting angles defined by reference to the tool shank

Fig. 5.3, based on BS 1296 Fig 21a, shows the main features of the **normal rake system** adopted as the basis for this specification. Note that the tool cutting edge is inclined to the assumed direction of primary motion (oblique cutting) but that angle λ is rather small and so would have little effect on the direction in which the chip would slide down the rake face. Angles α_n and γ_n, in a plane normal to the cutting edge (plane P_n), are the significant angles relative to the cutting action of the tool. Note that

$$\alpha_n + \beta_n + \gamma_n = 90°.$$

Cutting requires a small positive angle between the clearance face and the machined surface moving past it. The rate at which a wear land will develop below the cutting edge, and hence the life of the tool, depends upon this angle. Generally 3–5° is adequate and because the cut surface follows the line of cutting velocity the tool orthogonal clearance angle, α_0 on the diagram, is a satisfactory workshop measure of clearance.

Fig 5.4 represents the conditions when the cutting edge is not perpendicular to the cutting velocity (oblique). The cutting edge is at angle λ to plane P_r which is perpendicular to the cutting velocity. This causes the chip to slide down the rake face along line SU which is not perpendicular to the cutting edge as for orthogonal cutting.

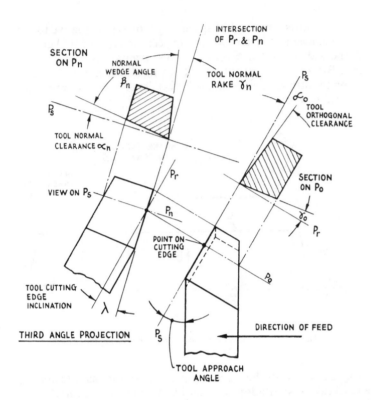

Fig. 5.3 Normal rake system of cutting tool angles based on BS1296

Direction of cutting velocity—perpendicular to tool shank base at the point shown on the cutting edge.
Planes passing through the selected point on the cutting edge are:

P_n, perpendicular to the cutting edge
P_o, perpendicular to the tool base and to plane P_s
P_r, parallel to the tool base
P_s, perpendicular to the tool base and containing the cutting edge.

Angle λ, tool edge inclination, can be either clockwise or anticlockwise from plane P_r.
BS1296 designates the condition shown as a negative angle

Experimental evidence obtained by G. V. Stabler shows that the angle lying in the rake face between a line perpendicular to the edge and the line of motion of the chip, shown as τ on the diagram, is, for all practical purposes, equal to the angle of obliquity λ.

$\tau = \lambda$ is sometimes referred to as the chip flow law. There are now two possible angles indicating the amount of rake: γ_n, the normal rake angle of BS 1296 lying in a plane perpendicular to the cutting edge, and the angle lying in a plane which contains:

    (i) the direction of the cutting velocity,
    (ii) the direction of the chip flow down the rake face, (line SU)

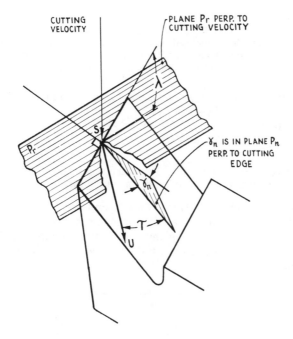

Fig. 5.4 Cutting angles in oblique cutting

Calling this angle γ_t (true or effective rake) it can be shown from the geometrical conditions and by putting $\tau = \lambda$ that:

$$\sin \gamma_t = \sin^2 \lambda + \cos^2 \lambda \sin \gamma_n \qquad (5.1)$$

See G. V. Stabler, "The Fundamental Geometry of Cutting Tools", *Proc. I.Mech.E.*, **165**, 1951

Most single-point tools operate under conditions closer to orthogonal than to oblique cutting. When operating with moderate positive or small negative normal rakes, angles of obliquity up to 10° have only a small influence on the value of γ_t and can be ignored. However, for cutting tests under laboratory conditions, such effects should be considered.

The main field of use of cutting tools with large angles of obliquity is in milling where they make possible the use of negative values for γ_n, which produces a strong tooth form but, by changing the direction of chip flow down the rake face, also make γ_t positive to give good cutting conditions (see Chapter 8).

Another important feature of oblique cutting is that the direction of chip flow can be so arranged that clogging of restricted tooth spaces or jamming of the chips in blind pockets of the component can be avoided by suitable choice of the angle of inclination of the tool edge.

Example 5.1

A cutting tool has a rake angle of 12° measured in a plane normal to the cutting edge. The cutting edge is inclined with respect to the direction of the cutting velocity by an amount which makes the rake, measured in the direction of chip flow, 13°. Find the angle of obliquity of the cutting edge.

Solution.

For oblique cutting $\sin \gamma_t = \sin^2 \lambda + \cos^2 \lambda \sin \gamma_n$ (Eqn 4.1)

Hence $\sin 13° = \sin^2 \lambda + \sin 12° \cos^2 \lambda$

$$0.2250 = 1 - \cos^2 \lambda + 0.2080 \cos^2 \lambda$$
$$\cos^2 \lambda = 0.7750/0.7920$$
$$\lambda = 8.4°$$

The result confirms that small angles of cutting edge inclination are not particularly significant in their influence on cutting rake.

The working angles of a cutting tool depend upon the positioning of the tool in the machine and upon the particular motions of the machine. Fig 5.5 shows how the working angles of a lathe tool mounted "above centre" should be measure; Fig 5.6 shows how the feed rate influences the cutting angles.

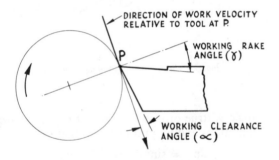

Fig. 5.5 "Working" rake and clearance angles

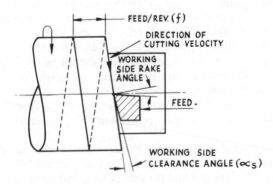

Fig. 5.6 Influence of feed on working cutting angles

5.2 Approach Angle and Rake Angles

Fig 5.7 shows the general conditions for roughing cuts. The relationship of cutting edge PQ to the axis of work rotation depends on the tool approach angle (see Fig 5.3) and also on the angle of the tool shank with respect to the axis of work rotation. For this reason the angle between PQ and the rotational axis, defined by the symbol ϕ, is here termed the working approach angle.

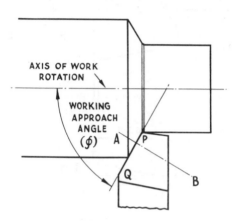

Fig. 5.7 General conditions for roughing cuts

For orthogonal cutting, the normal rake angle γ_n is a function of the side rake and back rake angles, and of the working approach angle. Fig 5.8 illustrates these relationships.

When the cutting edge PQ, Fig 5.7, lies in a plane containing the axis of rotation of the workpiece or cutter the relationship between the tool angles measured relative to the tool shank and the normal rake angle γ_n may be conveniently expressed trigonometrically. Fig 5.8 shows the geometrical relationships from which the trigonometrical relationships are derived.

The relationships $x \sin \phi$ and $x \cos \phi$ arise from triangle PTU as projected in the plane of the paper. Since the rake face of the tool slopes away from the plane of projection, point T is distance $x \sin \phi \tan \gamma_s$ below this plane (which also contains P), and point U is distance $x \cos \phi \tan \gamma_b$ below a plane parallel to the plane of the paper and containing point T. Triangle PP_1U, projected to show the slope of the rake face in plane AB, gives the relationship $\tan \gamma = \dfrac{P_1U}{x}$. From the above it can be seen that

$$P_1U = x \sin \phi \tan \gamma_s + x \cos \phi \tan \gamma_b,$$

hence $\qquad \tan \gamma = \sin \phi \tan \gamma_s + \cos \phi \tan \gamma_b \qquad (5.2)$

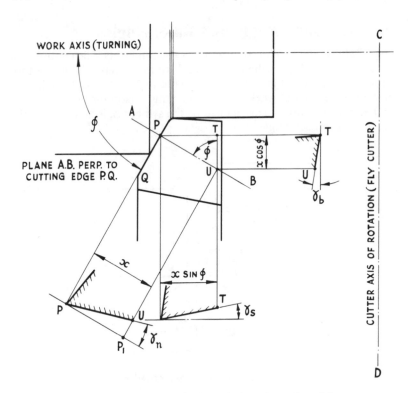

Fig. 5.8 Geometry of normal rake angle for orthogonal conditions

Angle γ, as defined above, is the "*cutting edge side rake angle*" of the German system.

The relationship given in Eqn (5.2) is true for negative rake conditions. It also applies if the cutter rotates about an axis CD to "face" a stationary workpiece, although the terminology then used to describe the cutting angles is different. (See Chapter 8—Principles of Metal Cutting—Milling.)

Example 5.2

Show that the working cutting clearance angle of a twist drill is lower towards the centre than at the periphery. A 25 mm dia drill, chisel edge 3 mm wide, is used with a feed of 0·64 mm/rev. If the nominal clearance angle is 7°, find the greatest and least working clearance angles.

Solution

Due to the feed motion of the drill, each point on the cutting edge travels in a helical path, the nominal clearance angle being reduced by the helix angle at the point being considered as indicated in Fig 5.9 on p. 177.

Since radius r is larger at P than at Q, the helix angle (δ) of the path travelled, given by $\tan \delta = \dfrac{f}{2\pi r}$, is smaller at P than at Q. The working clearance angle α is

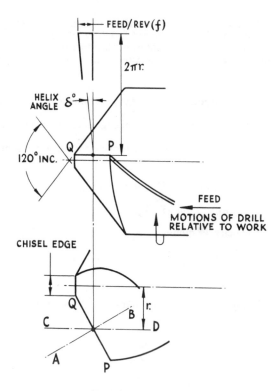

Fig. 5.9 Clearance angle of a twist drill

reduced due to the influence of the feed helix angle δ, hence it is lower towards the centre than at the periphery.

Angle δ lies in plane CD; its effect in the plane AB, which contains the working clearance angle α, depends upon the point angle of the drill. Assuming this to be 120° included, $\tan \delta_{AB} = \tan \delta \cos 30°$, the suffix AB indicating the magnitude in plane AB of the angle δ lying in plane CD.

At P, $\tan \delta_{AB} = \dfrac{0 \cdot 64}{25\pi} \times 0 \cdot 866 = 0 \cdot 0069$

$\delta_{AB} = 24'$ approx., and the effect on the cutting clearance at the periphery is negligible.

At Q, $\tan \delta_{AB} = \dfrac{0 \cdot 64}{3\pi} \times 0 \cdot 866 = 0 \cdot 0588$

$$\delta_{AB} = 3° \, 22'$$

The least working clearance angle is $= 7° - 3° \, 22' = \underline{3° \, 38'}$

Example 5.3

A tool used in a relieving lathe has its rake face in the plane of the axis or work rotation. The work rotates at 15 rev/min and the tool is displaced towards the work axis by the relieving cam at a velocity of 17 mm/s. Find, at a point where the work dia is 100mm, the cutting speed and the working rake angle in a plane perpendicular to the work axis. What front clearance angle relative to the tool shank is required to give a working clearance angle of 8° in this plane?

Solution

Fig 5.10 shows the relationships between the various velocities upon which the solution depends.

The velocity of work relative to the tool edge is represented by PR. $\angle SPR = 90°$, hence $\angle QPR = \gamma$.

The velocity of the work relative to the tool edge is the vector sum of PQ and QR

$$PQ = \pi \times \frac{15}{60} \times 100 = 78 \cdot 5 \, \text{mm/s}$$

$$PR = \sqrt{78 \cdot 5^2 + 17^2} = \underline{80 \, \text{mm/s}}$$

i.e. true cutting velocity 4·8 m/min

$$\tan \gamma = \frac{17 \times 60}{15 \times 100\pi} = 0 \cdot 2165 \quad \gamma = 12°$$

i.e. working rake angle = $\underline{12°}$.

The clearance angle relative to tool shank = $12° + 8° = \underline{20°}$.

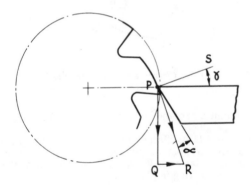

Fig. 5.10 Cutting angles of form-relieving tool

Example 5.4

A tool has a working approach angle $\phi = 55°$, a normal rake angle $\gamma_n = 22°$ and a cutting edge which lies in a plane parallel to the base of the tool. Find the side rake angle γ_s and the back rake angle γ_b (American system) for these conditions.

Solution

Equation (5.2), $\tan \gamma_n = \sin \phi \tan \gamma_s + \cos \phi \tan \gamma_b$, cannot be used to obtain a solution, since it contains *two* unknowns. The information that the cutting edge lies in a plane parallel to the tool shank can, however, be used to obtain a solution to the question. The geometry upon which the solution is based is represented, in plan view, in Fig 5.11

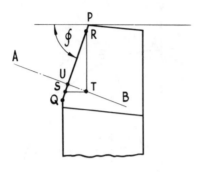

Fig. 5.11

From the diagram, $\angle RTU = \angle TSU = \phi$.

Point T in the rake face of the tool lies at distance UT $\tan \gamma$ below the horizontal plane containing the edge PQ.

Hence,
$$\tan \gamma_b = \frac{UT \tan \gamma}{RT} = \frac{UT \tan \gamma}{UT/\cos \phi}$$

$$= \tan \gamma \cos \phi$$

Similarly,
$$\tan \gamma_s = \tan \gamma \sin \phi$$

For the values given,

$$\tan \gamma_b = 0{\cdot}4040 \times 0{\cdot}5736 = 0{\cdot}2317$$
$$\gamma_b = 13° \, 3'$$

$$\tan \gamma_s = 0{\cdot}4040 \times 0{\cdot}8192 = 0{\cdot}3309$$
$$\gamma_s = 18° \, 19'$$

It is left as an exercise for the reader to show that the formulae derived above are consistent with Eqn (5.2).

Note on Solution to Example 5.4. The tool-angle relationships derived above may be solved graphically as shown in Fig 5.12.

AB is a circular arc, centre O, having a radius representing $\tan \gamma$ to a suitable scale: $\angle AOB = 90°$. Angle ϕ is set off as shown to intersect arc AB at point E; EC is drawn parallel to AO, ED is drawn parallel to BO. From the diagram it can be seen that

$$OC = \tan \gamma \cos \phi = \tan \gamma_b,$$
$$OD = \tan \gamma \sin \phi = \tan \gamma_s,$$

hence the values of $\tan \gamma_b$ and $\tan \gamma_s$ are represented to the same scale as $\tan \gamma$ was constructed.

If the axes OA and OB are graduated in proportion to the tangents of angles and each graduation marked with the actual **angle**, the tangent of which has been represented, values of γ_b and γ_s can be read off directly. This construction enables a very useful tool-angle chart to be drawn

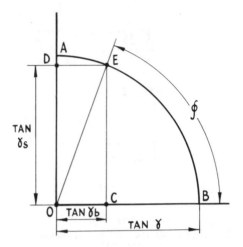

Fig. 5.12 Graphical solution of rake angles

covering a suitable range of γ and a range of ϕ from 0° to 90°. The "Rake Conversion Chart" by Dr. G. F. Galloway, is based upon this construction.

5.3 Chip Formation

Two experimental methods have been used in order to discover the way in which chips are formed. In one of these the cutting process is stopped suddenly to leave the chip attached to the workpiece and in contact with the tool. This gives a "still" picture of chip formation which probably suffers some distortion due to elastic recovery when the cutting stresses are released.

The second method is that of high-speed photography, which enables a "slow-motion" film of chip formation to be made. The method has been employed by Professor Loxham and his colleagues at the College of Aeronautics, Department of Production and Industrial Administration. In both methods the region around the cutting edge of the tool is viewed through a microscope so that chip formation may be examined in detail. Such experimental techniques have enabled ideas about chip formation to be clarified, thereby aiding the study of metal cutting.

Dr. Merchant, of the Cincinnati Milling Machine Co., took an idealised concept of chip formation for which a precise geometry may be derived as the basis for his studies of the mechanics of metal cutting.

Fig 5.13 illustrates the concept. Workpiece material advancing at velocity V towards the tool edge, is compressed at the tool rake face, causing failure to occur by plastic shearing along the plane PQ, called the

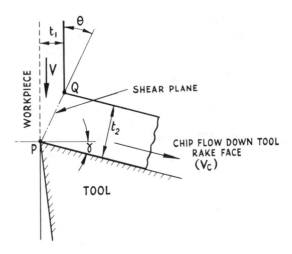

Fig. 5.13 Merchant's "idealised" concept of chip formation

shear plane. Under suitable conditions a continuous and steady rate of deformation occurs along the shear plane and the deformed material slides at a uniform velocity V_c down the rake face of the tool in the form of a continuous chip. Before deformation the thickness of the chip is t_1 and t_1 = feed/rev when $\phi = 90°$; during deformation the cut chip increases in thickness to t_2. The rake angle (γ) plays an essential part in the action and shearing occurs along some definite plane, the position of which is given by the shear plane angle θ. Since t_1 and γ are known, and t_2 may be measured for a chip cut under steady conditions, the shear plane angle θ can be found from a simple cutting test.

Direct measurement of t_2 is not practical because of the roughness of the upper side of the cut chip. The following method permits reasonably accurate values of t_2 to be found.

A small shallow saw notch is milled along the periphery of the bar to be machined (Fig 5.14). The depth of cut d is obtained by measuring the diameter of the bar before and after cutting and from these measurements the mean diameter of the bar D_m is also obtained. The mean length of the cut chip l_2, measured between two successive notches, is determined by measuring along the inner and outer edges of the chip and finding a mean value. (The distances may be stepped off in small units set as accurately as possible on toolmakers' spring dividers.) The mean distance before cutting $l_1 = \pi D_m$. Assuming no deformation occurs in the depth d, which is probably nearly true,

$$t_1 . l_1 = t_2 . l_2$$

and
$$t_2 = \frac{t_1 . l_1}{l_2}$$

The ratio t_1/t_2 is a measure of the amount of deformation occurring during cutting; it changes according to the particular material cut and the value of the effective rake angle employed. The higher the value of this ratio obtained from a cutting test, the lower the energy consumed in shearing along PQ. Efficient cutting lubricants tend to increase the ratio, and so reduce the total energy requirements for cutting. For this reason changes in the value of t_2, other factors remaining constant, may be used to test the relative effectiveness of various cutting lubricants.

θ may be obtained from a simple large-scale drawing once the values t_1, t_2 and γ are known. By calculation, $\tan\theta = \dfrac{\gamma_c \cos\gamma}{1 - \gamma_c \sin\gamma}$, where $\gamma_c = t_1/t_2$.

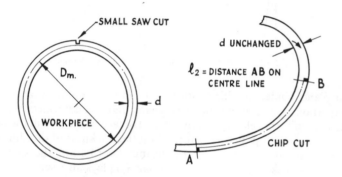

Fig. 5.14 Method of obtaining chip length l_2

Example 5.5

A bar 76 mm dia, is reduced to 71 mm dia by means of a cutting tool for which $\phi = 90°$ and for which the cutting edge lies in the plane containing the work axis of rotation. The mean length of the cut chip $l_2 = 73.9$ mm, the rake angle $\gamma = 15°$ and a feed of 0.2 mm/rev is used. Find the cutting ratio t_1/t_2 and the value of the shear plane angle.

Solution

$$t_2 = \frac{73.5\pi}{73.9} \times 0.2 = 0.63 \text{ mm}$$

$$t_1/t_2 = 0.2/0.63 = 0.32$$

θ may then be found by scale drawing as shown in Fig 5.15. Set off TP and PS such that $\angle\text{TPS} = 90° + 15°$; PS represents the rake face of the tool. To some convenient scale set off a line parallel to TP at distance 0.2 mm, and a line parallel to PS at distance 0.63 mm to intersect at Q. Join PQ and measure the resulting angle TPQ to obtain the value of θ.

By measurement $\theta = \underline{19}$ °.

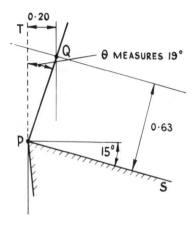

Fig. 5.15 Graphical solution of shear plane angle

Chip Types. The variables which influence the type of chip produced when cutting are:

(i) properties of the material cut, especially the ductility;
(ii) rake angle γ;
(iii) cutting speed V;
(iv) depth of cut d;
(v) feed rate f (mm/rev);
(vi) type and quantity of cutting fluid employed.

Additionally the surface finish of the tool faces, the coefficient of friction between the chip and the tool, and the temperature reached in the region of cutting, all have some influence upon chip formation, but are generally less-significant variables than those listed above.

Fig 5.16 illustrates distinctive chip types. In practice, there is a gradual

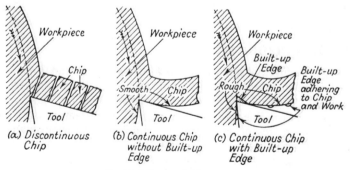

Fig. 5.16 Types of chip formation
(Courtesy I.Mech.E.)

change from one distinctive type to another which classification of chip forms cannot accurately represent.

(*a*) Shows a discontinuous chip without built-up edge. Conditions which give rise to this type of chip are: work material brittle, γ small, V low, d and f large (especially f), no cutting lubricant used. The machining of grey cast iron gives rise to this type of chip.

(*b*) Shows a continuous chip without built-up edge. Conditions which give rise to this type of chip are: work material moderately ductile, γ large, V high, d and f small (especially f), use of an efficient cutting lubricant, a good surface finish on the tool cutting faces and a tool material which does not tend to pressure weld to the work material. The machining of steels of moderate hardness, particularly during finishing cuts, gives rise to this type of chip. It is one of the easiest chip types to study, as instanced by Dr. Merchant's theory of the basic mechanics of metal cutting, because the cutting forces remain fairly steady during the cutting, which simplifies the experimental procedures.

(*c*) Shows a continuous chip with built-up edge. Conditions which give rise to this type of chip are similar to those under (*b*), but with a bias towards higher values of d and f (especially f) and lower values of V and γ, and towards poor lubrication properties of the coolant employed and a tendency to pressure welding of the workpiece material to the tool material. Built-up edge is caused by small particles of the cut chip pressure welding to the rake face of the tool. Surface finish of the machined bar is marred by small pieces of built-up edge which are eventually swept from the tool by the rotating workpiece and which remain attached to the machined surface. Some very ductile materials, e.g. annealed copper, give rise to excessive built-up edge at low values of γ and particularly high values (around $30°-35°$) may be necessary in order to cut such material satisfactorily.

The disposal of continuous-type chips may present practical difficulties and "chip-breakers" are generally necessary for production machining where conditions favour the formation of type (*b*) or type (*c*) chips.

5.4 Machinability

Chips may be cut from some materials with relative ease and from others only with the greatest difficulty. This difference may be attributed to the "*machinability*" of the respective materials. Machinability, however, is not a single measurable property of a material, and attempts which have been made to represent the relative machinability of various materials numerically are only partially successful.

The most significant variables indicating machinability are: tool life, and the quality of surface finish produced. Conditions of the material which determine machinability are: composition, heat treatment and microstructure. The measurable mechanical properties of hardness, tensile strength and ductility give some indication of the machining properties to be expected, but cannot distinguish between, say, the machinability of a free-cutting mild steel and of an austenitic stainless steel having somewhat similar mechanical test properties.

Some significant facts relating to machinability are given below:

(a) *Hardness*. Steels up to 300 HB do not present great machining difficulty unless large amounts of alloying material are present. Steels up to 350 HB are machinable with the superior grades of HSS, and with carbide tools. It is possible to hob splines on shafts of medium alloy steels following their heat treatment to somewhere near the above degree of hardness.

Some materials, notably manganese steel (manganese content 12–14%) and alloys of the Nimonic series, have pronounced work-hardening properties which influence machinability. Indentation hardness tests may give values below 200 HB, which does not suggest any difficulty will be encountered during machining. Reference to p. 201, however, shows that chip formation involves "working" of the material, and hardness may increase considerably from this cause. The increase of cutting power, due to work-hardening, gives rise to the generation of more heat; the resulting fall in tool life reveals an increased resistance to machining as compared with other materials of equivalent indentation hardness. An extensively worked manganese steel may rise in hardness value to 550 HB, in which state machining becomes impracticable. A dull cutting tool operating at too small a feed may fail to cut a chip and will then work-harden the surface of the material so that subsequent penetration with a reconditioned tool is impossible. The use of sharp, well-finished tools, at moderate depths of cut and feed, is the correct technique to employ when machining materials which work-harden rapidly.

The machinability of plain carbon steels falls steadily as the carbon content rises. Surface finish is better on the low-carbon steels if these have been cold drawn.

(b) *Micro-structure*. Banded structures, as shown in Fig 5.17, do not machine well. Surface finish is poor due to tearing of the ferrite-rich areas.

Fine-grained materials take a good surface finish but have an increased resistance to machining. High-carbon steels may be machined at greater metal-removal rates if annealed or spheroidised; the resulting surface finish is then not very good, so that the treatment is generally confined to roughing operations.

(c) *Composition*. High-nickel–chrome alloy steels are hard to machine due to their toughness, a combination of high strength with relatively

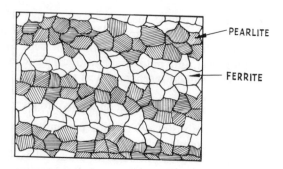

Fig. 5.17 Banded structure in a medium-carbon steel

high ductility. Under such conditions the amount of work to be done on the material necessary to cause plastic shear resulting in chips, as described on p. 180, must be large.

The 18.8 type of austenitic stainless steel is difficult to machine because the ductile austenite transforms to the harder martensite under cutting stresses. For such conditions the cutting edge of the tool must be kept beneath the surface of the workpiece; rubbing, without producing a chip, may so work harden the surface that it is almost impossible to get a tool to penetrate the hard skin formed.

(d) *Free Machining Properties.* Inclusions of a weaker insoluble material, such as manganese sulphide in a mild steel, considerably increase machinability both in regard to metal removal rates and the resulting surface finish. The inclusions give rise to local weaknesses which, under the cutting forces, increase stress concentration and thus cause failure at lower force values. Such inclusions cause a small reduction of mechanical properties only and the free machining steels are of considerable economic importance in bar turning on automatic lathes.

Numerous manganese sulphide inclusions occur in steels having higher than normal amounts of sulphur (0·2 % in place of 0·04 %) to which manganese of about five times this amount has been added to neutralise the sulphur. The addition of the manganese is necessary to prevent the formation of the very weakening ferrous sulphide at the grain boundaries. The microstructure is illustrated in Fig 5.18. The introduction of small amounts of lead, 0·15–0·35 % in steels, 1·0–3·0 % in brasses and bronzes, is effective in improving machinability for similar reasons.

Machinability Ratings. In their *Manual on Cutting Metals*, the American Society of Mechanical Engineers (A.S.M.E.) give numerical ratings indicating relative machinability. A.I.S.I. Steel No. B1112, carbon 0·13 % max, manganese 0·70–1·00 %, sulphur 0·16–0·23 % in cold-drawn condition, U.T.S. 82 000 lbf/in^2 (566 N/mm^2), 179 HB, is rated at 100.

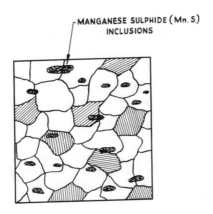

Fig. 5.18 Inclusions in a free-machining low-carbon steel

By comparison a $3\frac{1}{2}\%$ nickel, $1\frac{1}{2}\%$ chrome steel, heat treated to 375 HB is rated at 24; a leaded brass 82 HB is rated at 200; and a phosphor bronze 140 HB is rated at 40. The ratings are based on actual cutting tests and, as instanced by the values for the alloy steel and bronze, do reflect common experience in cutting such materials.

The Manual contains excellent information on microstructures suitable for machining and on many other special aspects of machinability.

Example 5.6
Compare the relative machining properties of a 70/30 brass and a free machining brass. Mention chip types, and any differences in the cutting conditions required.

Solution
70/30 brass: in the annealed condition, the elongation is approx 70%; in the cold-worked condition the elongation is approx 10%. Machining is only likely to be required to dress the edge of pressings or produce drilled holes. The material would be machined in the worked condition and before any annealing process which may be required. The chip will be continuous and chip disposal difficult. A rake angle of about 25° is suitable; a cutting lubricant and a fine feed should be used to produce good surface finish. Tool faces should have a very good surface finish to minimise built-up edge.

Free machining brass: 58% Cu, 39% Zn, 3% Pb, is a probable composition and the bar is likely to be extruded. Ductility is represented by an elongation of approx 30%, but the material machines easily due to the lead inclusions. It should be cut dry, using a small or zero rake angle, at moderate speeds and feeds. Discontinuous chips, very easily cleared from the tools, make this material suitable for turned work on bar automatics.

EXERCISES 5

1. A cutting tool has an approach angle of $\phi = 60°$ and rake angles of $\gamma_b = 12°$, $\gamma_s = 18°$. Find the normal rake angle on the assumption that the cutting is orthogonal.

If this tool is set 3 mm above centre turning bar of 100 mm dia, what change will be caused in γ_b and approximately what change will be caused in the normal rake angle?

2. The apparent rake and clearance angles of metal-cutting tools are measured from the plane of the base of the tool.

(*a*) Show by means of diagrams:

(i) two instances where, due to tool setting, the true tool angles are different from the apparent ones;
(ii) two instances where they are different due to the nature of the machining operation.

(*b*) Illustrate, and discuss briefly, the relative advantages and disadvantages of the Normal Rake system and the American system of defining rake angles.

3. A screw-cutting tool, Fig 5.19 is to have an included angle of 55° in plane AB and 10° front clearance angle as shown.

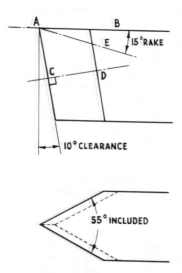

Fig. 5.19

Determine to the nearest minute:

(*a*) the angle to be ground in plane CD,
(*b*) the angle resulting in plane AE if a rake angle of 15° is afterwards ground on the tool.

4. A straight form tool is required to turn a concave, part-circular groove, of 13 mm radius. The tool is to have a front clearance of 12° and zero rake. Determine the shape to which a grinding wheel must be "trued" in order to grind the required form on the tool.

To what depth can the tool be advanced into the work if the minimum normal clearance angle round the form is not be less than 3°?

5. Define orthogonal cutting and show the geometrical conditions for which it will occur. Why are these conditions frequently used in experimental work on cutting?

Sketch the conditions of chip formation, and give brief notes upon them, for the production of continuous type chips:

(i) without built-up edge;
(ii) with built-up edge.

Why is the first of these chip types the most desirable one for experimental work on cutting?

6. A turning tool has rake angles of $\gamma_b = 10°$ and $\gamma_s = 16°$. For what value of the approach angle ϕ will the cutting be orthogonal?

If $\phi = 50°$, what change must be made in γ_s in order to achieve orthogonal cutting conditions? What is the value of the normal rake angle for this condition?

7. Show from the geometry of chip formation for a continuous type chip without built-up edge, that the shear plane angle θ is given by,

$$\tan \theta = \frac{r_c \cos \gamma}{1 - r_c \sin \gamma}$$

where r_c is the chip thickness ratio $\dfrac{t_1}{t_2}$.

8. A 100 mm dia bar is turned by means of a tool for which $\phi = 90°$ and $\gamma_s = 15°$. The depth of cut is 5 mm and the feed is 0·25 mm/rev.

If the mean length of a cut chip representing one rotation of the workpiece is 92 mm, find the shear plane angle.

9. You are required to test the relative machinability of two different alloy steels.

Indicate the information which you would require concerning these steels and the particular tests you would carry out in order to reach your decision.

10. (a) Outline the causes of built-up edge and its effects upon:

(i) tool life and the manner of tool failure;
(ii) the finish of the surface being machined.

(b) Describe two different methods by which continuous chips can be broken, for practical convenience, into short lengths.

11. The normal rake angle of a tool (as BS1296) is − 6°, i.e. negative rake. The angle of obliquity of the cutting edge with respect to the cutting velocity is 30°. Determine the rake angle lying in a plane containing;

(i) the line of cutting velocity
(ii) the line of flow of the chip·down the rake face.

12. Show that an angle of obliquity of the cutting edge of 20° has greater significance on the effective cutting rake angle when the normal rake angle is 10° negative than when it is 10° positive.

CHAPTER 6

Mechanics of Cutting— Single-point Tools

6.1 Units and Measurement

A considerable amount of useful data on metal cutting, e.g. the ASME *Manual on Cutting of Metals*, is available in imperial units as also in past production department records of manufacturing companies. Table 6.1 defines the symbols used in this book and gives imperial and metric S I units for each, together with a conversion factor. (Imperial unit × conversion factor gives metric unit).

TABLE 6.1

	Symbol	Imperial units	Conversion factor	Metric Units
Cutting speed	V	ft/min	0·305	m/min
Cutting force	T	lbf	4·45	newtons (N)
Depth of cut	d	in	25·4	mm
Feed/rev	f	in	25·4	mm
Metal removal rate	w	in³/min	273	mm³/s
Power consumed		hp	746	watts (W)
Power criterion $\left(\dfrac{\text{Power}}{w}\right)$		hp/in³/min	2·73	W/mm³/s
K factor $\left(\dfrac{w}{\text{Power}}\right)$	K	in³/min/hp	0·366	mm³/s/W
Specific cutting pressure	P	lbf/in²	0·0069	N/mm² (or MN/m²)

The cutting speed V is the relative velocity of the workpiece and tool at the tool edge. For any point on the tool edge it can be considered as a vector, and the cutting force T is measured along the line of this vector.

The following elementary relationships should be noted:

(a) energy/min consumed in cutting $= TV$ Nm/min;

(b) power consumed in cutting $= \dfrac{TV}{60}$ watts (W);

(c) metal removal rate,
$$w = df \frac{V}{60} \times 10^3 \text{ mm}^3/\text{s}.$$

The power required to remove a unit volume of material per minute is a measure of its resistance to cutting; it also gives an indication of the effectiveness of the cutting conditions. Typical values for common materials enable estimates of cutting power and cutting force to be made for specified metal removal rates. These values are of use to machine tool designers and production planning engineers.

$$(d) \quad \frac{\text{power}}{w} = \frac{TV}{60} \frac{60}{df V \times 10^3}, \quad \text{i.e. } \propto \frac{T}{df}. \qquad (6.1)$$

Hence the power criterion is independent of cutting speed except in so far as the cutting force changes with the cutting speed.

Units of the power criterion are $\text{W/mm}^3/\text{s}$ which is equivalent to J/mm^3. Some authorities quote values of the specific energy required for cutting, i.e. the energy required to remove a unit volume of material. However, at the practical level, machine tool users will tend to think in terms of the power available at the spindle of the machine. It should be recognised that for a specific energy of, say, 2 J/mm^3 it will require 2 W to remove metal at a rate of $1 \text{ mm}^3/\text{s}$.

Measurement of the input to the electric motor of a machine tool provides a convenient method of measuring the power consumed in cutting. If the value of the power supplied when the machine is running idle is subtracted from the power reading taken under the cutting load, a reasonable estimate of the power consumed in cutting is obtained. The method is an approximate one, because the efficiency of the drive under varying loads is not taken into account. Watt-meters are commonly used to measure the power; 746 watts = 1 hp. Many machine tools are equipped with motors rated in hp.

Example 6.1
The power required to turn a medium-carbon steel is approximately $3.8 \text{ W/mm}^3/\text{s}$.

If the maximum power available at the machine spindle is 5 hp, find the maximum metal removal rate. Also find, for a cutting speed of 36 m/min and feed rate of 0·25 mm/rev, the depth of cut and the cutting force which will occur when the metal removal rate is at the maximum value.

Solution

$$w_{max} = \frac{5 \times 746}{3 \cdot 8} = \underline{982 \text{ mm}^3/\text{s}}$$

$$T = \frac{5 \times 746 \times 60}{36} = \underline{6216 \text{ N}}$$

$$d = \frac{60 \times 982}{10^3 \times 36 \times 0 \cdot 25} = \underline{6 \cdot 55 \text{ mm}}$$

Example 6.2

A lathe running idle consumes 325 W. When cutting an alloy steel at 24·5 m/min the power input rises to 2580 W. Find the cutting force and torque at the spindle when running at 124 rev/min. If the depth of cut is 3·8 mm and the feed 0·2 mm/rev, find the power criterion.

Solution

$$\text{Power consumed in cutting} = 2580 - 325 = 2255 \text{ W}$$

$$w = 0\cdot2 \times 3\cdot8 \times 24\cdot5 \times \frac{10^3}{60} = 310 \text{ mm}^3/\text{s}$$

$$\text{Power criterion} = \frac{2255}{310} = \underline{7\cdot27 \text{ W/mm}^3/\text{s}}$$

$$\text{Torque at the spindle} = \frac{2255 \times 60}{2\pi \times 124} = \underline{174 \text{ Nm}}$$

$$\text{Cutting force } (T) = \frac{2255 \times 60}{24\cdot5} = \underline{5522 \text{ N}}$$

6.2 Specific Cutting Pressure

$$\text{Specific cutting pressure } (P) = \frac{T}{\text{cut area}} = \frac{T}{df}.$$

This concept is a useful one, since P is a measure of the resistance to cutting offered by the material. The term **specific** is employed to denote that P is not a true stress set up in the material cut; it is called a pressure because it has the form, force/area.

The cut area is given by $d \times f$ irrespective of the value of ϕ or of any nose radius on the tool (geometric property of figures on same base and between the same parallel lines); see Fig 6.1.

Unfortunately the value of P is not independent of the tool-plan shape or of the magnitude of f, and it also varies with the rake angle used. It is only slightly affected by changes in cutting speed within the conventional range. Fig 6.2 illustrates the variation in the value of P which arises from a variation in feed, other factors remaining constant.

Except for finishing feeds, the variation of P due to variation of f is insufficient to prevent useful estimates of the cutting force being made from average values of P for the material cut.

It is obvious that the cutting force is given by $T = Pdf$. The simplicity of this arrangement is attractive, but the variable nature of P is a disadvantage. More accurate estimates of T can be made by using empirical formulae of the form $T = C . d^x . f^y$, where C is a constant for the material cut (similar to P which it displaces) and x and y change as the shape of the cut area changes, the method is not independent of ϕ or of the magnitude of the nose radius of the tool. The values of x and y are also slightly influenced by the magnitude of the rake angle used. For

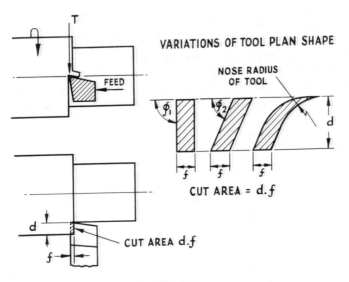

Fig. 6.1

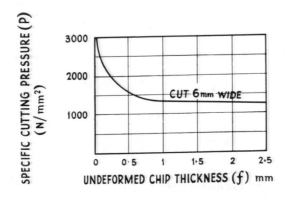

Fig. 6.2 Influence of feed on specific cutting pressure

these reasons the empirical formulae can be used only when values of x and y are known for the tool shape and conditions which apply. This makes the procedure too involved for general use.

The value of P is directly related to the power criterion for cutting.

From Eqn (6.1)

$$\frac{\text{power (W)}}{w} = \frac{T}{df} \times 10^{-3}$$

hence $P\left(\dfrac{N}{mm^2}\right) \times 10^{-3} = \dfrac{\text{power consumed (W)}}{\text{metal removal rate (mm}^3/\text{s)}} = \dfrac{1}{K}$ (6.2)

where K is the metal removal rate per watt.

As indicating the force and power involved in cutting, the specific cutting pressure and the power criterion (or K value) have the merit of simplicity, but both vary with the cutting conditions as shown in Fig 6.2 and Fig 6.3.

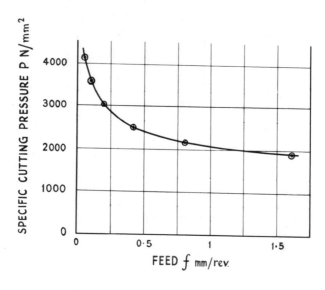

Fig. 6.3

Example 6.3

The given data relates to the rough turning of an alloy steel (SAE 3140) heat treated to 285 HB and having a U.T.S. of 986 MN/m².

Depth of cut 6·4 mm, approach angle (ϕ) 60°, nose radius 6·4 mm, side rake angle 14°, back rake angle 8°.

Cutting speed (V) m/min	55·5	35·4	22	14·3	9·5	6·4
Feed (f) mm/rev	0·05	0·10	0·20	0·40	0·80	1·60
kW consumed in cutting	1·27	1·42	1·50	1·64	1·87	2·16

Draw a graph to show the variation of specific cutting pressure with feed. Give the average value of the power criterion for cutting this material.

Solution

Feed (*f*)	0·05	0·10	0·20	0·40	0·80	1·60
Metal removal rate (*w*)	296	378	470	610	810	1093
$\dfrac{\text{Power (W)}}{w}$	4·29	3·76	3·19	2·69	2·31	1·98
P N/mm²	4290	3760	3190	2690	2310	1980

Note, $P = \dfrac{10^3 \times \text{power (W)}}{w}$ from Eqn (6.2)

The resulting graph is shown in Fig 6.3.
Average value of power criterion = 3·04 W/mm³/s

6.3 Variation of Specific Cutting Pressure with Rake Angle

As would be expected, practical tests show that *P* falls as the effective rake angle γ is increased. The relationship is not independent of speed, and for negative rake tools the cutting forces are often lower at high speeds than at low speeds. The graph, Fig 6.4, shows the approximate magnitude of the change in *P* for steels, due to these causes.

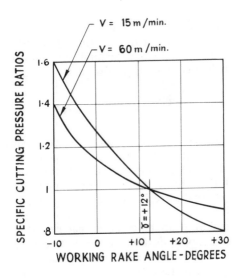

Fig. 6.4 Influence of rake angle on specific cutting pressure

6.4 Measurement of Cutting Forces

It is convenient to measure cutting forces in three mutually perpendicular planes related to the axis of work rotation and direction of
feed, as shown in Fig 6.5.

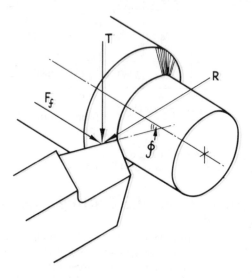

Fig. 6.5 Forces acting on a cutting tool

The vector sum of T, F_f and R is shown in Fig 6.6, from which it
can be seen that the resultant force acting upon the tool is given by
$\sqrt{(T^2 + F_f^2 + R^2)}$ and that it makes an angle θ with the projection of the
work axis in the plane containing the resultant. The value of θ is given by

$$\tan \theta = \frac{F_f}{\sqrt{(T^2 + R^2)}}$$

Measurement of the forces T, F_f and R is made using some form of
cutting-tool dynamometer. The principle frequently employed in such
instruments is that of measuring small deflections caused by the cutting
forces in each of the three directions. To simplify cutting tests, conditions
can be so arranged that force R is practically zero. If ϕ is made $90°$, and
the tool edge is made to lie in the plane containing the work axis and to
cut across the end of a tubular piece of material, R will be negligible.
   A sharp-pointed tool conforming to the above conditions may be used
to turn solid bar without causing significant values of R, an arrangement
more convenient for metal-cutting tests. Chip formation then occurs
under orthogonal conditions.

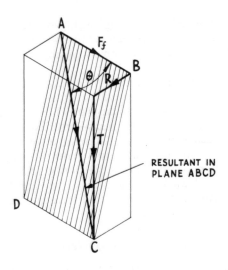

Fig. 6.6 Resultant cutting force

The general principle employed in deflection-type cutting-tool dynamometers is shown in Fig 6.7. A stiff member A, resting on a solid pivot, carries a cutting tool at one end and is attached to the frame B by means of a leaf spring at the other end. Force T deflects member A, relative to B, by an amount depending on the magnitude of T and stiffness of the spring. The load-deflection graph is a straight line, hence a dial gauge which measures the deflection can be calibrated to read T lb force. The

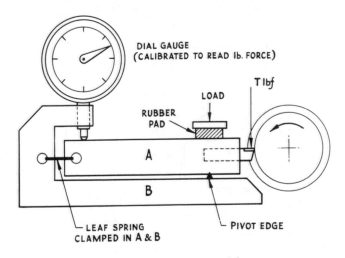

Fig. 6.7 Single-component cutting-tool dynamometer

instrument is calibrated by applying dead loads; matching of the dial-gauge calibration and dynamometer loading is achieved by grinding the thickness of the leaf spring, and finally by adjusting the load on the rubber pad.

The scheme illustrated operates in the vertical plane. To measure the feed force F_f, frame B must be housed in a further solid member so that it deflects in a plane perpendicular to the plane of the given projection. One further important condition must then be observed; the calibration for T must not be affected by the magnitude of force F_f, and vice versa. Member A must not deflect relative to B under the influence of force F_f, nor must the slope of the load–deflection graph be changed. This condition is not achieved in some types of two and three component cutting tool dynamometers and errors of force measurement may arise from this source.

6.5 Merchant's Analysis of Metal Cutting

By using the concept of chip formation described on p. 180 and by measuring the forces T and F_f with a cutting-tool dynamometer, Merchant was able to build up a picture of the forces acting in the region of cutting which give rise to plastic deformation and sliding of the chip down the tool rake-face. The theory assumes that a continuous-type chip without built-up edge is produced during the cutting, and the force system is illustrated in Fig 6.8.

The forces exerted by the workpiece on the chip are:

F_c = compressive force on the shear plane;
F_s = shear force on the shear plane.

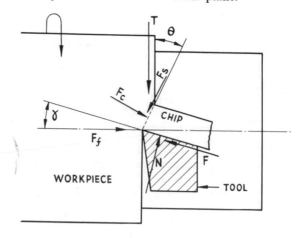

Fig. 6.8 Chip formation and force systems as postulated by Merchant

The forces exerted by the tool on the chip are:

N = normal force at the rake face of tool;

F = frictional force along the rake face of tool.

The forces acting on the tool, measured by the cutting-tool dynamo-meter, are the forces T and F_f shown in Fig 6.5.

As explained on p. 180 and illustrated by Example 5.5, the shear plane angle θ can be found from a simple cutting test. Since γ is known and θ can be determined, the directions of all the forces shown in Fig 6.8 can be found.

It is reasonable to suppose that the action of the workpiece on the chip is balanced by the reaction of the tool on the chip, hence the resultant of forces F_c and F_s, and the resultant of forces N and F, will be common in magnitude and direction (but opposite in sense). The action of the workpiece on the tool is measured by means of a cutting-tool dynamo-meter, and since T and F_f give rise to the other forces, their resultant is also common in magnitude and direction with the above.

Using the concepts illustrated in Fig 6.8, it is now possible to find graphically the magnitude of the mutually perpendicular pairs of forces F_c, F_s and N, F. Use is made of the geometrical property of the angle in a semicircle, and the required graphical construction is illustrated in Fig 6.9.

The vector diagram of forces is constructed as follows. Draw F_f and T to some convenient scale and join AB to obtain their resultant. Bisect AB and draw a circle having the resultant force as its diameter. Set off BE, making angle θ with force T, to cut the circle at E. Join EA. The magnitudes of F_s and F_c are now shown.

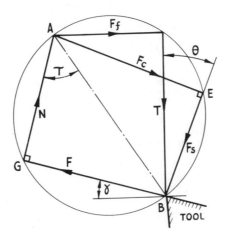

Fig. 6.9 Merchant's Circle

Set off a line BG, at an angle of $(90° - \gamma)$ from force T, to cut the circle at G. Join GA. The magnitude of forces N and F are now shown, as also the coefficient of friction at the chip–tool interface (F/N). Angle BAG is the angle of friction τ.

$$\tan \tau = \frac{F}{N}$$

Friction at the chip–tool interface appears to be of a different order of magnitude from that of normal sliding friction. For this reason the symbols μ and ϕ, as used for sliding friction, have been avoided.

The following expressions, derived from the geometry of Figs 5.13 and 6.9, enable the values from Merchants's analysis to be calculated.

Let $r_c = t_1/t_2$, generally called the chip thickness ratio.

Then $\tan \theta = \dfrac{r_c \cos \gamma}{1 - r_c \sin \gamma}$

~~Compressive~~ *Shear* force on the shear plane;

$$F_s = T \cos \theta - F_f \sin \theta.$$

~~Shear~~ *compressive* force on the shear plane;

$$F_c = F_f \cos \theta + T \sin \theta.$$

Friction force at the chip-tool interface;

$$F = F_f \cos \gamma + T \sin \gamma.$$

Normal force on the chip–tool interface;

$$N = T \cos \gamma - F_f \sin \gamma.$$

The coefficient of friction at the interface;

$$\tan \tau = (F_f + T \tan \gamma)/(T - F_f \tan \gamma).$$

Example 6.4
The following values relate to a cutting test under orthogonal cutting conditions and for a chip type as under (b) on p. 184.

$$T = 1500 \text{ N}, \quad F_f = 1000 \text{ N}, \quad \gamma = 10°, \quad t_1/t_2 = 0.37$$

Determine, using Merchant's theory, the cutting forces F_c, F_s, N and F, and also the coefficient of friction at the chip-tool interface.

Solution
Find the shear plane angle θ. Draw the Merchant Circle diagram as explained on p. 199. The following values found by this method are subject to normal graphical errors:

$$\theta = 21\tfrac{1}{2}°, F_c = 1504 \text{ N}, F_s = 1024 \text{ N}, F = 1260 \text{ N}, N = 1313 \text{ N}$$

Coefficient of friction at the chip–tool interface $= \dfrac{1260}{1313} = 0.96.$

The very high value of the coefficient of friction is typical of the results obtained using Merchant's analysis. Such results suggest that the normal conditions of sliding friction do not apply at the chip-tool interface. The fact that pressure welding may occur between the chip and the tool rake-face, as in built-up-edge conditions, gives further confirmation of this.

The theory does not give a completely satisfactory picture of metal cutting, and discussion of some of its weaknesses can be found in later research papers. The theory is, however, a useful step forward in the attempt to present an adequate picture of the chip-forming process, and it has been the stepping-stone to much of the subsequent research work in this field.

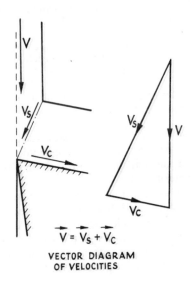

$$\vec{V} = \vec{V}_S + \vec{V}_C$$

VECTOR DIAGRAM
OF VELOCITIES

Fig. 6.10

6.6 Merchant's Analysis, Work Done in Cutting

This can best be illustrated by a worked example.

Example 6.5
When machining at 165 m/min, $T = 1080$ N, $F_f = 1000$ N, $\gamma = 10°$, the shear plane angle was found to be $19°$. Determine the velocity of shearing along the shear plane and the velocity of sliding at the chip–tool interface, and find the work done per min in shearing the metal and against friction. Show that the work input is equal to the sum of the work done in shearing and against friction.

Solution
First draw the vector diagram of velocities as shown in Fig 6.10.

The vector equation is:

Vel. of workpiece relative to the tool (V)

> = Vel. of workpiece relative to the chip (V_s)
> + Vel. of the chip relative to the tool (V_c)

From the vector diagram:

$$V_s = 164 \cdot 5 \text{m/min}, \ V_c = 55 \text{ m/min}$$

By drawing the Merchant circle diagram:

$$F_s = 690 \text{ N}, \ F = 1180 \text{ N}$$

Hence:

(i) Work done per min in shearing metal = $690 \times 164 \cdot 5 = 113\,500$ J

(ii) Work done per min against friction $= 1180 \times 55 \ \ = \ 64\,900$ J

Work input per min = $1080 \times 165 = 178\,200$ J $\quad$ Sum of (i) and (ii) $\quad \underline{178\,400 \text{ J}}$

It can be seen that the work input is equal to the sum of the work done in shearing the metal and the work done against friction, within the limits of accuracy to be expected from graphical methods.

It is left to the reader to decide whether the above example provides any verification of Merchant's theory.

Merchant's Constant (C). It seems reasonable to suppose that the angle at which the metal shears when forming a continuous-type chip is related in some manner to the cutting conditions and to the mechanical properties of the material cut.

By making a few assumptions about the relationships involved, Merchant deduced mathematically that the shear plane angle was dependent upon the rake angle, upon the angle of friction at the chip–tool interface and upon an angle (C) which is a constant for the material cut. Constant C represents in some manner the mechanical properties of the material at its point of failure in plastic shear. The relationship given by Merchant is:

$$2\theta + \tau - \gamma = C \tag{6.3}$$

Experimental results show that C is not strictly constant, and for additional reasons more recent researches tend to cast doubt on the validity of Eqn (6.3). Unfortunately there is no space here for a discussion of the assumptions made in deriving the equation. As, however, C is fairly constant for particular materials over the normal range of cutting conditions which arise in practice, Eqn (6.3) has a certain utility. This is illustrated by Exercises 6 numbers 9 and 10.

EXERCISES 6

1. State the approximate pressure in N/mm^2 of chip cross-sectional area likely to be exerted on a single-point H.S.S. tool when turning: (i) mild steel; (ii) brass.

Use the figures stated to determine the power at the motor necessary to turn these materials under the following conditions:

(a) Mild steel; $V = 24$ m/min, depth of cut = 6 mm, feed = 0·25 mm/rev.
(b) Brass; $V = 73$ m/min, depth of cut = 3 mm, feed = 0·36 mm/rev.
The overall machine efficiency may be taken as 70% in each case.

2. Steel is being cut on a centre lathe under the following conditions: $V = 30$m/min, $\gamma = 15°$, depth of cut = 3·8 mm, feed = 0·25 mm/rev. The cutting forces acting are:

Vertical (cutting) load, 1960 N;
Axial (feed) load, 935 N;
Radial load, 670 N.

(a) Find the magnitude of the resultant cutting force, the power consumed in cutting and the K factor $\left(\dfrac{w}{\text{power}}\right)$.

(b) Give the direction and approximate magnitude of the changes which would occur in the values obtained under (a):

(i) if the cutting speed were increased to 46 m/min;
(ii) if the rake angle were increased to 25°.

3. The following data relates to the rough turning of an alloy steel at a constant feed of 0.4 mm/rev, constant tool life 60 min.

Cutting speed (V_{60})	31	26	23	22	21	20·5	20
Depth of cut (d)	1·6	3·2	6·4	9·5	12·7	16	19
Power at spindle (kW)	0·67	1·1	2·0	2·9	3·9	4·8	5·7

Use the values to obtain graphs which show the variation in metal-removal rate and in specific cutting pressure with respect to the depth of cut.

4. For certain cutting conditions the cutting force is related to the depth of cut and feed by the empirical equation:

$$T = 2000\, d^{0.82} f^{0.68}$$

A lathe having 4 kW available at the spindle is used under these conditions to turn a 200 mm dia bar of metal, depth of cut 7·6 mm, feed 0·5 mm/rev.
Estimate the maximum spindle speed which may then be used.

5. (a) Explain, using diagrams, the general design of a dynamometer for measuring forces on a tool during the cutting process.

(b) In a test using such a dynamometer the following data were obtained: depth of cut = 7·5 mm, cutting speed = 30 m/min, feed rate = 0·12 mm/rev, tangential load on tool = 3·5 kN

Determine the efficiency of the machine tool if the input to the driving motor was 3 kW and its efficiency 85%. Find the specific cutting pressure and the rate of metal removal.

6. The given data relates to turning tests carried out on a medium nickel–chrome steel in a heat treated condition, 285 HB, U.T.S. = 980 MW/m².

The cutting speed is that for a tool life of 60 min; the power is that consumed in cutting.

Depth of cut, mm (d)	1·6	3·2	6·4	12·7	25·4
Feed, mm/rev (f).	1·6	0·8	0·4	0·2	0·1
Cutting speed m/min . . .	5·5	7·3	10·7	16·2	25
Power (kW)	0·67	0·75	1·12	2·09	3.88

Use this information to plot graphs which show the influence of the chip proportions, (ratio d/f) upon the following:

(a) the metal removal rate:
(b) the power consumed per unit volume of metal removed per second.

(The ratio d/f should be plotted to a logarithmic scale.)

Of what significance are the facts which may be deduced from these graphs?

7. During a metal-cutting test under orthogonal conditions a lathe knife tool, rake angle 20°, was used to machine the end of a steel tube of wall thickness 3·2 mm, at a feed of 0·38 mm/rev. The following data were obtained from the test:

Vertical (cutting) load, 2340 N;
Axial (thrust) load, 1000 N;
Average chip thickness, 0·9 mm.

Determine by graphical means, or by calculation:

(a) the coefficient of friction at the chip–tool interface;
(b) the angle of inclination of the shear plane;
(c) the shear stress on the shear plane.

8. The following data were obtained from a cutting test: $\gamma = 20°$, $\phi = 90°$, depth of cut 6·4 mm, feed 0.25 mm/rev, chip length before cutting 29·4 mm, chip length after cutting 12·9 mm. The cutting forces were: axial force 427 N, vertical force 1050 N.

Use Merchant's analysis to calculate:

(i) the direction and magnitude of the resultant force;
(ii) the shear plane angle;
(iii) the frictional force;
(iv) the friction angle.

9. (a) In orthogonal planing how can the shear plane angle and coefficient of friction along the rake face of the tool be found?

(b) How would the shear plane angle be affected if the coefficient of friction is decreased?

(c) If Merchant's machinability constant $C = 70$ when the rake angle $\gamma = 20°$ and the friction angle $\tau = 40°$, what will be the magnitude of the shear plane angle?

10. Determine Merchant's constant C for aluminium from the following information: $\gamma = 35°$; $T = 200$ N; $F_f = 90$ N; $t_1 = 0·125$ mm; $t_2 = 0·25$ mm; cutting speed = 30 m/min; width of cut = 2·5 mm.

What amount of work per min is done against friction at the chip–tool interface?

CHAPTER 7

Economics of Cutting—
Single-point Tools

7.1

While a study of the geometry and mechanics of metal cutting is necessary in order to achieve efficiency, metal cutting is primarily an economic activity. When roughing, the aim is to remove a particular volume of metal in minimum time or at minimum cost; when finishing, the area of finished surface produced is the criterion.

Throughout the following discussion the economics of cutting are developed in relation to the volume of metal removed, but the same principles are applicable to finishing cuts, where the area of surface produced is the decisive feature. The economics can be based either upon time or cost; the former is important when maximum output from the available plant is required, the latter is the more common condition where production costs must be kept as low as possible.

7.2 Variables Affecting Metal-removal Rate

Since the metal removal rate $w = df \times 10^3 \, V \, \mathrm{mm^3/s}$, any increase in cutting speed, depth of cut or feed will give a directly proportional increase in the metal removal rate. The power available at the machine spindle is one factor limiting the metal removal rate, as shown in **6.1**.

If a further condition is imposed and the tool is required to cut effectively for a specified tool life, there is a limit placed upon the cutting speed for each particular combination of depth of cut and feed employed. The following data, derived from cutting tests, illustrates these relationships.

Table 7.1 shows that an increase in feed causes a greater fall of V_{60} than a similar increase in depth of cut.

Tool life is not a very precise concept since a complete breakdown of the edge is not a reasonable or practical thing to allow. "Failure" can be more realistically identified using one of the following parameters;

    (i) an increase in cutting force of some defined amount,
    (ii) development of the wear-land on the clearance face to a defined magnitude.

TABLE 7.1

Rough Turning Hot-rolled Medium-carbon Steel

Tool HSS.; cut dry; tool life 60 min

(V_{60} is the cutting speed for a 60 min tool life)

Depth of cut, mm	Feed, mm per rev			
	0·2	0·4	0·8	1·6
	V_{60}	V_{60}	V_{60}	V_{60}
3·2	58	37	25	17
6·4	48	32	21	14
9·6	45	30	19	12.5
12·8	43	28	18	12

Either method may be used to standardise tool life tests. Under normal production conditions specifying tool changes in terms of the number of parts machined is a practical way of controlling the amount of tool wear.

For any given set of cutting conditions there is a relationship between cutting speed and tool life which is a vital one for the economics of the process. This relationship may be represented by the empirical law $VM^n = C$, where C and n are constants. It must be understood, however, that the law is true only if other possible variables, depth of cut, feed, rake angle, plan approach angle, etc., are kept constant. Any change in these will have a marked effect upon the value of C. The law, introduced by F. W. Taylor as a result of his experimental work on the cutting of metals, is illustrated graphically in Fig 7.1.

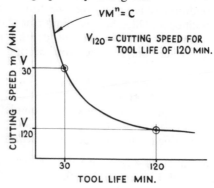

Fig. 7.1

The exponent n depends mainly upon the cutting-tool material and has values, when rough turning, of approximately $\frac{1}{8}$ for HSS tools and $\frac{1}{5}$ for TC tools. The constant C is related both to the tool material and to the material cut; it is also affected by other variables of the cutting process, as indicated above, i.e. proportions of the cut, tool geometry and the employment of cutting fluids. Since $VM^n = C$, the constant C has the value of V for a tool life of $M = 1$ min.

Values of n and C can be found only from cutting tests. The most comprehensive cutting-test data available are those published in the American Society of Mechanical Engineers handbook (1952).

Example 7.1 ✓
A tool-life cutting test of HSS tool material, used to cut a special die steel of 363 HB, gave the following values:

Cutting speed, V m/min	49·74	49·23	48·67	45·76	42·58
Tool life, M min	2·94	3·90	4·77	9·87	28·27

Use the values to obtain the constants of the tool life equation, $VM^n = C$.

Solution
To obtain satisfactory results from the test data a straight-line graph should be drawn. This can be obtained by plotting the equation,

$$\log V + n \log M = \log C$$
$$\log V = -n \log M + \log C$$

$\log V$	1·6967	1·6924	1·6873	1·6605	1·6292
$\log M$	0·4683	0·5911	0·6785	0·9943	1·4513

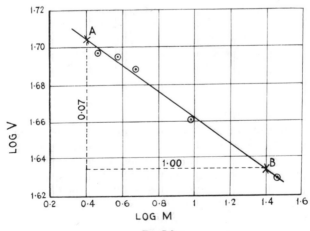

Fig. 7.2

Consider points marked A and B on the graph:

(i) the slope $-n$ $= -0.07,$
(ii) the value of $\log C$ $= 1.704 + 0.07\,(0.4)$
                         $= 1.732$

hence $C = 54$

Tool life equation is, $VM^{0.07} = 54$

Example 7.2

When turning 19 mm dia bar on an automatic lathe employing TC tools the value of n is $\frac{1}{5}$, and the value of V_{60} is 104 m/min.

At what speed should the spindle run to give a tool life of 6 hours? If a length of 50 mm per component is machined and the feed used is 0.16 mm/rev, what is the cutting time per piece and how many pieces can be produced between tool changes?

Solution

$$V \times 360^{1/5} = 104 \times 60^{1/5}$$

$$V = 104 \left[\frac{60}{360} \right]^{0.2}$$

$$= 73 \text{ m/min}$$

$$\text{Spindle Speed} = \frac{10^3 \times 73}{\pi \times 19} = \underline{1220 \text{ rev/min}}$$

$$\text{Cutting time per piece} = \frac{50 \times 60}{1220 \times 0.15} = \underline{16.5 \text{ s}}$$

$$\text{Number of components per tool change} = \frac{6 \times 60 \times 60}{16.5} = \underline{1300}$$

Example 7.3

Find the percentage change in cutting speed required to give an 80% reduction in tool life (i.e. reduce tool life to $\frac{1}{5}$ of its former value) when the value of $n = 0.12$.

Solution

$$V_1 M_1^{0.12} = V_2 M_2^{0.12}$$

$$\frac{V_2}{V_1} = \left[\frac{M_1}{M_2} \right]^{0.12}$$

$$\frac{V_2}{V_1} = \left[\frac{1}{1/5} \right]^{0.12} = 5^{0.12}$$

$$\frac{V_2}{V_1} = 1.214$$

Increase in cutting speed = 21.4%.

The solution of Example 7.3 draws attention to an important practical point respecting the spindle-speed ratios of machine tools. Because comparatively small changes in cutting speed give rise to large changes in tool life the spindle speeds of machine tools should rise in a geometrical progression of a suitable ratio (see p. 70). It can be seen from the example that, for a given diameter of work, an increase of spindle speed of approximately 21% causes a reduction of tool life of 80%. For many machine tools a spindle-speed ratio of the order of $\sqrt[10]{10}$ is used; this gives log (ratio) = 0·1, or a ratio of 1·259. The increase in spindle speed at each step is then approximately 26%.

7.3 Economic Cutting Speed ✓

An increase of cutting speed has two main effects upon the economics of cutting; the metal removal rate is increased, the tool life is decreased. An increase in the metal removal rate will lower the direct cost of metal removal; a reduction in the tool life will increase the costs of servicing and replacing worn-out tools. The two separate effects, and their combined influence upon the total cost of machining, are best illustrated graphically as shown in Fig 7.3. The following deductions can be made from the graphs:

(a) As V increases, the time required to remove the metal (and hence the cost of its removal) will fall. The cost of cutting $\propto 1/V$.

(b) As V increases, the tool life M falls. The costs of tooling $\propto 1/M$, but by Taylor's equation $1/M = [V/C]^{1/n}$ and since C is a constant, the costs of tooling $\propto V^{1/n}$.

(c) The inclusive costs of machining will be the sum of the separate costs, and by addition of the separate cost values for each value of V shown, a third graph showing the change of the inclusive cost with

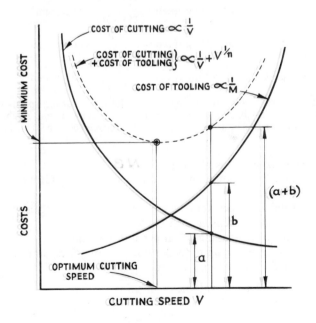

Fig. 7.3 Economic cutting speed

respect to changes in cutting speed is obtained. This graph has a minimum value for inclusive cost, and the ideal (or optimum) cutting speed is the value of V at the minimum point.

Since tooling costs can be seen to depend upon the value of n, it would appear that this exponent is important in relation to the economics of metal cutting.

Example 7.4 ✓

Under certain machining conditions the tool life equation is $VM^{0.2} = 180$. The time taken to change a tool is 10 min. Show that operating at a cutting speed of 90 m/min gives higher output than operating at either 120 m/min or 60 m/min, other cutting conditions remaining constant.

Solution

One way of demonstrating the superiority of a cutting speed of 90 m/min is to determine the **average** cutting speed where the time spent in tool changing (during which no cutting occurs) is taken into account. The output will be highest where the average cutting speed is highest because the remainder of the cutting conditions are constant.

$$\text{Tool life } M = \left[\frac{180}{V}\right]^5$$

When

$$V = 60, \quad M = 243 \text{ min}$$
$$V = 90, \quad M = 32 \text{ min}$$
$$V = 120, M = 8 \text{ min}$$

When $V = 60$, average cutting speed $= \dfrac{243 \times 60}{243 + 10} = 58$ m/min

$\quad V = 90$, average cutting speed $= \dfrac{32 \times 90}{32 + 10} = 69$ m/min

$\quad V = 120$, average cutting speed $= \dfrac{8 \times 120}{8 + 10} = 53$ m/min

On a time basis 90 m/min is the best of the three cutting speeds quoted. However, on a cost basis the servicing of the tool every 32 min might be too expensive, and on this basis a speed somewhere between 60 and 90 m/min might be more profitable.

Economic Relationships of Cutting   N B

Let H = hourly cost of running the machine, i.e. operators wage and overheads.

$\quad J$ = total cost per tool change; i.e. tool grinding, setting and eventual replacement costs.

$\quad P_m$ = cost of machining metal per unit volume.

$\quad P_t$ = cost of servicing tools per unit volume of metal cut.

$\quad P$ = total costs per unit volume of metal cut, i.e. $P_m + P_t$.

Time to machine a unit volume of metal is

$$\frac{1}{w} = \frac{1}{df \times 10^3 \, V} = \frac{k}{V},$$

where k is a constant. (Since we are only concerned with the influence of V upon the economics of cutting, d and f are regarded as constants.)
Cost of machining per unit volume of metal cut

$$P_m = \frac{Hk}{60\,V} \tag{1}$$

The number of tool changes in k/V min $= k/MV$, where M is the tool life in min, but from Taylor's equation $M = [C/V]^{1/n}$

Cost of tool servicing per unit volume of metal cut

$$P_t = \frac{Jk}{V}\left[\frac{V}{C}\right]^{1/n} = \frac{JkV^{(1-n)/n}}{C^{1/n}} \tag{2}$$

By addition of (1) and (2)

$$P = \frac{Hk}{60\,V} + \frac{JkV^{(1-n)/n}}{C^{1/n}}$$

Differentiating and equating to zero:

$$\frac{dP}{dV} = \frac{Hk}{60\,V^2} + \frac{1-n}{n}\frac{Jk}{C^{1/n}}V^{(1-2n)/n} = 0$$

$$\frac{H}{60V^2} = \frac{1-n}{n}\frac{J}{C^{1/n}}V^{(1-2n)/n} \text{ since } k \neq 0$$

$$\frac{H}{60} = \frac{1-n}{n}\frac{J}{C^{1/n}}V^{(1-2n)/n}V^2$$

$$= \frac{1-n}{n}J\left[\frac{V}{C}\right]^{1/n}, \text{ but } \left[\frac{V}{C}\right]^{1/n} = \frac{1}{M}$$

Hence,

$$\boxed{\frac{H}{60}\frac{M}{J} = \frac{1-n}{n}} \tag{7.1}$$

represents the economic cutting conditions.

Since $(H/60) \times M$ is the cost of operating the machine between tool changes (tool life of M min), and J is the total cost per tool change, the equation can be written:

$$\frac{\text{Cost of operating between tool changes}}{\text{Total cost of a tool change}} = \frac{1-n}{n} \tag{7.2}$$

The expression $(1-n)/n$ shows the significance of the exponent n of Taylor's equation in relation to the economics of cutting. The expression is sometimes called the **costs ratio** for economic cutting.

The relationship proved above has been obtained on the assumption that depth of cut (d) and feed (f) are constants. Since, however, the ratio of the costs depends only upon the value of n, and n is not significantly changed by normal variations of d and f, the costs-ratio relationship is valid regardless of the particular values of d and f being used.

As is evident from the equation for economic conditions, the tool life M is a most significant factor because the substitution, $1/M = [V/C]^{1/n}$, has been used to eliminate the constant C of Taylor's equation. The variables d and f have a marked influence upon the value of C, and it should be clear that for the economic value of the tool life, V will depend upon the particular values of d and f being used. Reference to Table 7.1 will confirm this. To summarise; the economic value of M (*economic tool life*) depends only upon the particular value of n relating to the cutting process and upon the operating and tooling costs involved. The appropriate cutting speed required to give this economic tool life depends upon the material of the tool and workpiece, upon the tool geometry and also upon the depth of cut and feed employed.

Example 7.5
For certain machining conditions the total cost of operating the machine is £6 per hour and the total cost of a tool change is £3·60. If, for the depth of cut and feed employed, $V_{60} = 36$ m/min and $n = 0\cdot14$, find the economic cutting speed.

Solution

$$\frac{6}{60} \cdot M \times \frac{1}{3\cdot6} = \frac{0\cdot86}{0\cdot14} \text{ from Eqn (7.1)}$$

$$M = 221 \text{ min (economic tool life)}$$

Since
$$V_{60} = 36 \text{ m/min for the cut employed,}$$
$$V_{221} \times 221^{0\cdot14} = 36 \times 60^{0\cdot14}$$
$$V_{221} = 36\left[\frac{60}{221}\right]^{0\cdot14} = \underline{30 \text{ m/min}}$$

When maximum output rather than minimum cost is required, the economic relationships have the form

$$\frac{\text{Operating time between tool changes } (M)}{\text{Time to change tool}} = \frac{1-n}{n} \qquad (7.3)$$

This relationship can be proved from first principles in the manner of Eqn (7.2).

Attention should be given to the significance of n in both Eqn (7.2) and Eqn (7.3). For HSS tools n is approximately $\frac{1}{8}$ and the cost (or time) ratio for economic conditions is 7; for TC tools n is approximately $\frac{1}{5}$ and the ratio is 4. These easily remembered figures provide some guidance for judging machining practice in workshops.

When rough turning with HSS tools an operator can regrind and reset a tool in under 3 min. The economic tool life is then around 20 min. Very few operators run their machines at cutting speeds high enough to achieve this condition. (In some machine shops the rate at which they would consume cutting tools might be questioned if they did so!)

When operating with TC tools special tool-grinding service is essential. The high cost of the tools and the high cost of servicing them on diamond-grit wheels make the inclusive cost of servicing a tool about $\frac{1}{3}$ of the cost of operating the machine for one hour. Under such conditions a tool life of 80 min is economic.

The use of cemented carbide in the form of "throw-away" tips is increasing. A square tip, with suitable clamping to the tool shank, may be indexed round the four edges of both faces as wear occurs. While the limited range of plan shape is a restriction, this arrangement greatly reduces tool servicing costs, leading to an economic tool life at relatively higher metal removal rate than for more conventional tools.

Servicing costs for the tools rise as tooling becomes more complex, and the economic cutting conditions will then occur at reduced cutting speeds. Given reasonably accurate cost figures, it is easy to check if these are in the ratio of $(1-n)/n$, as is required for economic cutting conditions.

7.4 Cutting-tool Materials

The economics of cutting are considerably influenced by the cutting tool material employed. The following materials are used.

(a) *Carbon Tool Steel.* Plain carbon steel of high quality (crucible cast generally), containing about 1 % carbon, has limited use. Special "non-shrink" types, for which the dimensional changes occurring in heat treatment are very small, have alloying additions of manganese (approx 1·5 %) and other elements, such as chromium, vanadium and tungsten, in smaller amounts. They are oil hardening and are useful for making form tools where the tool profile is not ground after heat treatment.

(b) *High-speed Steel.* Tungsten is generally the major alloying element, as in the 18–4–1 type; 18 % tungsten, 4 % chromium, 1 % vanadium. There are, however, HSS alloys in which a lower tungsten content is used, supplemented by larger additions of other alloying elements, generally molybdenum, cobalt and chromium.

(c) *Special (or Super) grade HSS.* Tungsten may be raised to 20 % or more, or other alloying additions made to improve the cutting properties. Better hot-hardness and wear-resistance properties are then obtained.

(d) *Cast Non-ferrous Alloys.* These are generally cobalt based, with alloying additions of chromium, tungsten and carbon; a typical analysis is 45 % cobalt, 35 % chromium, 18 % tungsten and 2 % carbon. They do not contain iron except as an impurity. The metal cannot be forged or readily cut to shape when cold; it must be cast to the required shape and then dressed by grinding.

(e) *Cemented (Sintered) Carbides.* The carbides of tungsten, titanium, tantalum and other rare metals are first prepared as very fine powders. They are then mixed with a "binder" in powder form, usually cobalt. The powder is compressed, which makes it into a compact form, and then sintered. Sintering is a high-temperature treatment (approx 1500°C) which causes the cobalt to fuse to the carbides, thus binding them together in a dense hard mass. The material cannot be worked except by grinding, preferably by means of diamond-grit wheels, on account of its extreme hardness. The powder must be pressed into the required form or the required tool shape cut from a billet of compressed powder, preparatory to the sintering process. An allowance (approx 20%) must be made for shrinkage during the sintering process. Cemented carbide is generally used in the form of a tool tip.

(f) *Ceramics.* Hard substances, such as aluminium oxide and silicon nitride can be prepared as tool tips for use with a suitable holder. The hardness exceeds that of cemented carbides, but the material is more brittle. An attraction of ceramic is lower cost and better wear resistance compared with cemented carbide; the tips cannot be serviced, but are supplied in "throw away" form.

When machining metals with ceramic tools exceptionally high cutting speeds may be used and very good finishes can be achieved. Due to their brittle nature difficulties arise when the metal to be cut is exceptionally tough, or when chatter or interrupted cuts are encountered, and as yet cemented carbide is superior in withstanding such conditions. Ceramics, due to their very high resistance to abrasive wear, may be attractive for machining non-metallic materials such as vulcanised rubber or compositions which contain gritty particles. Research may further improve these cutting materials.

(g) *Diamond.* Borts (crystalline diamonds) are used, as they may be split along distinct cleavage planes approximately to the required shapes before being finished by lapping with diamond powder. Diamonds are among the hardest known substances; incompressible, good heat conductors and of a low coefficient of friction. Due to the extremely keen edge which can be dressed on them, they are capable of producing very good surface finishes; they also can hold very close dimensional tolerances because of the absence of tool wear. Diamond boring of aluminium alloys or bronze will produce work superior in quality to that produced by internal grinding.

The chief properties which determine the usefulness of cutting materials are:

    (i) hardness, including the property of hot-hardness;
    (ii) mechanical strength, particularly shear strength;
    (iii) resistance to wear by abrasion;
    (iv) ease of "working" and of sharpening during service.

Fig 7.4 shows the relative hot-hardness values of the principal tool metals and clearly indicates the superiority of cemented carbide at both high and low cutting temperatures. It also shows the advantage of the

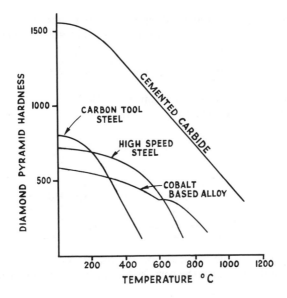

Fig. 7.4 Hot-hardness properties of cutting tool materials

cast non-ferrous alloy over HSS when high cutting temperatures are reached. The greater resistance of the cast alloy to abrasive wear than is possessed by HSS, and the greater resistance to shock loads than is possessed by cemented carbides, underlie the utility of this material. It can be sharpened on normal grinding wheels, which is a much cheaper method of sharpening than the use of diamond-grit wheels as required for cemented carbide. Further development of cast non-ferrous alloys can be expected, especially for the machining of the titanium and Nimonic alloys used in gas-turbine manufacture.

Ceramic material is cheaper to produce than cemented carbide and has superior hardness. It cannot be ground in the workshop and is generally used as a "throw-away tip". It is rather unreliable when used under severe cutting conditions due to its extreme brittleness, and this appears to be a limiting factor in its application.

HSS can be used in bar form, clamped in a tool holder, or may be butt-welded to a medium-carbon steel shank to form a "solid" tool. Cast non-ferrous alloy and cemented carbide is generally used as a "tip" which is brazed or "copper welded" to a steel shank.

Ceramic tips cannot be brazed and, like diamond tools, are frequently used mechanically clamped in a holder. Epoxy-resin adhesives are sometimes used as a means of securing ceramic tips to steel shanks.

The influence of tool material upon the economics of cutting can be measured in terms of tool life. The following values are derived from data given by J. Cherry (1960).

Material Cut, SAE 1050 (approx 0·5 % plain carbon) 201 HB, hot rolled.
Dimensions of cut, $d = 2·5$ mm, $f = 0·25$ mm/rev.
Cutting fluid, soluble oil of 1/15 ratio.

Material	Tool-life equation
HSS 18–4–1 type	$VM^{0·125} = 52$
HSS 18–4–1 5% cobalt	$VM^{0·135} = 57$
Cast non-ferrous alloy	$VM^{0·15} = 67$
Cemented (sintered) carbide	$VM^{0·25} = 181$

Assuming the value given on p. 212 for an 18–4–1 HSS tool, i.e. economic tool life 20 min, the permissible cutting speed for cutting steel, SAE 1050, is given by:

$$V_{20} = \frac{52}{20^{0·125}} = 36 \text{ m/min}$$

For a cemented-carbide tool, economic tool life 80 min, the permissible cutting speed for cutting steel, SAE 1050, is given by:

$$V_{80} = \frac{181}{80^{0·25}} = 60 \text{ m/min}$$

It can be seen that for optimum cutting conditions the metal removal rate is nearly twice as high for the cemented carbide as for the 18–4–1 HSS tool.

There are sound economic reasons to justify the use of each of the cutting-tool materials listed on p. 213 for particular workshop uses.

A toolroom turner will grind 18–4–1 HSS tools to do a variety of work for which standard-shape tipped tools of cemented carbide would be unsuitable. A low-cost easily ground material is economically the correct choice for such conditions.

Certain cutters, e.g. form-relieved hobs, cannot be made economically in cast alloy or by powder metallurgy methods. Tooth inserts would be prohibitive in cost and likely to fail in service unless exceptional precautions were taken. The use of a "super" grade of HSS is the best choice; the cutter can then be manufactured at reasonable cost and will have the best cutting performance of the "practical" materials available.

For long runs on automatic machines carbide tools are the obvious choice; expensive tool changes will be reduced to a minimum and the machine can be run at high cutting speeds to obtain a high output.

The machining of iron castings presents particular problems of tooling; local hard spots may fracture carbide tools, or may rapidly abrade HSS tools if these are used. Cast non-ferrous alloy withstands these conditions particularly well, and reasonably high metal removal rates can be maintained.

7.5 Cutting Fluids

These have two main functions:

(i) to remove heat generated in cutting and so limit the rise of temperature at the tool cutting edge;

(ii) to lubricate the area of contact between the tool clearance face and the workpiece, and between the tool rake face and the chip, thus reducing friction, abrasive wear and built-up edge, and so increasing the tool life and the quality of the surface finish.

An important subsidiary function of a cutting fluid is to wash away swarf. A basic requirement is that the fluid used must not cause corrosion of the machine tool or workpiece.

Example 7.6

The power required to cut a material under certain conditions is $1.97 \text{ W/mm}^3/\text{s}$. A cut 6·4 mm deep × 0·25 mm/rev feed is taken at a cutting speed of 25 m/min and the work is cooled by a flow of 2·3 litres per min of coolant, specific heat capacity 3·56 kJ/kg°C, which conducts away approximately 90% of the heat produced. The mass of 1 litre of coolant is 0·92 kg. Determine the rise in the temperature of the coolant due to this cut.

Solution

$$\text{Vol of metal removed per second} = \frac{0.25 \times 6.4 \times 25 \times 10^3}{60}$$

$$= \frac{40}{60} \times 10^3 \text{ mm}^3$$

$$\text{Power consumed in cutting} = \frac{40}{60} \times 1.97 = 1.3 \text{ kW}$$

Heat produced per min $= 1.3 \times 60 \text{ kW}$

Weight of coolant supplied per min $= 2.3 \times 0.92 = 2.12 \text{ kg}$

$$\text{Temperature rise} = \frac{1.3 \times 60 \times 0.9}{3.56 \times 2.12} = \underline{9.3 \text{ degC}}$$

The example gives some concept of the magnitudes involved when applying coolants. The temperature rise is dependent upon the flow of cutting fluid, and if straight cutting oils are used the flow must be large enough to keep the oil temperature below the point at which fumes are produced.

Heat absorbed by a cutting fluid must be subsequently radiated to the shop atmosphere, or a gradual rise of temperature will occur. A large coolant tank provides a large radiating area, and the larger the volume of coolant stored, the greater the amount of heat that can be absorbed for a limited temperature rise. In any process where high dimensional accuracy is important cutting-fluid temperature must be confined to reasonable limits; this is particularly true for cylindrical grinding of large diameters.

It can be seen from Fig 7.4 that control of the cutting-tool temperature is likely to limit the rate of tool wear. Example 6.5 draws attention to particular aspects of the mechanics of chip forming showing that work is done:

(i) by plastic shear on the shear plane;
(ii) by friction at the chip–tool interface.

Apart from the direct cooling effect of a cutting fluid, there is the possibility of lubrication between the tool and chip reducing the work done against friction. Any change in the coefficient of friction will influence the cutting ratio t_1/t_2, thus changing the length of the shear plane and hence the amount of work to be done in deforming the metal. Merchant (1950) has shown that a 10% reduction in friction would have the following effects.

The average temperature of the chip cut would be lower by about 81 deg F (27 deg C).

Tests made by Ernst and Merchant (1950) on a variety of cutting fluids show that these generally increase the cutting ratio t_1/t_2, but that the effect, within the normal cutting-speed range, falls as the cutting speed is increased. Fig 7.5 shows the relationships between cutting ratio, cutting speed and various cutting fluids. These results suggest that the depth of penetration of cutting fluid into the area of contact, where friction occurs, falls as the cutting speed increases.

Tests reported in the ASME *Manual on Cutting of Metals* (1952) give the following (converted) values for cutting SAE 3140 steel using 18–4–1 HSS tools cutting at 31 m/min, cutting fluid supplied at 22 litres/min, depth of cut 2·5 mm, feed 3·0 mm.

TABLE 7.2

Material cut, alloy steel; shear strength = 690 N/mm² (100 000 lbf/in²) machining constant 75°; effective rake 15°.

Condition	Coefficient of friction	Heat from friction *(kJ/kg of metal removed)	Heat from deformation *(kJ/kg of metal removed)
Dry	1·0	102·3	222·7
Cutting fluid	0·9	93·9	210·4
% decrease	10	19·1	12·8

* 1 kJ/kg = 0·428 Btu/lb

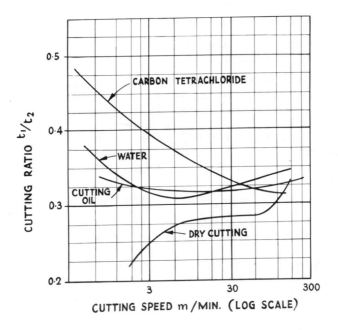

Fig. 7.5 Influence of cutting fluids on chip thickness ratio t_1/t_2
(Ernst and Merchant)

TABLE 7.3

Type of cutting fluid	Tool life (min)	Power (kW)
Dry	12	1·36
Sulphurised oil	27	1·3
Sulphurised and chlorinated oil	33	1.35

These values show clearly the improvement in tool life resulting from the use of a cutting fluid but do not confirm the prediction of Merchant that there is a reduction in the actual work done in cutting. However, the heavy feed of 3 mm/rev used in the tests is of a different order of magnitude from the feeds employed by Merchant, which were light in order to produce a continuous chip without built-up edge.

Types of Cutting Fluid. Cutting fluids are mainly required to carry away heat (e.g. rough turning) and swarf (e.g. grinding) are generally based on water. The addition of oils and emulsifying agents serves primarily to inhibit rusting, although when the oil concentration is raised some lubricating effects are achieved (e.g. milling, where each cutting edge is completely wetted with coolant before the cutting of each chip).

Typical concentrations are:

Grinding (oil/water), approx $\frac{1}{40}$ or $\frac{1}{50}$.
Turning and Milling, approx $\frac{1}{20}$.

Mixing must be done strictly to the makers' instructions. Hard water can be softened before mixing with the oil by the additon of 20 g of common soda to 10 litres of water. The main causes of oil separation after mixing are incorrect mixing procedure and excessive water hardness (in excess of 9° Clark's scale). Translucent soluble oils are sometimes preferred. These do not leave gummy deposits, and the engagement between the tool and the work may be observed while operating.

Straight cutting oils are blended from two basic types of oil:

(i) mineral oils, e.g. paraffin and other petroleum oils;
(ii) fatty oils, generally organic oils of animal or vegetable origin.

The fatty oils have very good lubricating properties and promote good finishes, especially on high-tensile steels (lard oil is an example). They are less stable than mineral oils and may decompose, becoming unpleasant if used in the natural state for a long time.

Mineral oils are cheaper and more stable than fatty oils, and for these reasons are generally blended with them.

Most cutting oils are "sulphurised". Chemically combined sulphur is introduced into the oil. This helps to prevent pressure welding of the chip to the tool (built-up edge) by forming between them a film possessing anti-weld properties. Sulphurised oils may cause dark staining of copper-rich alloys, and special sulphur-free grades are available for use on these materials. Chlorine-containing additives are employed for the same purpose, and some cutting oils contain both sulphur and chlorine compounds.

Despite their much higher cost, straight cutting oils have wide application for two principal reasons:

(a) They are employed on automatic machines, especially multi-spindle bar lathes, because water-base coolant (which is quite satisfactory for most turning operations) is likely to find its way into the headstock, contaminate the lubricating oil and so cause serious deterioration of the mechanism.

(b) They promote a superior surface finish when used for such process as gear cutting, honing, threading and broaching. Paraffin is sometimes used on aluminium alloys in preference to soluble oil because of its superior "wetting" property.

For operations such as tapping and reaming, greases which melt at the tool edge due to the heat generated in cutting may be more convenient than oils.

7.6 Other Variables Influencing the Economics of Cutting

Taylor's equation, upon which the economics of cutting primarily depend, is not independent of such variables as depth of cut, feed, rake angle and plan approach angle. Particular values of these may permit a higher metal removal rate at the optimum tool life than will other values. In its simplest form this may be noted by reference to Fig 7.6, which shows the effect of varying the rake angle.

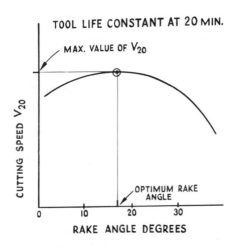

Fig. 7.6

The graph shows that, all else remaining constant, there is an optimum value for effective rake angle. The graph would not necessarily have the maximum cutting speed at the same value of γ if the feed were changed. However, the curve is fairly flat in the region of the maximum cutting speed, and the value of V_{20} is not likely to depart much from the maximum value on account of small changes in the other cutting conditions.

The general impact of other cutting variables can best be shown in sketch graphs:

(a) Fig 7.7 shows the effect of varying the depth of cut and feed upon the cutting speed, tool life constant.

(b) Fig 7.8 shows the effect of varying the depth of cut and feed upon metal removal rate, tool life constant.

Notice that in Fig 7.7 it can be seen that V_{20} falls as d or f is increased, but from Fig 7.8 it can also be seen that the metal removal rate (w) **rises**

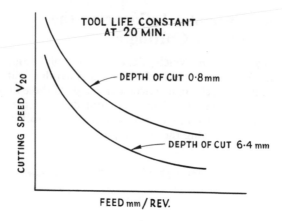

Fig. 7.7 *Influence of feed rate upon cutting speed, tool life constant*

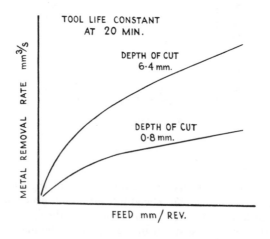

Fig. 7.8 *Influence of feed rate upon metal removal rate, tool life constant*

despite this fall in V_{20}. The use, when roughing, of full depths of cut and maximum feeds at cutting speeds which give the economic tool life for the selected conditions, is in accordance with the economics of the process.

(c) The effect of the plan shape of the tool upon cutting speed, tool life constant, is shown in Fig 7.9.

As angle ϕ falls below 90° the cut is spread over a longer cutting edge. The tool is less likely to fail if a small nose radius is used instead of a sharp point, and a small trailing angle gives good support to the cutting

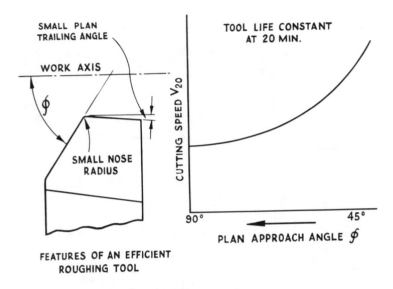

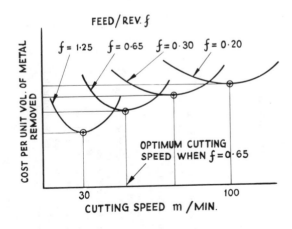

SMALL PLAN
TRAILING ANGLE

WORK AXIS

ϕ

SMALL NOSE
RADIUS

TOOL LIFE CONSTANT
AT 20 MIN.

CUTTING SPEED V_{20}

90°   45°

PLAN APPROACH ANGLE ϕ

FEATURES OF AN EFFICIENT
ROUGHING TOOL

Fig. 7.9 Influence of tool shape upon cutting speed, tool life constant

edge and increases the section through which heat can pass from the tool edge. All these features of tool plan shape tend to increase the value of V_{20}. The general impact of the two main variables of cutting, cutting speed and feed, on the economics of cutting is illustrated in Fig 7.10.

FEED/REV. f

$f = 1.25$ $f = 0.65$ $f = 0.30$ $f = 0.20$

COST PER UNIT VOL. OF METAL REMOVED

OPTIMUM CUTTING
SPEED WHEN $f = 0.65$

30   100

CUTTING SPEED m /MIN.

Fig. 7.10 Influence of feed and speed upon the economics of metal removal

TABLE 7.4
Recommended Cutting Speeds

Material to be cut	Approx tensile strength (N/mm²)	High-speed steel cutting tools (18% tungsten)				Stellite 0·40	Tungsten carbide and similar tools
		Turn, face and bore	Ream and screw	Form Rough	Form Finish	Turn, face and bore	Turn, face and bore
* Free-cutting bright mild steel	310–385	37–60	6·0–9·0	37	7·3	73–90	90–180
* Black reeled mild steel bar	340–385	28–30	4·5–6·0	28	4·5	55–60	75–150
* 0·20 Carbon steel bar	385–460	24–30	4·5–6·0	12	2·5	50–60	60–140
† 0·30 Carbon steel bar	430–540	24–30	4·5–6·0	4·5	1·8	50–60	60–140
† 0·40 Carbon steel bar	460–620	23–28	3·5–4·5	4·5	1·8	50–55	60–140
† 0·50 Carbon steel bar	700–770	21–24	3·5–4·5	3·5	1·8	43–50	60–110
† 3% Nickel steel bar	620–650	18–24	3·5–4·5	3·5	1·8	37–50	60–110
† Nickel-chrome case-hardening steel	700–770	18–24	3·5–4·5	3·5	1·8	37–50	60–110
* Mild-steel stampings	385–460	28–37	4·5–7·5	18	4·5	55–60	60–110
† High-tensile steel stampings	770–925	12–15	2·5–3·0	3·5	1·8	18–24	60–110
‡ Cast-iron castings, Brinell 150	—	18–24	3·5–4·5	15	3·0	28–37	60–75
‡ Cast-iron castings, Brinell 200	—	15–18	3·0–3·5	12	2·5	24–28	50–55
‡ Cast-iron castings, Brinell 230	—	9–15	1·8–3·0	2·5	2·0	15–23	30–35
‡ Malleable-iron castings	—	15–21	3·0–4·5	4·3	2·0	30–43	50–55
‡ Malleable-iron castings (well annealed)	—	24–34	4·5–6·0	18	3·5	50–70	60–90
* Mild-steel castings	385–460	15–25	3·0–4·5	12	4·5	23–37	50–110
‡ Brass bar	—	75–125	30–37	37	18	75–180	150–300
‡ Gun-metal castings	—	14–21	3·0–4·5	18	18	18–30	90–150
‡ Aluminium castings	—	75–125	15–24	75	15	75–180	185–300

Cutting speed for general purposes (m/min)

Metric conversion of data supplied by H. W. Ward Ltd

* Indicate that soluble oil is the most suitable coolant.
† Indicates that a straight cutting oil is the most suitable coolant.
‡ Indicates that a coolant is generally unnecessary.

7.7 Recommended Cutting Speeds

Anyone who has studied this chapter will appreciate the difficulty of compiling a table of recommended cutting speeds which refers only to two variables, cutting-tool material and material cut. Obviously the speeds will be too low for very fine finishing cuts and too high for heavy roughing cuts. Nevertheless, there must be some starting-point for setting the machining conditions of any actual piece of work, and for short-run work a choice somewhere near the optimum is good enough.

From information given on p. 222 it follows that maximum rates of metal removal at the economic tool life depend upon the values of ϕ, d and f. Working approach angles of 60° to 40° are advantageous, but as the angle is reduced the tendency for the longer cutting edge and thinner chip to set up vibration is increased, which sets a practical limit for ϕ. Depth of cut should always be as high as possible and feed as high as is consistent with the stiffness of the workpiece and tool and of the power available at the spindle. Experience with N. C. machines has shown it to be very desirable that feed rates can be adjusted during operating without changing the input data. This feature enables cutting rates to be optimised on the machine by raising the feed rate near to its practical limit.

Table 7.4 gives recommended cutting speeds for turning operations

For long runs of machining, modification of the initial values can be made as experience of cutting performance is gained. It is for this purpose that a sound knowledge of cutting principles should form part of the technical training of a production engineer. Do not stick to first choices, but learn to criticise performance, basing your analysis upon the theoretical concepts outlined in this chapter, and so learn to adjust cutting conditions until they are near the optimum.

As metal machining becomes automated there will be no operator to adjust cutting conditions where the initial choices are poor. For this reason an increased technical competence in specifying them will become necessary and only a thorough acquaintance with the subject will provide a satisfactory basis for the work. There will also be an increasing need for the publication of reliable cutting data, especially data relating to the more recently introduced work materials. This can be done only if research and testing continue on a fairly large scale and if the results are collated and published.

EXERCISES 7   N13

1. (a) What is the relationship between tool life and cutting speed?
(b) If chip thickness is increased, how would the value of C be affected?
(c) If $n = 0.2$ and $C = 30$, what cutting speed would give a tool life of 1 hour?
2. When machining on a lathe taking 2·5 mm depth of cut and 0·25 mm/rev feed, the vertical cutting force on the tool is 588N
(a) What volume of metal can be removed per minute per kW?
The speed/life relationship of a tool is given by $VM^n = C$ for a given set of

conditions. What would be the effect on C:
(b) If the chip thickness is increased?
(c) If the depth of cut is increased?
(Assume no nose radius.)

(*Hint.* Solution to (b) and (c) should include sketch graphs. Solution can vary according to the value of ϕ taken; $\phi = 90°$ is suggested.)

3. Use the values given in Table 7.1 to plot graphs showing the variation in cutting speed and metal removal rate which occur as the feed is increased. Take depth of cut = 6·4 mm, tool life = 60 min.

The tabulated values are for a tool, $\phi = 90°$, having a nose radius of 2·5 mm. In what way do you think the values in Table 7.1 will change if a tool for which $\phi = 60°$ having no nose radius is tested?

(See Fig 7.9; note that when $\phi = 60°$ the chip thickness normal to the cutting edge will be increased as the depth of cut is increased.)

4. It is required to assess the cutting qualities of a certain batch of HSS tools by means of a "short life" practical test. The following values of spindle speed (rev/min) and length of travel (L) of the lathe carriage up to the failure of each tool are applicable to such a test:

Spindle speed	395	343	256
L mm	26·5	64·8	398

Workpiece dia 90 mm, feed 0·5 mm/rev, depth of cut 1·4 mm.

From this data calculate the constants of the tool life equation $VM^n = C$. Determine the tool life to be expected when cutting at 45 m/min.

5. Find the optimum speed, and tool life for minimum cost, for turning cold-rolled shafts given the following information:

$$VM^{0.25} = 100$$

Tool changing cost   = 50 p
Cost of grinding tool   = 180 p
(Cost of labour + overheads)/min   = 13 p

6. If $VM^n = C$ is the tool-life equation representing the cutting conditions, show that the inclusive cost of machining (S) is given by:

$$S = kM^n \frac{H}{60} + kM^{(n-1)}J$$

where H = hourly rate of operating the machine;
J = the inclusive costs of a tool change;
k = a constant for the cutting conditions.

Use the above expression to show that the economic tool life is given by:

$$M = \frac{1-n}{n} J \frac{60}{H}$$

Find the optimum spindle speed for turning a 150 mm dia shaft if the ratio $H/J = 2·25$ and $VM^{0.12} = 50$

7. Illustrate in a sketch graph the economic factors involved in metal cutting and show that cutting speed has an optimum value.

When finish turning a 50 mm dia × 130 mm long bore in high-tensile steel at a feed of 0·13 mm/rev the tool life equation was $VM^{0.12} = 146$. The cost of regrinding the tool was 8 units and the tool changing time 10 min.

If the inclusive cost of operating the machine is 13·5 units/hr, determine:

(a) the economic machining time per component;
(b) the number of components to be produced between tool changes.

8. It is required to reduce 50 mm dia M.S. bar to 32 mm dia for 152 mm of length by means of a single operation on a lathe. The conditions are as follows:

Operator's hourly rate = 4·2 units
Machine hourly rate = 11·4 units
Time to remove, replace and reset the tool = 0·1 hr
Cost of regrinding the tool = 0·3 units
Initial cost of the tool = 10 units
Number of possible regrinds of the tool = 50
Number of parts to be turned = 10 000
Feed/rev of tool = 0·25 mm
*Operator constant = 1·15
Tool-life law, $VM^{1/5} = 60$

Evaluate the economic spindle speed for the lathe.

(* Assumed to mean that the operator is earning 15 % bonus.)

9. The tool-life equations for four different tool materials are given on p. 216. If, for these materials, the ratio of operating to tool grinding costs (H/J) has the values shown below, find the economic cutting speed for each material.

HSS $\dfrac{H}{J} = 7·5$;

HSS (super grade) $\dfrac{H}{J} = 6·8$;

cast non-ferrous alloy $\dfrac{H}{J} = 5·5$;

tungsten carbide $\dfrac{H}{J} = 3·8$.

If the specific cutting pressure is 2000 N/mm² for the material cut, find the power required at the spindle for machining at the optimum rate with each of the tool materials listed; depth of cut 6·5 mm, feed 0·25 mm/rev.

10. When turning under certain conditions the relationship between cutting speed, tool life and chip thickness could be expressed as

$$VM^{0·1} = Cf^{-0·5}$$

where f = chip thickness in mm. For a tool where $\phi = 90°$ cutting at 30 m/min, the tool life was 1 min. Estimate the cutting speed which would give the same tool life if $\phi = 30°$, the other cutting conditions being unchanged.

11. (a) Discuss the criteria by which the "durability" of cutting tools can be assessed. Compare the relative performance of HSS and TC tools.

(b) In what manner do modern cutting fluids assist the performance of cutting tools?

(c) Compare the effectiveness of a cutting fluid used for milling with one used for turning.

CHAPTER 8

Principles of Metal Cutting—Milling
PART A—PERIPHERAL MILLING

8.1 Milling on the Cutter Periphery

Cutters which present more than one edge to the work usually have a higher metal removal rate than single-edged tools, and also the life of the cutter between regrinds is raised by increasing the number of cutting edges. Table 8.1 shows two main groups of such tools. A further group of multi-edge tools which needs special consideration beyond the compass of the present volume includes threading cutters (taps, dies, chasers), broaches and hobs. A grinding wheel is a form of multi-edge cutter, and special consideration is given in Chapter 9 to the cutting action which occurs during grinding.

TABLE 8.1

Multi-edge Cutting Tools

Group	Machines	Cutters
1	Drills Capstan lathes Turret lathes	Twist drills Reamers Multi-flute core drills Counter-bores Spot-facing cutters
2	Milling machines	Saws and slotting cutters Side-and-face cutters Slab mills End mills Face mills Form-relieved cutters

BS 5533: Specification for geometry of the active part of cutting tools, may also be consulted.

The tools classified under group (1) above generally have their cutting edges in continuous engagement with the work and are fed axially at a uniform feed per revolution. The undeformed chip thickness is therefore constant and directly proportional to the feed/rev. The geometry and mechanics of cutting are then identical with those discussed for single-point tools in Chapters 5 and 6.

The tools classified under group (2) have their cutting edges intermittently engaged with the work, and are fed in a plane parallel or perpendicular to the cutter axis of rotation, as shown in Fig 8.1. The geometry of chip formation for these cutters is more complex than for the cutters in group (1), or for single-point tools.

The economic considerations of Chapter 7 are, however, applicable to all types of cutting tools. Where the equation $VM^n = C$ relates to the tool, and not to a single cutting edge of the tool, the values of C will increase as the number of cutting edges of the tool is increased.

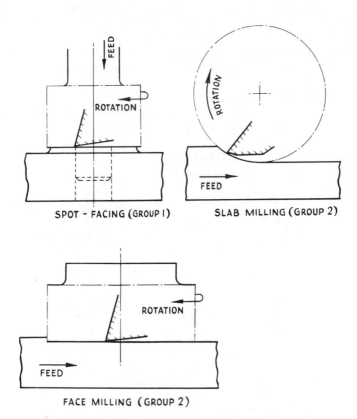

SPOT - FACING (GROUP I)   SLAB MILLING (GROUP 2)

FACE MILLING (GROUP 2)

Fig. 8.1 Relationship of feed and rotation in group 1 *and* group 2 *multi-edge cutting tools*

8.2 Peripheral Milling—Geometry of Chip Formation

The geometry of chip formation depends upon the path of the cutter edge across the workpiece. The cutter rotates with uniform angular velocity about a fixed axis; the work moves towards the cutter at a uniform feed rate and the path of the cutter relative to the workpiece is determined by a combination of rotary and feed motions. If the workpiece is regarded as stationary, and a motion equal and opposite to the feed motion is given to the cutter axis, the path of the tooth across the workpiece can be set out.

Fig 8.2 illustrates the cutting conditions: the cutter axis is imagined to lie at the centre of a disc of radius r (such that $r = f/2\pi$, where f = feed/rev) which rolls without slip along the straight edge ST. A point Q on the cutter periphery, at radius R from the axis of the disc, will trace out the path of the cutting edge relative to the workpiece. The curve described by Q is a **trochoid**. The chip cut lies between the trochoid AB, traced by the cutting edge, and the trochoid AC cut by the previous tooth. For **up-cut** milling the chip is cut from A to B; the undeformed chip thickness then increases from zero at A to a maximum (t_{max}) just before B is reached.

For a trochoid, the centre of curvature of Q is at U, the point where the rolling disc touches the straight edge, and the velocity óf Q relative to the workpiece is perpendicular to UQ and not to OQ.

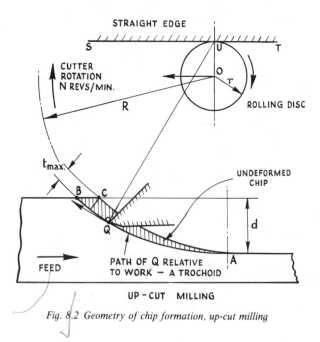

Fig. 8.2 Geometry of chip formation, up-cut milling

If the direction of the feed is now reversed, Fig 8.3 **down-cut** milling, the chip will be cut from B to A, and t_{max} will occur almost at the start of the cut. The curve BA is a different portion of the trochoid traced by the cutting edge Q, and the path length from B to A is shorter than the equivalent length A to B for up-cut milling.

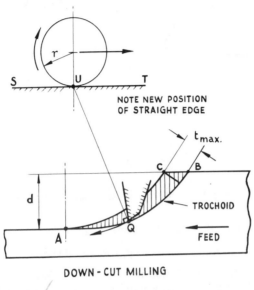

NOTE NEW POSITION
OF STRAIGHT EDGE

DOWN-CUT MILLING

Fig. 8.3 *Geometry of chip formation, down-cut milling*

machine
must have
hydraulic
drives
leadscrew + nut
is not
allowed

Because the path of the cutting tooth across the workpiece when down-cut milling comes from a different portion of the trochoid than for up-cut milling, there are small differences between the magnitudes of t_{max}, of chip length and of effective cutting clearance angle as between these methods, the cutting conditions being otherwise identical. The mathematics of the trochoid is involved and does not give exact expressions in a convenient form, but approximate solutions, which provide a sufficient demonstration of the above differences, may be found as follows.

Undeformed Chip Length (AB). Consider a small element of the trochoid AB (Fig 8.4) generated by rotation of the cutter through a small angle $\delta\theta$. The length of the element PQ depends upon two displacements:

    (i) $PT = R\,\delta\theta$, due to rotation of the cutter;
    (ii) $TQ = r\,\delta\theta$, due to the feed motion of the work.

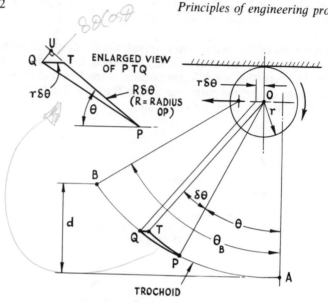

Fig. 8.4 Determination of undeformed chip length

The vector sum of these displacements is given by

$$\delta\theta[(R\cos\theta+r)^2+R^2\sin^2\theta]^{1/2},$$

and does not lead to a solution in a convenient form.

Extend PT (see enlarged view in Fig 8.4) to the point U such that TUQ is a right angle. Now, since r is very small in relation to R, length PQ is very nearly the same as length PU.

PQ $\simeq$ PU $\qquad \qquad \therefore$ PQ $\simeq R\delta\theta+r\delta\theta\cos\theta$

$$= (R+r\cos\theta)\delta\theta$$

Hence $\qquad \qquad$ AB $\simeq \int_0^{\theta_B}(R+r\cos\theta)\,d\theta$

$$= R\theta_B+r\sin\theta_B \qquad \text{(up-cut milling)} \quad (1)$$

Similar reasoning gives:

$$\text{BA} \simeq R\theta_B-r\sin\theta_B \qquad \text{(down-cut milling)} \qquad (2)$$

From Fig 8.5 it can be seen that

$$CD = r\sin\theta_F,$$

which is very nearly the same as $r\sin\theta_B$ $\qquad \qquad (3)$

Also, by similar triangles

$$CD = \frac{r}{R}(EF) \qquad \qquad (4)$$

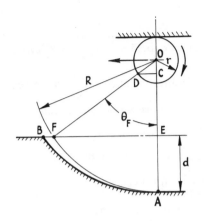

Fig. 8.5

and by Pythagoras' theorem

$$EF = [R^2 - (R-d)^2]^{1/2} = (2Rd - d^2)^{1/2} \qquad (5)$$

Let f = feed/rev of cutter, i.e. $f = 2\pi r$

hence $r = f/2\pi$ (6)

By substitution of (3), (4), (5) and (6) in (1) and (2):

$$AB \simeq R\theta_B + \frac{f}{2\pi R}(2Rd - d^2)^{1/2} \qquad \text{(up-cut milling)} \qquad (8.1)$$

$$BA \simeq R\theta_B - \frac{f}{2\pi R}(2Rd - d^2)^{1/2} \qquad \text{(down-cut milling)} \qquad (8.2)$$

Eqn (8.1) and Eqn (8.2) are given in the Cincinnati reference book, *A Treatise on Milling and Milling Machines*.

The difference in the undeformed chip length as between up-cut and down-cut milling is now seen to be $(f/\pi R)(2Rd - d^2)^{1/2}$, the length for down-cut milling being the shorter. This difference increases in direct proportion to the feed.

Although this difference is very small, it is a difference in the amount of **sliding** which occurs between the cutter edge and the material cut, and it leads to a slight reduction in the amount of cutter wear achieved by changing from the up-cut to the down-cut method. As will be shown later, it is not the most significant reason for the improvement in tool life normally resulting from this change.

Example 8.1

A 100 mm diameter cutter, having 8 teeth, cuts at 24 m/min. The depth of cut is 4 mm and the table feed 150 mm/min. Find the percentage reduction in sliding between the cutter edges and the material cut, which results from a change from up-cut to down-cut milling.

Solution

$$\text{Spindle speed} = \frac{10^3 \times 24}{\pi \times 100} = 76 \text{ rev/min}$$

$$\text{Feed/rev of cutter} = \frac{150}{76} = 1.974 \text{ mm}$$

Let $\qquad \theta$ = angle of engagement between cutter and work

$$\text{Cos } \theta = \frac{50-4}{50} = 0.920 \quad \theta = 23°$$

$$= 0.403 \text{ rads.}$$

$$r = \frac{1.974}{2\pi} = 0.314 \text{ mm}$$

Path length $AB = 50 \times 0.403 + 0.314 \sin 23°$

$$= 20.15 + 0.123 = 20.273 \text{ mm}$$

Reduction of path length resulting from change of method

$$= 2 \times 0.123 = 0.246 \text{ mm}$$

$$\% \text{ reduction in sliding} = \frac{0.246}{20.273} \times 100 = \underline{1.2\%}$$

The increase of cutter life on account of reduced sliding will be small, and the improvement usually achieved by a change from up-cut to downcut milling must depend upon additional factors.

Feed Rate and Cutter Wear. The life of a cutter is influenced by the amount of sliding which occurs between the teeth and the work. If a workpiece of length l mm is cut at a feed of f mm/rev the number of rotations of the cutter to remove the metal is l/f (approach distance neglected), and each tooth travels approximately $R\theta_B l/f$ mm through the material. It is obvious that high values of f reduce the amount of sliding per unit volume of material removed. For this reason milling should be done at moderate cutting speeds and high feed rates. The normal upper limit of feed rate will depend either upon the mechanical strength of the cutter or workpiece, or upon the power available at the machine spindle. Vibration may be a limiting factor.

Depth of Cut and Cutter Wear. The depth of cut (d) is also significant in relation to cutter wear. The volume of metal removed per pass $\propto d$; the cutter wear $\propto R\theta_B$. It can be seen from Fig 8.5 that θ increases as d increases according to the relationship $\cos \theta = (R-d)/R$. For typical values of R and d an increase in d is always proportionally greater than the accompanying increase in θ. The volume of metal removed per pass is thus seen to increase faster than the amount of sliding between the cutter and workpiece, for an increase in d. The best relationship between cutter life and volume of metal removed is achieved by taking one pass only at the full depth of cut required. Reference p. 249 shows a further advantage; the torque at the arbor gets smoother as d is increased.

Cutter life should also be considered in relation to the principles given on pp. 221–222, Figs 7.7 and 7.8. The main differences between cutting with single-point tools and milling are differences in the geometry of chip formation, which for milling involves intermittent engagement of the cutting edges with the workpiece.

Chip Thickness. As may be seen from Fig 8.2 and Fig 8.3, the chip thickness varies during cutting. The maximum thickness, t_{max}, occurs almost at the end of the cut for up-cut milling and at the start of the cut for down-cut milling.

A close approximation for the value of t_{max} can be obtained by reference to Fig 8.6.

By similar triangles,
$$\frac{f_t}{t_{max}} = \frac{L}{(2Rd - d^2)^{1/2}} \tag{1}$$

where f_t = the feed/tooth.

Also
$$L^2 = (R + r - d)^2 + 2Rd - d^2$$
$$= (R + r)^2 - 2rd \tag{2}$$

by substitution of (2) in (1)

$$t_{max} = f_t \left[\frac{2Rd - d^2}{(R + r)^2 - 2rd} \right]^{1/2} \quad \textit{for up-cut milling}$$

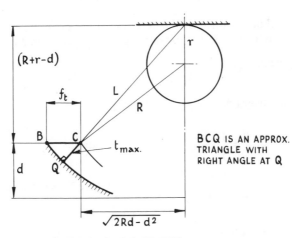

BCQ IS AN APPROX.
TRIANGLE WITH
RIGHT ANGLE AT Q

MAXIMUM CHIP THICKNESS

Fig. 8.6

Similarly, it can be shown that:

$$t_{max} = f_t \left[\frac{2Rd - d^2}{(R-r)^2 - 2rd} \right]^{1/2} \quad \textit{for down-cut milling}$$

These expressions are not very convenient, and by further approximations more suitable expressions for general use are obtainable.

(a) r is generally small and can be neglected, to give,

$$t_{max} = f_t \left[\frac{2Rd - d^2}{R^2} \right] \tag{8.3}$$

Any distinction between the values of t_{max} for up-cut or down-cut milling has now disappeared.

(b) If d is small relative to R (shallow cuts), d^2 can be neglected to give

$$t_{max} = f_t \left(\frac{2Rd}{R^2} \right)^{1/2} = 2f_t \left(\frac{d}{D} \right)^{1/2} \tag{8.4}$$

where D = diameter of the cutter.

(c) If d cannot be neglected (deep cuts),

$$t_{max} = f_t \left[\frac{d}{R} \left(2 - \frac{d}{R} \right) \right]^{1/2} \quad \text{by rearrangement of (8.3)}$$

$$= 2f_t \left[\frac{d}{D} \left(1 - \frac{d}{D} \right) \right]^{1/2} \quad \text{by substitution of cutter diameter}$$

$$= \frac{2}{D} f_t [d(D-d)]^{1/2} \quad \text{by rearrangement} \tag{8.5}$$

Eqn (8.4) can be obtained by the development of Schlesinger's formula for mean chip thickness. As shown in Fig 8.7, t_{mean} is assumed to occur at angular position $\frac{\theta}{2}$,

From the diagram, $t_{mean} = f_t \sin \frac{\theta}{2}$,   (1)

but $\sin \frac{\theta}{2} = \left[\frac{1 - \cos \theta}{2} \right]^{1/2}$, and $\cos \theta = \frac{R-d}{R}$

hence $\sin \frac{\theta}{2} = \left[\frac{d}{2R} \right]^{1/2} = \sqrt{\frac{d}{D}}$,   where D = cutter diameter

                                                                                                      (2)

Substituting (2) in (1),

$$t_{mean} = f_t \sqrt{\frac{d}{D}} \quad \text{(Schlesinger's formula)}$$

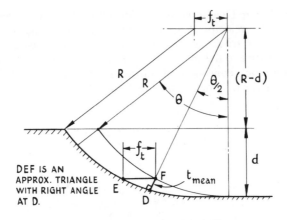

Fig. 8.7 Geometry of Schlesinger's formula for mean chip thickness

Since $t_{max} = 2t_{mean}$, Schlesinger's formula agrees with Eqn (8.4). It should be appreciated that Schlesinger's method is not as accurate for deep cuts as Eqn (8.5).

Example 8.2

A side and face cutter 125 mm diameter has 10 teeth. It operates at a cutting speed of 14 m/min and table feed of 100 mm/min. Find the maximum chip thickness: (i) for a cutting depth of 5 mm; (ii) for a cutting depth of 25 mm

Solution

$$\text{Spindle speed} = \frac{10^3 \times 14}{\pi \times 125} = 35 \text{ rev/min.}$$

$$f_t = \frac{100}{35} \times \frac{1}{10} = 0.286 \text{ mm}$$

From Eqn (7.4) (i) $t_{max} = 2 \times 0.286 \sqrt{\dfrac{5}{125}} = \underline{0.114 \text{ mm}}$

From Eqn (7.5) (ii) $t_{max} = \dfrac{2 \times 0.286}{125} \sqrt{(25 \times 100)} = \underline{0.229 \text{ mm}}$

It has been assumed so far that each tooth of a cutter cuts an equal chip, a condition unlikely to occur in practice due to the eccentric running of cutters and arbors. Where t_{max} is very small, some of the teeth may not cut a chip while others may cut chips of twice the estimated thickness. Eccentric running may cause cutter breakage by the overloading of some tooth; it may also cause unnecessary cutter wear because some of the teeth rub over the surface without cutting a chip. This rubbing is a serious disadvantage when cutting metals which work-harden rapidly.

Influence of Chip Geometry on the Cutting Angles. It has been shown in **8.2** that the velocity of a cutter edge relative to the workpiece is tangential to a trochoid. The nominal rake and clearance angles, measured relative to the cutter circumference, are thus slightly modified by the geometrical conditions of cutting. The extent of this modification can be approximately determined as follows; see Fig 8.8.

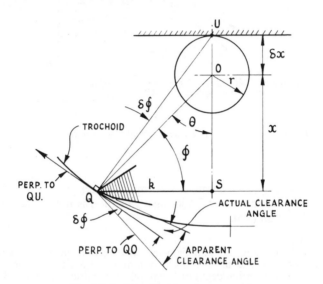

Fig. 8.8 Peripheral cutting clearance angle

From the diagram, $\tan \phi = \dfrac{x}{k}$

differentiating, $\sec^2 \phi \, d\phi = \dfrac{dx}{k}$

and $\qquad\qquad \delta\phi \simeq \dfrac{\delta x}{k} \cos^2 \phi$; since $\delta x (= r)$ is small.

$\qquad \therefore \quad \delta\phi = \dfrac{r}{R^2} k$; since $\cos^2 \phi = \dfrac{k^2}{R^2}$

now $\qquad\qquad k = (2Rd - d^2)^{1/2}$, as shown in Fig 8.6,

hence $\qquad\qquad \delta\phi = \dfrac{r}{R^2}(2Rd - d^2)^{1/2}$ radians

By substituting $r = f/2\pi$ and converting to degrees,

$$\delta\phi = \frac{90f}{\pi^2 R^2}(2Rd - d^2)^{1/2} \text{ degrees} \qquad (8.6)$$

The clearance angle is decreased by this amount due to the feed motion. The effect is maximum where $d = R$ (plunge cut or face milling) when

$$\delta\phi = \frac{90f}{\pi^2 R} = \frac{180}{\pi} \times \frac{f}{2\pi R} \text{ degrees}$$

a result which may be established directly from a vector diagram.

Example 8.3
A slot 32 mm deep, is milled with a cutter 120 mm diameter operating at a feed/rev of 5 mm. Find the maximum reduction of the nominal clearance angle caused by the feed motion.

Solution

$$\delta\phi, \text{ at 32 mm depth} = \frac{90 \times 5}{\pi^2 \times 60^2} [32(120 - 32)]^{1/2}$$

$$= 0{\cdot}0126 \times 53{\cdot}07$$

$$= \underline{0{\cdot}67^\circ}$$

It should be realised that an exceptionally heavy feed is involved. For more normal conditions the effect rarely exceeds $0{\cdot}25^\circ$ and may be neglected. However, the land width as well as the clearance angle enters into any consideration of rubbing at the clearance side of the tooth, and when very small nominal clearance angles are ground on cutters for the purpose of milling very tough steels it is possible for the feed motion to absorb much of the clearance provided.

8.3 Geometry of the Cutting Edge

The general form of cutting edge is represented by the tooth of a helical slab mill, Fig 8.9. The following symbols are used to indicate the rake angle in different planes:

γ_t = effective rake angle (angle in plane of chip flow);
γ_r = rake angle in plane perp to axis (radial rake angle);
γ_n = rake angle in a plane normal to PQ (normal rake);
also σ = spiral angle of cutting edge

A similar suffix notation is used to indicate the clearance angle (α) measured in different planes.

By projective geometry

$$\tan\gamma_n = \tan\gamma_r \sec\sigma$$

$$\tan\alpha_n = \tan\alpha_r \sec\sigma$$

The cutting conditions for the tooth shown in Fig 8.9 are termed **oblique** (see p. 173) and arise from the helical tooth form of the cutter.

Oblique cutting is illustrated in Fig 8.10, which shows the effect of an oblique edge in curling the chip. The direction in which the chip flows up

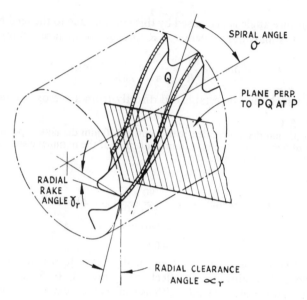

Fig. 8.9 Cutting angles of a helical slab mill

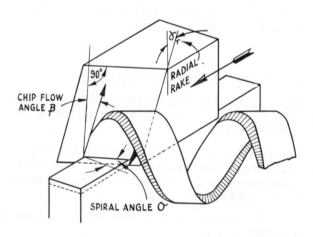

Fig. 8.10 Oblique cutting

the rake face of the tool is no longer perpendicular to the cutting edge, as
for orthogonal conditions; the chip flow angle β is now used to indicate
the direction of chip flow. An investigation of oblique cutting by Stabler
("The Fundamental Geometry of Cutting Tools", *Proc. I.Mech.E.*, **165**,
1951) has shown that the value of β is approximately the same as the
angle of inclination, i.e. the spiral angle of the cutter.

The direction of flow of the chip up the rake face of the tool is such that the effective rake angle γ_t is larger than the normal rake angle γ_n, depending on the value of the spiral angle σ. Stabler shows that

$$\sin \gamma_t = \sin^2 \sigma + \cos^2 \sigma \sin \gamma_n \qquad (8.7)$$

The geometry of the oblique cutting edge is also treated in chapter 5.

Example 8.4
A slab milling cutter has a radial rake of 7° and a spiral angle of 35°. Find the effective rake angle.

Solution

$$\tan \gamma_n = \tan \gamma_r \sec \sigma$$
$$= \tan 7° \sec 35°$$
$$= 0.1228 \times 1.221 = 0.1499 \quad \gamma_n = 8.5°$$
$$\sin \gamma_t = \sin^2 35° + \cos^2 35° \sin 8.5°$$
$$= 0.3291 + (0.6711 \times 0.1478)$$
$$= 0.4283$$
$$\gamma_t = \underline{25.4°}$$

The result shows that the introduction of the spiral angle has the effect of raising the value of the rake angle from $\gamma_r = 7°$ (when $\sigma = 0$) to $\gamma_t = 25.4°$. Since this large effective rake angle is achieved without producing a weak tooth section, the principle is of importance in cutter design. The resulting change in the direction of chip flow helps to prevent clogging of the tooth spaces of the cutter.

8.4 Cutting Forces and Power

Fig 8.11 shows those components of the force exerted by the work on a cutting tooth, which act in a plane perpendicular to the cutter axis. The axial load on the cutter will be treated separately.

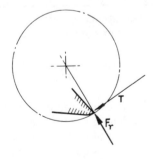

Fig. 8.11 Forces acting on cutter tooth

T, the tangential force, determines the torque on the cutter; F_r, the radial force, may be regarded as the rubbing force between the workpiece and the tooth. The value of T will depend upon the chip area being cut and on the specific cutting pressure. Work done in cutting a chip $= \int_0^l T \, dl$, where l is the undeformed chip length.

Direct measurement of forces T and F_r is difficult because they are oscillating rapidly during the cutting; a suitable dynamometer must be one capable of recording the fluctuations on a time base. From the general principles deduced from cutting data obtained when turning metals, it is possible to deduce the approximate trend of the forces which occur in up-cut and down-cut milling.

Fig 8.12 shows the trend of these forces, in relation to the undeformed chip section for up-cut milling. Note the upward surge of force F_r near the start of the cut. This is caused by cutting from zero chip thickness at A so that high elastic forces must be exceeded before the tooth edge penetrates the metal to be cut. Obviously at this point T has a value which includes the frictional resistance of the tooth to sliding over the metal. For this reason the values of T, and of the work done in cutting the chip, tend to be higher for up-cut than for down-cut milling. Comparison of Fig 8.12 with Fig 8.13 should make this clear.

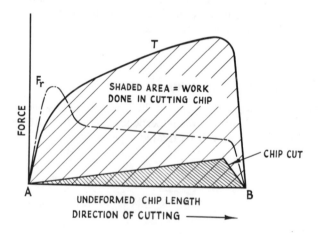

Fig. 8.12 Relationship between forces acting on cutter tooth and undeformed chip thickness, up-cut milling

The high initial value of F_r causes rapid wear of cutter edges, and this has the effect of work-hardening the surface which the following teeth must penetrate. In the milling of materials which work-harden readily the effect, as shown in Fig 8.14, is quite serious; the cutting edges on the clearance side of the teeth rapidly develop a polished land. If dull cutters

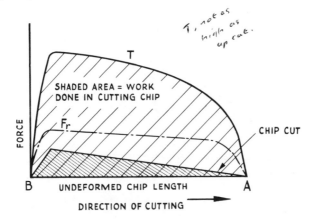

Fig. 8.13 Relationship between forces acting on cutter tooth and undeformed chip
thickness, down-cut milling

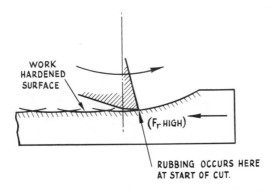

Fig. 8.14 Rubbing action caused by radial force

are kept in service F_r rises to a very high value and pieces of metal may
fracture from the rake face, as shown in Fig 8.15. It is obvious that such
conditions are unfavourable for the application of carbide tooth cutters
because of their brittleness.

Since down-cut milling avoids the conditions described in the above
paragraph, an improved cutter life should generally result from a change
to this method. It is normally employed when peripheral milling with
carbide tooth cutters (e.g. deep slot milling).

Total Forces Acting on a Cutter. Suppose three teeth are in engagement with the workpiece and the down-cut method of milling is
employed. Fig 8.16 illustrates these conditions and shows how the forces

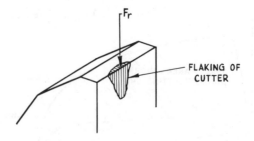

Fig. 8.15 Compression fracture at cutting edge caused by very high radial force

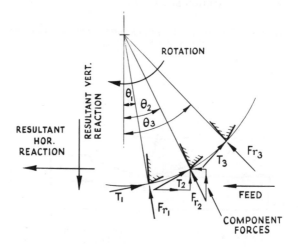

Fig. 8.16 Total reactions of cutter on workpiece, down-cut milling

acting may be resolved to give the magnitude of the reactions of the cutter on the workpiece.

The Vertical Reaction $= T_1 \sin \theta_1 + T_2 \sin \theta_2 + T_3 \sin \theta_3$
$$+ F_{r1} \cos \theta_1 + F_{r2} \cos \theta_2 + F_{r3} \cos \theta_3$$

For all possible values of θ the vertical reaction is downwards forcing the workpiece on to the machine table.

The Horizontal Reaction $= T_1 \cos \theta_1 + T_2 \cos \theta_2 + T_3 \cos \theta_3$
$$- F_{r1} \sin \theta_1 - F_{r2} \sin \theta_2 - F_{r3} \sin \theta_3$$

The horizontal reaction will be in the **same direction** as the table feed for small values of θ and will fall in value (may even become reversed in direction) as θ is increased. A feed drive with backlash eliminator, or a suitable hydraulic feed drive, must be employed in association with the down-cut method of milling.

A similar analysis of the reactions when up-cut milling will show that the direction of the reaction in the vertical plane depends upon the value of θ; it is possible for the work to be lifted from the table over unclamped sections, due to flexure of the workpiece, when deep slots are being milled.

Fig 8.17 shows the axial force acting on a cutter due to the spiral angle of the cutting edge. The value of T may be taken as the sum of the separate values T_1, T_2, etc. Helical cutters should be mounted so that force A pushes the arbor into the spindle nose. Milling machines have bearings designed to carry thrust loads in either direction. The arbor, however, is secured in a non-stick taper by means of a long slender drawbar. Elastic extension of the drawbar may become a source of vibration if force A, which varies during cutting, greatly increases the tensile load in the bar.

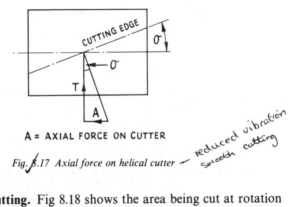

A = AXIAL FORCE ON CUTTER

Fig. 8.17 Axial force on helical cutter — reduced vibration smooth cutting

Work Done in Cutting. Fig 8.18 shows the area being cut at rotation angle θ when a straight-toothed cutter is employed. The value of T for this position is given by $T = Pbt$, where P is the specific cutting pressure. Fig 8.19 shows the variation of P which occurs with variation of chip thickness, but since t is a function of θ, P also is a function of θ.

The work done in cutting a chip (W_c) = torque × angle turned

$$W_c = Rb \int_0^{\theta_B} Pt d\theta, \text{ where } R \text{ is the cutter radius.}$$

The relationships between t and θ and between P and θ are complex, so that the above expression does not lead to practical solutions. An approximate solution is possible in terms of mean values of t and P.

Schlesinger's formula gives $t_{\text{mean}} = f_t \sqrt{(d/D)}$, and values of P for the mean chip thickness can be reasonably estimated from test data, hence,

$$W_c = R\theta_B b f_t \sqrt{(d/D)} P_{\text{mean}} \qquad (8.8)$$

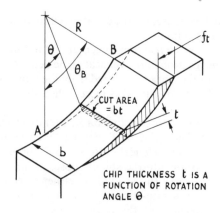

Fig. 8.18

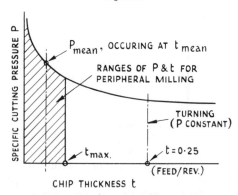

*Fig. 8.19 Range of specific cutting pressure involved in peripheral milling,
compared with turning (see also Fig 5.3)*

If a cutter has N teeth and rotates at S rev/min the total work done/min
in cutting $= W_c NS$, and from this expression a value for the power
required at the cutter can be estimated.

Example 8.5

A milling cutter is to produce a slot 20 mm wide and 12 mm deep. The
cutter is 100 mm diameter, has 10 teeth, cuts at 25 m/min, and a table feed of
125 mm/min is to be employed. If $P_{mean} = 4200 \ N/mm^2$, estimate the power
required at the cutter.

Solution

An expression for power can be deduced from the formulae developed on
p. 245.

$$\text{Power (watts)} = \frac{W_c NS}{60} \qquad W_c = R\theta_B bf_t \sqrt{\frac{d}{D}} P$$

$$\text{Power} = \frac{R\theta_B bf_t NS}{60} \sqrt{\frac{d}{D}} \times P$$

Examination of the units employed will show that R must be in metres.
Let F = table feed, mm/min. Then $F = f_t N S$

hence $\qquad$ Power $= \dfrac{R \theta_B b F}{60 \times 10^3} \sqrt{\dfrac{d}{D}} \times P,$ $\qquad$ for R in mm

For the given conditions, $\cos \theta_B = \dfrac{38}{50}$, $\theta_B = 0.707$ rads.

$$\text{Power} = \frac{50}{10^3} \times 0.707 \times 20 \times 125 \times \sqrt{\frac{12}{100}} \times \frac{4200}{60} \times 10^{-3} \, \text{kW}$$
$$= \underline{2.15 \, \text{kW}}$$

The method may appear to give the power at the cutter without taking the cutting speed into account. However, if the table feed remained constant, any increase in cutting speed would reduce the feed/tooth; the specific cutting pressure would then rise because the chip thickness would be reduced, and more power would be required. So long as the table feed F is unchanged the metal removal rate is unchanged and the power required for the cut will remain fairly constant for conventional values of cutting speed.

If the depth of cut (d) is considered as a variable, it can be shown that the power criterion $\dfrac{\text{watts}}{w}$ (where w = mm^3/s of metal removed) will be reduced by cutting at half the depth and at twice the feed. Proof is left as an exercise for the reader. The power saved is, however, of negligible importance, and as the total amount of sliding between the cutting teeth and workpiece is increased, the tool life will be reduced.

The chief uncertainty in making such estimates as Example 8.5 lies in the value of P because this varies with the sharpness of the cutter. P may rise to as much as twice the initial value during the period between cutter regrinds. As may be seen by reference to Fig 8.19, values of P for milling are higher than for rough turning, hence the power criterion $\left(\dfrac{\text{watts}}{w} \right)$ will be higher.

A convenient method of estimating the power required for a milling operation is provided by the power criterion $\dfrac{\text{watts}}{w}$, which may be tabulated as a constant for various materials. A comparison between milling and turning of SAE 1020 steel, based on this method, is as follows:

(i) Milling SAE 1020, H.S.S. slab mill, cut 125 mm wide × 6·4 mm deep × 76 mm/min feed.

$$\frac{\text{watts}}{w} = 4.64 \quad \text{(based on Cincinnati data)}$$

(ii) Turning SAE 1020, depth of cut 6·4 mm feed 0·38 mm

$$\frac{\text{watts}}{w} = 2\cdot6 \text{ (based on ASME data)}$$

K Values for Power Estimates when Milling. Both Cincinnati and the Kearney and Trecker Corporation have published values of an approximate constant (K) in relation to the power required for milling various materials.

TABLE 8.2
Typical Values of K ($mm^3/s/watt$)

Material cut	Brinell hardness	K
Steel	100	0·27
Steel	200	0·22
Steel	300	0·19
Steel	400	0·17
Aluminium		0·74
Brass		0·61
Bronze		0·47
C.I (average)		0.42
C.I (hard)		0.28

(converted from published values in Imperial units)

$K = w/$watts and is the volume of metal which can be removed per second by 1 W at the cutter. The values quoted are for cutters near the end of their tool life so that maximum power demands may be estimated.

Example 8.6

Estimate the power required to take a cut, 100 mm wide × 3 mm deep, at 80 mm/min feed, in a 60 t alloy steel for which $K = 0\cdot17$. If the cutter diameter is 90 mm, and a cutting speed of 14 m/min is employed, find the mean torque at the arbor and estimate the force required to drive the machine table (up-cut milling). If the cutter has a spiral angle of 40° estimated the axial thrust.

Solution

Power at the spindle,

$$\text{Power} = \frac{w}{K} = \frac{100 \times 3 \times 80}{60 \times 0\cdot17} = \underline{2353 \text{ W}}$$

Mean force at the periphery of the cutter,

$$T = 2353 \times \frac{60}{14} = \underline{10080\text{N}}$$

Mean torque at the arbor,

$$\text{Torque} = \frac{90 \times 10080}{10^3 \times 2} = \underline{454 \text{ Nm}} \qquad T = Fr$$

Estimated force to drive the machine table: reference to Fig 8.16 shows that the contact angle θ, and magnitude of forces F_r and T, are involved. Since for the cut being considered, θ_B is small, the force to drive the table (neglecting friction at the slide) is approximately equal to T (10·08 kN)

Estimated axial thrust:

$$A = 10·08 \, tan \, 40° = \underline{8·46 \, kN}$$

Note that the feed force of 10·08 kN estimated above is about 8 times the feed force required to achieve an equivalent metal removal rate on a lathe.

Smoothness of Arbor Torque. For a given breadth of cut (b) and depth (d) the torque at the arbor will fluctuate according to:

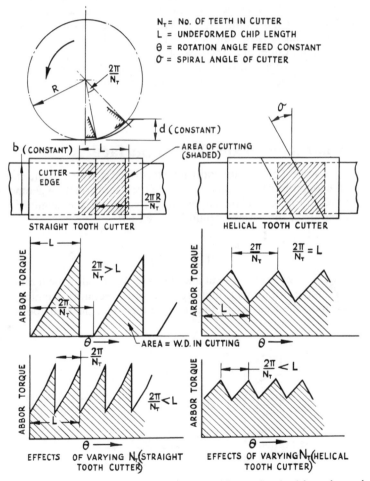

N_T = No. OF TEETH IN CUTTER
L = UNDEFORMED CHIP LENGTH
θ = ROTATION ANGLE FEED CONSTANT
σ = SPIRAL ANGLE OF CUTTER

Fig. 8.20 *Influence of number of teeth in cutter, and of the spiral angle of the teeth, on arbor torque*

(i) the number of teeth in the cutter (N_T);
(ii) the spiral angle of the teeth (σ).

Fig 8.20 illustrates the effect of increasing N_T for a straight-tooth cutter and for a spiral-tooth cutter. The progressive reduction in torque fluctuation should be noted. Since torque × angle turned = work done, the shaded areas of the graphs show the relative amounts of work necessary to achieve a common metal removal rate. The smoother the torque, the **lower** the maximum value required for equal amounts of work done in cutting.

Of the variables which may be employed to obtain a smooth arbor torque, N_T is the least effective due to eccentric rotation of the cutter (see p. 237) and the rise in P associated with reduced chip thickness, Fig 8.19.

The larger the spiral angle, the smoother will be the torque, and for cutters operating at low values of d there is a distinct advantage in employing high values of σ. Increase of the cutting depth (d) also results in a smoother torque and is an additional reason why cutters should be set to cut the full depth in one pass. Other reasons for doing this are given on pp. 234 and 245

8.5 Character of the Milled Surface

The cross-section of a peripherally milled surface is a copy of the cutter form, the longitudinal section is a result of the chip-formation geometry illustrated in Fig 8.21. If the cutter ran perfectly true the height of the tooth marks on the surface would be given by:

$$h \simeq \frac{f_t^2}{8[(R \pm f_t)N_T/\pi]}$$

where the +ve sign is for up-cut and the −ve sign for down-cut milling. More often the surface markings are the result of eccentric running and depend upon the feed/rev of the cutter rather than the feed/tooth.

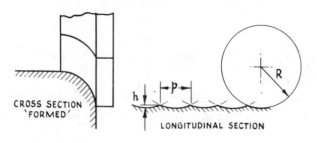

Fig. 8.21 Surfaces produced by milling

8.6 Cutter Application

It has been shown that peripheral milling is a complex cutting process. There is no easy route by which the optimum conditions for a specific piece of milling can be decided. The following summary draws attention to the main variables which influence the choices to be made when selecting cutting conditions.

Cutter Diameter. The larger the cutter, the more cutting teeth available and the longer the cutter life. A small cutter, however, will give rise to a smaller arbor torque than a large cutter for the same peripheral force T and will also be subject to smaller torque fluctuation. It is useless to mount large cutters on 27 mm dia arbors. A more general use of 32 mm and 40 mm dia arbors would improve milling performance by reducing the amplitude of the torsional vibrations caused by torque fluctuations.

Cutting Depth. Set the machine to cut the full depth at one pass wherever possible; exceptions are for saws and other delicate cutters which cannot stand the high tooth loads involved.

Table Feed. Use high table feeds in conjunction with moderate cutting speeds so that the chip thickness is as large as the tooth strength of the cutter and stiffness of the set-up will permit. Heavy milling machines should be fitted with wattmeters to show the power being consumed; the cutting conditions may then be selected so as to push this as high as possible within the machine capacity (see Table 16.3).

PART B—FACE MILLING

8/7 Relationships between Face and Peripheral Milling

In face milling the chips are cut on the periphery of the cutter and are bounded by trochoids as for peripheral milling; a different portion of the trochoid is, however, involved, as shown in Fig 8.22. The undeformed chip shapes for up-cut milling, face milling and down-cut milling lie within the crescent bounded by the trochoids. The machined surface is that left by the **face** of the cutter.

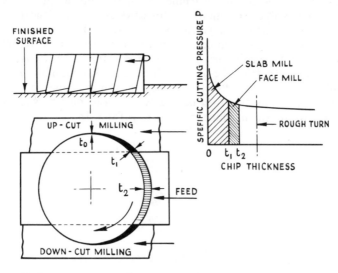

Fig. 8.22 Comparisons of undeformed chip thickness and specific cutting pressures involved in peripheral and face milling

Shaded portion $(t_0 - t_1)$ up-cut milling; portion $(t_1 - t_2)$ face milling; remaining shaded portion, down-cut milling.

The practical advantages are:

    (i) the power consumed in cutting is only about 70 % of the power required for slab-milling;

    (ii) cutter edges which produce the finished work surface make very little contact with any hard scale on the workpiece, the process is therefore most suitable for the machining of castings and forgings;

(iii) the finished surface is **generated** and a very high degree of flatness can be obtained;

(iv) torque at the arbor is fairly smooth due to the long undeformed chip length;

(v) the cutter can be designed to take inserted teeth, and tungsten carbide teeth may be used;

(vi) the cutter bolts directly on to the spindle nose (large face mills) and is much more rigidly supported than a slab mill in the middle of an arbor.

The general considerations of Part A are applicable to face mills, as may be seen from the following example.

Example 8.7

An 200 mm diameter face mill has 6 inserted teeth and is used to cut material 140 mm wide. The cutter operates at a speed of 30 m/min and table feed of 120 mm/min; the centre of the cutter is 58 mm from the edge of the work approached by the teeth. Find:

(i) the variation of undeformed chip thickness;
(ii) the influence of the cutting conditions on the clearance angle;
(iii) the angles at which the teeth approach and leave the workpiece;
(iv) the cutting time to mill a length of 460 mm;
(v) the maximum number of teeth in contact with the work.

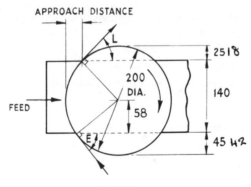

Fig. 8.23

Solution

$$\text{Spindle speed} = \frac{10^3 \times 30}{\pi \times 200} = 48 \,\text{rev/min}$$

$$\text{Feed/tooth}, f_t = \frac{120}{48 \times 6} = 0.417 \,\text{mm}$$

(i) Undeformed chip thickness, t_1 at entry, t_2 at exit, and by application of Eqn (8.5)

$$t_1 = \frac{2 \times 0.417}{200}(45 \times 155)^{1/2} \quad \text{(see Fig 8.23 and compare with Fig 8.22)}$$

$$= 0.348 \text{ mm}$$
$$t_{max} = f_l = \underline{0.417 \text{ mm}}$$
$$t_2 = \frac{2 \times 0.417}{200}(25 \times 175)^{1/2}$$
$$= \underline{0.276 \text{ mm}}$$

Note the comparatively small change in thickness as compared with slab milling.

(ii) Loss of clearance angle due to table feed, $\delta\phi$.

$$\text{From the vector triangle of velocities, } \sin \delta\phi = \frac{\text{Table feed}}{\text{Cutting speed}}$$

$$\sin \delta\phi = \frac{120}{30 \times 10^3} \delta\phi = \underline{0.23°}$$

(iii) Angles at entry and leaving (see Fig 8.23)

$$\cos E = \frac{58}{100} = 0.58, \underline{E = 54.5°}$$

$$\cos L = \frac{82}{100} = 0.82, \underline{L = 35°}$$

(iv) Cutting time. The approach distance can be found with sufficient accuracy from a scale drawing. Alternatively, approach dist. $= 100(1 - \sin 35°) = 43$ mm.

$$\text{Cutting time} = \frac{460 + 43}{120} = \underline{4.2 \text{ min}}$$

(v) Max number of teeth in contact,

Arc of engagement of cutter $= 180° - (54.5° + 35°)$
$$= 89.5°$$

$$\text{Angular spacing of teeth} = \frac{360°}{6} = 60°$$

Max number of teeth in contact $= \underline{2}$.

8.8 Geometry of Face Mills

Fig 5.8 shows that a single-point face cutter rotating about an axis has a tool-edge geometry identical with that of a turning tool. In extending these geometrical principles to the cutting edges of a face mill a new terminology is involved, as shown in Fig 8.24 and Fig 8.25. It is important to consider the impact conditions as the tool edge enters the workpiece; application of tungsten carbide requires that the initial impact be as far away from the cutting edge as possible.

Fig 8.25 illustrates the geometry of the cutting edge AB of an inserted tooth of a face mill. When AB lies in a plane containing the axis of

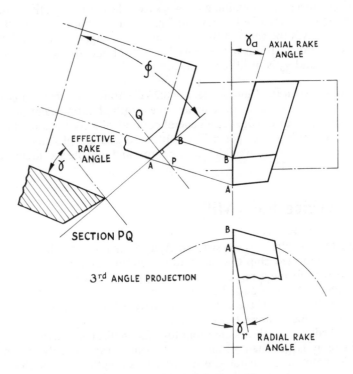

Fig. 8.24 Tool angles of a face mill

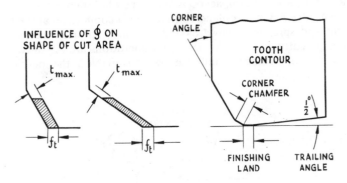

Fig. 8.25 Tooth contour for face mills

rotation the cutting conditions are **orthogonal** and by the principles of 5.2 the normal rake angle is given by:

$$\tan \gamma_n = \tan \gamma_r \cos \phi + \tan \gamma_a \sin \phi$$

The values of γ_r, γ_a and ϕ employed may, however, cause the edge AB to be inclined to a plane containing the work axis; the cutting condition are then **oblique**, as described in 8.3 and Fig 8.10. For oblique cutting the expression gives the value of the orthogonal rake angle γ_0 (see Fig 5.3). However for inclinations of the tool edge up to about 20° the difference between γ_n and γ_0 is of little significance.

Influence of ϕ on the Chip Shape. Fig 8.25 illustrates the effects of ϕ in changing the thickness of the chip and the length of engagement of the chip along the cutter edge. The general contour of a tooth as used on carbide face mills is also shown. The influence of changes of shape of the undeformed chip section on the cutting forces and tool life are discussed in 6.2 and on p. 223.

8.9 Carbide Face Mills

The similarity between the tooth of a face mill and of a single-point turning tool has already been stressed. Apart from a very small variation of the undeformed chip thickness during cutting, face milling can be equated with facing a rectangular piece of metal on a lathe, where an interrupted cut also occurs. Tungsten carbide tools may be successfully employed for both of these processes, provided the conditions at the tooth engagement (impact) are suitable.

Fig 8.26 illustrates these conditions for a face mill. So long as angle E is considerably larger than γ_r, impact will occur away from the cutting edge. Sometimes γ_r is made −ve in order to strengthen the tooth and ensure good conditions at impact. If AB, Fig 8.24, is in a plane containing the axis of rotation the impact occurs over the whole depth of cutting. By inclining edge AB in this plane, so that impact commences at the top of the cut and spreads downwards and outwards towards the face and peripheral cutting edges, the best entry conditions are obtained.

When using carbide face mills the power available at the spindle must

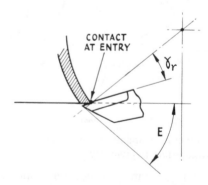

Fig. 8.26 Conditions of tooth entry, face milling

TABLE 8.3

Recommended Feeds per Tooth for Steel typically 0.3 per tooth.

Type of milling	Feed per tooth (mm)
Face	0·20–0·38
When ϕ exceeds 45°, correspondingly larger values may be used	
Side or straddle	0·20–0·30
Slab	0·20–0·30
Slotting	0·15–0·25
Saw	0·08–0·15

be adequate and feeds must be large enough for each tooth to take a definite cut. Where the power of a machine is low, cutters having very few teeth must be employed in order to maintain a sufficiently large feed/tooth. Stalling of the cutter, which would otherwise occur at appropriate feed rates, is almost certain to damage the carbide teeth.

Recommendations for Carbide Milling. The information in Table 8.3, kindly made available by the Cincinnati Milling Machine Co., is taken from their pamphlet *Recommendations for Carbide Milling.* Fig 8.27 shows the recommended cutting speeds.

Select the feed/tooth from the above table, remembering that for shallow slotting cuts the maximum undeformed chip thickness may only

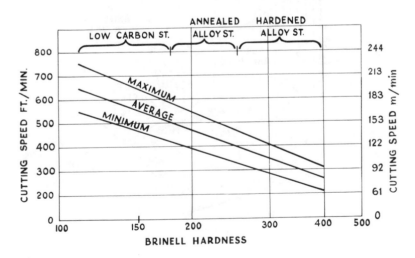

Fig. 8.27 Cutting speeds for carbide milling
(Courtesy of Cincinnati)

note

TABLE 8.4
Recommended Rake Angles for Steel

Face milling		Axial rake (γ_a)	Radial rake (γ_r)	Corner angle (ϕ)	Normal rake (γ_n)	Inclination angle (λ)
	Low-carbon and annealed alloy steels	$+5°$	$-12°$	$45°$	$-5°$	$+12°$
	Hardened alloy steels	$+5°$	$-18°$	$45°$	$-10°$	$+16°$

Courtesy Cincinnati Milling Machine Co. Ltd.

be 10 % to 50 % of the feed/tooth (see p. 235). On such cuts use the upper limits.

The geometry of carbide face mills is shown in Fig 8.28. The "inclination" angle (λ) shows that cutting edge AB does not lie in the reference plane, hence the cutting conditions illustrated are **oblique**. Where operating conditions permit the use of high feed rates, ϕ may be increased to 60°.

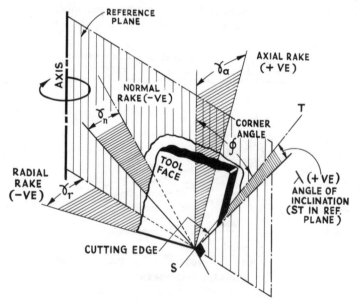

Fig. 8.28 Geometry of carbide face mills
(Courtesy of Cincinnati)

Power estimates can be based upon the values of K given in Table 8.2 (p. 248).

The angle of inclination λ will depend upon the values of the radial and axial rakes, and upon the corner angle.

Fig 8.29 illustrates these relationships. AB′ is the projection, in a horizontal plane, of the cutting edge AB shown in the main view. It will assist in the understanding of this diagram if it is compared with Fig 5.8.

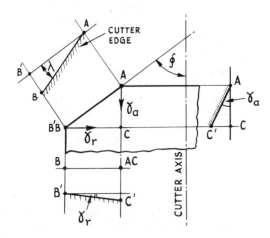

Fig. 8.29 Geometry of the oblique edge of a face mill

Let point C lie in this horizontal plane; then

$$AC = AB' \cos \phi \qquad (1)$$

$$B'C = AB' \sin \phi \qquad (2)$$

From the projection $\tan \lambda = \dfrac{BB'}{AB'} \qquad (3)$

but $BB' = AC \tan \gamma_a - B'C \tan \gamma_r$, and by substitution of (1), (2) and (3),

$$\tan \lambda = \cos \phi \tan \gamma_a - \sin \phi \tan \gamma_r \qquad (8.9)$$

Example 8.8

A 200 mm diameter face mill has 6 inserted carbide teeth of corner angle 45°, and takes a cut 6 mm deep across a steel slab 120 mm wide, of 300 Brinell hardness.

Select suitable cutting conditions for this work and estimate the power required at the spindle. Find the minimum chip thickness measured perpendicular to the corner edge.

Solution
   The graph, Fig 8.27, shows a suitable cutting speed to be 100 mm/min.

$$\text{Spindle speed} = \frac{10^3 \times 100}{\pi \times 200} = 160 \, \text{rev/min}$$

Feed/tooth, say 0·33 mm
Table feed required,

$$F = 0.33 \times 6 \times \frac{160}{120} = 317 \, \text{mm/min}$$

Metal removal rate,

$$w = \frac{317 \times 6 \times \frac{160}{120}}{60} = \frac{5068.8}{} = 2880 \, \text{mm}^3/\text{s}$$

Power consumed, $K = 0.19$

$$\text{Power at cutter} = \frac{2880}{0.19} = 15160 \, \text{W}$$

Min value of undeformed chip thickness perp to cutting edge: (assume cutter is positioned over centre of work). By Eqn (8.5) and since $\phi = 45°$,

$$t = \frac{2 \times 0.33}{\sqrt{2} \times 200} [40(200 - 40)]^{\frac{1}{2}}$$
$$= 0.00\,233 \times \sqrt{6400} = 0.186 \, \text{mm}$$

Example 8.9
   A carbide face mill has inserted teeth to provide radial rake $-12°$, axial rake $+5°$, and corner angle 45°. Find the angle of inclination of the cutting edge and the approximate values of the normal and the effective rake angles.

Solution
   By Eqn (8.9),

$$\tan \lambda = \cos \phi \tan \gamma_a - \sin \phi \tan \gamma_r$$
$$= \cos 45° \tan 5° - \sin 45° \tan(-12°)$$
$$= (0.7071 \times 0.0875) + (0.7071 \times 0.2126)$$
$$= 0.0619 + 0.1503 = 0.2122$$
$$\lambda = +12°$$

Approx value of normal rake angle (see 8.8),

$$\tan \gamma = \tan \gamma_r \cos \phi + \tan \gamma_a \sin \phi$$
$$\tan \gamma = \tan \gamma_r \cos \phi + \tan \gamma_a \sin \phi$$
$$= \tan(-12°) \cos 45° + \tan 5° \sin 45°$$
$$= (-0.2126 \times 0.7071) + (0.0875 \times 0.7071)$$
$$= -0.1503 + 0.0619 = -0.0884$$
$$\gamma = -5° \, \text{approx}$$

$$\sin \gamma_t = \sin^2 12° + \cos^2 12° \sin(-5°) \quad \text{(by Eqn (8.7))}$$
$$\gamma_t = -2 \cdot 3°$$

EXERCISES 8

1. Compare up-cut and down-cut milling processes with particular reference to chip formation and forces induced in component and cutter.

2. Illustrate the tooth path relative to the work for up-cut milling, and show:

(a) increase of the chip thickness t as the cut progresses;
(b) decrease of effective clearance angle as t increases.

A 100 mm dia side and face cutter has 10 teeth and cuts at 24 m/min, table feed 80 mm/min. If the depth of cut is 4 mm, find the maximum chip thickness.

3. Show for down-cut milling that the tooth path across the workpiece is a trochoid.

A 180 mm dia side-and-face cutter has 14 teeth; it is used at a spindle speed of 48 rev/min and table feed of 70 mm/min, to produce a slot 32 mm deep.

Find the length, and maximum thickness, of an undeformed chip. On what assumption are such values calculated?

4. Discuss the relationships between the number of teeth in the cutter, the cutting depth and the spiral angle of the teeth, which together determine the smoothness of the arbor torque when using a slab mill.

A slab mill has a radial rake of 5° and a spiral angle of 50°. Determine the effective rake angle.

5. Show that the power required to drive a milling cutter depends upon the mean chip thickness, the mean specific cutting pressure for the material cut, the angle of engagement between the cutter and the workpiece, the width of cut and the table feed.

If the cutting speed only is increased, what are the likely effects upon the forces and power required for cutting?

6. Illustrate by means of sketches:

(a) the direction of chip flow;
(b) the effective rake angle;
(c) how the magnitude direction and sense of the force acting on the tool may be measured for the following cutters—

(i) a side turning tool;
(ii) a cylindrical milling cutter 80 mm dia, 100 mm long, with cutting edges set at an angle of 20° to the axis of the cutter.

7. Two surfaces are to be milled (about 2 mm metal removal) at production rates.

(a) Steel forging, surface 40 mm × 70 mm
(b) Grey iron casting, surface 400 mm × 600 mm

Specify the method of milling and type of cutter you would use in each instance. Give brief reasons for your choice.

A face milling operation employs a 150 mm dia cutter having 5 inserted carbide teeth. The surface machined is 115 mm × 380 mm. Illustrate the positioning of the cutter for an angle of entry of 35°. Estimate a cutting time/piece given cutting speed = 180 m/min, feed = 0·25 mm/tooth. Sketch a suitable profile for the cutter teeth.

8. Explain, with reference to chip formation, why the power consumed per unit volume per min of metal removed is lower for face milling than for peripheral milling. (An analytical treatment is expected.)

Given the specific cutting pressure as 3100N/mm^2, estimate the max load/tooth for a slotting cutter 90 mm dia, of 12 teeth and 10 mm width, cutting a slot 8 mm deep at a speed of 24 m/min and table feed of 10 mm/min.

9. A 180 mm dia face mill is to cut steel of 350 HB. A cut of 5 mm depth across a slab 95 mm in width is to be taken at a cutting speed of 76 m/min. If the

feed/tooth is not to be less than 0·2 mm, and the power of the machine is limited to 7·5 kW at the cutter, find the maximum number of teeth which could be safely employed. (Use Table 8.2).

10. Discuss, with the aid of diagrams, the following aspects of the milling process.

(*a*) The reason why carbide-tooth slotting cutters are generally used with the down-cut milling technique.

(*b*) The reason why a slab mill should be mounted so that end thrust of the arbor is towards the spindle nose.

(*c*) The reason why the corner edges of an inserted tooth carbide mill are arranged to cut under oblique rather than under orthogonal conditions.

11. A face mill has inserted carbide teeth of axial rake 6° and radial rake–10°. The corner angle (ϕ) is 50°. In relation to impact at tooth entry, explain the advantage of the negative radial rake.

Find the angle of inclination of the cutting edge and the orthogonal rake angle γ_o. Show that γ_o is only slightly less than the normal rake angle γ_n. (see Fig 5.3).

Find the effective rake angle (γ_t) for these conditions.

CHAPTER 9
Principles of Metal Cutting—Grinding

9.1 Introductory Remarks

Grinding is used to improve geometric and dimensional accuracy and to improve surface finish. Under precision grinding conditions dimensional accuracy of 0.002 mm and surface finish of 0.05 μm R_a value can be achieved.

The process has a geometry of chip formation similar to that of milling. The grit edges which project from the surfaces of the wheel act as very small cutting teeth. When cutting on the periphery of the wheel, Fig 9.1, chip formation occurs under similar geometrical conditions to up-cut or down-cut milling, depending upon the direction of work speed relative to the direction of wheel rotation. When grinding on the face of the wheel, Fig 9.2, the geometrical conditions are similar to face milling.

Fig. 9.1 Surface grinding on wheel periphery

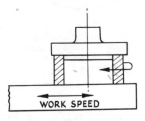

Fig. 9.2 Surface grinding on wheel face

The principal differences between the cutting action of grinding, and of milling, lie in the following:

(i) grinding grits are sufficiently hard to cut fully hardened steels of the order of 850 HV;

(ii) the cutting angles of the grits have a random geometry;

(iii) the pitch of the grit cutting edges is much smaller than the pitch of milling-cutter teeth;

(iv) the size of the chips cut is very small for grinding as compared with milling.

263

Any serious study of the grinding process is helped by examination of wheel structure, and of grinding swarf, under a low-power microscope. If a measuring microscope is available the approximate sizes of the grits, and of the chips cut, can be determined. A wide strip of transparent adhesive tape, wrapped sticky side outward round a steel rule and then held in the stream of sparks produced by grinding, may be used to collect a representative sample of the chips.

Figs 9.3 and 9.4, based upon microscopic examination of grinding swarf, show the form of the chip produced when surface grinding on a horizontal-spindle machine as compared with the longer chip formed when grinding on a vertical-spindle machine. The small spheres are chips that have coiled up and fused together.

Fig. 9.3 Grinding chips × 30 magnifications, surface grinding mild steel on wheel periphery, wheel—A 46 L 4 V

Fig. 9.4 Grinding chips × 30 magnifications, surface grinding mild steel on wheel face, wheel —A 36 G 10 V

9.2 Composition of Grinding Wheels

Fig 9.5 illustrates grinding grits cemented together by means of a bond material to make an abrasive wheel.

General information regarding standard methods of wheel specification is widely available, see BS 4481. The following points should be noted.

Abrasive Material

(a) Silicon carbide (SiC), specification 'C'. Hardness on Moh's scale 9·5 (diamond = 10). A rather brittle grit which tends to fracture under the forces which occur when grinding steels.

(b) Aluminimum oxide (Al_2O_3), specification 'A'. Hardness on Moh's scale 9. Tougher than silicon carbide and for this reason used to grind steel.

Grit Size

Artificially produced abrasive is crushed to produced sharp-edged grits which are graded for size by sieving. A 46 grit indicates that the abrasive particles will just pass through a sieve having 46 openings per inch (25·4 mm) in either direction.

Bond Material

rubber bonds — off hand grinders.
disc flexibility

Vitrified clay, specification 'V', is the material used to cement the grits of wheels employed for most precision grinding operations. A thin cut-off wheel, or a wheel subjected to shock loads or side forces as in fettling operations, requires a less brittle bond material. Bonds such as rubber or synthetic resin are then employed to reduce the chance of wheel fracture under the operating loads.

Bond Strength (Grade)

The amount of bond material surrounding the grits largely determines the force required to break a grit from the wheel, a property indicated by term **grade**. Grade is specified by letter symbol.

Soft —————————→ **Medium** —————————→ **Hard**

E F G H I J K L M N O P Q R S T U V W

The workshop terms, **soft** and **hard**, are used to indicate that a relatively small or large force is required to break a grit from the wheel.

Structure

This describes the relative spacing of the grits, e.g. closely packed together or a more "open" arrangement. For the same size of grit the pitch of the grits round the circumference of the wheel is greater for "open" than for "close" structure. The structure symbol is a number.

dense **Close** —————————→ **Open**

Structure Symbol 1   2   3   4   5 . . . 9   10   11   12

Fig 9.5 draws attention to open spaces in the bond of the wheel (**voids**). As the structure is made more open the voids tend to increase in number and size. The cutting life of an open-structure wheel is less than that of a close-structure wheel of the same dimensions, because there are less grits to become worn and be discarded. The increased pitch of the grits improves chip clearance. For certain grinding applications the heating effects of cutting are reduced by the employment of open-structure wheels.

Porosity

This term does not enter into the standard specification of a wheel but is used to indicate the combined effect of grit-size and structure. When the grits are large or the structure "open", the space between adjacent grits exposed at the wheel face into which a chip can recede during the passage of the grits over the work material, will be larger than when the

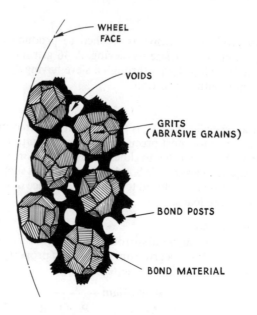

Fig. 9.5 *Composition of an abrasive wheel*

grits are small or the structure "close". The higher the porosity, the greater the chip clearance space between the grits and the more freely will coolant penetrate the wheel. It is sometimes arranged for coolant to enter a porous wheel at the central mounting, and be expelled by centrifugal force at the periphery. Such application of the coolant effectively dislodges swarf from between the cutting grits.

9.3 Force and Power in Grinding

very high in grinding

Cutting speeds for grinding are always high, the upper limit being imposed either by the safe centrifugal stresses of the wheel or by the upper limit of rotational speed of the spindle employed. Vitrified wheels may be used up to about 1800 m/min; elastic bonds may be used at much higher speeds, up to 4800 m/min for abrasive cut-off wheels. For the internal grinding of small bores cutting speeds may not exceed 760 m/min due to the speed limitations of belt drives and bearings. A 10 mm diameter wheel must rotate at approximately 25 000 rev/min to achieve this cutting speed. Bearings which operate up to speeds of 100 000 rev/min have been developed, but the bearing loads must be very light and special driving arrangements are necessary; compressed air-turbine drives achieve this.

Cutting forces in grinding are difficult to measure and at present it is possible only to estimate the forces which act on the individual grits. The same basic mechanics may be applied to the grinding process as are applied to single point cutting. Using the symbols of **6.2**, the force acting on a grit in the direction of its velocity is given by:

$$T = P \times \text{Cut area}$$

It is difficult to obtain accurate values of the cutting force on a grit, or of the cross-sectional area of the chip cut. The sections of the grooves cut by individual grits will vary in shape due to the random geometry of the grits, and any attempt to find the value of the maximum chip thickness, and hence the maximum force on a grit, is necessarily approximate.

The following expression for chip thickness when surface grinding has been derived (Backer *et al.* 1952):

$$\text{chip thickness } (t) = \left[\frac{4v}{VCr} \sqrt{\frac{d}{D}} \right]^{\frac{1}{2}}$$

where v = work speed, m/min.
V = cutting speed, m/min;
C = the number of effective grits per mm^2 of grinding wheel surface;
r = ratio of width to depth of a groove cut by a grit;
d = depth of cut, mm;
D = wheel diameter, mm;
C is measured by rolling the grinding wheel on a piece of smoked glass and counting, under a microscope, the marks left where grit points pierce the smoke film;
r is measured by taper sectioning of the ground workpiece so that the ratios of width to depth of the grooves cut by the grits can be estimated with reasonable accuracy.

It is possible to verify this expression for chip thickness as follows.

Consider a section through a grinding wheel in a plane normal to the axis of rotation, in which grits are imagined to lie with points projecting as indicated, Fig 9.6, spaced $1/N$ mm apart, where N is the number of

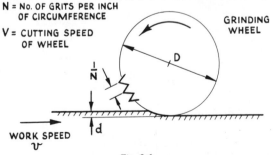

N = No. OF GRITS PER INCH
OF CIRCUMFERENCE

V = CUTTING SPEED
OF WHEEL

GRINDING
WHEEL

D

$\frac{1}{N}$

WORK SPEED
v

d

Fig. 9.6

grits per mm of the section circumference. By analogy with milling, Eqn (8.4), the maximum chip thickness is given by, $t = 2f_g \sqrt{(d/D)}$, where f_g is the feed of the work per grit and t a uniform thickness across the full width of cut. It can be shown very simply that f_g is given by v/NV, so that for surface grinding,

$$t = \frac{2v}{NV}\sqrt{\frac{d}{D}} \tag{9.1}$$

Consider the area of metal removed across a wheel of face width s at the position of maximum chip thickness.

$$\text{Area removed} = \frac{2vs}{NV}\sqrt{\frac{d}{D}} \tag{1}$$

This area is, in effect, removed by a succession of grits and Fig 9.7 represents a possible condition for the metal removed by a single grit. The area of the cut at maximum chip thickness is $tb/2$.

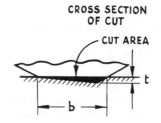

CROSS SECTION OF CUT

Fig. 9.7 Typical cross-section cut by a grit

Although the grits have a random geometry there are laboratory methods which enable the average ratio (r) of width b to depth t of the cut to be estimated from a grinding test.

By substitution of $b = tr$ the cut area shown in Fig 9.7 becomes $t^2r/2$.

The total area of metal removed across the wheel face depends upon N and s; the total area removed is therefore

$$\frac{Nst^2r}{2}. \tag{2}$$

Equating (1) and (2),

$$t^2 = \frac{4v}{N^2Vr}\sqrt{\frac{d}{D}}$$

but $N^2 = C$, by definition;

hence

$$t = \left[\frac{4v}{VCr}\sqrt{\frac{d}{D}}\right]^{\frac{1}{2}} \tag{9.2}$$

This expression is the same as that derived by analogy with micro-milling by Backer, Marshall and Shaw (see bibliography).

Example 9.1
The following conditions relate to a surface grinding operation carried out with a 46-grit wheel:

$$V = 1700 \text{ m/min}, \quad v = 9 \text{ m/min}, \quad C = 2\cdot95,$$
$$r = 17, \quad d = 0\cdot025 \text{ mm} \quad D = 200 \text{ mm},$$

estimate the maximum chip thickness.

Solution
$$t = \left[\frac{4 \times 9}{1700 \times 2\cdot95 \times 17} \times \sqrt{\frac{0\cdot025}{200}} \right]^{\frac{1}{2}}$$
$$= [0\cdot000422 \times 0\cdot0112]^{\frac{1}{2}}$$
$$= 0\cdot0022 \text{ mm}$$

The result clearly indicates the very small magnitude of the chip thickness which occurs when grinding. The depth of cut specified is about 10 times that used for finishing cuts on precision work, hence values much lower than the one determined can be expected for such operations. The very low value of chip thickness then occurring is obviously related to the high quality of surface finish produced by precision grinding operations.

The following data relating to the magnitude of forces and power which occur when precision grinding, has been extracted from a research paper by Grisbrook (1960):

Cutting speed 525 m/min
Work speed 10·98 m/min
Width of cut 12·7 mm
Depth of cut 0·0076 mm
Material cut, hardened steel of 800 HV
Wheel, **WA 46 JV**

Grisbrook developed a dynamometer for measuring the horizontal and vertical forces acting on the workpiece during a surface grinding operation. For the conditions quoted, the tangential force at the wheel was 62·3 N approx, varying slightly with the amount of grinding done since the previous dressing of the wheel.

From estimates of the area of contact between wheel and work, and from values of C for **46** wheel, it is probable that some 18 or so grits would be cutting at one time and that the **average** tangential force/grit would be about 3·47 N.

It is most unlikely that the force is so evenly distributed. A dull grit will have a higher force than average acting upon it if the normal considerations for single-point tools apply to grinding.

The metal removal rate achieved under the conditions quoted is given by:

$$w = 10.98 \times \frac{10^3}{60} \times 12.7 \times 0.0076 \text{ mm}^3/\text{s}$$

$$= 17.66 \text{ mm}^3/\text{s}$$

$$\text{Power at the wheel} = \frac{1525 \times 62.3}{60} = 1583 \text{ W}$$

$$\text{Power criterion} = \frac{1583}{17.66} = 89.7 \text{ W/mm}^3/\text{s}$$

This is a strikingly high value compared with the values for cutting with single-point tools, or for milling operations, on steels. It is shown in Grisbrook's paper that the value is almost as high for unhardened steel of 200 HV. For precision grinding of steel the power criterion watts/w does not appear to depend much on the hardness value of the material cut.

Some research workers tend to express the above relationship in terms of specific energy; i.e. the energy required to remove one mm^3 of metal, denoted by $U_s \left[\dfrac{\text{Work done}}{\text{Volume}} \right]$. The units of U_s are $\dfrac{\text{Nm}}{\text{mm}^3} = \text{J/mm}^3$ 89.7 W/mm^3/s converted to specific energy units as follows:

$$U_s = 89.7 \text{ J/mm}^3$$

Grisbrook was able to show that the value of U_s falls as the metal removal rate (w) is increased by an increase in work speed or in depth of cut, i.e. chip thickness (t) increasing. This fact should be compared with the observed fall of specific cutting pressure (P) with increase of chip thickness known to occur for single-point cutting.

A fall in the value of U_s as the metal removal rate is increased means that the power requirements for grinding at heavy metal removal rates will be lower than the 89.7 W/mm^3/s determined above, and an average figure of 30 W/mm^3/s is about right for steels. The size of motor provided on a modern grinding machine reflects the high power requirement of the grinding process. One theory put forward to explain the rise in U_s which accompanies a fall in chip thickness is that the tangential force on the wheel contains a fairly large element of friction due to the rubbing of grits on the workpiece. The frictional element does not fall as the chip thickness is reduced, hence the energy consumed in removing a unit volume of metal rises.

Heating Effects during Grinding. The high value of U_s is an indication of the large amount of heat generated relative to the amount of material removed.

For the example considered on p. 000 about 90 J of heat are produced per mm³ of metal removed.

If 20% of this heat were to go into the metal removed, which, being steel, weighs 7740 kg/m³ and has an average specific heat of around 0·2 over a temperature range up to melting point, the resulting temperature rise would be 2760 deg C.

Specific heat capacity, steel at high temperature, is about $4200 \times 0·2 = 840$ J/kg/°C

$$\text{Temp. rise} = \frac{90 \times 0·2 \times 10^9}{840 \times 7740} = 2760 \text{ deg C.}$$

Since steel melts at about 1530°C it is obvious that only a fraction of the heat produced enters the chip. It is also known that melting is a time-temperature effect; microscopic examination of grinding swarf shows that melting does not occur to the extent which the above figures appear to suggest, and the short duration of the heating is probably one reason for this. The presence of grinding sparks and of some heat-fused globules among the grinding swarf is evidence of the very high temperature reached by the chips. The harder the metal cut, the greater the number of globules to be found in the swarf.

Independent attempts to measure the temperature of the work at the point of contact with the grinding wheel confirm that instantaneous values of the order of 1050–1650 °C are reached.

9.4 Dressing and Trueing of Grinding Wheels

Dressing. This is a process used to clear the cutting surface of the wheel of any dull grits and embedded swarf in order to improve the cutting action. It may be done by means of a star-wheel dresser, by wheel crushing, or by means of a carborundum dressing stick.

Trueing. In this process a diamond is employed to bring the wheel to the required geometric shape, e.g. a true cylinder or a cylinder having a screw-thread form in an axial plane. It also restores the cutting action of a worn wheel as in dressing. The distinction between trueing and dressing is sometimes hard to draw; e.g. a wheel can be brought to the required "form" by crushing.

The processes are effected by:

    (i) dislodging whole grits from the bond;
    (ii) chipping the edges of the grits.

There is some difference in the manner of the achievement of (ii) as between diamond trueing and crush dressing. Abrasive grit, being crystalline, tends to frature along the most highly stressed crystallographic plane.

Diamond trueing tends to chip the grits along planes which make a small angle with respect to the direction of motion of the grit. Crush dressing may cause shear fractures along planes which make a large angle with respect to the direction of motion of the grit. As may be seen in Figs 9.8 and 9.9, crushed grit is likely to have more favourable cutting angles (greater clearance angles, lower negative rake angles) than diamond-trued grit.

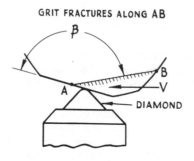

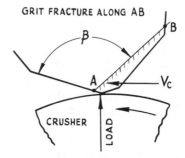

Fig. 9.8 Diamond dressing of
grinding wheel

Fig. 9.9 Crush dressing of
grinding wheel

Crush dressing tends to remove whole grits by fracture of the bond posts, especially in open-structure wheels where the "voids" provide space for the collapse of grits, and it also tends to provide sharp cutting edges on any fractured grits. A crush-dressed vitrified wheel will have free-cutting properties but will not produce a surface finish on the work equal to that of the same wheel when diamond trued.

Diamond trueing at large depths of cut tends to remove whole grits; if the wheel is finished by taking several passes, each with an infeed of about 0·005 mm, followed by several passes with no additional feed, the trued surface will have its grit edges chipped away to give a very "smooth" wheel which can then be used to obtain a fine surface finish on the work. The use of a somewhat rounded diamond for the final dressing of the wheel tends to result in a good finish on the work. Any heavy cuts taken with such a wheel will break down the fine surface of the grits (self-sharpening action), improve the cutting property and reduce the quality of the surface finish obtained.

Practical Examples of Dressing and Trueing. Fig 9.10 illustrates a type of radius dresser used for precision toolroom work. Concave and convex curves may be dressed to various radii by adjustment of the lower slide (A). This slide can be controlled to swing through a predetermined angle by means of stops; slide (B) may then be brought into operation in order to dress a flank tangential to the radius as illustrated.

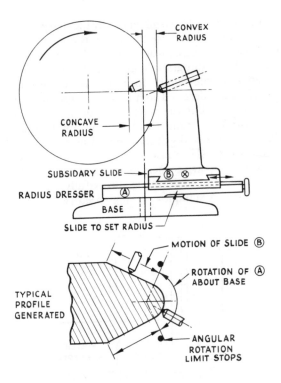

Fig. 9.10 Radius dresser for precision wheel trueing

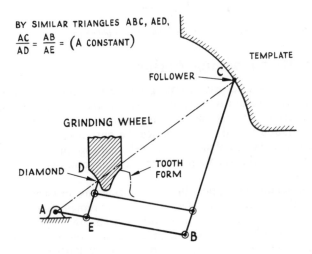

Fig. 9.11 Pantograph method of wheel trueing as used on gear-grinding machine

The accuracy of the work is influenced by the sharpness of the point of the diamond employed because the action is a **generating** one.

Fig 9.11 shows a pantograph device as used to dress formed wheels for gear grinding. The pantograph copies the template profile on to the wheel at a reduced scale. Similar form-dressing devices are available on toolroom surface grinders and are particularly useful in small press-tool manufacture for grinding the profiles of punches and segmental dies.

Fig 9.12 illustrates a form-crushing operation. Consideration of the various diameters involved will show that some relative sliding between the wheel and the crusher must occur and so cause crusher wear. It is difficult to maintain sharp corners of profiles by the crushing technique. Crushing of screw-thread forms is successfully employed on thread-grinding machines. A suitable crushing speed (V_c) is 25–30 m/min.

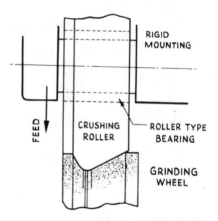

Fig. 9.12 Form-crushing of a grinding wheel

9.5 Self-sharpening Action

The cutting life of a grit operating on steel, or on a similarly tough material, is comparatively short. Dressing the wheel each time the exposed grits had lost their cutting efficiency would be very time consuming and would greatly reduce the output from grinding operations. If a suitable balance between the cutting forces and the bond strength of the wheel is obtained, the need for continual redressing can be avoided.

It is reasonable to suppose that the forces acting on a grit will increase as the cutting edge deteriorates, other factors remaining constant. This may be seen to occur during cutting tests on single-point tools. Gisbrook's work shows that increased cutting forces occur in surface grinding operations as the run proceeds. A particular set of the conditions investigated gave the following results:

(Newly dressed wheel)	T	F_N
Commencement of run	22·25 N	44·5 N
After 12·2 m of traverse	44·5 N	155·75 N

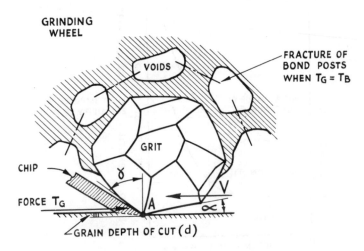

Fig. 9.13 *The cutting action of an abrasive grit*

T_B represents the limit of T_G imposed by the bond strength.

T and F_N, shown in Fig 9.14, are the components of forces acting on all the grits in contact with the workpiece. As these forces are seen to increase during cutting, increases in the force/grit must occur and the force/grit will rise for each particular grit as it gets duller. If the stress set up in the bond material by the cutting force is sufficient to fracture the bond posts (Fig 9.13, T_G reaching the limiting value T_B) the dull grit will be

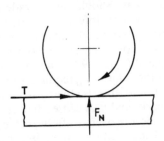

Fig. 9.14 *Components of grinding forces*

broken from the wheel and adjacent new sharp grits exposed for cutting. There will be a gradual loss of wheel diameter, and a continual replacement at the wheel cutting surface of dull grits by sharp grits. This is commonly called **self-sharpening action**.

An idealised concept of this action is represented in Fig 9.15.

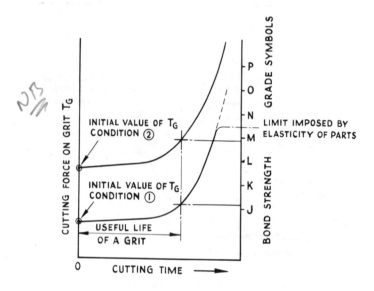

Fig. 9.15 Graphical representation of self-sharpening action

Suppose the point T_G (1) represents the force on a grit newly exposed to cutting. As cutting proceeds there will be a progressive fall in the cutting efficiency of the grit and a consequent rise in force T_G. If a J grade wheel is employed, T_G will reach the limit imposed by the bond strength of the wheel somewhere near the end of the useful cutting life of the grit. At this point the grit will break from the wheel.

If, however, an L grade wheel is used, T_G will rise considerably higher before the grit breaks away. Should an N grade wheel be used, even higher values of T_G must occur before the grit is fractured from the wheel, but now there is a further possibility. Due to the elastic nature of the wheel, wheel spindle, workpiece, etc., the presence of dull grits will give rise to a very high value of F_N (Fig 9.14) and the wheel may deflect away from the work so that the value of T_G required to release the grit cannot be reached. Such conditions give rise to excessive heating of the surface ground, cause burn marks and may cause small cracks in the surface of the metal which can be discovered afterwards by the use of crack-detection techniques. The condition is sometimes called "glazing" due to the glossy polished surface of the wheel which results.

When it is not a simple matter to change the wheel grade, e.g. on machines employing large and heavy wheels, the conditions of grinding can be adjusted so that the initial force is raised, as (2) in Fig 9.15, or if necessary lowered. In this way a correct self-sharpening action can be achieved provided the grade of wheel is not grossly out of relationship to the grinding conditions.

$t = \frac{2v}{NV}\sqrt{\frac{d}{D}}$

Influence of the Variables of the Grinding Process upon the Cutting Force per Grit. Reference to Fig 9.6 and Eqn (9.1) shows that the expression

t = chip thickness
V : cutting speed

$$t = \frac{2v}{NV}\sqrt{\frac{d}{D_G}}$$

v = speed of work
N = no. of grain per mm.
of circumference
d = depth of cut

relates to the chip thickness cut when surface grinding. Symbol D_G has been substituted for D in order to distinguish between the wheel diameter and the work diameter (D_W) of cylindrical grinding. Since for similar figures, the ratio of the areas equals the square of the ratio of one of the linear dimensions, the area cut by a grit is proportional to t^2:

force on grit

$$T_G = P \times \text{cut area}$$

and assuming that the specific cutting pressure (P) remains constant,

$$T_G \propto t^2 \propto \frac{v^2}{N^2V^2} \times \frac{d}{D_G}.$$

D_G and N can be varied only by changing the wheel. V is not normally a variable except due to wheel wear. (Some grinding machines provide for increase of the wheel spindle speed to compensate for reduction of diameter as the wheel wears to keep V reasonably uniform.) The only variables which can be used to change the force/grit are work speed (v) and the depth of cut (d); of these v is seen from the above to be the more effective. J. J. Guest deduced this by a study of the geometry of chip formation during grinding.

If the more refined expression for chip thickness of Eqn (9.2) is employed we have

$$T_G \propto \frac{v}{V}\sqrt{\frac{d}{D_G}}$$

which again shows v to be a more effective variable than d in changing the cutting force on a grit.

Most modern grinding machines have a large range of work speeds; some have infinite variation of work speed throughout the range, generally by hydraulic means. The part played by v as a variable in obtaining self-sharpening conditions can then be fully exploited in selecting the grinding conditions.

essentially $T \propto V$

9.6 Geometry of Contact between Wheel and Work—External Cylindrical Grinding

Apart from the significance of v and d discussed above, the force/grit will depend upon the work diameter (D_W) and the traverse rate.

Guest showed that for external grinding, force/grit varies as

$$v^2 d \left[\frac{1}{D_W} + \frac{1}{D_G} \right],$$

hence the smaller the work diameter or the wheel diameter, the higher the force/grit.

The same result as is obtained by Guest's theory can be derived from the geometry of the chip shape shown in Fig 9.16. To an exaggerated scale KLMN is the chip cut by a grit, and the maximum area will occur across LN, where the thickness is maximum.

By ignoring the very small amounts of curvature which occur, KLN may be treated as a right-angled triangle, the right angle at L. KN is the distance moved by the workpiece during the period between the passage

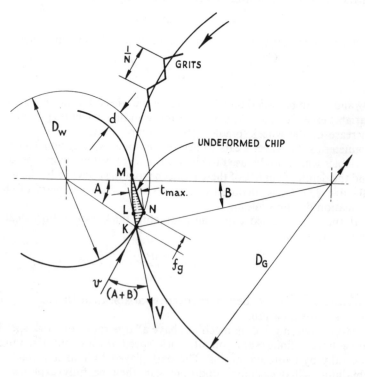

Fig. 9.16 Geometry of chip formation for cylindrical grinding

of successive grits, i.e. the feed per grit represented by f_g. It can be seen that

$$t_{max} = f_g \sin (A + B) \text{ to a high order of accuracy.} \qquad (1)$$

Fig 9.17 shows the geometrical relationships between D_W, D_G and the depth of cut d.

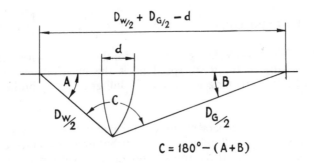

$$C = 180° - (A + B)$$

Fig. 9.17

Consider the triangle in Fig 9.17. By the cosine rule,

$$\left(\frac{D_W}{2} + \frac{D_G}{2} - d\right)^2 = \left(\frac{D_W}{2}\right)^2 + \left(\frac{D_G}{2}\right)^2 - 2\frac{D_W}{2}\frac{D_G}{2} \cos[180° - (A+B)]$$

Since d is very small, terms involving d^2 are negligible and omitted from the expansion below. Hence

$$\frac{D_W D_G}{2} \cos(A + B) = \frac{D_W D_G}{2} - dD_W - dD_G$$

$$\text{or } \cos(A + B) = 1 - 2d\left(\frac{D_W + D_G}{D_W D_G}\right).$$

$$1 - \sin^2(A + B) = \cos^2(A + B) = 1 - 4d\left(\frac{D_W + D_G}{D_W D_G}\right) + \text{terms} \quad \text{contain-}$$

ing d^2.

Hence $\sin^2(A + B) \simeq 4d\left(\frac{D_W + D_G}{D_W D_G}\right)$

$$\text{or } \sin(A + B) \simeq 2\left[d\left(\frac{1}{D_W} + \frac{1}{D_G}\right)\right]^{\frac{1}{2}}.$$

Feed per grit, $f_g = v/NV$, and by substitution of these results in Eqn (1) we have

$$t = \frac{2v}{NV}\sqrt{\left(d\frac{D_W + D_G}{D_W D_G}\right)}.$$

This is the form generally stated for the result of Guest's theory, but it may also be written as;

$$t = \frac{2v}{NV}\sqrt{\left[d\left(\frac{1}{D_W}+\frac{1}{D_G}\right)\right]}.$$

Considering the main variables in external grinding,

$$\text{Force per grit} \propto t^2 \quad \text{and} \quad t^2 \propto \frac{v^2d}{V^2}\left(\frac{1}{D_W}+\frac{1}{D_G}\right),$$

the pitch of the grits (N) being a constant for the grade of wheel selected. Clearly, raising of the work speed (v) is the most effective way of increasing self-sharpening action should dull grits not be broken from the bond.

Fig 9.18 shows the general conditions for external cylindrical grinding.
The traverse rate will influence the distribution of the cutting across the face of the wheel. If the traverse/rev of work (p) just exceeds $b/2$, where b is the width of the wheel, and cutting takes place in both

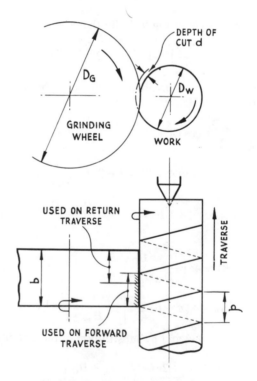

Fig. 9.18 Conditions for external grinding

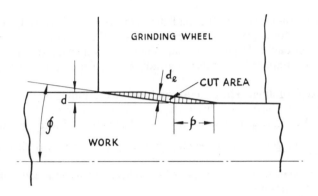

Fig. 9.19 *Effect of taper lead on cutting conditions*

directions of table reciprocation, wear is evenly distributed across the wheel. If $p < b/2$ a "taper lead" will be produced by wheel wear, Fig 9.19. The effective cutting depth d_e is now smaller than the infeed. The traverse rate now influences the chip thickness; the effective cutting depth is given by $d_e = p \sin \phi$ and there is a lower force/grit.

Internal Cylindrical Grinding. The conditions are shown in Fig 9.20. The force/grit varies as

$$\frac{v^2 d}{V^2}\left(\frac{1}{D_W} - \frac{1}{D_G}\right) \qquad \leftarrow \text{incorrect.}$$

and is much lower for internal than for external grinding for the same cutting speed (V). For internal grinding V is often much smaller than for

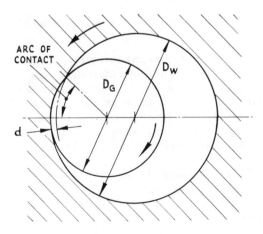

Fig. 9.20 *Arc of wheel contact, internal grinding*

external grinding due to the small diameters of wheel involved, see 9.3: as V falls the force/grit rises. Note that the arc of contact increases rapidly as D_G approaches D_w in magnitude. Generally somewhat softer grades of wheel are required for internal grinding than for external grinding.

Surface Grinding. The general conditions for grinding on the periphery of the wheel have been discussed (p. 280). Grinding on the face of the wheel, Fig 9.21, gives rise to much smaller values of force/grit due to:

(i) the geometry of the chip produced (compare with face milling 8.7);

(ii) taper wear at the edges of the wheel which reduces the effective cutting depth.

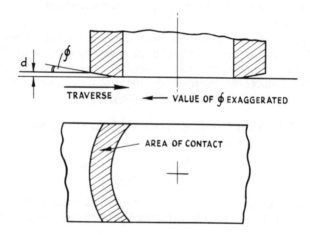

Fig. 9.21 Contact between wheel and work, surface grinding on wheel face

The cylinder wheels employed on a vertical spindle grinder need to be of a soft grade (G), large grit (36) and open structure (8 or 10); the two latter requirements help to provide chip clearance and also reduce the number of grits in contact with the work, thus increasing the force/grit. When a hard wheel has to be employed, e.g. to maintain a corner in slideway grinding, a saucer wheel having a thin edge is necessary in order to distribute the cutting load on fewer grits, Fig 9.22.

Cylindrical Work—Grinding of Shoulders. The wheel head of some cylindrical grinding machines may be swivelled so that the spindle axis is inclined to the work axis as shown in Fig 9.23. A section in plane AB shows that the contact between the shoulder of the workpiece and the wheel is similar to that of a surface grinding operation where the wheel periphery is used. Ideally the same force/grit is desired when grinding the

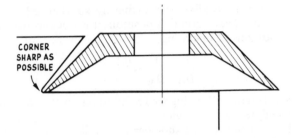

Fig. 9.22 Use of "saucer" wheel to reduce contact area

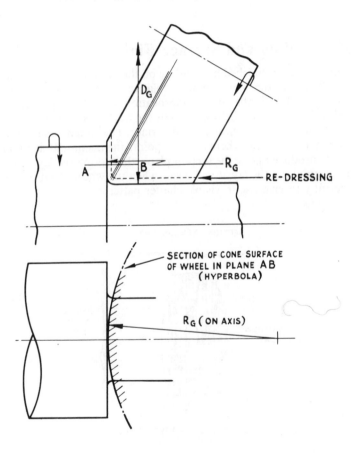

Fig. 9.23 Grinding of shoulders of cylindrical work by angular setting of wheel head

shoulder as when grinding the diameter, so that self-sharpening conditions occur at each grinding position. It is obvious that for most practical conditions of operating

$$\frac{1}{D_G} + \frac{1}{D_W} > \frac{1}{2R_G},$$

hence the force/grit will be higher for grinding on the work diameter than for grinding on the shoulder.

Excessive "glazing" at the shoulder is less likely to occur for these conditions than when "full contact" at the shoulder is made by using the wheel with its axis parallel to the work axis. A very important saving is made in wheel dressing, because both surfaces can be redressed continually without loss of the face width of the wheel as indicated in Fig 9.23.

need over.

9.7 Grinding and Surface Finish

When a surface is finished by grinding on the periphery of the wheel the **lay** will follow the work velocity relative to the wheel; for surface grinding it will be in the line of reciprocation of the table, for cylindrical grinding it will follow a helix defined by the work speed and traverse rate. Fig 9.24 illustrates a typical ground surface. The roughness is generally greater across the lay, where at some points the maximum depth of the grooves produced lie in the section plane, than along the lay. Waviness may occur along the lay; it will occur when the wheel is out of balance sufficiently to give rise to visible chatter patterns.

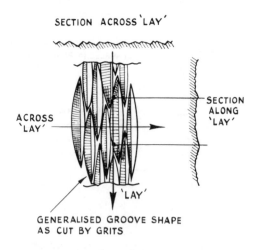

SECTION ACROSS 'LAY'

ACROSS 'LAY'

SECTION ALONG 'LAY'

'LAY'

GENERALISED GROOVE SHAPE AS CUT BY GRITS

Fig. 9.24 Surface characteristics producing by grinding

Example 9.1 shows that when surface grinding with a 46 grit wheel, depth of cut 0·025 mm, the chip thickness is 0·0022 mm. The maximum depths of the grooves cut in the work must be of this order, so that a peak-to-valley average reading of the surface finish across the lay will not exceed this value. Experience shows that for grinding, the surface finish average number (R_a) is between $\frac{1}{3}$ and $\frac{1}{5}$ of the peak-to-valley average number, and for the conditions of Example 9.1 a surface finish of between 0·8 μm and 0·4 μm is to be expected. Since the depth of the grooves cut will depend upon the value of t, where

$$ t = \left[\frac{4v}{VCr} \sqrt{\frac{d}{D}} \right]^{\frac{1}{2}} $$

it can be seen that a low work speed and small depth of cut will tend to improve the finish, as also will a smaller grit size (for which C is relatively higher). This supposes a perfectly true wheel spinning about a perfectly constant axis, conditions which are never exactly satisfied in practice. The necessity of high-quality bearings to achieve high surface finish is obvious, and there is a limit set by the condition of the bearings to the improvements in finish which can be obtained by a reduction of the grit size, of the depth of cut or of the work speed (see p. 88).

It is of interest to examine the relationship between the out-of-balance forces acting on the wheel bearings and the surface-finish defects which may arise. Suppose a grinding wheel, rotating at 1200 rev/min, is out of balance by 35 g acting at 200 mm radius.

$$ \text{Centrifugal force} = M\omega^2 r $$

$$ \omega = \frac{1200}{60} \times 2\pi = 40\pi \text{ rad/s} $$

$$ \text{Centrifugal force} = \frac{35}{10^3} \times \frac{200}{10^3} \times (40\pi)^2 = 110 \text{ N}. $$

The centrifugal force gives rise to a force acting in a plane through the wheel and work axes. This force has a maximum value of 110 N and is reversed in direction at each $\frac{1}{2}$ revolution of the wheel. It would require a very stiff machine structure to prevent some very small decrease and increase in the mean distance between the axes under such conditions. Fig 9.25 illustrates the resulting chatter pattern. This may show up more distinctly when the ground diameter has been caused to slide in a close-fitting hole. The pitch of the markings is given by $q = \dfrac{\pi v D_G}{V}$ mm, and will be much smaller when grinding with small-diameter wheels than with large-diameter wheels due to the higher spindle speed.

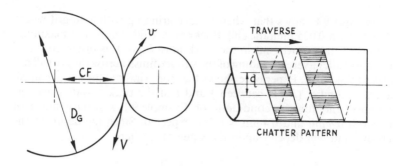

Fig. 9.25 "Chatter" pattern resulting from unbalanced grinding wheel

In general terms, the quality of surface finish which may be obtained from grinding operations is approximately as follows (R_a values).

(*a*) General work of moderate size: 0·8–0·4 μm

(*b*) Precision work of normal standard: 0·4–0·1 μm

(*c*) Fine grinding: below 0·1 μm and under very good conditions below 0·02 μm. It is necessary to have an efficient coolant filter system in order to achieve these very fine finishes.

9.8 Economics of Grinding

(*a*) Grinding has two principal economic advantages over other methods of metal machining for the finishing of surfaces:

(i) due to the large number of very small chips cut it is much easier to work to close tolerances and fine surface finishes;

(ii) due to the high work speed (compared with traverse rates for, say, milling) and to the very large number of cutting edges presented to the work, the time taken to produce a unit area of finished surface is lower than that for other machining processes.

(*b*) Grinding tends to be restricted to finishing processes because the volume of metal to be removed is then relatively small. The main reasons for this are:

(i) the large amount of power consumed per unit volume of metal removed by grinding as compared with alternative methods;

(ii) the relatively high cost of grinding wheels per unit volume of metal removed.

To compete in metal removal with a milling machine having a 7·5 kW motor, a grinding machine would require a 75 kW motor! It is generally uneconomic to remove large amounts of metal by grinding because the machines available lack the power and strength to remove the metal at time rates which compare with milling or turning.

Despite the drawbacks of high power consumption and wheel costs, certain developments in large quantity production techniques have been made in which grinding has replaced face milling. Datum faces may be prepared by such methods on castings and drop stampings, and the rotary table principle can be used to give a continuous output of such pieces. One advantage of such an arrangement is that the cutting tool can be serviced (dressed) on the machine spindle, so that loss of output from this cause is smaller than would arise from milling cutter changes.

EXERCISES 9   *do out.*

Note. See questions 6 and 7 for definitions of the symbols used in these exercises.

1. (*a*) A grinding wheel is specified as A 46 J 8 V. Give the meaning of each symbol and explain the significance of each in relation to the cutting action of a grinding wheel.

(*b*) Explain what is meant by self-sharpening action as applied to the grinding process and describe the various factors which give rise to this.

2. (*a*) Write short notes on the cutting action of a grinding wheel and state the factors affecting wheel selection.

(*b*) Give typical values of peripheral wheel speed for cylindrical, surface and internal grinding, and compare the area of contact of wheel and work for these processes.

3. (*a*) How is the choice of grinding-wheel grade influenced by: (i) the area or arc of contact, and (ii) the nature of the workpiece material?

(*b*) With the aid of a line diagram, explain how, in cylindrical grinding, the workface of the wheel may be preserved flat without recourse to dressing or crushing. Hence, find a suitable traverse rate for a 40 mm wide wheel grinding a 50 mm dia shaft, if the work speed is 18 surface m per min.

4. (*a*) Using diagrams, explain why "crushed" grinding wheels tend to be freer cutting than diamond dressed wheels.← *P. 272*

(*b*) Given Guest's criterion $v^2 t(D + d)/Dd$, explain the effect of a decrease of wheel diameter on cutting efficiency when surface grinding; surface speed of wheel to remain approx constant.

(*c*) What are the advantages of hydraulically operated table drives for reciprocating tables of surface grinding machines, as compared with rack and pinion drives?

5. (*a*) Explain the theory of the cutting action of a grinding wheel and define the characteristics by which the nature and action of a grinding wheel is assessed.

(*b*) Define diagrammatically the geometry of a tool-and-cutter grinding machine and show how it would set to grind a face mill with inserted blades and 250 mm in diameter.

6. Sketch the conditions of chip formation for cylindrical grinding and deduce from these that the maximum chip thickness is given by,

$$\frac{v}{NV} \sin (A + B).$$

first part of proof

Given that

$$\sin (A + B) \simeq 2 \sqrt{\left(t\frac{D + d}{Dd} \right)},$$

where t = depth of cut, D = wheel dia, d = work dia, show that the force acting on a grit is proportional to

$$\frac{v^2}{V^2} t \left[\frac{D+d}{Dd} \right].$$

What bearing has the expression for the force acting on a grit, upon the conditions required for efficient grinding?

7. (a) Derive an approximate expression for the maximum thickness of the chip when a grinding wheel of diameter D is grinding a cylindrical workpiece of diameter d with a depth of cut t, the peripheral speeds of wheel and workpiece being V and v respectively.

(b) Evaluate this maximum chip thickness if $D = 300$ mm, $d = 40$ mm, $t = 0.025$ mm, $V = 1500$ m/min, $v = 18$ m/min and the abrasive grains are 0·8 mm apart.

8. With reference to the grinding process, show how the wheel is prepared for:

    (i) the grinding of an accurate radius;
    (ii) thread grinding using a multi-ribbed wheel;
    (iii) thread grinding using a diamond-trued single-form wheel.

The geometry of the trueing and forming attachments should be given.

9. (a) Explain briefly why the mechanical efficiency of metal cutting by grinding is only about $\frac{1}{10}$ of the mechanical efficiency of metal cutting by turning. How does this fact influence the design of grinding machines?

(b) Why does grinding give surface finishes superior to most other metal-cutting processes?

(c) Compare the economics of the grinding process as a means of finishing cylindrical surfaces to close tolerances, with those of the turning process.

10. (a) Explain briefly why a cylindrical grinding machine should provide for a wide range of work speeds, preferably on an infinitely variable basis.

(b) Explain briefly the significance of Guest's criterion

$$\frac{v^2 t}{V^2} \left[\frac{D \pm d}{Dd} \right]$$

in relation to the grinding process.

(c) When rough grinding steel bars, work speed 12 m/min, depth of cut 0·05 mm, the wheel was found to wear excessively. Use Guest's criterion to show that the operating conditions can be changed to correct this trouble without lowering the production rate. Suggest suitable values for the new cutting conditions.

CHAPTER 10

Principles of Machining— Non-traditional Methods

10.1 Introduction to Non-traditional Machining

In traditional methods of machining, material is removed from the workpiece by means of a tool of superior hardness. However, this concept of a hard tool cutting a softer workpiece cannot be applied to certain machining processes developed in the last few decades.

Known scientific principles have been intensively developed and applied to material removal processes of unconventional nature in manufacturing industry. Chemical, electro-chemical and thermo-electric sources of energy are tapped and used in machining processes which, in certain circumstances, provide either technological or economic advantages over traditional methods. In particular, it is feasible

(i) to machine the "exotic" materials developed for high performance applications in the aerospace industry, e.g. very high-tensile alloy steels and heat resisting alloys; and

TABLE 10.1

Categories of Machining

Fundamental Energy Source	Mechanical		Thermo-Electric		Electro-Chemical
Principles of material removal techniques	Shear	Erosion	Vaporisation		Ion displacement
			(a)	(b)	
Medium employed for removal of material	Cutting Tool	Abrasive particles at high velocity	Electrons— high voltage discharge	Radiation amplified light	High density current— electrolyte
Process	Conventional Machining	Ultrasonic Machining	Electro-discharge Machining	Laser	Electro-chemical Machining

289

(ii) to produce design features which are costly, difficult or even impossible to make by traditional methods.

One very important feature of many of these newer processes is that the hardness of the workpiece material is of no significance from the machining point of view for it does not increase wear of the "tool", where one is needed, nor does it reduce the rate of metal removal. Indeed, hardened components are sometimes found to "machine" more readily than materials in a relatively soft condition. A number of industries have taken advantage of this characteristic. It is especially valuable in toolmaking, for the manufacture of dies and moulds, where greatly improved accuracy is achieved by finish machining after hardening, and expensive hand-working is reduced or eliminated.

Machining processes are categorised in Table 10.1 according to the fundamental energy source, with the exception of machining based on chemical sources of energy which has been omitted for reasons of space.

In addition to the processes shown in the table, a number of variants exist which are too numerous to deal with in this text.

ELECTRO-DISCHARGE
MACHINING (EDM)

10.2 Introduction

Electro-discharge machining is one of several processes employing thermo-electric energy to remove material from a workpiece through melting or vaporisation of selected areas. Other processes in this group are: electron-beam machining (EBM) which operates by transforming the kinetic energy of high speed electrons into thermal energy as they bombard and vaporise a local area of the workpiece; laser-beam machining (LBM), which is dealt with in **10.17**; and the lesser used plasma arc and ion beam processes. Of all these methods, EDM has the most practical advantages and is the one most widely applied in manufacturing engineering.

10.3 Basic Principles of EDM

Briefly EDM is a process for producing holes, external shapes, profiles or cavities in an electrically conductive workpiece by means of the controlled application of high-frequency electrical discharges to vaporise or melt the workpiece material in a particular area. The electrical discharges are the result of controlled pulses of direct current and occur between the tool electrode (usually negative) and the electrically conductive material of the workpiece (usually positive).

The tool and workpiece are separated by a small gap, say 0·01 to 0·5 mm and are submerged or flooded with a dielectric fluid, e.g. paraffin, white spirit or light oil. A voltage exceeding the breakdown voltage of the gap (determined by the size of gap and the insulating resistance of the dielectric) is applied to initiate a discharge. A channel is ionised at the two closest points between the electrode and the workpiece, Fig 10.1, and a massive current flow results causing erosion of a particle of metal. The ionised channel is formed of a plasma (i.e. gas ionised at very high temperature, in this case 8000–12 000°C) consisting of metallic atoms (M) vaporised from both the workpiece and the tool electrode, positive ions (M^+) and electrons (e^-) as shown in Fig 10.1 (inset). The instantaneous vaporisation produces a high-pressure bubble which expands radially into the dielectric. The discharge ceases with the interruption of the current. The metal is ejected leaving a small part-spherical crater in the workpiece and re-solidifies as globules in suspension in the dielectric. A sludge of black particles, mainly carbon, formed from the hydrocarbons of the dielectric is produced in the gap

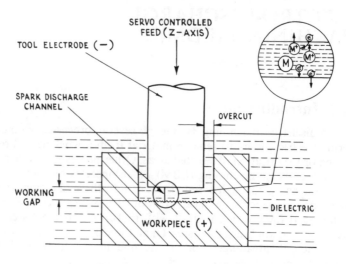

Fig. 10.1 Basic principle of EDM

and is expelled by the energy of the discharge, remaining in suspension until removed by filtering. Immediately following the discharge, the dielectric surrounding the channel deionises and once again becomes effective as an insulator.

The rate of material removal from the tool and workpiece is asymmetric, it depends on the polarity, thermal conductivity and melting point of the materials as well as the duration and intensity of the discharges. By suitable selection of parameters, the rate of erosion of the workpiece can be increased whilst that of the tool is decreased. Since metal is removed by vaporisation, physical properties of the workpiece which are important in the cutting of metals—e.g. hardness, toughness— are not significant and hard metals, e.g. tungsten carbides, can be eroded without difficulty.

10.4 The EDM Machine Tool

The general features of a basic EDM machine are shown in Fig 10.2. Essentially they comprise a bed, table, slides, dielectric system and a column on which is mounted a head provided with a servo-mechanism to control the rate of feed of the quill in which the tool-holder is mounted. Because the width of the working gap is of critical importance, the rate of feed is vital and control by a sensitive hydraulic servo-system or a directly coupled d.c. motor (which gives a faster response to signals) is essential.

The worktable is mounted on orthogonal slideways, often provided with optical scales for positioning it to an accuracy approaching that of

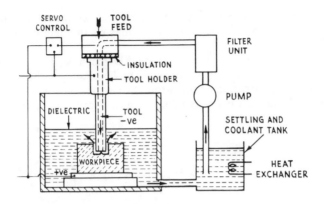

Fig. 10.2 General features of ED machine

jig-boring machines. The whole working area is surrounded by a tank to contain the dielectric which circulates from the machine to a storage tank in which suspended particles of the erosion process settle. It is then pumped back into the working zone through a filter. To remove heat generated during erosion the tank is provided with a heat exchanger to maintain a dielectric temperature of 20°c.

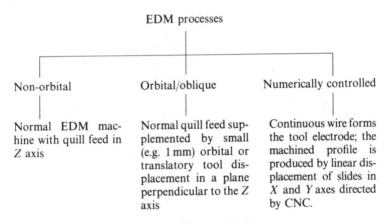

EDM processes

Non-orbital	Orbital/oblique	Numerically controlled
Normal EDM machine with quill feed in Z axis	Normal quill feed supplemented by small (e.g. 1 mm) orbital or translatory tool displacement in a plane perpendicular to the Z axis	Continuous wire forms the tool electrode; the machined profile is produced by linear displacement of slides in X and Y axes directed by CNC.

Fig. 10.3 Categories of ED machine tools

The performance of a basic ED machine can be improved by the provision of a small orbiting or translatory displacement of the electrode in a plane perpendicular to the feed vector. This lateral movement improves the dielectric flushing action in the working gap, significantly reducing machining times and electrode wear. Alternatively, or additionally, for producing holes of circular section, the electrode may be rotated around its own axis. For producing these motions, an attachment may be fitted to standard machines, or the device may be an integral part of the machine.

The CNC continuous wire electrode ED machine, Fig 10.4, is an important development for producing complex shapes in through-hole applications e.g. extrusion or press-tool die cavities. The wire electrode, typically 0·25 mm diameter, is taken from a supply spool containing

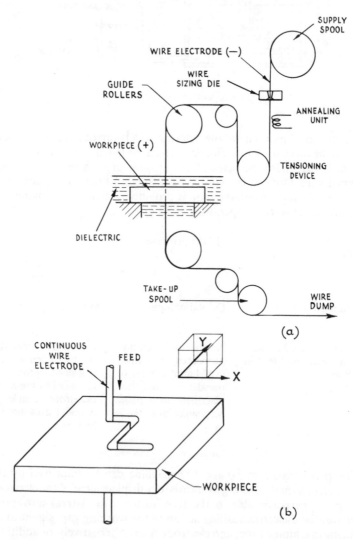

Fig. 10.4 Principle of continuous wire electrode CNC electro-discharge machine

sufficient wire for 24 hour continuous operation, at a velocity of 0·1 to 8 m/minute. For highly accurate work, the wire is drawn through a sizing die and reduced in diameter by 0·015 mm; it is then annealed and passed through sapphire guides to a device which stabilises the tension at 0·5–1·0 kg. In operation, de-ionised water is used as the dielectric and apart from its primary function, it may be used in a concentrated jet to carry the end of the wire, when setting up, through a pre-drilled hole in the workpiece and over the guide rollers to provide automatic operation. The electrode may be inclined at an angle of $1\frac{1}{2}°$ to the perpendicular to provide means for machining clearance in the profile of dies. Displacement of slides in the X and Y axes is under CNC control and is programmed as for conventional CNC machines.

Example 10.1
In a typical EDM operation on a CNC machine, a profile 100 mm long is machined in a steel extrusion die 20 mm thick by means of a 0·235 mm wire electrode. Given that the metal removal rate is 0·36 mm³/s and the radial overcut 5 μm, determine the erosion time in minutes and state the rate of linear erosion.

Solution

$$\text{Erosion time} = \text{Vol. to be removed/metal removal rate}$$
$$= 100 \times 20 \times (0·235 + 0·01)/0·36$$
$$= \underline{22·68 \text{ minute}}$$

Linear rate of erosion is $\underline{4·4 \text{ mm/minute.}}$

The capital cost of ED machines is comparable with traditional machines of the equivalent size and type. This factor renders comparison of economic performance with other machines fairly straightforward. A combination of the two methods is often practised, i.e. removal of bulk metal from the workpiece by drilling or milling, followed by roughing and finishing EDM processes.

10.5 Spark Generating Circuits

For metal to be eroded from the workpiece it is necessary for the ED machine to generate a spark whose characteristics can be controlled to provide the optimum conditions for a particular application, e.g. high metal removal rate or a fine surface texture. These requirements demand a voltage supply adequate to initiate and maintain the discharge process, also a system which provides the necessary control over the intensity, duration and cycle times of the discharges. These take place in the range from 2–1600 μs.

Many types of generator circuits have been devised. The resistance–capacitance (RC), i.e. relaxation circuit, was the original system. It is simple, reliable and provides fine surface textures, e.g. 0·25 μm R_a, but the discharges occur at relatively high voltages and are difficult to control, resulting in low metal removal rates and substantial tool wear. The most widely used system is the transistorised pulse generator which gives high metal removal rates and reduced electrode wear, through highly developed control of the machining parameters. To obtain both high machining rates and fine surface finishes, many machines are equipped with dual circuits.

10.6 The Relaxation (RC) Circuit

A basic form of RC circuit is shown in Fig 10.5(a). On commencing operation the capacitor is in the uncharged condition. Then it is charged from a d.c. voltage source (V_s) via the resistor which determines the rate of charging. The relationship between time (μs) and voltage is given in Fig 10.5(b), from which it will be seen that the voltage (V_c) across the capacitor increases exponentially as charging proceeds. When V_c has risen to the level of the breakdown voltage (V_b) existing in the working gap, the capacitor discharges across the gap and a particle is eroded from the workpiece. The spark is not sustained because the capacitor is discharged far more quickly than it can recharge via the resistor. The cycle is continuously repeated until the operation is complete.

This sequence can be examined in electrical terms since it is well known that the increase in voltage during the charging of a capacitor is given by the expression

$$V_c = V_s(1 - e^{-t/RC}),$$

where t = time (second)

     RC = resistance (ohm) × capacitance (farad)

        = time constant.

i.e. the voltage of the capacitor approaches the supply voltage with a time constant equal to RC, and the spark will be discharged when V_c reaches a value corresponding to V_b.

Example 10.2
(a) Show that if $t = RC$, the voltage of the capacitor is 63·2% of the supply voltage after the elapse of time period, t.
(b) What percentage of the supply voltage is reached by the capacitor when $t = 4RC$?

Solution
(a) $V_c = V_s(1 - e^{-t/RC})$

hence, when $t = RC$, $e^{-t/RC} = e^{-1} = 0.368$

    ∴ $V_c = V_s(1 - 0.368) = 0.632 V_s$

    i.e. $V_c = 63.2\%$ of V_s

(b) When $t = 4RC$, $e^{-t/RC} = e^{-4} = 0.0183$

    ∴ $V_c = V_s(1 - 0.0183) = 0.982 V_s$

    i.e. $V_c = 98.2\%$ of V_s

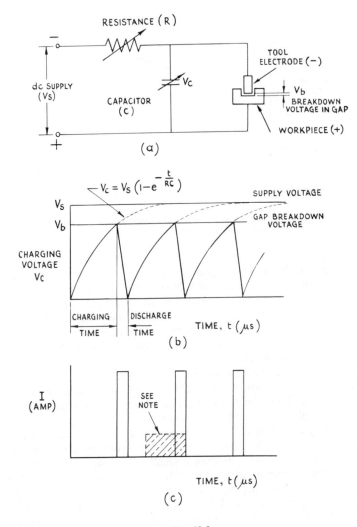

Fig. 10.5

(*a*) Basic relaxation (RC) circuit
(*b*) Relationship between charging voltage and time
(*c*) Characteristics of current in working gap

Note: The shaded portion represents a discharge of equal energy but of more desirable
characteristics resulting in a higher metal removal rate and reduced tool wear.

The theoretical energy (W joules) in an individual spark discharge is
given by the expression

$$W = \tfrac{1}{2} V_b^2 C,$$

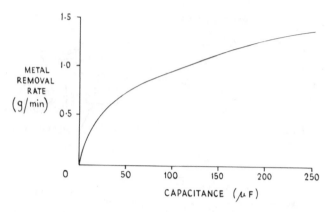

Fig. 10.6 Metal removal rate as a function of capacitance (after Rudorff) Brass electrode, hardened steel workpiece.

from which it follows that the greater the value of V_b with respect to V_s the greater the energy discharged. However, the exponential rate of charge exhibited by the curve, Fig 10.5(b), shows a marked decline as the value of V_c approaches that of V_s. Hence, if V_b were closer to V_s, fewer discharges would occur per unit time and in consequence the metal removal rate would suffer. The optimum value of V_b is usually taken at 73% of V_s for a high rate of machining.

Bearing in mind that the time cycle is important in allowing de-ionisation of the dielectric and for debris to be flushed from the working gap, it follows from the foregoing that there are optimum machine settings for voltage, R and C, for a given set of operating conditions.

The supply voltage usually lies between 200 and 400 V; an increase in V_s increases V_b and the machining rate, but produces a poor surface texture. A reduction in V_s enables a smaller working gap to be used, improving finish and accuracy, but reducing the machining rate. High rates of machining are obtained by reducing the time constant RC to give rapid charging; however, as R is reduced, the frequency increases and may reach a point at which de-ionisation is prevented from taking place and arcing occurs. Arcing causes effective machining to cease and creates thermal damage. Discharge energy (hence machining rate) and capacitance are related in the expression $W = \frac{1}{2}V_b^2 C$, indicating that an increase in capacitance increases the discharge energy. The relationship established by Rudorff* is shown in Fig 10.6. It follows that the machine settings for optimum performance in a given set of machining conditions involve a compromise in selecting the parameters of the process.

---

* D. W. Rudorff, Principles and Applications of Spark Machining, *Proc. I.Mech.E.*, **171**, 495 (1957).

10.7 The Transistorised Pulse Generator Circuit

The interdependence of parameters, a restricted choice of electrode materials and their high wear rate are among the disadvantages of the RC circuits. The introduction of semi-conductors has improved the design of pulse generators and allows the frequency and energy of discharges to be varied with a greater degree of control. Furthermore, the voltage of these machines is reduced to the 60–80 V range, permitting discharge characteristics with a lower profile, as shown in Fig 10.7, with the result that craters formed at each discharge tend to be shallower and wider.

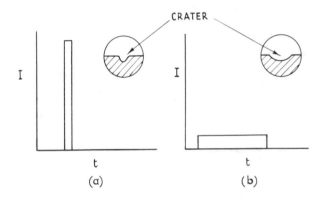

Fig. 10.7 Comparison of characteristics for discharges of equal energy produced by:

    (*a*) RC generator;
    (*b*) transistorised generator

In a simple form of the transistorised circuit, Fig 10.8(*a*), the discharges are controlled by a switching unit on a fixed frequency selected by reference to machining parameters. However, conditions in the working gap vary, causing lags in ignition to occur. Since the ON-time and the OFF-time are fixed, the useful discharge period X varies and efficiency is diminished, Fig 10.8(*b*). An improved arrangement incorporating feed back is shown in Fig 10.9(*a*). In this circuit the conditions at the spark gap are monitored by a detector unit which determines the exact moment of current flow after the ignition lag. The time base for the ON-time then becomes effective, providing a constant discharge period. The time base for the OFF period ensures a constant interval for de-ionisation and flushing away of debris by the dielectric. Consistency in the energy of discharge as shown in Fig 10.9(b) results in a much more efficient operation.

Generators of the type described above are typically 25 A or 50 A and

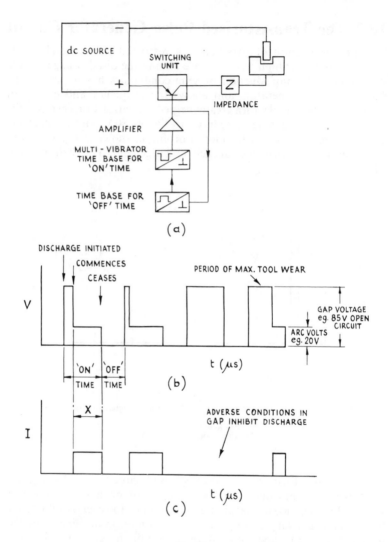

Fig. 10.8

(a) Basic transistorised pulse generator circuit
(b) and (c) Characteristics of discharges

details of the performance of a 25 A generator are given below (courtesy: Charmilles).

| Power | 2 kW | Interval OFF-time 2–1600 μS |
| Open gap voltage | 80 V | Minimum discharge energy 180 μJ |

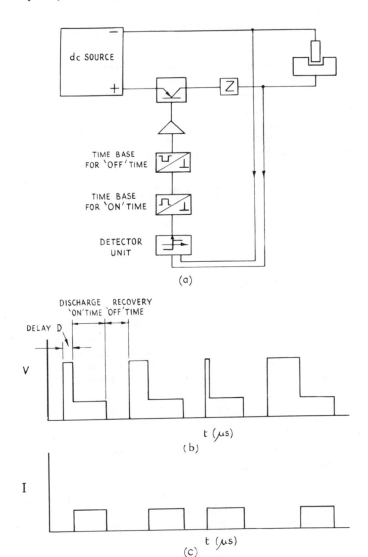

Fig. 10.9

(a) Principle of the Isopulse generator (*courtesy: Charmilles*)
(b) and (c) Discharge characteristics

Maximum average current	25 A	Maximum discharge energy 1.0 J
Discharge ON-time from	2–1600 μs	Finest surface finish 0·4 μm R_a

An extension of the control over the process through the introduction of full adaptive control of an ED machine:

(i) continuously monitors on-line machining performance;

(ii) provides on-line optimisation for machining parameters;

(iii) provides progressively increased electrical power as the effective machining area increases;

(iv) modifies characteristics of the discharge near the end of an operation to provide conditions for the finishing cut, which eliminates sub-surface damage and ensures the required surface finish is attained.

10.8 EDM Process Parameters

The Tool Electrode. Any material that is a good electrical conductor theoretically may be used as a tool electrode. Essentially the material should have

(i) rigidity;

(ii) low electrical resistivity;

(iii) a high melting point.

Low electrode wear is associated with a high melting point of the material: graphite has a very high value, 3500° C, followed by tungsten, 3400° C. However, in practice, considerations of cost (e.g. graphite is cheap, tungsten very expensive), rate of wear, ease of fabrication, availability, performance in terms of metal removal rate, surface texture produced, etc., combine to reduce the range of materials.

In view of the wear rate of electrodes, their replacement cost is an important factor. Tools are fabricated by a variety of methods—conventional machining, EDM, casting, etching, stamping, plating of moulded araldite, etc. In some applications, e.g. machining a forging die, inexpensive tools can be made from a previous component, i.e. an existing forging.

It is not possible to give firm data for tool wear rates. Manufacturers publish empirically derived tables for their machines, and the extract shown in Table 10.2 for three different settings of parameters when finish machining a steel component with a copper electrode illustrates the degree of variability, even within strictly limited conditions.

TABLE 10.2

Setting	R_a (μm)	Metal removal rate (mm^3/min)	Volumetric wear rate
1	0·40	0·2	20%
2	0·60	0·8	25%
3	1·60	2·1	26%

The choice of polarity on transistorised pulse generators has a very marked effect on wear of electrodes. The significance is shown graphically in Fig 10.10 for a machining operation using a 25 mm diameter graphite electrode on 1 % carbon steel. The band spread in each case is due to selecting different settings for the pause time.

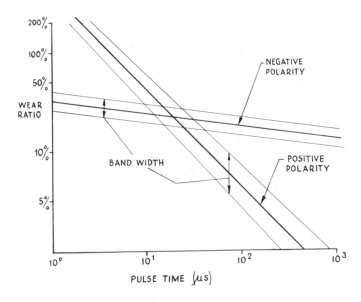

Fig. 10.10 *Effect of polarity on electrode wear*

Wear rates can be measured in linear or volumetric terms. In roughing operations, frontal wear of the tool is likely to be heavy and its expression in terms of a volumetric wear ratio would be appropriate. In finishing, a small loss of detail, significant in linear but not volumetric terms, may render the tool unsuitable for further use.

$$\text{Volume wear ratio, \% } = \frac{\text{volume of workpiece removed}}{\text{volume of electrode consumed}} \times 100$$

$$\text{end, side or corner wear ratio, \% } = \frac{\text{depth of machining}}{\text{end, side or corner wear}} \times 100.$$

An example of electrode wear resulting from the machining of a component pre-drilled to reduce EDM time is illustrated in Fig 10.11.

The Dielectric Fluid. In addition to providing suitable conditions necessary for discharges to take place, the dielectric fluid cools the

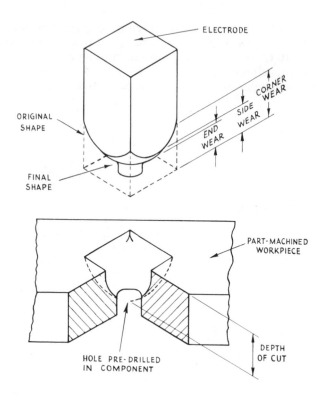

Fig. 10.11 Typical electrode wear in machining a pre-drilled component

electrodes and flushes away unwanted products of the process. The fluid must be of low unit cost and possess the following properties:

(i) low viscosity to ensure efficient flushing;
(ii) high flash point;
(iii) non-toxic;
(iv) non-corrosive;
(v) high latent heat;
(vi) a suitable dielectric strength, e.g. 180 V per 0·025 mm;
(vii) rapid ionisation at potentials in the range 40–400 V followed by rapid de-ionisation.

From the wide range of dielectric fluids available, three classes are principally used:

(i) hydrocarbons;
(ii) aqueous solutions of ethylene glycol;
(iii) de-ionised water.

Hydrocarbons are the major group and may be considered according to their viscosity, see Table 10.3. In finishing operations the working gap is small and the lighter oils are used to ensure flushing – a very important function – is performed satisfactorily. The gap is less restricted in roughing operations enabling higher machining rates to be achieved with heavier oils. Clearly, in EDM the flashpoint of the dielectric is important, also the machining rate is reduced if a low boiling-point fluid produces excessive gas on vaporising. The gases formed include hydrogen, methane, propane, acetylene etc. Deionised water is widely used for EDM on continuous wire CNC machines equipped with a deionising unit.

TABLE 10.3
Comparison of hydrocarbon dielectrics

Dielectric fluid	Flash point	Typical appli- cation	Comments
White Spirit	40°C	Small work, close tolerances, sharp definition, eg blanking tools with fine detail.	Low viscosity, useful in small working gaps or fine work not requiring high metal removal rate.
Paraffin	50°C	Medium work, eg plastic moulds, press tools, extrusion dies.	Good general purpose dielectric. Inexpensive.
Light Oil	130°C	Large work, heavy rough machining, eg drop forging dies.	Used in high power ED machines. Does not filter so readily.

Flushing Techniques. The correct circulation and filtering of the dielectric fluid is most important in EDM. At the beginning of an operation with a fresh supply of dielectric, it is clean and has a higher insulation strength than one containing particles. However, debris is created immediately spark discharges commence, and dielectric strength is diminished by particles acting as "stepping stones" in the tool–workpiece gap. If too many particles are allowed to remain, a "bridge" is formed resulting in arcing across the gap causing damage to tool and workpiece. Therefore, the degree of contamination in the gap must be controlled to provide optimum conditions in which machining can take place (Fig 10.12).

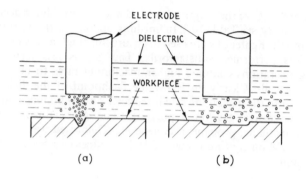

Fig. 10.12 Contamination by debris in the working gap

The main techniques are:

     (i) injection flushing (Fig 10.13);
    (ii) suction flushing (Fig 10.14);
   (iii) side flushing (Fig 10.15);

Additionally, pulsating flushing coupled with a reciprocating movement of the tool in the Z axis, is used in combination with these techniques.

    In the case of injection flushing, a slight taper is produced on the sides of the cavity due to the occurrence of lateral discharges as particles pass up the side of the tool. In Fig 10.13(a) the small "pip" must be removed if the machined area is not a through cavity. The use of porous graphite electrodes permits a most effective flushing action, particularly useful when machining deep cavities.

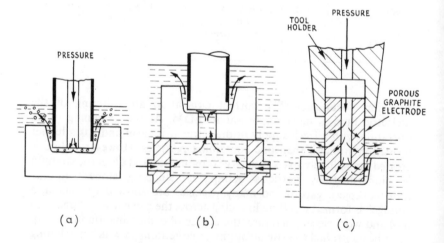

Fig. 10.13 Injection flushing techniques

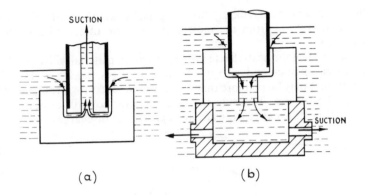

Fig. 10.14 Suction flushing techniques

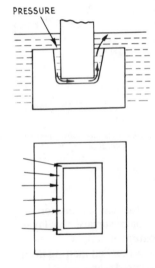

Fig. 10.15 Side flushing

Suction flushing avoids the tapered side effect of the previous method because the debris is not drawn past the sides of the tool and avoids the occurrence of lateral discharges. Generally, the suction effect is evenly distributed over the face of the tool, tending to give a more efficient machining action. Care must be taken to avoid trapping gases in recesses or in the pot. An example of side flushing—which must not be directed from opposing directions—is shown in Fig 10.15.

Surface Structure. Because the discharge temperature is of the order 8000–12 000° C, the nature of the workpiece surface layers may be affected in some materials, e.g. steels, especially as carbon will be present due to its release from the molecular structure of the hydrocarbon dielectrics.

The depth of the heat-affected zone for a given material will depend on the characteristics and energy of the discharges, e.g. in a finishing operation it may be no more than 0·002 mm, whereas for a roughing cut it may be 0·2 mm. Typically the machined surface will exhibit three layers, (Fig 10.16) after exposure to high-energy discharges.

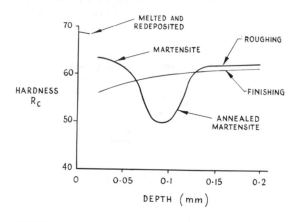

Fig. 10.16 Typical surface structure subsequent to roughing and finishing operations by EDM

    (i) a recast layer, formed by molten metal particles being re-deposited on the workpiece surface; this layer in steel workpieces may be harder than the parent metal;

    (ii) a layer which has reached melting point, but not dispersed, and which remains as a recast layer;

    (iii) an annealed layer, of hardness less than that of the parent material.

In many instances these effects will be minimised by the finishing cuts and will not be detrimental to the function of the component. However, for some components, e.g. in aerospace, the modification to the surface layers may be a critical factor, especially as micro-cracks may be present. Experimental findings indicate that fatigue endurance limits are less than would be expected from similar components not subjected to EDM (see Fig 10.17). In applications where the presence of a highly stressed surface layer is undesirable it may be relieved by shot-peening, grinding, electro-polishing or chemical machining.

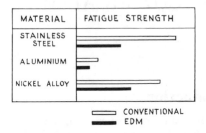

Fig. 10.17 Comparison of fatigue strength of identical components produced by conventional and electro-discharge methods

10.9 Summary of Approximate Operating Data

As a guide to the operational results in the application of ED machines the following data are given. It must be recognised that these values may not apply in specific instances, but they are included here in order to convey some idea of the magnitude of the values likely to be experienced in practice.

Metal removal rate	typically 1 mm^3/second, but since roughing and finishing operations with different electrode/workpiece materials are involved and machine sizes and powers cover an extremely wide range, the rate may occur in a range from 0·01 to 150 mm^3/s.
Overcut	typically 0·005 to 0·2 mm per side (minimum corner-radius = size of overcut).
Taper	typically 0·05–0·5 mm per 100 mm per side.
Accuracy of workpiece	tolerances of $\pm 0·05 - \pm 0·15$ mm easily achieved; tolerances of $\pm 0·005 - 0·01$ mm obtainable with close control.
Surface texture	1–2 μm R_a easily achieved; 0·25–1 μm R_a obtained with care.

ELECTRO-CHEMICAL MACHINING (ECM)

10.10 Introduction

Electro-chemical erosion techniques for machining metals in engineering manufacture have been developed in the last few decades, however, the basic principles employed in the process were established in the early nineteenth century. It is well known that if some metallic conductors are immersed in a suitable electrolyte and a direct current is passed, metal will be removed from the anode and will plate-out on the cathode. However, in ECM the anode, not the cathode is the workpiece, and is shaped by the selective loss of metal whilst deposition on the cathode is prevented by the flushing action of the electrolyte.

Whereas EDM is mainly confined to a single components or small batch work, ECM is particularly suited to the machining of large batches of identical components.

In essence, the ECM process involves passing direct current at 5–25 V through an electrolyte in the gap between the anode (workpiece) and the cathode (tool) at a current density ranging from 50 to 1000 A/cm^2. The tool material is a suitable conductor, eg copper or stainless steel, and is shaped to erode the workpiece to its reverse profile. Under properly selected conditions the tool does not diminish in size, i.e. 'wear', and is advanced toward the workpiece at a steady rate in the range of 0·001–1 mm/s, maintaining a constant working gap of say, 0·25 mm. Through this gap electrolyte will be passed at a velocity of 10–50 m/s. The electrolyte most commonly used is a 10% solution of sodium chloride (brine) and an EC machine tool must be constructed of materials able to withstand the corrosive action of this and other electrolytes. The need for such protection against corrosion is one of the reasons for the high cost of an ECM installation.

Plating-out on the tool does not occur and, unlike the case in nearly all other machining processes, no metallic particles are formed. However, depending on the electrolyte used, a sludge is precipitated in which are found salts or hydroxides of the metal elements of the workpiece material, and these solids are removed from the electrolyte by filtering.

10.11 Basic Theory

An electrolyte differs from a metallic conductor in that a current is carried, not by electrons, but by atoms which have either gained or lost electrons and in consequence have acquired either negative or positive charges. Such atoms are termed ions: those which carry negative charges pass through the electrolyte towards the anode and are called anions, and the positively charged ions move towards the cathode and are referred to as cations. As shown in Fig 10.18(*a*), the applied potential difference results in a flow of ions within the cell and a flow of electrons in the conductor in the opposite direction, external to the cell.

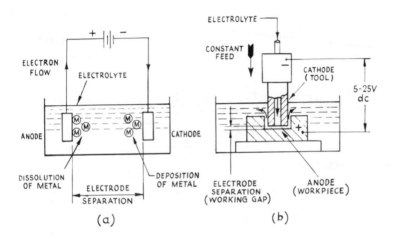

Fig. 10.18

(*a*) The basic electrolysis process
(*b*) The basic principle of ECM

The negative electrons on the cathode neutralise or discharge cations as they reach the cathode, and if copper is considered as the metal suspended in the electrolyte, the discharged cation is a positively charged atom of copper and is deposited on the cathode. This reaction may be expressed by

$$Cu^{++} + 2e \longrightarrow Cu, \quad \text{where } e = \text{one electron.}$$

The reaction is maintained by dissolution of the anode material to form cations and deposition of these cations at the cathode. Thus a passage of current through the cell results in a transfer of copper from the anode to the cathode.

The process is expressed in Faraday's two laws of electrolysis as follows:

1. The mass of any substance liberated in electrolysis is directly proportional to the quantity of electricity that liberated it.
2. The masses of different substances, liberated in electrolysis by the same quantity of electricity, are proportional to their chemical equivalent weights i.e. relative atomic mass ÷ valency.

To relate the electrolysis process more clearly to ECM, Fig 10.19 illustrates the electro-chemical process as applied to an iron workpiece in a suitable electrolyte. When the dc source is connected to the anode and cathode with the electrolyte flowing in the working gap, dissolution of the anode commences, and the reaction may be represented –

$$Fe \longrightarrow Fe^{++} + 2e.$$

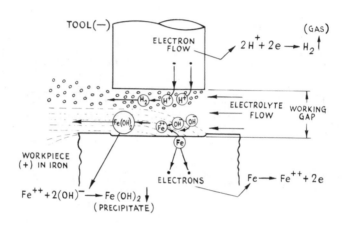

Fig. 10.19 *The electro-chemical process when applied to an iron workpiece in a suitable electrolyte*

The following reaction occurs at the cathode:

$$2H_2O + 2e \longrightarrow 2(OH)^- + H_2 \uparrow.$$

The hydrogen gas is evolved and the metal ions combine with the hydroxide ions to form a precipitate, ferrous hydroxide, $Fe(OH)_2$:

$$Fe^{++} + 2(OH)^- \longrightarrow Fe(OH)_2 \downarrow.$$

A further reaction of ferrous hydroxide may occur, not associated with the machining taking place at the working gap, but due to subsequent contact with water and oxygen in which ferric hydroxide $Fe(OH)_3$ is formed

$$4Fe(OH)_2 + 2H_2O + O_2 \longrightarrow 4Fe(OH)_3.$$

In more commonly used industrial applications of electrolysis, e.g. electroplating, the space between the electrodes is considerable (see Fig 10.18(a)), but in ECM it is normally less than 1 mm, and it is essential that hydrogen and the precipitated ferrous hydroxide are flushed from the working gap to ensure their presence does not interfere with the process. Considerable heat is generated in the gap and the flushing action ensures that it is quickly dissipitated. Provided the anode is fed toward the cathode at a rate commensurate with the rate dissolution is taking place, a steady state exists, and the gap under these conditions is termed the equilibrium gap.

It should be clear that since deposition is prevented by flushing, the reaction at the cathode results only in the generation of hydrogen, the shape and size of the tool remains unchanged, and it will be appreciated that this is a considerable advantage in practical machining applications of ECM.

10.12 Theoretical Rate of Metal Removal

Since the metal of the workpiece (anode) is removed by electrochemical action, the rate of machining is not dependent upon the hardness of either the tool or the workpiece but upon the following factors:

- (i) the current;
- (ii) time during which current passes;
- (iii) relative atomic mass of the metal;
- (iv) valency of the ions produced;

and Faraday's laws can be used to determine the theoretical metal removal rate, although in practice departures from the theoretical values are observed (see Fig 10.20). The two laws may be combined to give the following equation:

$$m = \frac{Aq}{vF} = \frac{AIt}{vF}, \tag{10.1}$$

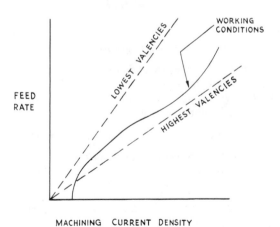

Fig. 10.20 Departure from Faraday's laws under typical working conditions

where m = mass of metal removed (grams)
  A = relative atomic mass (workpiece)
  I = current (amperes)
  t = time (seconds)
  $q = It$ = charge required (coulombs)
  v = valency of ions produced
  F = Faraday's constant (approximately 96 500 coulombs)

In the Table 10.4 the valencies quoted for some elements are those which are most likely to apply in ECM. For example, although the valency of iron and nickel is either 2 or 3, dissolution of both elements in ECM may be considered to occur in the divalent state.

TABLE 10.4

Element	Cr	Cu	Fe	Mn	Ni	Si	Ti
Relative atomic mass (A)	51·99	63·57	55·85	54·94	58·71	28.09	47·9
Valency (v)	3	2	2	2	2	4	2
Chemical equivalent (A/v)	17·34	31.78	27·93	27·47	29·36	7·02	23·95

The electro-chemical equivalent (Z) is the mass (m) of a substance liberated by 1 coulomb. For example, in the case of iron,

Electro-chemical equivalent, Z = chemical equivalent/F
  = 27.93/96 500
  = 0.000 29 g/C

It follows from this definition that

$$m = ZIt \text{ grams} \tag{10.2}$$

(since 1 coulomb = 1 ampere × 1 second) where Z is the electro-chemical equivalent of the anode.

However, in engineering it is more convenient to consider metal removal in terms of volume, hence

$$\text{volume of metal liberated} = ZIt/\rho \text{ mm}^3 \tag{10.3}$$

where ρ = density of workpiece material (g/mm³)
  Eqn (10.3) can also be expressed in terms of valency and relative atomic mass by substitution in Eqn (10.1).

$$\text{Volume of metal liberated} = AIt/Fv\rho \text{ mm}^3 \tag{10.4}$$

Similarly, metal removal rate, w, is given by

$$\text{metal removal rate, } w = AI/Fv\rho \text{ mm}^3/\text{s} \tag{10.5}$$

Example 10.3
Determine the theoretical metal removal rate in the electro-chemical machining of a zinc workpiece at 1000 A if the density of zinc is $7.13\,\text{g/cm}^3$ and its chemical equivalent $32.685\,\text{g}$.

Solution

$$w = 32.685 \times 1000/96\,500 \times 7.13 \times 10^{-3}$$
$$= \underline{47.5\,\text{mm}^3/\text{s}}$$

In practical manufacturing conditions the machining of a workpiece consisting of a single element is unusual; it is more likely that an alloy will be involved. The metal removal rate for an alloy may be calculated by considering each element individually and then combining the results on a percentage by mass basis.

For example, consider an alloy composed of elements P, Q, R in the proportion (by mass) $X_P\%$, $X_Q\%$, $X_R\%$ respectively, with the dissolution of the ions occuring in valency states of v_P, v_Q and v_R. The chemical equivalent of the alloy (A/v) is obtained by summing the chemical equivalent of each element in the alloy multiplied by its respective proportion by mass, as follows:

$$A/v \text{ of alloy} = \frac{1}{100}\left[X_P(A_P/v_P) + X_Q(A_Q/v_Q) + X_R(A_R/v_R) + \cdots \right]$$
$$(10.6)$$

The volume of alloy removed can then be found from Eqn (10.4) and the metal removal rate from Eqn (10.5).

The feed rate in equilibrium conditions, i.e. the rate of penetration of the tool, can also be calculated.

Let a = effective area of electrode (mm^2)
  f = rate of penetration (feed in mm/s)

Then

rate of penetration per unit time = vol. removed in unit time/a
i.e., from Eqn (10.3),

$$f = ZI/\rho a \text{ mm/s} \qquad (10.7)$$

Since the basic ECM process consists of two electrodes immersed in a water-based electrolyte and connected to a d.c. supply Ohm's law applies. The resistance (R) is dependent upon the specific resistivity (k in $\Omega^{-1}\,\text{mm}^{-1}$) of the electrolyte, the effective area (a) of the electrodes and the working gap or separation (δ). Substituting in Ohm's law:

$$I = \frac{V}{R} = \frac{Vka}{\delta} \text{ amperes} \qquad (10.8)$$

and substituting for I in Eqn (10.7)

$$f = \frac{ZVk}{\rho\delta} \text{ mm/s} \qquad (10.9)$$

Eqn (10.9) shows that if the rate of penetration is constant the voltage and the conductivity of the electrolyte (which is affected by temperature, see Fig 10.26) must be constant irrespective of load; otherwise the size of the working gap will vary and accuracy will be adversely affected.

10.13 The ECM Machine Tool (Fig 10.21)

From the foregoing consideration of the theoretical aspects of ECM a more detailed knowledge of the machine tool installation can be obtained. A rectifier provides the d.c. supply and the machine is rigidly designed in order to withstand the very high hydrodynamic forces associated with the flow of electrolyte. The ram of the machine is provided with a controlled linear displacement to give extremely accurate feed rates and rapid traverse rates together with power and stiffness adequate for the arduous machining conditions. Servo-controlled feed, as for EDM, is not needed for ECM.

In addition to the machine tool, the installation has an extraction system for the evolved hydrogen (with safeguards in the design against

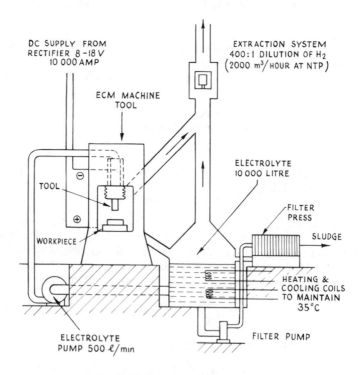

Fig. 10.21 Typical installation for ECM

the formation of pockets of gas), also a circulation system for the electrolyte which includes pumps, filters, tanks and heat exchangers. The electrolyte velocity in the working gap may be as high as 50 m/s and a flow rate of several hundred litres/minute is needed for a machining operation at 10 000 A. Energy from several sources is transferred to the electrolyte in the form of heat and must be removed by the heat exchangers to maintain the electrolyte at a constant temperature, usually about 35° C.

The electrolyte is clarified to remove solids, ensuring that the machining process is not adversely affected by their presence; e.g. if electrically conductive solids lodge in the narrow working gap a short circuit can occur, with very serious results. The solids include particles of the precipitated metal hydroxide and particles of intermetallic compounds released by the dissolution of the surrounding metal structure. Methods of clarification employ settling tanks, flotation, filtration, magnetic and centrifugal separation.

Brine has been mentioned as the most common electrolyte, but other solutions are used and may be acid, neutral or alkaline. It is necessary to protect EC machines against the corrosive effects of these substances. Protection can be afforded by the selection of suitable materials in the construction of the machine and electrolyte system—e.g. stainless steel, concrete lined with PVC, graphite. Structural members can be given organic coatings such as polyurethane, nylon, epoxy resin. Additionally, cathodic protection can extend to the whole framework of the machine by the application of a small electrical potential from an external source between an auxiliary anode and the machine tool. EC machine installations are often very large and are expensive to purchase, install and maintain.

10.14 Applications of ECM

Due to the high capital cost and expensive machine setting costs, standard ECM is mainly applied to large batch production work. The applications of the process may be divided into three groups:

(a) The machining of parallel sided shapes, internal or external, employing a linear displacement of the tool, i.e. the resulting surface has a constant section in a plane perpendicular to the feed axis; see Fig 10.22(a), (b), (c).

(b) The machining of 3-dimensional shapes, internal or external, employing a linear displacement of the tool. The machined surface will not possess a constant section perpendicular to the feed motion; see Fig 10.22(d).

(c) Deburring, see Fig 10.22(e).

Electro-chemical machining can be extended to embrace other techniques (see Fig 10.23) resulting in combined processes such as EC

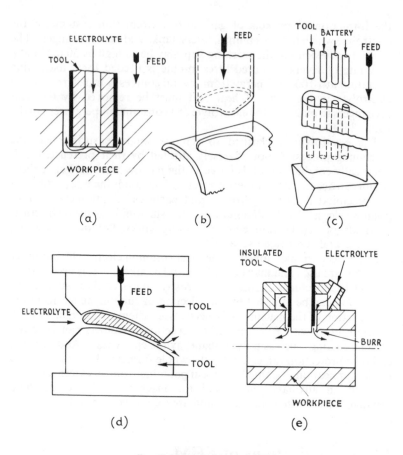

Fig. 10.22 Applications of ECM

(a) Drilling parallel-sided cavity
(b) Trepanning
(c) Deep hole drilling
(d) External forming
(e) Deburring

grinding (the simplest of all the ECM processes), EC turning, EC milling, EC honing, etc. As an example, electro-chemical grinding (ECG), Fig 10.24, is briefly discussed below.

Electro-chemical Grinding. In this process metal is removed by a combination of electro-chemical erosion and a mechanical abrasive action. The grinding wheel is usually metal-based and is faced with diamond abrasive particles or aluminium oxide grits. The wheel is the negative electrode and is connected to the d.c. supply through a spindle

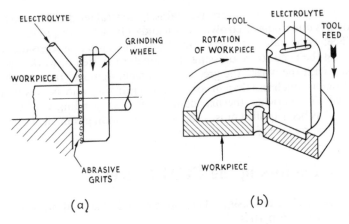

Fig. 10.23

(*a*) Electro-chemical grinding   (*b*) Electro-chemical turning

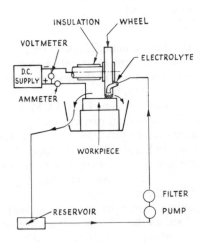

Fig. 10.24 Principle of ECG machine tool

insulated from the body of the machine. The workpiece is connected to the positive side of the supply.

The abrasive grains in the wheel are not electrical conductors and act as insulators in maintaining a constant gap between the metallic body of the wheel and the workpiece. The electrolyte is forced under pressure through the wheel/workpiece gap in the same direction as the wheel rotation. Erosion of the workpiece material occurs with the flow of current through the gap and the rate of decomposition is speeded up by the grinding action of the abrasive grains. In general terms, 90 % of metal removal is due to the electrolyte action and only 10 % is due to grinding.

Wheel wear rates are very low, thus eliminating or considerably reducing the need for re-dressing. The greater the area of workpiece in contact with the wheel, the greater is the metal removal rate. The heat generated is much less than in conventional grinding, and as a result it is unusual to experience thermal damage such as grinding cracks. The process has been applied most successfully in grinding cemented carbide die inserts, punches and cutting tools.

10.15 Factors in the ECM Process

Tool Materials and Design. The tool electrode material must possess the following properties:

- (i) good electrical conductivity;
- (ii) good thermal conductivity;
- (iii) chemical resistance to the electrolyte;
- (iv) stiffness to withstand electrolyte pressure;
- (v) machinability.

Copper and brass are the two materials most frequently used, although for certain electrolytes titanium or stainless steel have an improved resistance to corrosion. Other useful electrode materials include aluminium, copper–tungsten and graphite.

The initial cost of tools designed for ECM is often higher than electrodes for a similar operation carried out by EDM; however, any number of components can be produced by a single tool in ECM which is certainly not the case in EDM. Ideally, the tools should be designed to enable the electrolyte flow to be laminar at every position without eddies occurring, thus avoiding cavitation and achieving uniformity in the removal of metal from the workpiece.

Tools must be insulated if parallel sides are required in the cavity being machined. Fig 10.25 shows the effect of using a non-insulated tool. The parabolic shape of the workpiece cavity produced by such a tool clearly is to be expected if it is remembered that electrolytic action occurs whatever the distance between the electrodes; i.e. electrolytic action is continuing from the sides of a non-insulated tool as penetration proceeds. Tools should be carefully produced with all surface imperfections removed by polishing, otherwise these will be faithfully reproduced on the finished surface.

Composition of the Workpiece Material. Machinability in ECM is dependent on the chemical composition of the workpiece material and independent of its hardness or toughness. Almost any material that conducts electricity can be shaped by ECM. However, carbon is passive

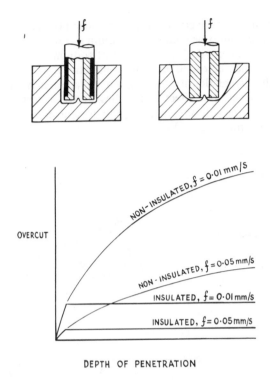

Fig. 10.25 *Relationships between overcut, depth of penetration, feed-rate, for insulated and non-insulated tools*

in electro-chemical reactions consequently cast iron, which contains free carbon, cannot be machined satisfactorily by ECM. The surface texture produced may be affected by the grain size of the material. Grain boundary material may erode at a rate different from that of the grain itself; where this occurs, fine grain materials tend to be less affected than coarse grain ones. Such intergranular erosion is likely to adversely affect the fatigue strength of the component. However, EDM does not result in a heat affected surface in the machined area.

The Electrolyte. Many ECM installations require large amounts of electrolyte, consequently, it should be cheap and additionally possess the following properties:

    (i) good electrical conductivity;
    (ii) non-toxic;
    (iii) as non-corrosive as possible;
    (iv) as safe to handle as possible.

Brine meets most of the criteria and is the most popular electrolyte, but its corrosiveness must be countered. Sodium nitrate is also widely used, but it has a conductivity less than that of sodium chloride. The more concentrated the electrolyte the more conductive it will be, and because of the high current density for a given voltage machining rates will increase; however, the effect diminishes above a certain level. The resistivity of brine solutions with respect to temperature and concentration is shown in Fig 10.26.

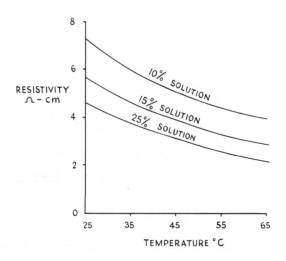

Fig. 10.26 Effect of temperature and concentrations on resistivity of NaCl solutions

10.16 Summary of Approximate Operating Data

The following data are given in order that some notion may be gained of the magnitude of values met in the ECM process:

Metal removal rate	(See section 10.12)
Overcut	0·02–0·1 mm per side
Accuracy of workpiece	±0·05 mm easily achieved, ±0·01 mm obtainable.
Surface texture	1 to 2 μm easily achieved, 0·1 μm obtainable.

LASER-BEAM MACHINING (LBM)

10.17 Introduction

Laser is the acronym for Light Amplification by Stimulated Emission of Radiation, infra-red and ultra-violet being included in the definition of light in this context.

There are two categories of laser:

(i) gas lasers—CO_2 is the gas most commonly used in lasers employed in machining processes, and He–Ne (helium–neon) is used in measurement and machine tool alignment applications;

(ii) solid state lasers, e.g. ruby (crystalline aluminium oxide), neodymium in glass (a concentration of up to 8 % of neodymium in glass).

Lasers in both categories are finding an increasing number of applications in engineering manufacture, especially for micro-machining, heat treatment, welding, cutting and many aspects of measurement including the provision of positional feedback information in the displacement of machine tool slides.

10.18 Principle of the Laser

The principle of the laser is the same irrespective of whether the lasing material is a fluid or a solid. In essence, the laser consists of a tube containing:

(a) the laser material with mirrors at either end;

(b) a separate source, e.g. xenon arc lamp, to inject energy into the laser for conversion into an output consisting of a light beam which has the following characteristics:

(i) highly collimated, i.e. a very small divergence of say, $< 10^{-3}$ radian;

(ii) monochromatic;

(iii) coherent, i.e. in phase.

The 'pumping' unit (see Fig 10.27) is usually a flash-lamp for solid state lasers and a device for providing an electrical discharge in the case of gas lasers. The energy from the pump excites atoms (Fig 10.28(a)) in the laser medium and their electrons move into higher energy levels, i.e. orbits farther from the nucleus. The atoms radiate the absorbed energy as light at the wavelength of the exciting energy as the electrons fall back to the lower state; this radiation is termed stimulated emission. The

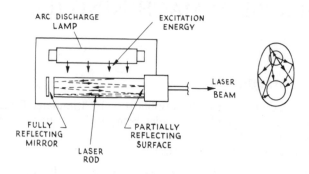

Fig. 10.27 Principle of the laser

emission of energy is amplified by the laser only when the excited atoms outnumber those in the normal state—the action of the pump is important in this connection. The power of the laser is determined by the number of excited atoms taking part.

Initially, the emissions of light energy take place in random directions, and energy is lost through the wall of the laser tube (Fig 10.28(b)). However, reflecting surfaces are placed at either end of the laser medium, one partially reflective, the other fully reflective. Some of the stimulated emissions are reflected by the mirrors longitudinally in the laser cavity and an oscillation builds up. Further atoms are excited and the stimulated emission increases, in phase and of the same wavelength, until the laser beam is established external to the laser rod through the one mirror which is only partially reflective.

The operation of the laser may be pulsed or continuous. In pulsed lasers the oscillation of light in the laser medium is interrupted by Q-switches, e.g. by cycled inclination of the reflective mirror. A typical pulse time is 10 μs, and by varying the period of the switching operation, power may be increased or decreased (the excited atoms increase in number during the period of interruption). In continuous wave gas lasers, power output is increased by an extension to the length of the laser cavity.

10.19 Application of the Laser

The principle of the application of the laser to industrial purposes is illustrated in Fig 10.29. The narrow beam emitted by the laser is expanded and directed through a lens to focus the beam in a con-centrated area of, say, 1–20 μm diameter to provide a spot of high power density which may then be used for its intended application, Table 10.5.

From the relationships which follow, it can be seen that to achieve spots of high peak power density it is desirable to have as large a radius as

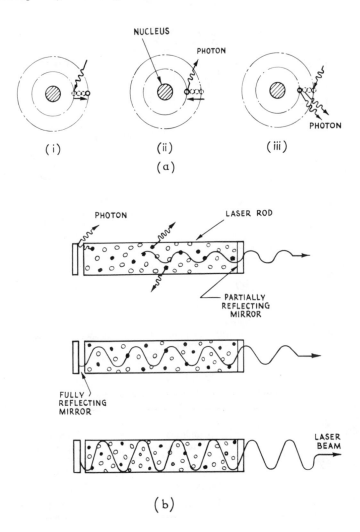

Fig. 10.28

(*a*) Excitation of the atom:
(i) absorbtion; (ii) spontaneous emission; (iii) stimulated emission
(*b*) Formation of coherent monochromatic laser beam

possible for the unfocused beam and the beam expander unit is introduced for this reason. The spot radius, r_s, is given by the expression

$$r_s = \frac{f\lambda}{\pi r_b},$$

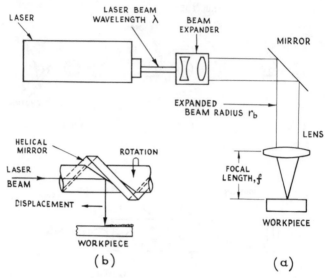

Fig. 10.29

(*a*) Principle of laser machining processes
(*b*) A method of displacing beam with minimum inertia for high speed linear welding or cutting

TABLE 10.5
Power densities and industrial applications

Power density (W/cm^2)	Condition of material	Typical application
$< 10^4$	Heat absorbed	Heat treatment
10^4–10^6	Molten	Welding
10^6–10^8	Vaporised	Cutting, drilling

where f = focus length of lens,
         r_b = radius of unfocussed beam
         λ = wavelength of radiation.

and the peak power density, P_d, is given by

$$P_d = \frac{2P}{\pi r_s^2},$$

where P = total power output.

By a choice of suitable power densities, the required condition of a metal workpiece in the area of the spot can be selected. It should be noted that the surface condition of the workpiece as regards reflectiveness will affect efficient absorption.

Although metal removal rates can be quite high, the extremely low efficiency of the laser, see Table 10.6, ensures that the input power requirement is also very high, making the process uncompetitive with traditional methods for the bulk removal of metal (note that conventional chip removal techniques require energy for mechanical shear whereas the cutting action of the laser requires energy for vaporisation).

TABLE 10.6

Characteristics of lasers used in production processes

Type	Electrical efficiency (%)	Wave length (nm)	Continuous power (W)	Focused peak power (W)	Applications in manufacturing
CO_2	> 10	10 600	up to 1000	10^8	Cutting, drilling, heat treatment, scribing, welding
He-Ne	< 0.1	633	0.002	10^{-3}	Alignment, displacements, interferometry
Nd in glass	> 1	1 060	up to 1000	10^9	Drilling, welding
Ruby	< 0.15	694	0.05	10^8	Drilling

10.20 Industrial Applications

Despite limitations, especially of low overall efficiency, the laser has advantages which ensures its increasing value and use. It will melt or vaporise any known material including diamond, produces narrow kerfs, and small heat-affected zones with negligible effect on adjacent areas. The beam is easy to control through optical systems or by CNC displacement of slides, and enables otherwise inaccessible areas to be machined or welded, or for these processes to be carried out in specially controlled environments. It can be applied to small batch production, e.g. the production of sheet metal parts in quantities too small to be economic for a press tool.

The laser has made a considerable contribution in two particular areas, in the cutting or scribing of difficult materials, e.g. ceramics, and in micro-machining, especially in the micro-electronics industry, producing circuits, transistors and diodes on silicon wafers.

The laser is a robust piece of equipment and provided suitable safety precautions are taken it can be used under normal operating conditions by skilled or semi-skilled workers.

ULTRASONIC MACHINING (USM)

10.21 Introduction

Unlike the processes previously described, USM removes material from the workpiece in the form of chips, and has the advantage that it is suitable for machining materials whether or not they are electrically conductive. In particular it provides a method for machining hard, brittle materials, e.g. diamond, ceramics, glass, and those with special physical or mechanical properties, e.g. titanium and heat resisting alloys. USM can be used for machining cemented carbide, but at the cost of a high rate of tool wear.

10.22 The Basic Principle of USM

A tool with a cross-section similar in shape to that required to be produced in the workpiece is axially vibrated at a small amplitude in the ultrasonic frequency range, Fig 10.30. Abrasive grits, suspended in a liquid carrier, are passed through the gap between the tool and workpiece. The vibrations of the tool tip transmit energy into the grits and on impact with the workpiece small particles, i.e. chips, are removed from the workpiece. A gradual downward feed of the tool maintains a static load between the tool and the workpiece during the cutting operation.

The material removal process is observed to be due to several factors:

(i) hammering by the tool of abrasive grits which are in contact with the workpiece;

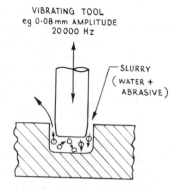

VIBRATING TOOL
eg 0·08 mm AMPLITUDE
20 000 Hz

SLURRY
(WATER +
ABRASIVE)

Fig. 10.30 Principle of ultrasonic machining

328

(ii) impact of free abrasive grits on the surface of the workpiece;
(iii) cavitation.

The mechanism of (i) is thought to account for the greater part of the material removal.

10.23 The USM Machine Tool

The machine tool is compact and may be floor or bench mounted. It has a table capable of orthogonal displacements in the X and Y axes on which a rotating table may be fitted. The tool vibrator spindle is mounted in ball or roller slides, usually in the vertical plane, with a feed mechanism controlled to provide a steady working force during operation and a woodpecker action to facilitate removal of retained grits or debris from the working cavity. The basic elements of an ultrasonic machine tool are as follows:

(i) main frame, table and slides;
(ii) acoustic elements;
(iii) slurry system;
(iv) feed mechanism.

The Acoustic Elements. The basic elements in the vibrating unit are illustrated in Fig 10.31 and comprise the generator, transducer unit with

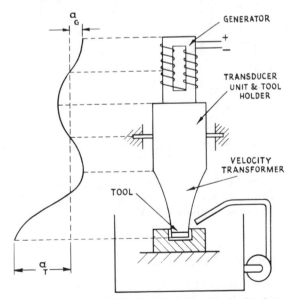

Fig. 10.31 Basic elements in the acoustic unit related to the distribution of the vibration amplitude in the system

tool-holder, velocity transformer and the tool. Magneto-strictive transducers are generally employed in USM, but piezo-electric transducers
may be used. The generator unit converts power from the supply at
50 Hz to high frequency energy in the range 20 000 to 25 000 Hz. The
audio threshold is approximately 15 000 Hz, hence the practical minimum working frequency for the machine is about 16 000 Hz with the
upper limit of frequency being imposed by considerations of heating in
the transducer.

In the magneto-striction transducer, the high-frequency vibration is
produced by passing a current at a particular frequency through a coil
wound around the transducer core. This core is composed of a stack of
nickel plates and small changes in dimension (i.e. magneto-striction) are
obtained when the laminae are magnetised. The dimensional change of
the transducer is of the order of 0.025 mm although both frequency and
amplitude may be adjusted within limits, and the tool-holder is so
designed that the transducer amplitude is increased by gains of up to six
or seven times. Maximum fatigue strength is obtained by interposing a
velocity transformer, manufactured from monel metal, between the
transducer and the tool. The transducer, transformer, tool holder and
tool must be in resonance to achieve optimum tool amplitude and power
output. The shape of the tool unit is important in this connection (see
Fig 10.32).

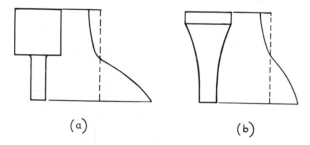

*Fig. 10.32 Examples of types of velocity transformers and their respective
vibration amplitudes*

The power input to the transducer is termed the machine power rating,
and ranges from 0.05 kW for a small USM drill to 4 kW; a typical
machine has a rating of about 0.5 kW.

10.24 Process Parameters

There are a large number of variables in USM and the results of research
investigations into their effects are inconclusive; however, the process
parameters may be grouped as follows:

(i) materials—tool and workpiece;
(ii) acoustic system—amplitude, frequency, working force;
(iii) abrasive slurry—abrasive material, size of grit, concentration of grits in slurry;
(iv) geometry of machined area.

The Tool. Carbon steels and stainless steels are frequently used for tool materials. When cutting hard materials, e.g. ceramics, a hardened tool steel would be used for roughing cuts and a medium carbon steel for finishing operations. Examples of some tool/workpiece wear ratios are given below in Table 10.7.

TABLE 10.7

Tool wear ratios

Tool material	Workpiece material	
	Glass	Cemented carbide
Brass	1 : 50	1:0·75
Copper	1 : 200	—
Mild steel	1 : 100	1 : 1
High carbon steel	1 : 250	1 : 3
Cemented carbide	1 : 1000	1 : 0·85
Stainless steel	1 : 150	1 : 2·5

A typical example of the characteristics of tool wear is illustrated in Fig 10.33. The working force exerted by the tool is closely controlled by hydraulic means and varies from about 1 N when machining fine holes to several hundred newtons for large work.

The Abrasive. The abrasive grits are suspended in water to form a slurry. The main materials used for the abrasive in ascending order of

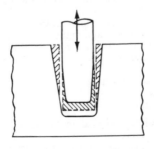

Fig. 10.33 Typical characteristics of tool wear and taper in workpiece

hardness, are aluminium oxide, silicon carbide and boron carbide, the latter being the most expensive. The machining rate, which ranges from, say, 0·01 to 2 mm/minute, is affected by the grain size. In general, the maximum rate is achieved as the grain size approaches the magnitude of the tool amplitude. The abrasive size also affects the surface finish; typical examples are:

$$280 \text{ grit} = 0·6 \ \mu\text{m R}_a$$
$$800 \text{ grit} = 0·25 \ \mu\text{m R}_a.$$

Material removal rate decreases as the sharpness of the grits declines and the abrasive must be replaced in order to maintain the machining rate.

EXERCISES 9

1. (a) Describe the principle of operation of a relaxation generator used for electrical discharge machining and explain how its disadvantages are overcome in other types of generator.

(b) Explain with reference to the relaxation generator why a servo-mechanism must be used to feed the tool and show how an error signal may be obtained when using either this generator or a pulse generator.   [CEI]

2. (a) Draw a graph to show the relationship between the breakdown voltage of the dielectric fluid used in a spark erosion machine and the distances between electrode and workpiece. Discuss the influence of this relationship upon the design and operation of such machines.

(b) Show that for a spark machine operating on a relaxation circuit the breakdown voltage, U, is given by

$$U = E(1 - e^{-t/RC}),$$

where E = supply voltage;
  t = charging time;
  R = resistance of circuit;
  C = capacitance of circuit.

Hence, determine for the above machine the average power output, given that the resistance $R = 3·2$ ohms; capacitance $C = 150 \ \mu\text{F}$; supply voltage $E = 200$ V and the breakdown voltage $U = 160$ V.   [CEI]

3. (a) Compare and contrast EDM and ECM with respect to

(i) principle of operation;
(ii) applications.

(b) When considering the use of electro-machining and the more traditional metal removal processes, what factors would influence the decision in deciding which techniques to apply?

4. (a) Explain the principles of metal removal by the EDM method and show by means of a well proportioned diagram the general features of an ED machine.

(b) Compare the following processes in terms of metal removal rate, surface finish and dimensional accuracy:

(i) electro-discharge machining;
(ii) electro-chemical grinding;
(iii) ultrasonic machining;

and for each process indicate a typical application which would justify its use, giving reasons for your choice.

5. (a) With the aid of diagrams, explain the principles of ECM.

(b) The approximate data in Table 10.8 are extracted from a table comparing

TABLE 10.8

Type of process	Max. metal removal rate (mm^3/s)	Power consumption ($W/mm^3/s$)	Max. rate of penetration (mm/s)	Accuracy (mm)	Surface finish (μm)
Abrasive ie. grinding	13 650	27	0·42	0·0025–0·25	0·125–250
ECM	550	82	0·21	0·005–0·125	0·125–1·25

the performance of various metal removal techniques. Relating your remarks to the data given, discuss the advantages of ECM which explain the reasons for its use as an industrial process.

6. In ECM, a relationship exists between the rate of feed and the current density employed. In a series of tests on steel and steel alloys the tool feed rate was recorded against various current densities. The results obtained for the maximum and minimum rates of penetration are given in Table 10.9. Plot the graphs for the two tests to establish the range in the tool feed rate when machining steel and its alloys.

(a) What is the max and min. value of the constant term in the equation $f = ZI/\rho a$.

(b) State the mean feed rate in an operation using 1000 A on a work area 10 × 25 mm.

7. Describe the process of ultrasonic machining and discuss the effects of the various parameters, showing the advantages and limitations of the process. [CEI]

8. (a) Describe the principle of ultrasonic machining.

(b) A table comparing the performance of various material removing techniques gave the information in Table 10.10. Consider the figures in the table

TABLE 10.9

Current density (A/mm^2)	1	2	3	4	5
Tool feed rate (max.) (mm/s)	0·05	0·11	0·16	0·22	0·27
Tool feed rate (min.) (mm/s)	0·04	0·08	0·12	0·16	0·20

TABLE 10.10

Type of process	Max. material removal rate (mm^3/s)	Power consumption ($W/mm^3/s$)	Max. rate penetration (mm/s)	Accuracy (mm)	Surface finish (μm)
USM	2·73	136	0·042	0·005–0·02	0·25–0·6
EDM	72·0	110	0·21	0·005–0·12	0·25–5

and discuss the advantages of USM which ensure its value in industrial applications.

9. (*a*) Discuss the process of electro-discharge machining with particular reference to the workpiece, surface finish, metal removal rate and tool wear. Quote typical applications of the process.

(*b*) Compare the foregoing process with electro-chemical machining and indicate graphically, and by description for the latter case, the general relationships which are known to exist between the working gap and the machining voltage. Indicate the effect of increasing the working gap on the permissible feed rate.

(*c*) Calculate the amount of titanium removed in an electro-chemical machining operation given that:

$$\begin{aligned}
\text{Relative atomic mass} &= 47{\cdot}9 \\
\text{Machining time} &= 2 \text{ min} \\
\text{Valency} &= 4 \\
\text{Work area} &= 12 \text{ cm}^2 \\
\text{Current density} &= 250 \text{ A/cm}^2 \\
\text{Faraday's constant} &= 96\,500 \text{ coulombs.}
\end{aligned}$$

10. Determine the metal removal rate in an ECM machining operation on an alloy of Ni–Cr–Mo at 10 000 A. The density of the alloy is $8{\cdot}91$ g/cm^3 and its composition (%) is as follows:

C 0·1, Cr 15; Fe 5·5; Mo 15·9; Ni 59·5; W4.

Neglecting carbon, which does not dissolve anodically, the atomic weights of the elements are 52.01, 55·86, 95·95, 58·69, 183·92 respectively. It may be assumed the following valencies will apply in the process—2, 2, 3, 2, 6 respectively.

CHAPTER 11

Forming of Metals

Note on S I units employed in this chapter. Where component dimensions are in millimetres it is convenient to use N/mm^2 ($= MN/m^2$) for stresses. As a practical unit for forces (punch loads etc) the newton is too small for convenience and the kilonewton has been used.

Force in kN = stress in N/mm^2 × area in mm^2 × 10^{-3} Presses are commonly rated in tons (force) or in the earlier metric unit of tonnes (force) which, for all practical purposes, may be regarded as of equal value. Since 1 ton force $\simeq$ 1 tonne force $\simeq$ 10 kN, the use of kilonewtons as the force unit makes it a very easy matter to select presses of suitable force rating for any work being planned.

11.1 Methods of Forming Metals

Hot and cold working of metals is of great importance in engineering manufacture. Processes such as forging, rolling and drawing predominate in the primary stages of manufacture and have been perfected largely through traditional developments based upon craft skills. From about 1920 onwards a more scientific study of the plastic working of metals has given impetus to technological developments, the fruits of which may be seen in a modern continuous strip rolling mill for the poduction of sheet steel.

At the secondary stage of engineering manufacture the conversion of sheet and bar forms of wrought materials into engineering components by metal forming processes has also passed through equivalent stages of development. Sheet-metal presswork has revolutionised automobile body manufacture; the extrusion process has led to some entirely new concepts in manufacturing; the rolling of spline shafts, screw threads, etc., has further extended the forming processes, so that it is now possible to convert the primary stage raw material into components by "chipless" machining methods. Such methods are important because:

(i) they result in a much higher percentage material utilisation and so reduce material costs;

(ii) they compete favourably with traditional machining and fabrication methods in the quality of the work produced, and in production costs.

335

There are a number of text-books which give a descriptive treatment of the principal metal-forming processes. In the present volume it seems appropriate to treat the secondary stage plastic working of metals in greater detail so that a deeper insight into the underlying principles is revealed. With this object in view it is proposed to concentrate on some aspects of metal plasticity, and upon the particular forming processes of sheet-metal presswork and extrusion.

11.2 Plasticity of Metals

Within their elastic range metals behave very closely in accordance with the well known mathematical laws. Once the yield point is exceeded the behaviour is less exactly predictable, especially for conditions of combined stresses. There is a growing volume of work on plasticity in which mathematical treatments are developed (see bibliography) but for most of the common metalworking processes semi-empirical methods still seem to be the most useful. The object of such methods is to enable the results of practical tests to be used as a means of predicting behaviour under processing conditions somewhat similar to those of the tests. Standard tensile and compressive tests are the simplest tests providing information about the behaviour of metals within the plastic range.

Fig 11.1 shows the load-extension graph of a tensile test of a ductile metal which has no distinct yield point. Up to the load represented by

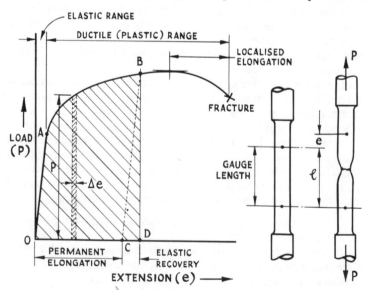

Fig. 11.1 Tensile test of a ductile metal

point A, the material is elastic. Consider the load to be raised slowly to point B, and then to be removed. During the unloading the load–extension graph will follow line BC parallel with AO; distance OC represents the permanent extension caused by the load, distance CD represents the elastic contraction (recovery) which occurs as the load is removed. The shaded area OABD represents the amount of work necessary to cause the deformation OC.

If the "overstrained" material is again loaded a new load-extension graph will have its origin at C, its yield approximately at B and its breaking point at approximately the same point as would have resulted in carrying the first test through to failure. The results of working the material to point B within the plastic range are:

(i) the yield point, and hence the safe working stress for the material, is raised; — cold working.

(ii) the ductility, measured by the amount of elongation occurring before fracture, is lowered.

Two important deductions relevant to metal deforming at room temperature can now be made:

(a) The elastic recovery which occurs on release of the deforming stresses is inevitable, and there will be minor changes of the dimensions when cold-deformed parts are ejected from the tools. "Spring-back" in sheet-metal presswork typifies this.

(b) During the plastic deformation each increment of elongation, Δe, will require a specific amount of work, as represented in Fig 11.1 by $P \times \Delta e$. From the shape of the graph between points A and B it can be seen that each successive increment of deformation will require a slightly larger amount of work to be done on the material; the resistance to "working" rises steadily during the deformation. An alternative way of looking at this is to regard the yield point as rising steadily from A to B as the permanent extension is increased from O to C.

If tests of material properties at elevated temperatures are conducted information relative to the hot working of metals may be similarly examined. Fig 11.2 illustrates, for a 0.09% mild steel, changes in the initial yield stress and changes in the ductility as revealed by a percentage elongation test, caused by heating the steel to various temperatures. Fig 11.3 illustrates successive changes in the load-extension diagrams of a similar steel, caused by heating. From Fig 11.2 it is obvious that by working the steel at temperatures around $800\,°C$ the following advantages accrue;

(i) the amount of work required, and the magnitude of the forces necessary to work the metal, are both greatly reduced;

(ii) the working (ductile) range of the metal is greatly extended;

338

Principles of engineering production

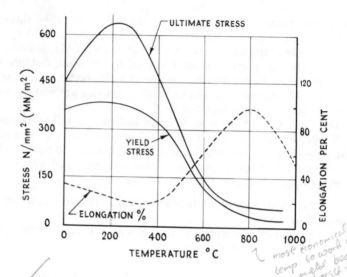

Fig. 11.2 Influcence of temperature on the properties of a 0·09% carbon steel
(after Lea)

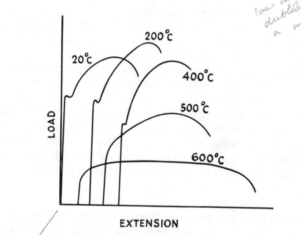

Fig. 11.3 Influence of temperature on the load–extension diagrams for a
low-carbon steel

(iii) the elastic recovery consequent upon the removal of the deforming stress is very small because of the low yield point.

Hot working is easier to perform than cold working, but as a secondary manufacturing process it is subject to the following disadvantages.

(*a*) The finished components contract on cooling. Since the finishing temperature may not be uniform throughout the component, and may not be accurately known, exact dimensional allowances cannot be made to counteract this. An accuracy better than IT 12, see Table 1.4 is difficult to attain by hot working of steels.

(*b*) Suitable working temperatures for steels give rise to oxidation and scaling. This results in rough component surfaces, particularly when the surface finish of the tooling begins to deteriorate.

(*c*) Dimensional changes occur in the tools due to heating; abrasive wear of the tools steadily reduces their accuracy.

For these reasons hot working cannot compete with cold working in regard to dimensional accuracy and to surface finish of the resulting product.

11.3 True Stress-Strain Curves

In Fig 11.1 the load is seen to fall as the breaking point is approached, a condition which is the reverse of that occurring between points A and B. The reason is to be found in the reducing cross-sectional area (necking) which precedes fracture. If the reduced area is taken into account the actual stress in the yielding material can be shown to rise continuously. Fig 11.4 shows a true stress-strain curve developed from the load-

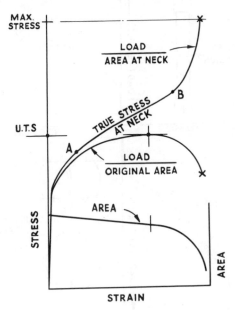

Fig. 11.4 True stress–strain curve for a tensile test on a ductile metal
(afer Salmon)

extension curve of Fig 11.1. Notice that the yield point rises progressively, and in approximate linear relationship to the strain between points
A and B. In the region of point B the ductility of the material peters out;
there is a further sharp rise of stress up to the breaking point,
accompanied by very little strain.

A much more complete picture of the plastic working properties of a
metal is gained by extending the tests into the compression range.
Fig 11.5 shows the compression curves for load-compression and for
true stress-strain. The curves are drawn in the third quadrant because
compressive stress and strain are regarded as of opposite sign to tensile
stress and strain. The nature of the ultimate failure of the material differs
as between tension and compression, a fact which has some bearing upon
the success of certain cold-deforming techniques.

Ductile metals deformed under compressive loads admit of a much
greater amount of deformation before failure than if they are deformed
under tensile loads. When such failures do occur they tend to be caused
by induced tensile and shear stresses. The stress at the expanding
periphery in the example of the cylindrical compression test specimen
illustrated in Fig 11.5 is a typical example.

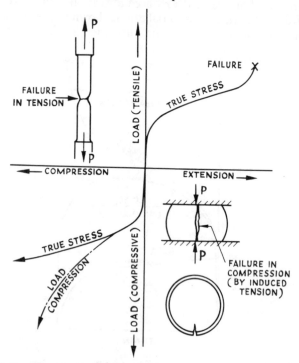

Fig. 11.5 Behaviour of a ductile metal under tensile and compressive loads

11.4 Work Done in Compressing a Perfectly Plastic Material

A first approximation to the work done in deforming a metal can be made, subject to two important basic assumptions:

(i) that the material is perfectly plastic, represented by the fact that the yield stress σ_y is a constant;

(ii) that there is no friction between the deformed material and the anvils which exert the deforming load and against which deforming displacements occur.

It follows from the second assumption that the deformed specimen will remain a parallel cylinder throughout the test and not exhibit the barrelling effect, caused by friction at the anvils, shown in Fig 11.5.

Fig 11.6 shows the deformation assumed to occur, and the resulting load-compression curve for the idealised compression test. Any change in volume during compression will be extremely small. If A = cross-sectional area of the specimen, h = length of specimen, V = volume of specimen and P = deforming load, then

$$\text{Original volume } (A_0 h_0) = \text{Final volume } (A_1 h_1).$$

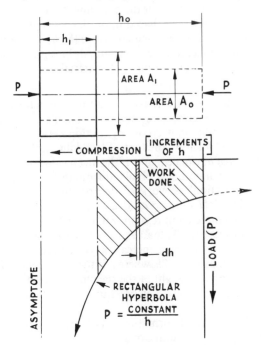

Fig. 11.6 Work done in deforming a given volume of perfectly plastic material, no frictional resistance occurring

The deforming load at any position is given by:

$$P = \sigma_y A; \quad \text{but } A = \frac{V}{h},$$

hence
$$P = \frac{\sigma_y V}{h} = \frac{\text{Constant}}{h},$$

and the graph is a rectangular hyperbola. The work done in deforming the material is represented by the shaded area under the graph.

$$\text{Work done} = \int_{h_1}^{h_0} P \, dh = \sigma_y V \int_{h_1}^{h_0} \frac{dh}{h}$$

$$= \sigma_y V \ln \frac{h_o}{h_1} \tag{11.1}$$

$$(\ln = \log_e)$$

Note on units: given σ_y in N/mm^3, V in mm^3, the work done will be in N mm. The energy equivalent of 1 N mm of work is 10^{-3} J.

This is an important result. Much of the experimental work done in order to obtain empirical data for the determination of the forces acting in plastic forming processes is based upon the concept of the principal logarithmic deformation represented by $\ln(h_0/h_1)$. If Eqn (11.1) is divided by the deformed volume the result, $\sigma_y \ln(h_0/h_1)$, represents the work done to deform a unit volume of material.

In order to relate Eqn (11.1) to true conditions for deforming metals, a realistic value must be given to σ_y and a reasonable allowance must be made for the work done in overcoming friction between the workpiece and the tools. Fig 11.7 shows the type of test data available, from which realistic estimates of σ_y can be made. If the mean value of σ_y for the range of deformation which occurs is obtained from test results, a reasonable estimate of the frictionless work of deformation can be made. (See Feldmann, H. D., *Cold Forging of Steel*).

The effect in a simple compression test, of friction at the anvils, is to give rise to an increase in the load P necessary to cause yielding. Siebel has shown that the approximate increase in yield stress caused by friction at the anvils is given by $\sigma_y \mu d/3h$, where μ is the coefficient of friction and d and h the diameter and height of the specimen respectively. A method of developing this approximate expression is as follows.

Let k = resistance to deformation when friction is neglected, i.e. $P_0 = kA$, and let k_f be the additional resistance to deformation caused by friction such that the true deforming load $P_1 = (k + k_f) A$. Suppose the load P_1 to be just sufficient to cause a small deformation Δh, during

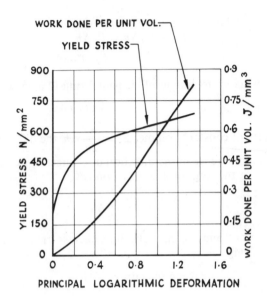

Fig. 11.7 *Plastic deforming properties of a 0·07% carbon steel (after Feldmann)*

which the elemental ring shown in Fig 11.8 moves outwards by an amount $\dfrac{x}{r}\Delta r$.

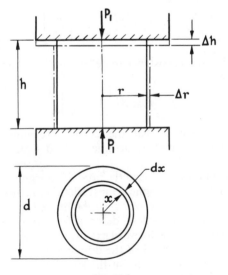

Fig. 11.8

Work done at the anvil in overcoming friction,
$$(P_1 - P_0)\Delta h = P_f \Delta h$$
$$= k_f \pi r^2 \Delta h \tag{1}$$

Frictional resistance to sliding of elemental ring (2 anvils)
$$= 4\pi k\mu x\,dx \tag{2}$$

By property of constant volume, $\Delta r = \dfrac{-r}{2h}\Delta h$, the difference in sign representing a difference in the direction of change, hence the outward displacement of the ring for a contraction Δh is,
$$\frac{x}{r}\frac{r}{2h}\Delta h = \frac{x}{2h}\Delta h \tag{3}$$

By equations (2) and (3), the work done against friction in displacing the elemental ring
$$= 4\pi k\mu x\,dx \times \frac{x}{2h}\Delta h \tag{5}$$

Total work done against friction, from equations (1) and (5),
$$k_f \pi r^2 (\Delta h) = \frac{4\pi k\mu(\Delta h)}{2h}\int_0^r x^2\,dx$$
$$= \frac{2\pi k\mu\,(\Delta h)r^3}{3h}$$
$$k_f = \frac{2\mu kr}{3h} = k\left[\frac{\mu d}{3h}\right]$$

It follows that for a resistance to deformation k, the total load on the anvils must be,
$$P = Ak\left[1 + \frac{\mu d}{3h}\right] \tag{11.2}$$

The solution assumes that the cylinder remains parallel during deformation which cannot occur unless $\mu = 0$, hence the proof is not rigorous.

It follows from Eqn (11.2) that the ratio d/h is significant in relation to the amounts of work to be done against friction. If h becomes very small in relation to d, much more work will be needed to overcome friction than to cause the frictionless deformation. For this reason it is impossible to continue the forward extrusion process to eject the entire billet. In sheet-metal presswork the drawing of relatively thin sheet is more difficult than the drawing of thicker sheet partly because of the relatively large frictional forces involved.

Example 11.1
A billet of aluminium 25 mm dia × 38 mm long is compressed between flat parallel steel anvils to a length of 19 mm. The initial yield stress is 65·4 N/mm² and after a 50% reduction the yield stress is 82·7 N/mm². Find the frictionless work done in deforming the material and the mean force which would produce this amount of work. If $\mu = 0.14$, find the maximum load to be exerted.

Solution

$$\text{Mean yield stress} = \frac{65\cdot4 + 82\cdot7}{2} = 74\cdot05 \text{ N/mm}^2$$

$$\text{Volume} = \frac{\pi}{4} \times 25^2 \times 38 = 18\,653 \text{ mm}^3$$

Frictionless work of deformation, by Eqn (11.1),

$$\text{Work done} = 74\cdot05 \times 18\,653 \times \ln\frac{38}{19} \times 10^{-3} \text{ J}$$

$$= \underline{958\,\text{J}}$$

Mean deforming force (neglecting friction)

$$P_{\text{mean}} = \frac{958}{19} \times 10^3 = 50\,420 \text{ N}(50\cdot42 \text{ kN})$$

Final diameter of work, assuming frictionless deformation,

$$d^2 \times 19 = 25^2 \times 38$$
$$d = 35\cdot36$$

Maximum deforming force occurring at the end of the compression,

$$P_{\text{max}} = 82\cdot7 \times \frac{18\,653}{19}\left[1 + \frac{0\cdot14 \times 35\cdot36}{3 \times 19}\right] \text{by Eqn (11.2)}$$

$$= 82\cdot7 \times 981\cdot7\,(1 + 0\cdot087) = \underline{88\,250}\ \text{N}(88\cdot25 \text{ kN})$$

The operation is within the capacity of a 10-tonne (force) press.

It would be wrong to expect high accuracy from such calculations; the theory employed is not rigorous, the yield stress (or more accurately the resistance to deformation) is not exactly known. However, such estimates as can be made are of considerable practical value; they enable presses of adequate capacity to be selected and provide data from which stresses in the tools can be reasonably apportioned.

11.5 Some Metallurgical Aspects of Hot and Cold Working

The effects of plastic deformation upon the structure of metals and alloys has been the subject of considerable metallurgical research. There is a trend towards explanation of the plastic behaviour of metals in terms of dislocation theory, and this may be profitably studied by students whose courses include Metallurgy as a separate subject. It seems desirable to include within this chapter a brief outline of some important metallurgical aspects of plasticity.

Commercial metals are polycrystalline. The crystals have an ordered arrangement of atoms which may be represented by a "lattice", Fig 11.9(a). Single crystals have considerable ductility and distort by "slip" along favourably oriented crystallographic planes when subjected to a sufficient stress, Fig 11.9(b). The crystals have a random orientation among themselves, and much of the strength of a metal is due to the fact that the slip planes lie in different directions in the different crystals and that at the crystal boundaries atoms are shared, i.e. have a position in the lattice of two or more crystals. Dislocations are "faults" in the atomic lattice, i.e. line discontinuities. Their density in an annealed material (total length of the lines of misfit per unit volume) is about 10^7 cm/cm^3.

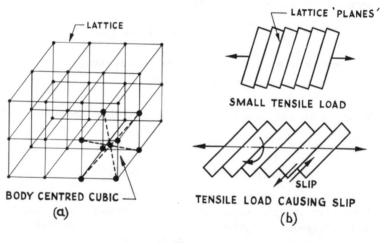

Fig. 11.9

(a) Lattice structure of a crystal   (b) Deformation by "slip"

Commercial metals are never "pure", and due to *minor* segregation at the ingot casting stage, a proportion of the impurities are deposited along the grain boundaries. It is one of the functions of hot working to break down the large crystals which form due to the slow cooling of the ingot, and to break up and disperse segregations. Fig 11.10 illustrates the effect of mechanical working and of the reheating of a metal. Large equi-axed crystals are distorted under the deforming load (by "slip"). The deformed crystals are unstable above a certain temperature, and on heating will recrystallise to form small equi-axed crystals. If the heating is

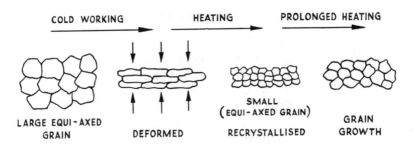

COLD WORKING   HEATING   PROLONGED HEATING

LARGE EQUI-AXED GRAIN   DEFORMED   SMALL (EQUI-AXED GRAIN) RECRYSTALLISED   GRAIN GROWTH

Fig. 11.10 Effects of mechanical working and o heating on the grain structure of a metal

prolonged, larger equi-axed crystals will "grow" from these small crystals.

In hot working the sequence is a continuous one, recrystallisation immediately follows severe distortion of the crystals. In cold working the temperature of the material remains below the recrystallisation temperature. Changes of mechanical properties which arise during cold working (pp. 336–338) are mainly the result of the deformation of the crystals by "slip", so that ultimately the number of "slip planes" remaining unused is small. An annealing process subsequent to cold working will change both the structure and mechanical properties of the material. Fig 11.11 shows the relationship between recrystallisation temperature and the degree of cold work; Fig 11.12 shows the relationship between the grain size resulting from an annealing process and the amount of cold work to which the material has been subjected. The very coarse grain is that caused by the *critical* amount of cold work. In sheet-metal presswork it is necessary to avoid the critical amount of cold work where subsequent heat treatments occur, otherwise a large-grained "orange peel" surface defect will result.

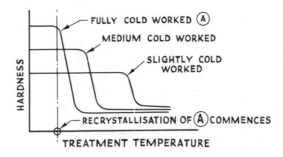

Fig. 11.11 Influence of the amount of cold work (as revealed by hardness) upon recrystallisation temperature

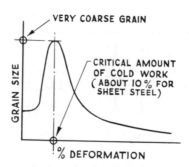

Fig. 11.12 "Critical" amount of cold work

One result of the dispersion of segregations during hot working is that commercial forms of metal tend to have directional properties. Sheet and strip metals used in presswork will bend across the direction of rolling more successfully than along the direction of rolling; sharp bends made along the direction of rolling may cause cracks to appear on the tension side of the bend. Deep-drawn cups frequently have localised elongations round their rim (ears) caused by differing properties of ductility along and across the strip. One of the advantages of cold forging p. 375, as compared with conventional machining, is that the flow pattern of the material may relate more satisfactorily to the stresses which the component has to carry.

The general metallurgical concepts stated above need to be modified when considering certain alloys. The solid-solution alloys behave very much as pure metals. More complex alloys do not conform to the simple pattern of the pure metals. Fig 11.13 shows the changes in the strength and ductility which occur in brasses as the zinc content is increased.

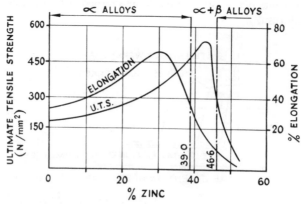

Fig. 11.13 Influence of percentage composition upon the properties of brasses

The α brasses are both hot and cold working.

The α + β brasses are hot working because at the working temperature of about 750 °C the α phase is entirely absorbed into the β phase. Any brass containing the γ phase is brittle and of little use except for low-grade casting.

Table 11.1 draws attention to the remarkable change in mechanical properties of a 70/30 brass subjected to cold work.

TABLE 11.1

Condition of 70/30 Brass	0·1 % Proof stress N/mm²	Tensile strength N/mm²	% Elongation
Cold-rolled—annealed	92	325	70
50 % reduction by cold working	510	570	8

11.6 Sheet-metal Presswork

There are three different ways of working sheet metal in presses:

(i) **shearing**—deforming to a shear failure in order to cut various contours from the sheet;

(ii) **bending**—a localised deformation within the plastic range;

(iii) **drawing**—a deformation within the plastic range involving considerable change of shape.

The researches of the late Professor H. W. Swift considerably advanced the understanding of (i) and (iii). A summary of the more practical aspects of Professor Swift's work, by J. Willis (see bibliography), has influenced the treatment of sheet-metal presswork given in this chapter.

Shearing. Fig 11.14 shows the progressive deformation and the development of a shear fracture during the shearing process, together with a typical load-penetration graph as obtained experimentally by Swift.

Fig 11.15 illustrates the effect of clearance on the piercing of a moderately ductile metal which work hardens and begins to develop cracks at an early stage of penetration. If the clearance is suitable the cracks run one into the other. The resulting hole is slightly tapered; the work done in shearing is somewhere near minimum, but the maximum load on the punch is almost independent of the clearance and is given by:

$$P_{max} = \text{metal thickness } (t) \times \text{perimeter} \times \text{ultimate shear stress of sheet}$$

Fig 11.16 shows the effects of varying the clearance upon the sheared edges of a blank. The amount of clearance required to give a reasonably

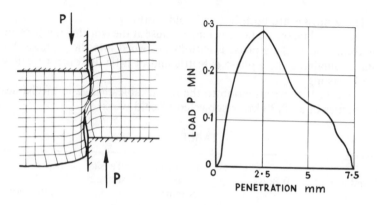

Fig. 11.14 Shearing of mild steel, no clearance employed

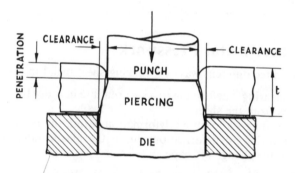

Fig. 11.15 Influence of "clearance" when piercing a hole

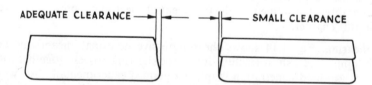

Fig. 11.16 Effects of varying the amount of clearance upon the edges sheared

clean edge varies with the thickness and hardness of the stock to be sheared. Swift suggested the values shown in Table 11.2.

Fig 11.17 illustrates a load-penetration curve for shearing where normal clearance is employed. It can be seen that a first estimate of the amount of work required for a shearing operation is given by,

TABLE 11.2

Clearance on Tools for Blanking and Piercing

Material	Hardness HV	Clearance as a % of thickness
Mild steel	94–144	5–10
70/30 brass	77–110	0–10
Copper	64–93	0–10
Zinc	61	0–5
Aluminium	21–28	0–5

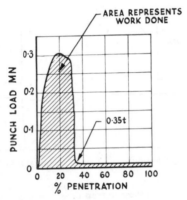

Fig. 11.17 *Load–penetration graph and work done in shearing, normal clearance*

work done = max punch load × % penetration × thickness

$$= P_{max}\, pt,$$

where the percentage penetration (p) represents the proportional depth to which the tools sink into the metal before cracks run one into the other. Table 11.3 gives some typical values for the resistance to shearing and percentage penetration which occurs under average conditions of clearance (σ_s is the ultimate shear stress).

In order to blank metal of substantial thickness or components of extensive contour, the work done in shearing may be spread over a larger length of press stroke by the introduction of *shear* on the tools. Fig 11.18 shows *shear* as applied to press tools.

Example 11.2

A hole, 100 mm diameter, is to be punched in steel plate 5·6 mm thick. The material is a cold-rolled 0·4 % carbon steel for which the ultimate shear stress is

TABLE 11.3

Percentage Penetration and Resistance to Shearing

Material	Annealed		Partially cold worked	
	σ_s N/mm^2	$p\%$	σ_s N/mm^2	$p\%$
Mild steel	240	50	297	38
Brass	220	50	360	20
Copper	150	55	195	30
Bronze	245	25	290	17
Aluminium	55	60	90	30

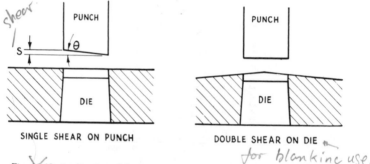

SINGLE SHEAR ON PUNCH   DOUBLE SHEAR ON DIE

Fig. 11.18 Application of shear *to press tools* s = *depth of shear on punch*

550 N/mm^2. With normal clearance on the tools, cutting is complete at 40%
penetration of the punch. Give suitable diameters for the punch and die and a
suitable shear angle for the punch in order to bring the work within the capacity
of a 30 t press.

Solution

Suitable clearance on tools say 10% of work thickness.
Punch diameter = 100 mm (determines smallest opening)
Die diameter   = $100 + 2(0.1 \times 5.6) = 101.1$ mm
Max load on punch (without shear)

$$= 550 \times 100\pi \times 5.6 \times 10^{-3}$$
$$= \underline{968 \text{ kN}}$$

Let s mm = the depth of shear required to reduce the punch load to 300 kN
Work available during shearing stroke = $(300 s)$ J
Work required to shear hole = $968 \times 5.6 \times 0.4 = 2168$ J
Equating the amounts of work,

$$300 s = 2168$$
$$s = \underline{7.23 \text{ mm}}$$

Angle of shear, $\tan \theta = \dfrac{7.23}{100} = 0.0723 \quad \underline{\theta = 4.2°}$

The assumption has been made that shear on the punch will spread the load uniformly over the working portion of the stroke. This is not strictly true for piercing a circular hole. Also there is an additional load, required to bend the piercing to the punch face contour, which has not been included. Since the amount of shear angle suggested is already fairly large, it would be advisable to transfer the operation to a slightly larger press if available, say 35–40 tonne.

Finish Blanking Technique. Swift investigated blanking conditions in which a close-fitting punch having a sharp edge was used in conjunction with a die having a radiused edge, as shown in Fig 11.19. It was discovered that very smooth-edged blanks were produced, probably due to the ironing effect as the material is forced into the die, but that considerably more energy was required than for conventional blanking. The Production Engineers Research Association (PERA) further developed this process, now referred to as the "finish blanking" technique.

Savings effected by this process in eliminating profile trimming of a copper blank, as reported by PERA, have been substantial.

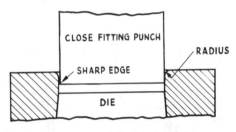

Fig. 11.19 "Finish blanking" technique

11.7 Bending

The bending of a metal strip or bar gives rise to plastic deformation in compression on one side, and in tension on the other side of a neutral plane. As the deformation proceeds the width on the compressed side of the bar increases, while that on the stretched side of the bar decreases and to maintain the moment of resistance for the area, the neutral plane displaces towards the compressed side of the metal. Fig 11.20 illustrates this. The shift of the plane must be taken into account when estimating lengths of material prior to bending; the principles are generally well known and are set out in engineering reference books under "allowances for bends".

Fig 11.21 shows the general arrangement of the tooling required to produce bends in strip metal. The load on the punch will vary during the operating cycle according to the work being done.

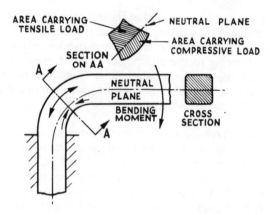

Fig. 11.20 Displacement of neutral plane during bending of a bar

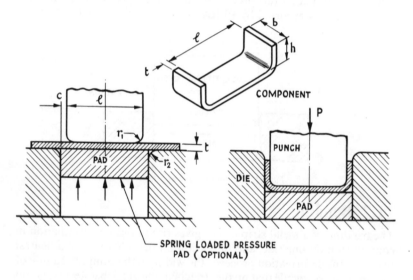

Fig. 11.21 Press-tool for a simple bending operation

A punch load P_B is required to produce the bends. The conditions are as represented in Fig 11.22. Once the material in the region of the bend is stressed to the plastic state the stress distribution can be represented with approximate accuracy as shown in Fig 11.22.

$$\text{Moment of resistance to bending} = \frac{bt}{2}\sigma_y\frac{t}{2} = \frac{bt^2}{4}\sigma_y$$

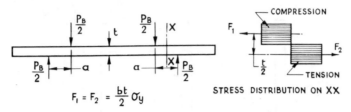

Fig. 11.22 Approximate stress distribution in a bending operation

The moment acting is obtained by assuming concentrated loads to occur at the points of tangency between the punch and die radii, and the strip, hence:

$$\text{Bending moment} = \frac{P_B}{2}a$$

Distance $a = r_1 + c + r_2$ (Fig 11.22) at the start of bending but reduces as the punch descends and may be taken as equal to the metal thickness t for estimating P_B.

$$\text{Equating moments,} \quad \frac{P_B t}{2} = \frac{bt^2}{4}\sigma_y$$

$$P_B = \frac{bt}{2}\sigma_y \tag{11.3}$$

The solution ignores the effects of friction.

As the metal strip is drawn into the die there will be friction between the component and the die walls which will rise to a high value if dimension c is made smaller than the strip thickness t. Assuming the material is stressed up to the yield point, and that the coefficient of friction is given by μ, the maximum punch load required to overcome this friction is given by:

$$P_F = 2\mu bh\sigma_y \tag{11.4}$$

If c is much smaller than t ironing will occur; the solution may then be obtained by reference to p. 364.

In order to "set" the bends, and flatten (planish) the workpiece, it is sometimes required to "bottom" the press. To do this effectively the punch load must be sufficient to take the material trapped beneath it just above the yield stress. The required force for planishing is given by,

$$P_P = bl\sigma_y \tag{11.5}$$

Example 11.3

Fig 11.23 shows the dimensions of a bracket required to be bent from a flat strip of mild steel of 450 N/mm² yield stress. If the work is drawn to a depth of 18 mm below the top surface of the die, find the punch force required for:

    (i) bending
    (ii) overcoming friction, assuming the sides of the component are very slightly ironed (take $\mu = 0.15$);
    (iii) planishing at the end of the stroke.

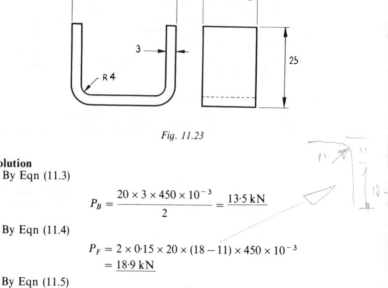

Fig. 11.23

Solution
By Eqn (11.3)

$$P_B = \frac{20 \times 3 \times 450 \times 10^{-3}}{2} = \underline{13 \cdot 5 \text{ kN}}$$

By Eqn (11.4)

$$P_F = 2 \times 0 \cdot 15 \times 20 \times (18 - 11) \times 450 \times 10^{-3}$$
$$= \underline{18 \cdot 9 \text{ kN}}$$

By Eqn (11.5)

$$P_P = 20 \times (32 - 14) \times 450 \times 10^{-3}$$
$$= \underline{162 \text{ kN}}$$

The results show quite clearly that for the planishing operation the press capacity must be much higher than is necessary to accomplish the bending operation. Because the force to overcome friction may exceed that required to bend the material, Eqn (11.3) does not satisfactorily indicate the press load capacity for bending.

Fig 11.21 and Fig 11.24 illustrate various types of bending tools. A feature of cold bending which frequently requires attention is the "spring-back" which occurs due to elastic recovery of the strained material, as illustrated in Fig 11.25. Ways of countering this effect are:

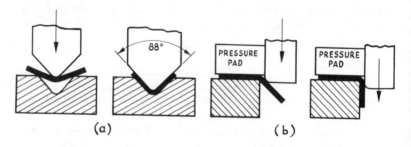

Fig. 11.24 *Various methods of bending by means of press-tools*

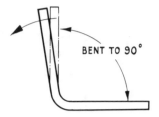

Fig. 11.25 "Springback" in sheet metal bends

(i) overbending, e.g. $\theta = 88°$ in Fig 11.24 (*a*) in order to produce 90° bend;

(ii) overbending by means of an "ironing" effect as illustrated in Fig 11.26;

(iii) slight ironing and planishing to "set" the bends as on p. 355.

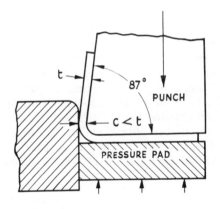

Fig. 11.26 Overbending by ironing

11.8 Deep Drawing   must be ductile metals

Swift has shown that stress analysis applied to deep drawing is an involved matter. Rules for deep drawing remain largely empirical, and research has been confined almost exclusively to the drawing of cylindrical cups. For other shapes a theoretical discussion of the deforming mechanics is too complicated to lead to any useful general rules.

Fig 11.27 shows the essential features of the "drawing" process. As the punch descends, material from the flange is drawn over the die radius and into the wall of the cup. The accompanying deformation is illustrated in

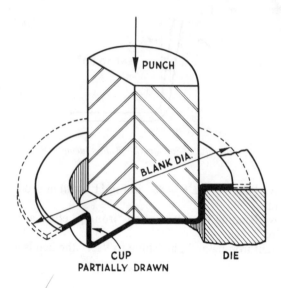

Fig. 11.27 Basic features of a metal-drawing operation

Fig 11.28. The drawing action induces a circumferential compressive stress in the flange. Except for relatively thick material, there is a tendency for the flange to wrinkle, and a pressure pad must then be used to prevent this. Fig 11.29 illustrates the tooling principles employed; the lower pressure pad is optional. Fig 11.30 shows the stresses acting upon a small element of material positioned within the flange, as depicted by Swift. It is clear that the element will tend to increase in thickness as it is drawn towards the wall of the cup. Fig 11.31 shows changes of thickness caused by the drawing process.

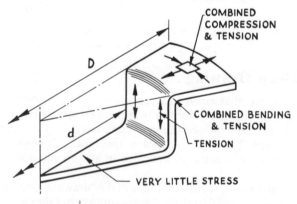

Fig. 11.28 Deforming stresses in metal drawing

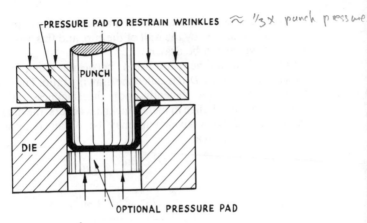

PRESSURE PAD TO RESTRAIN WRINKLES ≈ ⅓ × punch pressure.

Fig. 11.29 *Press-tool for drawing a cup*

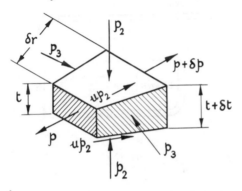

Fig. 11.30 *Stresses acting upon a small element of flange material during a drawing operation (after Swift)*

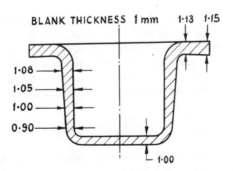

Fig. 11.31 *Plastic strain in a drawn cup*

The punch force in "drawing" is limited to the maximum tensile load which can be carried by the wall of the cup, and this sets a limit to depth of flange which can be drawn.

Fig 11.32 shows the relationships between a blank and the resulting drawn cup. The ratio D/d is called the drawing ratio. The maximum value of the drawing ratio depends upon the thickness ratio t/D. If it is assumed that no change in metal thickness occurs, the diameter of blank required to draw a given cup may be obtained approximately by equating surface areas.

$$\frac{\pi D^2}{4} = \frac{\pi d^2}{4} + \pi dh$$

$$D = \sqrt{(d^2 + 4dh)} \tag{11.6}$$

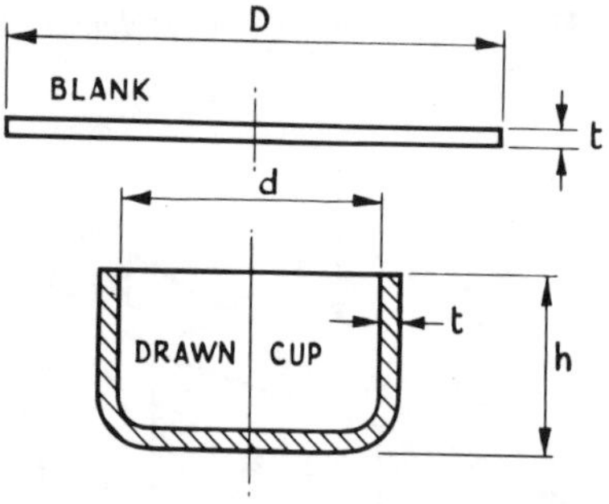

Fig. 11.32

From figures published by Crane (see bibliography), and by reference to test results given in Swift's researches, the following table has been constructed to show the maximum drawing ratios for high-grade sheet steel.

Both Swift and Crane show that $D/d = 2$ represents about the maximum drawing ratio likely to be achieved under good conditions, and under general manufacturing conditions somewhat lower first reductions are advised. Some materials relatively weak in tension, e.g. pure aluminium, cannot be drawn to quite the high ratio of sheet steel.

The material properties which principally determine how well a metal may draw are:

    (i) ratio of yield stress to ultimate stress (σ_y/σ_t), the lower the ratio the better;

    (ii) rate of increase of yield stress relative to progressive amounts of cold work; too rapid work hardening is usually an indication of low drawing property.

TABLE 11.4

Drawing Ratios for Sheet Steel (First Draw) where a Pressure Pad is Employed

Thickness ratio, $\frac{t}{D} \times 100$	Maximum drawing ratio, D/d
0·15	1·43
0·20	1·54
0·30	1·67
0·40	1·82
0·50	1·91
Above 0·50	2·00

Professor Swift was able to show that the maximum drawing ratio was achieved by observing the following rules:

(i) the drawing radius of the die to be $10t$;
(ii) the pressure pad force to be about $\frac{1}{3}$ of the punch force, more rather than less.

An empirical formula for the punch load during drawing can be developed from two basic facts established by Swift's researches:

(i) cups tend to fail by tearing of the wall near the bottom when the ratio $\frac{D}{d}$ exceeds 2;
(ii) the drawing load increases in an approximate straight line relationship with respect to the drawing ratio.

When $\frac{D}{d} = 2$ the punch force is given approximately by

$$P_{\max} = \sigma_t \pi dt$$

where σ_t is the UTS of the sheet.

For other drawing ratios,

$$P = \sigma_t \pi dt \left[\frac{D}{d} - 1 \right] \text{ according to (ii) above.}$$

Where P is required as a means of selecting press capacity, a degree of safety can be introduced into the expression and some allowance made for friction between the cup and the die walls, by adding 30% to the above,

i.e.
$$P = 1·3\, \sigma_t \pi dt \left[\frac{D-d}{d} \right]$$

$$= 1·3\, \sigma_t \pi t [D - d] \tag{11.7}$$

This expression does not make any allowance for ironing the walls of the cup and should be used without making such an allowance only where the clearance between the punch and die is about 5 % larger than the blank thickness.

Example 11.4

A cup, 105 mm inside dia. × 90 mm deep, is to be drawn from steel sheet of deep-drawing quality 1 mm thick. Determine the blank diameter and a suitable punch diameter for the first draw. Give the probable dimensions of the cup resulting from the first draw and estimate the press capacity required, assuming $\sigma_t = 415$ N/mm^2

Solution

By Eqn (11.6) $D = [105^2 + (4 \times 105 \times 90)]^{\frac{1}{2}} = 221$ mm

Thickness ratio, $\dfrac{t}{D} \times 100 = \dfrac{1 \cdot 00}{221} \times 100 = 0 \cdot 453$

By Table 11.4, safe drawing ratio = 1·82

Dia for first draw, $d = \dfrac{221}{1 \cdot 82} = 121$ mm

The cup cannot be produced by a single-stage draw, and the reduction must be divided between the operation here considered and a redrawing operation. If d is taken as 121 mm the amount of the reduction at the redrawing operation is rather small, and it would be better to have a somewhat lower reduction at the first draw. (See p. 364 for redrawing ratios.)

Let the diameter of first draw be $\underline{d = 130 \text{ mm}}$

$\dfrac{D}{d}$ for 1st draw = 1·7

$\dfrac{D}{d}$ for 2nd draw = 1·24, which is quite suitable.

Estimated depth of first draw when $d = 130$, by Eqn (11.6):

$$130^2 + (4 \times 130)h = 221^2$$
$$h = \underline{61 \cdot 43 \text{ mm}}$$

Estimated capacity of press required, by Eqn (11.7):

$$P = 1 \cdot 3 \times 415 \times \pi \times 1(221 - 130) \times 10^{-3}$$
$$= \underline{154 \cdot 3 \text{ kN}} \ (15 \cdot 43 \text{ t force})$$

If a double-action press is used it might just be possible to do this job on a press of 15 t capacity. However, since the maximum punch force is only available near the end of the stroke, the maker's capacity charts should be consulted. If a single-action press is used the punch load will be increased by the pressure-pad load (because there is no separate part of the press mechanism to provide this), and an increase of $\frac{1}{3}P$ must be made. It might then be just possible to do the job in a 20-ton single-action press, but again the maker's charts should be consulted.

Redrawing. Where it is impossible to obtain the required depth of cup at one draw, as in the above example, there are several ways of deepening the cup after the first draw. These are:

(i) redrawing, either by direct or by reverse redrawing methods;

(ii) ironing, which will restore a more uniform wall thickness to the cup;

(iii) pressure sinking, a method applicable to cups which are short relative to their diameter, and which increases the thickness of the cup walls. (See Willis under bibliography)

Fig 11.33 shows successive stages in producing a cup, and Fig 11.34 shows the normal form of a redrawing tool where a pressure pad is employed to prevent wrinkling of the work. Swift found that a throat angle of 10° gave the best results for most materials, but that 15° was superior for the redrawing of aluminium. Fig 11.35 illustrates reversed redrawing; the process does not permit of any greater reduction, but has

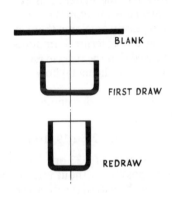

Fig. 11.33 Successive stages of deep drawing

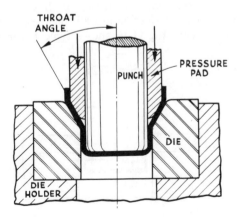

Fig. 11.34 Press-tool for redraw operation

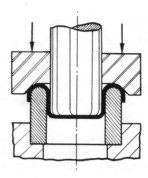

Fig. 11.35 Reversed redrawing

the advantage of "working" the material more uniformly than direct redrawing. For this reason it is sometimes used on brasses which have to be heat treated to avoid season cracking; there is then less likelihood of coarse grain developing due to critical amounts of cold work having occurred. Swift emphasised that the reverse redrawing die should have a single-radius curve over which the metal flows, not separate radii joined by a flat.

Redrawing is generally done in descending ratios for the subsequent draws given approximately by:

$$(D/d)\ 1{\cdot}43,\ 1{\cdot}33,\ 1{\cdot}25,\ 1{\cdot}19,\ 1{\cdot}14\ \text{and}\ 1{\cdot}11.$$

For thin material a first redraw of 1·33 or 1·25 may be sufficiently high. Several redraws may be possible without inter-stage annealing, but the total reduction made must be within the ductile range of the material as revealed by its percentage elongation.

Ironing.   This process is similar in principle to the cold drawing of tubes on a mandrel. There is a reduction in wall thickness and a consequent lengthening of the cup. Fig 11.36 shows typical ironing conditions.

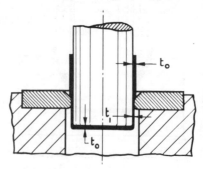

Fig. 11.36 "Ironing" of a cup

Annealed cups can be subjected to a wall-thickness reduction of about 50%, but in practice the amount of reduction is generally lower and the purpose of the process is generally to obtain uniform wall thickness.

If the wall thickness is small relative to the cup diameter, then by the property of constant volume,

$$\pi d t_0 h_0 = \pi d t_1 h_1, \text{ hence } \frac{t_0}{t_1} = \frac{h_1}{h_0} \text{ very nearly,}$$

and by Eqn (11.1) for frictionless work:

$$\text{Work done in ironing} = \sigma_y V \ln \frac{t_0}{t_1}$$

An allowance for friction can be made on the lines of Eqn (11.4).

Example 11.5

A drawn steel cup, nominal wall thickness 0·9 mm, is ironed on a 50 mm diameter punch through a die opening of 50 mm diameter. If the mean yield stress is 500 N/mm² and the coefficient of friction is 0·07, find the punch load. The parallel land of the die is 3·8 mm wide.

Solution

Let $\quad P_l =$ frictionless load of ironing.

$$P_l = \frac{\sigma_y \pi d_m t_0 h_0}{h_1} \ln \frac{t_0}{t_1}, \quad \text{but} \frac{h_0}{h_1} = \frac{t_1}{t_0}$$

Hence $\quad P_l = \sigma_y \pi d_m t_1 \ln \frac{t_0}{t_1} \qquad (d_m = \text{mean dia})$

$$= 500 \times \pi \times 49{\cdot}5 \times 0{\cdot}5 \times \ln \frac{0{\cdot}9}{0{\cdot}5} \times 10^{-3}$$

$$= \underline{22{\cdot}85 \text{ kN}}$$

This punch load causes tensile stress in that portion of the wall which has passed through the die; it must not raise the stress above the yield point or the metal will stretch further and may tear.

The additional load on the punch due to friction:

$$P_F = 0{\cdot}07 \times 500 \times 49\pi \times 3{\cdot}8 \times 10^{-3}$$
$$= \underline{20{\cdot}48 \text{ kN}}$$
$$\text{Total load on punch} = \underline{43{\cdot}33 \text{ kN}}$$

Lubrication. Operating speeds for drawing and ironing are within the range 8–16 m/min, although at the higher speeds there is sometimes a tendency for the material being worked to "pick up" on the die. This is a form of pressure welding caused by the high pressure and the local heating due to friction. Adequate lubrication lowers the operating forces and helps to prevent "pick up" of material on the tools.

Table 11.5 shows some of the lubricants used by Swift.

TABLE 11.5
Lubricants for Drawing and Ironing

Material	Drawing lubricants	Ironing lubricants
Mild steel	Graphite-bearing lubricants and soaps	Graphite-bearing lubricants
Brass	Soap lubricants	Graphite and kaolin
Aluminium	Graphite and tallow and soaps	Dry graphite

Not all lubricants are equally acceptable, some cause discoloration of the components worked. There is a large number of commercial products available which fulfil particular needs.

11.9 Extrusion

Extrusion, Fig 11.37, is rapidly becoming a metal-forming process of special interest to the production engineer. It has been in use as a primary forming process for bar sections since the beginning of the century, but considerable interest is now centred in its use as a secondary forming process capable of supplying components to reasonably close tolerances and at lower cost than the conventional machining method. Note the great increase in use of aluminium extrusions for building.

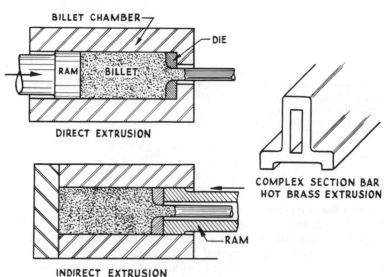

Fig. 11.37 Primary extrusion processes

Hot extrusion of copper alloy bar in a variety of sections, see Fig 11.37, dates from 1894, when George Alexander Dick took out a patent for his horizontal extrusion press (direct extrusion).

Typical hot extrusion temperatures are:

Magnesium and its alloys	280–320°C
Aluminium and its alloys	450–490°C
Brasses	700–750°C
Copper	800–880°C

Steels may be hot extruded in the 1000–1250°C range, but at these high temperatures problems of scaling and die wear occur. By the principles detailed on p. 338, hot working can be done at lower operating forces and power than cold working, but it cannot achieve the same high accuracy. This is particularly true for steels.

The flow pattern of extrusion has been studied by means of the slip-line field theory (Johnson and Mellor 1900) and also by practical tests. Slugs of soft material are divided axially on a diameter, and a square-mesh network is marked on the axial sections. After extrusion the halves of the slug are separated and the resulting distortion of the network examined. Fig 11.38(*a*) shows the flow pattern of a typical forward (or direct) extrusion. Note the "dead" metal zone at the corner of the billet chamber and the shearing of the billet resulting from this. Fig 11.38(*b*) shows the flow pattern of a typical backward (or indirect) extrusion to form a canister, where taper on the punch end, and the more limited extent of the deformation, have practically eliminated any dead metal at A.

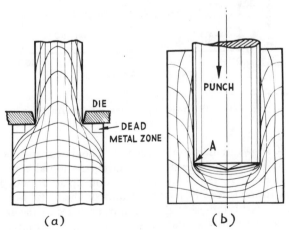

Fig. 11.38 Flow patterns in extrusion

(*a*) Forward extrusion (after Pearson)
(*b*) Backward extrusion (after Feldmann)

368   *Principles of engineering production*

Ram Forces in Extrusion. Experimental studies have been made by fitting pressure-recording equipment to hydraulic presses and plotting the pressure against the ram travel. Fig. 11.39 shows the curve for backward and for forward extrusion of aluminium at a temperature of 450°C. The curves from O to A and O to B show the initial build up of the load, during which there is elastic flexure of the press and a small yield of the billet necessary to force it against the wall of the billet chamber. Pressure for forward extrusion is seen to fall as the work proceeds from A to C, while for backward extrusion the pressure remains approximately constant. This difference is due to the friction which arises in forward extrusion, during which the entire billet must slide forward in the billet chamber. Both curves show a sudden rise from C to D. This occurs as the billet-end gets nipped between the punch and the die, and is due to the rise of yield stress caused by deforming and by the fact that the friction force depends upon the ratio d/h (see Eqn (11.2)). There is a small amount of the billet which cannot be extruded and which must be cut off as a discard from the end of the extrusion.

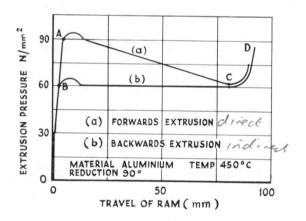

Fig. 11.39 Extrusion pressures (after Pearson)

Fig 11.40 shows an indicator diagram for a cold extrusion, of the type obtained by Feldmann. The diagram shows the initial spread of the billet up to point A, the elastic compression up to B and the fairly uniform extrusion force which is then required. The useful work done in extruding the part is represented by the area enclosed by the graph; area C represents work lost as the elastic strains in the component and equipment are released. The very high punch load necessary for a cold extrusion in steel should be noted.

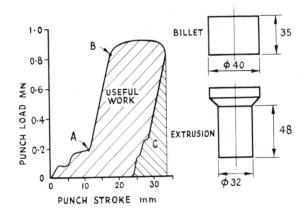

Fig. 11.40 Load–displacement diagram for a cold extrusion in steel
(after Feldmann)

Forces and Work Done in Extrusion. As with sheet-metal press-work, accurate calculation of extrusion forces is difficult because of the involved mechanics of the plastic yielding of metals. However, reasonable estimates are required in order to select press capacities and to design suitable tools. Since cold extrusion (forging) of steel makes the most severe demands on equipment, this topic will be considered further.

The following semi-empirical approach is widely used. Eqn (11.1) shows that the frictionless work of deformation can be calculated.

Work done $= \sigma_y V \ln(h_0/h_1)$, from which it is seen that the principal logarithmic deformation $\ln(h_0/h_1)$ gives a proportional indication of the work to be done.

Fig 11.41 shows a cylindrical billet and the extrusion which could be produced from it. If the frictionless work done on a perfectly plastic material is considered it can be shown that the work done in extrusion to reduce the diameter is equal to the work required in compression to

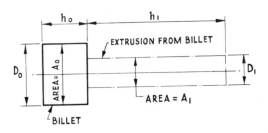

Fig. 11.41 Cylindrical extrusion from a cylindrical billet

return the metal back to the billet dimensions. By application of Eqn (11.1), substituting h_1/h_0 for h_0/h_1,

$$\text{Work done in extrusion} = \sigma_y V \ln \frac{h_1}{h_0}$$

By equating volumes,

$$\frac{A_0}{A_1} = \frac{h_1}{h_0}, \text{ where } A = \text{area of cross-section;}$$

hence,

$$\text{Work done in extrusion} = \sigma_y V \ln \frac{A_0}{A_1}$$

$$\text{Mean force on punch } P_E = \sigma_y A_0 \ln \frac{A_0}{A_1} \quad (11.8)$$

where P_E is the force required to extrude, friction neglected.

It appears from Eqn (11.8) that the load on the punch (or ram) required for extrusion is related to three main variables:

(i) σ_y, which will rise steadily according to the amount of deformation involved;

(ii) A_0, the area of billet to which the ram load is transferred;

(iii) $\ln(A_0/A_1)$, which is a measure of the extent of the deformation required.

Research work by Pugh and Watkins (see bibliography) has enabled the following empirical formulae for the cold extrusion of a number of non-ferrous metals to be established. The basic formula is:

$$p = a \ln \frac{A_0}{A} + b \quad (11.9)$$

where p is the extrusion pressure at the punch in N/mm^2 units:

$A_0 =$ cross-sectional area of the billet;

$A =$ cross-sectional area of the extrusion.

The constants a and b for various materials are shown in Table 11.6.

TABLE 11.6

Constants for the Pressure of Extrusion, Ram Speed 140 mm/min

Material	a	b
99·5% pure aluminium	223	106
ERHC copper	722	80
70/30 brass	1377	11
Tin	92	46
Zinc	325	177
Lead	42	39

Somewhat higher values of p generally occur as the speed of extrusion is raised.

The values of a and b automatically allow for the friction which occurs during the extrusions.

Fig 11.42 shows the experimental results in their graphical form for both forward and backward cold extrusion of a steel, En 2A, now 040A12. The empirical laws given above were formed by fitting equations to similar graphical results. Note that the backward extrusion of canisters does not give a graph quite the same as for forward extrusion. The reason for this lies partly in the fact that the ratio $\ln(A_0/A)$ is not the exact principal logarithmic deformation for producing canisters.

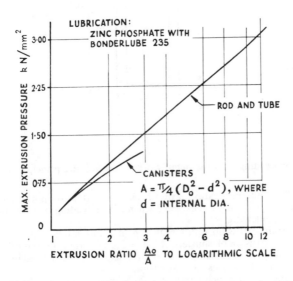

Fig. 11.42 Extrusion pressures for En 2A steel, current equivalent 040A12.
(after Pugh and Watkins)

Researches at PERA on the cold extrusion of low carbon steels have enabled Tilsley and Howard to construct a similar empirical equation for these steels,

$$p = \sigma_y \left(3\cdot45 \ln \frac{A_0}{A} + 1\cdot15 \right) \qquad (11.10)$$

where σ_y is the yield stress of the particular steel after annealing. Pugh and Watkins, and Feldmann, also give information from which the deforming pressures for steels can be determined. For any particular composition of steel other than low plain carbon steel (0·1–0·3% carbon), reference should be made to the available test date for that steel because the extrusion pressure rises with increase in carbon content and with alloying additions of nickel and chromium.

Example 11.6

Determine a procedure, and determine the extrusion pressures and loads, for producing a cold extrusion in 040A12 steel to the drawing Fig 11.43.

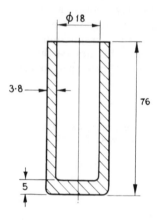

Fig. 11.43

Solution

Before proceeding with the detail work, a few guiding principles need to be stated.

(1) The slenderness ratio l/d of a backwards extrusion punch required to form a canister, should not exceed 3 when cold extruding steels, or the punch may fail by buckling.

(2) Certain extrusion ratios reduce p to a minimum value, and for the backwards extrusion of canisters, $A_0/A = 2$ is a desirable ratio for this reason.

(3) Generally, for canisters, a greater reduction can be effected by a forward extrusion than by a backward extrusion.

(4) A maximum punch stress of 3700 N/mm² should not be exceeded.

From the drawing, Fig 11.43, it can be seen that the outside diameter of the finished cup is 25·6 mm. It might be possible to start with 24 mm diameter bar, coin this out to 25·6 mm diameter, and then backward extrude the canister. The required extrusion ratio would be

$$\frac{A_0}{A} = \frac{25\cdot6^2}{25\cdot6^2 - 18^2} = 1\cdot98 \text{ (near to the ideal value)}$$

However, the required length of punch would be 71 mm, making the punch slenderness ratio $71/18 (= 3·94)$, which is too high.

For this reason it will be necessary to start by making a backward extrusion as a preform, and to increase the depth of this by a forward extrusion. Possible billet diameters are 28 mm or 32 mm. If, as seems probable, the 32 mm diameter will give a solution, calculations must be made to confirm this.

Final extrusion ratio, $\dfrac{A_0}{A} = \dfrac{32^2 - 18^2}{25\cdot6^2 - 18^2} = 2\cdot11$ which seems suitable.

Volume of component $= \dfrac{\pi}{4}[76(25{\cdot}6^2 - 18^2) + (18^2 \times 5)]$

$$= 21\,054 \text{ mm}^3$$

Required length of 32 mm diameter billet

$$= \dfrac{21\,054}{\dfrac{\pi}{4} \times 32^2} = 26{\cdot}18 \text{ mm}$$

It will not be possible to forward extrude the entire volume of material for reasons given on p. 368, so an allowance must be made for a discard and trimming of the top of the canister. A 10% allowance on the length of the billet is adequate.

The billet required is 32 mm diameter × 28·8 mm long and will be cut from bar stock and coined as shown in Fig 11.44(a). The coining operation assists in getting a symmetrical backward extrusion. The coined slug will be annealed, pickled, given a phosphate treatment (Bonderised) and then oiled. The phosphate coating, which itself acts as a lubricant, absorbs some of the oil and so further improves the lubrication.

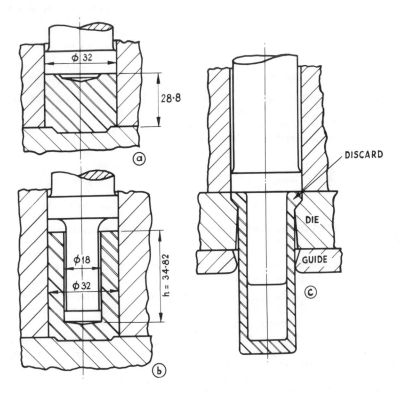

Fig. 11.44 Tooling for a cold extrusion in steel

The slug will then be backward extruded. Fig 11.44(*b*) shows the dimensions and tooling, dimension *h* must be calculated from the remaining sizes. By equating volumes:

$$h(32^2 - 18^2) = 32^2(28{\cdot}8 - 5)$$
$$h = 34{\cdot}82 \text{ mm}$$

The slenderness ratio of the required punch is $\dfrac{34{\cdot}82 + 2{\cdot}5}{18} = 2{\cdot}07$, which is quite satisfactory.

$$\text{The extrusion ratio is } \frac{32^2}{32^2 - 18^2} = 1{\cdot}463$$

This is an acceptable ratio.

For 040A12 steel in the annealed condition, σ_y is about 310 N/mm^2
By Eqn (11.10), extrusion pressure, $p_1 = 310 \, (3{\cdot}45 \ln 1{\cdot}463 + 1{\cdot}15)$

$$= \underline{764 \text{ N/mm}^2}$$

$$\text{Punch load} = \frac{\pi}{4} \times 18^2 \times 764 \times 10^{-3} = 195 \text{ kN.}$$

The canister so produced will now be forward extruded. The yield stress σ_y will be much higher than the 310 N/mm^2 used above unless the canister is annealed prior to the forward extrusion; however, the total amount of deformation required is quite possible without interstage annealing. Reference to load compression graphs show that after cold extrusion to a ratio of 1·463, σ_y will be about 560 N/mm^2.

[*Note:* The overall extrusion ratio, $\dfrac{32^2}{25{\cdot}6^2 - 18^2} = 3{\cdot}09$, is also the product of the separate extrusion ratios, i.e. $1{\cdot}463 \times 2{\cdot}11 = 3{\cdot}09$. Extrusion in steel may be taken to overall ratios of between 3 and 6, depending upon composition, without interstage annealing.]

Extrusion pressure $p_2 = 560(3{\cdot}45 \ln 2{\cdot}11 + 1{\cdot}15)$

$$= \underline{2087 \text{ N/mm}^2}$$

$$\text{Ram load} = \frac{\pi}{4}(32^2 - 18^2) \times 2087 \times 10^{-3} = 1147 \text{ kN}$$

(ie about 115 t force)

Fig 11.44(*c*) shows the arrangement for forward extrusion.

Extrusion Speeds. Experimental work reveals that there is generally some increase in the extrusion load accompanying an increase in extrusion speed, although the reverse may occur if the rise of temperature caused by the increased rate of working is sufficient to lower the yield stress of the material being worked.

Brasses and other non-ferrous alloys are extruded at speeds between 12 and 65 mm/s, the rate depending on the capacity and power of the equipment employed. Small extrusions carried out on crank-type presses may be done at relatively high speed, 150 mm/s, but bar extrusion by means of hydraulic presses tends to be at the lower rates.

Small slugs of aluminium, and tin–lead alloys, are extruded to form canisters by cold impact extrusion. The technique differs from other forms of extrusion mainly in the extrusion speed (100–350 mm/s) and in details of the tooling. Fig 11.45 shows a typical cold impact extrusion as carried out on a crank-type press, and the comparatively simple tooling involved. It is much simpler to produce a small deep canister in aluminium by impact extrusion than by deep drawing.

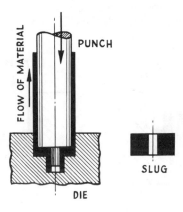

Fig. 11.45 Cold impact extrusion

Lubricants. These are particularly important in cold extrusion to ensure that there is no pressure welding of work material to the die or tool surfaces.

The non-ferrous metals may be lubricated with oils or tallow, or aluminium or zinc stearate; lanoline or powdered paraffin wax may also be used. For the brasses and copper, sulphonated oil or tallow is superior to the untreated lubricant. Lubricants favoured for cold impact extrusion are olive oil and powdered paraffin wax, or white vaseline and starch.

The most difficult lubrication problems are posed by steels. For hot extrusion, glass is used as a lubricant, and is effective in protecting the tools and reducing tool wear. The hot metal is rolled in glass fibre to coat the billet. Cold extrusion of steel requires a special surface coating of the billet and phosphating is the basis of most commercial methods of preparation. After phosphating, the work is lubricated with a sulphonated vegetable oil or tallow, which is partially absorbed into the phosphate coating.

Cold Forging of Steel. Extrusion techniques have been combined with hydraulic press techniques of squeeze-forging to give the process now

376 Principles of engineering production

generally described as cold forging of steel. The object is to form a component from a suitable billet without having to machine away surplus material; a cold-forged and thread-rolled socket screw is a typical product of the technique. The development is dependent upon special tool steels capable of withstanding compressive stresses up to 3700 N/mm², and upon presses such as the one installed by PERA, a 300 t double-action hydraulic extrusion press designed specially for this type of work. Fig 11.46 shows how backward and forward extrusion may be combined in a cold-forging operation, while Fig 11.47 shows a typical component produced by the cold forging technique.

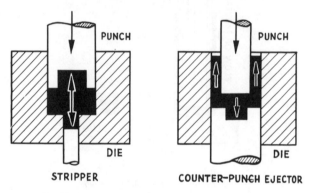

Fig. 11.46 Cold-forging operations (after Feldmann)

The economic advantages may be summarised as follows:

1. Material saving: this can be as high as 70% over conventional machining methods.
2. Reduction of process time: machining processes may be completely eliminated and the extrusion forging processes can be performed quite rapidly.
3. Dimensional accuracy: a tolerance of IT 11 is normal, but IT 9 can be achieved by introducing a "sizing" operation. By special coining or calibration operations, IT 8 or IT 7 can be achieved. The resulting surface finish, 0.6–0.8 μm R_a value, is superior to most single-point machining operations and equal to much commercially ground work.
4. Enhanced material properties: a 300 N/mm² UTS steel may cold work to 600 N/mm² UTS in the product, the hardness increasing from about 90–100 HB up to 200–250 HB. Fig 11.48 shows the changes in the mechanical properties of the material resulting from the process. There is, of course, some fall in ductility.

Economics of Cold Forging. Exploitation of the process depends upon adequate technical information at the design stage, and upon expensive

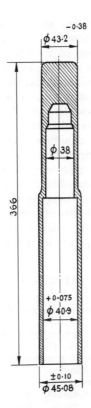

Fig. 11.47 Typical cold extrusion forging in steel

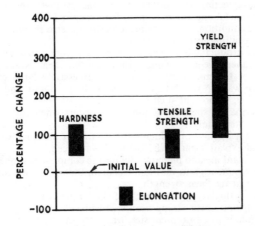

Fig. 11.48 Changes in the mechanical properties of steel produced by cold extrusion (after Galloway)

specialised tool design and manufacture. For these reasons the quantities required in order to compete with conventional machining methods are rather high, but the quantities required may fall as the process becomes more highly developed and more widely used.

For multi-purpose installations capable of handling a reasonable range of work, the economic minimum quantity is about 3000–10 000 components, depending upon the complexity of the part. Where highly specialised single-purpose installations are required (as in automobile manufacture) the economic minimum quantity will be 100 000–500 000 parts, depending upon complexity.

The maximum advantages cannot be obtained without complete reconsideration of component design, because a component originally conceived as a machined drop stamping may not be ideally suited to cold forging. Satisfactory exploitation of new manufacturing processes must start at the component design stage, hence the need for designers and draughtsmen to study the principles involved.

EXERCISES 11

1. Summarise the advantages of hot and cold forming of metals over production by machining methods under the following headings: material utilisation and properties, manufacturing costs.

What are the principle disadvantages? Some reference to typical components, tooling and other equipment is expected.

2. (a) What physical and mechanical properties control the suitability of an alloy for a deep-drawing operation?

(b) Give a list of the chief metals and alloys which can be deep-drawn and discuss briefly the stages in a deep-drawing operation.

3. A hollow cylindrical steel blank, inside dia 24 mm, outside dia 50 mm, thickness 24 mm, is compressed between parallel flat anvils until the thickness is reduced to 18 mm. The initial yield stress is 200 N/mm², the final yield stress is 350 N/mm² Neglecting friction at the anvils, estimate the work done in deforming the metal and the maximum load required.

For the true conditions of deforming, describe the stresses induced in the steel ring and the resulting axial section.

4. A factory producing brass sheet by the "cold-work and anneal" cycle finds that in subsequent deep-drawing operations the sheet is subject to tears. Examination of the microstructure showed excessively large grain. Explain clearly the two ways in which this effect could be produced, and so decide the steps to be taken to prevent such losses.

5. (a) Describe the shearing action which occurs when cutting sheet metal with hardened steel tools.

(b) Describe a method of reducing the maximum tool load during such an operation, and explain clearly why the load is reduced.

6. Design a blanking and piercing tool for the component shown in Fig 11.49 Dimension the punches and dies and calculate the max. press load, assuming 155 N/mm² ultimate shear strength.

7. (a) What is the largest diameter that can be pierced in 1.6 mm thick steel plate of 310 N/mm² shear strength on a 25·t press?

(b) If the hole is to be nominal size, what size should the punch be?

(c) If the blank is to be drawn into a cup, what would be the approximate diameter after the first draw?

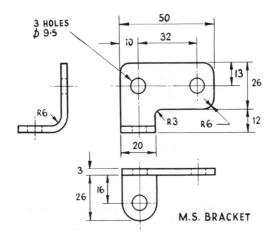

Fig. 11.49

8. The load–displacement graph of a drawing operation is shown in Fig. 11.50. The cup, of inside diameter 150 mm and depth 40 mm, is in steel sheet of thickness 3 mm. It is to be drawn on a double-action press of 80 t force (approximately 800 kN) capacity at 30° above bottom dead centre and 10 kJ continuous stroking capacity.

(a) Estimate from the graph approximately the amount of work needed, in kilojoules, to draw the cup.
(1 kJ = 1000 N m.)
  (b) (i) State whether or not the press specified is of adequate capacity.
      (ii) Justify your answer.
  (c) The press has a flywheel of moment of inertia 1200 kg m² rotating at 60 rev/min. How much energy can the flywheel supply for a 20% slowdown?
9. Fig 11.51 shows a cylindrical cup drawn from a disc. One formula for the maximum value of the drawing force (P) is

$$P = \pi d t \sigma (D/d - 0.7)$$

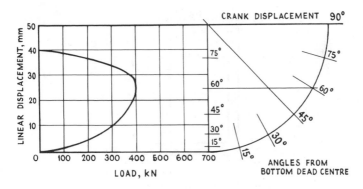

Fig. 11.50

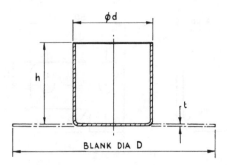

Fig. 11.51

where d, t and D are the dimensions shown on the diagram and σ is the yield stress of the material. The energy (W) required to draw the cup is given by

$$W = cPh$$

where h is the depth of the cup and c is a value depending upon the drawing conditions.

(*a*) A blank of diameter 500 mm and thickness 4·5 mm is drawn in one pass to a cup of diameter 300 mm.
Given $\sigma = 350$ N/mm^2, $c = 0·6$, find the maximum load and the energy required to draw this cup.

(*b*) A double-action press, load capacity 1500 kN and energy capacity 100 kJ when continuously stroking, is selected for the operation. Comment on the suitability of the press for this operation.

10.   A cylindrical cup of inside diameter 30 mm and depth 60 mm, is drawn from brass of thickness 0·8 mm.

(*a*) Calculate an approximate blank diameter.

(*b*) For the particular material the maximum ratio for successive draws (D/d) is 1·8, 1·4, 1·3 and 1·2. Calculate the minimum number of drawing operations for this cup.

(*c*) Explain why the drawing ratio (D/d) reduces for EACH subsequent draw.

(*d*) For the first drawing operation, the presses available are rated at 10 ton, 15 ton and 20 ton. The material has a tensile strength of 320 N/mm^2.

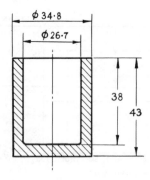

Fig. 11.52

Taking 1 ton force = 9·96 kN, find the lowest rated press which could be used.

11. With the aid of neat sketches, illustrate the principal features of the following processes:

    (a) Direct extrusion.
    (b) Indirect extrusion.
    (c) Impact extrusion.

12. Fig 11.52 shows a component required in 70/30 brass. It is proposed to make this by the following method:

    (i) shear billet from 25 mm dia bar;
    (ii) coin billet to 34·3 mm dia;
    (iii) anneal;
    (iv) backward extrude to form canister.

Estimate, making use of Eqn (11.9) where necessary:

    (a) the required length of bar to be sheared (allow 5 % for trimming the canister edge);
    (b) the shearing force required (ultimate shear 170 N/mm^2);
    (c) the maximum punch load for the coining operation;
    (d) the punch load for the backward extrusion.

CHAPTER 12
Precision Measurement

12.1

Engineering dimensional measurement involves the Euclidean concepts of the straight line and plane. Linear measurements are ratios expressed in terms of some arbitrary length standard, e.g. the Imperial Standard Yard or the International Prototype Metre. Other forms of length standard are possible, but present primary length standards are defined in terms of the wavelength of monochromatic light. The establishment of an absolute length standard belongs to the realm of physics rather than engineering.

Angular measurement involves the concept of a plane; the relationship between two non-parallel straight lines in space can only be expressed in terms of one angle if the lines lie in a common plane. The angle between intersecting planes can only be defined by reference to a third plane which intersects them: the fundamental (dihedral) angle between planes lies in a third plane which intersects both planes at right angles. These concepts are essential to the understanding of "solid angle" geometry such as the tool angle geometry of Chapters 5 and 8. An angle is measured in terms of its ratio to a natural standard, i.e. the circle (which may be subdivided into degrees), or the radian.

The international metre is defined in terms of the wave length of monochromatic light. The International Committee of Weights and Measures recommended Krypton 86 as the radiation source: under standard conditions the metre equals 1650763·73 wavelengths. The metre had its origin in the International Prototype Metre of 1889, a line standard of the form shown in Fig 12.1. The principal working standards of industry are the well-known slip (or block) gauges together with length bars and, less frequently used, precision line standards. Laser interferometry enables direct readings to be taken of the length of end standards (see p. 390).

12.2 Length Standards

The International Prototype Metre (Fig 12.1), is a **line standard**. The length is defined by two fine terminal lines. Fig 12.2 shows a form of line standard now commonly used in machines which employ an optical

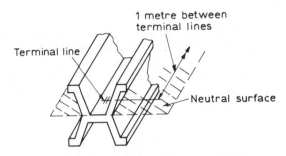

Fig. 12.1 International prototype metre of 1889

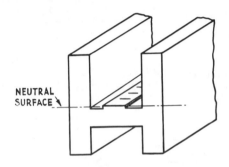

Fig. 12.2 Common form of line standard

measuring system. Sources of variation in the distance defined by the terminal lines of line standards are:

(i) temperature variations, due to normal expansion on heating;
(ii) flexure variations, caused by changes in weight distribution, i.e. by changing the points of support;
(iii) secular change, dimensional change occurring over long periods of time due to internal changes of the stress distribution and of the grain structure of the material.

To be suitable for use as a working line standard a material must have the following properties:

(i) take a high surface polish and be free of tarnishing;
(ii) have a suitable coefficient of expansion;
(iii) remain stable (in size) over long periods of time.

Standard length is defined at standard temperature; the International standard temperature for this purpose is 20 °C

Pure nickel is very stable, takes a suitable polish, does not tarnish and has a coefficient of expansion of $12 \cdot 8 \times 10^{-6}$ per deg C. An invar alloy of

58% nickel, 42% iron has similar properties, but has a coefficient of expansion of $11 \cdot 2 \times 10^{-6}$ per deg C in the temperature region of 20 °C, a figure very close to that for steels. Measurement of steel components by reference to such a line standard is obviously attractive; it is no longer necessary to work at exactly 20 °C, provided the work and the standard are at the same temperature. Many line standards are now made from this alloy.

TABLE 12.1

Coefficients of Linear Expansion

Material	Approx expansion per deg C, units $\times 10^{-6}$
Aluminium	22–24
Brass	18–20
Bronze	16–18
Cast iron (grey)	9–10
Copper	16–17
Magnesium	28–30
Nickel	12–13
Steel	11–12

Points of Support. Sir G. B. Airy was able to show that supporting a bar at two carefully determined points gave a condition for which the ends of the bar remain horizontal.

The relationship between the position of the two points of support and of the resulting deflection of bars of uniform cross-section has been fully discussed by Dr. Chree (see bibliography). Some of the points discussed are mathematically involved, but the gist of the matter is as follows.

With point O, Fig 12.3, as the origin of the x and y axes, the slope of the portion of the bar between A and B is given by:

slope,
$$\frac{\mathrm{d}y}{\mathrm{d}x} = \frac{W}{EI} \times \frac{1}{6}[l(l^2 - 3a^2) - (l - x)^3] \qquad (12.1)$$

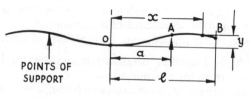

Fig. 12.3

deflection, $\quad y = \dfrac{W}{EI} \times \dfrac{1}{24}[4la^3 - l^4 + 4lx(l^2 - 3a^2) + (l-x)^4].$ (12.2)

where
$\quad\quad W$ = weight per unit length;
$\quad\quad E$ = Young's modulus, and
$\quad\quad I$ = second moment of area.

For the ends to be horizontal, $dy/dx = 0$, and from Eqn (12.1)

$$l(l^2 - 3a^2) - (l-x)^3 = 0$$

putting $x = l$, since we are dealing with point B,

$$l^2 = 3a^2, \text{ or } \frac{a}{l} = \frac{1}{\sqrt{3}} = \underline{0.577.}$$

The positions so defined are known as the "Airy" points of support.

It has been shown by Dr. Chree that minimum flexure occurs when the deflections at O and B are equal, i.e. when y is zero at B.

From Eqn (12.2), when $y = 0$,

$$4la^3 - l^4 + 4lx(l^2 - 3a^2) + (l-x)^4 = 0$$

and when $x = l$,

$$4la^3 - 12l^2 a^2 + 3l^4 = 0$$

or
$$4\left(\frac{a}{l}\right)^3 - 12\left(\frac{a}{l}\right)^2 + 3 = 0 \quad\quad (12.3)$$

Solving Eqn (12.3) by Newton's method gives,

$$\frac{a}{l} = \underline{0{\cdot}554}$$

The deflection, at its maximum value, is about twice as large for the "Airy" points of support $a/l = 0{\cdot}557$, as for supports at $a/l = 0{\cdot}554$.

End standards are supported at the "Airy" points so that the lapped end faces lie parallel. Ideally, line standards should be supported at $a/l = 0{\cdot}554$, so that the deflection is minimal. In view of the comparatively stiff sections used for line standards, it is unlikely that small changes in the position of the points of support will cause detectable changes in the length along the neutral plane.

Interferometry. Light is a form of energy radiation having wave properties. Suitable sources can emit monochromatic rays (rays confined to a very narrow spread of wavelength λ), which provide a basis for interferometric measurement.

As they leave a common source, rays are "in phase", but by causing them to traverse paths of differing length before they re-combine, two such rays can interfere. Newton's rings provide a well-known example of this principle. Fig 12.4(a) shows, in simplified form, optical conditions for interference. Rays PQR and PR emerge from a common source but travel by different paths to the eye. Ignoring phase change at the reflecting surface, the intensity of the re-combined rays depends upon the difference of their path lengths (PQR − PR) and their wavelength λ. Fig 12.4(b) illustrates graphically the results of re-combination.

(i) when the path difference is $N\lambda$ (i.e. in phase)
(ii) when the path difference is $(N + \frac{1}{2})\lambda$ (i.e. out of phase)

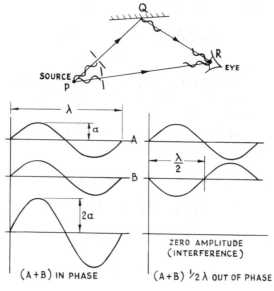

Fig. 12.4 (a)   (b)

The distinct dark bands caused by interference provide a physical basis for precision measurement.

The simplest practical method of using the interference effect is by means of an optical flat (or proof plane). This is a thick disc of either glass or quartz with parallel faces ground and polished flat to a very high order of accuracy. Usually only one face is of specified flatness; it may be coated to increase the light reflected from the surface (it then becomes a more efficient beam splitter).

Fig 12.5 shows an optical flat resting at a very small angle α (exaggerated in the diagram) to the upper lapped surface of a gauge block. Incident rays, R_1 R_2, . . . from a common monochromatic source are partially reflected at the lower (coated) face of the flat while the remaining portion of the beam is reflected at the surface of the gauge. The two reflected portions of each ray (af and bcd for R_2) re-combine on the retina of the eye, giving rise to apparent dark bands wherever the air

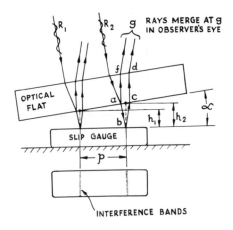

Fig. 12.5 Interfeence bands viewed through an optical flat

gap between the slip and the plane gives rise to a path difference of $\frac{1}{2}\lambda$. As the air gap is crossed twice, interference bands will be seen where the width of the air gap is $(N\lambda) + \frac{1}{4}\lambda, + \frac{3}{4}\lambda, + \frac{5}{4}\lambda$, etc.

Two deductions can be made from the appearance of the bands:

(i) as they are similar to contour lines on a map, any curvature or any irregularity in their successive pitches (*p*) indicates that the slip gauge surface is not flat,

(ii) from the pitch of the interference bands and know wavelength of the light, angle α can be determined:

$$\alpha \text{ radians} = \frac{\lambda}{2p}.$$

This principle is sometimes used for fine measurement of angles.

Fig 12.6 shows the optical arrangement of an NPL type of interferometer for testing the flatness and parallelism of slip gauges. The slip is wrung to a flat-lapped rotatable platen. Comparison of the interference bands on the face of the slip and on the platen monitors the parallelism of the slip gauge. Insets (*a*) (*b*) and (*c*) of Fig 12.6 show varying types of error deducible from a comparison of the two interference patterns.

Calibration of Length Standards. Fig 12.7 shows the principle of an NPL type length interferometer capable of measuring end standards of up to 100 mm to an accuracy of 0·025 μm (0·000 025 mm). Usually there are light sources providing monochromatic light of three different wavelengths with this system. Fig 12.8 shows how the interference bands are measured to obtain fractional increments of $\frac{1}{2}\lambda$, $a/b = f$.

The height of the gauge must be some multiple of the wavelength used,

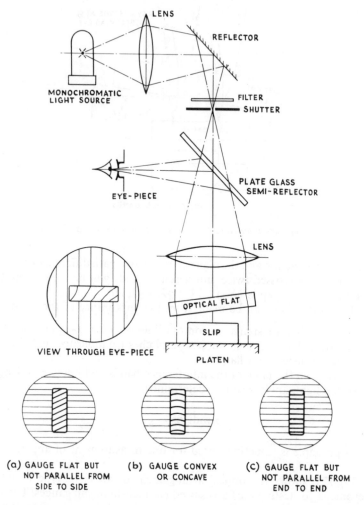

Fig. 12.6 NPL type interferometer for flatness and parallelism of slip gauges

which most probably incorporates a fractional element, so for the three different wavelengths,

$$h = \tfrac{1}{2}(N_1 + f_1)\lambda_1$$
$$= \tfrac{1}{2}(N_2 + f_2)\lambda_2$$
$$= \tfrac{1}{2}(N_3 + f_3)\lambda_3.$$

Before this stage is reached h should be known to a fairly high degree of accuracy, thus enabling the N values to be estimated. These values must be rounded to the nearest integers and the three equations then used to find new values for h. If they do not agree, change the values of N in

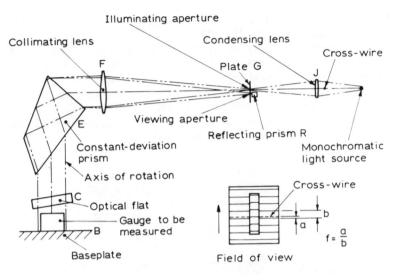

Fig. 12.7 Optical system of NPL gauge length interferometer (0–100 mm)

integer steps until all three results give, as closely as possible, the same value for *h*. Solutions can be obtained quickly by means of a special slide rule having three scales proportional to the three wavelengths used and a cursor which can be moved along to find the coincidence of *N* values when the scales have been displaced by the observed fractional amounts.

This somewhat slow and involved method is now being superseded by laser interferometry.

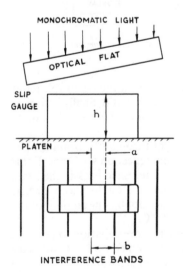

Fig. 12.8 a/b = f to give fraction of 1/2λ

Laser Interferometry (Laser = light amplification by stimulated emission of radiation) (see pp. 323–324).

A monochromatic laser source greatly increases the distance over which interference effects can be used; up to 50 m is possible. A helium–neon source, wavelength 0·6328 μm, is common. Coupled to a digital readout display the system can provide direct readings.

The equipment, shown in Fig 12.9, has three main items, a sensor unit, a reflector unit and a control display unit. The sensor is fixed; the reflector can be displaced horizontally as shown.

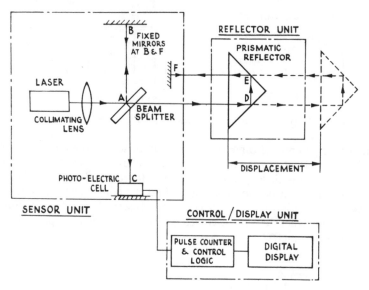

Fig. 12.9 Equipment for measurement by laser interferometer

A beam emitted from the laser source divides at the beam splitter at point A. One portion follows AB and, by reflection at B, finally arrives at the photo-electric sensor at C. The path length of this beam has to be kept constant.

A second portion of the beam passes right through the beam splitter and enters the prismatic reflector. By internal reflection via D and E this beam reaches the sensor unit at F, whence it is reflected back to the beam splitter, where a portion of it is finally directed to C on the photo-electric cell. Any displacement of the reflector unit will double the amount of the change in path length A D E F and back to C.

Both portions of the original beam return some radiation to point C. As explained on p. 386 the intensity of the combined rays at C will vary from a maximum to a minimum (interference) according to the phase difference of the combining rays. Displacement of the reflector unit will cause a series of electrical pulses to be generated by the photo-electric cell; these can be counted electronically and processed to give a digital display in any desired unit of length. A helium–neon source will give rise to a pulse for each 0·3164 μm displacement. This is not, of course, as fine a degree of resolution as is achieved by using sources of three different wavelengths and the method of coincidences. However, for many purposes, it provides a sufficiently accurate method of precision measurement.

As described, the system could not detect any difference between + ve or − ve shift of the reflector unit. By fitting two laser sources of phase difference $\frac{1}{4}\lambda$ and collecting pulses from each at separate photo-electric cells, the pulses being fed to a logic unit incorporating a time base, this limitation can be overcome. Incoming pulses have a different pattern relative to the time base according to the direction of the displacement, so enabling pulses to be added or subtracted as required. Such systems are sometimes incorporated as a means of measuring displacement for NC machines. The time base signals enable displacement rates to be controlled.

Slip Gauges: BS 888 and BS 4311. These are the working length standards of Industry and require no further description here. BS 888 contains a useful appendix on the care and use of slip gauges, and the advice given should be followed. There are also details of several useful accessories; measuring jaws for internal and external work, scribing and centre points, and holding devices, all of which contribute to a wide application of slip gauges in industry.

An appreciation of the accuracy to which such gauge blocks are manufactured can be obtained by noting the permissible errors laid down in BS 888. For gauges up to and including 25 mm the permissible errors are as shown in Table 12.2.

TABLE 12.2
*Maximum Permissible Errors of Slip Gauges up to and
Including 25 mm (Unit 0·000 01 mm)*

	Workshop grade	Inspection grade	Calibration grade	Reference grade
Length	+ 20 − 10	+ 20 − 10	± 12	± 5
Flatness	25	10	8	8
Parallelism	25	10	8	8

In the writer's experience few slip gauges of any new set supplied lie at the extreme limits. A set of workshop grade slips, calibrated immediate after purchase, contained only 3 gauges near the limits, and only one where the calibration was 0·000 02 mm above the high limit of length. If four gauges from a new workship grade set, each under 25 mm, are wrung together, then by the principles of p. 495, the overall size is unlikely to be outside limits of $+0.0005 - 0.0002$ mm.

12.3 Some Sources of Error in Linear Measurement

Accuracy in measurement depends as much upon method and cleanliness as upon the equipment available. Where slip gauges are used as a basis of reference, it is likely that errors arising from these sources exceed the error of the reference standard for a majority of the precision measurements made in average inspection departments.

Apart from temperature effects, errors can arise from the following causes:

    (i) flexure at contacting surfaces;
    (ii) errors of alignment
    (iii) errors of reading, i.e. parallax effects and vernier acuity.

Fig 12.10(*a*) illustrates the difference in the contact geometry between the flat anvils of a measuring machine or comparator, a slip gauge and a precision ball. Since there must be some contact force, there must be some deflection due to stress in each instance. For the same measuring force the reading obtained for the ball will contain a larger error, due to elastic deflections at the contact points, than will the reading obtained for the slip gauge. It is an important general principle in the use of sensitive comparators, that the measuring force must be maintained at a small constant value, and that the geometrical conditions of contact which occur for each of two comparative readings should be as alike as is possible. The first object is achieved for the bench micrometer, by the use

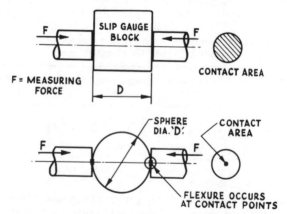

Fig.12.10(a) Geometry of contacting surfaces

of a fiducial indicator, and for comparators, by the spring load on the moving anvil; the second is achieved by providing different shaped measuring tips as part of the equipment of high-class measuring machines or comparators.

Fig 12.10(*b*) illustrates errors of alignment with respect to work measured between the flat anvils of a bench micrometer. These errors are frequently called the sine and cosine errors.

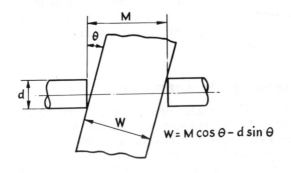

$$W = M \cos \theta - d \sin \theta$$

Fig. 12.10(b) Sine and cosine errors of mesurement

Fig 12.11 illustrates parallax error for the reading of scales. It should be obvious that errors from this source tend to fall as the magnification factor of the instrument rises. Reference to BS 887: Vernier Callipers, and BS 870: External Micrometers, will show that the dimension here indicated as *t* is controlled by the specification so as to limit parallax effects. One way of defeating the parallax effect is to project the scale and the index on to the same plane, as is done in most optical measuring equipment.

Fig 12.12 illustrates the well-known principle of double graticule lines and what is meant by vernier acuity. Most people can judge spaces *a* and

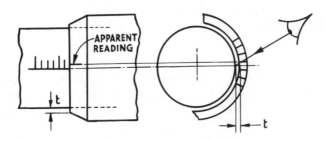

Fig. 12.11 Parallax error of micrometer reading

Fig. 12.12 Double graticule lines

b to be equal to a higher order of accuracy than that with which they could position one line directly over another. For a similar reason many people prefer to judge contour accuracy, tested by optical projection (shadowgraph), by leaving a very thin band of light between the shadow and the master outline.

12.4 Angular Measurement

The basis of most angular measurement is the divided circle as exemplified by the scale of a vernier protractor. In its most refined form this circle is a silver-coated or glass disc upon which the division lines are ruled or etched, and the scale is read through an optical system of considerable magnifying power. Optical dividing-heads and circular dividing-tables operating on this principle are now obtainable reading to 1 second of the arc, and of maximum cumulative error not exceeding 5 seconds of arc.

A sense of proportion is brought into precision angular measurement if it is realised that a new penny at 4 km distance subtends an angle of approximately 1 second of arc. The writer once saw a working drawing in which a taper shoulder of 3·2 mm depth, on a ground spindle, had been given an angular tolerance of ± 5 seconds of arc!

TABLE 12.3

Angle Slip Gauges

Degree series	1° 3° 9° 27° 41° 90° (square)
Minute series	1′ 3′ 9′ 27′
Second series	3″ 9″ 27″

As an alternative to the divided circle, angle slip gauges are available, generally made to a tolerance of 2 seconds of arc. Since they may be wrung together additively or subtractively, a small number of gauges can give a large range of combinations.

Fig 12.13 shows how an angle of 14°24′9″ can be built up from such gauges. The precision polygon Fig 12.14 is a further piece of basic

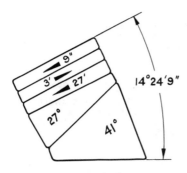

Fig. 12.13 Angle slip gauges

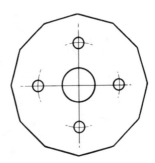

Fig. 12.14 Twelve-sided precision polygon

equipment in angular measurement; it is the solid angle equivalent of the divided circle, and has the advantage that the accuracy is independent of the axis about which it rotates, provided that this is parallel to the lapped faces.

There are two main sources of error in angular measurement:

(i) error of centring, e.g. of a divided scale;
(ii) error between the plane in which an angle is defined and the plane in which it is measured.

Fig 12.15 shows a circular scale correctly divided about axis A, and rotating relative to the index line about axis B at eccentricity (e) from A. It can be seen that the error, Δ radians, between the reading and the actual, angle of rotation is given by,

$$\Delta = \frac{e}{R} \sin \theta \text{ (very nearly)}$$

The sine curve of errors has been plotted.

There is a phase shift of the sine curve as the position of B moves with respect to the numbering of the divided scale.

Example 12.1

An accurately divided circular scale, 100 mm diameter, rotates about a centre displaced 0·0025 mm from the centre of graduation on a line joining the 150° and 330° positions, and is nearest to the 150° position. Draw a graph from which the errors due to the eccentric mounting of the scale can be read to the nearest second of arc.

Solution

$$\frac{e}{R} = 0·000\ 05 \text{ radians}$$

$$= 10 \text{ seconds of arc (very nearly)}$$

Fig 12.16 shows an easy graphical construction for the sine curve, and the method for positioning the phase shift involved.

The influence of such error of centring upon circular division is not confined to

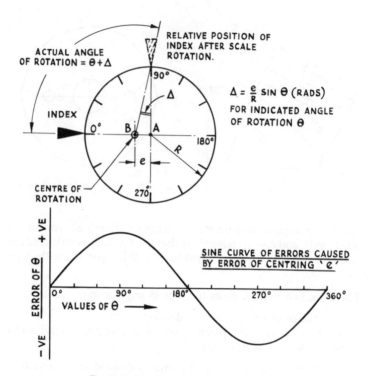

Fig 12.15 Centring error in circular division

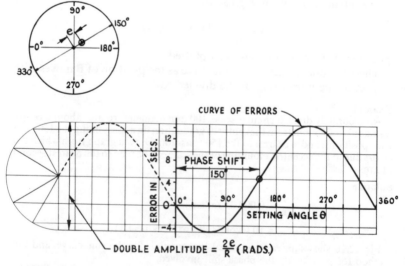

Fig. 12.16 Graphical construction of the curve of errors caused by an error of centring

circular scales; it is equally important in relation to gearing, and to spline and serration fitting.

Example 12.2

A vernier protractor is set to an angle of 60°. It is employed to set the angle between the face of an inclinable angle plate and a surface plate, but in so doing it is held 3° out of position measured in the horizontal plane. What is the maximum (dihedral) angle between the two planes so set? What error is caused?

Solution

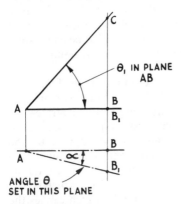

Fig. 12.17

The compound angle geometry is represented in Fig 12.17. The angle of 60° is set in plane AB_1 of the plan view; the dihedral angle lies in plane AB of the plan view and is the angle CAB of the elevation. It can be seen that the dihedral angle θ_1 is given by

$$\tan \theta_1 = \frac{BC}{AB} = \frac{BC}{AB_1} \sec 3°$$
$$= \tan 60° \sec 3°$$
$$= 1\!\cdot\!734\ 38$$
$$\theta_1 = 60°2'2\!\cdot\!5'' \quad \underline{\text{The error, } \Delta = 2'2\!\cdot\!5''}$$

The error calculation depends upon small differences. A 10 digit calculator has been used to obtain accuracy.

When $\alpha < 0\!\cdot\!5°$ it is more reliable to find the error directly.

$$\Delta\text{(radians)} = \frac{\alpha^2 \sin 2\theta}{4}, \quad \alpha \text{ in rads.}$$

Valid for small errors only, the expression shows the influence of α to be greatest when setting an angle of 45°. A proof is given in the earlier edition.

Where precision methods of angular measurements are used (e.g. autocollimator or Talyvel, etc.) it is most important to measure in the correct plane.

12.5 Measurement of Small Linear Displacements

A comparator is an instrument which magnifies small linear displacements in order to make them visible. Apart from high magnification, a comparator must have the following qualities;

    (i) it must be robust and give repeat readings consistently;
    (ii) the magnification factor must be constant;
    (iii) it must operate from a small uniform force exerted at the moving anvil.

There are many types of linear comparator now available, the main types are: **mechanical, optical, pneumatic and electrical.** Examples of each should be studied in a Metrology Laboratory and their relative advantages and disadvantages assessed. The following discussion of some of the main operating principles is not intended to be exhaustive, but is to draw attention to a few of the most important points.

Mechanical. Levers in some form or other are among the chief means of magnification. Crossed strip hinges, Fig 12.18, are frequently employed in place of pivots in order to avoid "play". Fig 12.19 illustrates the operating principles of one of the most successful types of mechanical comparator. The unit A is displaced against a light spring by the movement of the measuring anvil. The knife edge of this unit causes B to rotate about the centre of the "crossed-strip" hinge and so to rotate the long arms attached to it. These arms tension a bronze tape which is part wound round, and secured by screws, to the spindle which carries the pointer. The pointer moves against a suitably divided fixed scale. An interesting feature of the arrangement is the method of mounting the knife edge of A such that dimension l can be adjusted by means of the clamping screws E. This enables the desired magnification factor to be

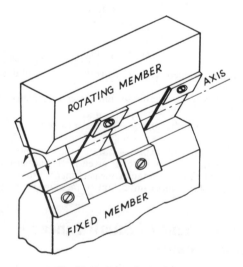

Fig. 12.18 Crossed strip hinge

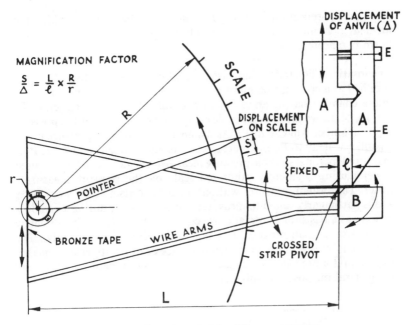

MAGNIFICATION FACTOR

$$\frac{S}{\Delta} = \frac{L}{\ell} \times \frac{R}{r}$$

Fig. 12.19 Operating principle of Sigma comparator

set. An electromagnetic eddy-current damping device (similar in principle to that fitted to domestic electric current meters) is attached to the pointer spindle and makes the instrument "dead-beat".

Optical. The main advantage of optical type comparators is that a beam of light, which can be used as a magnifying lever, has no inertia and may be contained within a compact space by reflecting it between mirror surfaces. Most of the comparators which use a beam of light are refinements of the optical lever illustrated in Fig 12.20. Since the change

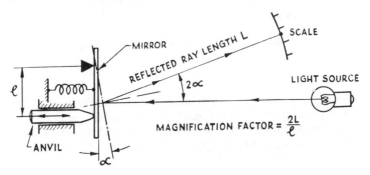

MAGNIFICATION FACTOR $= \frac{2L}{\ell}$

Fig. 12.20 Principle of the optical lever

of angle on reflection is twice the change of the angle at which the incident ray enters, there is a multiplying factor of two each time the beam is reflected.

Pneumatic. The underlying principle is illustrated in Fig 12.21. Air supplied at a constant pressure P_1 passes through a control orifice and into a chamber having an escape orifice called the measuring jet. If the surface of the workpiece closes the escape completely, $t = 0$, the pressure in the chamber will rise to P_1. As distance t is increased, pressure in the chamber will fall to P_2 and there a relationship between t and P_2. If P_2 is measured by some suitable pressure measuring device, t can be measured directly using a suitably calibrated scale on the pressure measuring meter. The system measures without metallic contact at the workpiece, and is particularly suited to measurement of the work during a grinding process as a basis for automatic size control. The scale is approximately linear over a small range of t (a few hundredths of a mm only). The special equipment needed for each bore-size or other application makes the method more suitable for use on long runs of repetition work than for general purpose measurement.

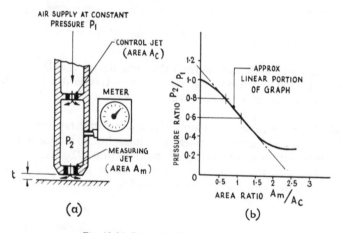

Fig. 12.21 Principle of pneumatic (air) gauging

Practical tests show the system has an approximate linear relationship between the dimensionless ratios. P_2/P_1 and A_m/A_c (see Fig 12.21(b)), where A_m is the area through which air escapes and A_c is the area of the control jet. Linearity extends approximately over a range of P_2/P_1 of 0·6 to 0·8. Over this range

$$P_2/P_1 = k A_m/A_c + 1·1. \qquad (12.4)$$

The sensitivity of the system is given by

$$\frac{\text{scale displacement } (\delta R)}{\text{change in } t \ (\delta t)} = \frac{\delta A_m}{\delta t} \frac{\delta P_2}{A_m} \frac{\delta R}{\delta P_2}$$

where $\delta A_m/\delta t$ is the sensitivity of the measuring head,

$\delta P_2/\delta A_m$ is the pneumatic sensitivity,

$\delta R/\delta P_2$ is the pressure gauge sensitivity.

Since $A_m = \pi d_m t$, $\qquad \delta A_m/\delta t = \pi d_m$,

and from Eqn (12.4), $\delta P_2/\delta A_m = k \, P_1/A_c$,

the pneumatic sensitivity is shown to be directly proportional to the supply pressure and inversely proportional to the area of the control jet.

For the middle of the linear range Eqn (12.4) becomes

$$0.7 = k\frac{A_m(\text{mean})}{A_c} + 1.1$$

or

$$A_c = \frac{-k \, A_m(\text{mean})}{0.4},$$

which shows that for high pneumatic sensitivity A_m must be small. This implies that linearity can only be obtained over a very small range of t. The linear range can be increased by fitting a measuring head with an orfice as shown in Fig 12.22. The parabolic end of the plunger maintains a linear relationship between A_m and t over an extended range of t.

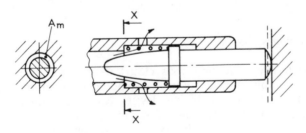

Fig. 12.22

Example 12.3

A back pressure air gauging system has a linear range between values of the pressure ratio from 0·6 to 0·8, the linear relationship being represented by

$$P_2/P_1 = -0.5 \, A_m/A_c + 1.1.$$

The control jet has 0·4 mm dia., the measuring jet 0·65 mm dia. Air is supplied at a pressure of 3 bars and the measuring indicator displaces 2 mm per 10^{-3} bar change of pressure.

    (i) Show that the linear range extends over 0·025 mm

    (ii) Find the overall sensitivity of the equipment within this range.

Solution
  Linear range

$$A_m = 0.65\pi t \qquad A_c = 0.2^2\pi$$

$$0.5 A_m/A_c = 8.125 t$$

$$0.6 = -8.125 t_1 + 1.1 \qquad t_1 = 0.062$$

$$0.8 = -8.125 t_2 + 1.1 \qquad t_2 = 0.037 \quad \therefore \quad \underline{\text{Linear range} = 0.025 \text{ mm}}$$

Sensitivity,

$$\frac{dR}{dt} = \frac{dA_m}{dt}\frac{dP_2}{dA_m}\frac{dR}{dP_2}$$

$$\frac{dA_m}{dt} = 0.65\pi \qquad t_{\text{mean}} = 0.0495$$

$$\frac{dP_2}{dA_m} = \frac{-0.4 P_1}{A_m(\text{mean})} \qquad A_m(\text{mean}) = 0.65\pi \times 0.0495$$

$$= \frac{-0.4 \times 3}{0.0322\pi} \qquad\qquad = 0.0322\pi$$

$$\frac{dR}{dP_2} = 2 \times 10^3 = 2000$$

$$\frac{dR}{dt} = 0.65\pi \times \frac{1.2}{0.0322\pi} \times 2000$$

$$= 48\,450$$

<u>Magnification is × 48 450</u>

Electrical. There are numerous electrical principles which can be applied to the measurement of small displacement, e.g. strain gauges may be used. Electronic amplifying devices can give magnifications of extremely high order. However, for stability and reliability the most successful comparator of this type operates on variable inductance measured via a bridge network. Fig 12.23 shows the measuring head. Displacement of the iron armature between the inductance coils L_1 and L_2 puts the bridge circuit out of balance, causing the ammeter to move and to indicate the magnitude of the displacement, Fig 12.24.

Optical Magnification of the Workpiece. The comparators described above magnify small linear displacements in order to make them visible; an alternative to this is to magnify the workpiece so that direct measurement may be made to a high order of accuracy. There are alternative ways of achieving this end, both of which have particular advantages.

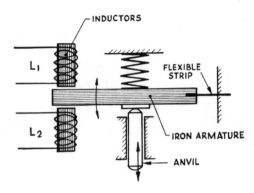

Fig. 12.23 Measuring head of electrical comparator

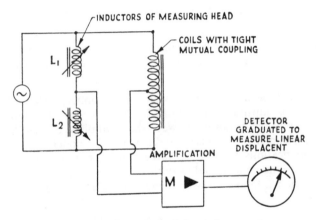

Fig. 12.24 Bridge network of electrical comparator

(1) *The Measuring Microscope.* Fig 12.25 shows the optical principle of a microscope. The objective lens is a magnifier which produces an image CD of workpiece AB; the eyepiece is a further magnifier which makes the image CD appear as the virtual image EF. If the objective lens magnifies 6 times, and the eyepiece 10 times, the virtual image will be 60 times full size.

In a toolmakers' or measuring microscope the work is mounted on a rectangular co-ordinate table having micrometer control of the displacements made by either slide. Cross lines in the focal plane of the eyepiece provide a datum against which displacements can be measured. Angular measurements can be made either by having a graduated circular table as part of the work stage, or by having a rotatable graticule line in the eyepiece (goniometric eyepiece). It is generally more convenient to

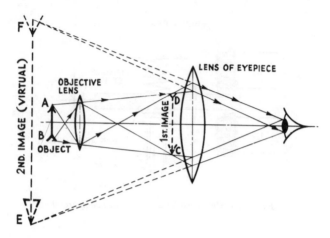

Fig. 12.25 Optical principle of a microscope

measure very small work by means of a measuring microscope than by contact methods, as instanced by the measurement of the smaller BA screw threads.

(2) *Optical Projection.* The somewhat simpler optical system of optical projection is illustrated in Fig 12.26. The degree of magnification depends upon the distance l between the focal plane of lens P, and the screen. Instruments which can handle work of a moderate size at 50 or 100 magnifications tend to be rather bulky, but optical projection, resulting in a magnified shadow outline of the workpiece, has a number of attractions. Direct measurements by rule can be made; at 50

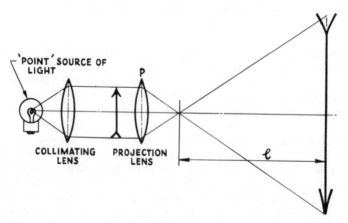

Fig. 12.26 Optical projection

magnifications 0·02 mm is represented by 1 mm on the rule. Profiles can be drawn at 25 or 50 times full sizes for such things as press tool dies, and this is the cheapest method of profile inspection. Most screw gauge profiles are checked by the method. At large magnifications small errors in the lens systems give proportionally large distortion, also the sharpness of the shadow outline is affected by the thickness of the workpiece projected, but such disadvantages are relatively small in relation to the general utility of the method for work where the accuracy required is not closer than about 0·02 mm. Angles can be measured by means of a suitably large vernier protractor.

12.6 Measurement of Small Angular Displacements

Fundamentally, the amplification of small angular displacements is not greatly different from the amplification of small linear displacements; mechanical, optical and electrical devices can be employed.

A mechanical dividing head is comparable in operating principle to a micrometer, a large angular rotation is used to cause a small angular displacement.

The optical device for amplifying an angular displacement most frequently employed is the autocollimator. There are versions of this instrument which read directly to minutes of arc without the aid of a measuring microscope, but in its most refined form the microscope is essential, and enables an accuracy of the order of one second of arc to be obtained. Fig 12.27 illustrates the optical principle upon which the instrument works. Suppose a ray of light is emitted from source S at the middle of the focal plane of the collimating lens. The lens will convert this into a parallel beam which is then reflected from some working surface such as CD. If CD is inclined at angle α, the reflected ray makes an angle of 2α with the incident ray. The reflected beam re-enters the collimating

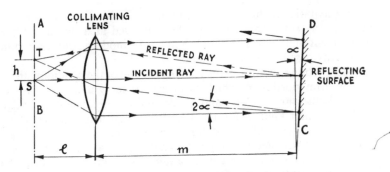

Fig. 12.27 Optical principle of the autocollimator

lens to be refocused at some new point in the focal plane such as T. Distance h is proportional to the angle, and measurements of h in plane AB enable values of small angles to be determined. Note that the value of h is independent of the distance m of the instrument from the reflecting surface, although of course it is directly dependent upon l (a constant for the lens) and upon α. The full optical system of a typical instrument is rather more complex and is represented in principle only by Fig 12.28. The autocollimator and angle slip gauges fulfil for angular measurement the same purpose as is fulfilled by the comparator and slip gauge blocks for linear measurement.

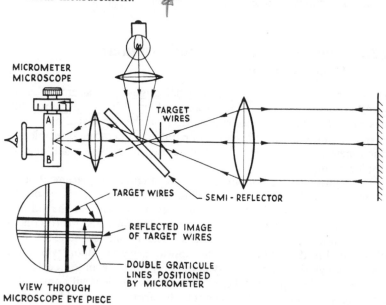

Fig. 12.28 Optical system of the autocollimator

The gravitational pull of the earth has a fixed direction for any comparatively small area, and may be employed as a datum for the measurement of angles. The plumb-bob has its modern counter-part in instruments based upon a pendulum.

Fig 12.29 shows such an instrument. At the end of the pendulum there is a soft iron portion A which displaces, under gravitational force, between inductance coils C_1 and C_2 depending on angle θ. A bridge circuit of similar kind to Fig 12.24 feeds a signal to the meter which measures displacement from a datum in either minutes/seconds of angle or millimetres per metre. The pendulum and indicating meter have a damping system; the instrument has a range of about $\pm 2°$ and can be read to increments of one second of arc.

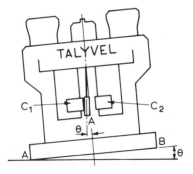

Fig. 12.29 Talyvel (courtesy of Taylor Hobson)

A spirit level is an alternative instrument for measuring small angular displacements relative to a horizontal datum, the level of a liquid at rest. Fig 12.30 shows the main features of this instrument. A 20 second level has a displacement of 2 mm for a tilt of 0·01 in 1000 and is representative of the precision class of this inexpensive and very useful piece of equipment. The principal use of both items of equipment is that of testing straightness and flatness as described on pp. 414 and 416.

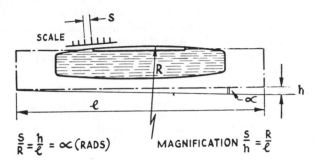

Fig. 12.30 Precision spit level

12.7 Indirect Measurement

Many measurements made in precision engineering work are obtained indirectly, generally by calculation from other directly determined dimensions.

Fig 12.31 illustrates an indirectly made measurement. A disc of known radius is placed in the vee, and dimension h is measured as a means of determining dimension l. There are two very important points to observe:

(i) since l is calculated from values of r, α and h (and the 90° corner angle also forms part of the solution), l cannot be accurately found

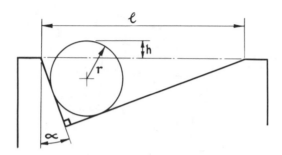

Fig. 12.31 Use of roller for measuring a dimension indirectly

unless all the features used in its determination are known to be correct;

(ii) error of $l(= \Delta l)$ is determined from the apparent error of $h (= \Delta h)$; if $\Delta h/\Delta l > 1$ the method is critical and a reliable result can be obtained, but if $\Delta h/\Delta l < 1$ the result is less certain, since the accuracy to which l is known is lower than the accuracy to which h has been measured.

For an indirectly determined dimension the geometrical conditions upon which the result depends should be carefully studied; calculations should be arranged to give values of high numerical accuracy, and the method should be analysed to show that the result is not greatly affected by small errors in the basic dimensions from which it is calculated. These points are best illustrated by a few worked examples.

Example 12.4

The dimensions of the arrangement shown in Fig 12.31 are: $\alpha = 20°$, $r = 11·996$ mm, $h = 5·208$ mm. Use these dimensions to determine dimension l correct to the nearest 0·002 mm and comment upon the geometric features which must be checked in order to prove the result reliable.

Solution

From triangles A, B, C and D of Fig 12.32.

$$l = (r - h)\tan\alpha + r\sec\alpha + r\operatorname{cosec}\alpha + (r - h)\cot\alpha$$
$$= r(\sec\alpha + \operatorname{cosec}\alpha) + (r - h)\,2\operatorname{cosec}2\alpha$$
$$= (11·996 \times 3·987\,98) + (6·788 \times 2 \times 1·555\,72)$$
$$= 68·9602, \text{ i.e. } \underline{68·960 \text{ to the nearest } 0·002 \text{ mm.}}$$

Geometric features which require testing in order to prove that the calculated solution is valid are:

(i) the straightness of the inclined edges on which the disc rests, and of the edges from which dimension h is measured;

(ii) the accuracy of the 20° angle, which should be tested between edges referred to in (i);

(iii) the accuracy of the right angle between the edges on which the disc rests.

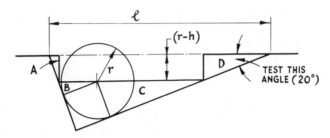

Fig. 12.32

Example 12.5

Fig 12.33 represents a bore of large diameter D measured by means of a pointed end bar, length L, which is swung about point A to touch the bore on the opposite side at two points distance W apart.

Obtain an approximate expression for D, in terms of L and W, which is sufficiently accurate when W is small relative to L. If $L = 500$ mm and the calculated value of D is required to be known to an accuracy of ± 0.01 mm., find the maximum value which W can have, assuming that this dimension is obtained by a rule measurement to an accuracy of ± 0.50 mm.

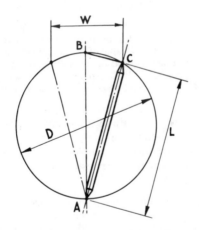

Fig. 12.33 Measurement of a large bore with a point gauge

Solution

From Fig 12.33,
Since ACB is a right angle (angle in a semicircle)

$$(AB)^2 = (AC)^2 + (BC)^2$$

If dimension W is small, $BC \simeq \dfrac{W}{2}$

hence

$$D^2 = L^2 + \frac{W^2}{4} \text{ (very nearly)} \qquad (12.5)$$

Let $D - L = \Delta$, then from Eqn (12.5)

$$(L + \Delta)^2 = L^2 + \frac{W^2}{4}$$

and

$$\Delta = \frac{W^2}{8L} \text{ if second powers of } \Delta \text{ are neglected}$$

$$D = L + \frac{W^2}{8L} \text{ (very nearly)} \qquad (12.6)$$

Calculation of the degree of approximation involved in any specific instance is left as an exercise for the reader.

We must now consider the influence of errors in the value of W upon the value obtained for D, by application of the above formula. By differentiation,

$$\Delta D \simeq \frac{2W}{8L} \Delta W \text{ (L regarded as a constant) or for small errors;}$$

$$\text{error in } D = \frac{W}{4L} \times \text{error in } W, \text{ very nearly.}$$

For the values given in the question, when $D = \pm 0{\cdot}01$ and $W = \pm 0{\cdot}50$.

$$W = \frac{4L \times \Delta D}{\Delta W}$$

$$= \frac{4 \times 500 \times 0{\cdot}01}{0{\cdot}5} = \underline{40 \text{ mm}}$$

i.e. Provided $L > 500$ and $W < 40$, a rule measurement for W, in error by $\pm 0{\cdot}05$ will not give rise to an error in the value of D calculated from Eqn (12.6) greater than $\pm 0{\cdot}01$ mm. By an exact method of calculation and assuming length W is known exactly, $D = L/\cos(\sin^{-1} W/2L)$ giving $D = 500{\cdot}4003$. Using Eqn (12.6), the same values of L and W result in $D = 500{\cdot}4$, showing the closeness of the approximation.

Methods such as the above are of importance in metrology, and the degree of accuracy obtained in the final result should never be taken for granted. Analysis of the method employed is an important step in deciding the validity of a particular result.

Example 12.6

Show, for a sine-bar, that the accuracy of the angle set is a function of the accuracy of the centre distance between the rollers and of the setting height. How should an angle of 80° be set up in order to minimise errors?

Solution

Fig 12.34 shows the usual arrangement of a sine-bar in which angle θ is obtained from dimensions h and l. It will be assumed that the rollers are of identical diameter and have their centre line exactly parallel with the edges of the sine-bar.

From the diagram $\sin\theta = \dfrac{h}{l}$

Assuming h to vary, by differentiation

$$\cos\theta \, d\theta_1 = \frac{dh}{l} \quad \text{or} \quad \Delta\theta_1 \simeq \frac{\sec\theta}{l} \Delta h \qquad (12.7)$$

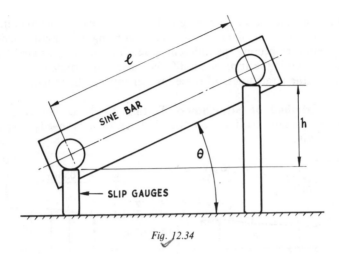

Fig. 12.34

assuming l to vary,

$$\cos\theta d\theta_2 = -\frac{h}{l^2}dl \quad \text{or} \quad \Delta\theta_2 \simeq -\frac{\tan\theta}{l}\Delta l \qquad (12.8)$$

from Eqn (12.7) and (12.8)

Total error in θ: $\qquad \Delta\theta = \dfrac{\sec\theta}{l}\Delta h - \dfrac{\tan\theta}{l}\Delta l \text{ (radians)} \qquad (12.9)$

a result which can be obtained more directly by the use of partial differentiation. The following deductions can be made from Eqn (12.9):

(i) the higher the value of l, the greater the accuracy of angular setting, other things remaining constant;

(ii) the higher the value of θ, the lower the setting accuracy, since as $\theta \longrightarrow 90°$, $\sec\theta \longrightarrow \infty$ and $\tan\theta \longrightarrow \infty$, and it is unlikely that dimensions l and h are entirely free of error.

The most satisfactory method of setting up an angle of 80° is to set the sine-bar to 10°, clamp it to the face of a high-grade cube and then to rotate the cube through 90° in a vertical plane, from its initial position on the surface plate.

The relationships between linear and angular dimensions discussed in this example illustrate another aspect of the relationships between errors with which one is concerned when making indirect measurements.

12.8 Straightness Testing

BS5204 parts 1 & 2, refer to the two principal forms of straight edge, the cast-iron and the rectangular steel types. The cast-iron type is of "fish-back" shape to minimise flexure; it has a scraped surface of from 30 mm to 100 mm wide according to length. The steel type is of a deep uniform rectangular section, 6 mm to 13 mm according to length. General information respecting the different **grades** and their associated tolerances is given in the appropriate BS. There are three principal methods by which the straightness of these instruments can be tested.

Wedge Method of Straightness Testing. Fig 12.35 illustrates the method generally used to test the accuracy of a bevel-edge type of straight edge.

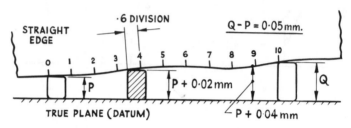

Fig. 12.35 "Wedge" method of straightness testing

The straight edge is supported from a surface of known accuracy at points P and Q (for choice of supporting points, see p. 385) such that a very slow taper is produced between the surface plate and straight edge. The space between P and Q along the edge is marked off into a convenient number of intervals and checks made, as shown, in the region of each by using a suitable nominal-sized build-up of slip gauges. The diagram has been drawn for specific values and shows the following errors of straightness:

(i) straight edge **low** by 0·0003 mm at point (4);
(ii) straight edge **high** by 0·0004 mm at point (8).

The method is simple and fairly rapid; known errors of the datum surface can be taken into account.

Fundamental Method Based upon the "Wedge" Principle. This is an interesting example of fundamental technique in Metrology because no assumption that the datum surface is flat is made, and the method reveals all the errors of straightness in the edges employed. It is, however, very slow and is unlikely to give reliable values unless the test is conducted with very great care.

An approximately parallel rectangular straight edge is divided into suitable intervals along its length and measurements taken across the width at each interval; measurements w_1, w_2, w_3, etc., between edges A and B as illustrated in Fig 12.36.

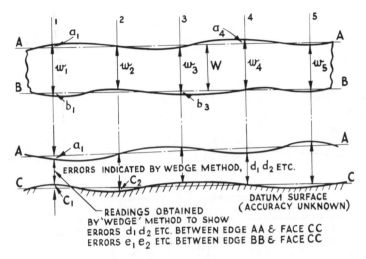

Fig. 12.36 Fundamental method of straightness testing

Edges A and B are then separately tested for straightness against the same portion of a surface plate employing the wedge methods described on p. 412. The apparent errors of edge A are called d_1, d_2, d_3, etc., and of edge B are called e_1, e_2, e_3, etc., while the true errors of these edges have the symbols a_1, a_2, a_3, etc., for edge A and b_1, b_2, b_3, etc., for edge B. The true errors of the datum surface C are c_1, c_2, c_3, etc.

Let $W =$ mean width between edges A and B,

then
$$a + b = w - W \tag{1}$$

also
$$a + c = -d \tag{2}$$

and
$$b + c = -e \tag{3}$$

Since a and c have been assumed $+$ ve, d and e must be $-$ ve. The actual results must be evaluated with due regard to signs.

We now have three equations relating the three unknowns, a, b and c; a suitable method of evaluating these is as follows:

From (2) and (3)
$$d + e = -a - b - 2c$$
$$= -(a + b) - 2c$$

Substitute (1)
$$d + e = -(w - W) - 2c$$
$$c = -\tfrac{1}{2}(w - W + d + e)$$

From (2)
$$a = -d - c$$

From (3)
$$b = -e - c$$

A suitable tabular form of working is shown below.

Position	$(w-W)$	d	e	$c = -\frac{1}{2}(w-W+d+e)$	$a = -d-c$	$b = -e-c$
1						
2						

Level Method. This method is frequently used for cast-iron straight edges; it is also suitable for testing the straightness of the "ways" of machine-tool beds. A level of appropriate sensitivity is mounted upon a "bridge-piece" as shown in Fig 12.37. The vee grooves in the ends of the "bridge-piece" enable it to be used on the inverted vee guides of machine-tool slides when required.

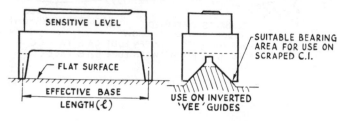

Fig. 12.37 Mounted level for straightness and flatness testing

Fig 12.38 shows the method of working. The "bridge-piece" and level are placed in consecutive positions along the work, and the "slope" at each position determined from the reading of the level. It is necessary to convert these values into linear distances, the heights h_1, h_2, etc., at the ends of length of the base representing the "slope" indicated by the level. It can be seen from Fig 12.38 that the readings must be summated (added with due regard to sign), because although the slope of the second reading is zero, the distances of points 1 and 2 of the surface below the horizontal datum through 0 are equal.

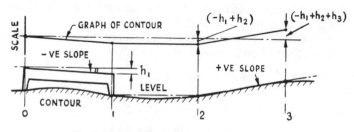

Fig. 12.38 "Level" method of straightness testing

There are two methods of presenting results:

(i) graphically, which has the advantage of giving a pictorial impression of the errors but is subject to considerable scale distortion;

(ii) in a tabular form, in which the values are treated in a manner similar to (i) but without the actual drawing of a graph.

Example 12.7
A 20-seconds level, used on a bridge-piece for which $l = 130$ mm, is employed to test the straightness of a surface 650 mm long. The level readings obtained are: $+0.2, +1.4, 0, -1.2, +2$, where unit displacement of the bubble represents a slope of 20 seconds of arc. Find the errors of straightness of the surface.

Solution
Let h be the height at the end of a 130 mm length to produce a slope of 20 seconds of arc.

$$h = \frac{20}{3600} \times \frac{2\pi}{360} \times 130 = 0.0125 \text{ mm (very nearly)}$$

Fig 12.39 shows a graphical solution. It is clear that the surface tested is somewhat inclined to the horizontal and that a straight line through the end points is a more reasonable datum from which to express the errors of straightness.

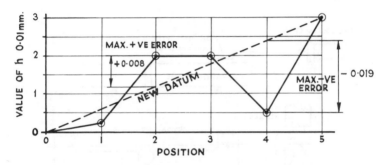

Fig. 12.39

The tabular method of solution is easy to follow once it is realised that the process is equivalent to the above graphical one. The heights of the points are first obtained using a horizontal datum. The heights of points on a straight-line datum passing through the end points of the surface are then written down; the final column gives the differences between points on the surfaces tested and this new straight line datum.

TABLE 12.4
Values of h, and Subsequent Values, Unit = 0.01 mm

Position	0	1	2	3	4	5
Reading	—	+0.20	+1.40	0	−1.20	+2.00
Value of h	—	+0.25	+1.75	0	−1.50	+2.50
Summation of values	0	+0.25	+2.00	+2.00	+0.50	+3.00
New straight-line datum	0	+0.60	+1.20	+1.80	+2.40	+3.00
Errors from new datum	0	−0.35	+0.80	+0.20	−1.90	0

Straightness testing may be done in a similar manner by employing alternative types of instrument to measure the slopes. Fig 12.40 shows an arrangement for testing a rectanglar-type straight edge by means of an autocollimator. A "level" operating on the pendulum principle of p. 406 may be substituted for the spirit level, and this instrument will give readings much more rapidly.

Other practical methods of testing straightness for which there is no space to give detailed explanation here are:

  (i) the beam comparator;
  (ii) the alignment telescope;
  (iii) the taut wire;
  (iv) the water trough;
  (v) the electronic level (see p. 407).

Some of these methods have special advantages where the surfaces involved are very large, e.g. for testing the beds of very large planing machines.

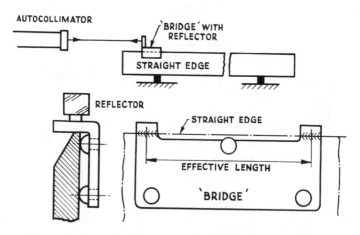

Fig. 12.40 Autocollimator method of straightness testing

12.9 Flatness Testing

BS817 gives details of cast-iron surface plates, including the tolerances relative to the various grades and the definition of the mean true plane from which the errors are measured. Apart from the three-plate method of generating and testing flat surfaces, tests of flatness can be made by an extension of the principles already described for straightness testing.

Fig 12.41 shows a surface 1250 mm × 850 mm suitably divided for flatness testing by means of a grid network. Tests for straightness are

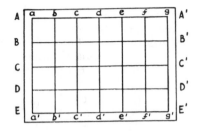

Fig. 12.41

made along lines AA′, BB′, CC′, etc. Tests are then made along aa′, bb′, etc., so as to orientate the first set of values. Ultimately the heights of all points (Aa, Ab . . . Ef, Eg) from the mean true plane are obtained. The main problem is one of orientation; it is obvious that all the values for the straightness tests must be taken from the same datum and that values from new datum positions can be inserted only by considering a change of inclination of the whole surface relative to the horizontal plane (not a change for one straight line only). An example should make this clear.

Example 12.8

The following values were obtained from a series of straightness tests made to assess the flatness of a surface. The unit is 0·1 mm, the results have already been summated, and they are all given with reference to the same datum. Determine, for the intersecting points of the grid, the errors of flatness of the surface tested measured form a mean true plane.

A–A′	0	+0·2	+0·6	+1
B–B′	0	−0·1	+0·4	+0·7
C–C′	0	+0·3	+0·5	+0·9
D–D′	0	−0·2	+0·3	+0·6
a–a′	0	+0·2	−0·2	+0·3

Solution

From the results along a–a′, the points on D–D′ are shown all to be +0·3 higher, with respect to the datum used, than the points on A–A′. Correct this by tipping the plane about A–A′ as follows:

a–a′	0	+0·2	−0·2	+0·3
New datum	0	+0·1	+0·2	+0·3
New values	0	+0·1	−0·4	0

Correct rows BB′, CC′, etc., by raising or lowering all the points in accordance with the true value of the **first** point in the row as shown by the new values for a–a′

	a	b	c	d
A–A′	0	+0·2	+0·6	+1
B–B′	+0·1	0	+0·5	+0·8
C–C′	−0·4	−0·1	+0·1	+0·5
D–D′	0	−0·2	+0·3	+0·6

It can now be seen that a further improvement is possible by tipping the plane about a–a′ so as to bring point Dd to zero. The correction to be made to each line of values is:

0   − 0·2   − 0·4   − 0·6   to give:

	a	b	c	d	Sum of values	
					+ ve	− ve
A–A'	0	0	+0·2	+0·4	+0·6	0
B–B'	+0·1	−0·2	+0·1	+0·2	+0·4	−0·2
C–C'	−0·4	−0·3	−0·3	−0·1	0	−1·1
D–D'	0	−0·4	−0·1	0	0	−0·5
					+1·0	−1·8

Difference = − 0·8

Three corners of the surface now lie in a common plane from which the error at the remaining points on the surface has been expressed. The maximum effect of angular change of datum has been achieved. The **mean true plane** could be either above or below this datum plane (although parallel with it). To test for this it is necessary to find any difference between the total + ve and − ve values of the errors shown at this stage. The difference between + ve and − ve errors is seen to be − 0·8.

Since 16 positions are involved, raise all the values by $\frac{0·8}{16}$ (= 0·05) to get the errors measured from the mean true plane. the errors are:

	a	b	c	d
A–A'	+0·05	+0·05	+0·25	+0·45
B–B'	+0·15	−0·15	+0·15	+0·25
C–C'	−0·35	−0·25	−0·25	−0·05
D–D'	0	−0·35	−0·05	+0·05

The maximum errors from the mean true plane are +0.045 mm at Ad, and −0·035 mm at Ca and Db.

This example has a small number of values so that the principles are not lost in a mass of detail. Values along lines b–b', c–c', d–d' could be taken and used to confirm the accuracy of the above result. Sometimes plots across the diagonals of the surface are taken as a further check upon the results.

Straightness and flatness testing involve the setting of a line or surface datum from which error is measured. An arbitrary choice of datum will result in differing error values from different tests. Using the principle of least squares of errors will give a standard datum but the numerical work is considerable. Digital computing is an obvious method for such situations; eventually one may expect to see the development of instrumentation combined with the use of a mini computer, to give direct errors from the instrument readings.

12.10 Measurement of Surface Texture

The measurement of surface texture is fairly complicated, and only a general outline can be given here. It is advisable to study BS1134 Parts 1 & 2 in order to get some appreciation of the difficulties involved, and of the terminology applied to surface finish measurement.

Surface finish measurement is complex, because the character of a machined surface involves the three dimensions of space. Any attempt to express the quality of a surface by means of a number is necessarily rather limited. Fig 12.42 shows, grossly exaggerated, some of the main features of a machined surface; note the primary texture of short wavelength, usually termed **roughness**, the secondary texture or **waviness** and the directional nature of the texture pattern which is covered by the term **lay**. Any numerical assessment of a surface finish will be influenced by the direction in which measurements are taken relative to the lay, and by an arbitrary distinction between roughness and waviness.

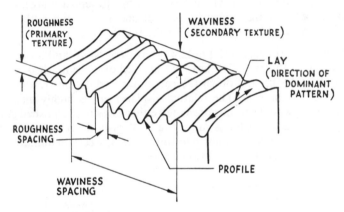

Fig. 12.42 Elements of the surface character of a machined surface

There are three main methods for the assessment of surface texture.

(1) *Comparison with Roughness Standards.* Flat and cylindrical sample surfaces, finish machined by the common workshop processes and then calibrated, are used as a basis of comparison. Work produced is compared visually and by "feel" with the sample surfaces acting as "standards". The method depends upon individual judgement and lacks precision on this account, but it is relatively cheap to apply and is a convenient one for general purposes.

(2) *Interferometry Method.* Fig 12.43 shows the type of surface pattern produced by viewing a finished surface through a microscope system which incorporates an interferometer. The method is useful for viewing

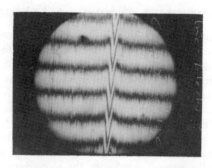

Fig. 12.43 Interferometry pattern showing scratch on a slip gauge approx
0·000 25 mm deep as seen through a surface finish microscope

(*Courtesy of Hilger & Watts*)

very highly finished surfaces, such as slip gauges. The chief advantage occurs in examining work where the surface finish blemishes are less than 0·004 mm wide, so that a probe-type instrument, tip radius of the probe about 2 μm, would not penetrate to the full depth of the grooves.

(3) *Probe-type Instruments.* Fig 12.44 shows the "skid" and probe of an instrument of this type. The head is traversed over the finished surface; the probe rides up and down the roughness undulations relative to a datum set by the skid. The relative displacement is highly magnified electronically and the results presented either as a surface finished graph, Fig 12.45, or as a roughness value. Fig 12.46 gives details of one widely use instrument for surface finish testing. There are certain limitations of the method which are not always appreciated.

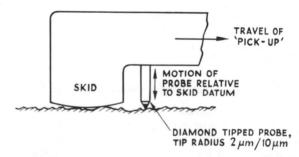

Fig. 12.44 "Pick-up" of surface-finish recording instrument

(*a*) Use of a skid for setting the datum is convenient, as it is then not necessary to line up the work to a high order of accuracy, but in riding over the surface undulations the skid modifies, in some small degree, the wave pattern recorded by the probe.

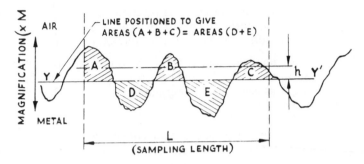

Fig. 12.45 Surface-finish graph

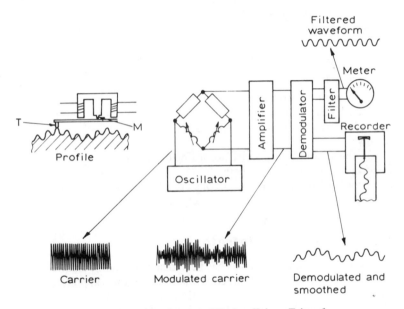

Fig. 12.46 System diagram of Taylor–Hobson Talysurf

(b) The probe must have a point of finite radius, and so cannot penetrate to the full depth of the finest scratches, a fact which is significant in the measuring very high-grade finishes.

(c) Graphs produced by such instruments are subject to considerable scale distortion, e.g. vertical axis × 50 000, horizontal axis × 100. They do, however, give a reasonable impression of the character of the surface tested if this fact is kept in mind.

(d) Instruments which give numerical readings are influenced by the sampling length traversed by the measuring head (pick-up) and by the particular starting and finishing positions used. The greater the wavelength of the main roughness markings, the longer must be the sampling length in order to give a satisfactory value.

Surface finish numbers cannot show the differences of texture as between surfaces of equal roughness value produced by different methods, e.g. between, say, grinding and honing. For such purposes a graph is essential.

R_a **Values.** The numerical form of assessment given in BS1134 is known as the arithmetical mean deviation R_a value. The physical meaning of an R_a value depends upon the graphical form of the surface tested. Fig 12.45 shows a typical surface finish graph with the sampling length L marked off. To obtain the R_a value, the line YY′ must be drawn so that the shaded areas above and below it, enclosed by the graph, are equal in value, i.e. areas $A + B + C$ = areas $D + E$. The required value is then determined from,

$$h = \frac{A + B + C + D + E}{L} \times \frac{1000}{V} \mu m$$

where V is the vertical magnification of the graph and L the actual measured base of the graph, i.e. 100 mm to represent 1 mm. Instruments of the type shown in Fig 12.46 make this calculation electronically.

R_a values should be specified according to the "preferred" series shown in BS1134, the finer values being 0·025, 0·05, 0·1, 0·2, 0·4 etc. Numerical assessment of surface finish is not of so great a precision that a difference between, say, 0·05 and 0·06, has much significance.

12.11 Practical Metrology

Precision measurement such as has been discussed in this chapter is best studied in conjunction with practical measurement work, preferably in a Metrology Laboratory. Reference to the appropriate British Standard is always advisable. Development of equipment is continuous, and equipment manufacturers generally provide full technical information concerning the operating principles and applications of their products. For this reason, the information in this chapter has been restricted very largely to fundamental principles which remain valid, even if future changes in the design of the equipment modify the methods employed.

The working of numerical examples serves a useful purpose by making sure that the principles have been understood, but in no sense can this type of exercise be a satisfactory substitute for practical measurement work.

EXERCISES 12

1. A slip gauge, nominal size 8 mm, measured on an NPL-type interferometer, gave the following results:

Wavelength (λ)	Fraction displacement (f)
0·643 851 μm	0·85
0·508 586 μm	0
0·467 818 μm	0·50

(i) Find the values of f for a gauge of exact size.
(ii) Show that the above measurements satisfy conditions for a gauge 0·000 2 mm undersize.
(Use an 8-digit calculator)

2. (a) Explain the following sources of error which may arise when using a sensitive comparator: (i) parallax; (ii) elastic deflection at measuring contacts; (iii) sine and cosine errors. How may the effects of such error sources be reduced to a minimum?

(b) Use a diagram to describe the operating principle of either an optical or a mechanical type of comparator. Derive an expression for the magnification of the system which you describe.

3. (a) Discuss the particular merits of cabinet-type projectors, as compared with a toolmaker's microscope not equipped with a projection screen, for examination of gauges.
Give reasons why the overall accuracy of such an instrument is rather limited.

(b) Make an optical diagram of a projector, showing how the relative positions of the screen, projection lens and object, affect the magnification and definitions of the image.

4. (a) Explain the essential differences between linear measurement and circular dividing.

(b) Describe the dividing instrument known as a circular division tester and show the effects of eccentricity of the divided circle and how these are eliminated. State the average accuracy of this type of instrument.

5. A 150 mm diameter circular divided scale is mounted with a slight eccentricity. When tested against a 12-sided precision polygon, the errors in minutes of arc read from an Angle Dekkor were:

Position	0	30°	60°	90°	120°	150°	180°
Error	0	+ 1·8	+ 2·6	+ 1·8	0	− 2·5	− 5
Position	210°	240°	270°	300°	330°	360°	
Error	− 6·8	− 7·5	− 6·8	− 5	− 2·5	0	

Determine the amount and the angular position of the eccentricity.

6. Describe with the aid of a sketch the optical principle of an autocollimator.
When testing the straightness of a surface 1550 mm long, a reflecting surface supported vertically on a "bridge" having feet at 150 mm apart is used in conjunction with an autocollimator, and the following results are obtained:

LH   RH

Position	1	2	3	4	5	6	7	8	9	10
Reading (sec)	+ 12	+ 16	0	− 24	− 20	− 8	0	− 12	+ 16	+ 12

The + ve sign indicates work rising towards RH end.

Find the maximum errors of straightness of the surface from a datum line through the end points.

7. The following results were obtained from a test on a straight edge using a 125 mm–10 seconds precision level. Slip gauges of equal size were wrong on the base of the level at a pitch of 25 mm

Reading position	1	2	3	4	5	6	7	8	9	10
Divisions on level	+4	+1	0	−1	−3	+1	0	+2	+2	−1

Obtain the linear equivalent per division and hence plot a graph showing the variations of the edge from true straightness.

8. (a) Illustrate the use of calibrated balls, rollers and slip gauges for the measurement of:

(i) plain internal diameters ranging from 6 mm to 25 mm;
(ii) taper plug gauges having a large taper;
(iii) radius gauges above 300 mm radius.

(b) Develop the geometry for one of these examples and comment on the need for sufficient checks to give a good knowledge of the overall accuracy of the gauge.

9. (a) The 32 mm dimension of the profile shown in Fig 12.47 is checked, using a standard 25 mm roller, by measuring dimension h. Find this dimension correct to the nearest 0·002 mm.

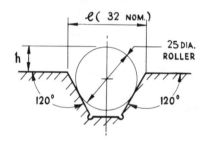

Fig. 12.47

(b) For a certain gauge, made to this profile, h was found to be correct, but the 120° angles were both 4 min of arc oversize. Find, to the nearest 0.002 mm, the error introduced into l.

10. Fig 12.48 shows a method used to determine the radius R of a circular arc. If h measures 17.120 mm find R.

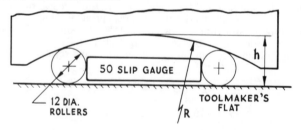

Fig. 12.48

If the reliability of the measurement of h is ± 0.005 mm, to what degree of accuracy has the value of R been found?

11. (a) Show, for a sine-bar, that the error of angular setting θ arising from errors of the dimensions l and h is given by:

$$\Delta\theta \text{ (rads)} = \frac{\sec\theta}{l}\Delta h - \frac{\tan\theta}{l}\Delta l$$

(b) If, for a 100 mm sine-bar, the setting error $\Delta\theta$ is not to exceed 15 seconds of arc when $\Delta l = +0.004$ mm and $\Delta h = -0.002$ mm, what is the maximum value of θ to which the sine-bar may be set?

12. (a) What is the meaning of the following terms: surface texture; surface waviness; arithmetical mean deviation; root mean square; peak to valley; 0·8 mm and 2·4 mm wavelength?

(b) What are the relative merits of a stylus type and an interferometric type of surface finish measuring instrument?

13. A pneumatic comparator has a linear characteristic given by $P_2/P_1 = -0.5\,A_m/A_c + 1.1$ over the range P_2/P_1 from 0·55 to 0·85 and is supplied with air at 2·5 bar. The control jet is 0·6 mm dia. and the magnification factor of the meter used is 2000.

(i) What diameter measuring jet should be fitted so that a range of 0.03 mm is just within the linear range stated?

(ii) What will be the mean position of the work from the measuring jet at the middle of the linear range and what will be the overall magnification of the system?

CHAPTER 13

Dimensional Control

13.1 Limit Gauging

Consider a bore of 50·046/50·000 mm diameter and 50 mm long. As explained in **1.6**, the limits define a zone within which the surface of the bore must lie. It is possible to test the bore, to see if it does comply with the specification, by means of a simple **go** and **not-go** gauging system, Fig 13.1.

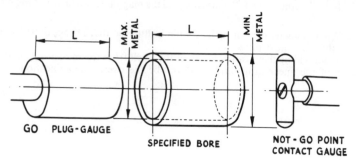

Fig. 13.1 Limit gauging a bore

To check the work completely by direct measurement would be much more difficult, because, not only has the diameter to be tested, but the roundness and straightness of the cylindrical bore as well. A correctly designed and made limit gauge checks geometrical and dimensional features simultaneously; it can show the work to be correct, but it cannot completely reveal the particular errors which may render it incorrect.

Advantages of the limit gauging method are:

(i) it is generally much quicker than direct measurement, and may be carried out by less skilled labour;

(ii) it automatically takes into account combinations of errors such as errors of work diameter and roundness.

Disadvantages of the method are:

(i) particular sources of error are less easily revealed;

(ii) gauges cannot be manufactured entirely without error, and they are subject to loss of accuracy from wear;

426

(iii) practical considerations, such as weight, flexure and manufacturing complexity, restrict gauging to certain gauge sizes and types known to be successful;

(iv) the manufacturing cost of the gauges may not be recovered from a small quantity of work.

Taylor's Principles of Gauging. Fig 13.1 illustrates **go** and **not-go** gauges made as closely as possible to these principles. The **go** end of the gauge must be of perfect form made to the maximum metal condition of workpiece. It must completely cover the surface to be tested. A gauge which conforms to these conditions is termed a **full-form gauge.** The **not-go** end of the gauge ideally comprises points, which explore the surface being tested in order to detect any position outside the minimum metal condition. The two points at the ends of the bar gauge shown in Fig 13.1 come as near to these ideal requirements as possible.

For practical reasons the **go** gauge may not be full-form, e.g. the weight or length of such a gauge may not be convenient; similarly the **not-go** gauge will depart from the ideal because point contact leads to rapid gauge wear and may also involve a more expensive design of gauge. Generally, where machine-tool alignments and bearings are satisfactory, the geometric errors of machining are relatively small and a common type of gauge, e.g. calliper-type diameter gauge, checks the size only. Where components are easily deflected, e.g. thin-walled tubing, a gauge based on Taylor's principles is desirable; a **go** type calliper gauge might then accept work which would not enter a **go** ring gauge.

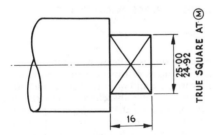

Fig. 13.2 Square-ended shaft

Example 13.1
Design gauges suitable for the full inspection of the square end to be straddle milled on the shaft illustrated in Fig 13.2.

Solution
A solution is shown in Fig 13.3.

Note the significance of the MMC specification Ⓜ included in the work limits. If the work is on top limit it must be exactly square, and the full-form **go** ring will test this feature. If the work is below top limit errors of squareness are acceptable provided the work is passed by **both** gauges. A serious error of squareness might pass the **go** gauge if the work size were small enough; the

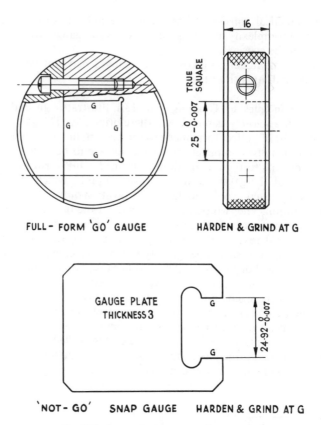

FULL- FORM 'GO' GAUGE   HARDEN & GRIND AT G

'NOT- GO'   SNAP GAUGE   HARDEN & GRIND AT G

Fig. 13.3 Gauges for inspection of square end

not-go gauge, having only limited contact on opposite faces, would then reject the work. Reference to p. 24 gives other examples of this important principle.

The full-form gauge would be expensive to make and would not be justified for a short run of work. Indexing mechanisms are generally reliable, and straddle milling produces faces which are closely parallel, so that a calliper-type limit gauge for the size only could be satisfactory. For "incoming parts" inspection, where there is no knowledge of the quality of the manufacturing equipment employed, the ring gauge is desirable; also one such gauge might be supplied, along with several calliper-type limit gauges, in order to control a long run of work in a general machine shop.

Work Specification in Relation to Gauging. Consider the problem of designing a gauging system to control the hole diameter and its position, specified in Fig 13.4(*a*). The specification requires the centre of the hole to be within limits of 32·1/32·0 mm from the edge, whatever the actual size of the hole. To achieve this, a position gauge designed around some form of expanding location pin is required. Such a gauge would be expensive to make and slow in use.

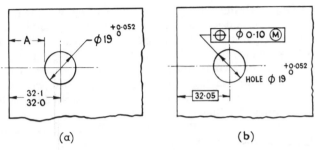

Fig. 13.4 Work specification

Alternatively, consider a method of gauging for position based upon dimension A. As the component drawing stands, A is subject to tolerance build up; it can vary by 0·126 mm, and a limit gauge for A based upon this figure could accept work outside the stated conditions.

If the dimensioning is changed to that shown in Fig 13.4(b) this is overcome because the positional tolerance now applies only to a bore at MMC. The gauge represents the conditions of the mating part; the increase in the positional tolerance due to the increase in bore size will still allow the parts to assemble.

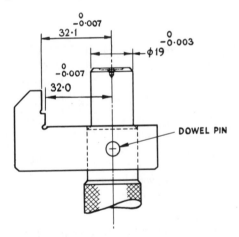

Fig. 13.5 Gauge for 32·1/32·0 dim, bore at MMC

The MMC specification changes the drawing to make it conform to a simple gauging method. The main reason for doing this is that agreement between the two is exact, whereas for the original dimensions an exact gauging method would be unreasonably expensive in equipment, and in inspection time. As so often in production engineering, the ultimate justification for the suggested change in specification is an economic one.

Standard Gauge Designs. An excellent series of designs for gauges in common use, such as doubled-ended plug gauges, ring gauges, calliper gauges, etc., is given in BS1044. There are two principal advantages to be gained by employing standard designs; quantity-produced gauge blanks may be purchased at much lower cost than they can be made in the average tool-room, saving both time and money; also, because there is no need to make special drawings for gauges illustrated in the British Standard, considerable time is saved in the tool design office.

Certain standards, such as BS3550: *Involute Splines*, contain complete information on the gauges required for controlling work to the specification: sizes of the gauge blanks, dimensions of the gauging faces and the appropriate gauge tolerances. Fully worked out systems of gauge inspection, stating roller dimensions required to check the gauges, are given. Very great savings can be made in technical departments, and in tool-making and inspection, if full use is made of such information.

Gauge Tolerances. BS969 gives a complete coverage of the recommended tolerances for plain gauges. (Screw thread gauges are discussed in Chapter 14.) The system is illustrated in Fig 13.6.

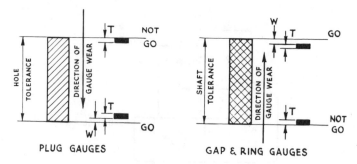

Fig. 13.6 Gauge tolerances to BS 969

The magnitudes of the gauge tolerance T, and of the wear allowance for the **go** gauge W, depend upon the workpiece tolerance as shown in BS969.

BS969 gives no distinctive tolerances of "workshop" or "inspection" gauges. Gauges are made to a common tolerance and, where required, are sorted on final inspection. Those having the largest amount of metal for wear on the **go** dimension are marked **workshop**, the remainder are marked **inspection.**

Certain expensive type receiver gauges, e.g. the **full-form go** gauges for splines and serrations, have rather more generous gauge tolerances and wear allowances than are specified for plain limit gauges. Tolerancing of the more complex type of gauge requires experience and discretion, because special difficulties of tolerance build-up and of manufacturing methods are involved. Examples are given later in this chapter.

Limitations of the Gauging Method

(a) *Rigidity*. Calliper gauges are easily "sprung" over a work diameter; also they vary in size, when held in the hand, due to temperature changes. For these reasons BS969 suggests that they are only suitable where the work tolerance exceeds 0·018 mm. This is reasonable where small work diameters are involved, but becomes impractical at work diameters of 75 to 100 mm due to flexure and temperature distortion. The alternative method, using a calibrated standard and bench type comparator, is far superior for inspecting external diameters to very close tolerances.

Plug gauges are relatively free from flexure effects, and for this reason may be used on a **go, not-go** basis where the work tolerance is as low as IT6.

(b) *Weight*. Plug gauges for large bores are heavy and awkward to handle, unless attention is paid to weight reduction, Fig 13.7 shows how weight may be reduced. Spherically ended bar gauges are more suitable for bores of 120 mm diameter and above.

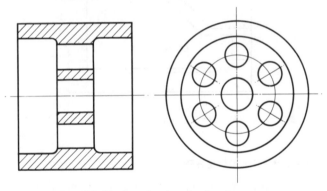

Fig. 13.7 Weight-reduced section for plug gauge

(c) *Profile Gauging*. Sighting methods, as shown in Fig 13.8, introduce discretionary judgements into inspection and are not always acceptable on that account. The "size" of any gap between the component and the gauge, as it appears when held up to the light, depends upon the thickness of the gauging edge, upon surface finish of the work and upon cleanliness, especially freedom from oil films. If the gauge edge is reduced to about 0·8 mm thickness, a gap of about 0·013 mm can be seen. The alternative is to make a more costly form of gauge and to use feeler gauges, or **go** and **not-go** limit plug gauges, to eliminate the discretionary element. A typical gauge of this type is shown in Fig 13.9. Such gauges can precisely control a profile to a tolerance zone specified in accordance with BS308.

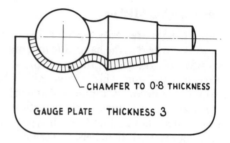

Fig. 13.8 "Sighting" method of profile gauging

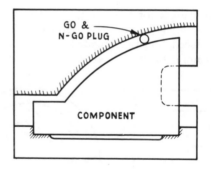

Fig. 13.9 Limit gauging of a profile

13.2 Gauging of Tapers

Taper cone gauges are in common use and can effectively control a diameter in a specified plane perpendicular to the work axis on a **go** and **not-go** basis. They are less effective in their control of included angle. "Blueing" methods may be employed to test the accuracy of the taper angle, but the method is discretionary. The elaborate set of gauges sometimes described for control of taper angle on a **go** and **not-go** basis is rarely employed; the gauges are both costly to make and slow in use.

Example 13.2
   Fig 13.10 illustrates a taper fit. Tests show that when the nut is tightened, the 6·35 mm nominal gap closes by an average amount of 0·13 mm. Design a set of limit gauges which will control the assembly to the required limits, given that the taper hole is to be bored and the shaft end to be ground.

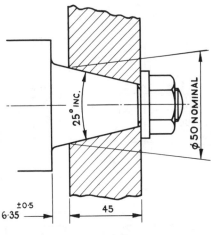

Fig. 13.10

Solution
Let d = component diameter at any position on the taper, and
l = length along the axis of the taper.

For 25° included angle, $\dfrac{\Delta d}{2\Delta l} = \tan 12\tfrac{1}{2}° = 0{\cdot}222$

i.e. $\Delta d = 0{\cdot}444\,\Delta l$

The tolerance on the 6·35 nominal dimension = $\pm0{\cdot}5$

$$\Delta d = 0{\cdot}444 \times 1 = 0{\cdot}444\ \text{mm}$$

i.e. the total tolerance on taper diameter is 0·44 mm (say)

A suitable division of this tolerance is:

(i) bored hole, say 0·27
(ii) ground shaft, say 0·17

The limit steps required on the taper gauges are:

Plug gauge for hole, $\Delta l_h = \dfrac{0{\cdot}27}{0{\cdot}444} = 0{\cdot}61$ (say)

Ring gauge for shaft, $\Delta l_s = \dfrac{0{\cdot}17}{0{\cdot}444} = 0{\cdot}39$ (say)

If a unilateral hole-based system is employed the nominal diameter of the taper at the large end is 50 mm.
Fig 13.11(*a*) shows the plug gauge required.
Fig 13.11(*b*) shows the ring gauge and **go** and **not-go** slip gauge required.
The dimensions of the **go** and **not-go** slip gauge are determined as follows:

Nominal value of the gap, $x = 6{\cdot}35$ mm
Allowance for closure on bolting, add 0·13 mm
Bore on **top** limit absorbs 0·61 mm of the tol on x.
Go size of slip; bore on top limit, shaft on bottom limit;

$$x_1 = 6{\cdot}48 - 0{\cdot}5 + 0{\cdot}61 = \underline{6{\cdot}59\ \text{mm}}$$

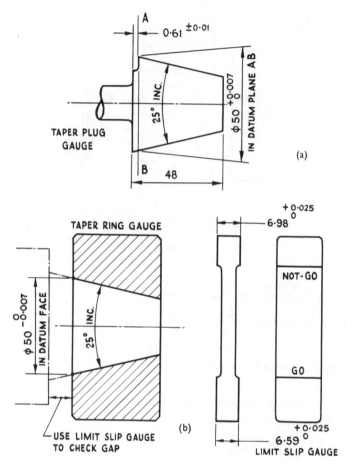

Fig. 13.11

(a) Taper plug gauge (b) Taper ring and slip gauge

not-go size of slip; bore on bottom limit, shaft on top limit,

$$x_2 = 6.48 + 0.5 = 6.98 \text{ mm}$$

Check $x_2 - x_1 = 0.39$, which agrees with Δl_s above.

Two comments can be made on the above solution:

(a) The ± 0.5 tolerance on the 6·35 dimension could easily be held under average machine shop conditions. Should the 6·35 dimension have a closer tolerance, say ± 0.13, it would be necessary in order to hold the limit, to machine the face of the taper bore after a trial assembly. Production methods are in part determined by the design tolerances.

(*b*) The given solution is based upon algebraic association of tolerances. If the principles of **15.10** can be employed because the probability of a very few assemblies lying outside the specified limits is acceptable, somewhat wider tolerances could be permitted.

Limit Gauging of Taper Angle. Taper cone gauges do not give positive control of taper angle. For external cylindrical work a much more effective method is to support the work so that the upper edge lies parallel with a plane surface, and to gauge for parallelism by means of dial gauges as illustrated in Fig 13.12. When grinding "on-centres" sine centres provide the most suitable means of support. For centreless ground work a special angle block may be made and the work located on this between two guide strips, or alternatively, it can be supported in a vee-block tipped to the appropriate angle. One attraction of the method is that the straightness of the sides of the taper can be checked.

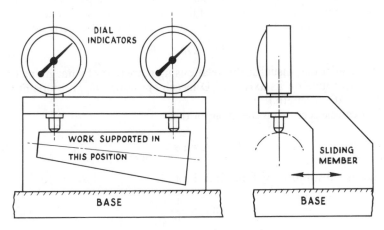

Fig. 13.12 Gauging of taper angle

Fig 13.13 illustrates the geometry upon which the relationships between the various angles depend.

Let α = angle of inclination of the centre-line of the cone with respect to the vee;

θ = semi-angle of the cone;

ϕ = semi-angle of the symmetrical vee.

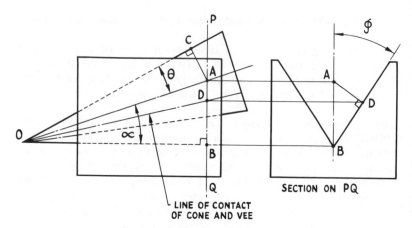

Fig. 13.13 Geometry of cone and vee

The cone contacts the vee flank along the line OD. The normal AD to the point of contact at D lies in the plane PQ, which is perpendicular to the line of intersection of the flanks of the vees. AD is perpendicular to BD, as shown in the sectional view on plane PQ, and is also perpendicular to OD.

$$AD = OA \sin \theta \qquad (1)$$

(The reader may visualise this relationship more easily by imagining the cone to rotate on its axis until D has the position shown by point C; AD = AC in length.)

It can be seen from the diagram that

$$AB = OA \sin \alpha = \frac{AD}{\sin \phi} \qquad (2)$$

and by substitution of Eqn (1) in Eqn (2)

$$\sin \alpha = \frac{\sin \theta}{\sin \phi} \qquad (13.1)$$

To test any particular angle, θ and ϕ will have known values and α can be found from Eqn (13.1). The vee block can then be inclined to an angle $(\alpha + \theta)$ to bring the top edge of the cone parallel with the surface plate on which the vee block rests. A dial indicator test will reveal any error of parallelism, and this may be restricted to a specific amount, depending upon the accuracy to which θ must be produced.

It would be possible to extend this principle in order to make a semi-automatic gauging system, as illustrated in Fig 13.14, which would control taper-angle and diameter. If automatic loading and ejection were used, and coupled with gauging heads which would sort the work according to signals produced by its accuracy, an automatic method of inspection could be developed. Such methods are necessary in conjunction with high-output automatic machines, e.g. centreless grinder, where the work is required to be 100% within the specification, so that statistical quality control cannot be used. If signals from the automatic gauging equipment are fed back to the machine, to cause it to make corrective adjustments, the basis of automatic size control is established. Control methods of this kind are now being used for very high-output work of a precision character. They represent the ultimate development in gauging technique, the gauge "instructs" the machine. Automatic size-control of grinding operations is desirable because of the fine tolerances set, and of the steady drift of size due to wheel wear.

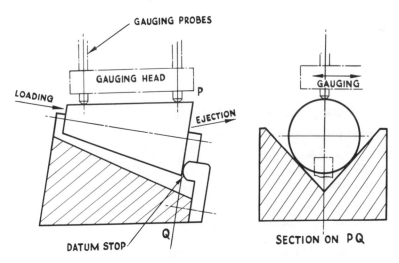

Fig. 13.14 Design study of semi-automatic gauging system

Gauging Fixture for Bevel Gears. Fig 13.15 shows a scheme developed for the inspection of the cone angle, and the diameter in a datum face, of a bevel gear blank. The fixture is used on a surface plate, and a dial gauge reading over the setting pin, and over the work, gives an easy control of angle and diameter. Any alternative gauging method would be slow, require much more equipment and might be less reliable. A taper ring gauge would not be effective due to the large included angle of the taper.

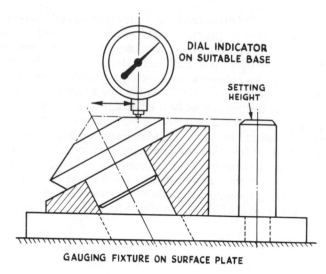

GAUGING FIXTURE ON SURFACE PLATE

Fig. 13.15 Gauging fixture for bevel-gear blanks

13.3 Gauge-making Materials

The chief properties required are:

    (i) hardness, so that the gauging surfaces are not easily damaged;
    (ii) stability, so that dimensional changes do not occur;
    (iii) wear resistance, so that the wear life is reasonable.

The material must also take a high-grade surface finish, generally by the processes of grinding and lapping.

The main materials used for gauges are:

(a) *Carburised and Hardened Mild Steel.* Available in a wide range of sizes and easily machined; a case depth of about 0·2 mm obtained by carburising is hardened to about 850 HV prior to the final grinding. A relatively cheap material for large gauges.

(b) *High-carbon Steel.* Generally oil hardening steel of around 0·9% to 1·0% carbon is used for small plugs or gauges made from plate. Only the gauging surfaces should be hardened.

(c) *Special Wear-resistant Materials.* A small diameter screw plug gauge used on a cast iron component will lose its size very rapidly due to abrasive wear. For situations like this improved wear resistance can be obtained from:

(i) high-speed steel (better wear resistance than carbon steel);

(ii) "hard" chromium plating on hardened steel, a "flash" of plating on thread ground gauges, a moderate thickness of plating finally ground to size for plain gauges;

(iii) tungsten carbide, sintered metal powder-mouldings ground with diamond grit abrasive and so very expensive, but having a greatly improved wear life.

The heat-treatment of all steel gauges should include a stabilising process after hardening to reduce the small dimensional changes which normally occur over a period in the finished gauge. This is very important for gauges of large size or where very high accuracy is involved (e.g. slip gauges).

Fig 13.16 gives details of the construction and manufacturing method for a receiver type gauge for checking the location of four holes relative to a bored diameter.

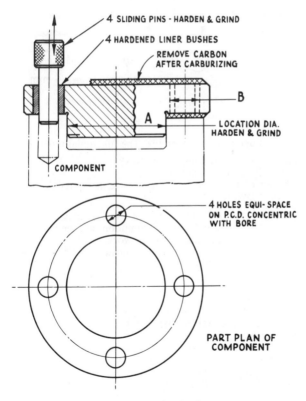

Fig. 13.16 Manufacturing details of receiver gauge

13.4 Component Tolerancing and Gauge Design

Many of the principles given in Chapter 1, Specification and Standardisation for Production, are linked with problems of maintaining accuracy during manufacture. It is difficult to treat all the practical aspects of this which may arise in process planning or gauge design, in a textbook. An attempt is made in the following worked examples to show how such problems can be tackled. There are, of course, many possible alternatives to the solutions presented, which are only intended to give an insight into some aspects of tolerancing and gauge design.

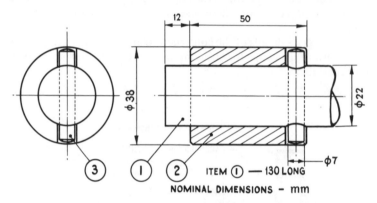

Fig. 13.17 Assembly showing nominal dimensions

Example 13.3

Fig 13.17 gives details of an assembly. The functional requirements are:

(i) pin (3) to be an interference fit in shaft (1);
(ii) sleeve (2) to be a slide fit on shaft (1);
(iii) the slot of (2) to engage pin (3) in either possible position with a minimum of "play".

Tolerance the functional dimensions of the assembly in accordance with BS4500, as far as possible, and on the assumption that the manufacturing costs are to be typical of average machine-shop work.

Design suitable gauges for the control of the limits set, assuming that there is to be a fairly long production run.

Solution

Selection of the Main Fits

(a) Pin (3) in shaft (1), H7/p6 is a suitable interference fit.
Reamed hole in shaft (1), $\phi\,7\cdot015/7\cdot000$
Centreless ground pin (3), $\phi\,7\cdot025/7\cdot015$
(b) Sleeve (2) on shaft (1) (it is assumed that the shaft will be centreless ground), H7/g6 is a suitable close-clearance fit.
Reamed hole in sleeve (2), $\phi\,22\cdot021/22\cdot000$
Ground shaft (1), $\phi\,21\cdot993/21\cdot972$
(c) Position of hole in shaft (1) and of milled slot in sleeve (2). The positional tolerances are shown in Fig 13.18.

(*d*) Limits for the milled slot of sleeve (2). If the slot is to engage the pin in both possible positions its minimum width will depend upon the positional tolerances given in Fig 13.18.

Let w = minimum width of the slot

then
$$\frac{w}{2} = \text{rad. of pin at MMC} + \tfrac{1}{2}(t_1 + t_2)$$

$$w = 7 \cdot 025 + 0 \cdot 200 = 7 \cdot 225 \text{ mm}$$

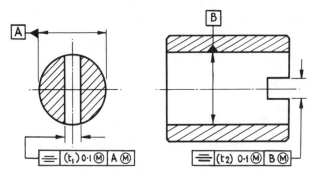

Fig. 13.18 Tolerances controlling the relationships of the pin and slot

A suitable tolerance for the milled slot is 0·08 and the limits are 7·305/7·225.

Since BS4500 gives no suitable limits for a basic size of 7 mm and there is no good reason to change this basic size, it seems best for the **special** limits to remain. The slot can be produced by means of a cutter of 8 mm (standard) thickness, specially reduced in width to cut the required size, i.e. cutter grind to $7 \cdot 230 \, {}^{+0.02}_{0}$ mm thickness.

(*e*) Fig 13.19 shows a component drawing for the sleeve (2). Provision has been made to accommodate the burr and swollen edge which will arise when the pin is driven into the shaft.

(*f*) The standard type gauges required are as follows:

    (i) 7H7, D/E plain plug (D/E = double ended);
    (ii) 22H7, D/E plain plug.

The 7p6, and 22g6, limits, will be controlled by means of slip gauges and a measuring comparator, because calliper type gauges are unsuitable for such close tolerances, see p. 431, item (*a*).

(*g*) Special gauges:

    (i) Fig 13.20 shows the special D/E slip gauge required for the width of the milled slot.

    (ii) Fig 13.21 shows a receiver-type gauge for the position of the hole in the shaft. While such a gauge would be relatively expensive, it would be desirable for a long production run. The position of the hole would depend upon the accuracy of the jig provided for drilling it. The jig may function satisfactorily for a time, but wear of the drill bush will occur, and the position of the hole drilled will vary from this cause. The position of the hole must be checked at regular intervals. It would be possible to dispense with the gauge, provided a "first-off" inspection of each batch was made to check the position of the hole.

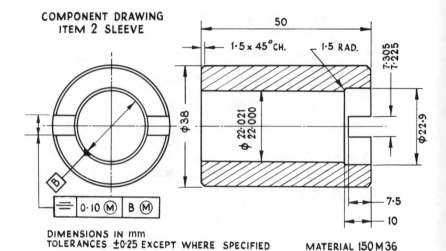

Fig. 13.19 *Production drawing of sleeve*

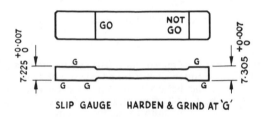

Fig. 13.20 *Double-ended slip gauge for milled slot*

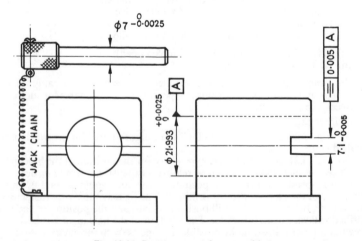

Fig. 13.21 *Position gauge for reamed hole*

A skilled inspector would be required for this work; if a "viewer" or unskilled operator is to do the inspection the receiver gauge must be provided.

The width of the gauge slots is shown as $7 \cdot 1 ^{\,0}_{-0.005}$ mm, a figure arrived at as follows. The positional tolerance of the hole, item (1), is (0.05×2) wide, the nominal diameter 7mm; the nominal width of the slot is therefore $7 \cdot 100$ mm. The gauge has to control the **position** of the hole to a tolerance of (0.05×2), and a reasonable gauge tolerance is 10% of this, or 0.01, opposite to the direction of gauge wear (i.e. minus). The gauge maker needs a positional tolerance and a width tolerance, so the 0.01 has been split as shown in Fig 13.21. As arranged, it is possible for one side of the slot to lie at $\left(\dfrac{7 \cdot 1}{2}\right) + 0.0025$ from the centre-line of the datum hole, i.e. to be just outside the specified work tolerance.

(iii) Fig 13.22 shows a **full-form** receiver gauge, designed in accordance with Taylor's principles, for checking the position of the milled slot. If this gauge accepts the work, and if separate **not-go** gauges for the bore and for the width of the slot also pass the work, the component inspected has been proved to lie within the tolerance zones specified. The $7 \cdot 125 ^{+0.005}_{0}$ width of the tongue is determined as follows:

Nominal width of the tongue = Minimum width of the slot

$-$ Positional tolerance of the slot $= 7 \cdot 225 - 0 \cdot 1 = 7 \cdot 125$ mm

The 10% gauge-making tolerance has again been divided between the positional and width dimensions of the tongues.

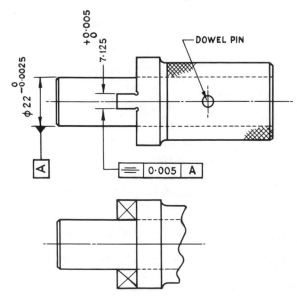

Fig. 13.22 Receiver gauge for position of milled slot

Example 13.4
A taper cone, nominal included angle 25°, rests in a symmetrical vee of included angle 90°. To what angle must the vee be inclined for the upper edge

of the taper cone to be parallel with the surface plate upon which the vee-block rests?

If dial indicator readings taken over the taper cone show a difference of 0·03 mm over a length of 50 mm, lower at the large end of the taper, what error of included angle is indicated?

Solution
By Eqn (13.1),
$$\sin\alpha = \frac{\sin\theta}{\sin\phi}$$

From the given conditions $2\theta = 25°$, $2\phi = 90°$ and α is required.

$$\sin\alpha = \frac{\sin 12\cdot5°}{\sin 45°}$$

$$= 0\cdot306\,09$$

$$\alpha = 17°\,49\cdot5'$$

Angle of inclination required $= 17°\,49v5' + 12°\,30'$

$$= \underline{30°\,19\cdot5'}$$

Angular error of $(\alpha + \theta)$ indicated $= \dfrac{0\cdot03}{50}$ radians

$$= 0\cdot0006 \text{ radians or } 2\cdot06'$$

α is however a function of θ. By differentiation of Eqn 13.1, ϕ being regarded as a constant,

$$\cos\alpha\,.\,\Delta\alpha = \frac{\cos\theta}{\sin\phi}\,.\,\Delta\theta \text{(very nearly)}$$

$$\Delta\alpha = \frac{\cos 12\cdot5°}{\cos 17°\,50' \times \sin 45°}$$

$$= \frac{0\cdot9763}{0\cdot952 \times 0\cdot7071}\Delta\theta$$

$$= 1\cdot45\Delta\theta$$

But
$$(\Delta\alpha + \Delta\theta) = 2\cdot06'$$

$$\therefore\; 2\cdot45\Delta\theta = 2\cdot06'$$

$$\Delta\theta = 0\cdot84' \text{ or } 50\text{sec of arc}$$

Error of included angle $= \underline{-0°\,1'\,40''}$

13.5 Alternatives to Limit Gauging

Refinements in machine tool control (see Chapter 4) and better instrumentation, mainly due to electronics have had the following impact on the machining of components:

(i) output rates are raised;
(ii) dimensional and geometric accuracy has become more reliable.

Due to (i) manual inspection by limit gauging becomes a disproportionately large element of the production cost. Due to (ii) dimensional control is more easily integrated with the machining process so that inspection can be limited to "first off" checks supplemented by sampling methods for important dimensions (see Chapter 15).

Such technical improvements have almost eliminated the need for expensive receiver gauges to check dimensional and geometric features as required by Taylor's principles of gauging. However, limit gauging is still the cheapest and most convenient method of control for such things as small plain bores and both internal and external screw threads. Full sets of gauges based on Taylor's principles remain an economic form of dimensional control for such items as splines and serrations, where the alternative of 100% inspection by measurement requires standards room equipment and highly skilled labour.

13.6 Multi-gauging Based on Comparators

A pre-set comparator has advantages over a calliper-type limt gauge; one instrument can cover a wide range of sizes and the actual departures from the ideal size can be detected. By building a number of comparator units into a type of gauging fixture rapid inspection of a number of dimensional features can be performed simultaneously.

Fig 13.23 illustrates schematically how a back pressure air gauging system operating as explained on p. 400 can be developed for multigauging. Back pressure P_b determines displacement h of the manometer

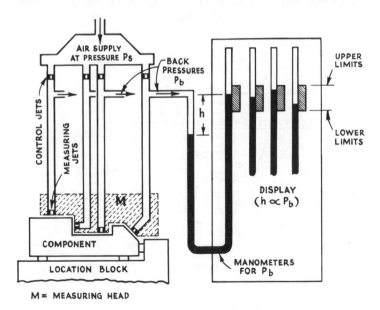

Fig. 13.23 Multi-gauging fixture, based on air gauging

associated with each measuring element. If the control and measuring jets are suitably chosen and a small adjustable air bleed is incorporated in each line, it is possible to have common limits for *h* on the display, even where different limits of size apply to the workpiece. The system involves certain specially manufactured elements, namely:

(i) the measuring head;
(ii) the component locating block;
(iii) a "master" component for setting up and subsequent checking.

These parts need not be manufactured to the same high precision as gauges because adjustments can be made, via the air bleeds, during setting up. It is very easy to see at a glance if all the columns of coloured liquid terminate within the limits for *h*, an arrangement ergonomically superior to that of reading separate dials. Electronically operated comparators are now available which employ a column of light (neon discharge) in place of the manometer of the air gauging system. By further processing the output signals from electronic comparators, it is possible to operate just one indication lamp at each pass: green light—accept, red light—reject.

13.7 In-process Measurement

A machine tool fitted with a control system may be suitably adapted to measure and control a particular dimension during the machining. Fig 13.24 illustrates such a system developed by Ferranti for control of

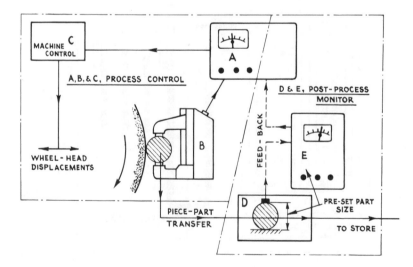

Fig. 13.24 In-process gauging with feed-back

an external diameter during a grinding process. This system incorporates post-process measurement with feedback to give greater reliability.

Item A is the primary control unit receiving a signal from the calliper-type measuring head B which it compares with a pre-set value in A. When "size" is signalled, the information passes to the machine control C, the grinding wheel head retracts and the ground part is transferred to a post-process measuring unit D operating in conjunction with E, where the diameter required is pre-set. Any error detected at E is fed back to A to adjust the size setting. The post-process monitor is away from disturbance factors of the grinding and gives a more reliable reading from which to control the size. Both B and D are adjustable for diameter, as also the size target analogues of A and E, making the equipment adaptable to a range of work provided parts are compatible with the transfer mechanism B to D.

13.8 Inspection Machines

The NC inspection machine is a development made necessary by the NC machine tool. Fig 13.25 illustrates a three axis type of inspection machine fitted with digital readout and control cabinet. Print-out facilities are available and some machines incorporate a mini-computer to save the operator doing calculations. An accuracy of 0·025 mm over 500 mm is an

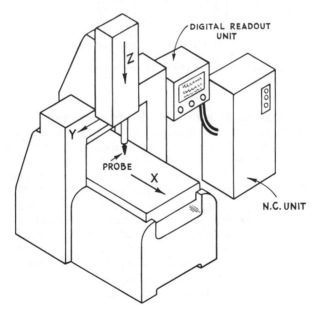

Fig. 13.25 Inspection machine with NC positioning and digital read-out

average for such machines although some are made to greater precision. As the diagram shows, the machine is similar in construction to a portal frame jig-borer, but without the boring head. A probe replaces the boring head and is linked to the read-out/print-out and computing facilities. The slideways may have either NC positional control, or continuous control (for contour checking), this fitted to at least the X and Y axes, and often to all three.

Consider a plate with bores positioned, using an NC machine tool. If a similar program is fed to the inspection machine and the plate suitably located, the centre of each bore can be aligned with the probe head. If the probe is then located in each bore (see Fig 13.26) positional errors can be read directly by digital read-out. By zeroing on the first hole a mini-computer can relate the error readings to the actual bore position, so simplifying part location on the machine.

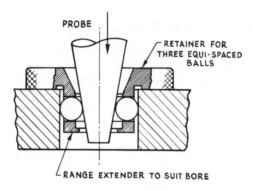

Fig. 13.26 Location of probe of Inspection machine in a bore

Such machines are likely to have considerable further development. Using special probes, some operating at 90° to the vertical axis, and circular tables, also by adding mini-computing facilities, the range of such machines will develop to match the sophistication of NC machine tools. Their principal merit is that they can provide the independent assessment of dimensional features produced on NC machine tools, profiles, hole positions, angular displacements etc. The reliability of NC machine tools is such that once the program is proved in this way, the major geometrical and dimensional features are reproduced consistently. The main cause of dimensional variation when machining is tool wear, and frequent checks are necessary to monitor this, for which reason simple limit gauges for hole diameters, screw threads, width of milled slots etc., are likely to remain as the economic method for these features.

EXERCISES 13

1. Make a drawing of a limited plug gauge which would be suitable for inspecting the 25·025/25 mm bore of a bush, 63 mm long, in accordance with the Taylor principle.
The drawing should indicate:

(*a*) The tolerance to which the **go** and **not-go** ends of the plug should be manufactured.
(*b*) The tolerance to which the measuring anvils will be subsequently inspected to control the degree of permissible wear.
(*c*) The material for which the measuring anvils of the gauge will be made.
(*d*) The sequence of operations used in making the measuring anvils.

2. Make sketches, in good proportion, of a suitable set of length gauges for use by a capstan-lathe operator on the shoulder lengths of the component given in Fig. 1.14(B). Give the gauging dimensions and their tolerances.
3. Design an inspection gauge suitable for checking the 6·05/6·00 mm dimension of item 2 of the assembly shown in Fig 1.15 (as dimensioned from the functional datum surface).
Make your own choice of diameters for the component, and dimension your gauge accordingly.
4. State the principles which govern the design of limit gauges giving examples of such gauges to check:

(i) length;
(ii) diameter;
(iii) depth;
(iv) distance between an internal and an external face.

5. Design all the gauges necessary for the inspection of the component shown in Fig 1.27 as far as this has been dimensioned. The design sketches must show the appropriate gauge-making tolerances.
6. The part shown in Fig 13.27 is to be inspected on all linear dimensions by limit gauging. The angle of the taper bore is not important, but the distance from the φ 20 mm ball must be held.

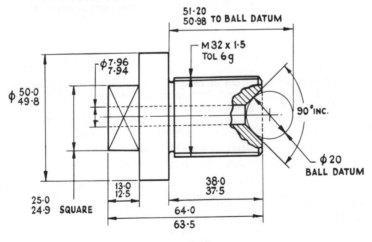

Fig. 13.27

Specify all the gauges you would require. Make dimensioned sketches of the gauges you would use for:

(a) the 38/37·5 mm shoulder length;
(b) the 25·0/24·9 mm square projection;
(c) control of the 51·20/50·08 mm dimension.

Show the gauge tolerances on these sketches.

7. A static coarse clearance fit for ease of assembly, is required between a shaft and hole of 100 mm nominal diameter. The fit is designated H8-c9 and the hole limits are $^{+54}_{+0}$ in 0·001 mm units. The extremes of fit are $^{321}_{180}$ clearance.

(a) Determine the limits of the shaft, and design and dimension a gauge to check it.

(b) Draw up a detailed manufacturing sequence for the gauge.

8. Fig 13.28 shows a bush in which a slot has to be milled. For convenience in manufacture the slot position must be redimensioned, working from the new datum face shown, without causing any departure from the previous specification. Give the required new dimensions.

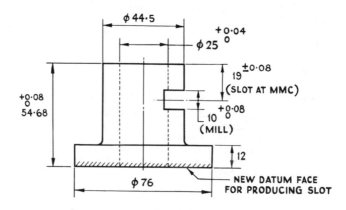

Fig. 13.28

Make dimensioned sketches of the gauges required to control the overall length of the component, and the width and position of the slot (as re-dimensioned). Show the gauge-making tolerances.

9. A sectional view through a valve block is shown in Fig 13.29. Design gauges on the flush-pin principle suitable for checking the following:

(i) the $33^{+0·25}$ mm depth of the $45^{+0·13}$ mm dia hole;
(ii) the $87·6^{-0·38}$ mm dimension of the taper cone seating.

10. A taper shaft, basic taper 0·25; 1 is 63·5 mm long and the diameter at the large end is $44·5^{-0·076}$ mm. If the shaft rests in a 60° included-angle vee block, to what angle must this be tipped for the upper edge of a shaft to be horizontal?

If the taper angle is inspected by means of two dial gauges placed 50 mm apart, what difference in their readings will occur for the maximum permissible error of the shaft taper? (Assume parallel tolerance zones.)

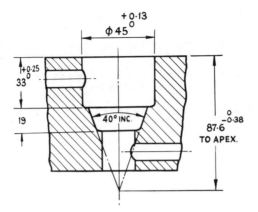

Fig. 13.29

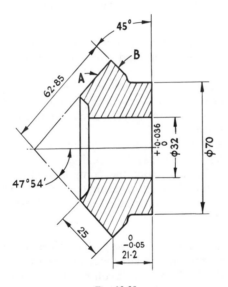

Fig. 13.30

11. Fig 13.30 gives the principal dimensions of a bevel gear blank.

Design a gauging fixture which checks the faces marked A and B by means of a sliding element carrying a profile plate gauge. Also dimension the fixture so that the cone apex position is tested by taking a dial-gauge reading over face A, and over a suitably positioned height-setting pin. What is the maximum acceptable variation of reading of the dial gauge when checking the cone apex position?

CHAPTER 14

Screw Threads Specification, Tolerancing, Gauging and Measurement

14.1

Manufacturing methods for screw threads exemplify the principles of cutting and forming previously described; the main methods are summarised below.

(1) *Taps and dies.* The tap is a fluted screw of hardened steel with its leading threads tapered off and ground back to provide cutting clearance. It cuts threads in a plain hole generally drilled somewhat larger than the minor thread diameter. The threads of the tap which follow the cutting portion have no cutting clearance and act as a guide to control the pitch. Dies, based upon a circular nut, cut external threads using similar principles.

To reduce the idle time needed to unscrew a tap or die, the cutting portions (generally four) may be fitted into a suitable holder and automatically withdrawn from the component thread before rapid retraction of the tool. The self-opening diehead has no lower limit of component diameter; the collapsible tap is only feasible for the larger internal threads.

(2) *Screw cutting and thread chasing.* The principles are of historical significance; the screw-cutting lathe was an important development of the early machine tool. The method controls the two basic elements of a thread independently; the pitch by the kinematics of the lathe, $z = k\theta_w$ (see Chapter 2) and the form by the plan shape of the cutting tool.

Disadvantages which make the method relatively slow are:

(i) waste material is removed in long thin strands at relatively low cutting speeds and a lot of idle return motions are necessary.

(ii) a vee-form tool cannot be advanced radially to cut a chip round its entire form because material from both flanks crowds onto the tool rake face causing torn component material and possible tool breakages. To overcome delays due to (i) many production lathes incorporate threading cycle mechanisms which give automatic retraction of the tool at the end of the cut and rapid return and advance (including the required element of in-feed) for the subsequent cut. Control elements of the more sophisticated NC lathes often incorporate 'canned-cycles' for screw cutting.

Problems associated with (ii) can be overcome by in-feeding the tool in a direction inclined by the semi-angle of the vee, instead of perpendicularly to the component axis. This results in one flank being 'formed' and the other 'generated' so that a chip is cut from one flank only.

(3) *Thread milling.* By replacing the single point tool of method (2) by a form milling cutter (hob) set to cut the full depth of thread, short chips will be cut as described in Chapter 7 and the thread completed in one pass. For short lengths of thread, especially on large diameters, a form relieved cutter with a number of threads (annular grooves) can be advanced to the depth of cut while the work is held stationary. The component can than be rotated about $1\frac{1}{3}$ times while the cutter is traversed at the appropriate rate of thread pitch. This, known as the 'plunge-cut' method, is much faster than thread chasing for work of large diameter or of coarse pitch; however the faceted milled surface is unlikely to be acceptable for work of high quality or precision.

Single form cutters, e.g. Acme, can be used to rough out long transmission screws such as machine tool leadscrews. The axis of cutter rotation needs to be inclined to the screw axis by the mean helix angle of the thread to minimise interference effects. Interference effects arise whenever helical grooves are cut with tools having the form of a rotating disc because mutual contact does not lie in an axial plane of the screw. Thread milled transmission screws are generally finished by thread chasing on a screw-cutting lathe.

(4) *Thread Grinding.* The process originated in early attempts to finish grind pre-cut hardened blanks for use as screw gauges. Modern taps are ground from pre-fluted hardened HSS blanks in a single pass, which illustrates subsequent progress. Kinematically the methods are either 'pass-through' or 'plunge-cut' as for thread milling.

Important stages in the development of thread grinding have been:

(i) manufacturing of grinding wheels of composite structure capable of removing large amounts of material while also retaining accurate thread form and giving a good surface finish;

(ii) development of techniques for dressing thread forms on single and multi-ribbed wheels in which diamond dressing or crush dressing may be used (see Section 9.4);

(iii) provision of adequate power at the grinding wheel spindle coupled with arrangements for varying wheel and work-head rotation speeds. Thread grinding can achieve very high pitch accuracy on hardened components (e.g. micrometer screws) and is now the basic method for completing the manufacture of the essential equipment for screw thread production.

(5) *Thread rolling.* By deforming a plain cylinder within the plastic range, threads can be produced without cutting away waste material. The flat plate method, rolling the blank under pressure between two suitably profiled flat plates, is a rapid method of producing bolts of relatively low quality such as ironmongery bolts. If the flat plates are replaced by cylindrical rollers (two or three according to the system employed) the rolling time can be extended and tougher metal worked to closer tolerances and better surface finish.

Only a brief summary of screw-thread manufacture is possible here as an introduction to the more specialised topics of this chapter. Full descriptive treatments and explanatory diagrams will be found in books listed in the general section of the bibliography.

Screwed assemblies have more complex fitting requirements than plain assemblies but basic size, tolerance and fundamental deviation remain the controlling factors. The principles outlined in Chapter 1 (specification) Chapter 12 (measurement) and Chapter 13 (gauging) are further exemplified by a consideration of their application to screwed assemblies.

14.2 Nomenclature and Specification

BS2517: *Definitions for Use in Mechanical Engineering* gives the standard definitions applicable to threads. Details of the principal thread forms are contained in;

   BS3643: *ISO Metric Threads,*
   BS4827: *ISO Miniature Threads,*
   BS4846: *ISO Trapezoidal Threads,*
   BS21: *Pipe Threads for Tubes and Fittings.*

Because they are likely to remain in use for servicing purposes the following are also of interest;

   BS 84: *Whitworth Form Threads,*
   BS 93: *British Association (BA) Threads.*

The well-known *Machinery's Screw Thread Book* is another handy reference.

Certain ideas about specification, tolerancing, gauging and measurement of screw threads of vee form (with a few minor exceptions) are common to all the above thread systems; these will now be explained with special reference to ISO Metric threads.

Fig 14.1 shows general features of screw threads of vee form. The **nominal** diameter is generally the **major** diameter of the basic form (exception, pipe threads). The "form" of a thread lies in a section plane along the axis.

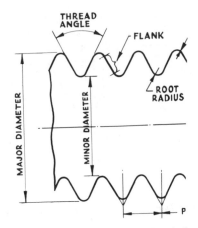

Fig. 14.1 General features of a screw thread of vee form

Fig 14.2 gives the basic form for ISO Metric threads and proportional dimensions in terms of the pitch (p). For bolts (external threads) the actual form lies on or below the basic form; for nuts (internal threads) it lies on or above basic form. The design form of the external thread is shown in Fig 14.3. The root of the vees is rounded, an important factor in relation to impact loading and fatigue strength; it also has relevance to the cutting tools. The crests may be either flat or rounded as shown. Die-threading and thread-rolling produce rounded crests, but for single-point thread cutting, the flat crest involves less trouble. In terms of pitch these radii are;

Root radius $0.1443p$

Crest radius $0.1082p$ (also the minimum radius allowed by tolerance at the root)

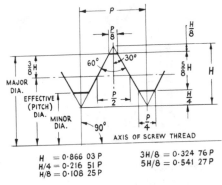

Fig. 14.2 Basic form of ISO metric threads

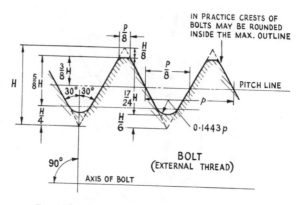

Fig. 14.3 Design form of ISO metric external thread

A reasonable tolerance at the root is necessary in order to allow for normal tool wear.

The design form of the internal thread as given in BS3643 has a radius at the major diameter (root of the vees for a nut). This radius is large enough to clear the flat crest of the basic form and provides for wear of screwing taps at their major diameter. Essentially vee threads are dimensioned to fit along the flanks of the vees, the most important dimension being the **effective** (or pitch) diameter.

Fig 14.4 shows the three essential dimensions which determine the fit of mating threads. The **effective diameter** (or pitch diameter) is defined as the diameter of the pitch cylinder. This is an imaginary cylinder, co-axial with the thread, which intersects the thread flanks in such a manner

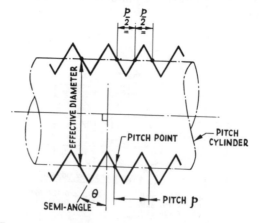

Fig. 14.4 Dimensions which control the fitting of vee threads

that the intercept on a generator of the cylinder, between the points where it cuts the opposite flanks of the thread groove, is equal to half the basic pitch.

The combined significance of the semi-angle, pitch and effective diameter in determining the relative position of adjacent flanks is shown in Fig 14.5. The pitch may be measured along any line parallel with the axis and intersecting the flanks, such as AB; dimensions p_{AB}, p_{CD}, etc., determine the relative position of points on the flanks along the thread. A dimension of similar significance to the effective diameter may be measured along any line perpendicular to the axis and intersecting the flanks, such as EF; dimensions E_{EF}, E_{GH}, etc., determine the relative position of diametrically opposed points on the flanks of the thread. It is important to realise that the common elementary concept of screw-thread dimensions given in Fig 14.1 is inadequate as a specification for manufacturing purposes.

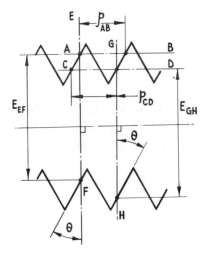

Fig. 14.5 Dimensions which determine the relative positions of the flanks of a vee thread

The helix is a three-dimensional curve, and the geometry of a screw thread cannot be completely specified by reference to a section plane containing the screw axis, as shown in Fig 14.4. It is an implied condition that the developed helix follows a straight line. Departures from this condition are often referred to as **drunkenness** (see Fig 3.22). Equipment capable of measuring small drunkenness errors is somewhat elaborate and treatment of this topic may be found in specialised texts on metrology.

ISO Metric–Designation. BS3643 provides three main thread group-ings, a COARSE thread series, a FINE thread series and a CONSTANT

PITCH series. Nominal sizes showing 1st, 2nd and 3rd choices and ranging from 1 mm to 300 mm are derived from a preferred size series (see p.000). For average work, coarse pitch series, each nominal size has its designated pitch (range 0·25 mm to 6 mm). The fine pitch and constant pitch series enable the choice of pitch to be varied to suit different design conditions. The fine pitch series does give a tremendous range of ostensibly standard sizes but it will be a very long time, if ever, before threading equipment and screwed parts for all these sizes are available from stock. Wherever possible thread sizes should be selected from the coarse pitch series.

BS3643 also provides for different **qualities** of screwed work as below:

Close fit	designation 5H (nut) 4h (bolt)
Medium fit	designation 6H 6g
Free fit	designation 7H 8g

Numbers relate to tolerance magnitude, letters to the deviation from basic size.

The full designation M8 × 1·25—6H/6g stated on a drawing would imply an ISO Metric thread, nominal diameter 8 mm, pitch 1·25 mm, nut to 6H tols, bolt to 6g tols. (i.e. medium fit).

14.3 Tolerance for ISO Metric threads

Fig 14.6 illustrates tolerance zones for the close fit (5H/4h). The H/h symbols are for zero deviation so the maximum material condition is controlled by the basic form. Notice also:

(a) The tolerance zones are greater at the root and crest than along the flanks.

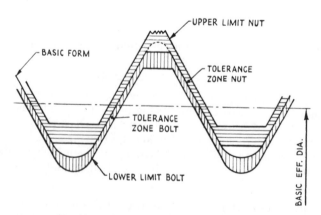

Fig. 14.6 Tolerance zones for close fit (5H/4h)

(*b*) **A unilateral** system is used, bolt tolerance below the basic size, nut tolerance above.

(*c*) *A clearance exists at the minor diameters.*

(*d*) The upper limit of major diameter of the nut is not specified; it is controlled by tap dimensions conforming to BS949.

(*e*) Because the basic form is not symmetrical about the pitch line ($\frac{3}{8}$H above, $\frac{1}{4}$H below) relatively large diameter tapping holes are permissible, which reduces the torque when tapping and so minimises breakages. Fig 14.7 shows the large amount of extra material which needs to be removed to tap a symmetrical form. (This is the principal difference between the ISO Metric form and the earlier Metric SI thread form.)

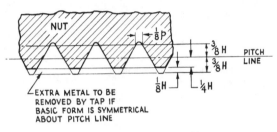

Fig. 14.7 Material to be removed by a tap

(*f*) From the tolerance zones shown in Fig 14.6 it follows that three different types of error are allowed:

(i) error of the flank angle;
(ii) error of pitch over the length of fitting;
(iii) error of effective diameter.

It is equally necessary to realise that any combination of these errors should not cause the profile to lie outside the tolerance zone at any point along the fitting length of an assembly.

Magnitudes of Tolerances and Deviations. As for plain work, tolerances and deviations are in proportion to the basic size to maintain constant quality for different work sizes. The rational basis of the system used is complicated by the fact that the coarser the pitch the more serious flank angle error becomes, and the greater the fitting length of screwed parts the more serious any progressive pitch error becomes. It is not possible to relate tolerances only to the work tolerance as for plain work.

The tolerances and deviations given in BS3643 are based on ISO specification 965/1–1973(E) and are derived as shown in Table 14.1.

The value of *d* in tolerance formula $90\,p^{0.4}\,d^{0.1}$ is the geometric mean of the diameter range; see p. 12 and Fig 1.6. The calculated values have

TABLE 14.1
Screw Thread Tolerances

	Tol grade	Major dia. (μm)	Effective dia. (μm)	Minor dia. (unit as shown)
BOLTS	4	0·63 × grade 6	0·63 × grade 6	(i) Upper limit nom $- (1{\cdot}2268p \times FD)$ mm (ii) Tolerance $0{\cdot}072p + \left[\begin{array}{l}\text{eff. dia. tol}\\ \text{for the grade}\end{array}\right]$ mm
	6	$180p^{2/3} - 3{\cdot}15/p^{1/2}$	$90p^{0\cdot4}d^{0\cdot1}$	
	8	1·6 × grade 6	1·6 × grade 6	
NUTS	5	(i) Lower limit = basic size	1·06 × grade 6 bolt	0·8 × grade 6 μm
	6	(ii) Upper limit undefined (Controlled by tap)	1·32 × grade 6 bolt	(i) pitches 0·2–0·8 mm $433p - 190p^{1\cdot22}$ μm (ii) pitches 1 mm and above ‿ ·0$p^{0\cdot7}$ μm
	7		1·7 × grade 6 bolt	1·25 × grade 6

FD (deviation) g (for bolts), $FD = 11p\,\mu$m   (p = pitch)

The above apply where the nominal length of engagement L_N has limits of:
L_N minimum $2{\cdot}24pd^{0\cdot2}$ mm
L_N maximum $= 6{\cdot}7pd^{0\cdot2}$ mm
where d is the smallest dia. of the range for which the tols. are common.

to be rounded according to the R40 series. However, the information given here is to show the fundamentally logical basis of a screw thread system of limits and fits and reference to BS3643 should always be made to obtain actual dimensions.

Fig 14.8 shows the three different grades of work by tolerance zones drawn to scale. The "close" class should only be used where the highest quality is essential because it is relatively expensive to produce. The "medium" class is suitable for most work; the "free" class meets conditions where quick and easy assembly is required and where threads may become dirty or damaged.

Example 14.1.
Working from basic principles, find limits for the three important diameters of an M36 × 4 "free" class screw thread assembly. The diameter falls within the range 30–39; the length of engagement is within L_N limits. Find the least possible depth of engagement and express this as a percentage of the basic depth.

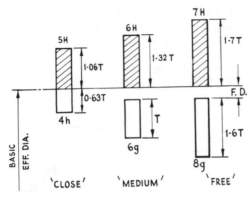

Fig. 14.8 Three classes of fit represented to scale

Solution

The required assembly is 7H/8g.

Bolt dimensions. $FD = 15 + (11 \times 4) = 59\,\mu m$
(rounded value 0·060 mm)

Mean dia of range $(d) = \sqrt{(30 \times 39)} = 34\cdot2$ mm

Effective dia. tol, grade $6 = 90 \times 4^{0\cdot4} \times 34\cdot2^{0\cdot1} = 223\,\mu m$

Tolerances (grade 8)

$$\text{Major diameter} = 1\cdot6\left(180 \times 4^{2/3} - \frac{3\cdot15}{\sqrt{4}}\right) = 724\,\mu m$$
(rounded value 0·750 mm)

Effective dia. tol $= 1\cdot6 \times 223 = 357\,\mu m$
(rounded value 0·355 mm)

Minor dia. tol $= (0\cdot072 \times 4) + 0\cdot355 = 0\cdot643$ mm

Upper limit, minor dia of bolt $= 36 - \{(1\cdot2268 \times 4) + 0\cdot060\}$
$= 31\cdot033$ mm.

Nut dimensions

Tolerances (grade 7)

Effective dia tol $= 1\cdot7 \times 223 = 379\,\mu m$
(rounded value 0·375 mm)

Minor dia tol $= 1\cdot25(230 \times 4^{0\cdot7}) = 758\,\mu m$
(rounded value 0·750 mm.)

Limits for M36 × 4 − 7H8g thread assembly.

Diameter	Nut	Bolt
Major	36·000 +	35·940/35·190
Effective	33·777/33·402	33·342/32·987
Minor	32·420/31·670	31·033/30·390

These limits are shown to scale in Fig 14.9.

Least depth of engagement $= \frac{1}{2}(35\cdot190 - 32\cdot420)$

$$= 1\cdot385 \text{ mm}$$

Depth of basic form $= 0\cdot5413p = 2\cdot165$ mm.

$$\text{Minimum depth ratio} = \frac{1\cdot385}{2\cdot165} \times 100 = \underline{64\,\%}$$

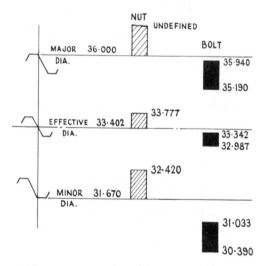

Fig. 14.9 Screw-thread tolerances drawn to scale

14.4 Screw-thread Gauging

Due to the complex geometry of a helical groove, a full assessment of the accuracy of a screw thread by direct measurement is a lengthy procedure. For this reason, and especially during manufacture, the accuracy of screw threads is generally controlled by limit gauging. Fig 14.6 illustrates the tolerance zones within which the parts must lie. A gauging system based upon Taylor's principles (p. 427) may be employed to restrict the work to the tolerance zones. Screw gauges, limits and tolerances are given in BS919.

If a tapped hole is considered, the gauges required are seen to be:

(i) a **full-form go** gauge, made to basic sizes;
(ii) an **effective diameter not-go** gauge;
(iii) a **minor diameter not-go** gauge.

The full form **go** gauge is a screw plug of length equal to the work length of engagement; it defines the maximum metal condition of the tolerance zone. The effective **not-go** gauge has restricted contact with the workpiece, as shown in Fig 14.10; it defines the minimum metal condition at the pitch points of the flanks.

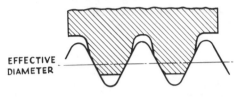

EFFECTIVE DIAMETER

Fig. 14.10 Truncated form of effective not-go gauge

The full truncated form is rather expensive to manufacture, and is used only for very coarse pitches where, due to the longer length of thread flank, angle error is of greater significance than for fine pitches. Ideally, the effective **not-go** gauge should not be influenced by errors of pitch or angle of the thread gauged; in its practical form these effects are minimised, but not entirely eliminated.

The minor diameter **not-go** gauge is a plain cylindrical plug sometimes called a **core not-go** gauge, or **core plug.**

Reference to Taylor's principles of gauging will show that the following gauges are required for a complete check of an external thread:

  (i) a **full-form go ring** gauge;
  (ii) an **effective diameter not-go** gauge;
  (iii) a **major diameter not-go** gauge;
  (iv) a **minor diameter not-go** gauge.

Screw ring gauges are expensive and rather slow in use; they have a limited application for final inspection purposes, and for gauging screw threads on thin-walled components which distort easily under the contact forces exerted by a calliper-type gauge. Calliper-type gauges having roller or "edge" type anvils are more commonly used.

The effective diameter **not-go** gauge must be of a calliper type, and have a thread form similar to that shown in Fig 14.10 in order to conform to Taylor's Principles. For the reasons given above there is an occasional need of ring-type **not-go** gauges where the walls of the workpiece are very thin.

The major diameter can be gauged by using a plain calliper gauge, made to the lower limit of size, as the **not-go** gauge; alternatively, blanks may be limit gauged for size prior to threading, a method which generally provides sufficient control.

The minor diameter of the thread is rarely tested by means of a separate **not-go** gauge. Optical projection of the thread form will show whether the root radius of the thread is being satisfactorily produced relative to the flanks. If this is so, work lying within the effective diameter limits is bound to lie within the minor diameter limits.

The common form of calliper gauge for external screw-thread work is shown in Fig 14.11. For very large work this type of gauge becomes unwieldly, and gauges which measure effective diameter in terms of the radius of an arc are then substituted.

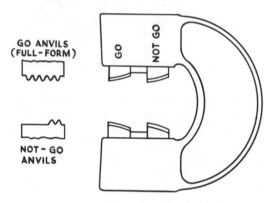

Fig. 14.11 Screw-thread calliper gauge

The Effectiveness of the Gauging Method. The gauging methods described restrict the work to the tolerance zone, because the magnitude of the zone is fixed by the major diameter, minor diameter and effective diameter limits. Gauging methods do not, however, enable the particular sources of error to be distinguished, and for this purpose direct measurements are necessary.

Figs 14.12 and 14.13 illustrate the effect upon the fitting conditions of errors of pitch, and errors of flank angle. Parts having such errors will assemble, provided there is a sufficient difference between the simple effective diameters to absorb these errors.

Such errors give rise to the concept of **virtual effective diameter**. As defined in BS2517, virtual effective diameter is the effective diameter of an imaginary thread of perfect form and pitch, having full depth of thread but clear at the crests and roots, which will just assemble with the actual thread over the prescribed length of engagement. This diameter exceeds the simple (measured) effective diameter by an amount relating to the combined effects of errors of pitch and errors of flank angle.

The gauging value of a screw plug or ring will be influenced by errors of pitch or flank angle so both must be very accurately measured, pitch directly on a special type of measuring machine, angle by optical projection or measuring microscope.

It follows directly from the geometry of Fig 14.12 that for errors of pitch

$$\text{virtual change in effective diameter} = \delta p \cot \theta,$$

where δp is the maximum pitch error over the length of engagement and θ the semi-angle of the vee. For ISO Metric the virtual change in effective dia is $1 \cdot 732 \, \delta p$.

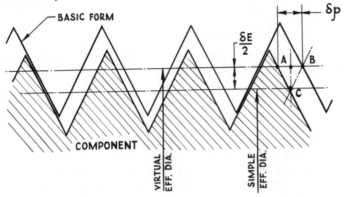

Fig. 14.12 *Influence of pitch error on the effective diameter required in a mating part*

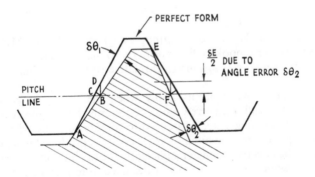

Fig. 14.13 *Influence of angle error on the effective diameter required in a mating part*

Fig 14.13 shows the effects arising from angle errors $\delta\theta_1$ and $\delta\theta_2$. Because the depth of thread is not symmetrical with respect to the pitch line the effects will differ slightly according to whether contact is made at A or E.

Considering point A, $\qquad$ AB $= 0 \cdot 25p$ from the basic form.

$$\text{BC} \simeq \text{AB} \times \delta\theta_1 \text{ rad} \qquad \text{BD} = 2\text{BC}$$

hence BD $\simeq 2 \times 0 \cdot 25p \times \delta\theta_1$ rad.

Separation by amount BD would occur on both flanks of the thread form and so accommodate an error $\delta\theta$ on *both* flanks.

It follows from the geometrical conditions of error $\delta\theta_1$ on *both* flanks that the resulting change of effective diameter would need to be

$$\delta E_1 = 2 \times 0 \cdot 25p(\delta\theta_1 + \delta\theta_1)\frac{\pi}{180} \text{ (angle error in degrees)}$$
$$= 0 \cdot 0087p(2\delta\theta_1). \tag{1}$$

If angle error of opposite direction is considered, the contact point will be at E and the expression changes to

$$\delta E_2 = 2 \times 0 \cdot 375p(\delta\theta_2 + \delta\theta_2)\frac{\pi}{180}$$
$$= 0 \cdot 0131p(2\delta\theta_2) \tag{2}$$

This higher value can only arise if the crests of the thread are not rounded as allowed by the specification.

In general the non-symmetrical aspect is ignored and positive or negative angle errors are regarded to have equal effect; hence, from Eqns (1) and (2),

$$\delta E \text{ (average value)} = \tfrac{1}{2}(0 \cdot 0087 + 0 \cdot 0131)p(\theta_1 + \theta_2)$$
$$= 0 \cdot 0109p(\delta\theta_1 + \delta\theta_2).$$

Flank angle errors are to be measured in degrees and added together regardless of their direction.

Note: The formula $E = 0 \cdot 0115p(\delta\theta_1 + \delta\theta_2)$ quoted for Metric SI threads in the NPL booklet *Notes on Screw Gauges* is based on the early thread form which was symmetrical relative to the pitch line.

Clearly the above concepts apply when measuring or gauging a screwed part. A full form screw gauge represents the imaginary form of perfect pitch and angle etc. introduced in BS2517 to define virtual size.

If a component having pitch or angle errors is produced it is possible to change the effective diameter sufficiently for the full form **go** gauge to accept the work, by cutting beyond the maximum metal condition an amount equal to the effective diameter equivalent of the errors, as given above. If, however, the pitch and angle errors are too large, the effective diameter equivalent to be removed is sufficient to enable the effective **not-go** gauge to pass over the work, and thus reject it.

14.5 Measurement of the Effective Diameter

Screw-thread measurement, as distinct from gauging, is a large topic, and one aspect only can be treated here, the measurement of the effective diameter. The handbook *Gauging and Measuring Screw Threads*, prepared by the National Physical Laboratory (NPL), Metrology Division, and published as *Notes on Applied Science No. 1* by HMSO, remains one of the most useful and authoritative sources of information, and should be available in every standards room and metrology laboratory. Some of the more significant points relating to the measurement of effective diameter set out here, exemplify principles of measurement already discussed in Chapter 12.

Fig 14.14 shows an NPL type screw thread measuring machine of floating carriage construction. Certain features incorporated in this design are of interest.

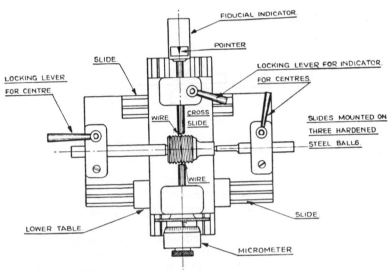

Fig. 14.14 Thread-diameter measuring machine

(1) The machine has two kinematic slides to give displacements along AA and BB, as shown in Fig 14.15. When work is supported on-centres, its axis lying along AA, the micrometer lying along BB must be correctly aligned so that there are no sine or cosine errors introduced (see Fig 12.10). In order to achieve this, the lower slide has one of the location pins which slide in the vee groove eccentrically mounted; a small rotation of this pin causes the slides to rotate relative to AA, and in this manner BB can be aligned at an exact right angle to AA. After adjustment, this pin is sealed and stamped to prevent tampering.

(2) The micrometer has a drum of large diameter which enables readings to be made direct to 0·002 mm, and by vernier scale to 0·0002 mm. Parallax error of reading is very small indeed. As a result of this high magnification factor, the system has a very large mechanical advantage: a very small torque applied at the drum produces a considerable force at the measuring contacts. A fiducial indicator is fitted to the "fixed" anvil so that the force at the measuring contacts is a

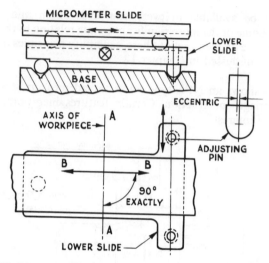

Fig. 14.15 *Adjustment of kinematic slides of screw-thread diameter measuring machine to obtain true alignment*

small and constant one. The "moving" anvil of the micrometer does not rotate, the position of the measuring cylinder in the thread vee is then not affected by any tendency to turn, as the drum is finally adjusted.

(3) The NPL procedure for effective diameter measurement requires that the machine is set from a plain cylindrical standard held between the machine centres. The thread measuring cylinders are included in the setting dimension, as shown in Fig 14.16. The geometry of the contact points for setting the machine is thus similar to the geometry of the contact points when measuring the effective diameter

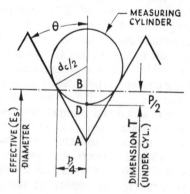

Fig. 14.16 *Setting and measuring on an NPL type screw-thread diameter measuring machine*

(see **12.3**). Any error due to dissimilarity of contact geometry, arising from elastic compression at the contact points, is thus very small. The contact points for setting and measuring are shown in Fig 14.16. A correction for the difference in contact geometry can be made, by using the information given in the NPL screw thread book (correction for elastic compression).

Fig 14.17 shows the basic geometry of the NPL *P* value method of effective diameter measurement. The dimension from the underside of the measuring wires, taken on each side of the thread, is denoted by the letter *P*. If this value is added to the value representing the setting standard when the micrometer is first set, i.e. the micrometer set to read $(S + P)$, the machine will automatically read the measured effective diameter of the thread.

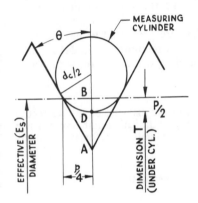

Fig. 14.17 Geometry of "P" value

Let d_c = the mean diameter of the pair of measuring cylinders employed, p = pitch of the thread, θ = semi-angle of the vee, E_s = the simple (measured) effective diameter;

from Fig 14.17

$$\frac{P}{2} = AB - AD \qquad\qquad AB = \tfrac{1}{4}p \,.\, \cot\theta$$

$$= \tfrac{1}{4}p \,.\, \cot\theta - \frac{d_c}{2}(\operatorname{cosec}\theta - 1) \qquad AD = \frac{d_c}{2}\operatorname{cosec}\theta - \frac{d_c}{2}$$

$$P = \tfrac{1}{2}p \,.\, \cot\theta - d_c(\operatorname{cosec}\theta - 1)$$

$E_s = (T + P)$, where T is the dimension under the cylinders.

A further advantage of the NPL procedure is now revealed. The value of d_c cannot be known exactly, but when the machine is set, the actual cylinders are incorporated into the dimension (see Fig 14.16). The error in E_s arising from uncertainty in the value for d_c has a value represented by

$$\delta E_s = (\operatorname{cosec}\theta - 1)\delta d_c$$

which is smaller by $2\delta d_c$ than the error would be if the machine were set without including the measuring cylinders.

It is hoped that the reader will ponder over the points discussed on pp. 467 and 469. Accurate measurement depends upon the design of the equipment and upon the methods employed; accurate trigonometrical calculations cannot of themselves do more than provide numerical values, the accuracy of which may not be reflected in the practical measurement.

Best-size Cylinders. Ideally, the cylinders chosen for the measurement of the simple effective diameter should contact the flanks at the pitch points (Fig 14.4), because this will make the value obtained for E_s independent of flank angle error. The required diameter is given by $\frac{1}{2}p\sec\theta$. In practice, **best-size cylinders** are permitted to have a small manufacturing tolerance, as will be seen by reference to the NPL screw thread book, and for such cylinders the effect of flank error on the value of E_s can be safely ignored.

Example 14.2

"Best-size" cylinders for measuring the effective diameter of an ISO Metric thread are required to touch the flank within $\frac{1}{20}$ of the flank length on either side of the pitch point. Determine the upper and lower limits of size for such cylinders in terms of the pitch of the thread.

Solution

From Fig 14.18, by properties of the fundamental triangle,

$$AB = 5/8p$$
$$= 0.625p$$
$$\tfrac{1}{20}(AB) = 0.0313p$$

Ideal size cylinder, dia $= \frac{1}{2}p\sec 30°$
$$= 1.1547p/2 = 0.577p$$

Limits of best size cylinder $= 0.577p \pm (2 \times 0.0313p \times \tan 30°)$
$$= 0.577p \pm 0.036p$$
$$= 0.613p/10.541p$$

Note: A tolerance of $\pm 0.043p$, often quoted, relates to the Metric SI thread. The ISO Metric thread has a shorter flank length.

The above account of screw-thread effective diameter measurement by means of cylinders is not exact, because the conditions represented in Fig 14.17 could occur only if the vee groove of the thread were annular instead of helical. For an M24 × 3 screw, a discrepancy of about 0.0023 mm on E_s is introduced on account of the helix angle effect. For

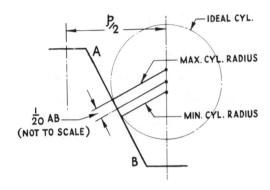

Fig. 14.18 Geometry of "Best-Size" cylinder

combinations of pitches and diameters which give rise to large helix angles a correction will be necessary; the correction formulae are given in the NPL Screw Thread book. For most threads the correction due to the difference in contact geometry mentioned in item (3), p. 468 is approximately equal and opposite to the correction required on account of the helix angle effect, and for work where an accuracy of ± 0.0025 mm is sufficient, both effects may generally be neglected.

The measurement of effective diameter by means of cylinders, should not be used on **acme** or **buttress** thread forms without reference to the NPL Screw Thread book, because of the large errors which may then arise from the helix angle effect.

EXERCISES 14

1. Fig 14.3 gives the design form of the ISO Metric external threads. Show that:

nominal depth of thread $= 0.613\,44p$
allowable crest radius $\quad= 0.0361p$
effective diameter $\quad\quad= $ nominal dia. $- 0.649\,52p$

2. (a) Write, in symbolic form, the three tolerance grades and fundamental deviations applicable to ISO Metric threads as specified in BS3643. Show how they are associated to provide three different classes of fit.

(b) Using the information given in Table 14.1 show, for an M80 × 3—8g thread, that the major and minor diameter tolerances are 0.600 mm and 0.551 mm respectively, the effective diameter tolerance being 0.335 mm.

(c) Why does the formula for effective diameter tolerance have terms in both p and d?

3. (a) Show diagrammatically the tolerance zones associated with a nut and screw of Whitworth form and explain why the tolerance on the effective diameter is less than that on the other elements of the thread form.

(b) How does the gauging of external screw threads present special problems in the design of gauges? Illustrate a design which meets the requirements, commenting on the special features necessary.

4. (a) What is understood by the term "Taylor's principle of inspection"?
(b) How is this principle employed in the inspection of external and internal screw threads?
(c) Briefly describe the methods used for inspecting screw ring and screw plug gauges.

5. What is meant by "virtual" or "compound" as applied to the effective diameter of screw threads?

The basic form of the British Association (BA) thread is shown in Fig 14.19. Show that an error of pitch of 0·01 mm requires an adjustment of 0·0227 mm at the eff. diam. and that flank angle errors of $+0·5°$, $-1·5°$ respectively on a 0BA screw (pitch = 1 mm) require an adjustment of $+0·018$ mm to accommodate them.

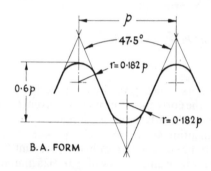

Fig. 14.19 Basic form of B.A. thread

6. A special form of buttress thread has a sharp crest and root, and an included angle of 50°. The leading flank is inclined at 5° and the trailing flank at 45° to a line perpendicular to the thread axis. If this thread is measured by the NPL method show that the P value is given by

$$P = 0·9195 \times \text{pitch} - 1·2233 \times \text{cylinder dia.}$$

7. (a) Outline the NPL method for measuring the effective diameter of a screw plug gauge. What are "best-size" cylinders and why are they used?
(b) Derive an expression for the P value for measuring ISO Metric threads. Find the P value for measuring an M8 × 1·25 thread with cylinders of 0·7160 mm mean diameter.
(c) Indicate why rake angle correction is necessary when measuring some threads.

8. (a) Describe, with sketches, the method used to check the simple effective diameter of a plug screw gauge on a floating carriage micrometer.
(b) For the expression $E = T + P$, state what the letters represent and explain why it is not used in this form when measuring the effective diameter of a precision screw.
(c) Two thread measuring needles having diameters of 0·8761 mm and 0·8733 mm respectively, have a value of the constant $P = 0·5051$ mm when used to check a screw of 16 tpi BS Whit. Why will the value of this constant be different if the needles are used to check a screw of any other form? Find the new value for a screw of 1·5 mm pitch with an included angle of 60°.

9. Working from first principles, show that the limits of diameter for "best-size" cylinders for measuring threads of BA form are $(0·546 \pm 0·019)p$, and that for No 1 BA the limits are 0·5085/0·4743 mm.

see fig N

CHAPTER 15
Statistical Methods of Process Control

15.1 Variability in Manufacturing Processes

When a large number of similar events occur, arising from procedures which are very nearly identical, they tend to follow a particular pattern. This is true of most manufacturing processes. The conditions which determine a particular feature of a product, e.g. the surface finish, are subject to small variations from a variety of causes, and these variations give rise to small variations in the product. When the quantity involved is large the pattern of variation can be studied on a statistical basis; it then becomes possible to assess the quality achieved by the process without testing every piece produced. A statistical method which reveals the pattern of variation in a product provides a more certain basis for the assessment of the quality of a large volume of work than would a detailed inspection of sample parts made without reference to the pattern of variability present.

Consider a 200 lot of 12·5 mm dia. pins taken at random from a large batch. If these are measured on the shank diameter they will be found to vary either side of a mean-size. There will be similar variations for each of the remaining dimensions; also there will be variations of the mechanical properties of the material as between one pin and another. For every manufacturing process it is accepted that such variations in quality will occur, and *tolerances* are generally introduced into the specification in order to define the acceptable amount of variation.

If we wish to test the quality of the pins in respect of shank diameter the 200 items can be limit gauged. This is a *sorting* process; any work varying more than the permitted amount is separated from the acceptable work. Limit gauging isolates the "defectives", it gives no information about the pattern of variability of the parts produced.

Alternatively, the shank diameter of the 200 pins could be individually measured and their sizes recorded. This procedure will yield a large amount of data which, when suitably arranged, can reveal the pattern of variability. The arrangement and analysis of such data, in order to obtain a clear picture of the pattern of variability, is based upon statistics, a mathematical science for the study of variability.

15.2 Statistical Concepts and Variability

For an introductory treatment of the mathematics employed in this section see 'Modern Applied Mathematics' by J. C. Turner (Hodder and Stoughton, 1970).

Suppose the measured shank diameters of the 200 rivets to be as given in Table 15.1

TABLE 15.1

Diameter (mm)	Mid-size (mm)	Frequency
12·1 up to 12·2	12·15	4
12·2 up to 12·3	12·25	21
12·3 up to 12·4	12·35	50
12·4 up to 12·5	12·45	72
12·5 up to 12·6	12·55	41
12·6 up to 12·7	12·65	12

The groupings of Table 15.1 are made so that a part measuring 12·2 exactly would be in the first group, a part measuring 12·3 in the second group, etc.

If the results shown in Table 15.1 are plotted as a bar-chart (histogram), Fig 15.1, a picture of the variability is obtained. If a smooth curve is now drawn through the highest point of the mid-ordinate of each strip a graphical representation of the variability is obtained. The graph, called a frequency distribution curve, would tend to have the same general shape if the number of pieces measured was increased, or if the groupings were varied in some small degree.

Suppose now that a very much larger number of pieces was measured, and the results arranged in at least twice as many groups so that the size-range of the groups became smaller; a frequency distribution curve of more closely defined shape would emerge and would reveal the variability pattern of the production process with greater certainty.

The shape of a frequency distribution curve (or simply "distribution curve" as it is generally called) is influenced by two important features of variability:

(i) the frequency with which parts close to the mean-size occur;
(ii) the "spread" either side of the mean-size, called the range.

Mean-size (the Arithmetical mean of all the sizes). The mean-size can be conveniently calculated from a set of values, such as Table 15.1, by the following method.

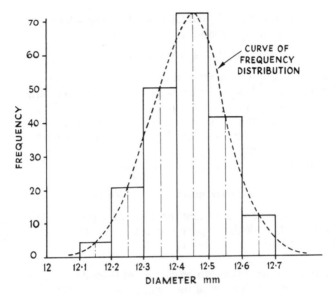

Fig. 15.1 Histogram and frequency distribution curve

Let x_1, x_2, etc., be the mid-size of the groups.
Let f_1, f_2, etc., be the frequency of pieces in the groups.
Let N be the total number of pieces.

Select some value of the size near to the anticipated mean-size, the fictitious mean to be represented by A. Subtract A from the mid-size of a group and multiply the result by the group frequency, i.e. $f_1(x_1 - A)$, $f_2(x_2 - A)$, etc. Take the sum of all these values, paying due regard to the sign of each; divide this sum by N. The arithmetic mean, represented by $\bar{x}$, is now given by the expression:

$$\bar{x} = \frac{f_1(x_1 - A) + f_2(x_2 - A) + f_3(x_3 - A) + \cdots}{N} + A. \quad (15.1)$$

A convenient tabular method of working is shown in Table 15.2, columns 3 and 4.

Range. This is the difference between the largest and the smallest part, e.g. 0·6 mm (or slightly less) for the measurements given in Table 15.1.

Standard Deviation (σ). Variability is revealed by the amount of the departure from the mean-size. It is roughly indicated by the range, but since range is a comparison between the sizes of two pieces only, it cannot give an accurate measure of the variability of *all* the pieces. The standard deviation is a more accurate measure of variability because the size of every part produced is taken into account.

If we are to take the size, and the frequency with which it occurs, into account in measuring variability, an expression of the form

$$f_1(x_1 - \bar{x}) + f_2(x_2 - \bar{x}) + \cdots$$

might conceivably give what is wanted. Due to the fact that $\bar{x}$ is the arithmetic mean, however, the positive and negative terms of this expression will be equal, and the sum of the terms zero. The difficulty is overcome by squaring the values $(x_1 - \bar{x})$, $(x_2 - \bar{x})$, etc., so that there are no negative signs. The resulting value is called the **variance**.

$$\textbf{Variance} = \frac{f_1(x_1 - \bar{x})^2 + f_2(x_2 - \bar{x})^2 + f_3(x_3 - \bar{x})^2 + \cdots}{N} \quad (15.2)$$

$$\textbf{Standard deviation} = \sqrt{\textbf{Variance}}$$

Both quantities are important measures of variability. The standard deviation is of particular importance because of its relationship to the **normal** distribution curve.

The standard deviation can be calculated from data such as given in Table 15.1, by an extension of the methods already given on p. 475 for finding $\bar{x}$.

The fictitious mean-size (A) is first employed to find a fictitious value (S) for the standard deviation.

$$S^2 = \frac{f_1(x_1 - A)^2 + f_2(x_2 - A)^2 + f_3(x_3 - A)^2 + \cdots}{N} \quad (15.3)$$

The process is conveniently carried out in tabular form, as shown in Table 15.2, columns 5 and 6. It can be shown mathematically that

$$\sigma^2 = S^2 - (\bar{x} - A)^2 \quad (15.4)$$

where σ represents the standard deviation.

Tabular Method for Finding $\bar{x}$ and σ. The data given in Table 15.1 is used to illustrate a convenient method of finding the required values.

$$\bar{x} = \left[\frac{65 - 104}{200} + 124 \cdot 5 \right] 10^{-1} \text{ by Eqn (15.1)}.$$

$$= 12 \cdot 43 \text{ mm (to the nearest } 0 \cdot 01)$$

$$S^2 = \tfrac{259}{200} \times 10^{-2} = 1 \cdot 295 \times 10^{-2} \text{ by Eqn (15.3)}$$

$$\sigma^2 = S^2 - (\bar{x} - A)^2 \text{ by Eqn (15.4)}$$

$$= 1 \cdot 295 \times 10^{-2} - (0 \cdot 2 \times 10^{-1})^2$$

$$= (1 \cdot 295 - 0 \cdot 04) 10^{-2}$$

$$= 1 \cdot 255 \times 10^{-2}$$

$$\sigma = 1 \cdot 12 \times 10^{-1}$$

$$= 0 \cdot 11 \text{ mm (to the nearest } 0 \cdot 01).$$

TABLE 15.2

(*Note*: The unit tabulated is × 10 mm in order to simplify the working)

1	2	3	4	5	6
Mid-value x	Frequency f	($A = 124.5$) $x - A$	$f(x - A)$	$(x - A)^2$	$f(x - A)^2$
121·5	4	−3	−12	9	36
122·5	21	−2	−42	4	84
123·5	50	−1	−50	1	50
124·5	72	0	0	0	0
125·5	41	1	41	1	41
126·5	12	2	24	4	48
	N = 200		65 − 104		259

The diameters of the pins can now be represented numerically in a way which indicates both the size and variability resulting from the manufacturing process.

Mean diameter = 12·43 mm

Range of diameters = 0·6 mm

Standard deviation = 0·11 mm.

15.3 Normal Curve of Distribution

The 200 pins considered will be taken from a much larger quantity manufactured. If very many more pins were measured and then grouped into smaller intervals, say 0·02 mm, it would be possible to draw a histogram from which a much smoother curve of frequency distribution would result, because by greatly increasing the number of pieces considered the influence of any exceptional sizes which have occurred will be reduced. At very large quantities, and where the causes of variation are strictly random, the distribution curve will tend to be **normal**.

It is possible to arrive at this **normal** form of distribution by mathematical reasoning; the resulting equation of the normal curve is

$$y = \frac{1}{\sigma \sqrt{(2\pi)}} e^{-(x - \bar{x})^2 / 2\sigma^2}$$

where σ is the standard deviation.

The equation can be simplified by putting $t = (x - \bar{x})/\sigma$. For the condition where $\bar{x} = 0$ the curve will have its axis of symmetry on the *y* axis instead of at the mean value, and for this condition $t = x/\sigma$, so that *t* now represents *x* to some scale depending on the value of σ. If, in order to represent the curve as simply as possible, we now put $\sigma = 1$, the equation to the curve becomes

$$y = \frac{1}{\sqrt{(2\pi)}} e^{-t^2/2}$$

The term $1/\sqrt{(2\pi)}$ is included to make the area under the curve equal unity. The areas bounded by the curve and by different values of *t*, expressed as a fraction of unity, then represent the probability of parts lying between those values of *t*. Table 1 of BS2564: 1955, p. 59, gives the area relationships at 0·2 intervals of the value of *t*.

The term $1/\sqrt{(2\pi)}$ can be ignored in plotting a curve of normal distribution, since it only causes a change of scale on the *y* axis. The shape of the curve may be obtained quite accurately by plotting the equation $y = e^{-t^2/2}$, and the area properties referred to above can be estimated by counting squares. Mathematical tables which give values of e^{-x} over a reasonable range of *x*, facilitate the plotting of such curves.

Example 15.1
Plot a curve of normal distribution and use this to estimate the number of pins. Table 15.1, having diameters outside the limits $12·43 \pm 0·1$ mm.

Solution
Equation to be plotted, $y = e^{-t^2/2}$

t	$t^2/2$	$e^{-t^2/2}$
± 0	0	1
$\pm 0·6$	0·18	0·835
± 1	0·50	0·606
$\pm 1·6$	1·28	0·278
± 2	2·00	0·135
$\pm 2·6$	3·38	0·034
± 3	4·50	0·011

Fig 15.2 shows the normal curve. This should be plotted on squared paper as accurately as possible. Estimate by counting squares, or by means of a planimeter, the area bounded by the curve and by the ordinates of $t = \pm 3$.

For the equation used to plot the curve, $\bar{x} = 0$ and $t = \bar{x}/\sigma$. It has been shown on p. 476 that σ for the pins is approximately 0·11 mm; we also know that the limits given in the question are $\pm 0·1$ either side of the mean-size ($\bar{x}$).

Hence, for the range of diameter expressed in the limits, $t = \pm 0·1/0·11$, i.e. $t = \pm 1$ roughly. Estimate the area between the curve and the ordinates $t = \pm 1$, and express this as a ratio of the area between $t = \pm 3$. As shown in Fig 15.2, approximately 68% of the area is enclosed between $t = \pm 1$. From the area property of the distribution curve it can now be estimated that $0·68 \times 200$ pins lie between the limits stated, i.e. 136 out of 200.

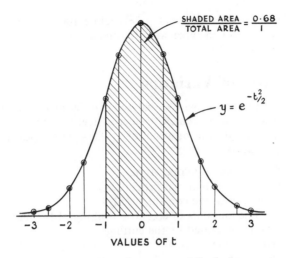

Fig. 15.2 Curve showing normal distribution

The significance of the area property of the normal distribution curve is revealed by the above example, and Fig 15.3 illustrates this property in terms of σ. It should be noted that ordinates of $\pm 3 \cdot 09\sigma$ do not enclose the entire area beneath the curve, because the "tails" of the curve extend to infinity. Since production patterns do not follow normal distribution

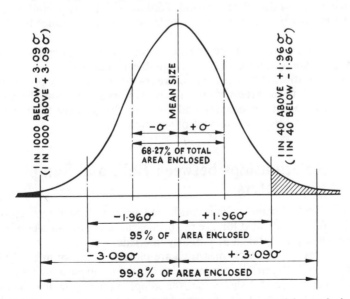

Fig. 15.3 Area properties of the normal distribution curve in terms of the standard deviation (σ)

exactly, the approximations that $\pm 3\sigma$ enclose 100% of the area, and $\pm 2\sigma$ enclose 95% of the area, are often made.

15.4 Causes of Variation

A manufacturing process may be analysed in order to identify the causes of the variations which occur. Consider a steel bar turned to a given diameter on a capstan lathe by means of a roller-box. Causes of variation of diameter could be:

(i) fluctuations of temperature;
(ii) variations in material properties;
(iii) variations in the coolant supply;
(iv) variable amounts of eccentric running of the bar;
(v) vibrations caused by the cutting;
(vi) errors of tool setting;
(vii) tool wear.

Items (i) to (v) are unlikely to follow any regular pattern and may be regarded as the causes of the *inherent process variation*. It will not be possible to relate these causes to specific changes in component diameter because their operation is of a random character.

Items (vi) and (vii) are *assignable causes* of variation. An error of tool setting will give rise to a discrepancy between the mean-size achieved and the mean-size of the tolerance band. Tool wear will cause a gradual drift of the mean-size of consecutive samples across the tolerance band.

Sampling methods have the advantage that, to a considerable extent, they separate variation due to assignable causes from the inherent process variation. It is possible to make reasonably accurate predictions of the distribution pattern of the bulk from information about the mean-size and variability of samples, and this is the basis of the technique of quality control by measurement of samples.

15.5 Relationships between Bulk and Sample Parameters

Suppose the diameter we have considered as being turned on a capstan lathe is to be controlled for size by the measurement of samples of four consecutive pieces, taken at $\frac{1}{2}$-hourly intervals.

If the sizes of the parts measured are plotted as shown in Fig 15.4 a comparison between the samples and the distribution pattern of the bulk can be made. Fig 15.4 shows that the sample range is smaller than the bulk range, and that the mean-sizes of samples do not spread so far either side of the bulk average as do the sizes of individual pieces.

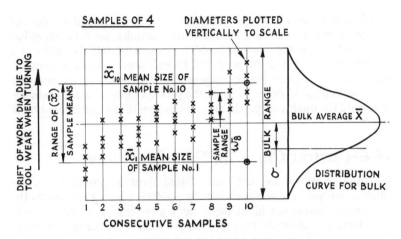

Fig. 15.4 Relationship between sizes of parts in a sample and the bulk distribution curve, roller-box turning

The most significant parameters of variability are average value and standard deviation. In order to show the relationships of these values, as between the samples, and the bulk of which they form a part, the following symbols will be used.

	Bulk	Sample
Average value	$\overline{X}$	$\overline{x}$
Standard deviation	σ	s
Number of parts	N	n
Range of sample	—	w
Average of sample ranges	—	$\overline{w}$

The following mathematical relationships link the above parameters:

(i) Mean value of sample averages,

$$\text{Mean of } \overline{x} \text{ values} = \overline{X}$$

(ii) Standard deviation of $\overline{X} = \dfrac{\sigma}{\sqrt{n}}$ \hfill (15.4)

(often called the standard error of $\overline{x}$)

(iii) Mean value of the square of sample ranges,

$$\text{Mean of } s^2 \text{ values} = \frac{n-1}{n} \times \sigma^2 \hspace{1cm} (15.5)$$

(iv) Standard error (deviation) of $s = \dfrac{\sigma}{\sqrt{(2n)}}$ \hfill (15.6)

If $\overline{X}$, σ and n are known it is possible to predict the spread of values of $\bar{x}$ to be expected from the measurement of samples, provided there has been no change in the inherent process variation. Should the values of $\bar{x}$ for the samples exceed the predicted spread, some assignable cause of variation, such as tool wear or tool-setting error has occurred, and this must be rectified in order to bring the process under control again; i.e. to restore the quality of production to the conditions represented by $\overline{X}$ and σ.

15.6 Control Chart for Sample Average

It is usual to set *warning* limits for $\bar{x}$ based upon the probability of one value in 40 lying outside each limt ($p = 0{\cdot}025$, where p represents the probability) and *action* limits based upon a probability of one value in 1000 lying outside each limit ($p = 0{\cdot}001$). Reference to Fig 15.3 shows that these conditions are achieved at ordinates of $\pm 1{\cdot}96\sigma$ and $\pm 3{\cdot}09\sigma$.

The control limits of $\bar{x}$ are given by:

$$\text{Outer control limit} = \overline{X} \pm 3{\cdot}09\,\frac{\sigma}{\sqrt{n}} \qquad (15.7)$$

since $\dfrac{\sigma}{\sqrt{n}}$ is the standard deviation for $\bar{x}$ by Eqn (15.4).

$$\text{Inner control limit} = \overline{X} \pm 1{\cdot}96\,\frac{\sigma}{\sqrt{n}} \qquad (15.8)$$

Example 15.2

Use the information on p. 477 to construct a control chart for sample averages suitable for a sample size of 6 pieces.

Solution

From
$$\bar{x} = 12{\cdot}43,\ \sigma = 0{\cdot}11$$

$$\text{Outer Control Limits} = 12{\cdot}43 \pm \frac{3{\cdot}09}{\sqrt{6}} \times 0{\cdot}11 \text{ by Eqn (15.7)}$$

$$= 12{\cdot}43 \pm 0{\cdot}14 \text{ mm}$$

$$\text{Inner Control Limits} = 12{\cdot}43 \pm \frac{1{\cdot}96}{\sqrt{6}} \times 0{\cdot}11 \text{ by Eqn (15.8)}$$

$$= 12{\cdot}43 \pm 0{\cdot}09 \text{ mm}$$

The chart is shown in Fig 15.5. The operator should be warned when a value of $\bar{x}$ lies outside the inner control limits.

It is often more convenient to set the limits for $\bar{x}$ from a knowledge of the average range of samples ($\bar{w}$). The relationship between σ and $\bar{w}$ depends upon the number in the sample, and σ may be reasonably estimated from $\bar{w}$ if n is small, by means of the expression:

$$\sigma = \frac{1}{d^n} \times \bar{w} \qquad (15.9)$$

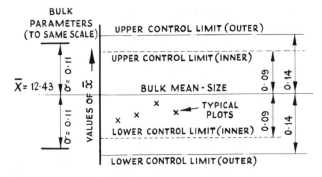

Fig 15.5 Control chart for sample average

where d_n has a value depending on the value of n. Values of d_n, given in BS2564, Table 3, are as shown.

The control limits are then given by:

$$\overline{X} \pm \frac{3 \cdot 09 \, \overline{w}}{d_n \sqrt{n}} \quad \text{and} \quad \overline{X} \pm \frac{1 \cdot 96 \, \overline{w}}{d_n \sqrt{n}}$$

Values of $3 \cdot 09/d_n \sqrt{n}$ and $1 \cdot 96/d_n \sqrt{n}$ are given in BS2564, Table 2, under the symbols $A'_{0 \cdot 001}$ and $A'_{0 \cdot 025}$, the suffixes indicating the probability of sample averages outside these limits (see value of p on p. 482).

TABLE 15.3

n.	2	3	4	5	6
d_n	1·13	1·69	2·06	2·33	2·53

Control Chart for Range. The control chart for sample average is a sufficient check on the quality of the work only if it is certain that the inherent process variation remains constant. It is desirable to test whether the work still being produced has the same value of σ as was used to set the limits for $\bar{x}$. The standard error of the standard deviation of the samples (s) is given by $\sigma/\sqrt{(2n)}$ Eqn (15.6). A control chart for s can thus be drawn in much the same way as a control chart for $\bar{x}$. This control chart will indicate any exceptional values of s and thus show if σ for the process is changing. One serious disadvantage of a control chart based upon s is the arithmetical work necessary to determine its value for each sample taken. When n is small $(n < 10)$ there is a predictable relationship between s and the sample range (w) of sufficient accuracy to enable a chart based upon values of w to be used to monitor σ. The control chart limits for **range** are:

Upper control limits—

Outer limit $= D'_{0.999} \times \bar{w}$;

Inner limit $= D'_{0.975} \times \bar{w}$.

Lower Control limits—

Outer limit $= D'_{0.001} \times \bar{w}$;

Inner limit $= D'_{0.025} \times \bar{w}$.

The suffixes relate to the probability of values lying outside the limits of 1 in 1000 and 1 in 40 as previously discussed. Lower control limits for range are rarely charted because the purpose is to detect any increase in the inherent process variation, as indicated by an increase in σ.

BS2564, Table 3, gives the required values of D'.

TABLE 15.4

n	2	3	4	5	6
$D'_{0.999}$	4·12	2·98	2·57	2·34	2·21
$D'_{0.975}$	2·81	2·17	1·93	1·81	1·72
$D'_{0.025}$	0·04	0·18	0·29	0·37	0·42
$D'_{0.001}$	0·00	0·04	0·10	0·16	0·21

It can now be seen that control charts for **average** and for **range** depend upon the value of σ for the process, or upon an estimate of σ based upon $\bar{w}$. To start a control chart, values of $\bar{x}$ and w should be plotted for about 10 samples (not less than 40 separate measurements) without making any attempt to determine the control limits. When this stage has been reached an initial estimate of $\bar{w}$ can be made, and limits set on a provisional basis. After a further 10 values have been plotted a better estimate for the value of $\bar{w}$ can be made, and new and more accurate values of the control limits set. Eventually, sufficient data will be available for an accurate assessment of $\bar{X}$ and σ to be made. Normal inspection methods should be continued until sufficient data has been collected from which reliable control limits can be set.

Example 15.3

Use the information on p. 477 to construct a chart for controlling the inherent process variation, based on samples of 6 pieces.

Solution

From p. 477 $\sigma = 0.11$

Standard error of $s = \dfrac{\sigma}{\sqrt{(2n)}} = \dfrac{0.11}{\sqrt{12}} = 0.032$

Control Limits for s;
 Outer Limits $= 0.11 \pm 3.09 \times 0.032$ by principles of p. 482
 $= 0.11 \pm 0.1$

Inner Limits $= 0.11 \pm 1.96 \times 0.032$ by principles of p. 482
 $= 0.11 \pm 0.063$

A chart, similar to Fig 15.5, can be constructed for values of s.
The more usual chart for range may be constructed as follows.
By Eqn (15.9), $\sigma = \bar{w}/d_n$ and a probable value of $\bar{w}$ can be estimated from this.

$$\bar{w} = 0.11 \times 2.53 = 0.278$$

The upper control limits are:

Outer limit $= D'_{0.999} \times \bar{w} = 2.21 \times 0.278 = 0.61$ mm
Inner limit $= D'_{0.975} \times \bar{w} = 1.72 \times 0.278 = 0.48$ mm

The control chart for range is shown in Fig 15.6.

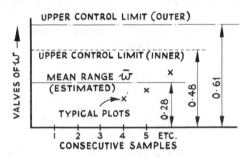

Fig. 15.6 Control chart for sample range

It can be seen that the upper limit for range just exceeds the bulk range of 0.6 mm. This arises because the initial data of Table 15.1 does not conform strictly to normal distribution, and because the strict meaning of "sample range" is involved.

For the range chart drawn "sample range" means the difference between the largest and smallest diameter of any six pieces selected at random from the 200. However many times six pieces are selected from a much larger bulk having the same inherent process variation, the range should not exceed 0.61 mm more than once in 1000 times!

More generally, samples collected during a production run are taken consecutively. This tends to give smaller values of sample range than for samples selected at random from the bulk. The drift of sample average, due to tool wear, is the main reason why samples taken from the bulk will have a greater range than samples collected consecutively during the production run. Fig 15.4 illustrates this point.

15.7 Control to a Specification

So far, it has been shown that the technique generally referred to as quality control by measurement can be used to maintain an established quality as more parts are produced. It is generally necessary to relate the quality produced to a specification.

For present purposes a tolerance band may be regarded as fixing the permissible variation on either side of a mean-size. Let $\overline{X}$ be the bulk average required, and a tolerance (T) be the bulk range; the dimension to be controlled is then specified in terms we have already employed.

Fig 15.7 relates a process distribution curve to three tolerance bands of common mean-size, but varying range. From the area property of the distribution curve, it is clear that the process represented by the curve can produce to tolerance band F with certainty, to tolerance band E provided there is no drift of the mean-size, but that for tolerance band G some scrap is bound to occur. It is useless to try and produce to tolerance band G unless a proportion of scrap is permitted; the inherent process variation must be reduced by an improvement of the equipment, or of the method, before scrap can be eliminated. It is one advantage of quality control methods that any inadequacy of the equipment or process is revealed at an early stage of production.

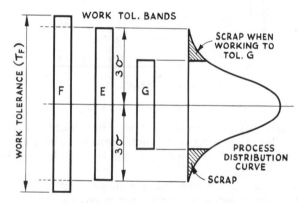

Fig. 15.7 Relationship of process variation to work tolerance

Let T = tolerance magnitude. The maximum value of σ for which the probability of work outside the limits is 2 per 1000, is given by $\sigma = T/2 \times 3\cdot09$. A specification and manufacturing process are reasonably matched if $T \geqslant 6\sigma$.

In BS2564 a relationship of similar importance between T and $\overline{w}$ is called the relative precision index (RPI).

RPI = $T/\overline{w}$, and BS2564, Table 4, gives values related to the number of pieces in the samples and to the degree of precision, classified as **low, medium** and **high**

Medium relative precision means that the quality of work produced is just good enough to meet the quality specified.

Since by Eqn (15.9) $\bar{w} = d_n \times \sigma$, it is possible to show from the values given in BS2564, Table 4, that in round figures:

$T < 6\sigma$ represents **low relative precision.**
T between 6σ and 8σ represents **medium relative precision.**
$T > 8\sigma$ represents **high relative precision.**

The methods of Example 15.2 are suitable for the construction of control charts for sample average when the relative precision index is **medium** or **low**. For low relative precision, however, defective work is bound to occur. An estimate of the proportion of the work likely to be defective can be made as follows:

Estimate σ from $\bar{w}$; i.e. $\sigma = \dfrac{\bar{w}}{d_n}$.

Let $\dfrac{T}{2\sigma} = k$; find k.

Now if $k = 3\cdot09$ the chance of rejects is 1 per 1000 either side of tolerance band, provided that $\bar{X}$ is at the middle of the tolerance band.

Suppose k is found to be $1\cdot8$. From the area properties of the normal distribution curve, Fig 15.2, when $t = \pm 1\cdot8$ there are $3\cdot6\%$ of the parts above and $3\cdot6\%$ below the limits set by t. Fig 15.8 illustrates the relationships and shows the percentage scrap to be expected.

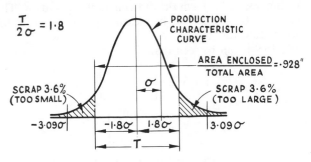

Fig. 15.8 Rejects when relative precision is "low"

When the RPI is **high** the bulk of work produced, if it is controlled by means of a chart for sample average constructed according to **15.6**, will be well inside the tolerance band. Some drift of size, as revealed by a change in sample average, might then be allowed without serious risk of producing scrap; the resultant longer run between tool adjustments would increase output. In order to do this it is necessary to set the control limits by a different method.

Fig 15.9 shows the relationships for $T > 8\sigma$ between the bulk distribution curve, the distribution curve of samples and the tolerance band. The new principle used in setting the control limits is examined in terms of the outer control limit on one side of $\overline{X}$ only; the same principle will apply for the other control limits.

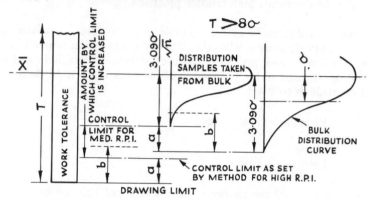

Fig. 15.9 Method of setting control limits for "high" relative precision

If the work tolerance $= \pm 3 \cdot 09\sigma$ the control limits for simple average would normally be set at $\pm 3 \cdot 09\sigma/\sqrt{n}$. The difference between $3 \cdot 09\sigma$ and $3 \cdot 09\sigma/\sqrt{n}$ is represented by dimension "a" in Fig 15.9. Now supposing the work tolerance is $8 \cdot 5\sigma$, the outer control limit for $\bar{x}$ could be set by measuring dimension "a" from the drawing limit towards $\overline{X}$. The inner control limits can be similarly set by measuring dimension "b" from the drawing limits towards $\overline{X}$.

From Fig 15.9 it can be seen that

$$a = 3 \cdot 09\sigma \left[1 - \frac{1}{\sqrt{n}} \right] \qquad (15.10)$$

and

$$b = \sigma \left[3 \cdot 09 - \frac{1 \cdot 96}{\sqrt{n}} \right]. \qquad (15.11)$$

Values of "a" and "b" can be found from a known value of $\bar{w}$ by substituting $\bar{w}/d_n$ for σ, Eqn (15.9).

BS 2564 Table 5 give values from which "a" and "b" can be determined directly:

$$a = A''_{0 \cdot 001} \times \bar{w}; \; b = A''_{0 \cdot 025} \times \bar{w}.$$

The suffixes indicate probability as previously explained (p. 482)

Example 15.4

Sample ranges for the first 12 samples of 5 pieces, taken at $\frac{1}{2}$-hourly intervals, during the production of a turned diameter $48 \pm 0 \cdot 1$ mm on an automatic lathe, are given.

Unit of Range = 0·1 mm

Sample No	1	2	3	4	5	6	7	8	9	10	11	12
Range (w)	0·2	0·4	0·2	0·5	0·7	0·2	0·5	0·6	1	0·5	0·2	0·3

Determine the relative precision index and construct a control chart for sample averages.

Solution

$$\bar{w} = \frac{\Sigma w}{12} = \frac{5 \cdot 3}{12} = 0 \cdot 44 \qquad RPI = \frac{T}{\bar{w}} = \frac{2}{0 \cdot 44} = 4 \cdot 6.$$

Reference to BS2564 shows this to be high relative precision. Alternatively, $\sigma = \dfrac{\bar{w}}{d_n} = \dfrac{0 \cdot 44}{2 \cdot 33} = 0 \cdot 19$, by estimation from $\bar{w}$, since $d_n = 2 \cdot 33$ when $n = 5$,

Hence

$$\frac{T}{\sigma} = \frac{2}{0 \cdot 19} = 10 \cdot 5 \qquad (T > 8\sigma)$$

To construct a control chart for $\bar{x}$:

$$a = 3 \cdot 09 \times 0 \cdot 19 \left(1 - \frac{1}{\sqrt{5}}\right) = 0 \cdot 32 \qquad \text{by Eqn} \qquad (15.10)$$

$$b = \left[3 \cdot 09 - \frac{1 \cdot 96}{\sqrt{5}}\right] \times 0 \cdot 19 = 0 \cdot 42 \qquad \text{by Eqn} \qquad (15.11).$$

The chart is illustrated in Fig 15.10, where a series of possible values of $\bar{x}$ have also been plotted.

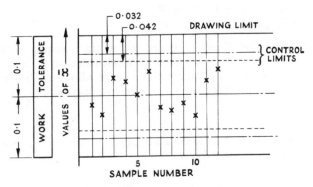

Fig. 15.10 Control chart for "high" relative precision

15.8 Control Chart for Attributes

Limit gauging sorts work into two classes—"good" and "bad". A similar classification may arise where practical conditions do not permit precise measurement, e.g. blow holes in castings or bubbles in glass. Provided a criterion is set distinguishing the lowest acceptable quality, it becomes possible to plot the proportion of defectives in batches on a control chart and to use the chart for detecting a decline in the general quality being produced, before a large quantity of scrap has occurred. The method is of course equally applicable where a direct measurement, e.g. linear size or electrical resistance, determines the outer limits of acceptable quality.

The number of defectives found in random samples of n pieces enables enables the "fraction defective" to be calculated.

$$\text{Fraction defective } (P) = \frac{\text{number defective per sample}}{n}$$

When a reasonable number of samples have been taken it is possible to obtain the mean value for P.

$$\text{Mean value of fraction defective } (\overline{P}) = \frac{\text{total defectives found}}{\Sigma\, n}$$

Since random factors underlie the variation in quality, the value of P varies from sample to sample and for such conditions it can be shown that P tends to follow a binomial distribution and have a standard deviation given by

$$s = \sqrt{\left(\frac{\overline{P}(1-\overline{P})}{n}\right)}$$

Having found s, it becomes possible to set limits for P which can then be marked on the control chart.

Outer limits (1 in 1000) are $\overline{P} \pm 3{\cdot}09s$
Inner limits (1 in   40) are $\overline{P} \pm 1{\cdot}96s$

It can be seen that these limits are set on the assumption that the distribution is "normal" while s has been calculated on the assumption that the distribution is "binomial". This is allowable because, for conditions where n is large and $nP > 5$ the two distributions are similar.

Example 15.5

The following data relates to the daily output of a foundry producing small castings. The sample size is 150.

Day	1	2	3	4	5	6	7	8	9	10	11	12	13	14	15
Defectives in sample	4	3	1	4	5	2	3	3	4	3	3	2	3	2	4

Draw up a control chart for the fraction defective. What number of defectives could be expected to occur once in forty samples?

Solution

Number of defectives	1	2	3	4	5	Sample size
Fraction defective	0·007	0·013	0·020	0·027	0·033	150

$$P = \frac{46}{15 \times 150} = 0.020\,44$$

$$s = \frac{0.020\,44\,(1 - 0.020\,44)}{150} = 0.011\,55.$$

Upper limits, (1 in 1000) $P + 3s = 0.055$
(1 in 40) $P + 2s = 0.044$

(lower limits not applicable).

Possible defectives per sample occurring once in forty times

$$= 0.044 \times 150 = 6.6.$$

That is, 7 defectives should not occur as frequently as once in 40 samples.

Note: Sometimes a specification gives the allowable "average" percentage defectives, e.g. 2%. If so, this should be used for calculating the standard deviation to be met, i.e. $\bar{P}$ would take the value 0·02.

15.9   Sampling of Incoming Goods

When regular deliveries of goods are received in large batches and the supplier is using a reasonable system of quality control, it is wasteful to submit the work to 100% inspection unless there are very special requirements. Sampling methods enable a check on the incoming quality to be made. The principles are similar to those under **15.8.**

A brief consideration of the statistical basis of sampling will indicate what is involved.

Let p be the probability of a defective, then $1 - p = q$ is the probability of a "good" part. If a sample of n pieces is taken at random from the batch, the probability of there being 0, 1, 2, 3 or more defective depends upon:

(i) the general level of quality being supplied,
(ii) successive terms of the binomial expansion of $(q + p)^n$.

Example 15.6

A large batch of components contains 8% defectives. If a sample of 50 pieces is taken, what will be the probabilities of finding 0, 1, 2, 3, 4 and 5 defectives in the sample? What is the probability of there being less than 4 defectives in a sample of 50 pieces?

Solution

$p = 0.08$ $q = 1 - 0.08 = 0.92$

$$(0.92 + 0.08)^{50} = 0.92^{50} + 50(0.92)^{49}(0.08) + \frac{50 \times 49}{2!}(0.92)^{48}(0.08)^2 + \cdots$$

$$= 0.016 + 0.067 + 0.144 + 0.199 + 0.204 + \cdots$$

It follows from successive terms of the expansion that the probability of there being less than 4 defectives is given by addition.

Defectives	Probability
0	0·016
1	0·067
2	0·144
3	0·199
Less than 4	0·426

Less than 4 defectives should appear in about 43 % of samples taken.

Example 15.6 shows that the binomial expansion is not very convenient for calculation. However, when n is large and p small, a Poisson distribution gives a reasonably close approximation to the binomial and is much more convenient to calculate. The Poisson distribution is based on the exponential functions e^x and e^{-x}

$$e^{-x} \times e^x = 1 = e^{-x}\left(1 + x + \frac{x^2}{2!} + \frac{x^3}{3!} + \cdots\right)$$

$$= e^{-x} + xe^{-x} + \frac{x^2 e^{-x}}{2!} + \frac{x^3 e^{-x}}{3!} + \cdots.$$

If x is given the value of the expected average number of defectives per sample, the successive terms of the Poisson series will be found to approximate quite closely to those of the binomial series. Considering example 15.6.

$$x = 0·08 \times 50 = 4$$

The probabilities given by this series are;

$$e^{-4} + 4e^{-4} + \frac{4^2 e^{-4}}{2!} + \frac{4^3 e^{-4}}{3!} + \cdots,$$

giving $0·018 + 0·073 + 0·147 + 0·195 + 0·195 + \cdots$

By this series the probability of there being less than 4 defectives per sample is seen to be 0·433 (the sum of the first four terms as before).

For sampling purposes there is no serious difference between the result obtained from the Poisson distribution and the binomial distribution.

Operating Characteristics of Sampling Systems. A commercial arrangement between a supplier and a purchaser can be operated as follows. Both agree on a permitted proportion of defectives and presumably the supplier will have some quality control system designed to maintain this quality. The purchaser operates as follows. From each incoming batch a random sample of n parts is taken. If this sample contains less than k defectives, accept the batch; if it contains more than k defectives submit the batch to 100 % inspection and return defective items; if more than k defectives appear in successive batches reject and return all the work to the supplier.

To successfully achieve its objective of minimising the purchaser's inspection costs while ensuring a reasonable standard of quality the system must;

(i) give a high chance of acceptance at the agreed proportion of defectives,

(ii) give a high chance of rejection if the proportion of defectives exceeds the agreed figure.

The Poisson distribution (p. 492) shows that, for 8 % defectives, chances of acceptance at this quality when $k = 2$ are $0.018 + 0.073 + 0.147 = 0.238$ (about 24 %)

This is low, if only 24 % of batches are likely to satisfy the customer a great deal of work would be returned to the supplier. However, suppose the agreed proportion defective was set at 2 %.

The Poisson distribution then becomes

$x = 0.02 \times 50 = 1$ and the first three terms of expansion are $0.368 + 0.368 + 0.184 = 0.92$. For 2 % proportion defective, where acceptance depends upon there being no more than 2 defectives in a batch of 50, the probability of acceptance is 92 %. Summarising the above considerations.

Sample number $(n) = 50$ Maximum permitted defectives $(k) = 2$.

Proportion defective	Probability of acceptance
2 % (0.02)	92 % (0.92)
8 % (0.08)	24 % (0.24)

If these principles are followed it is possible to develop a graph to show the probability of acceptance for differing quality levels for specified values of n and k. Fig 15.11 shows such a graph, commonly called an **operating characteristic**. It follows from the above considerations and from Fig 15.11 that:

(i) the producer's risk of having work containing no more than 2 % defectives rejected is $1 - 0.92 = 0.08$ (8 %)

(ii) the consumer's risk of accepting work containing no more than 6 % defectives is 0.42 (42 %).

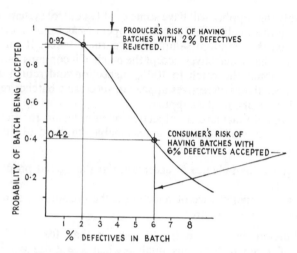

Fig. 15.11 Operating characteristic for $n = 50, k = 2$

Economics of Single Sampling. Since it would be normal practice to give 100 % inspection to a batch rejected by sampling as on p. 493, and since the reliability of the sampling method increases as the sample size is increased, it is possible to decide upon a sample number (n) such that the total amount of inspection is near the minimum. Clearly, as n is increased, k can be increased for the agreed values of producer and consumer risk. For any sample size the total amount of inspection I depends upon n and the producer's risk P_1.

$$I = n + (N - n)(1 - P_1),$$ where N is the total number in the batch from which sample n is taken.

The matter has been investigated by Dodge and Romig and their *Sampling and Inspection Tables* (Wiley) enable economic sampling sizes to be found for specified conditions.

Alternative Sampling Methods. Basically the criterion in sampling is to increase the discriminating power of the sampling without greatly increasing the amount of inspection involved. Two developments in this direction are as follows:

(a) *Double sampling.* Proceed as in single sampling, sampling size n_1, acceptable defectives per sample k_1. Whenever k_1 is exceeded take a further sample of n_2 pieces. Should the cumulative result, sample size $(n_1 + n_2)$, have total defects of less than k_3 ($= k_1 + k_2$) accept the batch; if k_3 is exceeded reject the batch. (See Dodge and Romig—double sampling.)

(b) *Sequential Sampling.* The procedure is based on a chart such as Fig 15.12, drawn on squared paper. Values of h and slope θ are available from tables or may be calculated as shown by Morney, *Facts from Figures*, Pelican. As the inspection proceeds the cumulative result is plotted on the squared paper until eventually a point is obtained outside the middle band, above for "good" work, below for "bad". The system is said to give a decision with the minimum amount of inspection but the statistical concepts involved are rather complicated.

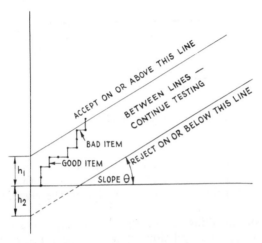

Fig. 15.12 Sequential sampling

While both these systems have attractions, their greater sophistication means that a higher level of supervisory work is involved and single sampling is more satisfactory where those operating the control system have only a modest appreciation of the statistical basis of their work.

15.10 Tolerance "Build-up" in Assemblies

Fig 15.13 shows the tolerance build-up which may occur if two bars of length $l_1 \pm \frac{1}{2}t_1$ and $l_2 \pm \frac{1}{2}t_2$ are placed end to end, where t_1 and t_2 represent the tolerances. The overall length is seen to be $(l_1 + l_2) \pm \frac{1}{2}(t_1 + t_2)$, the tolerance on the assembly being the sum of the tolerances of the separate parts, a principle more fully discussed in Chapter 1.

Suppose, however, that the two bars are taken at random from two large groups for which the distribution curve is somewhere near **normal**. The chance of two bars, one at the maximum-metal condition and one at the minimum-metal condition, being selected for the assembly is very remote, more so than the chance of selecting one bar at the extreme

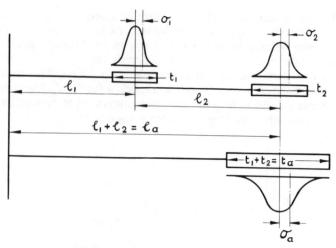

Fig. 15.13 Tolerance "build-up" in assemblies

tolerance condition. The frequency curves sketched in relation to the tolerance bands, Fig 15.13, illustrate this fact. Notice the long "tails" of the assembly distribution curve in relation to the algebraic tolerance of $\pm \frac{1}{2}(t_1 + t_2)$.

The important thing about the relationships illustrated, is the magnitude of σ_a, and its relationship to the magnitudes of σ_1 and σ_2. It can be shown mathematically that provided a random selection of the parts is made from bulks having normal distributions of standard deviations σ_1 and σ_2, the assemblies will also follow a normal distribution of standard deviation σ_a, where

$$\sigma_a = \sqrt{\sigma_1^2 + \sigma_2^2}.$$

The principle may be extended to any number of separate items of an assembly such that:

$$\sigma_a = \sqrt{(\sigma_1^2 + \sigma_2^2 + \sigma_3^2 \ldots \sigma_n^2)} \qquad (15.12)$$

Since, for the production characteristic curve discussed, the tolerance are approximately $\pm 3\sigma$, a similar rule applies to the tolerances, viz:

$$t_a = \sqrt{(t_1^2 + t_2^2 + t_3^2 \ldots t_n^2)} \qquad (15.13)$$

The value of t_a, obtained by the statistical method of associating tolerance, is seen to be lower than the value obtained by algebraic association. An important corollary for quantity production is that the assembly tolerance t_a could still be met if the component tolerances t_1 and t_2 based upon algebraic association were somewhat increased.

Example 15.7
Five components of equal tolerance are associated in an assembly, to build up a length for which the maximum permissible variation is 0·42 mm. What increase in component tolerance is possible when statistical concepts of tolerance build-up are used to replace the normal algebraic considerations?

Solution
Let t = tolerance on components.
For tolerance build-up considered algebraically:

$$t_1 = \frac{0·42}{5} = 0·084 \text{ mm}$$

For tolerance build-up considered statistically:

$$t_a = \sqrt{5t_2{}^2} \quad \therefore \quad t_2 = \frac{0·42}{\sqrt{5}} = 0·188 \text{ mm}$$

Permissible increase of tolerance $= 0·188 - 0·084$
$$= 0·104 \text{ mm}$$

The increase is about 120%. The very big increase is due to the large number of items in the assembly.

It is possible to extend these principles in order to widen tolerances on individual components, provided a known risk of assemblies falling below a specified standard is accepted. Use must be made of a simple law of probability.

Let p_a be the probability of an assembly lying outside certain limits. A suitable probability is $p_a = 0·001$, i.e., a chance of 1 per 1000 not meeting the specification. Let p_1, p_2, p_3, etc., be the probabilities of the separate parts lying outside certain limits. Then from the multiplication theorem of probability,

$$p_a = p_1 \times p_2 \times p_3, \text{ etc.}$$

If two parts only are to be assembled, and the probabilities of these parts lying outside certain limits are to be equal, $p_1 = p_2 = \sqrt{p_a}$. Values can be found for p_1 and p_2, in terms of the probability of assemblies lying outside a specified condition. Limits can then be set for the parts, so that the production will have probabilities of p_1 and p_2 amounts of work lying outside the limits, by making use of the area property of the normal curve.

Example 15.8
A hole-and-shaft assembly is required to provide a close running fit, nominal diameter 32 mm, minimum clearance 0·015 mm, maximum clearance 0·05 mm. The hole tolerance is to be 1·5 times the shaft tolerance. A risk of 1 in 1000 is to be taken of assemblies lying outside the specified clearances, and it may be assumed that the parts, produced in quantity, follow a normal curve of distribution. The assemblies are built by random selection of the mating parts. Find suitable hole and shaft limits and compare them with limits set to give 100% perfect assemblies. (Use a unilateral hole-base system.)

Solution

$$p_a = 0.001 \qquad \therefore \quad p_h = p_s = \sqrt{0.001} = 0.0316$$

The hole and shaft tolerances must be set so that approximately 3% of the parts lie outside the limits required for 100% perfect assemblies.

For 100% perfect assemblies:

$$t_h + t_s = 0.05 - 0.015 = 0.035$$
$$t_h = 1.5\,t_s \qquad \therefore \quad 2.5\,t_s = 0.035 \qquad t_s = 0.014\,\text{mm}$$
$$t_h = 0.035 - 0.014 = \underline{0.021\ \text{mm}}$$

Reference to Table 22 of BS 600 shows, that for a risk of 3% of the work outside the ideal limits (97% "good" work), the required limits are $\pm 2.2\sigma$. It is usual to assume that $\pm 3.09\sigma$ will just contain all the work produced, hence the component tolerances representing assemblies having the risk of defectives as stated will be those for 100% good assemblies increased in the ratio of 3.09/2.2.

The required tolerances are:

$$t_h = 0.021 \times \frac{3.09}{2.2} = 0.03$$

$$t_s = 0.014 \times \frac{3.09}{2.2} = 0.02$$

The limits of size must now be set.

For 100% good assemblies these are:

Hole   32·021/32·000 mm
Shaft   31·985/31·971 mm

Limits for 99·9% good assemblies (1 per 1000 defective) must be set so that the same mean-fit is achieved.

Hole   32·030/32·000 mm

The mean-fit required is 0·0325 clearance.

The mean-size of the shaft is $32.015 - 0.0325 = 31.9825$ (say 31·982)

Shaft   31·992/31·972 mm

The "fits" are illustrated to scale in Fig 15.14

The clearances possible for the second set of tolerances have extreme values (on an algebraic basis) of 0·008 mm minimum and 0·058 mm maximum. However, it is not likely that the specified assembly condition will be exceeded more frequently than 1 in 1000 assemblies. For this small risk, a 40% increase of component tolerance has been gained ("rounding" the figures has made this appear to be somewhat larger).

If the sizes are controlled by the quality control chart technique a watch can be kept on the distribution pattern, which must, of course, be something approaching "normal" for the consideration made above to apply.

It is possible to test the above solution by applying Eqn (15.13)

$$t_a = \sqrt{(0.03^2 + 0.02^2)} = 0.036\ \text{mm}$$

The limits set for the hole and shaft could be expected to give an assembly tolerance of 0·036 mm which would be exceeded not more than

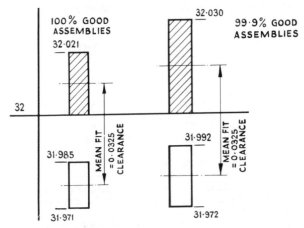

Fig. 15.14 Diagram of fits showing increase of work tolerances for 1 per 1000 assemblies outside the desired condition

1 in 1000 times. The result compares favourably with the required tolerance on the assembly of 0·035 mm.

The production engineer is always faced with the problem of controlling the quality of the goods produced, although the time spent in doing this does not contribute directly to the output. Skilled inspection is slow and expensive; semi-skilled viewing by means of limit gauges tends to fall in effectiveness as quantities are increased, due to the monotonous nature of the task and the unavoidable wear of equipment. Process control, which neither wastes skill nor fails in its objective as quantities are increased, is best effected by either the employment of automatic gauging equipment or by quality control based on statistical methods. The latter method has the advantage that a large expenditure on special equipment is avoided.

EXERCISES 15

1. Plot a normal distribution curve and use it to estimate the percentage of the total area under the curve lying between the following limits:

$$\pm 0.8\sigma, \quad \pm 1.28\sigma, \quad \pm 1.64\sigma, \quad \pm 1.96\sigma.$$

2. From the information given in **15.6** determine, for samples of 5 pieces, the values of $A_{0.001}$, $A'_{0.001}$, $A_{0.025}$ and $A'_{0.025}$.
On a particular control chart it is required to draw control limits for average which are likely to be exceeded 1 in every 20 times. If samples of 4 are taken, find the constants required to set these limits: (i) assuming $\bar{w}$ is known; (ii) assuming σ is known. (i.e. find $A'_{0.05}$ and $A_{0.05}$.)

3. After a machining operation on the diameter of a component specified as 47.500 ± 0.025 mm, a sample of 300 components was inspected the dimension being measured to the nearest 0·001 mm. The readings have been grouped into

discrete classes having equal intervals and the frequencies of occurrence are
tabulated below:

Dia of components (mm)	Frequency
47·480–84	8
85–89	21
90–94	38
95–99	54
47·500–04	66
05–09	52
10–14	34
15–19	20
20–24	7

Calculate (i) the arithmetic mean, (ii) the standard deviation, of the diameter
for the batch and draw a histogram of the distribution. (iii) What degree of
relative precision is indicated?

4. During the grinding of a large batch of components three modifications
were made to the operating conditions with the object of improving the surface
finish produced.

Measurements were made on components processed by the original method
and after each modification.

Surface finish CLA	Number of components			
	Method 1	Method 2	Method 3	Method 4
1μ	90	70	116	110
2μ	124	164	190	240
3μ	178	94	64	92
4μ	240	100	130	100

Determine if the changes in method produced any improvement in surface finish.

5. (a) To what kind of manufacturing process is statistical quality control
specially suited? Describe the steps which should be taken in applying statistical
quality control to a typical manufacturing process.

(b) Write down the formula for each standard deviation of a group of parts
when:

(i) the whole of the parts are measured;
(ii) a sample batch is inspected.

(c) Make a drawing of a normal distribution curve and show the percentage of
parts included in variations from the average of $\pm\sigma$, $\pm2\sigma$, and $\pm3\sigma$.

6. A certain dimension of a component produced in quantity on an automatic
lathe is specified as $84\cdot60\pm0\cdot05$ mm. A 5% inspection check resulted in the
following variation of the dimensions measured to the nearest 0·01 mm.

Dimension (mm)	84·56	84·57	84·58	84·59	84·60	84·61	84·62	84·63	84·64
Frequency	1	8	54	123	248	115	44	6	1

Calculate the mean value and standard deviation for the sample check and draw the frequency curve. Show that for practical purposes the variation of the dimension for the whole batch would be expected to fall within the prescribed limits.

7. (a) What is the significance of the RPI when considering the suitability of a process to produce to a particular specification?

(b) Give the relationship between σ and the process tolerance for low and high relative precision.

(c) When producing under low RPI conditions, show how the % scrap may be estimated.

(d) Why can the control limits for average be widened when the RPI is known to be high?

8. For a controlled operation on a lathe, a particular dimension of a part is specified as 55 ± 0.25 mm. Samples of five components were each measured to the nearest 0.001 in at 10 equal time intervals and the following readings obtained:

Sample No.	1	2	3	4	5	6	7	8	9	10
Dimension (in)	55·21	55·13	55·11	54·93	54·88	55·22	55·11	55·02	55·12	55·02
	54·99	55·03	55·01	55·12	55·14	55·15	55·07	55·06	55·03	54·97
	55·10	54·98	54·99	55·04	55·05	54·97	54·99	54·97	54·95	55·06
	55·02	54·96	54·97	54·98	55·11	54·95	54·93	54·99	54·98	54·99
	54·95	55·04	54·98	54·91	54·97	55·02	55·00	54·01	54·93	55·01

Calculate: (i) the relative precision index (RPI); (ii) the control limits on means and ranges, given that the RPI corresponds to medium relative precision.

From the given data and calculated limits construct control charts for means and ranges of operation. What do you deduce from your charts?

For samples of 5; $A'_{0.025} = 0.38$ $D'_{0.975} = 1.81$

$A'_{0.001} = 0.59$ $D'_{0.999} = 2.21$

9. The table gives the number of defectives found in 30 consecutive samples.

10	7	9	12	8	11	10	17	13	6
8	11	8	10	9	6	12	14	7	3
9	11	4	15	11	17	5	9	11	8

(i) Using information from the first 20 samples, draw a control chart for fraction defective.

(ii) Plot the remainder of the results and comment upon the quality of work which they indicate.

10. A sampling scheme is operated from the following instructions:

"From incoming batches take samples of 50 and inspect. If the sample contains no more than 3 defectives accept the batch; if it contains more than 3 defectives reject the batch."

Using the Poisson distribution, plot the operating characteristic for up to 10% defectives in a batch. State the producer's risk of having batches containing 2% defectives rejected, and the consumer risk of having batches containing 8% defectives accepted.

11. The required quality of a mass produced assembly is obtained by using the following limits because the permitted extremes of fit are just acceptable: bore 25·020/25·000 mm dia, shaft 24·992/24·980 mm dia.

During manufacture it is found that excessive scrap is produced because of the very close limits required, and in order to widen these, it is decided to accept a chance of 1 assembly per 1000 falling below the desired standard.

Given that the range for 99·8 % good work is $\pm 3\cdot09\sigma$ and for 97 % good work is $\pm 2\cdot2\sigma$, estimate suitable new limits on a statistical basis, and illustrate both sets of conditions in a conventional diagram.

Why is it desirable to use quality control methods when the new limits are introduced?

CHAPTER 16
Time And Cost Estimates

16.1 Manufacture Costs

Production engineering is an economic function, since manufacture must be carried out at the lowest cost consistent with the quality and functional needs of the product. The cost of an article has three main elements:

    (i) material cost,
    (ii) labour cost,
    (iii) overhead costs,

and, additionally, if special tooling is required for production purposes, a proportion of this cost is recovered in the cost of each article.

The overheads of a factory may be defined as "all the costs of running the factory, less the cost of direct labour and direct materials". The cost of direct materials is the cost of the raw materials from which parts in the finished product are made, plus the cost of purchased parts, e.g. ball bearings; direct labour costs are the wages paid to employees who work on the product or one of its components to change the raw material into the finished article.

Overheads include items such as rent, lighting, power, general supplies, wages of maintenance staff, typists, draughtsmen, salaries of departmental heads, managers, directors, etc. These are spread over the products of a firm by a method chosen because it gives the fairest spread of costs. A number of different methods are available for this purpose, but in general for the type of production covered by this book, the proportion of overheads borne by a product may be considered as being proportional to the labour cost of manufacture.

The labour cost for a machining operation depends upon the wage-rate of the worker and the time spent on the operation; overheads are then added, perhaps on a percentage basis, e.g. If an operation takes 12 minutes and is performed by an operator earning £2 per hour, then

$$\text{Labour cost} = 12/60 \times 2 = £0.4$$

If the overhead rate is assumed to be 400%, then

Overhead cost $= 0.4 \times 400/100 = £1.6$, hence

Total cost $=$ Labour cost $+$ Overhead cost $= 0.4 + 1.6 = £2$

The above example shows that any savings made in the cost of direct labour bring a reduction in the overheads added to the cost of the job, hence reducing the final cost of the product and its selling price, or alternatively, increasing the profit margin.

The percentage quoted above is not unrealistic for the overheads of some machine shops, but it will vary considerably according to the industry and its product. For example, a simple product—say a metal belt buckle—can be made by a firm with a simple organisation and low overheads because there will be low costs of design and development, little advertising and a small sales department, etc. In contrast, an assembly used for an important function on an aircraft will require much time spent in research and design, careful checking and stressing of the detail designs to ensure against failure in service, metallurgical examination of materials used, rigid control over manufacture and inspection, and perhaps the maintenance of a world-wide servicing organisation for the benefit of the users of the aircraft. In circumstances such as these it is understandable that the overheads will be much higher than for a firm making a simpler, less sophisticated product.

The ways by which overheads can be kept to a minimum are not our immediate concern, but the reader may be assured that alert managements are aware of the impact of overheads on the cost of the product and constantly make efforts to keep down such costs while still maintaining the staff and organisation necessary to give a good service to customers. Our object is to consider methods for estimating the time taken in machining operations, and from this information estimates of machining cost can be made.

16.2 Times for Machining Processes

The time for performing a machining operation comprises:

(i) manipulating time (including loading time);
(ii) cutting time, i.e. time the tool is actually in contact with the component.

Of these two elements, cutting time is more readily determined; it requires a knowledge of the machining method, tool and workpiece materials, and speeds and feeds of the machine used. This information can be factually established and the data used to calculate a cutting time.

Time spent in setting and manipulating the machine depends on many indeterminate factors such as the degree of skill, dexterity and speed of the operator. As a result, it cannot be calculated. The nearest approach to a rational basis for forecasting handling times is by the use of charts giving specimen times (often called synthetic times) for elemental tasks performed by the operator. These are discussed and examples are given in **16.7**.

Floor-to-Floor Time (FFT). This is the time which elapses between picking-up a component to load for a machining operation and depositing it after unloading. A floor-to-floor time, therefore, includes time for loading, manipulation, metal cutting and unloading the component. Allowances for tool changing, fatigue and for personal delays are added to the FFT to give the basic production time for the operation.

16.3 Calculation of Cutting Time

The determination of a cutting time depends on the correct selection of values for the two variables, cutting speed and feed rate, each of which depends on other factors such as depth of cut, rigidity of set-up, power available, etc. Once the variables have been established, the calculation is straightforward.

Tool and machine-tool manufacturers publish tables of recommended speeds and feeds to be used with their equipment; an example is given in Table 16.3 and in practice tables such as these should be consulted when estimating a cutting time.

Calculations for the cutting times of a wide range of basic machining processes can be covered by grouping according to the cutting action as follows:

(a) continuous (rotary), e.g. turning, drilling;
(b) intermittent (rotary), e.g. milling, hobbing;
(c) intermittent (reciprocating), e.g. planing, slotting.

The calculation of cutting time for many operations covered by the above groups can be carried out by identical procedures, e.g. the calculation for such diverse operations as turning, reaming and tapping uses the same principle in each case.

16.4 Formulae for Estimating Cutting Times (Fig 16.1)

Let

A = Approach distance for milling cutter (mm)
D = Diameter of cutter or workpiece (mm)
L = Length of stroke or length of cut (mm)
N = Spindle speed (rev/min)
N_T = Number of teeth in milling cutter
V = Cutting speed (m/min)
b = Width of cut (mm)
d = Depth of cut (mm)
f = Feed/stroke or Feed/rev (mm)
f_t = Feed/tooth of a milling cutter (mm)
t = Time for 1 cut (min)
S = Offset (mm), cutter centreline to workpiece centreline.

(a) *For Continuous (Rotary) Cutting Processes*

$$\text{Spindle speed, } N = \frac{10^3 V}{\pi D}. \tag{16.1}$$

$$\therefore \quad \text{Cutting speed, } V = \frac{\pi D N}{10^3}. \tag{16.2}$$

$$\text{Time for 1 cut, } t = \frac{L}{Nf}. \tag{16.3}$$

Or, substituting for N,
$$t = \frac{\pi D L}{10^3 V f}. \tag{16.4}$$

(b) *For Intermittent (Rotary) Cutting Processes (Milling, etc.)*
Spindle and cutting speeds are calculated using Eqns (16.1) and (16.2), the feed rate is then obtained as follows:

$$\text{table feed rate} = N \times N_T \times f_t \text{ mm/min} \tag{16.5}$$

hence, time for 1 cut,

$$t = \frac{\text{total length of cut}}{\text{feed rate}} = \frac{L}{N \times N_T \times f_t}. \tag{16.6}$$

When milling, the approach distance (A) must be added to the length of the machined surface to give the total length of cut (L). Reference to Fig. 16.1 will show that the approach distance may be calculated as follows.

For peripheral milling,

$$A = \sqrt{\left[\left(\frac{D}{2} \right)^2 - \left(\frac{D}{2} - d \right)^2 \right]}$$

$$\therefore \quad A = \sqrt{[d(D - d)]}. \tag{16.7}$$

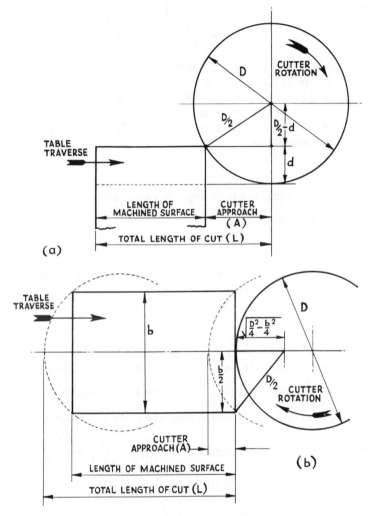

Fig. 16.1 Approach distance for milling cutters

(*a*) Peripheral milling
(*b*) Face milling

For face milling, cutter on workpiece centreline,

$$A = D/2 - \sqrt{\left(\frac{D^2}{4} - \frac{b^2}{4} \right)}. \tag{16.8}$$

For face milling, cutter centreline offset distance (S) from workpiece centreline,

$$A = D/2 - \sqrt{\left[\frac{D^2}{4} - \left(\frac{b}{2} + S\right)^2\right]}. \qquad (16.9)$$

The number of teeth (N_T) in a milling cutter must be known before Eqn (16.5) can be used. Cincinnati recommend as a general rule that cutters should have just enough teeth to ensure not more than two teeth are engaged at any time and give the following formulae (see p. 136 of *Treatise on Milling*, published by Cincinnati Milling Machine Co.):

For peripheral milling,

$$N_T = \frac{4\pi D}{D + 4d}\cos\alpha \qquad (16.10)$$

(where α = helix angle of cutter, degrees).

For face milling,

$$N_T = \frac{2\pi D}{b}. \qquad (16.11)$$

Alternatively, if the power available at the spindle is known the following expression may be used:

$$N_T = \frac{60K \times \text{watts consumed}}{f_t \cdot Ndb} \qquad (16.12)$$

Values of K are given in Table 8.2.

(c) *For Intermittent (Reciprocating) Cutting Processes (Shaping, etc.)*

Time for forward stroke $= \dfrac{L}{10^3 V}$, where V = average cutting speed.

If the forward and return strokes are made at the same average cutting speed:

$$\text{Time for one complete cycle} = \frac{L}{10^3 V} + \frac{L}{10^3 V} = \frac{2L}{10^3 V}$$

Since the speed of the return stroke is usually greater than the speed of the forward stroke:

$$\text{Time for one complete cycle} = \frac{L}{10^3 V} + \frac{L}{10^3 V_1} = \frac{L(V + V_1)}{10^3 V V_1},$$

where V_1 = average speed of return stroke.

Hence, time for one cut over work of breadth b, at a feed/stroke of f, is given by:

$$t = \frac{\text{width of work}}{\text{feed/stroke}} \times \text{time per complete cycle}$$

i.e.

$$t = \frac{Lb(V + V_1)}{10^3 f V V_1} \qquad (16.13)$$

It has been stated in 16.3 that cutting speeds recommended by tool and machine-tool makers should be used in estimating cutting time. Where this information is not available for processes other than turning, the following approximations may be useful as a guide:

Cutting speed for drilling = 0·9 × turning speed
Cutting speed for milling = 0·75 × turning speed

An approximate relationship between cutting speeds for HSS and cemented carbide tools is:
Cutting speed for cemented carbide tools = 3·5 × cutting speed for HSS tools.

16.5 Estimates of Cutting Times—Continuous (Rotary) Processes

Example 16.1
Estimate the time required for a **single cut** in each of the following machining operations:

(a) Turn 25 mm dia × 150 mm long. $V = 30$ m/min; $f = 0.25$ mm/rev.
(b) Turn 3 mm deep recess in a 50 mm dia shaft using a 6 mm wide form tool. $V = 14$ m/min; $f = 0.03$ mm.
(c) Tap M 8 × 1 pitch thread 14 mm deep. $V = 6.5$ m/min.
(d) Screwcut 64 mm dia × 6 mm pitch Acme thread 600 mm long. $V = 5$ m/min.
(e) Drill 12 mm dia × 40 mm deep. $V = 28$ m/min; $f = 0.18$ mm
(f) Ream 22 mm dia × 50 mm deep. $V = 15$ m/min; $f = 0.6$ mm
(g) Spotface 32 mm dia × 3 mm deep. $V = 17$ m/min; $f = 0.1$ mm.

Solutions

(a) Time per cut, $t = \dfrac{\pi D.L}{10^3\, Vf}$ (Eqn 16.4)

$$= \frac{\pi \times 25 \times 150}{10^3 \times 30 \times 0.25}$$

$$= 1.57 \text{ min}$$

(b) $$t = \frac{\pi \times 50 \times 3}{10^3 \times 14 \times 0.03} = 1.12 \text{ min}$$

(c) $$t = \frac{\pi \times 8 \times 14}{10^3 \times 6.5 \times 1}$$

$$= 0.06 \text{ min}$$

(d) $$t = \frac{\pi \times 64 \times 600}{10^3 \times 5 \times 6}$$

$$= 4.02 \text{ min}.$$

(e) $$t = \frac{\pi \times 12 \times 40}{10^3 \times 28 \times 0.18} = 0.3 \text{ min}.$$

(f)
$$t = \frac{\pi \times 22 \times 50}{10^3 \times 15 \times 0.6} = \underline{0.38 \text{ min}} .$$

(g)
$$t = \frac{\pi \times 32 \times 3}{10^3 \times 17 \times 0.1} = \underline{0.18 \text{ min}} .$$

If cutting times are being determined for actual components, to obtain accuracy estimates must be based upon those spindle speeds and feeds which are available on the particular machine used. This means that it is necessary to calculate a spindle speed (N) and then modify this calculated value to suit speeds available on the machine before substituting for N in Eqns (16.3) or (16.5).

Spindle speeds and feed rates are shown in machine capacity charts or data sheets; these are normally compiled in a firm's planning department and circulated to the staff likely to need them. A typical example of a capacity chart (for radial drilling machines) is given in Table 16.1, and an example of the abbreviated data sheet for speeds and feeds only (for milling machines) is given in Table 16.2.

To illustrate the way in which the principles of estimating shown in elemental form in Example 16.1 are used in building-up an estimate for a typical component, the following example is worked in detail. For clarity, each element of cutting time is separately calculated, and then all are summed; if the turning were to be carried out on a turret or automatic lathe however, some operations would be "overlapped" (see p. 526). For the present, this method of reducing machining times will be ignored. One point which will bear restating is that the **cutting time is the time the tool is actually in contact with the component during the metal removal process;** it does not include time for handling, measuring, tool changing, fatigue and personal allowances etc.

Example 16.2
Estimate a cutting time for machining on a centre lathe the screwed shaft, Fig 16.2, from 50 mm dia × 157 mm cold-drawn bar.

The cutting speeds and feeds based on the use of HSS tools are as follows:

Turning and facing	$V = 28$ m/min	$f = 0.315$ mm/rev
Drilling and centreing	$V = 23$ m/min	$f = 0.125$ mm/rev
Centre drilling	$V = 28$ m/min	$f = 0.05$ mm/rev
Forming	$V = 4.5$ m/min	$f = 0.063$ mm/rev
Tapping	$V = 4.5$ m/min	$f = $ lead of thread
Screwcutting	$V = 6$ m/min	$f = $ lead of thread

The available speeds and feeds are based on ISO Recommendation R229 (Tables 3.2 & 3.3)

Spindle speeds (rev/min):

28, 35.5, 45, 56, 71, 90, 112, 140, 180, 224, 280, 355, 450, 560, 710, 900.

TABLE 16.1

Capacity Chart for Radial Drilling Machines

	ABC Co. Ltd. 1 m Type "P"	LMN Co. Ltd. 1·4 m Type "Q"	XYZ Co. Ltd. 1·8 m Type "R"
Number of machines	2	2	1
Spindle:			
Effective radius	680 mm	900 mm	1400 mm
Horizontal traverse	680	900	1400
Vertical traverse	330	230	350
Max. distance:			
Spindle to base	1200 mm	1050 mm	1500 mm
Spindle to table	700	350	1000
Vertical adjustment of			
arm	680	700	670
Table size	760 × 890	760 × 1100	900 × 1300
Table height	480	680	500
No. and width of Tee			
slots (base)	Nil	Nil	Nil
No. and width of Tee			
slots (table)	Top 5 × 22 Side 2 × 22	Top 4 × 22 Side 3 × 22	6 × 28
Size of Morse taper in			
spindle	No. 4	No. 4	No. 5
Max size of drill (for MS)	32 mm	38 mm	64 mm
Max size of drill (for CI)	38	44	76
Max size of tap (for MS)	M24	M30	M48
Spindle speeds (rev/min)	113, 156, 212, 304, 420, 571, 730, 1007, 1370	62, 102, 132, 188, 216, 250, 307, 532, 760	31, 42, 57, 72, 100, 134, 190, 262, 355, 443, 615, 830
Feeds (mm/rev)	0·32, 0·21, 0·14	0·42, 0·32, 0·20	0·67, 0·44, 0·30, 0·21

Solution

The machining sequence is reduced to elemental operations, the numbers of which are shown in Figs 16.3–7; the estimated number of cuts is also shown.

Calculated spindle speed for Ops 1, 2 and 3

$$= \frac{10^3 V}{\pi D} = \frac{10^3 \times 28}{\pi \times 50} = 178 \text{ rev/min}$$

From data, corrected spindle speed, $\underline{N = 180 \text{ rev/min}}$

∴   Based on Eqn (16.3)

$$\text{Time for Op 1} = \frac{L}{N \cdot f} \times \text{No. of cuts} = \frac{40}{180 \times 0 \cdot 315} \times 3$$

$$= \underline{2 \cdot 12 \text{ min}}$$

TABLE 16.2
Available Spindle Speeds and Table Feed Rates—Milling Machines

ABC Co. Ltd. Type "P" (Horizontal)	rev/min	26	39	59	90	136	206	313	—
	mm/min	35	63	100	140	224	355	560	—
LMN Co. Ltd. Type "Q" (Vertical)	rev/min	46	65	88	125	175	230	310	460
	mm/min	16	22	32	45	63	80	112	160
XYZ Co. Ltd. Type "R" (Horizontal and Vertical)	rev/min	18	22	27	34	41	51	63	78
	mm/min	25	32	40	50	71	90	112	140

Note: On machines manufactured by XYZ C. Ltd.: Transverse feed rates × 0·75 = Table feed; Vertical feed rates = 0·6 × Table feed.

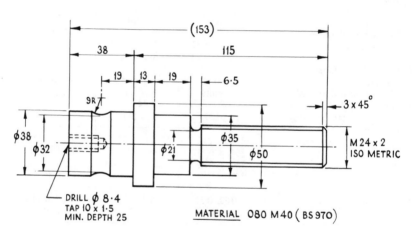

Fig. 16.2 Screwed shaft

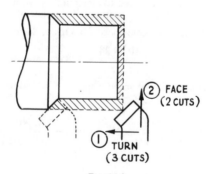

Fig. 16.3

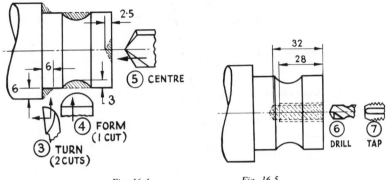

Fig. 16.4

Fig. 16.5

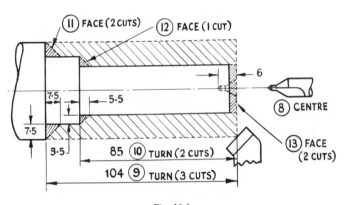

Fig. 16.6

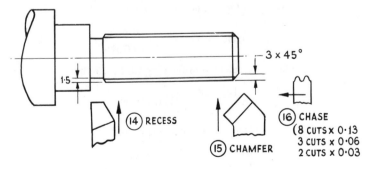

Fig. 16.7

$$\text{Time for Op 2} = \frac{19}{180 \times 0{\cdot}315} \times 2 = \underline{0{\cdot}67 \text{ min}}$$

$$\text{Time for Op 3} = \frac{(6+6)}{180 \times 0{\cdot}315} \times 2 = \underline{0{\cdot}43 \text{ min}}$$

$$\text{Spindle-speed calculation, Op 4} = \frac{10^3 \times 4{\cdot}6}{\pi \times 38} = 38 \text{ rev/min}$$

$$\therefore \text{ From data, } \underline{N = 35{\cdot}5 \text{ rev/min}}$$

$$\text{Spindle-speed calculation, Ops 5 and 6} = \frac{10^3 \times 23}{\pi \times 8{\cdot}4}$$

$$= 871 \text{ rev/min}$$

$$\therefore \text{ From data, } \underline{N = 900 \text{ rev/min}}$$

$$\text{Time for Op 4} = \frac{3}{35{\cdot}5 \times 0{\cdot}063} = \underline{1{\cdot}34 \text{ min}}$$

$$\text{Time for Op 5} = \frac{2{\cdot}5}{900 \times 0{\cdot}125} = \underline{0{\cdot}02 \text{ min}}$$

$$\text{Time for Op 6} = \frac{32}{900 \times 0{\cdot}125} = \underline{0{\cdot}28 \text{ min}}$$

$$\text{Spindle-speed calculation, Op 7} = \frac{10^3 \times 4{\cdot}6}{\pi \times 10} = 146 \text{ rev/min}$$

$$\therefore \text{ From data, } \underline{N = 140 \text{ rev/min}}$$

$$\text{Time for Op 7} = \frac{28}{140 \times 1{\cdot}5} = \underline{0{\cdot}14 \text{ min}}$$

For centre drilling, use maximum speed, i.e. $N = 900 \text{ rev/min}$

$$\text{Time for Op 8} = \frac{6}{900 \times 0{\cdot}05} = \underline{0{\cdot}14 \text{ min}}$$

Spindle speed for Ops 9 and 11 = Spindle speed for Op 1

$$\therefore \text{ Time for Op 9} = \frac{104}{180 \times 0{\cdot}315} \times 3 = \underline{5{\cdot}5 \text{ min}}$$

Spindle-speed calculation for Ops 10, 12, 13 and 15

$$= \frac{10^3 \times 28}{\pi \times 35} = 255 \text{ rev/min}$$

$$\therefore \text{ From data, } \underline{N = 224 \text{ rev/min}}$$

$$\text{Time for Op 10} = \frac{85}{224 \times 0{\cdot}315} \times 2 = \underline{2{\cdot}41 \text{ min}}$$

$$\text{Time for Op } 11 = \frac{(7\cdot5 + 7\cdot5)}{180 \times 0\cdot315} \times 2 = \underline{0\cdot53 \text{ min}}$$

$$\text{Time for Op } 12 = \frac{(5\cdot5 + 5\cdot5)}{224 \times 0\cdot315} = \underline{0\cdot16 \text{ min}}$$

$$\text{Time for Op } 13 = \frac{12}{224 \times 0\cdot315} \times 2 = \underline{0\cdot34 \text{ min}}$$

$$\text{Spindle-speed calculation for Op } 14 = \frac{10^3 \times 4\cdot6}{\pi \times 24} = 61 \text{ rev/min}$$

$$\therefore \text{ From data, } N = 56 \text{ rev/min}$$

$$\text{Spindle-speed calculation for Op } 16 = \frac{10^3 \times 6}{\pi \times 24} = 80 \text{ rev/min}$$

$$\therefore \text{ From data, } N = 71 \text{ rev/min}$$

$$\text{Time for Op } 14 = \frac{1\cdot5}{56 \times 0\cdot063} = \underline{0\cdot43 \text{ min}}$$

$$\text{Time for Op } 15 = \frac{3}{224 \times 0\cdot315} = \underline{0\cdot05 \text{ min}}$$

$$\text{Time for Op } 16 = \frac{76\cdot5}{71 \times 2} \times 13 = \underline{7\cdot0 \text{ min}}$$

From the above calculations, *Total Cutting Time = 21·56 minutes*

Note: If the required quantities of the screwed shaft were sufficient to warrant the use of more productive machines and tools the process sequence could be rearranged to considerably reduce the cutting time. For example, the use of roller-box tooling on a turret lathe would reduce the number of cuts, overlapped operations would eliminate some time elements and thread rolling or thread milling could replace screw cutting for the M24 × 2 thread. It is suggested that, as an exercise, a further example based on Fig. 16.2 be worked as indicated above but substituting different conditions.

16.6 Estimates of Cutting Times— Intermittent (Rotary) Processes

The cutting time for a milling operation is dependent on the length of cut and the rate of table travel.

(a) *Length of Cut.* It has been shown in Chapter 8 that milling operations are most efficiently carried out when the maximum depth of cut is machined at the appropriate feed rate. The length of cut must include the cutter approach distance, which may be obtained by a scale drawing, or calculated by using Eqn (16.7), (16.8) or (16.9). The time allowed for cutter approach is minimised by the use of string (or line) milling and eliminated by the plunge cut technique, see Fig. 16.8. The latter method will leave a curve at the bottom of a slot: this is often

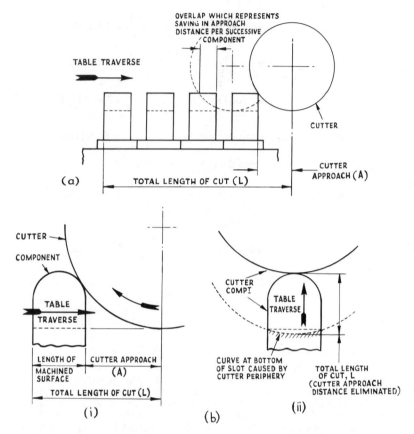

Fig. 16.8 *Methods for reducing total length of cut in peripheral milling operations*

(*a*) String (or line) milling technique

(*b*) Comparison between (i) conventional and (ii) plunge milling showing the elimination of the cutter approach distance in the latter instance

functionally acceptable, and in such cases, if the curve is not shown in the original design, its introduction could be the subject of a worthwhile design modification.

(b) *Rate of Table Travel.* Unlike some other machine tools, the table traverse rate of a milling machine is usually independent of the spindle speed, i.e. a change in rev/min of cutter rotation does not alter the table speed. In determining the traverse rate, provided sufficient power is available and the workpiece is rigid, the limiting factor is the load imposed upon each cutter tooth, which in its turn depends upon the strength of the material being cut and upon the chip thickness. A table of feeds/tooth is shown; Table 16.3 by courtesy of the Cincinnati Milling Machine Co.

TABLE 16.3
Suggested Feeds/Tooth for Milling Cutters (mm)

Material	S and F mills		Helical mills		Face mills		Circular saws		End mills		Form-relieved cutters	
	HSS	Carbide	HSS	Carbide	HSS	Carbide	HSS	Carbide	HSS	Carbide	HSS	Carbide
Aluminium and alloys	0·33	0·30	0·45	0·40	0·56	0·50	0·13	0·13	0·28	0·25	0·18	0·15
Medium brasses and bronzes	0·20	0·18	0·28	0·25	0·35	0·30	0·08	0·08	0·18	0·15	0·10	0·10
Cast iron (180–220 BH)	0·18	0·25	0·25	0·33	0·33	0·40	0·08	0·10	0·18	0·20	0·10	0·13
Malleable iron	0·18	0·20	0·25	0·28	0·30	0·35	0·08	0·10	0·15	0·18	0·10	0·10
Low-carbon steel	0·15	0·20	0·20	0·28	0·25	0·35	0·08	0·10	0·13	0·18	0·08	0·10
Medium-carbon steel	0·15	0·20	0·20	0·28	0·25	0·35	0·08	0·10	0·13	0·18	0·08	0·10
Alloy steel (annealed) (180–220 BH)	0·13	0·20	0·18	0·28	0·20	0·35	0·05	0·10	0·10	0·18	0·08	0·10
Alloy steel, tough (220–300 BH)	0·10	0·18	0·13	0·25	0·15	0·30	0·05	0·08	0·08	0·15	0·05	0·10
Stainless steels	0·10	0·15	0·13	0·20	0·15	0·25	0·05	0·08	0·08	0·13	0·05	0·08

Based on values published by Cincinatti Milling Machine Co. Ltd.

The above table provides a basis for the feed/tooth; in practice these values may be scaled down to take into account variations in cutting conditions such as sharpness of cutter, fragility of component, method of holding workpiece, power at spindle of machine, etc. The number of teeth in a cutter suitable for use with the above feed rates may be obtained from Eqn (16.10) or (16.11).

Example 16.3
Given the following cutting conditions, determine the nearest available table traverse rate:

(a) HSS peripheral slotting cutter, 100 mm dia; 12 teeth; 0·10 mm feed/tooth; $V = 26$ m/min;
(b) HSS end mill, 20 mm dia; 6 teeth; 0·08 mm feed/tooth; $V = 16$ m/min;
(c) Cemented carbide face mill, 250 mm dia; 14 teeth; 0·30 mm feed/tooth; $V = 72$ m/min.

Available spindle speeds (rev/min):

28, 40, 56, 80, 112, 160, 224, 315, 450, 630.

Available feed rates (mm/min):

12·5, 18, 25, 35·5, 50, 71, 100, 140, 200, 280, 400, 560, 800.

Solution

(a) Calculated spindle speed $= \dfrac{10^3 V}{\pi D} = \dfrac{10^3 \times 26}{\pi \times 100} = 82·8$ rev/min

Nearest available spindle speed, $N = 80$ rev/min

∴ From Eqn (16.7),

Calculated table feed $= N \times N_T \times f_t$
$= 80 \times 12 \times 0·10 = 96$ mm/min
Nearest available table feed $= 100$ mm/min

(b) Calculated spindle speed $= \dfrac{10^3 \times 16}{\pi \times 20} = 255$ rev/min

Nearest available speed spindle speed, $N = 224$ rev/min
∴ Calculated table feed $= 224 \times 6 \times 0·08 = 107$ mm/min
Nearest available table feed $= 100$ mm/min

(c) Calculated spindle speed $= \dfrac{10^3 \times 72}{\pi \times 250} = 92$ rev/min

Nearest available spindle speed, $N = 80$ rev/min
∴ Calculated table feed $= 80 \times 14 \times 0·30 = 336$ mm/min
Nearest available table feed $= 280$ mm/min

When it is functionally permissible to mill a flat surface using either a slab or a face milling cutter, a decision must be made as to which method to use. For short components the helical mill method is usually the quicker; for longer components face milling is quicker, the approach distance being important in this connection. This problem will be examined in the following example, which for reasons of comparison is based on the use of HSS cutters and single-piece loading.

Example 16.4
Calculate the cutting times for each of the following, and hence determine whether helical (slab) milling or face milling is the quicker process:

(a) Workpiece—grey cast iron; $V = 18$ m/min; depth of cut, $d = 2·5$ mm; dimensions of surface to be milled, 50 mm long × 76 mm wide.
Cutters: (i) helical mill, 63 mm dia × 45° helix; (ii) face mill 100 mm dia.

(b) Workpiece—grey cast iron; $V = 18$ m/min; depth of cut, $d = 5$ mm; dimensions of surface to be milled, 510 mm long × 100 mm wide.

Cutters: (i) helical mill, 100 mm dia × 45° helix; (ii) face mill, 160 mm dia.

Solution

(a) (i) *For Helical Milling*

No. of teeth in cutter, $N_T = \dfrac{4\pi D}{D + 4d} \times \cos\alpha$ (Eqn (16.10))

$$= \frac{4 \times \pi \times 63}{63 + (4 \times 2\cdot5)} \times \cos 45°$$

gives 8 teeth.

Feed/Tooth, $\quad f_t = 0\cdot25$ mm (Table 16.3)

Approach distance, $\quad A = \sqrt{[d(D - d)]}$ (Eqn (16.7))

$$= \sqrt{[2\cdot5(63 - 2\cdot5)]}$$

$$= 12\cdot3 \text{ mm}$$

Spindle speed, $\quad N = \dfrac{10^3 V}{\pi D} = \dfrac{10^3 \times 18}{\pi \times 63} = 91$ rev/min

Table feed $= N \times N_T \times f_t$ (Eqn (16.5))

$$= 91 \times 8 \times 0\cdot25 = 182 \text{ mm/min}$$

Time for 1 cut, $t = \dfrac{L}{N \times N_T \times f_t}$ (Eqn (16.6))

$$= \frac{50 + 12\cdot3}{182}$$

$$= 0\cdot35 \text{ min}$$

(ii) *For Face Milling*

No. of teeth in cutter, $N_T = \dfrac{2\pi D}{b}$ (Eqn (16.11))

$$= \frac{2 \times \pi \times 100}{76}$$

gives 8 teeth

$$f_t = 0\cdot33 \text{ mm (Table 16.3)}$$

$$A = \frac{D}{2} - \sqrt{\left(\frac{D^2}{4} - \frac{b^2}{4}\right)}$$ (Eqn (16.8))

$$= \frac{100}{2} - \sqrt{\left(\frac{100^2}{4} - \frac{76^2}{4}\right)}$$

$$= 17\cdot5 \text{ mm}$$

$$N = \frac{10^3 \times 18}{\pi \times 100} = 57 \text{ rev/min}$$

Table feed $= 57 \times 8 \times 0\cdot33 = 150$ mm/min

$\therefore$ Time for 1 cut, $t = \dfrac{50 + 17\cdot5}{150} = 0\cdot45$ min

(b) (i) *For Helical Milling*

$$N_T = \frac{4 \times \pi \times 100}{100 + (4 \times 5)} \times \cos 45°$$

$$\text{gives 7 teeth}$$

$$f_t = 0·25 \text{ mm}$$

$$A = \sqrt{[5(100-5)]} = 22 \text{ mm}$$

$$N = \frac{10^3 \times 18}{\pi \times 100} = 57 \text{ rev/min}$$

Table feed $= 57 \times 7 \times 0·25 = 100 \text{ mm/min}$

Time for 1 cut, $t = \dfrac{510 + 22}{100} = \underline{5·32 \text{ min}}$

(ii) *For Face Milling*

$$N_T = \frac{2 \times \pi \times 160}{100} \text{ gives 10 teeth}$$

$$f_t = 0·33 \text{ mm}$$

$$A = \frac{160}{2} - \sqrt{\left(\frac{160^2}{4} - \frac{100^2}{4}\right)} = 18 \text{ mm}$$

$$N = \frac{10^3 \times 18}{\pi \times 160} = 36 \text{ rev/min}$$

Table feed $= 36 \times 10 \times 0·33 = 119 \text{ mm/min}$

Time for 1 cut, $\therefore$ $t = \dfrac{510 + 18}{119} = \underline{4·44 \text{ mm}}$

The above example serves to illustrate the general rule stated earlier that helical milling is suitable for short lengths of cut (compare times for part (a)), but for generating long surfaces, face milling is quicker (compare times for part (b)).

16.7 Work Handling and Machine Manipulation

In small quantity batches of work the proportion of the floor-to-floor time required for handling and manipulation is usually high, but for large-quantity batch work the greatest proportion of time should be spent as productive cutting time with handling and manipulation time at a minimum. If the latter activities take up too great a proportion of the time the method of processing should be examined with a view to finding a quicker and cheaper way of doing the work.

The elements involved in handling and manipulation are as follows:

(i) initial setting-up of machine;
(ii) loading and unloading of component;

(iii) manipulation of machine during its operation (e.g. winding cross-slide by hand, gear changing);
    (iv) measuring and gauging;
    (v) changing and re-setting tools.

In addition to the above items, allowances are made for contingencies, fatigue and personal reasons. The magnitude of these allowances will depend upon the demands made on the operator by the work being performed. In many cases agreed allowances are applied as a routine measure each time a new estimate is made, but more consistent results will be achieved by the use of charts or graphs, such as the Merrick allowance curves, which indicate the percentage to be added to handling times to cover contingencies.

If the FFT for a component is 15 min, of which 3·15 min is handling time and the remainder cutting time, the allowance for contingencies may be derived from the Merrick Allowance Curves shown in Fig 16.9, as follows:

$$\text{Handling time as a percentage of FFT} = \frac{3 \cdot 15}{15} \times 100 = 21\%$$

hence the 20% Curve of Fig 16.9 is used.
From the graph, contingency allowance for 3·15 min handling time = 43%

$$\therefore \quad \text{Contingency Allowance} = 3 \cdot 15 \times \frac{43}{100} = 1 \cdot 35 \, \text{min}$$

$$\therefore \quad \text{Total Time} = 15 + 1 \cdot 35 = \underline{16 \cdot 35 \, \text{min}}$$

As mentioned in **16.2**, the most rational basis for estimating handling times is a series of charts giving "synthetic" times. These may be readily compiled for a given machine by practical time studies, examples of charts compiled in this way are given in Tables 16.4, 16.5 and 16.6.

Setting Times. The time allowed for the preparatory work prior to the commencement of a machining operation may, in practice, be in the form of a standard allowance, but where it is necessary to build-up estimates for setting times this can be done by using synthetic times for each element of the setting operation. Charts for this purpose can be readily compiled or reference can be made to published data. *Estimating Machining Times*, by T. W. Gorgon (Machinery Publishing Co.) gives many useful charts and tables in this connection.

Measuring and Gauging Allowances. Where measuring or gauging of a component has to be carried out during the period covered by the floor-to-floor times, time allowances may be estimated by reference to charts such as those mentioned above.

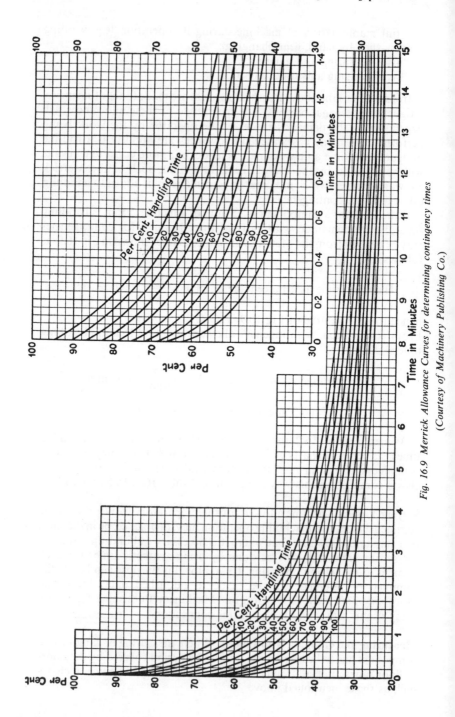

Fig. 16.9 Merrick Allowance Curves for determining contingency times
(Courtesy of Machinery Publishing Co.)

TABLE 16.4

Handling and Manipulating Times for a 350 mm Centre Lathe

No.	Element		Time	
			Sec	Min
1	Load/unload between centres with driving carrier	Weight, 1 kg	20	0·33
		Weight, 2	30	0·50
		Weight, 4	40	0·67
		Weight, 8	50	0·83
2	Load/unload in self-centring chuck	Weight, 1 kg	30	0·50
		Weight, 2	40	0·67
		Weight, 4	50	0·83
		Weight, 8	60	1·0
3	Start/stop spindle		2	0·03
4	Reverse spindle		2	0·03
5	Change speed		3	0·05
6	Change feed		4	0·07
7	Engage/disengage feed		1	0·02
8	Index toolpost		2	0·03
9	Approach tool, set to mark, return (turning)		3	0·05
10	Approach tool, set to mark, return (boring)		5	0·08
11	Wind cross-slide 50–100 mm		6	0·1
12	Wind main saddle 75–150 mm		3	0·05
13	Wind main saddle 150–500 mm		6	0·1
14	Fit/remove tool in tailstock		10	0·17
15	Approach/remove tailstock		15	0·25
16	Advance/return tailstock barrel 50 mm		8	0·13

Tooling Allowances. If a single cutting tool is in use during an operation, establishing the time allowance per component for tool changing is a simple matter. Where a number of tools are in use (as, for example, in a capstan lathe) the calculation becomes more involved, and an estimate sufficiently accurate for most practical purposes may be made as follows:

Let C = Total cutting time per component (min)
M = Average tool life per tool (min)
N = Number of tools in set-up
t = Average time to reset one tool (min)

Then, assuming tools operate consecutively,

$$\text{Total tool life} = M \times N \text{ (min)}$$

also,

$$\text{Number of components for a complete set of tool changes} = \frac{MN}{C}$$

TABLE 16.5

Handling and Manipulating Times for a Plain Milling Machine
(250 × 1250 mm *Table*)

No.	Element	Time	
		Sec	Min
1	Switch motor, on/off	5	0·08
2	Start/stop spindle	3	0·05
3	Engage/disengage feed	4	0·07
4	Change spindle speed	6	0·1
5	Change feed rate	5	0·08
6	Approach component to cutter, set to dial reading	6	0·1
7	Approach component to cutter, use feeler gauges, set table to position	12	0·2
8	Wind table, 100 mm table-slide	6	0·1
9	Wind table, 100 mm cross-slide	12	0·2
10	Wind table, 100 mm vertical slide	36	0·6

Note: Rapid traverse for table and knee movement is available on most milling machines and is normally at a constant rate for each direction.

TABLE 16.6

Handling and Manipulating Times for a Capstan Lathe
(50 mm *Diameter Bar Capacity*)

No.	Element		Time	
			Sec	Min
1	Load/unload in self-centring chuck	Weight, 1 kg	30	0·50
		Weight, 2	40	0·67
		Weight, 4	50	0·83
		Weight, 8	60	1·0
2	Feed bar to stop—self-centering chuck		15	0·25
3	Feed bar to stop—collet		8	0·13
4	Load/unload in collet (per component)		6	0·10
5	Start/stop spindle		2	0·03
6	Reverse spindle		2	0·03
7	Change speed (two levers)		3	0·05
8	Change feed		4	0·07
9	Engage/disengage feed		1	0·02
10	Index tool-post, advance to workpiece, set to mark, return		8	0·13
11	Index turret, clamp, advance to workpiece, return, unclamp		5	0·08
12	Wind cross-slide, 50–100 mm		5	0·08
13	Wind saddle, 75–150 mm		3	0·05
14	Set self-opening diehead (double setting + and −)		4	0·07

$$\therefore \quad \text{allowance/component/tool} = \frac{C}{MN} \times t \text{ min}$$

Hence, $\quad$ allowance/component for N tools $= \dfrac{Ct}{M}$ min. $\quad$ (16.14)

This may be extended to cover machining operations in which combined tooling is used, e.g. a turret-lathe operation involving the use of a knee toolholder supporting several tools.

Let N_1 = number of operations involving the use of single point tools

$\quad N_2$ = total number of single point tools used

Then, $\qquad$ tool allowance/component $= \dfrac{Ct \, N_2}{M \, N_1}$. $\qquad$ (16.15)

Example 16.5
Determine the allowance per component for tool changes on a turret lathe, given the following conditions:

(a) Total cutting time/component, $\quad C = 8$ min
$\quad$ Average tool life, $\qquad\qquad M = 60$ min
$\quad$ Number of tools, $\qquad\qquad\;\, N = 11$
$\quad$ Average time to reset 1 tool, $\quad t = 10$ min.

(b) As above, but with combined tooling set on 11 tool positions and using a total of 15 tools.

Solution

(a) From Eqn (16.14)

$$\text{Tool allowance per component} = \frac{Ct}{M} = \frac{8 \times 10}{60} = 1\tfrac{1}{3} \text{ min}$$

(b) From Eqn (16.15),

$$\text{Tool allowance per component} = \frac{Ct \, N^2}{M \, N_1}$$

$$= \frac{8 \times 10}{60} \times \frac{15}{11} = 1\cdot82 \text{ min}$$

16.8 Economic Comparision of Alternative Processes

A valuable use of an estimate is in making a comparison between the manufacturing costs of two or more rival production methods and selecting the most profitable; or alternatively, determining at what quantity one method ceases and another begins to be the cheapest process. This is termed the "break-even point".

A typical example of a break-even point is in deciding at what quantity to change from machining a component on a centre lathe to machining it on a capstan lathe, see **16.9**.

The advantages of a centre lathe are its universality and adaptability in turning a wide variety of components to a good degree of accuracy, but inevitably there are some turned components which can be produced equally well on capstan or turret lathes. The advantages of these latter machines can be summarised as follows:

(*a*) After the initial set-up the time spent in tool changing is reduced (there are 11 tool positions available, and combined tooling can be mounted on the turret faces). For small quantity work a simple basic set-up should be used.

(*b*) Trips for auto-feed and fixed stops on cross-slide and longitudinal saddle movements ensure consistent work, reduce gauging and eliminate the use of a rule.

(*c*) Accurate diameters are achieved by tool-setting, e.g. roller box, Fig 16.10, or—if the cross slide is being used—by means of large dials, indicator tabs, or a dial gauge as shown in Fig 16.11.

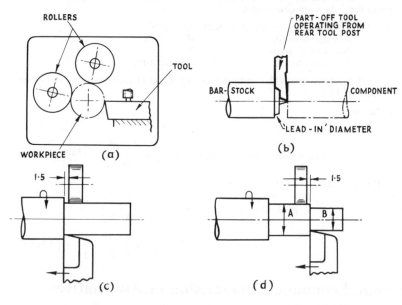

Fig. 16.10

(*a*) Principle of roller-steady turning box
(*b*) Method of providing "lead-in" for roller-box
(*c*) Normal roller setting to produce burnished finish
(*d*) Roller setting to produce concentricity between diameters A and B

(*d*) Overlapped operations can be introduced, i.e. the operator can perform work from the cross-slide while the hexagon turret is on automatic feed.

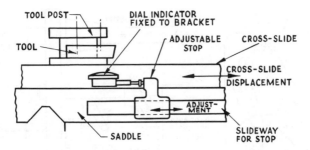

TOOL POST

DIAL INDICATOR
FIXED TO BRACKET

TOOL

ADJUSTABLE
STOP

CROSS-SLIDE

CROSS-SLIDE
DISPLACEMENT

ADJUST-
MENT

SADDLE

SLIDEWAY
FOR STOP

Fig. 16.11 Production of work-piece diameters to close tolerances may be achieved by accurate tool positioning using a dial indicator fixed to the lathe cross-slide

(*e*) Rapid spindle-speed changes can be made—often without stopping the machine; where the machine has a pre-selective head-stock, speeds can be changed with the cut still engaged without detriment to the tool.

Example 16.6
A turret lathe set-up using combination knee tooling is shown in Fig 16.12, the material being cut is a nickel alloy steel for which the specific cutting pressure (P) is 2070 N/mm². The relevant dimensions are tabulated below:

Dimension	Dia (mm)	Length (mm)	Depth of cut (mm)
A	200	98	3·8
C	150	50	3·8
C	76	58	4·5
Chamfer on C dia		9·5 × 45°	
D	58	108	3·0

If the turret feed rate is 0·22 mm/rev and the tooling permits a maximum cutting speed of 45 m/min, find:

    (*a*) cutting time;
    (*b*) power required at the chuck;
    (*c*) torque at the chuck and the tangential force at each jaw assuming 3 jaws are gripping at 90 mm radius.

Solution
    (*a*) The cutting time will be governed by the time taken to traverse the greatest length at a spindle speed which ensures that no tool is cutting at more than 45 m/min. Clearly, the maximum cutting speed will occur at *A* dia.

$$\therefore \quad N = \frac{10^3 V}{\pi D} = \frac{10^3 \times 45}{\pi \times 200} = 72 \text{ rev/min}$$

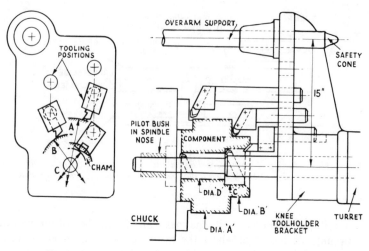

Fig. 16.12 Combination knee tooling on a capstan or turret lathe

The maximum length of cut is 108 mm; hence, using Eqn (16.4),

$$\text{Cutting time, } t = \frac{L}{N \cdot f}$$

$$= \frac{108}{72 + 0.22}$$

$$= 6.82 \text{ min}$$

(b) The force acting on a cutting tool is given by

$$\text{Force} = \text{Depth of cut} \times \text{Feed} \times \text{Specific cutting pressure}$$

Force (N) = Pdf, where P is in N/mm² d and f in mm

$$\text{Force} = 2070 \times 0.22 \times d$$

$$= 455.4d \text{ newtons}$$

$$\text{Power (W)} = \frac{\text{Force} \times \pi DN}{10^3 \times 60} \qquad (N = 72 \text{ rev/min, } D \text{ is in mm})$$

$$= \frac{455.4\, d \times \pi D \times 72}{10^3 \times 60}$$

$$= 1.717dD \text{ watts.}$$

Hence, total power $= 1.717\left[(3.8 \times 200) + (3.8 \times 150) + (4.5 \times 76) + (9.5 \times 76)\right.$
$$\left. + (3 \times 75)\right]$$

$$= 1.717 \times 2620$$

$$= 4496 \text{ W } (4.5 \text{ kW}).$$

(c) Power (W) = torque (Nm) $\times \theta$ (rad/s) $\left(\theta = \dfrac{72\pi}{30}\right)$

$$\therefore \quad \text{torque} = \frac{4496 \times 30}{72 \times \pi}$$

$$= \underline{596 \text{ Nm}}$$

$$\text{Tangential force} = \frac{596 \times 10^3}{90}$$

$$= 6630 \text{ N}$$

Tangential force per jaw = $\underline{2210 \text{ N} \ (2\cdot21 \text{ kN})}$.

16.9 "Break-even" Quantities

The component shown in Fig 16.13 could be machined on either a centre or capstan lathe. The question arises, what is the smallest quantity that could be economically turned on a capstan lathe? This can be solved on a time basis—or, better still, on a basis of cost, provided the monetary values of the hourly rates are available.

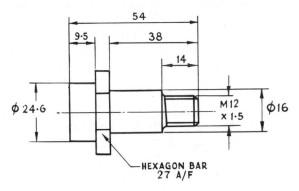

Fig. 16.13

Example 16.7
Find the "break-even" quantity if the estimated cost for producing the component shown in Fig 16.14 by alternative methods is as follows:

Method	Initial setting time	FFT	Cost/hour of setting	Cost/hour of operating
Capstan lathe	2 h	4 min	£10	£7
Centre lathe	$\frac{1}{2}$ h	25 min	£8	£8

(a) On a time basis, the break-even quantity will occur when the time for producing x components by each method is equal, i.e. when

time for producing x components on capstan lathe
= time for producing x components on centre lathe

i.e. capstan setting time + (capstan FFT × x)
= lathe setting time + (lathe FFT × x)

$$\therefore \quad 120 + 4x = 30 + 25x$$

$$\therefore x = 90/21 = 4 \cdot 3 \text{ components.}$$

$\therefore$ **On a time basis, it is quicker to produce up to 4 components on a centre lathe. For batches of 5 components or more the capstan lathe is the quicker machine to use.**

(b) On a basis of cost, the break-even point occurs when

  cost for producing x components on capstan lathe

        = cost for producing x components on centre lathe

i.e. cost of setting on capstan + ($x \times$ cost each on capstan)

        = cost of setting on lathe + ($x \times$ cost each on lathe)

$$(2 \times 10) + \left(7 \times \frac{4}{60}\right)x = (\tfrac{1}{2} \times 8) + \left(8 \times \frac{25}{60}\right)x$$

$$20 + \frac{7}{15}x = 4 + \frac{10}{3}x$$

$$\therefore \quad x = 5 \cdot 6 \text{ components.}$$

$\therefore$ **On a cost basis, batches of up to 5 components should be produced on a centre lathe; above this quantity the capstan lathe provides the cheaper method.**

The same principle as used in the foregoing example can be applied when deciding between using a capstan or an automatic lathe for a given component. In such cases, since the setting time is more costly than operating time, the appropriate rates should be taken into consideration.

Example 16.8

What would be the break-even quantity when considering the choice of a multi-spindle auto-lathe against a capstan lathe given the following information?

Element	Capstan lathe	Auto-lathe
Set-up time	1 h	6 h
Operating time	10 min	2 min
Set-up labour costs	£2·8/h	£2·8/h
Operating labour costs	£2/h	£0·8/h
Tooling cost	Nil	£80
Machine overheads	£6/h	£11·2/h

Solution

Total cost (C_c) of producing x components on capstan lathe (£):

$$C_c = \text{tooling cost} + \text{set-up cost} + x \text{ (cost/component)}$$

$$= 0 + (2 \cdot 8 + 6) + x\left\{\frac{10}{60}(2 + 6)\right\}$$

$$= 8 \cdot 8 + \tfrac{4}{3}x.$$

Total cost (C_A) of producing x components on auto-lathe (£):

$$C_A = \text{Tooling cost} + \text{Set-up cost} + x \text{ (Cost/component)}$$

$$= 80 + 6(2 \cdot 8 + 11 \cdot 2) + x\left\{\frac{2}{60}(0 \cdot 8 + 11 \cdot 2)\right\}$$

$$= 80 + 84 + \tfrac{2}{5}x$$
$$= 164 + \tfrac{2}{5}x.$$

Break-even point occurs when $C_c = C_A$

i.e. $\qquad\qquad 8\cdot8 + \tfrac{4}{3}x = 164 + \tfrac{2}{5}x$

$$\therefore \quad x = 166\cdot3.$$

∴. **The capstan lathe would provide the cheaper method for quantities up to 166 components; for greater quantities than this the multi-spindle automatic lathe would provide the cheaper method.**

In both the foregoing examples the quantity of components required for the costs of the alternative methods to break-even is lower than general practice on these types of machines would suggest. There are several reasons for this:

(i) The time taken per component for the first few of a batch is usually greater than the standard time. This applies particularly to capstan lathes (with automatic lathes the cycle time fixed).

(ii) The scrap rate may be higher for the first components produced.

(iii) Small batches on capstan and auto-lathes require a skilled operator; semi-skilled operators usually prefer a continuous flow of the same component.

(iv) Where piece-work is practised, large quantity batches usually provide good monetary earnings for the operator. High earnings are difficult to achieve on small batches unless the management is prepared to make an extra allowance for this class of work.

However, from the economic analysis it is clear that where alternative machines are available for a given operation relative costs should be carefully compared and the cheapest process chosen.

EXERCISES 16

1. Using data from Example 16.6 (page 527), determine for the tools which are cutting diameters A, B, C and D in Fig 16.13, the following:

(a) metal removal rate in mm^3/s
(b) power (W) per mm^3/s of metal removed.

2. Finish-turned steel bushes 0·25 kg in weight are to have a single hole drilled and reamed through their 6·5 mm thick wall on a two-spindle drilling machine. The jig used weighs 3 kg and has spigot location with C-washer clamping. Select suitable feeds and speeds for drilling and reaming and prepare an estimated time for the complete operation, making suitable allowances for manipulation and contingencies.

3. (a) Briefly state the economic advantages of the capstan lathe as compared with the centre lathe. What function does the centre lathe fulfil which explains its continued usefulness?

(b) Explain with the aid of sketches the essential differences in the processes used for turning the component shown in Fig 16.14 when:

(i) ONE is required;
(ii) 500 are required.

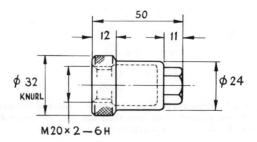

Fig. 16.14

4. Prepare a process layout for producing the duralumin housing. Fig 16.15, on a capstan lathe designed to use cemented carbide tooling.

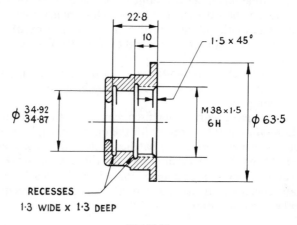

Fig. 16.15

5. Estimate a production time for machining the housing, Fig 16.15, in accordance with the layout prepared for Question 4 above and the following data.

Available spindle speeds: 550, 660, 800, 960, 1150, 1380, 1650, 2000 (a reduction ratio of $\frac{1}{5}$ of these speeds is available for screwing operations).

Available feeds (turret only): 0·3, 0·2, 0·15, 0·10 mm/rev

Cutting speeds: roughing 120 m/min; finishing 180 m/min; tapping 12 m/min.

Allow an average life per tool of 100 min with an average time for tool changing of 10 min/tool. The allowance for contingencies should be based on the Merrick Curves, Fig 16.9

6. (a) State the factors which affect the establishment of metal cutting speeds, explaining the meaning of the term "tool life".

(b) Estimate the total production time for a batch of 300 components to be milled two at a time in a fixture on a horizontal milling machine given that:

Length of each workpiece = 230 mm (assume held end-to-end)
Approach   = 32 mm
Over-run   = 20 mm
Feed/tooth   = 0·25 mm
Number of teeth in cutter = 10
Rev/min of cutter   = 80

Assume that the time allowed for loading, unloading and cleaning is $1\frac{1}{2}$ min/cycle and that other allowances amount to $\frac{1}{2}$ min/cycle.

7. Estimate the FFT per gear from the following data referring to the generation of teeth at one cut on a pinion-type cutter machine.

Gear Data (product)
  60 teeth, 4 module, depth of tooth = 9 *mm*
Machine Data
  Cutter feeds to depth.

Feed/stroke   = 0·05 mm
Stroke/min   = 250
Strokes/mm of PCD = 8

Assume that the idle time is 15% of the cutting time.

8. In a milling operation it is required to remove metal to a depth of 6·5 mm from a face 100 mm wide at a cutting speed of 60 m/min. A face milling cutter is used with 12 teeth and outside diameter 150 mm, the tooth loading being 0·10 mm/tooth.

(a) Determine the spindle speed and table feed rate.
(b) What is the rate of metal removal at full load?
(c) Calculate the approach distance of the cutter and state the significance of this value in estimating operation times.

9. Vice screws as shown in Fig 16.16 are to be produced in batches of 500 from diameter BDMS on a suitable sized capstan lathe using HSS tools.

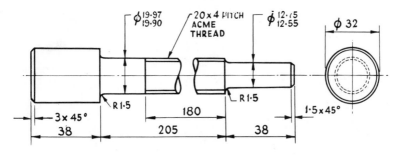

Fig. 16.16

(a) List the operations required in correct sequence, naming the tools and stations used.
(b) Choose suitable speeds and feeds and calculate the machining time. Estimate the times for all other operations and so arrive at the "floor-to-floor" time.

10. (*a*) Describe the purpose and use of a machine capacity chart as used in a tool drawing office, stating clearly any advantages likely to be gained from the use of charted information.

(*b*) Prepare a machine capacity chart for a range of medium-size horizontal milling machines.

11. Determine the production quantity at which the manufacturing costs of the following two alternative methods break-even:

	Numerically controlled miller	Conventional miller
Depreciation/h	£8	£2
Overheads/h	£6	£4
Setter operator rate/h	£2·8	£2·8
Programming cost	£8	—
Computer cost	£12	—
Machining time	$\frac{1}{2}$ h	$1\frac{1}{2}$ h
Set-up time	$\frac{1}{2}$ h	1

CHAPTER 17
Principles of Planning And Tool Design

17.1 Production Planning

Planning the manufacture of an assembled product may be straight-forward or complicated, depending upon the product. Consider the following assemblies:

    (a) simple drill jig;
    (b) retractable ball-point pen;
    (c) saloon car.

Only one jig, item (a), would be required, and since it is a simple jig, there would be few component parts. The manufacture of each part would be carried out by skilled men following conventional practices, and the co-ordination necessary to bring the components together upon their completion, ready for assembly, would be easily achieved. Planning is minimal.

Item (b) is essentially a mass-produced article built up from six to eight components. Since the manufacture of each part is repeated hundreds of thousands of times, it is worthwhile considering every conceivable method of manufacture to keep down costs. The design of each component of the pen would be analysed to see whether savings could be made by making modifications to simplify and cheapen manufacture without affecting the functioning of the pen. However, since so few parts are involved, the co-ordination necessary to bring them together for assembly would be simple to arrange.

The production of (c) is much more complex. In the first place, the main assembly (i.e. the car) is composed of major sub-assemblies—engine, gearbox, rear axle, etc., and in each of these there are smaller sub-assemblies—carburettor, clutch plate, differential, etc., which in turn involve smaller sub-assemblies. The number of different components is very great, the manufacture of many of them is complicated and involves a lot of operations. To co-ordinate the multiplicity of components and sub-assemblies for the assembly lines requires a complex organisation, especially when it is remembered that the parts must be delivered at the right place at the right time, and in the right order—it is useless for, say, a red wheel to arrive at the assembly line if a green car is being assembled.

535

The Basic Principle. Even though wide differences exist in products and in problems of production, the same principles are applied in planning production—but the extent of the preparatory planning will vary widely according to the economic benefit which can be derived from it. *The basic principle in all cases is to break down the assembly into sub-assemblies, and then into component parts*; once this is done, the task is of manageable proportions and the manufacture of an individual component can be considered in detail.

General Factors in Production Planning. Questions to be answered when planning the production of manufactured articles include the following.

(a) How many articles are required? Upon the answer to this question depends the methods used in manufacture and the amount of money which can be spent on tooling and equipment.

(b) What time is available for—

(i) preparation, i.e. material ordering, planning, design and manufacture of tooling;
(ii) manufacture of the components?

Those components requiring the greatest length of time in planning and production, and needing most tooling, must be dealt with first of all. If the available time is short it may not be possible to embark on a full tooling programme, and relatively simple tooling which is quickly made will be used. Using such methods, machining costs will be increased, and this is one-reason why rushed jobs are expensive to produce.

(c) What types of machines are available for the work?

(d) What form and size of raw material is most economic for a given component? E.g. if castings are required should these be sand castings, shell mouldings, gravity or pressure die castings?

(e) Are there any uneconomic features or foreseeable difficulties involved in manufacturing the component?

Note: This particular question is best dealt with in the design office before the components reach the point of manufacture. Many firms employ production specialists to co-operate with the drawing-office staff at the design stage to ensure the designs are suitable for economic production. Designers and Production Engineers are specialists in their own field, but they share a common duty—to pool their ability in a co-operative effort to market an efficient, functionally sound article at a reasonable cost. Unnecessary elaboration in design increases production cost, and the customer pays extra for a feature which adds nothing to the value of the article concerned. Fig 17.1 illustrates how a simple change in design can produce economies in production.

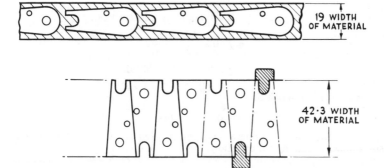

19 WIDTH OF MATERIAL

42·3 WIDTH OF MATERIAL

Fig. 17.1. An example of a design modification which reduces cost/component without adversely affecting functional performance

(a) Material utilisation = 54·3 %
   Number of components/stroke = 1
   Rate of production = 0·024 hour/100
   Cost of tool = £1100
(b) Material utilisation = 88·9 %
   Number of components/stroke = 2
   Rate of production = 0·012 hour/100
   Cost of tool = £870

(*f*) Will the entire quantity be manufactured as a single batch, or will there be several batches spread over a period of time? The customer may require deliveries to be evenly spaced over, say, twelve months: in these circumstances the most economical batch to produce should be determined. This may be calculated using the expression

$$\text{Batch size} = \sqrt{\frac{2CP}{I}} \qquad (17.1)$$

where C = rate of consumption (units/unit time);
      P = preparation costs;
      I = cost of interest on articles in stock per unit time (cost per unit/unit time).

Example 17.1
   Determine the minimum-cost batch size for producing an assembly costing £50 to produce, which is sold at the rate of 1000 per year, if the setting-up and general preparation costs are £25 per batch and the interest rate per annum for articles in stock is 10%. Assume a 5-day week and 50 working weeks/year.

Solution
   Let unit time = 1 day
   Working days/year = 5 × 50 = 250 days
   Rate of consumption of product/day, C = 1000/250 = 4

Interest Cost/unit time, I = Cost/assembly × Interest rate × $\dfrac{1}{250}$

$$= £\,50 \times \frac{10}{100} \times \frac{1}{250}$$

$$= £\,0.02 \text{ per assembly/day.}$$

From Eqn (16.1), Batch Size $= \sqrt{\dfrac{2CP}{I}} = \sqrt{\dfrac{2 \times 4 \times £\,25}{£\,0.02}}$

$$= \underline{100 \text{ assemblies}}.$$

Notes: The simple example above is given to emphasise that choice of batch size should be determined by rational methods and not by guesswork. Detailed treatment of optimum batch sizes occurs in *Elements of Production Planning and Control*, by S. Eilon (Macmillan).

17.2 Process Planning

With the product assembly separated into individual components, planning of the manufacturing processes for each part is carried out and the tooling requirements stated. Particulars of the material requirements and the standard tools and gauges needed for production are given to the purchase department, so that orders may be placed for them. Requests for the special jigs, fixtures, tools and gauges are passed to the tool design office so that the design of such equipment may commence. During the process of tool design, advantages arising from an alternative production method may make a modification to the planned sequence desirable. Consultation with the Planning Department is necessary to effect such a change.

Example 17.2

Consider the manufacture of the Pipe Connection, Fig 17.2, in alternative quantities of (*a*) 10 off, (*b*) 1000 off, and prepare process layouts showing the sequence of operations. Material: Al. Alloy. Form of material unspecified.

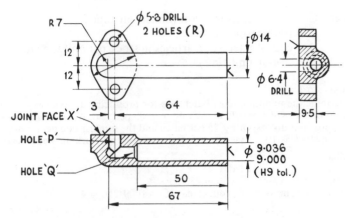

Fig. 17.2 Pipe connection in aluminium alloy (machine where marked √)

Solution (*a*) 10 Pipe Connections

Form of Material Supply. The form in which the material is required must first be chosen. The choice can be made from: solid bar, forging, sand casting, shell moulding, gravity die casting, pressure die casting.

Solid bar: Very lengthy machining operations would be necessary, and this would make the cost prohibitive.

Forging: The necessary dies required to produce forgings are too costly for them to be employed on small-batch-quantity work.

Sand Casting: Pattern required. This is a very simple pattern and would be inexpensive.

Shell Moulding: Gravity Die Casting; Pressure Die Casting: The tool costs for these forms of material would not be justified for 10 castings. These methods of producing the casting are suitable for larger quanties and will be considered for part (*b*) of this question.

From the above considerations it is clear that sand castings would be the most suitable form of materials to supply for a quantity of 10 components.

Machining. The operations for producing the pipe connector fall into three groups, i.e. producing

(i) the flat surface (X) on the flange;
(ii) the holes co-axial with the 14 mm diameter cylinder;
(iii) the holes perpendicular to the flange face.

A number of different procedures can be employed, but the choice is narrowed because it is necessary to produce a machined surface which can be used as a datum for the subsequent operations.

Method I—By first producing the flat surface (X)

Once the joint face (X) has been machined it provides an accurate surface from which the other operations may be performed.

The quantity (10 off) is insufficient to justify drill jigs, and the position of the holes must be marked-out.

Hole P breaks into *one side* of hole Q, and if it were machined first it would interfere with the drilling of Q, therefore the reverse procedure must apply, i.e. hole Q must be produced *before* hole P.

Holes P and R are perpendicular to the joint face (X), and if their positions are marked-out they may be drilled in a single operation. The sequence would then be as shown in Table 17.1.

Method II—By first producing the 9·036/9·000 mm dia hole

As an alternative to drilling the 9·036/9·000 dia hole on a drilling machine, it can be produced on a lathe. This method eliminates marking out for this hole (but not for the others) and has an advantage if the aluminium castings are not homogeneous, i.e. if "blow holes" or other inconsistencies are present in the metal structure. Such defects would cause the drill to deflect from its true path when using a drilling machine due to the resistance to cutting being unequal about the axis, but when drilling on a lathe *the defects will rotate-around the drill*, and deflection of the drill is less likely to occur (see Fig 17.4). The operation sequence would then be as shown in Table 17.2.

Summary

Method I is simpler than Method II for the following reasons:

(i) Setting the drilling machine to produce the 9·036/9·000 hole is simpler than setting the lathe, and does not involve making a split ring.

TABLE 17.1

Op. No.	Description of operation	Machine	Method of holding component
1	Mill face "X" using end mill	Vert. mill	Support on parallel in vice, Fig 17.3(*a*)
2	Mark out holes, P, Q and R	Fitting bench	
3	Drill 8·3 dia × 50 deep, 6·4 dia × 67 deep, ream 9·036/9·000 dia and spotface to 64 dimension	Drilling m/c	Grip in vice, joint face against fixed jaw, small vee block against 14 dia cylindrical surface, Fig 17.3(*b*)
4	Drill 1 hole P and 2 holes R	Drilling m/c	Vice

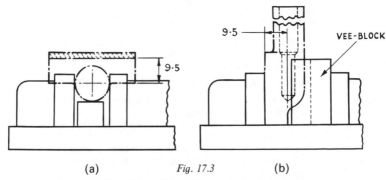

(a)   *Fig. 17.3*   (b)

(*a*) Set-up for milling pipe connection joint face
(*b*) Component held for drilling

Note that the machined flange face is positioned against the fixed vice jaw, thus avoiding inaccuracy caused by the moving vice jaw "lifting" (due to wear in the vice slides) when the vice is tightened

(ii) Milling the joint face *after* producing the hole means that considerable care must be taken to set the hole horizontal and a 9 mm dia test bar has to be used.

The only advantage of Method II is the one concerning homogeneity mentioned above and Method I would be used unless difficulty was experienced in producing a straight hole.

Solution (*b*) 1000 Pipe Connectors

Form of Material Supply. For the required quantity of 1000 pipe connectors, forging, shell moulding and gravity die casting can be considered as suitable methods for forming the component material; pressure die castings would require very expensive tooling and cannot be considered for quantities less than,

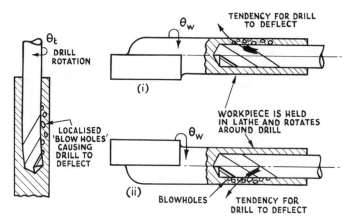

Fig. 17.4

(*a*) Non-homogeneous metal structure provides asymmetrical resistance to cutting, and as a result the drill deflects

(*b*) When the workpiece is rotated around a stationary drill the tendency for the drill to deflect is balanced and a straighter hole produced

TABLE 17.2

Op. No.	Description of operation	Machine	Method of holding component
1	Face 14 dia to 64 length, centre drill, drill 8·3 dia × 50 deep,6·4 dia × 67 deep, ream 9·036/9·000 hole	Lathe	Grip on 14 dia in 3-jaw chuck using split ring if necessary, Fig 17.5(*a*)
2	Mill face X using end mill	Vert. mill	Grip on 14 dia in vice, set horizontal using test bar in 9·036/9·000 hole, Fig 17.5(*b*) support with jack.
3	Mark-out holes P and R	Fitting bench	
4	Drill 1 hole P and 2 holes R	Drilling m/c	Vice

say, 10 000 castings. Technically, all of the suggested methods are acceptable; for the casting processes, accuracy of form would be ± 0.08 mm or less and the surface finish would be better than for sand castings. Since all methods are technically acceptable, the choice should be made on economic grounds, i.e. which method is the cheapest? The answer to this question can be resolved—not as a matter of opinion—but as a matter of fact. Quotations should be obtained from suppliers for the alternative forms of material and the cheapest type chosen, consistent with reliability in quality and delivery dates. With a high standard of

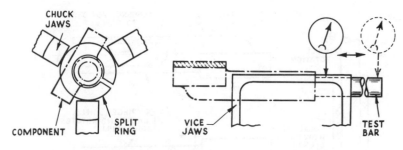

Fig. 17.5

(a) Use of split ring to adapt component to a three-jaw chuck
(b) Setting axis of 9·000/9·036 mm diameter hole level, prior to machining flange

general accuracy in forming the materials it is often possible to eliminate some machining, e.g. the two holes "R" or the face "X". The savings thus made in machining time and tooling costs can be set against the extra cost of precision forming methods, further justifying their use.

In this example we will assume shell mouldings are selected, with the two clearance holes "R" being cored in the casting. The operation sequence could then be as shown in Table 17.3

TABLE 17.3

Op. No.	Description of operation	Machine	Location surfaces	Tooling
1	Mill face "X" using end mill	Milling m/c	14 dia	Milling fixture or special vice jaws
2	Face 14 dia to 64 length centre drill, drill 8·3 dia × 50 deep and 6·4 dia × 67 deep. Ream 9.000/9.036	Capstan	Face "X" and 14 dia	Turning fixture
3	Drill 1 − 6·4 dia hole	Drilling m/c	Face "X", 9·036/9·000 bore and end face of 14 dia	Drill jig

17.3 Economic Basis for Machining Methods

Apart from eliminating the marking-out and drilling of holes "R", the main difference between the procedure for machining 10 and 1000 components is in the use of special tooling. The quantity at which tooling is *economically* justifiable (see p. 000) can be determined by calculating the break-even points for alternative methods. Break-even points were calculated in **16.9** for the capstan lathe and its alternatives, and this is now extended to include the economics of purchasing tools and new machines.

Tooling is economically justified when:

Total machining cost per piece without tooling
> **Total machining cost per piece using tooling + Tooling cost per piece.**

where,

Total machining cost per piece
= Labour cost per piece + Machine and overhead cost per piece.
= (Rate/hour × Time per piece in hours) + (Machine and overhead rate/hour × Time per piece in hours).
= **(Time per piece in hours) × (Labour rate/hour + Machine and overhead rate/hour).**

Example 17.3

Three different methods of production utilising three different grades of labour have been suggested for the manufacture of a component. The manufacturing information is given in Table 17.4.

TABLE 17.4

Method	Tool cost	FFT (min)	Hourly rate	Number of set-ups per annum	Set-up time (h)	Hourly rate for setting-up
A	Nil	24	£4	12	2·25	£7
B	£200	15	£6	10	2·50	£6
C	£990	10	£7·5	5	3·25	£7·5

Assuming all time saved can be gainfully employed, show at what quantities methods A and B cease to be the most economic.

Solution

Let x = Number of components produced.

Method A

Total cost/annum = cost of set-ups + machining cost

$$= £\left(12 \times 2\cdot25 \times 7\right) + £\left(\frac{24}{60} \times 4\right)x$$

$$= £189 + £1\cdot6x \tag{1}$$

Method B

Total cost/annum = tooling cost + cost of set-ups + machining cost

$$= £200 + £(10 \times 2\cdot5 \times 6) + £(15/60 \times 6)\,x$$
$$= £200 + £150 + £1\cdot5x$$
$$= £350 + £1\cdot5x \tag{2}$$

Method C

Total cost/annum = tool cost + cost of set-ups + machining cost

$$= £990 + £(5 \times 3 \cdot 25 \times 7 \cdot 5) + £(10/60 \times 7 \cdot 5) \, x$$
$$= £1112 + £1 \cdot 25x \tag{3}$$

The "break-even" point between Methods A and B occurs when total cost/annum of Method A = total cost/annum of Method B

i.e. when

$$£189 + £1 \cdot 6x = £350 + £1 \cdot 5x$$
$$(1 \cdot 6 - 1 \cdot 5)x = 350 - 189$$
$$0 \cdot 1x = 161$$
$$x = 1610 \text{ components}$$

From the linear equations (1) and (2), it can be seen that the slope of the line representing the cost of Method A is greater than the slope of the line representing Method B.

Hence above the break-even point where $x = 1610$ components, Method A would cease to be the most economic method of production.

Similarly, the "break-even" point between Methods B and C occurs when

total cost/annum of Method B = total cost/annum of Method C

i.e. when

$$£350 + £1 \cdot 5x = £1112 + £1 \cdot 25x$$
$$(1 \cdot 5 - 1 \cdot 25)x = 1112 - 350$$
$$0 \cdot 25x = 762$$
$$x = 3048 \text{ components}$$

Method B ceases to be economic when more than 3048 components are required per annum.

Example 17.4

What would be the minimum production quantity to justify the milling machine given the following information?

	Shaping	Milling
Set-up time	30 min	60 min
Operation time	12 min	6 min
Labour rate	£2 hour	£2 hour
Machine rate	£4 hour	£6 hour
Tooling cost	£45	£160

Solution

Let x = number of components produced

C_s = total cost ($£$) of x components produced by shaping
C_m = total cost ($£$) of x components produced by milling

C_s = Tooling cost + Set-up cost + Machining cost of x components

$$= 45 + \left(\frac{30}{60} \times 6\right) + \left(\frac{12}{60} \times 6\right) x$$

$$= 45 + 3 + 1.2 \, x$$

$$\therefore \quad C_s = 1 \cdot 2x + 48 \tag{1}$$

C_m = Tooling cost + Set-up cost + Machining cost of x components

$$= 160 + \left(\frac{60}{60} \times 8\right) + \left(\frac{6}{60} \times 8\right) x$$

$$= 160 + 8 + 0.8x$$

$$\therefore \quad C_m = 0.8x + 168 \tag{2}$$

Equating (1) and (2) to find the value of x at the break-even quantity we get

$$1.2x + 48 = 0.8x + 168$$

$$\therefore \quad x = 300$$

Minimum production quantity to justify the milling machine under given conditions is 300 components.

Additional Factors Affecting the Use of Tooling. In addition to economic reasons for using jigs and fixtures, it may be desirable to use tooling even below the strictly economic quantity because it ensures:

(*a*) workpieces within close limits;

(*b*) consistency of product.

The existence of a tolerance may help justify the use of tooling, since the scrap rate would be reduced and fitting, assembly and interchangeability facilitated.

17.4 Jig and Fixture Design

The principal considerations in jig and fixture design include:

(*a*) Positioning the component in the jig or fixture, i.e. **locating** the component.

(*b*) Securing the component in the jig or fixture while machining operations are carried out, i.e. **clamping** the component.

(*c*) Positioning fixtures correctly relative to the machine tool, Fig 17.6

(*d*) Positioning the cutting tool correctly relative to the component, Fig 17.6

(*e*) The design should ensure maximum safety for operator particularly when clamping, loading and unloading.

(*f*) Idle machine time whilst loading and unloading must be kept to a minimum.

Principles of Location. (*a*) Apply the kinematic principles of location given in on pp. 98–99, i.e. six locations without redundant constraints, Fig 17.7.

(*b*) Use three-point location to position rough unmachined surfaces in 1st operation jigs.

(*c*) Avoid locating from cored holes (position unreliable).

(*d*) Locate from the same machined surfaces for as many operations as possible.

(*e*) Ensure location method is "foolproof", i.e. that component can only be loaded into the jig in the correct position.

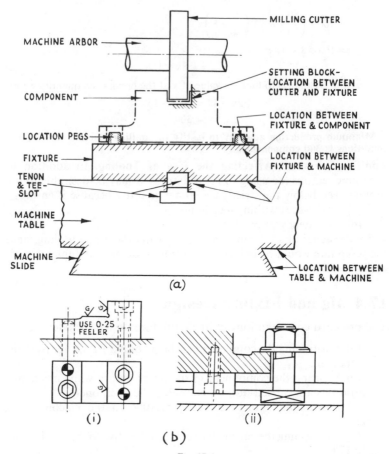

Fig. 17.6

(*a*) Location surfaces which position the cutter relative to the component and the fixture
relative to the machine slide movement on a milling machine
(*b*) Detail of (i) cutter setting block, and (ii) tenon and bolting arrangement for a milling
fixture

(*f*) Ensure location points are visible so that the operator can see they
are free from swarf, and can more easily load the component.

(*g*) Location points to be as far apart as possible to minimise
inaccuracies.

Kinematic principles are modified in practice for jig and fixture
applications, because of the need for supporting work to prevent
deflection and distortion caused by cutting and clamping forces.

An example of a component not fully constrained is given in Fig
17.8(*a*). The spigot provides two restraints (translational), but permits a

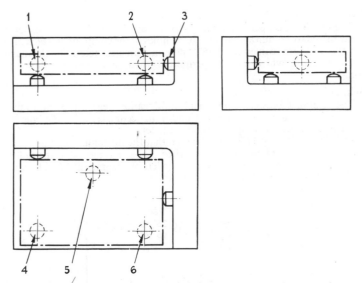

Fig. 17.7 *The six-point location principle applied to jig design*

The component is located by six restraints; to secure the component and prevent its movement, a closing (clamping) force is required.

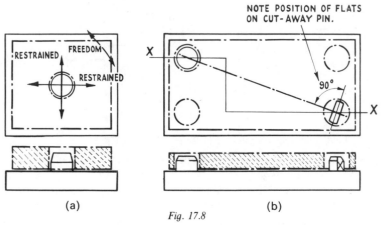

Fig. 17.8

(a) Component not fully located
(b) Component fully located

The six restraints are provided thus: 1 (R) by cut-away pin; 2 (T) by full location pin; 3 (2R, 1T) by flat base

rotational freedom; the flat surface provides three restraints (two rotational and one translational). A component fully constrained by the addition of a radial location is shown in Fig 17.8(b). The second location peg is flatted to allow for error in the pitch of the holes.

Example 17.5
The two location pegs in a milling fixture are 25·30/25·27 mm diameter, one being milled to 7·6 mm across flats. If the holes of the component which fit on the location pegs are reamed to 25·45/25·40 mm diameter, determine the maximum pitch variation which can be permitted when producing the holes in the component.

Solution
The clearance between component and location pegs will be at a minimum when MMC (Maximum Material Condition) occurs, i.e. when the hole is 25·40 diameter and the location peg 25·30 diameter.

By reference to Fig 17.9 it will be seen that the maximum tolerance from the true position of the holes will be absorbed if hole Y is moved to the right by an amount CD and if hole X is moved to the left by an amount EF. The holes can also move closer together by a similar amount.

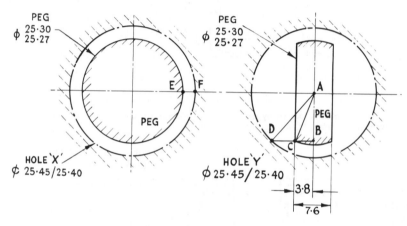

Fig. 17.9

$\therefore$ Total tolerance on pitch of holes $= \pm (CD + EF)$

Now EF = radial clearance between peg and hole

$$= \frac{25\cdot4 - 25\cdot3}{2}$$

$\therefore$ EF = 0.05 mm

$$CD = BD - BC$$

$$= \sqrt{[AD^2 - (AC + BC)(AC - BC)]} - BC$$

$$= \sqrt{\left[12\cdot7^2 - \left(12\cdot65 + \frac{7\cdot6}{2} \right)\left(12\cdot65 - \frac{7\cdot6}{2} \right) \right]} - \frac{7\cdot6}{2}$$

$$= \sqrt{15\cdot707 - 3\cdot8}$$

$$= 0\cdot163 \text{ mm}$$

$\therefore$ Maximum pitch variation $= \pm (CD + EF) = \pm 0\cdot213$ mm

Examples of Location Methods. Of the many methods of locating components in a jig or fixture, two are shown in Fig 17.10 and a third in Fig 17.11. When the main positional requirement for a hole drilled in the cast (or forged) boss of a component is that it shall be centrally situated, a cone is used to locate the boss co-axial with the drill bush; it may also aid clamping, as shown in Fig 17.10 (*a*). To provide a machinist with the means for visually setting a component with an irregular profile in a symmetrical position in a jig, a profile plate or recess may be used, see Fig 17.10(*b*).

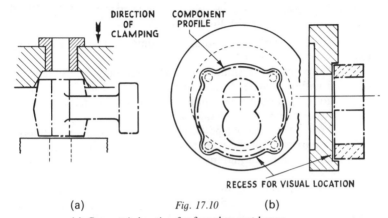

(a)   *Fig. 17.10*   (b)

(*a*) Concentric location for forged or cast bosses
(*b*) Turning fixture with location from component profile

This type of location ensures that the machining carried out in the jig or fixture (e.g. drilling of holes) matches the profile of the component.

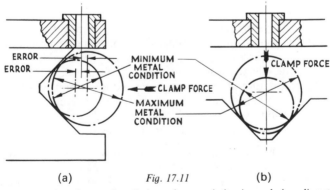

(a)   *Fig. 17.11*   (b)

(*a*) Incorrect vee location on close limit work—a variation in workpiece diameter will cause the hole to be drilled off-centre
(*b*) Correct application of vee location—variations in workpiece diameter do not affect position of drilled hole relative to component centre line, also workpiece is positively supported against cutting and clamping forces

For locating cylindrical components, the vee is extensively used and is made to be either fixed or adjustable—the adjustment providing a clamping force in addition to the location of the vee. When using vee locations they should be so arranged that a variation in diameter does not result in an inaccurate component, see Fig 17.11 (*a*) and (*b*).

Principles of Clamping. Elasticity as a design concept is not applicable to jig and fixture design, i.e. rigidity is needed to avoid strain and inaccurate workpieces. This is particularly true of clamping, where, for example, a force approaching 10 kN may be applied by means of a M 12 thread. (The clamping force between the jaws of a standard 150 mm milling-machine vice was found, by experiment, to be 40 kN)

(*a*) Clamping should absorb as little time as possible (use rapid-action clamping devices).

(*b*) Clamps must be situated so that they may be tightened or loosened without danger to the operator.

(*c*) Clamping should make minimum demands upon the operator's energy, otherwise his fatigue rate will increase.

(*d*) Clamp forces should be exerted only on positively supported (or very rigid) parts of the workpiece, see Fig 17.12(*a*).

(*e*) Clamp forces should not distort locations or tool guiding surfaces, see Fig 17.12(*b*).

(*f*) Reaction to cutting and clamping forces should be provided by the main frame of the jig or fixture. An exception to this rule occurs in simple turn-over type drill jigs used for drilling small holes, i.e. where cutting forces are small.

Machining Operations and Clamping Forces. The magnitude of clamping forces varies with the type of operation and the rate of metal removal.

(a) *Milling.* This process gives a rapid metal removal rate, and the cutting forces are of high magnitude. With conventional up-cut milling, the cutting force has a vertical component which tends to "lift" the work and reduce the effectiveness of the clamping force (see p. 245).

The cyclical nature of the cutting force induces vibration which may loosen certain types of clamp, e.g. cam clamps. Therefore clamps for milling operations should be carefully selected, strong and suitably positioned to secure the workpiece without distortion.

(b) *Drilling.* The cutting forces are more constant than in milling. The axial cutting force usually increases the normal pressure between component and jig (except with turn-over jigs), and thus the frictional resistance to the rotation of the workpiece under cutting torque from the drill is increased. This continues until the "chisel edge" of the drill breaks through, immediately reducing the axial force, which may even be reversed by the vertical force component shown in Fig 17.13(*b*) (most

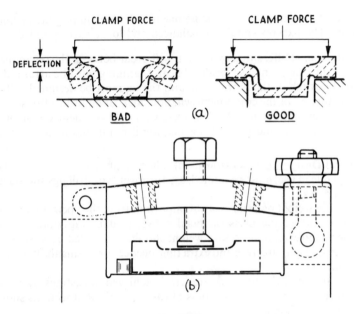

Fig. 17.12

(*a*) Method of supporting component to avoid deflection by clamping force
(*b*) Jig member deflected by clamping force—this will cause holes drilled to be incorrectly positioned and to have non-parallel axes

Observe how the positional error of the drilled holes will be increased by the excessive distance between component and drill bushes.

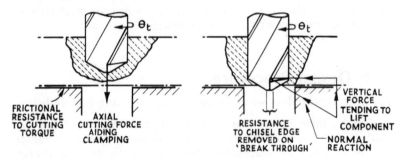

Fig. 17.13 Cutting forces in drilling

drill breakages occur at this point, when hand feed is being used). Light jigs have a tendency to lift from the machine table and spin round with the drill.

(c) *Turning.* Centrifugal force must be considered in relation to the clamping arrangements on Turning Fixtures, especially where small diameters or light alloys are being machined, necessitating high spindle speeds. The fixtures should be balanced and loose parts avoided.

(d) *Welding.* Differential expansion will occur between the component and the jig due to intense localised heat. Clamping must be arranged to avoid buckling of the fabrication, and the jig must be designed so that any distortion of the component will not "lock" it on its locations in the jig and prevent its removal. Clamp screws should be shielded from weld spatter, which would prevent unclamping if it adhered to the screw.

General Design Considerations. (*a*) The weight of *jigs*, to be moved by hand while in use, must be limited, e.g. turnover type drill jigs should not exceed 5–6 kg.

(*b*) The weight of *fixtures* is not important from the operational point of view, indeed the mass of metal assists in damping vibration and chatter. However, unnecessary weight should be avoided because of the extra cost of manufacture and extra time needed for setting the fixture on the machine.

(*c*) Optimum rigidity and strength is achieved in castings by ribbed construction. Maximum thickness of cast-iron ribs and sections should normally be 18 mm.

(*d*) There must be adequate arrangements for swarf and coolant disposal.

(*e*) Parts subject to wear or breakage should be easy to replace.

(*f*) Manufacture is cheapened if standard components are used in the design. The specification BS5078: *Jig and Fixture Components* and makers' catalogues specify ranges of standardised jig and fixture parts, e.g. drill bushes, clamps, spherical washers, etc., which are much cheaper to purchase than to make in small quantities.

17.5 Design Procedure

The general procedure when designing a jig or fixture is given below:

(*a*) Examine the essential features of the component, giving special attention to those drawing dimensions which have small tolerances.

(*b*) Consider all machining operation on the planned Process Layout and observe the sequence in which they appear.

(*c*) Study in detail the operation for which the tooling is required.

(*d*) Decide on location points, position and method of clamping.

(*e*) Produce a DESIGN STUDY in sketch form (see p. 553).

(*f*) Synthesise the design study into a general arrangement of the jig or fixture. Dimensions which can be established only on final assembly should be shown on the arrangement drawing, e.g. position of setting blocks for milling-cutter location.

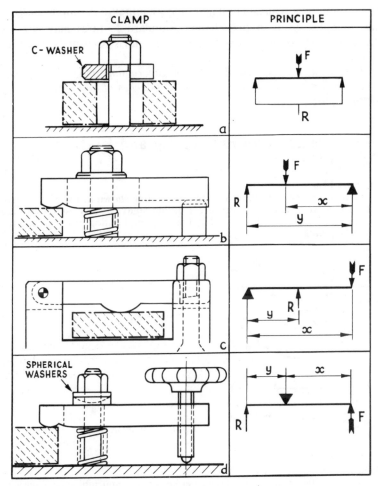

Fig. 17.14 Elementary clamping devices and the comparable lever principles

Note: The mechanical advantage for (*b*), (*c*) and (*d*) is given by the relationship, $MA = y/x = F/R$, where F = Applied force and R = Reaction of component to the clamping force.

In each of the above examples, the force F could be applied by means of a quick-action device (e.g. cam or toggle) instead of the screw thread illustrated, or by air or hydraulically operated devices.

Design Studies. Before the design of a jig or fixture is commenced, simple sketches are made to show important features such as in the selected location surfaces, clamp positions, tool guidance or setting arrangements and methods for coolant or swarf control. On these diagrams the component should be drawn in a distinctive colour to distinguish it from the tooling. Parts of the jig or fixture requiring special design should be sketched to illustrate the method of design (in some of the examples given in this chapter, standard features may also be sketched; this is for illustrative purposes only and is not usually necessary in a design study).

The basic idea behind a design study is to formulate and make clear the general scheme of the design, with detail sketches of any part of the jig which requires amplification.

17.6 Worked Example in Jig and Fixture Design (1)

Example 17.6

The first operation on the malleable iron casting shown in Fig 17.15 is face milling the two flange faces. Prepare a **design study** for single-piece loading showing the location method based on the six-point location principle, and the clamping points.

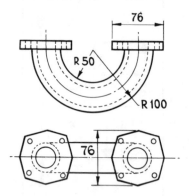

Fig. 17.15 Manifold (*malleable iron*)

Solution

The face-milling can be carried out on either a horizontal milling machine with the face mill bolted to the spindle nose and the component flange faces vertical, or on a vertical milling machine with the flange faces horizontal. For ease of loading, better visibility from the operator's position and ease of keeping the fixture free of swarf, the vertical milling machine is chosen.

Location

(i) The flange faces require to be machined perpendicular to the plane containing the axis of the U-shaped pipe. Location will be taken from the pipe, and since it has a cast surface, three-point location must be used.

(ii) To keep the three locations of (i) in position on the full diameter of the pipe, end movement of the manifold must be prevented by a single location.

(iii) Both flanges should be the same thickness after machining, hence the under-faces will provide location surfaces. To keep the component horizontal, two location points are needed.

The six-point location scheme is shown in Fig 17.16.

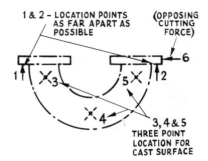

1 & 2 – LOCATION POINTS AS FAR APART AS POSSIBLE (OPPOSING CUTTING FORCE)

3, 4 & 5 THREE POINT LOCATION FOR CAST SURFACE

Fig. 17.16 Six-point location of manifold

Clamping Points. Clamping forces must be applied on positively supported surfaces, i.e. directly above location points. Since the surfaces above locations 1 and 2 are to be machined, these points cannot be used—and of the remaining locations, 3 and 5 are obvious choices.

Note: Many different types of clamps could successfully be used for this fixture, ranging from a simple lever clamp with screw and hexagon nut to pneumatic or hydraulic rapid-action devices. The method selected would depend on the quantity of components to be made and the economic factors of cost and time saved.

The general layout of the fixture is shown in the Design Study, Fig 17.17. Notice that the details are limited to the essential features (the clamp is omitted for reasons given above), but that sufficient information is provided to enable a competent draughtsman to produce a fully detailed design.

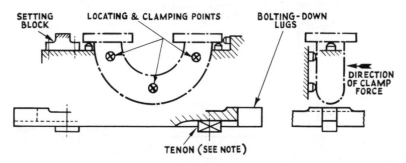

SETTING BLOCK   LOCATING & CLAMPING POINTS   BOLTING-DOWN LUGS

DIRECTION OF CLAMP FORCE

TENON (SEE NOTE)

Fig. 17.17 Design study of milling fixture for Manifold

Note: Tenons are usually essential for milling fixtures, but in the above case they could be omitted, since the face milling need only be parallel to the fixture base.

17.7 Worked Example in Jig and Fixture Design (2)

Example 17.7
The rocker arm shown in Fig 17.18 is to be machined from a forging in 150 M36 alloy steel in a batch of 1000 off. The operation layout is as shown in Table 17.5. Draw a diagram of the capstan set-up for Op. 1 and prepare design studies for the milling fixtures for Ops. 2 and 4, and drill jig for Op. 5.

TABLE 17.5

Op. No.	Operation	Machine	Special tooling
1	Face one side 50 dia boss. Centre, drill, bore, ream 28 dia.	Capstan lathe	Special jaws in two jaw chuck
2	Straddle mill 22 ± 0·05 dimension	Hor. mill	Milling fixture
3	Mill 50 dia boss face to 28 ± 0·05	Vert. mill	Milling fixture
4	Straddle mill 9 radius boss to 47·6	Vert. mill	Milling fixture as for Op. 2
5	Drill and ream 12 and 9 dia holes	Turret drill	Drill jig
6	Sawcut 3 wide	Hor. mill	
7	Deburr		

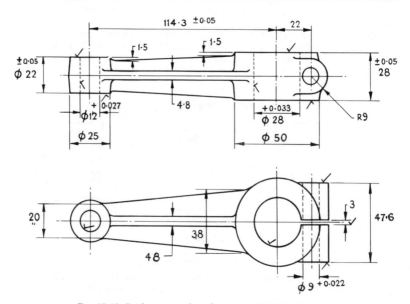

Fig. 17.18 Rocker arm—drop forging in 150M36 alloy steel

Solution

Op. 1 Capstan Set-up, Fig 17.19. Special chuck jaws are an effective and inexpensive way of holding the component. To assist in setting, two stop pads are provided; (i) a hollow bung in the chuck bore to prevent the work slipping while drilling takes place, and (ii) a stop pad into the chuck face to support and assist in the visual location of the small boss of the rocker arm.

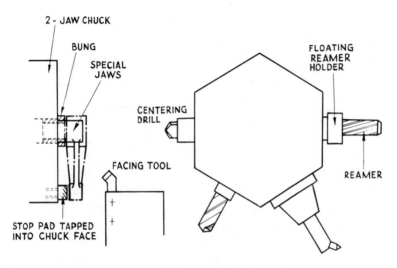

Fig. 17.19 Capstan lathe set-up for Op 1 on rocker arm

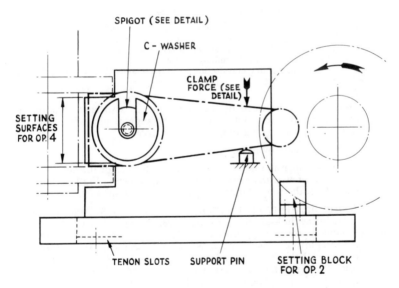

Fig. 17.20 Design study of milling fixture for Ops 2 and 4 on rocker arm

Ops. 2 and 4 Milling Fixture, Fig 17.20. Expense is saved by using one fixture for two similar operations. The main location is provided by a spigot fitting into the 28 mm dia bore. The location surfaces of spigots should normally be short, to facilitate rapid loading, but if the spigot is extended an anti-jamming device should be incorporated as shown in Fig 17.21(*b*).

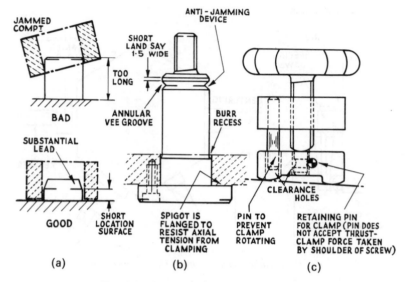

Fig. 17.21 Details of milling fixture (Fig. 17.20)

(*a*) Examples of good and bad location spigots. Jamming occurs when a spigot is too long, this is avoided by using a short spigot having a substantial lead. If a long location is necessary, an anti-jamming device—as shown at (*b*)—should be used
(*b*) Detail of location spigot for the milling fixture
(*c*) Detail of hand clamp with compensating pad for use above the support pin on the milling fixture

Five restraints are provided by the spigot and its associated location face (3T and 2R); the sixth restraint is given by the support pin, which is domed because it is in contact with a rough forged surface.

Clamping is effected by means of:

(i) the C-washer and hexagon nut fitted to the spigot thread;
(ii) a hand screw with compensating pad, as shown in Fig 17.21(*c*), which accommodates the rough tapering surface of the component.

Op. 5 Drill Jig, Fig 17.22. Location is again based on the large bore and its adjacent face using the locating spigot and C-washer method. The radial location in this instance is provided by a cam-actuated sliding vee; this method is preferred to the support pin as used in the previous example, because the vee centralises the small boss beneath the drill bush and improves the appearance of the component by ensuring the 12 mm hole is central with its surrounding boss. Cam action for the vee, Fig 17.23(*a*), is chosen because of its quick action.

Liners, see Fig 17.23(*b*), are used at each drilling position because separate slip bushes must be provided for the reaming-size drill and for the reamer at each hole. To "foolproof" the jig by preventing the slip bushes being inserted in the wrong liners, the liner for the 9 mm hole must have a different bore size from that of the liner used for the 12 mm hole.

The latch-type drill plate, Fig 17.24, must be accurately located and fitted to ensure positional accuracy of the drill bush. The hinge pin must be a close fit, and side location of the latch must be provided at its end by an accurate fit into the body of the jig. To keep the axis of the drill bush vertical, the latch must be

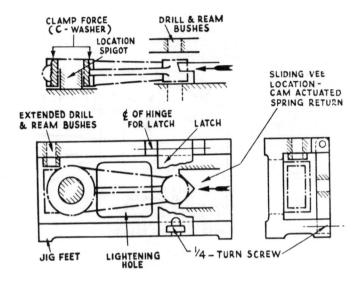

Fig. 17.22 Design study for drill jig for Op 5 on rocker arm

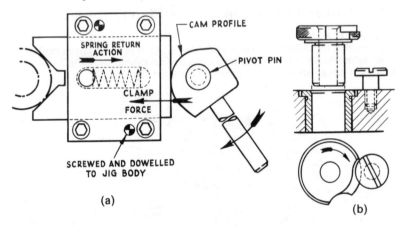

Fig. 17.23 Details of drill jig shown in Fig 17.22

(*a*) Cam-operated vee location

(*b*) Liner, retaining screw and slip-bush arrangement

located in a horizontal position by the bottom face of the slot in the jig body at the free end of the latch. **This is very important, and is a point often overlooked, particularly when using a latch for both a drill plate and for clamping the component.** The $\frac{1}{4}$-turn screw is a simple device for securing the latch: on final assembly of the jig the underface of the screw is adjusted so that when the screw is tightened, the flat head is at right angles to the slot in the latch; a $\frac{1}{4}$-turn of the screw lines up the head with the slot, enabling the latch to be lifted for unloading the component.

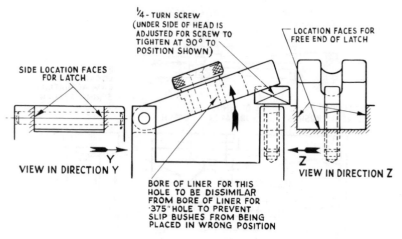

Fig. 17.24 Detail of latch for drill jig (Fig. 17.22)

17.8 Worked Example in Jig and Fixture Design (3)

Example 17.8

Given that the calliper for a disc brake, Fig 17.25, is produced from malleable iron castings in accordance with the sequence of operations shown in Table 17.6, prepare a design study for the turning fixture for Op. 7.

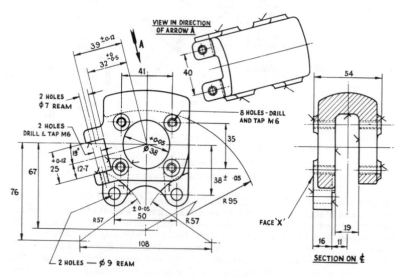

Fig. 17.25 Brake calliper in malleable cast iron

TABLE 17.6

Op. No.	Operation	Machine	Location	Special tooling
1	Mill Face "X"	Vert. mill	Opposite face to "X"	Milling fixture
2	Rough bore to 36·5 + 0·08 and face to 54 dimension	Turret lathe	Face "X" and profile	Turning fixture
3	Drill and ream 2–9 dia holes	2-spindle drill	Face "X" bore and profile	Drill jig
4	Mill slot, 95 radius × 19 wide	Hor. mill	Face "X", bore and 9 dia. hole	Milling fixture
5	Mill 2–57 radii to 16 dimension	Vert. mill	Face "X", bore and 9 dia. hole	Milling fixture
6	Mill slot 25 + 0·12 wide to the 32 − 0·5 dim.	Hor. mill	Face "X" bore and 9 dia. hole	Milling fixture
7	Finish bore 38 + 0·05 dia	Turret lathe	Face "X", bore and 9 dia. hole	Turning fixture
8	Drill and tap eight M 6 holes	2-spindle drill	Face "X", bore and 9 dia. hole	Drill jig
9	At 15° angle in side lugs—drill two M 6 tapping size holes, drill two 6·7 dia holes, ream two 7 dia holes, tap two M 6 holes	4-spindle or turret-type drill	Face "X", bore and 9 dia. hole	Drill jig

Solution
Notes on the Planned Operation.

(i) The 1st Op. produces a flat surface which is used as a location for all future operations.

(ii) The main bore is machined on the 2nd Op., but not to its finished size. The bore is functionally important and is also an important location feature in manufacture, but since the casting is to be machined subsequently on a number of other surfaces, distortion through the release of stresses in the material may occur. A further operation to finish bore the component will restore accuracy particularly in the alignment of the two 38 mm holes.

(iii) Ops. 1 and 2 have provided five restraints for location purposes: by drilling and reaming the two 9 mm dia holes in Op. 3 radial location will be possible from one of these holes—this is better than using the cast profile. Thus, six restraints are provided, and these locations may be used for *all* further operations.

Op. 7 Turning Fixture, Fig 17.26. The fixture is bolted to the flange of the turret lathe spindle, locating in the accurately machined recess (to provide means for checking concentricity of turning fixtures, a clocking groove, as shown in the diagram, may be used).

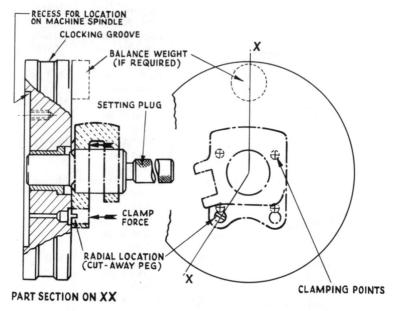

PART SECTION ON XX   CLAMPING POINTS

Fig. 17.26 Design for turning fixture for Op 7 on brake calliper

The component is located on the machined surfaces established for this purpose in the early operations, using a setting mandrel for centralising the calliper, and a cut-away peg for radial location. After clamping on the four positively supported points shown, by means of two strap clamps, the setting mandrel is removed, leaving the central bush in the fixture to support the pilot end of the boring bar used to finish machine the 38 mm holes.

Balancing of turning fixtures is essential, particularly when high spindle speeds or large out-of-balance masses are concerned. The balance weights may be either cast integral with the backplate, or separately secured in position—precautions being taken to ensure that the weight cannot loosen and fly-off the fixture while it is rotating. Final balancing is carried out (with a component clamped in position) by removing surplus metal from the balance weight.

EXERCISES 17

1. Design Studies are given for jigs and fixtures required for the components shown in Figs 17.15, 17.18 and 17.25. Use the design studies as a basis for drawing general arrangements of the jigs and fixtures.

2. The turning fixture shown in Fig 17.27 was designed by a student for boring an aluminium-alloy component.

(*a*) Assume the fixture was rigid and did not distort under the clamp force (approx 20 kN), discuss the effect of distortion on the workpiece.

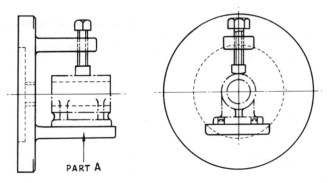

PART A

Fig. 17.27

(b) Assume the component was rigid and did not distort, state what effect deflection of part A of the fixture would have on workpiece accuracy.

(c) Design an alternative clamping method which avoids distortion of both fixture and workpiece.

3. A component is located on a milling fixture by means of two location pegs of equal diameter, one fully cylindrical and the other with flats 8 mm across. If the holes in the component are reamed to 25·05/25·00 mm diameter at 250·12/249·88 mm in pitch, determine the maximum permissible diameter of the location pegs.

4. Illustrate a sliding-vee type locator. State the circumstances under which this is used, and distinguish between its function and that of the fixed vee locator.

5. Sketch in detail location methods to be used when:

(a) drilling the hole in Lever, Fig 17.28(a);
(b) milling the slot in Hub, Fig 17.28(b).

6. (a) Describe the conditions when it is necessary to incorporate floating members in the design of a jig or fixture.

(b) Illustrate the use of this design principle with reference to two of the following:

(i) faceplate turning fixture;
(ii) milling fixture;
(iii) drilling jig.

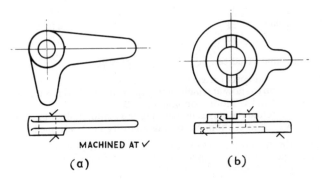

MACHINED AT ✓

(a)   (b)

Fig. 17.28

7. (a) What are the principal features to be examined when selecting the most suitable processes for manufacturing a component?

(b) Given the following particulars, what quantity would justify the use of the broaching machine?

	Milling machine	Broaching machine
First cost	£10 000	£25 000
Annual depreciation	£1 000	£2 500
Oncost/hour	£6	£6
Equipment cost	£100	£2 500
Setter's rate/hour	£2·50	£2·50
Operator's rate/hour	£2	£1·60
Set-up time	2 h	½ h
Operating time	20 min	5 min

8. A component can be produced to the required limits by horizontal milling or surface broaching; determine the quantity that would economically justify the allocation to the broaching machine when manufacturing in lots of 240, given the following:

	Horizontal mill	Broaching machine
Machine hour rate	£7	£7
Tooling cost	£800	£2 400
Operating time/piece	5 min	1 min
Set-up time	1 h	30 min
Labour rate	£2 per h	£1·80 per h

9. Three different methods of tooling are being discussed for the milling of a component required in large quantities. The production data has been assessed as follows:

Method	Tool cost	Time in min	Hourly rate	Set-ups per annum	Set-up time (h)	Hourly cost of set-up
A	£320	25	£8	12	2·5	£18
B	£960	21	£8	8	4·0	£18
C	£2 400	15	£9	4	5·0	£16

Assuming all time saved can be gainfully employed:

(a) tabulate total costs for each method; and

(b) plot a graph to show at which annual quantity method B is more economic than A, and method C more economic than B.

10. (a) Enumerate the stages in planning the manufacture of a new product.

(b) How would an economic ordering quantity be determined?

11. State the main principles of jig design. Outline the sequence of operations for the manufacture in medium lots of the component shown in Fig 17.29 and sketch the jig for drilling and reaming.

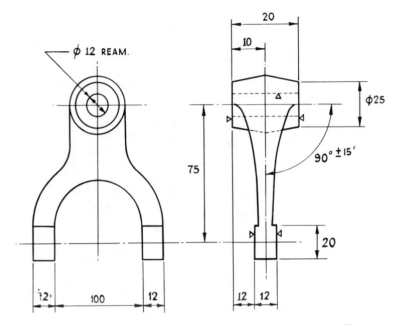

Fig. 17.29 Fork lever—mild steel stamping—machine where marked ∇

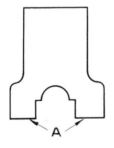

Fig. 17.30

12. A cast-iron single cylinder block as shown in Fig 17.30 is to be located to enable the joint faces "A" to be face milled first.

Sketch the ideal positions for the locations and illustrate a suitable clamping method for small batch production.

13. The component shown in Fig 17.31 is to be produced on a capstan lathe in large quantities using a fixture and a single loading per piece.

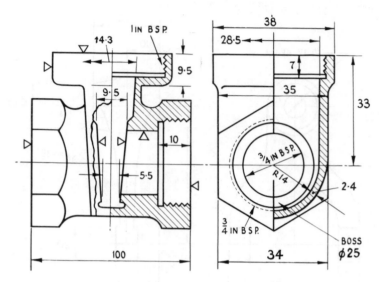

Fig. 17.31 Valve body—machine where marked ▽

(a) Draw up a sequence of operations, indicating tool positions and stating clearly where operations are simultaneous.

(b) Make an *outline* design of the fixture to be used.

BIBLIOGRAPHY

The following publications contain information likely to be of interest to readers of this book. Sources of the references made in the text are included in the list.

1 General
Boothroyd, G. Fundamentals of Metal Machining and Machine Tools. McGraw-Hill 1975
Chapman, W. A. J. Workshop Technology Part 3. 3rd Edition. Edward Arnold 1975
Radford, J. D. and Richardson, D. B. Production Engineering Technology. 3rd edition. Macmillan 1980
Wright Baker H. (Editor) Modern Workshop Technology Part 2. 3rd Edition. Machine Tools and Manufacturing Processes. Macmillan 1967

2 Specification and Standardisation
The management of design for economic production. PD 6470: 1975. British Standards Institution 1975
Handbook No. 18 Metric Standards for Engineering. British Standards Institution 1972
Machinery's Screw Thread Book 20th Edition. Machinery Publishing Co. 1972
Woodward, D. W. (Editor) Standards for Industry. Heinemann 1965

3 Machine Tools
Chironis, N. P. (Editor) Machine Devices and Instrumentation. McGraw-Hill 1966
Leslie, W. H. P. (Editor) Numerical Control Users Handbook. McGraw-Hill 1970
Martin, S. J. Numerical Control of Machine Tools. Hodder and Stoughton 1970
A Management Guide to Numerical Control Machine Tools. Institution of Production Engineers 1978
Schlesinger, G. Testing Machine Tools 7th Edition. Machinery Publishing Co. 1970
Town, H. C., Design and Construction of Machine Tools. Iliffe 1971
Tobias, S. A. Vibrations of Vertical Milling Machines Under Test and Working Conditions. Institution of Mechanical Engineers (173) 1959

4 Metal Cutting

Manual on Cutting of Metals 2nd Edition. American Society of Mechanical Engineers 1952
A Treatise on Milling and Milling Machines 3rd Edition. Cincinnati Milling Machine Co. 1951
Armarego, E. J. A. and Brown, R. H. The Machining of Metals. Prentice Hall 1969
Black, P. H. Theory of Metal Cutting. McGraw-Hill 1961
Kronenberg, M. Machining Science and Application. Pergamon 1966
Shaw, M. C. Metal Cutting Principles 3rd Edition. MIT Press 1968
Stabler, G. V. The Fundamental Geometry of Cutting Tools. Proceedings I.Mech.E. Vol. 165 1951
Cherry, J. Economics of Cutting Processes. Journal I. Prod. E. Feb. 1960
Backer, W. R. Marshall E. R. and Shaw, M. C. The Size Effect in Metal Cutting. Trans. ASME Vol. 74 1952
Gisbrook, H. Precision Grinding Research. Journal I. Prod. E. May 1960
Guest, J. J., Proceedings I. Mech. E. page 543 Oct. 1915
Sémon, G. A Practical Guide to Electro-Discharge Machining. Ateliers des Charmilles S. A. (Geneva)
Wilson, John F. Practice and Theory of Electro-Chemical Machining. Wiley-Interscience
Springborn, R. K. (Ed.) Non-Traditional Machining Processes. American Society of Tool & Manufacturing Engineers
Harry, J. E. Industrial Lasers and Their Applications. McGraw-Hill

5 Metal Forming

Calladine, C. R., Engineering Plasticity. Pergamon 1969
Crane, E. V. Plastic Working in Presses. Wiley 3rd Edition 1944
Feldmann, H. D. Cold Forging of Steel. Hutchinson 1961
Grainger, J. A. Presswork and Presses 2nd Edition. Machinery Publishing Co. 1952
Makelt, H. Mechanical Presses. Edward Arnold 1968
Rowe, G. W. An introduction to the Principles of Metalworking. Edward Arnold 1965
Schuler, L. Metal Forming Handbook 4th Edition. Louis Schuler – Göppingen Wuertt 1964
Willis, J. Deep Drawing. Butterworth 1954
Pugh, H. Ll.D. and Watkins, M. T. Experimental Investigation of the Extrusion of Metals. I. Prod. E. Brighton Conference 1961
Tilsley, R. and Howard, F. Cold Extrusion of Ferrous and Non-Ferrous Materials. I. Prod. E. Brighton Conference 1960

6 Dimensional and Quality Control

Handbook of Industrial Metrology. Society of Manufacturing Engineers. Prentice Hall 1967

Adams, L. F. Engineering Measurements and Instrumentation. Hodder and Stoughton 1975

Caplen, R. H. A Practical Approach to Quality Control 3rd Edition. Business Books 1978

Galyer, J. F. W. and Shotbolt, C. R. Metrology for Engineers. Cassell 1964

Miller, L. Engineering Dimensional Metrology. Edward Arnold 1962

Town, H. C. and Moore, H. Inspection Machines, Measuring Systems and Instruments. Batsford 1978

Chree, Dr. Proceedings of the Physical Society of London. Vol. XVIII p. 35

Evans, J. C. The Pneumatic Gauging Technique in its Application to Dimensional Measurement. Journal I. Prod. E. 1957

7 Planning Costing and Tooling

Eilon, S. Elements of Production Planning and Control. Macmillan 1962

Kempster, M. H. A. An Introduction to Jig and Tool Design. 3rd Edition. Hodder and Stoughton 1974

Parsons, C. W. S. Estimating Machining Costs. McGraw-Hill 1957

Parsons, S. A. J. Production Tooling Equipment. 3rd Edition. Macmillan 1966

Wage, H. W. Manufacturing Engineering. McGraw-Hill 1963

Answers to Exercises

Exercises 1

4. (a) 1, $1\frac{1}{4}$, $1\frac{1}{2}$, 2, $2\frac{1}{2}$, $3\frac{1}{4}$, 4 (kW)
   (b) G7/h6; hole 44·525/44·500; shaft 44·491/44·475
7. $D = 31·92$ mm, $+0·149 - 0·147$ close control of taper dia. at ball contact without close angular tolerance
8. 0·0078 mm; posn. tol., cylinder 0·0078 mm dia
9. (b) (i) 35·405 mm; 39·101 mm;
   (ii) $+0·02$ mm at min.material
10. Before plating 57·590/57·555; after plating 58·150/57·955; max. plating thickness 0·125 mm

Exercises 2

2. 210 mm; 8
5. 67 N; 59 N in plane of 50 kg load
10. (a) 0·0157 mm, tool below centre line
    (b) (i) 0·2667 mm;   (ii) 0·0801 mm; hole 37·84 mm dia
12. Drivers/driven; 5·28, 3·68, 2·57, 1·80, 1·26, 0·88
16. No 2

Exercises 3

5. 0·273 mm

6. $\dfrac{56 \times 48}{64 \times 100}$; $k = 16·043$

7. 7°14′

8. 167°55′; 26°47′

9. OA

$$\begin{array}{cc} x & y \\ 50 & 15 \\ \downarrow & 15 \\ 38 & 15 \end{array} \Big\} \text{St. line}$$

$$AB\begin{bmatrix} x = 38 - 18\sin\alpha \\ y = 33 - 18\cos\alpha \end{bmatrix}_{\alpha=0}^{\alpha=120°}$$

$$BC[y = 1·732x - 3·182]_{x=22·412}$$

11. Gears for 172·8 mm lead, $\dfrac{72 \times 24}{100 \times 24}$

Spindle elevations; 65°34′, 39°58′, 61°36′

Exercises 5

1. 21°11′; increases; $\gamma_b + 3°26′$, $\gamma_n + 1°34′$
3. (a) 55°34′;   (b) 51°12′

570

4. Ellipse; major axis 26 mm, minor axis 25·432 mm; depth 9·727 mm
6. $\phi = 48°24'$; change in γ_s, $-4°8'$; $\gamma = 15°20'$
8. 17°55'   11. 9°52'

Exercises 6

1. (a) 1950 N/mm^2; 1672 W   (b) 1100 N/mm^2; 2065 W
2. (a) 2273 N; 931 W; $k = 0·51$
   (b) (i) Force and power rise approx 50%; K unchanged
       (ii) Force and power fall slightly; K rises slightly
4. 60 rev/min
5. (b) 69%; 3900 N/mm^2; 450 mm^3/s
7. (a) 0·94   (b) 25   (c) 659 N/mm^2
8. (i) 1134 N at 22°;   (ii) 26°;   (iii) 760 N   (iv) 42°
9. (b) θ increases   (c) 25°   10. 84; 2837 J/min

Exercises 7

1. (a) $VM^n = C$ (b) C falls as f is increased   (c) 13·2 m/min
2. (a) $6·38 \times 10^4$ mm^3/min;   (b) C decreases;   (c) C increases slightly
4. $VM^{0.14} = 84$; $M = 88$ min (high accuracy not possible from given data)
5. 53 min; 37 m/min   6. 56 rev/min
7. 2·2 min; 152   8. 190 rev/min
9.
V (m/min)	31·5	33	36	69
Power (kW)	1·71	1·79	1·95	3·74
10. 42·4 m/min

Exercises 8

2. 0·042 mm   3. 78·48 mm; 0·088 mm   4. 40°
7. Centre of cutter 61·5 mm from edge of work; 0·85 min
8. 181 N   9. 6 teeth
11. $\lambda = 11°27'$; $\gamma_0 = -1°52'$; $\gamma_n = -1°54'$; $\gamma_t = -0°7'$

Exercises 9

3. Traverse rate $> 2·3$ m/min
7. 0·000 05 mm, using Guest's method
10. $v_1 t_1 = v_2 t_2$ to maintain metal removal rate but $v_1^2 t_1 > v_2^2 t_2$ to lower force/grit;
    $v_2 = 10$ m/min, $t_2 = 0·06$ mm are possible values

Exercises 10

2. (b) 2500 W   6. (a) 0·04; 0·055; (b) 0·19 mm/s
9. (c) 44·7 g   10. 341·4 mm^3/s

Exercises 11

3. 2870 J; 0·705 MN   6. 135 KN
7. (a) 160 mm (b) punch dia = nom. size of hole (c) 86·5 mm, assuming $D/d = 1·85$

8. (*a*) 11.5 kJ;   (*b*) energy capacity too low for continuous stroking;   (*c*) 17 kJ
9. (*a*) 1435 kN; 115 kJ
10. (*a*) 104 mm;   (*b*) draws   (*d*) 15 tons
12. (*a*) 38·6 mm;   (*b*) 79 kN   (*c*) 290 kN   (*d*) 730 kN

Exercises 12

5. 0·1133 mm at 330°   6. +0·02 mm; −0·03 mm
7. h = 0·0012 mm
9. h = 9·788 mm; error of l = +0·028 mm
10. 102·408 mm; ±0·089 mm   11. (*b*) 47° 18′
13. 1·8 mm dia.; 0·04 mm; × 50 000

Exercises 13

7. 99·820/99·733 mm dia.
8. T. P. centre line of slot from new datum 35·684 mm new posn. tol. for slot
   ±0·04 at MMC (alternatives possible)
10. 21° 30′; 0·0908 mm
11. 0·037 mm

Exercises 14

7. 0·3665 mm   8. 0·4243 mm

Exercises 15

3. (i) 47·502 mm;   (ii) σ = 0·009;   (iii) medium precision
4. Method 4; $\overline{X}$ = 2·34 μ, σ = 0·98 μ
6. $\bar{x}$ = 84·599 mm; α = 0·011 mm; $T > 8\sigma$ high precision
8. (i) RPI = 2·84;   (ii) mean, 55 mm ±0·104/±0·067; range, 0·389/0·319 mm
10. Producer's risk, 0·02; consumer's risk 0·42
11. Hole, 25·028/25·000 mm dia.; shaft 24·9985/24·9815 mm dia.

Exercises 16

(*Note*: as time estimates vary according to the speeds and feeds chosen, answers
can vary)

1. 1530 mm³/s; 2·07 W/mm³/s
2. 1 min   5. 2·2 min
6. 11¼ hours   7. ½ hour
8. (*a*) 127 rev/min; 152·4 mm/min   (*b*) 1650 mm³/s   (*c*) 19·1 mm
9. 7 min   11. Between 4 and 5 components

Exercises 17

3. 24·922 mm   7. (*b*) 1142
8. 2568   9. 1172; 2360

Index

BRITISH STANDARD SPECIFICATIONS

The following standards, which relate to the subject matter of this book, may be purchased from the British Standards Institution at 2 Park Street, London, WIA 2BS. For certain standards, a shortened form of title is given.

(It is important to consult the *current* standard, as revisions are made from time to time.)

Machine Tools

BS 46 & 4235	*Keys and Keyways and Taper Pins*
BS 292	*Dimensions of Ball Bearings and Cylindrical Roller Bearings*
BS 426	*Lathe Centres*
BS 436	*Machine Cut Gears, Spur and Helical*
BS 587	*Motor Starters and Controllers*
BS 721	*Machine Cut Gears, Worm Gearing*
BS 1089	*Workhead Spindles for Grinding Machines*
BS 1131	*Plain Metal Bearings (Including Oil-retaining Bushes)*
BS 1440	*Endless V-belt Drives*
BS 1660	*Machine Tapers, Reduction Sleeves and Extension Sockets*
BS 1983	*Chucks for Machine Tools*
BS 2059	*Straight Sided Splines and Serrations*
BS 2485	*Tee Slots, Bolts, Nuts and Tenons*
BS 2771	*Electrical Equipment of Machine Tools*
BS 2917	*Graphical Symbols for Fluid Power Transmission Diagrams*
BS 3027	*Dimensions for Worm Gear Units*
BS 3134	*Dimensions of Tapered Roller Bearings*
BS 3550	*Involute Splines*
BS 3635	*The Numerical Control of Machines*
BS 3641	*Symbols for Machine Tools*
BS 3979	*Dimensions of Electric Motors*
BS 4185	*Machine Tool Components*
BS 4656	*The Accuracy of Machine Tools and Methods of Tooling*
BS 5063	*Lubricants for Machine Tools*

Cutting Tools

BS 122	*Milling Cutters and Reamers*
BS 328	*Twist Drills, Combined Drills and Countersinks*
BS 949	*Screwing Taps*
BS 1296	*Single Point Cutting Tools*
BS 4193	*Dimensions for Throwaway Carbide Tips*

Grinding

BS 620	*Dimensions of Grinding Wheels and Wheel Segments*
BS 1089	*Workhead Spindles for Grinding Machines*
BS 2064	*Diamond Abrasive Wheels and Tools*
BS 4481	*Bonded Abrasive Products*

Metal Forming and Presswork

BS 18	*Methods for Tensile Testing of Metals*
BS 224	*Steel for Die Blocks for Drop Forging*
BS 240	*Brinell Hardness Test*
BS 427	*Vickers Hardness Test*
BS 860	*Table of Approximate Comparison of Hardness Scales*
BS 1639	*Methods for Bend Testing of Metals*
BS 3855	*Method for Modified Erichsen Cupping Test*
BS 4184	*Power Press Nomenclature*
DD 45	*Press Tool Die Sets*

Specification and Standardisation

BS 308	*Engineering Drawing Practice*
BS 970	*Wrought Steels*
BS 1916	*Limits and Fits for Engineering*
BS 1991	*Letters, Symbols, Signs and Abbreviations*
BS 2517	*Definitions for Use in Mechanical Engineering*
BS 2045	*Preferred Numbers*
BS 4500	*ISO Limits and Fits*
See also PD 6470:	*The Management of Design for Economic Production.*

Measurement

BS 817	*Surface Plates and Tables*
BS 870	*External Micrometers*
BS 888	*Slip (or Block) Gauges and Accessories*
BS 907	*Dial Gauges for Linear Measurement*
BS 958	*Precision Levels for Engineering Workshops*
BS 1054	*Engineers Comparators*
BS 1134	*Methods for the Assessment of Surface Texture*
BS 3064	*Sine Bars and Sine Tables*
BS 5204	*Specification for Straight Edges*
BS 5317	*Metric Length Bars and Their Accessories*

Gauges

BS 919	*Screw Gauges, Limits and Tolerances*
	Pt 1 *Unified form*; Pt. 2 *Whitworth and BA*; Pt. 3 *ISO Metric*
BS 969	*Plain Limit Gauges: Limits and Tolerances*
BS 1044	*Gauge Blanks*

Screw Threads

BS 21	*Pipe Threads for Tubes and Fittings*
BS 84	*Parallel Screw Threads of Whitworth Form*
BS 93	*British Association (BA) screw threads*
BS 3643	*ISO Metric Screw Threads*
BS 5346	*ISO Metric Trapezoidal Screw Threads*

Quality Control

BS 600	*Application of Statistical Methods to Quality Control*
BS 1313	*Fraction-defective Charts for Quality Control*

BS 2564	*Control Chart Technique*
BS 6000	*Guide to the Use of BS6001*
BS 6001	*Sampling Procedures and Tables for Inspection by Attributes*

Tool Design

BS 1098	*Jig Bushes*
BS 1935	*Spindle Noses and Adaptors, Multi-spindle Heads*
BS 5078	*Jig and Fixture Components*
DD 45	*Press Tool Die Sets*